BLOOD, METAL AND DUST

OSPREY
PUBLISHING

BEN BARRY

BLOOD, METAL AND DUST

HOW VICTORY TURNED INTO DEFEAT
IN AFGHANISTAN AND IRAQ

OSPREY PUBLISHING
Bloomsbury Publishing Plc
Kemp House, Chawley Park, Cumnor Hill, Oxford OX2 9PH, UK
1385 Broadway, 5th Floor, New York, NY 10018, USA
E-mail: info@ospreypublishing.com
www.ospreypublishing.com

OSPREY is a trademark of Osprey Publishing Ltd

First published in Great Britain in 2020

A catalogue record for this book is available from the British Library.

ISBNs: HB 9781472831019; PB 9781472831040; eBook 9781472831026;
ePDF 9781472831002; XML 9781472831033

20 21 22 23 24   10 9 8 7 6 5 4 3 2 1

Maps by www.bounford.com
Index by Zoe Ross

Typeset by Deanta Global Publishing Services, Chennai, India
Printed and bound in Great Britain by CPI (Group) UK Ltd, Croydon CR0 4YY

Editor's note
The appearance of US Department of Defense (DoD) visual information does not imply or constitute
DoD endorsement.

Osprey Publishing supports the Woodland Trust, the UK's leading woodland conservation charity.

To find out more about our authors and books visit **www.ospreypublishing.com**. Here you will find
extracts, author interviews, details of forthcoming events and the option to sign up for our newsletter.

Contents

List of Maps

List of Illustrations

Preface

Iraq and Afghanistan have been the dominant experience of this century for the land and air forces of the US and many of its allies. As a result, these forces have changed a great deal, as much as they changed in each of the previous century's world wars. The wars have also resulted in changes to the key non-state actors, particularly the Taliban, Al Qaida and its offshoot ISIS. Thirteen years of fighting inflicted over 56,000 killed or seriously wounded casualties on the forces of the US. The wars probably caused about quarter of a million civilian casualties. The two wars cost the US alone over $1.5 trillion in additional military funding over and above the Pentagon's annual budget.

The US-led attack on Afghanistan in 2001 was a direct result of the Al Qaida attacks on the United States on 11 September 2001. Although the US had no previous plans for war in the isolated landlocked country, the unforeseen requirement to remove the Taliban government from Afghanistan initially challenged US military capability. But a highly innovative campaign combining CIA and Special Operations Forces teams working alongside the Northern Alliance militias and US air attacks with precision weapons destroyed the Taliban forces with unexpected speed. The US succeeded in deposing the Taliban regime and evicting most of Al Qaida from the country, but they almost certainly missed an opportunity to trap Osama Bin Laden in the Tora Bora mountains.

Throughout 2002, the US made extensive preparations to remove Saddam Hussein from power in Iraq, to eliminate a perceived threat from weapons of mass destruction (WMD). Regime change in Iraq had been thoroughly planned and drew upon the full range of US military capability. The initial attacks by US, UK and Australian forces saw a numerically inferior, but much better trained and equipped, attacking force mount a joint air–land offensive campaign in which rapid land manouevre and precision air attack destroyed much larger, but less modern and less well led Iraqi forces and caused Saddam Hussein's regime to collapse.

Regime change operations in both countries thus produced stunning military successes, succeeding in much less time and with far fewer Coalition casualties than many had anticipated. These successes were followed by public declarations that major combat operations had ended.

But post-conflict stabilization of both countries saw the US and its allies struggle to align the ways and means necessary for military, reconstruction and political activity to generate the operational effects that would achieve strategic objectives. Initial optimism and hopes of political and security progress were thwarted when the conflicts assumed the character of prolonged, complex and bloody insurgencies.

Initial efforts to counter these insurgencies achieved only partial and local success that was insufficient to reverse the deterioration of security. This deterioration was only averted by surges, short-term deployments of additional US and international troops to conduct counter-insurgency, which achieved some security improvements, followed by the assumption of security leadership by the Baghdad and Kabul governments. After both these transitions, however, security deteriorated. Contributory factors included weaknesses in both governments, including corruption, and weaknesses in both nations' security forces, as well political failure to reduce the root causes of the insurgencies.

In Iraq, post-conflict operations were much more difficult than the US government had anticipated. Initial political errors led to a sub-optimal effort to stabilize the country. Although US and UK troops won numerous tactical victories against Iraqi militias and insurgents, many political and military mistakes made Iraq less rather than more stable. An impending descent of the country into inter-ethnic civil war was only averted by President Bush's decision to 'surge' additional US forces to Iraq. Using counter-insurgency (COIN) tactics, they were able to temporarily reverse the deterioration in security. But political progress proved more elusive and the hard-line autocrat Prime Minister Nouri al-Maliki persecuted the Iraqi Sunni minority, a significant factor in the rise of ISIS in Iraq. The US withdrew its forces from Iraq in 2011, only for them to return to the country in 2014 to help it repel attacks by ISIS, the nihilistic terror group that had evolved out of Al Qaida.

As the case for the 2003 invasion was based on a US perception of a non-existent WMD threat, the war was widely seen as unjustified. And US conduct, particularly in the first three years of the war, made matters worse and greatly damaged its reputation and influence, particularly in the Muslim world. The war weakened US power and influence, in the Middle East and beyond. Thus the US did not win the Iraq war; in fact it failed to achieve the great majority of its strategic objectives in Iraq. If any country did, it was Iran, which skilfully exploited the war to increase its influence in Iraq and deter any US regime-change operation against Tehran. By 2020, it was clear that by supporting Iraqi Shia and militias, Iran had achieved much more long-term influence in Iraq than had the US.

Meanwhile in Afghanistan, after 2001 the US, their allies and Afghan forces succeeded in preventing Al Qaida from re-establishing any significant footprint in Afghanistan. The international community, particularly the US and its allies, all sought a positive future for Afghanistan. But their combined efforts were insufficient to reform the Afghan government and reverse an increasingly capable Taliban insurgency. And the perceived illegitimacy of the war in Iraq contaminated much of the international legitimacy that initially applied to the US-led effort to stabilize and reconstruct Afghanistan. Before 2009, the US preoccupation with Iraq also reduced Washington's ability to apply leadership and resources to the reconstruction and stabilization of Afghanistan.

President Obama ordered a surge of additional US forces to conduct intensified COIN operations in 2010 and 2011. He also authorized the successful US commando raid that killed Osama Bin Laden. In many tactical actions the Afghan Taliban were comprehensively defeated by US and NATO troops, particularly when they were able to bring overwhelming airpower to bear on insurgent fighters. But neither these military efforts, international attempts to make the Afghan government more effective and less corrupt, nor a US-led programme to greatly increase the capability of the Afghan security forces was sufficient to create an enduring increase in the Afghan people's support for the Kabul government.

These factors meant that once the US and NATO withdrew from combat operations in 2014, the Taliban was able to re-establish a significant footprint and regain considerable military initiative over Afghan government forces. From a position of weakness, the US negotiated a ceasefire deal with the Taliban, with no guarantees that the Taliban would stick to their side of the agreement, nor that the elected Kabul government's interests would be protected. As a result, the 2001 defeat of the Taliban has been almost completely reversed by the insurgents. At this moment no one has 'won' the war in Afghanistan but an emboldened Taliban could well overwhelm the current Afghan government and its forces, imposing a victors' peace that would give it the ability to reverse much of the last two decades of socio-political development.

The bleak conclusion is that for all the blood and money expended since 9/11, the US and its allies did not win the war in Iraq and have failed in the longer term to achieve almost all of their objectives in Afghanistan. The ferocity of the armed opposition in both countries was a strategic shock to the US and its allies, particularly for nations whose armed forces were unable to fight, or whose governments would not allow them to fight, either because of aversion to casualties arising from an unpopular conflict, or an unwillingness to be seen to engage in combat, as opposed to peacekeeping operations. For the US, UK and more widely in the West, the widespread perception of illegitimacy and intractability of the conflicts, the difficulty in achieving strategic success and the cost in blood and treasure resulted in a loss of confidence in the West in the utility of force. The political and military credibility and confidence of the US and its allies were damaged. These consequences live with us today.

WHAT THIS BOOK IS

This book explains the military dimension of these strategic failures. It is a story of many hard-fought tactical victories by US, Coalition and NATO troops and of equally hard fighting by insurgents and militias against international forces. These wars have been described by many journalists. There is no shortage of memoirs, from those of heads of government and top-level political and military leaders to those of company commanders, pilots and front-line soldiers. But there has been much less discussion of how the character of the wars evolved, and of the key battles and campaigns.

Both wars are full of lessons and of implications for the future of war. There were many battles that can usefully inform thinking about the capabilities required for future wars. This book seeks to fill these gaps, helping the reader see the military dimensions of the conflicts and their implications from fresh perspectives.

This book is an accessible military history of the two wars that shows how the character of both conflicts changed between 2001 and 2020. It seeks to illuminate the factors that explain the ebb and flow of the military campaigns identifying lessons, as necessary. As far as practicable, the book attempts to understand the decisions that were made in the context of the situation at the time. The book's centre of gravity is the military dimension of the wars. But, as with many other recent conflicts, these wars featured an intimate connection between the fighting and politics, in Iraq and Afghanistan, in Washington DC, in the other capitals of troop-contributing nations, in the Brussels Headquarters (HQ) of the NATO alliance, and in Damascus, Tehran and Islamabad. So, as well as covering the fighting, it explains relevant political developments that influenced the character of the armed conflicts and considers why it was that after the government forces of Taliban Afghanistan and Saddam Hussein's Iraq collapsed so rapidly, subsequent stabilization operations proved so difficult, and US, Coalition and NATO strategic objectives proved so hard to achieve.

Despite the fact that the forces of the US and its allies 'won' many tactical battles, the book judges that the wars must be considered strategic failures. It shows that the most important reason for this failure was that it took several years for the US and its allies to recognize that the ways and means being employed in both countries were inadequate to meet the strategic objectives set. This factor, combined with failures at every level to adapt quickly enough to unforeseen circumstances, provided opportunities that were exploited by insurgents and militias.

Both wars were led by the US and the great majority of forces were provided by Washington. Throughout the Iraq war the Coalition comprised the US and a variable constellation of allies. The US led this grouping, but the other members did not participate in a Coalition-wide decision-making body, so had no veto over US decision making.

Initially a similar approach was applied to the command and control of international forces in Afghanistan, but from 2003, an increasing proportion of troops came under command of NATO. In 2006 NATO assumed command of the bulk of international forces in Afghanistan and the Alliance's military plans were formulated and approved by consensus between NATO's member states, although some US and Coalition troops worked to a separate US led chain of command until 2010.

The UK played the key secondary role, as one of the two 'occupying powers' in Iraq in 2003–04 and the second-largest contributor of troops to both wars. This is reflected in the weight of discussion in the book. Other countries that contributed forces are not ignored, but the US and UK military experience makes up the bulk of the book.

A military history of these wars could have different perspectives, for example, the viewpoint of the Afghan Taliban, the commander of Quds Force (Iran's secretive proxy warfare organization), a Shia militant in Iraq, a leader of Al Qaida, a former warlord of the Afghan Northern Alliance, or of the defence ministry of a small European member of NATO. But to quote Christopher Tyerman's analysis of the Crusades, a series of wars that had equally disruptive effects on the Middle East and that also ended in strategic failure:

> the essential contours of the subject would, if observed dispassionately, look much the same, because the study is intended as a history, not a polemic …
>
> to look at a subject from a particular vantage point is to adopt a position in order to more clearly inspect the view. It does not mean taking sides.[1]

THE KEY COMPONENTS OF MODERN WARFARE

The reader will find it useful to understand some key concepts of modern armed conflict. War is a state of armed conflict between countries, or between armed groups within a country, or both. Warfare is the overall conduct of war by states or non-state actors. The German military thinker Carl von Clausewitz outlines two facets of war: its nature, which remains constant under all circumstances; and its character, the variable ways and means by which war is fought. This alters according to context.

Clausewitz showed that war's enduring nature is that of an inherently human activity that is always dangerous and is often chaotic. He saw that waging war is an act or expression of policy, undertaken to sustain a position of advantage, create a more advantageous situation, or change the attitudes or behaviour of another party. The simplest measure of the success of any war is the extent to which belligerents deem its political outcomes to be favourable. Armed actors are likely to employ a wide variety of military and non-military ways and means to achieve success.

All of these factors applied to both the Afghanistan and Iraq wars. The conflicts also demonstrated that war is a dynamic activity in which the opponents are constantly seeking to gain advantage over each other. Successful use of new technology or tactics by one actor usually resulted in their opponents attempting to develop counter-measures. If these succeeded, they provoked fresh adaptations by the enemy. So, these wars featured complex action/reaction dynamics, resulting in constant changes to their character.

THE LEVELS OF WAR

The military forces of NATO, the US and most other Western countries use the idea of *levels of war* to help show the way in which war is planned and conducted. In order of diminishing size of forces employed the levels are: strategic, operational and tactical.

At the highest level of government, a nation determines a national strategy that sets out strategic objectives or end states and assigns national ways and means to achieve them. These can be military actions, but also include diplomacy, intelligence and development activities. This is known as the national strategic level. In the US it is represented by the President, key Cabinet members such as the Secretary of Defence and Secretary of State, and top officials such as the Chairman of the Joint Chiefs of Staff, the senior serving officer in the Pentagon. The National Security Council provides a strategic forum to assist the President, run by the National Security Advisor.

US doctrine considers that below the national strategic level comes a military 'theater strategic level'. For the US this level is represented by 'combatant commands'. Throughout the period covered by this book Iraq and Afghanistan were the responsibility of US Central Command, universally known as CENTCOM. With its main base in Tampa,

Florida, CENTCOM was also responsible for US military operations in Egypt, the whole Arabian peninsula, Jordan, Syria, the Gulf, Iran, Pakistan and Central Asia.

Below the strategic level comes the operational level. Commanders at this level link strategy with tactics by establishing the military objectives needed to achieve the strategic objectives, including the required actions and the sequence in which they are to be conducted. This is where commanders and their staff develop campaigns to organize and employ military forces by integrating ends, ways and means. Campaigns aim to achieve strategic and operational objectives within a given time and space. The breadth, depth and complexity of the operational level requires commanders and their supporting staffs to draw on all of their knowledge, experience, creativity, judgement and military planning skills.

The operational level has been described by retired British General Lord David Richards as the 'vital gearing between tactical activity and the strategic level at which politicians and Chiefs of Defence operate. It is the level at which campaigns are run and where political intent is analysed and turned into military effect; it is where wars are won or lost, and it is demanding stuff'.[2]

Below the operational level sits the tactical level, the foundation level of war. Tactics is the employment of forces arranged in relation to time, space and each other. This level of war is where battles and engagements are planned and executed to achieve the military objectives assigned to tactical units. In the Iraq and Afghan wars the land tactical level extended downwards from divisions, through brigades, to battalions, their companies down to platoons, squads and individual soldiers, fighting vehicles and aircraft.

The term 'operation' is used by armed forces in several different ways. It is usually used to describe a sequence of tactical actions with a common purpose or unifying theme. This can include the movement, supply, attack, defence and manoeuvres needed to achieve the objective of any battle or campaign. A major operation is a series of tactical actions – such as battles, engagements and strikes – conducted by combat forces co-ordinated in time and space to achieve strategic or operational objectives.

The term is also used at the operational and strategic levels to describe designated tactical and operational activities and entire campaigns. International forces, their Iraqi and Afghan allies and NATO often gave campaigns and operations names. Some such as Operation *Iraqi Freedom,* the US name covering all combat operations in Iraq, applied to whole campaigns. At the other end of the spectrum names might cover a single battle, such as Operation *Medusa,* the 2006 Canadian-led attack on Taliban forces outside Kandahar.

This blurring of the meanings of the word 'operation' illustrates that during these wars there was often a considerable difference between theoretical and actual military practice. In reality, the boundaries between the levels of war often blurred and shifted. And events could often have simultaneous implications at all levels. The popular image from television and films of land battles is of fighting in a geographically small area lasting a day or several days, and these often give an appearance of linear dynamics where an effect follows on from an identifiable cause. Some of the battles in Iraq and Afghanistan conformed to this image: their contours would have been familiar to veterans of World War II. Others did not and were much more complicated non-linear operations and activities.

There is much description of fighting in the book. But it also sets out to explain the broader factors that led to the battles and operations of these wars. Such factors include the decisions made by military commanders and strategic leaders and the planning of operations. These were influenced by many considerations, including the actions of the enemy and the intelligence that suggested what the enemy was doing next; practical considerations of geography, time and logistics; and actual and anticipated friendly and civilian casualties. Where necessary, the book analyses these, to better explain why key battles happened when and where they did.

SOURCES

The seeds of this work were sown in 2009, when I was asked by the British Army to analyse land operations in Iraq, identifying lessons, particularly those relevant to the then ongoing British operations in Afghanistan. Basing myself at the Land Warfare Centre, hard by the bleak training areas of Salisbury Plain, I made extensive use of its large archive of post-tour reports and interviews.

As well as having discussions with many British officers who served in Iraq during the period, I sought input from the US Army and the

UK's other multinational partners. The Australian and Italian armies provided particularly useful insights. Key findings were discussed at the Iraq Lessons Conference held at the Land Warfare Centre in January 2010. This lasted for two days and had over a hundred participants. The lessons and insights were validated by a reference group of serving and retired general officers with extensive experience of the campaign. The report was also calibrated against the testimony of all the witnesses who gave evidence to the UK's Iraq Inquiry up to 29 July 2010. A redacted version of the report was released by the UK Ministry of Defence in 2016. From October 2010, when I joined the International Institute for Strategic Studies (IISS), I have been analysing the continuing wars in Iraq and Afghanistan. This has included discussions with US, UK and NATO politicians, officers and officials, as well as field trips to Pakistan and Afghanistan.

This work gave me a good understanding of the dynamics of the Iraq war. And the UK's independent Iraq Inquiry provides a cornucopia of testimony by politicians, officials and military officers that illuminates the higher management of the war. It gives a detailed and brutally unflattering picture of the strategic leadership and management of the British war in Iraq by Prime Ministers Tony Blair and Gordon Brown, as well as the roles of the UK Ministry of Defence, Chiefs of Staff, Foreign and Commonwealth Office and Department for international Development. There is also an abundance of US primary and secondary source material about both wars. This spans from the national strategic to tactical levels.

There is no shortage of reportage about the various militia and insurgent groups. And they all produced a vast amount of propaganda. But there is comparatively little authoritative research on these groups. And though the intelligence services of the US and its allies collected a great deal of intelligence about their opponents, much of this remains classified.

So, this book inevitably prioritizes the actions of US and international forces. It could be seen as similar to military histories of Germany's 1941–45 war on Russia that were written in the Cold War, before Moscow opened its state archives. Despite not having the full picture of Soviet planning, there were many good accounts that well explained how Germany lost that war. I'd ask readers to think of this book in the same way.

I am British, so the book uses English spelling. But the US spells some words differently. For example, the UK has a Ministry of Defence, whilst the US has a Department of Defense. Where I discuss US formations or units, I use US spelling.

All military operations in Iraq and Afghanistan were subject to great friction and uncertainty. The disintegration of Iraqi society and governance after the war contributed. Many Iraqis felt intensely frustrated that the Coalition was taking too long to improve their lot. And similar frustration was felt by many Afghans. The vast deserts of Iraq and southern Afghanistan and the harsh mountains of eastern Afghanistan were forbidding areas in which to move and live, let alone fight. In both countries the summer heat was an oppressive force of nature that can only be fully appreciated by those who soldiered through it – especially armoured vehicle crews. That so many members of the armed forces of the US and its allies achieved as much as they did in such difficult circumstances and in a war that was increasingly unpopular at home, is tribute to their training, leadership, ethos and dogged ability to soldier on in adversity. And we should not forget that many of those who fought for insurgents and militias often did so with great bravery, against Coalition forces who deployed vastly superior military technology.

Acknowledgements

Some of the ideas expressed in the book have already been aired in the British Army's Iraq Lessons report and in publications by the International Institute of Strategic Studies (IISS): the Adelphi books, *Survival*, *Strategic Survey* and *The Military Balance*. I am grateful to the editors of all three: Dana Allin, Alex Nicoll and James Hackett. I would particularly like to thank my IISS colleagues: General (retired) Lord David Richards, Lieutenant General (retired) H.R. McMaster, Jack Baker, Philip Barton, Desmond Bowen, Toby Dodge, Douglas Barrie, Nick Childs, Dr Bastian Giegerich, Maxime Humeau, Antoine Levesques, Nigel Inkster, Emile Hockayem, John Raine, Rahul Roy-Chaudhury, Viraj Solanki, Professor Sir Hew Strachan, Michael Tong and the IISS' excellent librarians. Especial thanks are due to General (retired) Dick Applegate and General Sir Nick Carter for sponsoring field trips to Afghanistan and to Colonel (retired) Alex Alderson PhD and Professor Theo Farrell for mentoring my research on both wars. And to Marcus Cowper and Laura Callaghan at Osprey and Robert Dudley, my excellent agent. Finally, to my wonderful family, Liz, Charlotte and Jamie for putting up with the opportunity costs of my writing. It's been far too long …

MAP 1: AFGHANISTAN, 2001

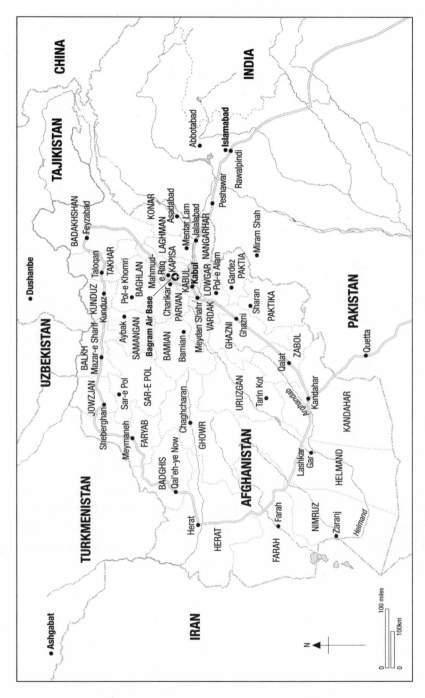

MAP 2: IRAQ, 2003

Before the Fall

The military experience of the US and its allies before 9/11

THE LEGACY OF VIETNAM

The Vietnam War became a national trauma for the US. It deeply divided the country and triggered an ever-increasing number of protests both against the war itself and against the conscription of young men. Many of those who protested the draft would probably have willingly fought against Nazi Germany or Imperial Japan in World War II. The war destroyed the career of US President Lyndon Johnson and deeply damaged the domestic reputation of the US Department of Defense – the Pentagon – and the US armed forces.

The signature of the 1973 Paris Peace Accords saw US forces withdraw from South Vietnam. Congress subsequently asserted itself by withdrawing funding for US support to the Saigon government. When in early 1975 North Vietnamese forces mounted all-out attack on South Vietnamese forces, the southern forces quickly collapsed. Amid scenes of panic, US diplomats and Marines were evacuated by helicopter from the roof of the US embassy in Saigon: US military humiliation was complete. The confidence of the US military was shaken, and its domestic standing and morale reached all-time lows. The US media, politicians and public lost confidence in the utility of military force.

At the same time, the rest of the US military was changing itself. The draft ended and the services changed into 'all volunteer' forces. Whilst

Vietnam had been the top priority for the best part of a decade, the US armed forces had of necessity reduced the priority they afforded to fulfil the roles assigned to them in a potential conflict between NATO and the Warsaw Pact.

As the US armed forces began to refocus on these missions, the 1973 Yom Kippur War erupted between Israel and an Arab coalition of Egypt and Syria. Taken by surprise, Israel was evicted from its well-prepared defensive positions along the Suez Canal and nearly lost control of the Golan Heights. Counter-attacks by the Israeli Army restored the status quo ante and ended the war. But it had been a close-run thing. As US officers analysed the conflict they noted the unprecedented intensity of the fighting. Although outnumbered, Israeli forces prevailed through superior training, tactical leadership and some superior equipment, especially that rushed to Israel by United States Air Force (USAF) transports after the war began.

Analysis of the Yom Kippur war deeply influenced the leadership of the US Army. It rebuilt its leadership, confidence and sense of self-worth. This included an increasing willingness to remove inadequate leaders. Seeking to improve training, it created training centres where laser weapons effects simulators and expert 'observer-controllers' greatly increased the realism and effectiveness of field exercises. The National Training Center in Fort Irwin, California allowed complete brigades to train against a dedicated opposing force. Equipped with vehicles visually modified to simulate Soviet armoured vehicles, a dedicated opposing force regiment employed Soviet tactics and often beat the visiting US troops.

Before the Vietnam War, the US Army's main effort had been preparing for a major war in Europe between the Soviet Union and its Warsaw Pact allies and the US and its NATO allies. For over a decade Vietnam had taken priority, but from 1975, the US Army's priority returned to preparing for the Cold War turning hot. The Army determined to rebuild its conventional military capabilities and doctrine to better prepare it for when the confrontation between the two blocs might turn to armed conflict. This saw the development of new operational and tactical doctrine.

The US Army's Training and Doctrine Command (TRADOC) and its commander General Don Starry were instrumental in providing both the leadership and energy to lead the many changes that the US Army had to make. There was increasing interest in the operational level of war and the planning and conduct of campaigns. This interest saw the US Army set up a School of Advanced Military Studies. Here a small number of specially selected mid-ranking officers would have a year's intensive education in military history and campaigning. They would form a cadre of high-level planners.

A key agent of change was to be doctrine. New overarching doctrine for US Army operations was contained in Field Manual 100-5 'Operations'. Initially published in 1982, its central message was the need for the US Army to prevail against the much larger Soviet Army by being able to 'fight outnumbered and win'. Central to this was the concept of the Air Land Battle. This envisaged an aggressive defence where the US Army and Air Force used their superior technology and training to offset their likely enemy's numerical advantage to achieve a level of attrition that would break up attacking Soviet formations.

The numerically superior Soviet ground forces were seen as less thoroughly trained than the US Army, with a more rigid command style and much military technology that the US considered was inferior to theirs. These weaknesses would be exploited by the factors that the US Army considered its strengths: superior training, more flexible commanders and superior technology. It would be particularly important for the US Army to be able to exploit the increasingly modernized US Air Force – not only providing close support to US Army units, but also interdicting the Soviet reinforcements as they moved west.

Following lessons learned on US and NATO exercises the Field Manual was revised in the 1986 edition to place much more emphasis on manoeuvre than on attrition. The differences between the two approaches to war would be important factors in both Iraq and Afghanistan.

Attrition is a simple form of war in which both sides directly fight each other, seeking to inflict maximum damage. Both sides are directly pitting their strengths against each other, with physical destruction being the primary means of success.

Manoeuvre is a more dynamic form of war, which seeks to pit strength against weakness. It emphasizes initiative, the destruction of enemy will and cohesion, surprise and deception. For land forces to achieve this they must be able to rapidly move around the battlefield, dispersing to avoid enemy air and artillery attacks, but rapidly concentrating forces to attack enemy vulnerabilities. This requires well-trained commanders who are willing to take risks and decide and act quickly. Hence the emphasis on increasing the realism of training in simulated battle conditions against an unforgiving enemy.

Of equal importance to the new doctrine was the way in which the Air Land Battle concept informed the development of new fighting equipment for the US Army, whose inventory of 1950s and 1960s vintage equipment was increasingly obsolete, with insufficient mobility, protection and firepower to manoeuvre against Soviet forces. The Army took advantage of the increase in defence spending by the government of new US President Ronald Reagan to launch a major programme of equipment modernization. The US Army prioritized its 'Big Five' new weapons: these included the M1 Abrams tank and the M2 Bradley, a fighting vehicle for mechanized infantry with a 25mm Bushmaster cannon and turret-launched TOW anti-tank missiles. The third weapon was a new artillery capability: the Multiple Launch Rocket System (MLRS), a self-propelled lightly armoured rocket launcher. Each launcher fired 12 227mm rockets. A single launcher could blanket an area about half a mile square with its firepower. A battery of nine MLRS launchers firing simultaneously could have the same firepower effect as 33 battalions of conventional gun artillery.

The final two systems of the 'Big Five' were helicopters. As a result of the Vietnam War the US Army had more helicopters than any other army in the world. The fighting had demonstrated the great utility of transport helicopters and the potential utility of helicopters armed with anti-tank missiles. The ubiquitous Huey utility helicopter would be replaced by the Black Hawk assault helicopter, with a much higher level of protection. And the Huey Cobra attack helicopters that had been rushed into service for the Vietnam War would be replaced by the formidable Apache attack helicopter, probably the most sophisticated fighting system in US Army service in Iraq and Afghanistan.

At the same time the US Air Force was also modernizing itself. The final stages of the Vietnam War had seen the use of the first laser-guided bombs. These were shown to have considerable utility, not least in destroying bridges in North Vietnam that US air attacks had failed to destroy with conventional 'dumb' bombs. After Vietnam these capabilities were further developed.

The US Air Force had also had many aircraft shot down by North Vietnamese anti-aircraft missiles. Soviet forces in Europe had large numbers of radars and anti-aircraft weapons, both guns and missiles.

A side effect of this was that the North Vietnamese captured many airmen who had successfully ejected from their stricken aircraft. These became another source of unwelcome pressure on the White House and Pentagon.

The US Air Force adopted two complementary approaches to countering Soviet air defences. The first was to continue to field dedicated aircraft and missiles for the suppression of enemy air defences. So-called Wild Weasel aircraft were dedicated to this mission. The second was to develop aircraft that could evade detection by radar. An enormous effort was made to develop 'stealth' technology. This was first fielded on the specially designed F117 Nighthawk fighter-bomber and later on the B2 Spirit intercontinental bomber.

Another initiative was the development of unmanned aerial vehicles (UAVs). So-called 'drones' had long been used as targets for guns and missiles during training. And thousands of sorties by unmanned reconnaissance aircraft had been flown over North Vietnam to photograph potential targets. About 10 per cent were shot down, but with no pilot to capture, the US Air Force judged the risk to be acceptable. During the 1980s the US Air Force, US Navy and the Central Intelligence Agency (CIA) all experimented with a variety of UAVs, some developed indigenously, others purchased from Israel.

In parallel with the improvement of US Army and Air Force capabilities, the capabilities of US special operations forces were being expanded and improved. This began inauspiciously with an operation to rescue US hostages in Iran that failed. The operation was mounted in response to the taking of US hostages by the newly formed Islamic Republic of Iran. In 1980 President Jimmy Carter authorized an operation to rescue the US diplomats and civilians held hostage in Tehran. The US had recently formed a special forces unit for countering terrorism and rescuing hostages. Modelled on the British Special Air Service (SAS), the Special Forces Operation Detachment Delta, known as 'Delta Force'.

Delta Force developed an audacious plan to rescue the hostages, Operation *Eagle Claw*. But it required the Delta Force commandos to be delivered to Tehran in helicopters, which the unit had not worked with before. These would be refuelled by C130 Hercules tankers from another unit at the isolated airstrip christened Desert One. In the event, a helicopter collided with a Hercules at the air strip. Troops and aircrew were killed and the mission abandoned. Iranian media coverage of the site, including displaying the charred remains of US servicemen, created another military humiliation. It contributed to President Carter's defeat in the 1980 US presidential election.

In the Philippines, Stanley McChrystal as a young US Army Special Forces officer was asked by a Philippine Army colleague to explain how the most powerful country on earth botched Operation *Eagle Claw*. At the time McChrystal could not do so. Later, answers came from an independent special commission.[1] Its report assessed that whilst the plan to rescue the hostages in Tehran was feasible, the joint task force formed to conduct the operation was too ad hoc. It failed to carry out a full mission rehearsal for all the components of the task force in the US, prior to deployment. These factors meant that the chances of overall mission success were greatly reduced. Reflecting later on the mission McChrystal assessed that the operation was:

America's first attempt at a new type of special operations warfare characterised by politically sensitive, complex, fast, joint operations. Its failure largely owed to insufficient bandwidth of every type … The assembled teams were not a bonded joint force, as they had not operated, or even fully rehearsed, together before crossing into Iranian airspace … The calamity of Desert One was not a failure of political or military courage. The failure occurred beforehand when the military failed to build and maintain the force necessary to accomplish these kinds of missions.[2]

The Pentagon got the message and the US Special Operations Command (SOCOM) was established. This was a permanently constituted unified joint command that contained all US Army, Navy and Air Force Special Operations Forces (SOF) and helicopters and transport aircraft dedicated to their support. It also had dedicated US Army and USAF helicopters and C130 Hercules aircraft. Delta Force and an elite team of US Navy sea, air and land (SEAL) commandos were incorporated into the Joint Special Operations Command (JSOC), a secretive organization whose primary role was counter-terrorism and hostage rescue. By the later 1980s considerable resources had been invested and extensive training conducted. Specialist equipment had been procured, including satellite communications and a family of helicopters that could be carried inside transport aircraft, and rapidly prepared to carry commandos to attack terrorists and rescue hostages. This meant that JSOC was not only capable of conducting hostage rescue missions as demanding as that planned in 1981 but was also in a position to perform a demanding range of precision strikes on terrorists and other targets.[3]

INCREASING EMPHASIS ON JOINT OPERATIONS

Throughout the 1980s there was increased emphasis on the need for the four US Services to work better together. This had been highlighted by the failure of Operation *Eagle Claw*. And a brief operation in 1983 in which Marines, Rangers, SOF and paratroops intervened to overthrow the pro-Cuba left-wing government in Grenada, although successful, had highlighted considerable weaknesses in co-operation between the four services. This reflected an old-fashioned approach where such co-operation was essentially voluntary.

A major consequence was the passage of new legislation to modernize US military strategic command and control, the 1986 Goldwater-Nichols Act. This simplified strategic command, with the Chairman of the Joint Chiefs of Staff now appointed by the Secretary of Defense, instead of being elected by the service chiefs themselves. The individual service chiefs would be responsible for force generation: forming, equipping, manning and training their forces. They would still be members of the Joint Chiefs' committee, but their role would be limited to advising the Chairman.

Standing 'combat commanders' would be created, who, using their HQs, would have authority over large regions of the globe. As standing joint commands, they would employ the forces assigned to them by the Pentagon. One of these was US Central Command (CENTCOM), responsible for US operations in the greater Middle East.

New legislation strengthened the role of the Defense Secretary and the Pentagon, making the Chairman of the Joint Chiefs of Staff the sole military advisor to the President, National Security Council and Defense Secretary. It also established that the chain of command ran from the President as commander in chief of the US armed forces, through the Defense Secretary to the commanders of the combatant commands. The Chairman of the Joint Chiefs would only direct the combatant commander if the Defense Secretary wanted him to do so.

A late-1989 operation to remove Panamanian president Noriega from power saw these arrangements tested operationally for the first time. Army General Max Thurman, commander of US Southern Command, exercised full operational control over US Army, Navy, Marine Corps, Air Force and special operations forces assigned to him. In a well-planned and rapidly executed operation Thurman's forces rapidly achieved their military objectives, demonstrating that inter-service co-operation had greatly improved since Operation *Eagle Claw* and the invasion of Grenada.

THE BRITISH EXPERIENCE

These US developments were followed with keen interest by many of their allies and by the NATO alliance. The development of the US Army had a major influence on the British Army, which saw itself as the preferred partner for US land operations. The British land forces had spent much of the 1970s deploying large numbers of troops to counter insurgents and terrorists in Northern Ireland. Between 1970 and 1977, the army was the only effective security force in the areas of Northern Ireland that had a predominantly Catholic working-class population. This required deployment of a large division-sized land force in Northern Ireland, with many of the required units taken out of the formations they were assigned to and deployed to Northern Ireland on short operational tours. This greatly reduced the ability of the army to train for its NATO role. In 1977 a UK security strategy for Northern Ireland was agreed among the British government, the British Army and the Royal Ulster Constabulary (RUC). The so-called 'Way Ahead' aimed to 'normalize' security in the province, with the police increasingly taking the lead for security. This strategy succeeded with police capability increasing and the requirement for army units gradually reducing.

This allowed the army to improve its effort to prepare its units and formations for their NATO role. The emerging US Army concept of Air Land Battle was closely studied by the British. Under the leadership of General (later Field Marshal) Sir Nigel Bagnall, the army's plans for its role in a prospective NATO/Warsaw Pact war in Europe placed less emphasis on attrition and more on manoeuvre. Bagnall directed that army tactical doctrine be rewritten to reflect this increased emphasis on manoeuvre, a key concept that applied to British operations after the

Cold War. It became easier to execute as 1960s-era armoured vehicles were replaced in the late 1980s by the new Challenger tank and Warrior armoured infantry fighting vehicle.

Bagnall was the most reformist peacetime British Army chief of the 20th century. He sought to make the army approach to command much more flexible and responsive, particularly stressing the importance of simpler and more agile command and control, the philosophy of 'mission command'. This was to improve the Army's agility and speed of decision making and action in war.

It is quite possible in peacetime for commanders to use modern communication systems to micro-manage the activities of their subordinates. But in war the enemy will attack communications and HQs and will seek to move at a tempo faster than the speed at which the other side can react. The alternative to micro-managed command is 'mission command', a philosophy of command that is more flexible and less prescriptive. It encourages commanders to give their subordinates not only a simple, clear mission, but also the maximum freedom of action to conduct it, allowing them to make full use of their greater knowledge of the local situation than any higher HQs. The concept sought to reduce the time to plan and then implement military missions, thus increasing tempo.

Bagnall initiated a wide range of reforms, for example in the training and selection of senior commanders. A new Higher Command and Staff Course was created to educate the brightest and best officers in the higher-level conduct of war, particularly at the operational level. It was greatly informed by the US School of Advanced Military Studies.

THE 1990S – AFTER THE COLD WAR

The November 1989 fall of the Berlin Wall symbolized the end of the Soviet Union's political and military hegemony over its satellite states in Eastern Europe. This was rapidly followed by the break-up of the Soviet Union itself.

The unexpected 1990 Iraqi invasion and occupation of Kuwait was a strategic shock. The US allied with countries across Europe and the Middle East for Operation *Desert Shield*, the protection of Saudi Arabia from further Iraqi aggression. Not since the Korean War had such a broad international military alliance been assembled.

In practice there were two separate military coalitions. The multi-national Arab force of formations from Saudi Arabia, Kuwait, Egypt, Syria, Oman, Qatar and the United Arab Emirates was commanded by a Saudi Arabian prince. The US was joined by other international forces including Argentina, Belgium, Canada, France and the UK, the UK being the second-largest contributor of ground, maritime and air forces. This second coalition was directed by US CENTCOM and its commander, the indomitable US General Norman Schwarzkopf. US Defense Secretary Dick Cheney chose to exercise strategic command through Chairman of the Joint Chiefs General Colin Powell.

After Iraq refused to withdraw its forces, Operation *Desert Storm* began with an air campaign that saw widespread use of precision weapons, especially cruise missiles and laser-guided bombs. The aircraft and air defences of the Iraqi Air Force were quickly overmatched by the US, UK and Saudi air forces, whose aircraft, crews and commanders were far better equipped, trained and led.

After five weeks of air attacks, a ground offensive of little more than 100 hours' duration evicted Iraqi forces from Kuwait and destroyed many Iraqi ground forces in southern Iraq. About 20,000 Iraqi troops were thought to have been killed, with over 50,000 taken prisoner, at a cost of fewer than 250 Coalition personnel killed.

The decisive role was played by two US Marine divisions, seven US Army divisions, five of which were armoured or mechanized, and a smaller UK armoured division. All had fighting vehicles, weapons and equipment that were more modern and capable than their Iraqi Army equivalents. There were even greater differentials of doctrine, leadership and training.

Nowhere was this better displayed than in the battle of 93 Easting. This was a clash between the US Army's 2nd Armoured Cavalry Regiment and two Iraqi Army brigades. In a fierce six-hour battle, the greatly outnumbered US unit destroyed large numbers of Iraqi tanks, other armoured vehicles and infantry positions.[4]

Coalition ground forces lacked numerical superiority over Iraqi ground forces. Under such circumstances the Iraqis should have been able to impose far higher casualties than they did. Instead Coalition casualties were remarkably light, but all Iraqi units and formations attacked by US and British formations were destroyed. Part of the reason for this was technological superiority. Particularly important were long-range thermal sights on Coalition tanks, which allowed Iraqi vehicles and positions to be destroyed from ranges beyond the Iraqis' ability to return effective fire. And the US Global Positioning System (GPS) greatly assisted navigation across the featureless flat deserts of southern Iraq and allowed artillery strikes to be fully integrated with ground manoeuvre.[5]

The other key factor was a considerable differential in military skill. US and British forces were much better trained than their Iraqi equivalents. Although the campaign was very different in character to the potential war between the Warsaw Pact and NATO for which US and UK forces had trained and prepared, many of the capabilities and approaches employed in Iraq and Kuwait were those that had been developed for that scenario. Just as importantly, US and UK leaders, from corporal to general, had rapidly adapted to the unfamiliar environment and novel plan. In contrast, Iraqi military leadership was weak and appeared wedded to an over-centralized command system and defensive tactics that had worked in the Iran–Iraq war of the 1980s.

Many in the US military considered that Operation *Desert Storm* had laid to rest the ghosts of the Vietnam War. The US forces had displayed considerable fighting spirit and had defeated the Iraqi forces with far fewer US casualties than expected. And the defeat of a numerically larger Iraqi Army in little more than a hundred hours was recognized as a victory of historic proportions.

Many of the weapons developed by the US Air Force played key roles in Operation *Desert Storm*. These included cruise missiles, laser-guided bombs and stealth aircraft. The US Army considered that the 'Big Five' key systems fielded in the 1980s had been essential to its success. Both services also considered that their success had vindicated the doctrines that the two services had developed to exploit the capabilities of their modernized forces. The US military assessed that the campaign had vindicated the post-Vietnam effort to improve the ability of the armed forces to operate together in a single joint campaign planned and executed by a joint commander and joint HQ. The investments made in developing realistic training and joint doctrine and in understanding the operational art had repaid themselves, with interest.

But in achieving the remarkable military transformation in the 1980s that made this possible, the US Army had deliberately walked away from some of the hard lessons of Vietnam. The revolution in training and doctrine of the 1980s deliberately emphasized state versus state warfare, and de-emphasized insurgency and counter-insurgency. Interest was maintained in US Army SOF and in the US Marine Corps, who had always seen 'small wars' as a core role. But for most of the US Army's leadership it seemed that Vietnam was an exceptional case that could be safely set aside while the US Army prepared for large-scale conventional war fighting.

Operations *Desert Shield* and *Desert Storm* had been unexpected. Equally unpredicted was the US mission to Somalia. Launched in late 1992 as a US intervention to protect the delivery of humanitarian aid to the failed state on the Horn of Africa, it created the conditions for the subsequent deployment of a United Nations (UN) force. A US military contingent remained. Its mission evolved into an armed conflict between a US SOF task force and General Aideed, a Somali warlord.[6]

As vividly depicted in the film *Black Hawk Down*, a US SOF raid in October 1993 to capture General Aideed ran into unexpectedly heavy opposition where the Somali militias' sheer numbers and willingness to fight and die overmatched the elite Delta Force and US Rangers. The resulting US casualties prompted withdrawal of the US force, but not before these events had resulted in the resignation of President Clinton's first defense secretary. This, along with the controversy surrounding Clinton's electoral pledge to allow gay and bisexual people to serve in the US military and a perception that Clinton had dodged the draft, all made it less, rather than more, likely that Clinton would deploy the US military, other than for missions where the chances of US casualties were minimal. This influenced the US military's approach to subsequent missions during the 1990s. Protection of the troops became the top priority of the missions. They would deploy into heavily fortified bases. Troops leaving the bases would wear the maximum amount of personal protective equipment: helmets and body armour. This policy of 'force protection' was to apply to US overseas deployments for the next quarter of a century.

In 1991 and 1992 the state of Yugoslavia broke up in a series of complex and overlapping wars. These were of a vicious character, where the international media showed abundant evidence of 'ethnic cleansing', prisoner abuse, war crimes and resulting large-scale flows of refugees. Such scenes had not been seen in Europe since the end of World War II and public and political opinion in the US and NATO and EU states was outraged.

Between 1992 and 1995 the best efforts of the international community seemed utterly incapable of negotiating a political settlement to the apparently intractable war in Bosnia. A UN force was deployed, initially to protect delivery of humanitarian aid. It was successful in this but was unable to change the fundamental drivers and dynamics of an increasingly intractable civil war.

British and French troops played a leading role in the so-called UN Protection Force (UNPROFOR). They soon found themselves operating beyond the narrow boundary of the mandate, seeking to reduce tension and limit the consequences of fighting. They did this by acting both to face down ruthless and unscrupulous warlords and to promote local ceasefires and negotiations between the sides.

By May 1995 UNPROFOR's position had become unsustainable. Fighting was intense. During the summer the Bosnian Serbs took UN troops hostage and attacked the Bosnian Muslim enclave of Srebrenica. Thousands of captured men and boys were deliberately massacred. The UK, France and the Netherlands created a rapid reaction force capable of combat, as opposed to peacekeeping, operations.

In late August, Bosnian Serb military positions were attacked by British, French and Dutch artillery of the UN Rapid Reaction Force. NATO aircraft joined the attacks. These strikes and changes on the battlefield brought about a ceasefire and created a unique window of opportunity for US diplomat Richard Holbrooke to negotiate the Dayton Peace Agreement, which set the political and military framework that has remained in place ever since. The agreement required the forces of the three warring factions to disengage and withdraw from the front line. NATO was to supervise and, if necessary, enforce this. The tensions and uncertainties of 1995 and the apprehension about NATO's very first land operation are now largely forgotten. Would the warring armies comply with the agreement so hastily negotiated at Dayton? Would NATO troops suffer the same non-co-operation, harassment and attacks as UN forces? Would NATO have to use force? Would there be casualties?

In the event the deployment of 60,000 NATO ground troops over December 1995 and January 1996 proceeded successfully. The Bosnian warring factions were given the confidence they needed to withdraw from the frontline, disarm and demobilize. There was no armed opposition to NATO troops and thus no NATO combat casualties, although land mines and the hazards of Bosnia's extremely dangerous roads took their toll. This was NATO's first ever land operation and its nations and their armies took satisfaction from the success of the operation.[7]

Whilst NATO's military mission had large numbers of troops and practically unlimited military authority, the complementary civilian mission mandated by the Dayton Agreement was much less well resourced. Carl Bildt, the first civilian High Representative to take charge of the civilian mission sought to move Bosnian politics away from the previous toxic nationalism towards the interethnic polity envisaged in the Dayton Agreement. A particular issue was that whilst the Bosnian Serb republic's legal government in Banja Luka was relatively liberal and co-operative, in 1997 Bosnian Serb nationalist hard-line supporters of the previous president and indicted war criminal Radovan Karadzic mounted direct challenges both to their government in Banja Luka and to NATO and the High Representative's authority. They attempted to stage a coup and Bosnian Serb government radio spewed out vicious propaganda. British troops acted to block the buses full of hard-line agitators and mounted raids on people and organizations that supported Karadzic, seizing arms and ammunition. US troops blocked the hostile radio stations. British and US troops had thwarted an extremist coup. But they had pushed close to the limit of their mandate.

The crisis had seen NATO troops successfully act in support of a clear political objective. But it revealed that the civilian High Representative lacked any tools to influence Bosnian politics. He therefore was granted additional powers, including the ability to impose laws and to dismiss public officials.[8] These tools proved essential in achieving progress in terms of both politics and security over the next decade, particularly when wielded by High Representative Paddy Ashdown, although after his tenure progress stalled.

A UN civil police mission was the focus of international efforts to root out extremists from the various Bosnian police forces and to reform law enforcement throughout the country, turning the various police forces from paramilitary militias to modern police forces. This was successful and by 2003 the Bosnian Police was certified by the UN as meeting minimum international standards.

Soon afterwards the situation in the Serbian province of Kosovo deteriorated. An independence movement amongst the Muslim Kosovars was met with violent repression by the Serb security forces and increasingly took on the character of an insurrection. European nations and the US saw the seeds of another violent civil war. Determined to do better at preventing another Balkan war, they brokered negotiations for a peace deal. These failed and in March 1999, NATO began air and missile strikes to compel Serb president Slobodan Milosevic to change the behaviour of his government's forces.

NATO anticipated that the campaign would be over relatively quickly. But Serb forces in Kosovo made effective use of dispersal, camouflage and deception and it took much longer than NATO had expected to impose the necessary punishment to get the Serbs to negotiate a withdrawal of Serb forces from Kosovo and their replacement by NATO's Kosovo Force (KFOR). When in mid-June 1999 KFOR entered Kosovo, they were greeted as liberators by the Muslim majority population. But NATO found that most local governance and security institutions had collapsed. The UN Mission in Kosovo (UNMIK) was brought in to fill the gap, taking the lead for civil administration, policing and justice. It also provided a UN civilian police force.

US troops again deployed on a stabilization mission. But in both Bosnia and Kosovo their troops put considerable effort into protecting themselves, much more so than did other NATO contingents. This greatly reduced the number of US troops that could deploy onto the ground outside their lavishly appointed bases. These measures reduced their ability to interact with the local people and thus undermined their operational effectiveness. The situation reflected great caution in the Clinton government, born of the political damage inflicted by the 1994 US defeat in Somalia. Some perceptive US commanders worried that force protection was not supporting the mission, rather it had become part of the mission.[9]

The next year the UK intervened in Sierra Leone. Despite deployment of a UN peacekeeping mission a violent civil war had almost destroyed the former British West African colony. Freetown, the capital, was on the verge of falling to the brutally violent Revolutionary United Front. Initially British SOF and a parachute battalion were deployed to evacuate British civilians.

Having completed this mission Brigadier David Richards, the commander of the joint task force, saw an opportunity to tip the balance of the conflict in favour of government forces. By retaining a visible presence of boots on the ground around Freetown, pushing special forces patrols forward of the city and aligning British troops with remaining pro-government forces, he was able to intimidate the various anti-government forces and restore the confidence of the UN contingent.

This success was reinforced by demonstrations of force by a Royal Navy task group which also landed Royal Marines. Threats of the use of force had great effect. These were reinforced by the destruction of an advance party of rebels by the parachute pathfinder platoon and by a subsequent special forces raid to rescue British soldiers taken hostage by the West Side Boys militia.

The intervention had featured rapid reaction at long range, calculated risk taking, integration of land, sea, air and special forces, information operations and the selective use of force. The British military were praised by Prime Minister Tony Blair and by many US military commentators.

The Bosnia, Kosovo and Sierra Leone interventions all succeeded. Casualties to the intervening forces were relatively low. Throughout the armed forces and defence ministries of the US, UK and their allies that had contributed troops there was a sense of pride that the interventions had made a positive difference. Together with obvious professional satisfaction and pride displayed by the armed forces that had participated, this contributed to widespread support from the public, media and politicians.

In this warm glow of satisfaction, the international forces involved conducted little objective analysis of why they had succeeded with so few casualties. Perhaps the most important factor was the great differential of military capability, where the advantage was overwhelmingly with the international forces. The Bosnian factions' military and the various rebel forces in Sierra Leone were of lower overall military effectiveness and were easily overmatched by the superior capabilities, leadership, training and quality of the intervening western forces.[10]

This assessment was notably absent from discussion and analysis within the armed forces of the US and UK. Instead they were confident that Bosnia, Kosovo, and Sierra Leone represented the kind of operations that they were most likely to have to conduct in the future.

Largely absent also was recognition that, important as the role of NATO's forces in Bosnia and Kosovo had been, political action had been equally important. Discussion on the character of future conflict tended to assume the primacy of the military and downplay or ignore the political dimension. There developed a tendency in the militaries of both the US and UK to assume that achieving political effects was the responsibly of politicians. These attitudes widened the gap between the military and politicians, leading to a lack of government-level discussion about how both could better work together in future stabilization operations, and particularly about how diplomats and development agencies could best co-operate with the military in an operational theatre.[11]

By 2001 the British military displayed a great deal of professional satisfaction. It was pleased with itself that following Operation *Desert Storm* its interventions in Bosnia, Kosovo and Sierra Leone had succeeded and had been supported by politicians the public and the media. It thought that future operations were most likely to be peace enforcement. At the newly created Joint Services Command and Staff College, the teaching of insurgency and counter-insurgency was largely abandoned, displaced in the syllabus by the teaching of doctrine for peace enforcement.

THE REVOLUTION IN MILITARY AFFAIRS

Although defence budgets of the US and its NATO allies were reduced after the end of the Cold War both armed forces and defence manufacturers continued to press for further modernization. Many armed forces, defence manufacturers and military theorists assessed that the US and its allies were in the midst of a 'Revolution in Military Affairs' (RMA). The central proposition of the persuasive advocates of the RMA concept was that the considerable improvements being made in reconnaissance and surveillance, digital communications and precision strike weapons would act together to produce superior intelligence of the enemy, and more accurate and effective strikes and manoeuvre.

Equally important was development of reconnaissance and surveillance capabilities, ranging from satellites through airborne radars to signals intelligence. Also required would be improved digital command and control systems to allow commanders to lead and staffs to co-ordinate the complex military choreography necessary to safely deploy both large land forces and hundreds of aircraft. Increased networking, it was felt, would increase the military advantages enjoyed by the US and its allies. A modernized networked force exploiting RMA technologies would gain decisive advantage over a less modern one.

Operation *Desert Storm* in Iraq in 1991, the 1995 employment of NATO airpower against Bosnian Serb forces and the 1999 Kosovo air campaign were all considered to have reinforced the RMA approach. The UK and many European nations held that the Bosnia air strikes and subsequent NATO land operation and the Kosovo intervention had both re-affirmed the importance of the NATO alliance.

But many key US military leaders and commentators felt that the Kosovo war had exposed considerable weaknesses in the NATO alliance. It had, they believed, added limited military value, and had instead imposed friction and delay. For example, the European members of NATO lacked the necessary drone, satellite reconnaissance, precision weapons and air defence suppression capabilities. These deficiencies had to be made up by the US. The Pentagon also found that NATO's consensual decision making constrained the prosecution of the war. A frustration for US commanders was that all the member states had the right to veto military decisions, including selection of targets, even if they were not taking part in the war.

INTERVENTION AND NATION BUILDING — TRANSATLANTIC DIVERGENCE

The experiences of Bosnia and Kosovo were interpreted differently on both sides of the Atlantic. This was vividly illustrated by the stark differences in approach by UK Prime Minister Tony Blair and newly elected President George W. Bush.

In April 1999 at the height of the Kosovo war Blair made a speech in Chicago to explain that he saw NATO's Kosovo intervention as:

a just war based not on any territorial ambitions but on values. We cannot let the evil of ethnic cleansing stand. We must not rest until it is reversed. We have learned twice before in this century that appeasement does not work. If we let an evil dictator range unchallenged, we will have to spill infinitely more blood and treasure to stop him later.[12]

He then set out his doctrine for military intervention:

> So how do we decide when and whether to intervene? I think we
> need to bear in mind five major considerations.
>
> First, are we sure of our case? War is an imperfect instrument for
> righting humanitarian distress; but armed force is sometimes the
> only means of dealing with dictators. Second, have we exhausted
> all diplomatic options? We should always give peace every chance,
> as we have in the case of Kosovo. Third, on the basis of a practical
> assessment of the situation, are there military operations we can
> sensibly and prudently undertake? Fourth, are we prepared for the
> long term? In the past we talked too much of exit strategies. But
> having made a commitment we cannot simply walk away once the
> fight is over; better to stay with moderate numbers of troops than
> return for repeat performances with large numbers. And finally, do
> we have national interests involved? ...
>
> I am not suggesting that these are absolute tests. But they are the
> kind of issues we need to think about in deciding in the future when
> and whether we will intervene.

Blair's view that international forces could not simply walk away
after intervention would not be shared by the government of new
US President George W. Bush and his key advisors. As presidential
candidate, Bush had repeatedly made his aversion to nation building
clear. For example, at an October 2000 debate he had said:

> I think what we need to do is convince people who live in the lands
> they live in to build the nations. Maybe I'm missing something here.
> I mean, we're going to have kind of a nation building corps from
> America? Absolutely not. Our military's meant to fight and win war.
> That's what it's meant to do. And when it gets over extended, morale
> drops.[13]

Defense Secretary Donald Rumsfeld had also declared himself viscerally
opposed to the US conducting 'nation building'. He and Bush sought
to reduce the use of US armed forces for such missions. They felt that
long-term stabilization operations such as Bosnia and Kosovo had
locked the US military into long-term open-ended commitments that

greatly reduced military strategic flexibility. These missions were seen as symbolizing the Clinton administration's strategic incompetence and vacuous liberal values. They wanted to make US forces more agile and rapidly deployable and responsive, by exploiting the RMA and by withdrawing from nation-building commitments. For example, Bush called for European troops to replace US forces in the Balkans so that 'we can withdraw our troops and focus our military on fighting and winning war'.[14] Bush and Rumsfeld also wanted to free up resources for the US military to transform itself by exploiting the revolution in military affairs.

Testifying to Congress in January 2001 Rumsfeld stated that 'I don't think it's necessarily true that the United States has to become a great peacekeeper'.[15] In a subsequent 2003 speech 'Beyond Nation Building', he articulated a view that an extended US troop commitment had created a culture of dependency in Kosovo and that, having conducted an intervention operation, US troops should depart as soon as possible.[16] But Bush, Rumsfeld and other advocates of US military disengagement from stabilization missions never convincingly explained how necessary political progress in Bosnia and Kosovo would have been achieved without US and NATO troops and supporting political action.

Strategic Shock and Response

Afghanistan from 9/11 to Operation *Anaconda*

SURPRISE ATTACK AND UNEXPECTED COUNTER-ATTACK

The attacks came out of clear blue sky. It is easy to forget the shock of the hijacked airliners flying into the twin towers of the World Trade Centre at the tip of Manhattan Island, in full view of the Statue of Liberty, both locations turned into icons by countless films, television series and the mental, physical and electronic images carried away by the millions of US and foreign tourists who visited New York every year. Then there was the airliner that struck the side of another US icon, the Pentagon. Throughout that terrible, shocking day bad news accumulated: a mixture of facts, rumours, soundbites, video grabs, headlines, news anchors interviewing experts, commentators and talking heads. There were phone calls made by people trapped on the floors of both towers, images of people jumping to escape the flames, to achieve a momentary respite before certain death, and the phone calls and voicemails from passengers in the four doomed flights.

There was also a slowly dawning realization that amongst the shock, horror, carnage, smoke, fire, choking dust and destruction there were stories of courage, duty and heroism. New York's Mayor Rudy Giuliani striding through the dust and chaos to take charge of the city and its response. Defense Secretary Donald Rumsfeld and many others in the Pentagon rushing from their offices to assist the injured. Firefighters going into both towers to ascend the emergency staircases, never to return.

The most significant story to emerge was that of flight United 93. Piecing together phone calls, voicemails, text messages and radar tracks to the huge crater in a Pennsylvania field, a story emerged of Al Qaida failure. After seizing control of the airliner, the hijackers had diverted the plane. But as the media and security officials analysed the fragments of communication by the passengers of the flight a picture emerged of the first counter-attack by the US. In this case it was launched by some of the 44 people who made up the crew and passengers of the airliner. They had learned of the other attacks from telephone calls and text messages. The full details will never be established, but it was clear that enough people came forward with the will and capability to fight back, in certain knowledge that the chances of their surviving were extremely thin.

The victory of the passengers had other effects. Many commentators have suggested that Flight 93 had been hijacked to be crashed on another iconic target in Washington DC, most likely the White House or the Capitol Building. If this was the case, the flight would probably have struck its target, as the mobilization of USAF fighter planes was not rapid enough to prevent the aircraft attacking the nation's capital.

This was the first battle between the US and Al Qaida. And it was mounted by civilians, in the knowledge that their efforts would probably result in their death. Such a counter-attack does not seem to have been anticipated by Bin Laden or those who planned the hijackings. This should have given the Al Qaida leader pause for thought. That doomed US civilians fought back should have been the first of many clear warnings that the US would stop at little to neutralize Al Qaida and capture or kill Bin Laden and the other leaders of the movement. In this, as in so much else, Bin Laden underestimated the US desire for retribution, to hold him personally to account, and to ensure that such a terrible attack could never be visited on the US again.

The first reaction of the US government was to order all other airliners flying over the country to land. It closed its airspace to all civilian air traffic. Canada did the same, as did many European countries. An unexpected and uncanny quiet settled over the many cities and their suburbs. This did little to mask a gathering sense of threat and unease, amplified by incessant rolling coverage of the atrocity on television news, with endless re-runs of footage of the attacks and their aftermath.

The air defences of the country were mobilized. Many of the fighters sent to patrol US airspace were from the Air National Guard, part-time pilots and aircrew. The US Navy put its ships stationed on the Eastern Seaboard to sea, including Aegis air defence destroyers and two aircraft carriers with their air wings. In New York City part-time National Guard soldiers and officers self-mobilized and made their way to the site of the attack to assist the police and emergency services. Elsewhere in the country the National Guard was mobilized by state governors for security duties, to assist overstretched state police and other security agencies. A US Navy hospital ship was sent to the city.

For the first time in its history the NATO alliance invoked Article V of the North Atlantic Charter, initiating collective self-defence. Even at the height of the many Cold War crises between NATO and the Warsaw Pact this provision had never been exercised. This was but one manifestation of a massive outpouring of international support. Many nations and their citizens had been stunned by the atrocity, which could so easily have been targeted at the gleaming towers of so many city centres. This was reinforced by the emerging reports of the identities of the dead. It would eventually be revealed that alongside 2,606 US citizens who died in the twin towers 372 came from 61 other countries, a reflection of New York's importance as a global hub for finance, business and culture.

AFGHANISTAN

To understand why Al Qaida had established their base in Afghanistan, it is necessary to understand the recent history of the country. It had always been difficult to govern, invade or occupy. Landlocked and bordered by Central Asia, China, Pakistan and Iran, its location and harsh terrain of mountains and desert were challenges to both rulers and invaders. Its ethnic mix was another challenge. Pashtuns in the south, Uzbeks and Tajiks in the north made central government even more challenging.

The British-ruled empire in South Asia, the Raj, covered modern-day India and Pakistan. But imperial rule ended amongst the forbidding ramparts of the Hindu Kush and the harsh bleak deserts and rocks of Baluchistan. Motivated by perceptions of Imperial Russian expansion southwards towards the Arabian Gulf, in 1837, as part of the so-called

Great Game between the two powers, the British sent an expedition to Kabul, the Afghan capital, aiming to install a pro-British ruler.

This easily reached Kabul, brushing aside the Afghan Army. But the British troops in the city became seen as occupiers. Amid staggering displays of both indecisiveness and incompetence by the force's commander, the elderly and infirm General Elphinstone, the British contingent, which now included a considerable number of wives and camp followers, was forced from Kabul and retreated towards India. This too was badly led and only one member of the expedition reached the British forward base at Jalalabad. A subsequent punitive attack was mounted in 1842. It reached Kabul, where part of the city was destroyed.

The Second Anglo-Afghan War began in 1878. Although the Afghan ruler, Mohammed Yaquab Khan, agreed to the British demands, there was a rebellion against the British. A counter-offensive, led by General Roberts, defeated Afghan forces at Herat and Kandahar and Afghanistan ceded to British demands for control over Afghan foreign policy. In 1893, the Afghans agreed a line of demarcation between their country and the Raj: the Durand Line. On the British side, the mountainous north-west bordering Afghanistan was the domain of fiercely independent Pashtun tribes. The combination of harsh terrain and the fighting spirit of the Pashtuns made it impossible for the British to establish the same level of control as they had over the rest of the Raj.

An accommodation was reached with the tribal elders, the Maliks. Their tribes were allowed to govern themselves, subject to the powers of the British political agents. This was cemented by the 1867 Murderous Outrages Regulations. From then on occasional uprisings or raids into the Raj would be met by punitive expeditions into the North West Frontier Province.

In 1919 there was a third Anglo-Afghan war. An effort to exploit civil unrest in the Raj, by invading through the Khyber Pass, was defeated by the British. A counter-offensive was mounted through the pass towards Kabul, complemented by another advance from Quetta towards Kandahar and the bombing of Kabul by the newly independent Royal Air Force (RAF). A negotiated settlement saw Amanullah, the Afghan leader, recognize the Durand Line and the British cede control of Afghan foreign affairs back to Kabul.

The special status and laws of the North West Frontier Province continued. There were still occasional British punitive expeditions. For example, there was a major campaign in Mohmand in 1934–35, and a brigade-sized punitive expedition in North Waziristan in 1936–37.[1] The British had tacitly accepted that whilst Afghan forces might be defeated by British troops, any occupation of Afghanistan was unlikely to succeed. And the special status of the North West Frontier Province was explicit recognition of the great difficulties of subduing the fiercely independent Pashtun tribes.

In 1947, exhausted and reduced to near-bankruptcy by World War II, the British withdrew from their Indian empire, the newly independent country immediately splitting into Hindu-majority India and the Islamic Republic of Pakistan. Pakistan chose to continue the special regime applied to the North West Frontier Province, which was named the Federally Administered Tribal Areas (FATA).

Afghanistan continued in its relative isolation. In the 1950s and 60s both the Soviet Union and the US attempted to influence the country. The Soviets contributed considerable sums in economic aid, while the US funded the irrigation of the Helmand River Valley, which turned a large area of desert in southern Afghanistan into irrigated farmland.

THE WAR BETWEEN THE SOVIETS AND THE MUJAHEDEEN

From the 1970s Afghanistan's politics became increasingly turbulent and bloody. In the 1980s and 1990s the country became a theatre of military intervention by outside powers. These sowed the seeds of Al Qaida's surprise attack on the US.

A republican *coup d'état* against the Afghan monarchy in 1973 was followed by a communist takeover in a 1978 coup. At the same time, armed opposition by Afghan insurgent groups, known as Mujahedeen, against the Kabul regime grew. Their principal ally, the Soviet government of Leonid Brezhnev, became increasingly concerned that its communist allies in Kabul were changing Afghanistan at such pace that popular opposition was rising too fast for the communist government to survive.[2]

In late 1979, Soviet special forces mounted a coup. The incumbent Afghan president was killed and replaced by Hafizullah Amin, who the Soviets hoped would be a more pragmatic leader. Soviet airborne forces were airlifted into Kabul airport and rapidly seized control of the city. Soviet motor rifle divisions moved south from Central Asia and rapidly seized control of the other major cities: Mazar-e Sharif, Herat, Kandahar and Jalalabad. Bagram, north of Kabul, was rapidly developed into a major Soviet air base.

Some in the Soviet government, KGB and military had doubts about the feasibility of this intervention. For example, applying classic Marxist revolutionary theory to the situation in Afghanistan pointed to the difficulties of implementing revolutionary change; analysis from a Marxist point of view suggested that the country was not ready, that it was predominantly rural and underdeveloped and that communist zealots in Kabul were antagonising the mullahs and the tribes. Afghanistan was most definitely not Russia in 1917. But these doubting voices were over-ridden by the key Kremlin decision makers.

The Soviets embarked on nation building, providing considerable civilian assistance to the new Afghan government and its agencies and attempted to improve the capabilities of the Afghan security forces. But the US, UK and Saudi Arabia sided with the anti-government Mujahedeen. Large amounts of money, weapons, ammunition, land mines and military supplies were provided. A credible estimate is that the CIA spent much as $9 billion supporting the Mujahedeen. This was matched by Saudi Arabia. Wealthy Saudis and individuals from the Gulf contributed more money. Pakistan insisted that all operational, financial, material and logistic support to the Afghan insurgents be disbursed by its intelligence agency Inter-Services Intelligence (ISI). Some 80,000 fighters are thought to have passed through ISI-sponsored training camps in Pakistan during the 1980s.

As well as hosting about three million Afghan refugees, ISI developed the means by which it would support and direct the Mujahedeen.[3] A number of large ammunition dumps were established to hold the considerable quantities of arms, ammunition and other supplies flowing into the country from the US, Saudi Arabia and the UK. Hospitals were established to treat the wounded. Camps were established where Mujahedeen fighters and armed groups were trained in the use of these new military capabilities.

ISI attempted to direct the Mujahedeen's military operations. Many groups were not amenable to this, so ISI incentivized them;

favouring guerrilla groups that were more militarily effective, and particularly those that were willing to follow ISI's direction. Some groups were supplied with intelligence and trained to attack specific important targets.

This was a long-term activity, as the time it would take to travel from Pakistan to targets deep inside Afghanistan would be often measured in months. Some of these attacks were extremely ambitious. They included Mujahedeen bands attacking Soviet air bases in Central Asia, an operational gambit that ISI was forced to suspend after the Soviets threatened retaliatory raids in Pakistan. An important consequence of ISI's role in supporting and advising the Mujahedeen was that Pakistan established strong contacts with many of the diverse array of armed groups that would be major actors over the next three decades.

The Soviet military campaign sought to protect Afghanistan's cities. The Soviets intended that Mujahedeen were to be held sufficiently at bay in rural areas and the mountains so that they could not disrupt key populated areas. To achieve this, raids and offensives were mounted, maximizing Soviet forces' advantages, including large numbers of armoured vehicles and artillery pieces. Initially the Soviets had the advantage of air superiority, which allowed them to bomb Mujahedeen at will and sow the Durand Line with air-dropped anti-personnel mines. Soviet helicopters were extensively used to insert special forces and to mount air assault operations where troops would be landed in up to brigade strength.

But despite these offensives, the effort to increase Afghan government control of the Afghan population proved difficult. In the deeply conservative rural areas, the modernization of Afghanistan was usually rejected in favour of support of the jihad against the infidel. This was reinforced by civilian casualties and collateral damage inflicted by the Soviets, and by corruption and predatory behaviour exhibited by both Soviet and Afghan forces. For example, Soviet paratroopers based in Kandahar would use highway checkpoints to rob Afghans travelling in cars, radio/cassette players being frequently plundered.

Soviet and Afghan forces found it difficult to stabilize areas outside the relatively well-protected cities and the immediate vicinity of their bases. Their large-scale offensives could often clear Mujahedeen from the targeted areas, but unless Soviet and Afghan forces remained in strength, control would over time be lost.

Soviet air superiority was challenged in late 1986 when the Mujahedeen began downing aircraft with the US Stinger shoulder-launched anti-aircraft missiles. Soviet bombers could counter the missiles by flying much higher, at the cost of reduced accuracy of bombing, but the weapon was effective against helicopters, making their use riskier and more difficult.

The effect of Stinger missiles on the Soviet military campaign is controversial. The Mujahedeen's supporters in the US claimed that their use was decisive. But the Stingers' introduction into the war coincided with a change of strategy by new Soviet president Mikhail Gorbachev. Anxious to reduce the financial, human, political and diplomatic cost of the war, he directed that the Soviet military transition responsibility to the Afghan government forces. A narrative grew within the Pakistan Army that the ISI had defeated a superpower.

Under the reforming President Gorbachev, the Soviet Union negotiated an international peace agreement for Afghanistan, the Geneva Accords. In February 1989, as it withdrew its forces, it left an Afghan government under President Mohammad Najibullah. The Soviets transferred leadership of the war back to the Afghan government and its conduct to their armed forces. Moscow advised Kabul to cut deals with the tribes and Mujahedeen who were amenable to ending the conflict. When the Soviets troops departed in 1989 the Afghan regime disappointed its enemies by failing to immediately collapse. Much to the surprise of many Western governments, the Kabul regime kept the Mujahedeen at bay for three years. But the dire economic condition of the rapidly disintegrating Soviet Union resulted in Moscow suspending its economic aid to Najibullah's government. Shortly afterwards, one of Najibullah's most capable fighters, the Uzbek warlord General Dostum, defected along with 40,000 Afghan troops. When he allied himself to the forces of Tajik commander Ahmad Shah Masood, the two warlords rapidly defeated Najibullah's forces and seized Kabul. This alliance quickly disintegrated, and Afghanistan was ravaged by another civil war between Mujahedeen factions. Kabul was devastated and the war generated over half a million refugees. A Mujahedeen government was eventually established under the leadership of ethnic Tajik leaders, Burhanuddin Rabbani and Ahmad Shah Masood. But the country soon descended into chaos with rampant infighting between former Mujahedeen commanders and other warlords.

The Taliban formed itself from former Mujahedeen. Initially a very small group defining itself by opposition to the rampant exploitation of civilians by warlords, it developed links to black market trade interests. In late 1994 it captured Kandahar, seizing large quantities of arms and ammunition. Pakistan's ISI decided to support the Taliban. They fielded a combined arms force consisting of infantry carried in ubiquitous 4x4 pick-up trucks, tanks and artillery, often attacking from multiple directions. Their tactics were flexible and aggressive, outfighting but not totally defeating militias of the previously successful warlords, such as Ahmad Shah Masood. Dominated by ethnic Pashtuns and supported by advice, training and supply of arms the Taliban overthrew the government in Kabul in September 1996.[4]

Initially welcomed by a proportion of Afghans as a force restoring security and stability, the Taliban leadership, madrassa-educated and with little knowledge of the outside world, would over the next five years impose an increasingly isolationist and fundamentalist Islamic regime over the country, but it was never able to eradicate the alliance of the warlords who styled themselves the Northern Alliance. These held out against the Taliban in parts of northern Afghanistan, exploiting their access to Central Asia to sustain their forces.

Pakistan was one of only three countries to officially recognize the new Taliban government. The other two were the United Arab Emirates and Saudi Arabia.

THE GROWTH OF AL QAIDA

The 1978 Israel–Egypt peace agreement, the 1979 Iranian revolution, the use the same year by the Saudi Arabian government of foreign troops to defeat militants who seized control of Mecca's Grand Mosque and the 1979 Soviet invasion of Afghanistan all stoked an upsurge of frustration in Muslim countries. This was often expressed as an increase in religiosity. Saudi Arabia felt particularly threatened by the new regime in Tehran and its ideology. Accordingly, Riyadh embraced the Muslim fundamentalist doctrine of Wahhabism, entrenching its principles in the fabric of the nation. It also provided considerable support to the proselytization of the doctrine beyond the kingdom.

The Soviet invasion of Afghanistan was seen by Riyadh as an opportunity to demonstrate a leading role in the Muslim world by supporting the Afghan Mujahedeen. The Saudis encouraged and supported a flow of Muslim volunteers to fight the Soviets. These included Osama Bin Laden, the wealthy son of a Saudi civil engineering magnate. By the mid-1980s he was well established in the Pakistani city Peshawar, just across the Afghan border, using his considerable wealth to fund the building of roads across the Durand Line. In 1986 he established a Mujahedeen camp near Jalalabad. A Soviet attack was repulsed by his fighters, which included many Arabs. The success of this defensive battle greatly enhanced Bin Laden's reputation as a jihadist. Al Qaida is thought to have been founded the year after. The withdrawal of Soviet forces from Afghanistan was seen by jihadists as a strategic victory in which they, not the US or Pakistan, had played the leading role.

Some jihadists moved on to other wars, including those in Bosnia and Chechnya. Others who had married Afghan or Pakistani women settled in those countries. Bin Laden returned to Saudi Arabia, but, expelled from that country, in 1992 he moved on to Sudan.

After 1989 the US had lost interest in Afghanistan. But the 1992 bomb attack on the World Trade Centre in New York and the thwarted 1995 plot to assassinate the Pope in the Philippines, to blow up airliners over the Pacific and crash an airliner on the headquarters of the CIA, were all evidence of a growing threat from violent Sunni extremists. Bin Laden and Al Qaida increased in importance as targets for US intelligence gathering, the Pentagon and CIA recognizing the serious potential danger posed by Bin Laden. In 1996 the US persuaded the Sudanese government to expel him. Bin Laden moved to Kandahar in southern Afghanistan, where his previous support to the Mujahedeen and deployment of his wealth to influence the Taliban government made him welcome.

By the end of 1997 the Clinton administration was sufficiently concerned about the potential threat posed by Bin Laden's group to instigate covert CIA operations against al Qaida, some in co-operation with other countries' intelligence agencies. Concurrent efforts were made to engage the Taliban government. Some 20 meetings between US and Taliban officials took place and Pakistan was pressured to help. Intelligence also showed that whilst Al Qaida was the wealthiest jihadist group based in Afghanistan, there were many others in the country. These included Uzbek, Turkish and Pakistani groups. Arab jihadist groups came from Libya, Egypt, Morocco, Algeria, Tunisia, Jordan and Palestine.

Many of these groups sought to conduct terrorism in their countries of origin, whilst Bin Laden's ideology increasingly focused on attacking the US. Influenced by the thinking of both jihadist movements and the Muslim Brotherhood, Bin Laden concluded that the 'near enemy' of apostate regimes such as Egypt and Saudi Arabia should be overthrown, by striking at the 'far enemy' that supported them: the US and its allies. In 1998 the Egyptian radical Ayman al Zawahiri merged his jihadist group with Al Qaida, becoming its deputy leader.

Following the August 1998 Al Qaida bombings of US embassies in Tanzania and Kenya by terrorists trained and prepared in Bin Laden's camps, Clinton ordered retaliatory strikes against al Qaida training camps in Afghanistan and a chemical installation in Sudan. Some 70 Tomahawk cruise missiles were fired from US Navy ships and submarines. Some damage was caused, and some Al Qaida members were killed, but the disruption inflicted on Al Qaida appears to have been minimal. And the US was not able to provide enough evidence to convince international media that the target struck in Sudan represented the chemical weapons facility that the US alleged it to be.

There is evidence that some in the Taliban regime were tiring of Bin Laden, and that the Saudi government was attempting to persuade Kabul to hand Bin Laden over to Riyadh. But the cruise missile strikes in Afghanistan made Mullah Omar, the Taliban leader, determined not to give up his guest. Bin Laden had also proved himself invaluable by deploying his men to help the Taliban fight the Northern Alliance. He provided the 055 Brigade, an elite unit of foreign jihadists – brave and determined fighters, whom the Taliban's army could ill-afford to give up.

After this strike, US intelligence gathering and military planning continued. On several occasions further cruise missile attacks were planned, but there was insufficient intelligence to justify launching the missiles. Plans for raids by US SOF to kill or capture Bin Laden were considered and rejected. But actionable intelligence was in extremely short supply and the risks of acting always seemed to outweigh the potential gains. In 2000, the CIA had begun using the Predator drone for surveillance and intelligence gathering. There were launched in secret from Uzbekistan. Concurrently, both the Pentagon and the CIA mooted the arming of Predator.

The new administration of President George W. Bush did not appear to afford a high priority to countering Al Qaida. New National Security Advisor Condoleezza Rice commissioned a policy review. Options examined included the use of armed Predator unmanned aerial vehicles, inserting a proxy force, possibly of US armed and trained militia, or supporting an attack on Al Qaida by Northern Alliance forces. But by September 2001 none of these had been approved.

On 10 September Al Qaida fighters posed as journalists conducting an interview on the Northern Alliance leader Ahmad Shah Masood. Explosives concealed in their camera detonated, killing them and seriously wounding Masood, who died aboard a helicopter evacuating him to Tajikistan.

PLANNING THE US MILITARY RESPONSE

On 9/11 President Bush had been in Florida visiting a school. On learning of the attack, he was taken to Air Force One. An emergency National Security Council meeting was held by video conference while the President was at Offutt Air Force Base, Nebraska. The CIA Director George Tenet assessed with 'near certainty' that Bin Laden had initiated the attacks.[5] Returning to the White House the President addressed the nation. His speech included a clear warning to any states that might be harbouring anti-US terrorist networks: 'We have made the decision to punish whoever harbours terrorists, not just the perpetrators.'[6]

The 9/11 attacks were the greatest strategic shock for the US since Pearl Harbor. Thousands of its citizens had been killed, the majority civilians. These attacks could just be the first of many others that Al Qaida could have planned at home or abroad on US citizens, diplomats or forces abroad, as well as US allies or wider interests. This put immense pressure on US President George W. Bush. Another such attack, which might well have included the use of weapons of mass destruction, would not only have been a catastrophe, but would also have been politically lethal to his government. This was also a deep concern for governments of the US' close military allies, including the UK.

The US was now faced with three unforeseen security and military requirements. First, it had to step up its domestic security. Any further Al Qaida cells had to be found and neutralized. And it had to rapidly improve airline and transportation security, as well as making sure that no further terrorist groups slipped into the US undetected.

Secondly, Al Qaida's previous attacks and global ambitions meant that the US had to formulate and execute a plan to tackle the terrorist group globally. In time this would evolve into an international counter-terrorism campaign mounted by a coalition of intelligence and security agencies led by the CIA.

Thirdly, it had to rapidly neutralize the threat from Al Qaida's main base: Afghanistan. It would be highly desirable to bring its leadership to face US justice, but neutralizing the threat had to take priority. Ideally this would be achieved diplomatically, but the isolated and introverted behaviour of the Taliban government suggested that the chances of a diplomatic settlement were low. There was no contingency plan for any military activity in Afghanistan in CENTCOM, the Pentagon, the CIA or anywhere else in the machinery of the US government.

It would in theory be possible to use the strategy that had been applied in Operation *Desert Storm* – building up an overwhelming ground and air force around Afghanistan, and at some stage launching first an air campaign and then a ground invasion by conventional forces. But the imperative of neutralizing the remaining Al Qaida threat from Afghanistan, along with public, political and media pressure to be seen to act against this new enemy, was considerable. Internationally the US needed to deter further terrorist attacks, not just from Al Qaida in Afghanistan, but more widely. So there were strong arguments to be seen to be taking rapid and decisive action against both the terrorist threat and the state that harboured it.

Top US political leadership was involved from the outset. From then on, until the end of 2001, Bush, Rumsfeld, Tenet, General Tommy Franks, the commander of CENTCOM, and other senior political leaders would be consumed by planning and then conducting operations in Afghanistan. There would be considerable discussion and interaction. This was assisted by the technology of secure video conferencing, which would allow individuals to join the meetings from any suitably equipped US government installation anywhere in the world. Video conferencing had been used by US commanders during the Bosnia and Kosovo wars, but it came into its own after 9/11.

The initiation, leadership and management of the war would also be greatly influenced by the leadership styles of Rumsfeld and Franks. For operations *Desert Shield* and *Desert Storm* the then-Defense Secretary Dick Cheney had chosen to lead both wars through the Chairman of the Joint Chiefs of Staff, General Colin Powell. On his second appointment as Defense Secretary Rumsfeld was confident enough to deal directly with Franks at the CENTCOM HQ in Tampa. Sidelining of the Chairman of Joint Chiefs and the Joint Chiefs themselves streamlined the passage of information and decision making and improved operational security. But it reduced the amount of internal scrutiny and challenging of the plans developed and decisions made in the Pentagon.

The day after the attacks, 12 September, saw the first meeting of the subset of the National Security Council that became known as the 'War Cabinet', Rumsfeld posing a key question about the role of any prospective US-led military coalition , 'It is critical how we define goals at the start, because that's what the coalition signs on for … Do we focus on Bin Laden and al Qaeda or terrorism more broadly?' Bush directed that initially the US should 'Start with Bin Laden, which Americans expect. And then if we succeed, we've struck a huge blow and can move forward.'[7]

Chairman of the Joint Chiefs of Staff General Hugh Shelton explained that the only pre-existing military plans were for firing cruise missiles against Al Qaida camps. Bush rejected this option as inadequate. In fact, straight after the attacks US military planners in the Pentagon, SOCOM, CENTCOM and in CENTCOM's subordinate HQs began considering the novel situation and potential military responses. Even before direction on specific war aims, it was clear that a military operation in Afghanistan would be required. This in turn would require US forces to establish bases closer to Afghanistan, in Pakistan and Central Asia.

Rumsfeld directed the formulation of 'credible military options'. At this stage, war aims for either Afghanistan or the global terrorist threat did not exist. At his news conference the same day Bush described the attacks as 'acts of war'. He told the leaders of Congress that 'This is not an isolated incident. This is war.'

On 13 September Bush was reported as telling his staff that, 'I want a plan – costs, time. I need options on the table … I want decisions quick.' Both he and Rumsfeld pressed for the fastest possible development of military options, Rumsfeld stating that 'We need new options. This is a new mission'. At the same time at a Pentagon briefing for reporters,

Deputy Secretary of Defense Paul Wolfowitz stated that US objectives included 'ending states who sponsor terrorism'.[8] There is evidence that Wolfowitz subsequently pressed for attacking Iraq.[9]

The War Cabinet gathered on 17 September at the President's rural retreat, Camp David, Maryland. Bush directed that attacking Al Qaida in Afghanistan would influence countries that supported terrorism to change their behaviour by ending that support. CIA Director Tenet explained Operation *Initial Hook*, the CIA's overall plan to tackle Al Qaida in Afghanistan. Unlike many European intelligence agencies, the CIA's role was more than just intelligence gathering and assessment; it also included covert armed action and supporting indigenous forces. For this purpose, the organization had paramilitary teams of CIA officers, many of whom were former US SOF operators and its own air wing of transport planes, helicopters and Predator drones. On that day Bush authorized the CIA to conduct covert action against Al Qaida and its allies.

The CIA initially refrained from armed attacks, holding back until the air war started. The CIA retained relationships with some warlords and anti-Taliban groups in Afghanistan. Its paramilitary teams would be deployed to Northern Alliance and other opposition forces. Those willing to fight the Taliban would be provided with funds, weapons, ammunition and supplies. These would be followed by US Army SOF teams who would further support opposition groups, especially in co-ordinating US air attacks. On 20 September the first CIA team was directed to deploy to Uzbekistan and from there to Afghanistan. In the Panjshir Valley the CIA and Northern Alliance intelligence staff set up a joint intelligence cell. The CIA team brought with them $10 million in cash.

On the same day President Bush addressed a joint session of Congress, setting out the US government's demands on the Taliban:

> Deliver to United States authorities all the leaders of al Qaeda who hide in your land. Release all foreign nationals, including American citizens, you have unjustly imprisoned. Protect foreign journalists, diplomats and aid workers in your country. Close immediately and permanently every terrorist training camp in Afghanistan, and hand over every terrorist, and every person in their support structure, to appropriate authorities. Give the United States full

access to terrorist training camps, so we can make sure they are no longer operating.

These demands are not open to negotiation or discussion. The Taliban must act, and act immediately. They will hand over the terrorists, or they will share in their fate …

Our war on terror begins with al Qaeda, but it does not end there. It will not end until every terrorist group of global reach has been found, stopped and defeated.[10]

A plan was rapidly developed for the CIA and US SOF teams to support anti-Taliban Northern Alliance forces. The US negotiated basing and overflight rights, initially with Pakistan and then with Uzbekistan, Tajikistan and Kyrgyzstan. A US Navy Amphibious Group carrying the 15th Marine Expeditionary Unit (MEU) deployed to the North Arabian Sea, south of Pakistan, as did the aircraft carrier USS *Kitty Hawk*. This giant ship had its customary air wing of fast jets removed, to be replaced by US SOF and a specially assembled wing of long-range special operations helicopters.

Initially, the CIA would deploy teams to arm, fund and supply the anti-Taliban Northern Alliance forces. CENTCOM envisaged US Special Operations Forces (SOF) linking up with the CIA and Northern Alliance, leveraging both the CIA and Northern Alliance's efforts by integrating them with a US air campaign against the Taliban's military capability and leadership. US ground troops would be introduced to complete the destruction of the Taliban and Al Qaida. Once this was complete there would be stabilization operations.

General Franks briefed the President on the CENTCOM plan on 21 September and the National Security Council four days later. Franks explained that unless Uzbekistan allowed the US to use its airfields, the air attacks and SOF insertions would have to be confined to the southern portion of Afghanistan. This restriction would greatly reduce the impact of the operation as the Northern Alliance was active in the northern half of the country.

Rumsfeld, CENTCOM, the Pentagon and the diplomats of the State Department redoubled their efforts with the Uzbek government to negotiate basing and overflight rights for US aircraft. They were eventually successful and helicopters for both SOF and for combat search and rescue transports and fighter bombers were based there.

This was a period of intensive political, diplomatic and military planning. The full weight of US intelligence collection was applied to Afghanistan. This included the signals intelligence capabilities of the National Security Agency and the US Air Force, giving access to static electronic listening posts, eavesdropping satellites and the giant flying listening stations of the Rivet Joint aircraft, a converted Boeing 707 transport full of radio interception equipment and expert operators.

Just as important was the effort to collect images of the country, to locate Taliban and Al Qaida forces and military installations. It was also necessary to understand the environment around these potential targets, to allow the risk of civilian casualties and collateral damage to be assessed.

The US had a large array of reconnaissance satellites. Some gathered images using powerful cameras. Others listened to the radio spectrum. Prior to 9/11 these were deployed to meet US strategic intelligence priorities. These had now changed, so the orbits of many of these satellites needed adjustment. At some stage the US began to fly unmanned aerial vehicles over Afghanistan. These included the US Air Force's Global Hawk and Predator platforms and the CIA's own Predators. The UK also deployed RAF photo reconnaissance aircraft, the elderly Canberra PR9 – a jet bomber of late 1940s vintage but equipped with modern cameras. These were complemented by USAF and RAF electronic reconnaissance aircraft listening in to Taliban communications. By the end of 2001 almost 50 US and allied surveillance and reconnaissance aircraft were supporting CENTCOM.

This intelligence-gathering effort was continuous. Once bombing and missile strikes began, the effectiveness of each attack would need to be assessed, to confirm that the target had been fully neutralized. And as the Taliban and Al Qaida were attacked both from the air and from the ground some of their forces were likely to move and these would need to be tracked. Also, both enemies' ability to attack aircraft, particularly the slower-moving transports and helicopters, would need to be assessed. Given that helicopters flew more slowly and less high than fixed-wing aircraft, those carrying CIA and SOF teams into Afghanistan were especially vulnerable but were also the most crucial aircraft sorties of all. So a significant portion of intelligence and surveillance systems would need to be tasked to support of these flights.

The US government demanded unconditional support from Pakistan. President Musharraf agreed to allow US aircraft to transit the country's airspace and provided access to some Pakistani military airfields. On 28 September, US Marines deployed to the airfield at Jacobabad, Pakistan to secure it for the deployment of US combat search and rescue aircraft.

At the start of October, US and British military liaison teams deployed to Pakistan to co-ordinate passage of US and allied aircraft and access to Pakistani air bases. Bush and Rumsfeld gave final approval to General Franks' detailed plan. On 3 October, Rumsfeld issued the Top Secret direction *Strategic Guidance for a Campaign Against Terrorism*. This stated that the campaign would be a global war on terrorism, involving multiple different operations and using 'all tools of national power'.

It seems that the War Cabinet had by then agreed that the campaign should result in the removal of Afghanistan's Taliban government, although the possibility of the Taliban changing its mind and surrendering Al Qaida and Bin Laden was acknowledged. There was debate over the name of the operation. Initially it had been called Operation *Infinite Justice*. When Rumsfeld learned that some Muslim scholars would likely object to the title as it appeared to assume some of Allah's powers, the name was changed to Operation *Enduring Freedom*.

It would be important that US intervention did not make the situation in Afghanistan worse. This included exacerbating the long-term suspicions and rivalries between the Pashtuns in southern Afghanistan and the Northern Alliance. And every warlord prepared to co-operate with the US had their own interests and agendas.

'Jawbreaker', the first CIA team to deploy to Afghanistan, was flown in a CIA-owned Russian Mi17 helicopter to the Panjshir Valley. Here it was met by Northern Alliance officers, and established a base and direct communications to the CIA. On 27 September the team met the Northern Alliance's commander, General Mohammed Fahim. The team set up an electronic listening post to eavesdrop on Taliban communications and began mapping the Northern Alliance and Taliban front-line positions, in preparation for the forthcoming US air offensive.

US military planners considered it unlikely that the campaign would succeed during the Afghan winter. Snow would make many mountain passes impassable to ground forces and the likely clouds, winds and storms would restrict the use of all types of aircraft.

So, any US troops deployed into the country by air had to have access to enough supplies to last out any interruption to supply due to adverse weather.

The closest military partnership was between the US and the UK. Both nations had a long-standing military and intelligence partnership, the latter founded on the 'five eyes' intelligence collaboration arrangement between the two states, Australia, Canada and New Zealand. There was also a particularly close working relationship between UK and US SOF. Prime Minister Tony Blair had a long telephone conversation with President Bush on 12 September, immediately followed up by a five-page paper sent to the White House later that day. This recommended demanding that the Taliban hand over Bin Laden and close Al Qaida's camps. British military planners rapidly deployed to CENTCOM.

The British rapidly began collecting intelligence on Afghanistan and sharing it with the US. Although the British military presence in the Gulf and Indian Ocean was usually small, by coincidence a large joint task force was in Oman and the seas around it. A long-planned exercise, Saif Sareea II, was testing Britain's ability to project its Joint Rapid Reaction Force to Oman where it was conducting combined training. Under the HQ of 1st Armoured Division was an armoured brigade and the RAF deployed Tornado bombers, helicopters and transport aircraft.

Commanded by the UK joint HQ, a maritime task group of one of the UK's pocket-sized aircraft carriers was joined by some of the Royal Marines amphibious forces, 3 Commando Brigade. Quietly, with no publicity, an army brigade HQ was flown out to Oman to replace the joint HQ that had been running the exercise. The UK also moved two of its nuclear submarines into position to fire Tomahawk cruise missiles at Afghanistan, as well as air to air refuelling and intelligence-gathering aircraft. After the exercise ended in mid-October a small flotilla of amphibious ships, destroyers and frigates were reassigned to Operation *Veritas,* the UK name for its operation to support the US campaign in Afghanistan. The aircraft carrier HMS *Invincible* and Royal Navy amphibious ships became a floating base for helicopters, Royal Marines and SOF.

This British force had over 4,000 personnel. It was dwarfed by the US military capability in the Gulf and Indian Ocean, which itself was growing every day, but its value was as much political as military.

The same was true of the effort to garner international political and diplomatic support that Prime Minister Blair had thrown himself into.

As planning continued apace many nations offered military assistance. Offers of intelligence gathering and combat capabilities by Australia were gratefully accepted. Others were politely declined, as the US doubted that the forces offered would add value to the campaign. The Pentagon and State Department were overwhelmed with offers and most were declined. Many were not even acknowledged.

This was in part a product of the herculean tasks that faced US diplomats and military planners. But it was also a manifestation of a deep-seated mistrust of alliances. The considerable complications of the Kosovo war, the limited added value of many European military capabilities and the way NATO had appeared to slow down US decision making and constrain its military options led to a considerable body of distrust in the Pentagon and US military. Donald Rumsfeld was to summarize this in a sound bite; the approach of the Kosovo war was to be reversed. This was not to be a coalition of equals: it was to be a US-led mission and the 'mission was to determine the coalition'.

General Franks exercised command and control from CENTCOM's main HQ in Tampa and decided to retain tight control over the operation. He would make extensive use of secure video conferencing for planning, command and co-ordination. The air operation was controlled from a Combined Forces Air Component Command (CFACC) based at Prince Sultan air base in Saudi Arabia. US SOF would be commanded from an HQ in Doha, Qatar. Naval operations would be commanded from CENTCOM's maritime HQ in Bahrain. The CENTCOM land component HQ based in Kuwait would not be initially used. The option of setting up a dedicated US joint task force HQ for Afghanistan was rejected, in part because of the lack of time.

Whilst US forces could access northern Afghanistan by air from Central Asia, they also needed access to the south of the country. As relations between the US and Iran had been extremely strained since 1979, this could only come through Pakistan, President Musharraf having granted the US access to about two-thirds of the country's airspace.

US and British liaison officers had deployed to the country in early October. There was much to arrange with the Pakistani authorities.

For example, the passage of fighters, bombers, refuelling aircraft, transports and helicopters through Pakistani airspace required extensive communications and 'deconfliction measures' arranged between Pakistani civilian and military air traffic control, US air bases in the Gulf and elsewhere, US and British aircraft carriers and amphibious ships in the Indian Ocean and the three Pakistani airfields being used as Coalition air bases. At the height of the campaign there were over 50 aircraft and 2,000 troops based in the country, to which Pakistan was providing 100,000 gallons of fuel every day.

TOPPLING THE TALIBAN

A US ultimatum to the Taliban government of Afghanistan to hand over the Al Qaida leadership was ignored by Kabul. On its expiry on 7 October 2001 President Bush announced that the US was conducting:

> carefully targeted actions to disrupt the use of Afghanistan as a terrorist base of operations and to attack the military capability of the Taliban regime … Our military action is also designed to clear the way for sustained, comprehensive and relentless operations to drive them out and bring them to justice.[11]

He also stated that US aircraft would drop humanitarian aid to the Afghan people.

US air and missile strikes were launched against the Taliban's conventional military capability. Royal Navy submarines fired some of the UK's small stock of Tomahawk cruise missiles. Air drops of humanitarian aid were made by giant C17 transport aircraft flying from USAF bases in Germany. Over 70 such missions would be flown between the start of the campaign and mid-December. US Marines and SEALS deployed to provide security for a second airfield in Pakistan at Shamsi.

CENTCOM's air component was required to provide air support for anti-Taliban forces. Initial air and cruise missile strikes targeted the Taliban's air defences, its surface to air missile sites, radars, airfields and military aircraft. Although these were no match for US fighters, they could pose a threat to the more vulnerable helicopters and transport aircraft. It took only a few days for the US to gain air superiority over the country. The air attacks then turned to Taliban command, control and communications, camps and training sites, with its tanks and artillery being priority targets.

All of this was being conducted in a mountainous landlocked country, in the teeth of winter weather. This made getting helicopters over the mountains of Pakistan and Afghanistan especially difficult. And every single CIA agent, special operator, soldier or marine delivered into Afghanistan by air had to be supplied with rations, ammunition, batteries for the numerous radios, night viewing devices and laser target designators. Moreover, copious quantities of hard cash were needed to purchase vehicles and pay local warlords for their services.

All the military and CIA personnel and all these supplies had to be delivered by air, putting additional demand on the finite number of helicopters and transport aircraft and crews capable of operating at range and over the mountainous terrain. The British, for example, supplied their SAS forces using parachute air drop, requiring the full-time commitment of their single air despatch squadron of specially trained logistic soldiers who prepared the loads for parachute despatch, packing, rigging the British special forces' Hercules transport aircraft and finally pushing the loads from the aircraft. This was hard back-breaking work from start to finish. And finding the drop zones at night challenged even the most highly trained pilots and aircrews.

Afghanistan is not a small country, but unless the air space above the country was controlled, the ever-increasing number of aircraft over it meant there was a chance of air to air collisions between Coalition aircraft. Tight control was essential by day, when bombers and fighters flying from the USA, the island of Diego Garcia, US bases in the Gulf and aircraft carriers in the Indian Ocean all needed placing to best effect in order to support SOF and CIA parties on the ground, attack Taliban forces and react to any targets of opportunity. At night, while the fighters and bombers continued their deadly work, offering the Taliban no respite, they were joined by slow-moving transport aircraft delivering supplies and lower-flying more vulnerable helicopters that clandestinely delivered people and supplies. Their missions were often constrained by both weather and geography. For example, there were only a finite number of mountain passes that helicopters could transit through.

One night a flight of Black Hawk helicopters flew over a ridge to discover an unexpected group of fighters sitting around campfires. Both parties were equally surprised to encounter each other, but the fighters were quick to reach for their weapons and put a hail of tracer fire into the sky. This was not the only such chance encounter.

These factors put a premium on managing the airspace above Afghanistan. CENTCOM's air component HQ in Saudi Arabia was the focus for this. Its principal tool was the US Air Force's giant Airborne Warning and Control Systems (AWACS) aircraft. These were airborne radar stations; they featured a huge revolving radar antenna in a disc-shaped housing perched ungainly above a modified Boeing 707 airliner. As important as the radar were the computers, radar operators, airspace controllers and air battle managers carried in an austere cabin beneath. The use of AWACS had been essential in Operation *Desert Storm* and over Bosnia and Kosovo, and would be indispensable in this campaign too.

Two weeks after the campaign had started, the Taliban forces facing the Northern Alliance were still in the defensive positions they had held when the strikes started on 7 October. The Northern Alliance asked that the air campaign shift more effort to attacking these forces. This had been anticipated in the air component's plan. But now there were US 'boots on the ground', in the form of small parties of US SOF.

THE NORTHERN ALLIANCE ATTACKS

From early October the US began attempting to insert CIA and SOF teams into Afghanistan. Doing so required helicopter crews to overcome considerable practical difficulties caused by distance, the mountainous terrain of central Afghanistan, the presence of Taliban air defences and the deteriorating weather. By mid-October detachments of SOF were inserted by helicopter, linking up with anti-Taliban forces, mainly from the Tajik and Uzbek-dominated Northern Alliance. These were supported with finance and logistics. Some of this improvised campaign has been publicly described. Much has not.

Afghanistan became the main effort for US SOCOM. This brought together the US Navy's maritime special forces, the SEALS and supporting small boat squadrons. The Army provided 'green berets' SOF who were trained and equipped to support, assist and fight alongside indigenous forces behind enemy lines. The Army also provided three battalions of Rangers, elite light infantry.

The 160th Special Operations Aviation Regiment provided elite aircrew flying a range of helicopters from the small 'Little Bird' gunships through medium-sized Black Hawk assault helicopters to giant twin-rotor Chinook heavy-lift helicopters. The US Air Force also provided huge CH53 helicopters, as well as Hercules transport aircraft. The Hercules was also used as platform for a fire support aircraft, the AC130. This is a gunship, bristling with sophisticated sensors and fitted with a 40mm cannon and modified 105mm artillery gun.

Part of SOCOM was the secretive Joint Special Operations Command (JSOC). Containing the US Army's Delta Force, originally modelled on the UK SAS, and a team of Navy SEALS, the command had originally been formed to conduct hostage rescue missions after the failure of the 1980 US raid in Iran. Its role had gradually expanded from hostage rescue to encompass the most challenging special missions. JSOC teams from Navy SEALS and Delta Force comprised part of the first US SOF into action, Task Force 11, also known as Task Force Sword. The unit had also been allocated Ranger infantry and supporting intelligence and CIA personnel.

All the US SOF were an elite. The special operators of Delta Force, the Army special forces and the US Navy SEALS were all volunteers from the US services. They had been selected through physically demanding tests of physical and mental endurance. The small proportion of men who passed these tests were then given a long period of specialized training in the skills needed for their roles: close-quarter battle, survival, advanced medical skills, parachuting and foreign languages. The SEALS were specialists in amphibious missions, including operating from submarines and small boats. The Rangers were elite infantry, a specialist raiding force that often supported the other US SOF.

On 19 October, after an anti-Taliban militia marked the site with a transponder device, almost 200 of the Task Force Sword's Rangers parachuted from C130 Hercules aircraft on to a landing strip in desert to the south and west of Kandahar: Objective Rhino. It was captured without resistance. This provided a temporary forward operating base from which the rest of the task force could launch other raids.

The task force was probably raiding locations in Kandahar Province that intelligence suggested were linked with Bin Laden. The results of this ambitious parachute and helicopter operation were not clear. But it was filmed on video and the resulting TV broadcasts of Rangers parachuting in darkness seen through the blurred and grainy monochrome images of night vision devices were exciting and demonstrated that the US had an ability to deliver Rangers and SOF at strategic distance. These images were aimed as much at the US people and politicians, and the US' allies and other opponents, as they were at the Taliban, most of whom lacked the capability to receive them. It was a vivid example of the 'propaganda of the deed'.

THE BATTLE OF MAZAR-E SHARIF

At the Karshi Kanabad air base in Uzbekistan the 5th Special Forces Group had assembled the Joint Special Operations Task Force – North (JSOTF-N), also called Task Force (TF) Dagger. Commanded by Colonel John Mulholland, they were joined by US Army special operations helicopters and USAF special tactics teams. They were to assist the Northern Alliance in removing the Taliban. Many of their US Army special operators and dedicated helicopters were based on the aircraft carrier USS *Kitty Hawk*, which had been turned into a floating launchpad for helicopter-borne special forces raids into Afghanistan.

Mulholland planned to help the Northern Alliance forces push the Taliban back sufficiently to establish secure bases which the US could use during the winter. Mazar-e Sharif, with an estimated population of 200,000, was the largest city in northern Afghanistan. Seizing it would allow the US to use its airfield and make it easier to establish a line of communication with Central Asia, allowing the US to supply its forces and the Northern Alliance. A CIA team inserted into the area in early October had assessed that the Taliban defending the city would probably be unable to withstand US air strikes.

Mulholland planned to secure Mazar-e Sharif by linking up with the Northern Alliance's most powerful military commanders: Fahim Khan, Mullah Daoud and General Abdul Rashid Dostum. Dostum, an ethnic Uzbek, controlled the largest force involved in the battle, estimated at up to 8,000 fighters. These were a mixture of light infantry and cavalry, but lacked heavy weapons. A burly man with a reputation for brutality, Dostum had previously fought against the Northern Alliance.

All three were rivals and it was essential that the US was not seen to be favouring one group over another. So, the insertion of SOF teams had to balance military with political factors, which influenced the order in which SOF teams deployed from Uzbekistan.

In the second week of October the Northern Alliance began advancing towards the city. After they had seized the city's airfield, the Taliban counter-attacked, halting the Alliance's advance. Over the night 19/20 October Task Force Dagger infiltrated two teams into Afghanistan. The small group of US SOF had the best small arms that money could buy. They carried satellite radios that enabled them to communicate with their bases in Central Asia and the Gulf and ground to air radios that linked them with the aircraft. They also had laser designators that shone an infrared laser beam at a target. The reflected laser light would be used by sensors on precision bombs to guide them to impact.

The first, Tiger 2, comprising ODA 595 and two combat air controllers, landed to the south of Mazar-e Sharif where it intended linking up with General Dostum. His fighters at the landing site were mounted on horses. They had mounts waiting for the SOF. Tiger 2's commander had grown up on a ranch, but the rest of the team found the six-hour ride an exhausting experience. Dostum welcomed the SOF, understanding the way they could help his forces. As most Northern Alliance fighters wore no uniform, the special forces personnel dressed in mixture of civilian clothes and US uniforms. They had grown beards, to avoid being singled out by the Taliban.

Splitting into smaller teams, the soldiers quickly began calling in US aircraft to support Dostum's fighters by attacking Taliban forces. Their trenches, bunkers, gun emplacements and armoured vehicles were all targeted. Attacking aircraft included US Navy F18s flying from aircraft carriers. USAF heavy bombers, the giant B52 and smaller B1, came into their own, as they could carry a much larger bomb load and fly for much longer than the smaller fighter bombers flying from the Gulf and from aircraft carriers in the Indian Ocean. At night these would be joined by orbiting AC130 Spectre gunships, circling overhead for hours at time, the Taliban fighters showing up as ghostly images on the aircraft night sights. And the Taliban had no defences that could withstand the aircraft's firepower.

The laser-guided bombs carried by US fighters and bombers had first been used against North Vietnam in the early 1970s. Used extensively in Operation *Desert Storm* and in the Bosnia and Kosovo air campaigns, the technology was mature and well understood. A new type of bomb was the Joint Direct Attack Munition (JDAM). Developed in the 1990s, this took a conventional, unguided 'iron' bomb and added a guidance system that used the signals from US Global Position System (GPS) satellites combined with an inertial navigation system. JDAMs were able to deliver precision strikes to targets obscured by smoke, dust and weather and did not require the target to be constantly illuminated by laser beams. They were to be used in great quantities after 9/11.

As well as Dostum's forces there were fighting groups commanded by Mohammed Atta, a Hazara, and Mohammad Mohaqiq, a Tajik. The three commanders met on 23 October to plan the attack on the city. As air strikes continued the three groups pushed away Taliban forces blocking the roads to Mazar-e Sharif, the US supplying Northern Alliance forces by air drop and helicopter.

Atta and Dostum had a long history of enmity, friction, suspicion and mistrust. This resulted in a lack of co-ordination between the two different militias. The US made efforts to persuade the two warlords to reconcile and continue their advances and attacks.

On 6 November, the three warlords mounted a joint assault supported by US air strikes. The attackers included infantry travelling by horse. These were more mounted infantry than they were true cavalry, but no less effective for that. There was heavy fighting on the approaches to the city but by the afternoon of 9 November the Taliban defences collapsed. Many of their fighters fled the city, but the Northern Alliance captured about 3,000 Taliban prisoners.

The heavy bombers were decisive in breaking the will of Taliban forces defending Mazar-e Sharif. This was the first significant victory of the informal coalition between the Northern Alliance and the US. It disrupted the Taliban's ability to move and supply their forces. It gave access to a functioning airport, providing new opportunities for bringing US troops and supplies into Northern Afghanistan.

There was a bloody postscript. About 600 Taliban captives were detained in a 19th-century fortress to the south-west of the city. On 25 November these staged a revolt, seizing the fortresses' armoury and capturing a corner of the complex. Heavy fighting resulted as the Taliban, US SOF, some British SOF and a US Army infantry platoon sought to recapture the citadel, supported by the weight of US airpower.

The Taliban fought with a savage desperation. Airstrikes were called 'danger close', that is with friendly troops on the ground being within the normal safety distances of the weapons. At one stage US SOF were injured by the blast of one of these strikes. There was an attempt to flush the prisoners out by flooding, but this failed, and fuel was used to burn them out. Only about 80 prisoners survived.

THE FALL OF KABUL

The Taliban seemed to have little in the way of a defensive strategy. They seemed to want to hold on to all the main towns and cities, partly because the Northern Alliance held the Salang Tunnel which make it difficult for forces to move north from Kabul. It could not counter the ability of the Northern Alliance to tactically defeat Taliban forces in defensive positions. The Taliban rapidly lost the battlefield initiative.

The second team from Task Force Dagger that infiltrated on 19/20 October sought to assist the Northern Alliance forces closest to Kabul. The former Soviet air base at Bagram was controlled by Northern Alliance forces and ringed by minefields, which the Taliban found impossible to penetrate. Here the SOF team met with militia fighters commanded by Masood's successors, Generals Bismullah Khan and Fahim Khan.

From the airfield control tower the team could see the Taliban defensive positions spread out across the Shamli Plain. Like many of the fighting positions the Taliban had established, these were well known to the Northern Alliance forces facing them. For three weeks the SOF directed air strikes against these positions. As at Mazar-e Sharif, the Taliban had no effective defences against the high-flying bombers and growing number of fighter bombers. Hundreds of Taliban were killed and increasing numbers surrendered to the Northern Alliance, as their forces began to capture Taliban bunker and trench complexes.

The very visible destruction of Taliban troops and positions greatly impressed the Northern Alliance forces, particularly their commanders, who visibly grew in confidence. After the fall of Mazar-e Sharif, the CIA, SOF and Northern Alliance planned for an attack to capture Kabul.

On 13 November the Northern Alliance began a series of deliberate attacks, which were intended to culminate in the capture of Kabul. But the Taliban forces guarding the route to the city had been badly battered by the incessant US air attacks. Their defence quickly collapsed and little more than 24 hours later Kabul fell to an unopposed advance by Northern Alliance troops.

Taliban forces in Northern Afghanistan fell back on the town of Kunduz. Pounded by US air strikes, their defences against Northern Alliance forces did not last long. Concurrently Taliban forces in western Afghanistan collapsed. The remnants of Taliban forces that could evade the Northern Alliance and US airpower fled, either south-west towards Kandahar or south-east towards Pakistan.

SOUTHERN AFGHANISTAN, KANDAHAR AND KARZAI

Another SOF task force had been formed to operate in southern Afghanistan: Combined Joint Task Force (CJTF) South, for which US SOF were joined by the SOF of seven nations, including Norway, and the Canadian SOF unit, Joint Task Force 2. Deploying by air directly into south-east Afghanistan, it found the Norwegian SOF, who were trained to operate through the Norway's Arctic winter, had a level of skill in operations in Afghanistan's mountains that the SOF of neither the US nor the other nations could match.

The Northern Alliance had no presence in the Pashtun-dominated south of Afghanistan. Not only were its Uzbek and Tajik leaders disinclined to move into the south, but also the US considered that their doing so could politically destabilize the region. But US and British diplomats and intelligence agencies struggled to identify Pashtun military leaders who could incite uprisings against the Taliban. They eventually fastened on to Hamid Karzai, a Pashtun former mujahedeen leader, based in Pakistan. On 9 October Karzai and a few associates drove into southern Afghanistan, on motorcycles, carrying with them a CIA-provided satellite telephone. He sought to raise a rebellion against the Taliban in Tarin Kowt, the capital of Uruzgan Province.

So close to the Taliban heartland of Kandahar this action produced a furious counter-attack by Taliban troops. Karzai appears to have been evacuated by US SOF, returning to Uruzgan Province on 14 November. A Task Force Dagger team, Texas 12, flew into southern Afghanistan, its army MH60 Black Hawk helicopter being supported by Predator drones and AC130 gunships. It linked up with Karzai and his forces at Tarin Kowt, Uruzgan's provincial capital. The next night, weapons and ammunition were air dropped for Karzai's forces, after which the undefended town fell to them. The Taliban counter-attacked in battalion strength, but this force was destroyed by US air strikes directed by Texas 12. This was fortunate as many of Karzai's fighters had fled. But Karzai had now established a base north-east of Kandahar.

Between 19 and 25 November another SOF team, Texas 17, was flown to the south of Kandahar and contacted the forces of Gul Agha Sherzai. These turned out to be little more than an armed mob, albeit about 600 strong. The militia was persuaded to support the offensive against Kandahar and moved to block the road between Kandahar and the border town of Spin Baldak. From there the SOF could see all the way to Kandahar airport and air strikes were directed against Taliban and Al Qaida parties moving by road.

In the initial planning for intervention in Afghanistan General Franks had rejected an offer from the US Marines to assist in Afghanistan. Franks believed that the distance of almost 300 miles from the shore of Pakistan to the southern edge of Afghanistan made it impossible for the Marines to deploy from amphibious shipping in the Indian Ocean to the landlocked country. But Frank's understanding of Marine capabilities was out of date. The Marines had long been developing an ability to strike at range from the sea. During the previous decade the Marines had not only equipped themselves with giant CH53 transport helicopters able to refuel in the air, but also fitted a proportion of their C130 Hercules transports to act as air refuellers. They had also provided themselves with Sea Cobra attack helicopters and wheeled light armoured vehicles with 25mm cannon, to make themselves more lethal.

US Navy Vice Admiral Willy Moore, the commander of US ships in CENTCOM's area, saw an opportunity to unbalance Taliban defences in southern Afghanistan and threaten control of Kandahar. Moore requested that CENTCOM authorize the planning of raids into southern Afghanistan by Marines. To conduct these operations Moore selected Marine Brigadier General James Mattis to lead Task Force 58, comprising US Navy amphibious shipping and a Marine Expeditionary Brigade of two Marine Expeditionary Units (MEUs). It was organized, trained and equipped to deploy at speed from US Navy amphibious shipping and operate independently.

MAP 3: US-LED ATTACKS IN AFGHANISTAN, 2001/2

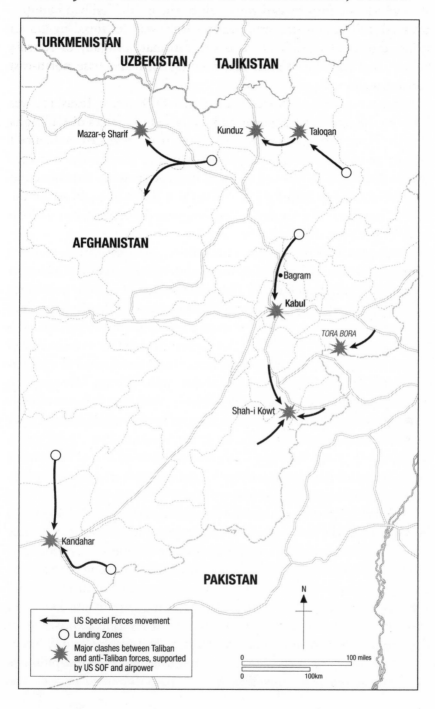

The two expeditionary units, 15th MEU and 26th MEU, each had at their core a US Marine infantry battalion. The brigade had a high degree of independence from external support, with its own combat support, including combat engineers and artillery, expeditionary logistic support and its own air wing with its own helicopters, including AH1 Cobra gunships, UH-1 Huey utility aircraft and CH53 transports.

Mattis co-opted a unit of US Navy SEAL commandos that had been left out of the SOF task forces already deployed to Afghanistan. He also sought advice from the commander of JSOC. Together they identified that for the Marines to seize a base in Kandahar Province would both disrupt Taliban defences and provide a secure launch pad for raids by both SOF and Marines.

Mattis selected as their first objective the airstrip south of Kandahar, Objective Rhino, that had previously been briefly held by the Rangers of Task Force Sword at the start of the campaign. This positioned them to both interdict Taliban movement and seize Kandahar airfield. A covert reconnaissance team of SEALs had been clandestinely inserted by helicopter a few days before to check that there were no Taliban in the area.

The night of 25 November, US Marine helicopters were launched from the Indian Ocean to seize the airstrip. The first wave of Marines clambered into six of the giant CH53 helicopters. These flew over 440 miles direct to the objective, being refuelled in the air by Marine KC130 tanker aircraft. The flight to Objective Rhino was the furthest inland that any amphibious force had ever struck.

Objective Rhino was rapidly secured, a team from a USAF special tactics squadron quickly establishing air traffic control and setting out landing lights. Marine C130 Hercules transports landed 400 more Marines. They were rapidly joined by Marine Cobra and Huey helicopters, which had stopped at Shamsi airfield in Pakistan to refuel. Shortly afterwards USAF C17 transports began flying in more Marines, their vehicles and a medical unit. A 125-strong contingent of 'Seabees', US Navy construction engineers, were flown in to maintain and improve the airstrip. The Marine helicopter and ground patrols sought to identify and attack Taliban within 120 miles of Camp Rhino. As they deployed, a stockpile of supplies was built up at the base. The US Navy's P3 Orion maritime patrol aircraft were operating over Afghanistan to provide persistent aerial surveillance, using powerful surveillance devices to search for the Taliban and Al Qaida. On several occasions columns of Taliban vehicles were detected approaching Rhino. These were destroyed by the Marines and US aircraft.

Mattis was now commanding Task Force 58 from the bleak, dusty airfield at Rhino, steadily reinforcing it with Marines. He had intended that his Marines reach out to attack the Taliban, and several times he offered CENTCOM the opportunity to use Task Force 58 to destroy the Taliban HQ in Kandahar. He was frustrated and perplexed when CENTCOM vetoed his proposals. Although the Marines were using their armoured vehicles and helicopters to mount long-range patrols, these operations only used a fraction of the combat power assembled at Rhino.

Meanwhile Karzai's forces were advancing from Tarin Kowt towards Kandahar. A battle developed around a bridge south of the town of Sayd Alim Kalay. Air strikes destroyed a convoy of enemy vehicles, but small arms fire prevented Karzai's fighters from capturing the bridge. The US SOF deployed on both sides of the road. A pitched battle developed, with several Taliban attacks across the riverbed being repulsed. Often the attackers were too close to the Americans to allow US aircraft to intervene. But the next day the attackers were nowhere to be seen and Karzai's advance continued.

On 5 December, Karzai's forces were about 20 miles from Kandahar. While they were halted to allow Karzai and the SOF to plan future moves against the city a combat air controller was attempting to bring bombs to bear on Taliban fighters to the south, assisted by a B52 bomber. Suddenly there was an enormous explosion. As the dust settled it emerged that three people had been killed and 20 injured. A 2,000-pound bomb had struck the group. The combat controller had been calling in a JDAM bomb. But an error made while changing the batteries of his GPS navigation device meant that instead of passing the co-ordinates of the Taliban fighters' position, the crew of the B52 were passed the co-ordinates of the controller instead.

Improbably, Karzai survived, albeit lightly injured. He showed remarkable composure. As the wounded were being tended by the survivors, Karzai learned from a satellite telephone call that he had been selected as the Chairman of the Interim Afghan Government. A subsequent satellite conversation revealed that the Taliban commander in Kandahar was willing to surrender the city. This was accomplished on 7 December.

Shortly afterwards the Marines of Task Force 58 secured Kandahar airfield. They were supported by their attack helicopters and Harrier jets. A Predator unmanned aerial vehicle flying overhead provided real-time video. Viewers included the CENTCOM land component HQ in Doha, Qatar. As at Camp Rhino, the airfield was rapidly secured and put into working order, this time with the assistance of a local anti-Taliban militia. By mid-December C130s and C17s were delivering supplies.

From 12 September the CIA, the National Security Agency and the many US military intelligence agencies had been attempting to locate Osama Bin Laden. In mid-November the CIA received reports that he was in Jalalabad, along with large numbers of retreating Al Qaida and Taliban fighters. Shortly afterwards intelligence suggested that he, along with many fighters, had fled the city southwards and taken refuge in the Tora Bora mountains. These were forbidding and difficult mountainous terrain, very close to Pakistan, where the Afghan Mujahedeen were said to have made considerable use of natural cave complexes.

COMMAND, CONTROL AND PLANNING FOR ANOTHER WAR

CENTCOM was controlling the military campaign from its permanent HQ in Tampa. Command was being delegated to the air component HQ in Qatar, the maritime HQ in Bahrain and the two US SOF HQs for northern and southern Afghanistan. In addition, the CENTCOM land component HQ in Kuwait was commanding the conventional land forces in Central Asia and Afghanistan. Franks chose not to designate an overall joint force commander for all operations in Afghanistan, preferring to exercise command himself from Tampa. He appeared confident that by a combination of video teleconference, emails and occasional visits to Afghanistan he and CENTCOM would be able to direct and supervise all military operations in the country.

Previously US theatre commanders had deployed their HQs to the operational theatre. General Schwarzkopf had done so in Saudi Arabia in 1990, when he had moved his HQ to the Saudi capital in Riyadh. And in 1996 Admiral Leighton Smith, the US and NATO theatre commander for NATO operations in Bosnia, had set up his

HQ in Sarajevo. In both cases they had put themselves and key staff in the political centres of gravity of the theatres. But in 2001 and 2002 General Franks chose to remain in Florida ten time-zones away from Kabul, relying on regular video conferences with subordinate HQs.

One factor preventing Franks from visiting Afghanistan and Central Asia and keeping him in the US was probably the initiation of military planning to attack Iraq. In late November Rumsfeld informed Franks that President Bush wanted both of them to start looking at options for dealing with Iraq and that Franks was to brief Rumsfeld in early December. To command and plan operations in Afghanistan, the key staff at Tampa were routinely working 16 hours a day for seven days. It seems likely that the additional task overloaded the HQ.

THE BATTLE OF TORA BORA

In early December teams from the CIA and Task Force Sword infiltrated the Tora Bora area. They confirmed the presence of both Taliban and Al Qaida fighters. The CIA became increasingly concerned that Bin Laden and other Al Qaida leaders would quickly flee from Tora Bora into Pakistan. This fear was amplified by the relative ease with which fighters could infiltrate to Pakistan. There was only a limited presence of Pakistani security forces in the rugged mountainous tribal areas. To prevent this the CIA requested that a battalion of Rangers be deployed to Tora Bora to seal escape routes and then to assault the caves in which Bin Laden was believed to be sheltering.

General Franks disagreed, rejecting the CIA's request. He and Rumsfeld agreed that the US should only have a 'light footprint' in Afghanistan, so as to avoid a Soviet-style occupation. US airpower, Task Force Sword and Northern Alliance militias would be used. This approach had worked in Mazar-e Sharif, Kabul and Kandahar, so why would it not work again? The US was to use the same approach to tackle Tora Bora. Two different Northern Alliance militias commanded by Hazrat Ali and Haji Zaman would advance into the area. These two commanders were rivals, whose only common interest appeared to be leveraging US support, money and supplies to bolster their influence. It is doubtful that they had much true interest in the destruction of Al Qaida. The destruction of the Taliban had removed the common purpose that had united the Northern Alliance's warlords.

On 5 December the militias began advancing, pushing aside Al Qaida fighters at the edge of the mountains. SOF called in US bombers to attack identified enemy. As the militias, backed by US SOF, slowly advanced they encountered bunkers and caves. Additional Afghan fighters with some aged Soviet-made tanks joined the operation as did German and British SOF. Air strikes intensified. That week over 2,000 US bombs and missiles were used to attack ground targets in Afghanistan.

Some Al Qaida fighters negotiated a truce with Zaman, offering to surrender to the UN. This was contrary to the US forces policy of killing or capturing Al Qaida. US commanders would only accept an unconditional surrender of the jihadists, and air attacks continued. This truce may have been a ruse to allow time to escape into Pakistan. Ali's forces continued to advance.

So far in the campaign, the US had only asked Pakistan for the use of its airspace and airfields. But as US troops deployed to Tora Bora, the US asked Pakistan to deploy forces to its side of the border that faced Tora Bora, to stop militants escaping into Pakistan. This happened slowly, the US turning down a request by the Pakistani Army for Pakistani troops to be lifted into the mountains by US helicopters. And it took time for the Pakistan Army to gain the consent of tribal elders, which it considered essential to the success of any military operation in the tribal areas. In the event some Pakistani troops were deployed into the tribal areas towards the end of the operation. Some Al Qaida fighters were captured.

The Afghan militia claimed to have killed 200 Al Qaida fighters and captured 25, some of the prisoners being Chechen jihadists. But Bin Laden was not found. The operation ended in mid-December. Later estimates were that between 1,500 and 2,000 Afghan, Arab and Chechen Al Qaida fighters had been in Tora Bora before the attack. Perhaps two-thirds of these made it across the border into Pakistan. Other Taliban and Al Qaida fighters crossed the border elsewhere along its 1,200-mile length. Both Mullah Omar, the Taliban leader, and Osama Bin Laden successfully fled to Pakistan.

Could the escape of Bin Laden and so many Al Qaida fighters have been prevented? The forbidding mountainous terrain probably made it impossible to prevent *all* the fighters escaping from Tora Bora into Pakistan. But deploying a US Ranger battalion, as the CIA had requested, would have made that escape much more difficult.

US Marine Brigadier General Mattis, commanding Task Force 58 on Kandahar airfield, was increasingly chafing under CENTCOM's apparent unwillingness to exploit the firepower and mobility of his force. Together with the Navy SEALS based at Kandahar, the Marines had combined forces to use Marine helicopters and infantry to conduct raids on the Taliban. Mattis' Marine expeditionary unit had also been resubordinated away from the Naval HQ at Bahrain to the CENTCOM Army HQ, ARCENT, an HQ that made many more demands on Mattis' small HQ and did not appear enthusiastic that the Marines be used any more aggressively.

Monitoring the US intelligence and operational picture, Mattis considered that the Marines could have assisted greatly at Tora Bora. Not only did they have their formidably tough infantry; they also had rapidly deployable light armoured vehicles and a full complement of combat support and expeditionary logistics. In addition they had attack and transport helicopters that could rapidly transport Marines and SOF to eastern Afghanistan, where they could have made a real difference. Mattis developed a plan to use the forces he had in southern Afghanistan to assist. US SOF, Marine infantry, light armour and attack helicopters would move by road and air to cut off the mountain passes interdicting the routes south from Tora Bora to Pakistan. This plan was put to ARCENT. The HQ did not respond. Increasingly frustrated at the opportunity that was being missed, Mattis offered to subordinate his force to the US SOF, but to no avail.

Afloat on amphibious shipping in the Indian Ocean there were more US Marines and British Royal Marines, both forces with organic helicopters that could have deployed direct to Tora Bora. And the US Army's 82nd Airborne Division based in Fort Bragg had an entire airborne brigade of paratroops at very high readiness for worldwide operations. Indeed, in the late 1990s the US had demonstrated the ability to use their C17 strategic transport aircraft to deliver a parachute battalion from Fort Bragg to Central Asia, conducting a battalion parachute drop to join a regional exercise. This capability could easily have been used to insert Rangers or paratroops into a drop zone close to Tora Bora.

It appears that the principal obstacle to putting an effective block of conventional forces between Tora Bora and Pakistan was the US military commanders' reluctance to do so. For this responsibility lies with General Franks at CENTCOM and Donald Rumsfeld. By not doing more at this crucial juncture they made it easier for Al Qaida to reconstitute its capability, credibility and narrative. So it was easier than it could have been for Al Qaida fighters to make their way to Pakistan and then on to Iraq and other countries.

INITIAL STABILIZATION OPERATIONS IN AFGHANISTAN

US, UK and other international troops who arrived in Afghanistan in the autumn and winter of 2001 and in 2002 were, without exception, shocked at the state of the country. Many of them had served in Bosnia, both during the civil war or after it ended, when the scars of that savage conflict were all too visible. The accumulated damage to Kabul was much greater than that inflicted on Sarajevo, the Bosnian capital. Many of Kabul's population had survived on international food aid for the previous five years. Most government ministries were hollow shells. Competent staff had mostly fled the Taliban's Kabul. Afghanistan's national capability as a state was at a very low level.

Afghan industry, agriculture and state institutions had been very badly damaged by two decades of war. The only telephones that worked were satellite phones. Western troops, diplomats and development staff were shocked to see how poor and isolated many rural agricultural communities were. And discovering that, other than in a very small elite centred on Kabul, Afghan society treated women as utterly subordinate to men was another shock to international sensibilities. To some it seemed that the further they travelled from Kabul, the further they went back in time, in both agriculture and linkages to the modern world. For example, it was not hard to find Afghans who had not heard of 9/11. British special forces patrols in rural regions would sometimes be asked if they were Russian troops.[12]

Embassies and international organizations established themselves in a very austere environment. The CIA set itself up in a ramshackle hotel where 'Bearded special operators and case officers with Glock pistols strapped to their thighs tromped in and out. The atmosphere was a cross between a central Asian organized crime clubhouse and a decrepit hotel in a muddy street in an old western.'[13]

In the Cold War the CIA had been very active in the developing world, seeking to constrain Soviet influence. It would use cash, intelligence feeds and advice to influence national leaders to support the US. And the Special Activities Division, its paramilitary wing, would raise local forces, to protect CIA agent handlers and to conduct covert armed action. These activities were a deeply ingrained part of the CIA's operational culture. Within the panoply of US national security actors, the CIA was independent and free-standing, considering itself equal to and not subordinate to the State Department and US military.[14]

The CIA, supported by US SOF, established a chain of small bases along the border with Pakistan. Typically located in small mud brick forts, their primary functions were to gather intelligence on Al Qaida and the Taliban. Also based in the forts were signals intelligence teams searching radio frequencies for evidence of both groups. In addition, the bases housed human intelligence teams. These attempted to recruit Afghan and Pakistani civilians as their eyes and ears. There were no telephones of any type in the frontier areas and agents would be despatched on missions of several weeks. These Afghans would be paid $50 or $100 for intelligence, but analysts found it very difficult to differentiate between fact, fantasy and rumour.

In the regions around the forts, as elsewhere in Afghanistan, local strongmen and militia leaders sought to capture US resources and military support. With inadequate understanding of the complex local dynamics, US and Coalition forces unknowingly allowed themselves to be manipulated. This included being provided with intelligence about Taliban and Al Qaida supporters, which on too many occasions led to raids on local actors who were nothing to do with the insurgents or jihadists, but who happened to be rivals of the group providing the information.

Some of those detained by US troops or the CIA were totally innocent of Taliban or Al Qaida sympathies or involvement. Some were sent to the US military prisons at Bagram air base in Afghanistan or Guantanamo Bay. Others disappeared into the CIA's secret prison network. There is overwhelming evidence that some Afghan prisoners were subject to cruel and inhumane treatment amounting to torture. Some died of their injuries, others of deliberate neglect. This did not apply to all detainees, but enough were abused to stoke the fires of resentment and humiliation.

These flames were also fanned by the way US and Coalition vehicles and convoys drove around Kabul and other towns and cities. They would often bully civilian vehicles off the roads making liberal use of warning shots. Many were under instructions not to stop in the event of an accident, no matter how serious. The numerous private security companies hired by the US military and many embassies were if anything less restrained than US troops. A particularly egregious example was the knocking down and killing of an Afghan woman by a private security team on their way to meet Hillary Clinton at Kabul airport.

In December 2001 as US-led forces continued to hunt down remnants of Taliban and Al Qaida forces, warlords' armed militias staked out territory that they controlled, the boundaries marked by checkpoints. Meanwhile an international conference convened under UN auspices in Bonn sought to assist the stabilization and reconstruction of post-Taliban Afghanistan. The Bonn Agreement was brokered between prominent Afghan leaders by the United Nations. Hamid Karzai was appointed interim Afghan president and inaugurated on 22 December. A committee was assembled to draft a new constitution.

At an international conference in Tokyo in early 2002, billions of dollars of international aid were pledged as was international assistance with reconstruction, development, building new security forces and countering the narcotics industry. There was to be an international effort to conduct security-sector reform and field new security forces.

THE INTERNATIONAL SECURITY ASSISTANCE FORCE (ISAF)

The Bonn Agreement noted that it would take time to develop Afghanistan's new security forces, so a UN-mandated force would deploy to 'assist in the maintenance of security for Kabul and the surrounding area'.[15] British Prime Minister Tony Blair was very keen that the UK lead this force. A reconnaissance party of British officers was despatched to Kabul where they found a city with few people, with no cars on the streets and in almost total darkness at night.

Over December and January, the UK-led International Security Assistance Force (ISAF) deployed by air to assist the Afghan authorities in the maintenance of the security of Kabul. As it was established by the UK, its HQ was based on that of the 3rd UK Division. It controlled a British-led multinational brigade of three battalions, one a British parachute battalion, with major French and German contributions. Many other nations offered to contribute forces. Most of these offers were of infantry, of which ISAF already had enough, but there were insufficient offers of engineers and logistic units, as well as helicopters.

The British wanted ISAF to be subordinated to CENTCOM. They sought to maximize co-operation between ISAF and the US-led Operation *Enduring Freedom* forces in Afghanistan and to be able to call on US forces, should the mission encounter any threats that it could not handle on its own. This was vetoed both by Donald Rumsfeld and by Germany, the latter stating that ISAF was a peace-keeping, not a combat force. This was an early harbinger of the differing national appetites for risk that would create political and military friction throughout the Afghan and Iraq wars.

ISAF's commander, British Major General John McColl, ordered ISAF to 'create a secure environment within Kabul, within which the developing Afghan government can gain traction'.[16] Anticipated threats of a Taliban counter-attack or armed conflict between rival militia groups failed to manifest themselves, although there were some exchanges of small arms fire with armed criminal gangs. ISAF's infantry spent much time patrolling the city alongside Northern Alliance troops.

McColl did all he could to support the new Afghan interim administration in general and Karzai in particular, as well as the UN diplomat Lakhtar Brahimi, whom McColl treated as de facto head of the international community in Kabul. The British contingent of ISAF also provided instructors for the training of the first battalion of the new Afghan National Guard. Along with ISAF, this provided security for the Loya Jirga that elected Karzai as head of the Afghan Transitional Government.

Karzai and many Afghans wanted ISAF to expand both in size and by deploying outside Kabul. McColl produced a plan to show what might be achieved with a fourfold increase in the size of the force to 20,000 international troops. This was opposed by Rumsfeld and rejected by the US National Security Council. With British military planners turning their eyes to Iraq, London too had no appetite for ISAF expansion. The British handed leadership of ISAF to Turkey in mid-2002.[17]

OPERATION *ANACONDA* — THE BATTLE OF THE SHAH-I KOWT VALLEY

After the battle of Tora Bora, US intelligence resources searched for any remaining Taliban, Al Qaida and jihadist forces remaining in Afghanistan. In early 2002, the US forces and the CIA began picking up multiple indications of jihadists concentrating in the Shah-i Kowt Valley, a mountainous region in south-east Afghanistan near the Pakistan border. This included agent reports of Chechen and Uzbek Al Qaida fighters manning checkpoints and the capture and execution of some Afghans who were acting as US informants. Analysis of agent reports and signals intelligence suggested the presence of up to 1,500 jihadist fighters.

The terrain was forbidding. The valley floor was over 6,500 feet above sea level. It was surrounded by mountain ridges up to 5,000 feet higher. Reaching the valley by helicopters launched from Bagram would be challenging enough; the intervening distance of approximately 90 miles, much of it mountainous, would restrict the time for which helicopters could remain aloft in the target areas. And the altitudes of the valley and surrounding ridges would reduce helicopter payloads.

Commanded by the CENTCOM land component HQ in Kuwait, the HQ of 10th Mountain Division had originally been deployed to Central Asia to help protect the US bases there. It was subsequently moved to Bagram airfield, becoming the US main conventional land force in the country. The troops available to it comprised an air assault brigade HQ of the 101st Airborne Division with two of its own battalions and a single infantry battalion of the 10th Mountain Division. The division assumed that the large amounts of fixed-wing aircraft available over Afghanistan would be able to provide all the fire support needed. So it left its artillery in the US. In late February the division was designated as CJTF Mountain.

Commended by US Army Major General Franklin Hagenbeck, the division planned Operation *Anaconda* to encircle and destroy

MAP 4: THE PLAN FOR OPERATION *ANACONDA*, FEBRUARY–MARCH 2002

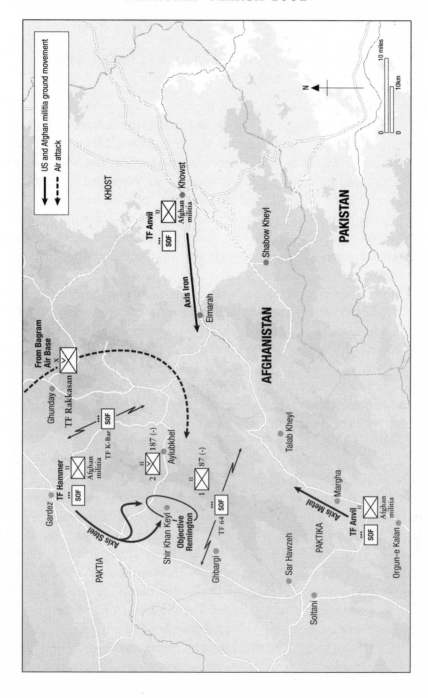

the concentration of Al Qaida fighters. The plan was that US SOF would lead up to a thousand Afghan militia fighters that they were supporting into the valley floor, while positions blocking the enemy's likely withdrawal routes would be seized by the division's infantry, landing by helicopter onto the commanding heights of the surrounding ridges. It anticipated that, once attacked, the fighters would attempt to escape towards Pakistan, being attacked by US airpower as they did so.

At its very beginning on 2 March the operation ran into unexpected difficulties. The combined force of Afghan militia led by US SOF was delayed by a traffic accident; it was then attacked by a AC130 gunship before running into unexpectedly effective enemy gunfire. The Afghans' morale was badly damaged and they became very reluctant to advance towards the jihadists. Concurrently the US infantry on the ridges were also subject to effective enemy fire from well-prepared dug-in fighting positions that were difficult to locate. Air support proved more difficult to co-ordinate than anticipated and unexpected bad weather delayed the arrival of reinforcing infantry. Lacking organic artillery, large numbers of air strikes and sorties by attack helicopters were needed just to keep the US troops alive. This unexpectedly heavy opposition caused the US infantry to withdraw from its exposed positions.

On 4 March, US SOF attempted to establish observations posts that overlooked the enemy. A US Navy SEAL, Petty Officer Roberts, fell from a helicopter and was captured and killed by the enemy. Not knowing of his death, the SOF attempted to land more operators to rescue him. During the ensuing fighting six more US troops were killed and a helicopter was shot down. This part of the battle became known as the battle of Roberts Ridge.

Very heavy use was made of US airpower to take the pressure off the infantry, SOF and Afghan militia. The US air HQ in Qatar had not been involved in the planning of Operation *Anaconda* and there was initially much confusion and friction in the command and control of fixed-wing aircraft. It took five more days for the ground forces to achieve control over the key terrain. Many of the Al Qaida and jihadist defenders had been killed by bombs. The US troops were astonished to find that they had dug well-protected trenches and bunkers, often with strong overhead cover and stocks of food, water and ammunition. They were also supported by similarly well-constructed observation posts sited to detect attackers forming up. None of these positions had been detected by drones, air reconnaissance or satellites.

Subsequently, US performance in the battle has come in for a great deal of criticism, not least in official histories commissioned by the US Army itself. The operation suffered from inadequate intelligence, insufficient organic fire support and unrealistic expectations, including over-reliance on warlords' militias. A major weakness was air–land integration. This arose as a result of a mutual lack of understanding between the CJTF Mountain HQ at Bagram air base and the US air HQ in the Gulf. Before the operation there had been little joint planning between General Hagenbeck's HQ and the air component HQ in Qatar. So, when urgent air support was needed in the first few days of the operation, it was not as effective as it should have been. And CJTF Mountain had no organic artillery which could have brought immediate suppressive fire onto the enemy. General Hagenbeck's ability to fight the battle was also complicated by his HQ having no authority over some of the US SOF and their helicopters that took part.

Planning of Operation *Anaconda* had been greatly influenced by the US military's ever-increasing capabilities to link up commanders and HQs by secure video, to allow them to interact by video conference. This was insufficient to prevent a major disconnect between the land component HQ in Bagram and the air component HQ in the Gulf. Video conferences lacked the many informal and social dynamics of physical meetings. A more conventional approach to command, control and planning and less reliance on video conference might have led to better planning of air–land integration.[18] It is likely that had there been a properly constituted joint task force HQ, commanding all US forces in Afghanistan, the battle would have been better planned and executed. The responsibility for this capability gap, along with the previous failure to interdict jihadist fighters escaping from Tora Bora to Pakistan lies at the door of General Franks.

THE AUDIT OF WAR

In World War II the US and UK had armed and supported resistance movements in Europe and Asia. During the Vietnam War, the US had supported indigenous groups in both Vietnam and Laos. Various clandestine and special forces as well as air supply and direct support by air strikes had been employed. But none of these operations had decisive strategic impact.

In contrast the US campaign after 9/11 to support anti-Taliban armed groups was decisive. It had succeeded much more quickly than was envisaged. Despite the difficulties posed by the lack of US knowledge of Afghanistan, compressed planning timeframe, mountainous terrain and demanding distance, this approach succeeded more rapidly than anyone suspected. Why was this?

The Taliban's rudimentary air defences having been easily neutralized at the outset, the US had air superiority over the country. The Taliban's static defensive positions of trenches and bunkers were relatively easy to identify from the air, opening them to devastating air attack. As Taliban forces collapsed there was plenty of opportunity for them to discard their military accoutrements and fade into the population.

At the start of the war, the Taliban forces were assessed as greatly outnumbering the Northern Alliance. But the great majority of Taliban units were of limited military quality; they were ill-trained and equipped with obsolete and poorly maintained equipment. Their standard of military leadership was low. There was also a vast differential of military technology. The Taliban had few systems procured after the 1980s and much dated from the 1950s and 60s. The US had dropped over 12,000 bombs. Sixty per cent of these had precision guidance.

In contrast, Al Qaida fighters displayed greater fighting spirit. Many of them were Arabs who had less chance of blending into the Afghan towns and villages and who could expect little mercy from the Northern Alliance if captured. Many were better trained than the average Northern Alliance fighter, with a higher standard of tactics, and often fought with a savage and desperate determination.

However, there was a huge differential of capability between them and the US forces. The SOF opposing them, the US Army 'green berets', Delta Force, and Navy SEALS, were all elite operators, carefully selected, rigorously trained and with tried and tested leaders with immense experience in special operations. The same applied to the allied special forces from the UK, Canada and Norway that the US permitted to join them. In the Rangers and Marines, the US was deploying elite infantry forces, some of the world's best.

The same applied to the crews of the SOF dedicated helicopters and transport aircraft, again selected for high levels of airmanship to deliver and supply parties at range, at night and at the limits of their aircrafts' envelopes. And the Marines and SOF displayed a very high standard of air–land integration, both in delivering troops and supplies at range with their organic helicopters and transport aircraft and in being able to direct air strikes onto the Taliban. The main body of pilots and aircrew of the fighter jets and bombers of the US Air Force, Navy and Marine Corps flying high above had also been no less rigorously selected and just as extensively trained.

All the US and allied soldiers, sailors, marines and airmen had high morale. The 9/11 attacks were an outrage and there was a universal feeling that justice should be served on Al Qaida. And as the Taliban forces crumbled under the relentless onslaught of both the Northern Alliance and US airpower, morale rose. In contrast Taliban morale declined under the relentless pressure of US air strikes and the Northern Alliance attacks.

The Taliban had also been outmanoeuvred. It had been unable to move reserves to reinforce the defenders of Mazar-e Sharif. As the campaign went on, movement of Taliban troops by road was increasingly subject to interdiction by US aircraft.

US airpower had a decisive effect. Neither the Taliban nor Al Qaida had any way of countering the US Navy's ability to launch combat jets from the enormous aircraft carriers in the Indian Ocean. Carrier-borne airpower was particularly important in October and November 2001 when the US Air Force lacked enough airfields close enough to Afghanistan to bring more than a fraction of their aircraft to bear.

Aircraft carriers and amphibious ships also played a decisive role as floating platforms from which SOF and amphibious forces could be projected by helicopter from the Indian Ocean over Pakistan and into Afghanistan. Without these capabilities, the Taliban would have controlled southern Afghanistan for longer and more of their fighters would have escaped into Pakistan. There would have been more chance of trapping Bin Laden and more Al Qaida fighters in the US and Afghan attack on the Tora Bora mountains if CENTCOM had chosen to deploy the US Marines of Task Force 58 from Kandahar to eastern Afghanistan.

The US had taken advantage of an army in being, the Northern Alliance. Incentivized by US money and supplies, the Alliance's advance had been made possible by the application of US airpower, the whole integrated by the CIA and US SOF teams. At the height of the fighting in December, numbers of US and allied SOF on the ground were probably less than a thousand.

This remarkable example of integration between ground troops and precision air strikes and between the Northern Alliance and the US overwhelmed the enemy. The harsh rule of the Taliban had also alienated many Afghans who welcomed their defeat.

CENTCOM and many military commentators were rightly impressed with the success of the campaign and the differential in casualties: 12 US military personnel and one CIA officer had died but hundreds of Taliban and Al Qaida fighters had been killed. The Pentagon and US government's sense of satisfaction was justified. But there were some characteristics of the conflict's character that attracted less attention.

The militias that fought on the US side did so in accordance with an 'Afghan way of war'. This included ceasefires and switching sides. And the militias and the warlords who led them would usually put their own interests first. Secondly, whilst there had been much fighting there had been comparatively little close combat where Taliban and pro-US groups closed with each other. The close combat that did occur often featured resolute groups of US and coalition SOF. Apart from Tora Bora, the difference between the Afghan and US ways of war had not caused friction, but time would tell if the interests of the US and its allies and those of the various anti-Taliban groups would converge or diverge.

These were factors that contributed to the failure to trap Bin Laden and Al Qaida fighters at Tora Bora. Important as they were, however, the main factor that led to the missing of this opportunity was Rumsfeld's and Franks' failure to deploy enough US or Coalition troops into the area.

After the fall of the Taliban, the British-led ISAF performed a vital role in helping to stabilize Kabul and reinforce the authority of President Karzai. The US chose to maintain a 'light footprint' in the country. The military limitations of this approach were exposed by the failure of Operation *Anaconda to* encircle and destroy a concentration of Al Qaida fighters. The principal reason for this was that the Al Qaida fighters were in well-prepared fighting positions and stood and fought, neither of which had been predicted by US military intelligence. Additional factors were an unwillingness of Afghan militias to close with Al Qaida, insufficient organic fire support and air–land integration resulting from a mutual lack of understanding between the US land component HQ at Bagram air base and the US air component HQ in the Gulf. Abundant secure email and video conference links were no substitute for the lack of a properly constituted joint task force HQ, commanding all US forces in Afghanistan.

Economy of Force

Stabilizing Afghanistan 2002–05

US STRATEGIC PRIORITIES CHANGE

CENTCOM was under direction from the Pentagon to keep its troop presence in Afghanistan to a 'light footprint'. Rumsfeld was concerned to avoid the US and its allies being seen as an army of occupation, like the Soviet forces in the 1980s. From late 2001, Rumsfeld and Franks were increasingly engaged in planning to attack Iraq. They both identified that any attack on Iraq would need considerably more ground troops than had been used to remove the Taliban from power so US force levels in Afghanistan needed to be minimized. CENTCOM's main effort became planning for the attack on Iraq. From early 2002 Iraq displaced Afghanistan as the strategic priority of the US and its allies.

Afghanistan became an 'economy of force' theatre. About 10,000 US and Coalition conventional forces and SOF remained in the country to hunt any remaining Al Qaida and Taliban forces. They would be assisted by US-funded warlords' militias. In April 2002 President Bush announced that:

> peace will only be achieved when we give the Afghan people the means to achieve their own aspirations. Peace ... will be achieved by helping Afghanistan develop its own stable government. Peace will be achieved by helping Afghanistan train and develop its own

national army. And peace will be achieved through an education system for boys and girls which works ... We're clearing minefields. We're rebuilding roads. We're improving medical care. And we will work to help Afghanistan to develop an economy that can feed its people without feeding the world's demand for drugs.[1]

The same month saw the US establish a new CJTF HQ to command US forces in Afghanistan and co-ordinate with ISAF. The HQ of 18th Airborne Corps became CJTF 180, commanding US and allied forces to counter residual Taliban and Al Qaida presence in Afghanistan. It sought to mount 'search and destroy' missions to locate and then attack Al Qaida and Taliban remnants, anywhere in Afghanistan where intelligence indicated promising targets.

Whilst these operations were sometimes successful, the resulting civilian casualties and collateral damage increasingly alienated Afghan civilians. As there were no US HQs subordinate to the single HQ at Bagram, aggrieved Afghans lacked a local Coalition military HQ where they could seek resolution to these grievances. With the exception of ISAF's operations in Kabul, no US or international forces were assigned a specified area of Afghan territory as their own area of operations.

The US and international reconstruction and development effort was almost entirely focused on Kabul. And CENTCOM and Rumsfeld made it clear that there were no extra military resources to spare for Afghanistan. How then was Afghan government capability outside Kabul to be developed?

The CJTF Chief of Plans, British Colonel Nick Carter,[2] had visited a US SOF team in Gardez in eastern Afghanistan. Manned by reservists, it included a vet and doctor, whose expertise had made them very popular with local Afghans. Carter proposed that similar teams be deployed throughout the country to help the Afghan government extend its reach into the provinces. Initially these were called Coalition Humanitarian Liaison Centres. Manned by staff from US Army Civil Affairs units they were to assess humanitarian needs and conduct small-scale reconstruction projects.

By the end of 2002 the concept was expanded to include US government civilians and the teams were re-named as provincial reconstruction teams (PRTs); these were multi-agency groups of military and civilian personnel, including diplomats and development agency staff and experts in other fields such as policing, agriculture and justice. Located at provincial capitals they were intended to support Afghan civilian reconstruction efforts as well as increasing the local population's consent to the activities of international forces. By the end of 2003 there were nine PRTs in Afghanistan.

Most teams were provided by the US, but New Zealand, Germany and UK also deployed PRTs. This initiative was adopted by ISAF as well. Teams varied considerably in size, from 50 to 100 people in a US PRT, to a German PRT with about 300 people. The capabilities and operational approaches of the PRTs also varied greatly according to the lead nation, reflecting different national attitudes to development, its synchronization with the military, and national attitudes to force protection of civilians. US PRTs were multi-agency in character: the military provided security, while the US Agency for International Development (USAID) ran reconstruction and development programmes, and the State Department provided diplomats to monitor and influence local Afghan politics.[3]

Although they had initially called for ISAF to expand its footprint outside the capital, many international aid agencies and non-government organizations were uncomfortable with the PRT concept and the way the teams operated. They felt that the teams' disbursement of aid and reconstruction contracts was something that should better be done by impartial international organizations, who, in theory, could deal with both sides on the conflict. This was reinforced by the wearing of civilian clothes by US military staff engaged in reconstruction. The civilians also claimed that in areas where PRTs operated, armed attacks on international civilians increased as insurgents could not distinguish between PRT staff and international civilians. These concerns were largely ignored by the US, who argued that the reconstruction teams were getting things done that no other organizations could. And some post-war research has challenged the contention that civilian reconstruction personnel were more at risk in areas where PRTs worked.[4]

A NEW US APPROACH

In late 2003, a new US-led theatre command for Afghanistan was formed: Combined Forces Afghanistan (CFC-A). In order both to counter an already deteriorating security situation, where Taliban attacks were slowly increasing, and to better assist the Afghan authorities and the UN, its commander, Lieutenant General David Barno, developed a fresh concept for Coalition operations. His approach was based on the principles of counter-insurgency. It had five pillars:

- Engage Regional States.
- Enable Reconstruction and Good Governance by building Afghan infrastructure and government institutions.
- Defeat Terrorism and Deny Sanctuary. This comprised SOF operations against Al Qaida, conventional forces operations against Taliban insurgents, negotiations with rival groups and reconstruction.
- Enable Afghan Security Structures by building the Afghan security ministries, army and police, and using them on operations, to improve popular support and legitimacy.
- Sustain Area Ownership.

This last pillar allocated responsibility for areas of Afghanistan to US military commanders. The restive southern and eastern parts of Afghanistan were made the responsibility of US brigades. US conventional forces would cease their episodic deployment of 'search and destroy' raids and be based in key areas of southern and eastern Afghanistan where the Al Qaida and Taliban threats were greatest. US forces were very thinly spread, but would increase stability by focused combat operations, partnering with the increasing number of Afghan forces, and use development projects conducted by PRTs to promote popular support.

Barno also sought to fully integrate the US military activity with the political and development work being conducted by the US and its allies. He moved himself and his key staff into the US embassy in Kabul, to better integrate his work with that of US Ambassador Khalilzad.

But with the March 2003 launch of Operation *Iraqi Freedom*, Iraq was increasingly becoming the US government's over-riding strategic priority. In May 2003, as President Bush declared an end to major combat operations in Iraq, Donald Rumsfeld told journalists that in Afghanistan, 'we're at a point where we clearly have moved from major combat activity to a period of stability and stabilization and reconstruction activities.'[5]

International assistance to Afghan development continued, as did an effort to reform and expand the Afghan National Police (ANP) and the formation of a new Afghan National Army (ANA). Outside Kabul Karzai's government's writ was weak. He often relied on the co-option and empowerment of local strongmen and warlords and their militias. Some of these were also funded and employed by the US, often the CIA. They frequently preyed on local civilians.

Both the US and NATO considered that political and security progress was being made. And a large number of nations were providing troops, funding and development assistance to the stabilization and reconstruction of the country, albeit with US funding being much lower than the ever-increasing sums being spent on the faltering efforts to stabilize Iraq. By then the ISAF Force included troop contingents from 23 different nations. And the US-led Operation *Enduring Freedom* forces included contingents from 18 nations. Whilst US forces and a number of international special forces' contingents were trained and equipped for combat against the Taliban and Al Qaida, many nations sent troops only capable of peace-keeping and supporting reconstruction. A British-led effort to co-ordinate security sector reform saw responsibilities allocated to lead nations as follows:

- US: Afghan National Army
- Germany: Afghan National Police
- UK: counter-narcotics
- Japan: disarmament, demobilization, and reintegration of militias
- Italy: judicial and legal system

The US-led efforts to build a new Afghan Army initially had some effect, but the new Afghan National Guard and Ministry of Defence quickly fell under control of the warlord General Mohammed Fahim. The US had them disbanded and the Ministry of Defence rebuilt from scratch.

The Japanese provided funding for a programme to disarm, demobilize and re-integrate militias. This had some success in getting warlords to hand over some of their heavy weapons. But it did not significantly reduce the capabilities of warlords, some of whom remained on the US payroll.

In this period, President Karzai had little real power and authority, beyond that bestowed on him by the US and ISAF forces. He had no choice but to appoint powerful warlords to many of the key ministerial positions in his government. General Barno masterminded efforts to counter warlords' militias that often acted to block political progress and the writ of the Afghan government. In 2004 public disorder broke out in Faryab Province, with protests against a provincial governor appointed by Karzai. These protests were thought to have been generated by Dostum. An Afghan Army battalion was sent to restore order. With it went US military advisors. Dostum was told by US Ambassador Khalilzad that any attack on the Afghan troops would be considered an attack on US forces. A B1 bomber was called in to make sonic booms over Dostum's home.

Later in 2004, Karzai decided to replace the newly promoted Marshal Fahim, a former warlord, as vice president. Anticipating that Fahim might retaliate by mounting a coup d'état using his personal militia, which included armoured vehicles, General Barno deployed NATO troops outside all the compounds containing Fahim's fighters, ostentatiously displaying their anti-tank weapons. This gambit was successful. Using Japanese funding, there was some limited progress in the disarmament of militias, but there was so much ordnance in the country that any warlord who wanted could easily arm their followers with small arms and other light weapons.

The Italian efforts to modernize Afghanistan's judicial and legal system had little effect outside Kabul. And many of the Italian-led reforms were intended to impose a European-style justice system on a country that had no appetite for such an approach. German-led efforts to rebuild the Afghan National Police were even more problematic. The Germans deployed 17 officers to a police academy in Kabul to run a course of three years in length. Unsurprisingly this very slow approach failed to meet the desperate need for police. The US State Department took over the effort, but the civilian contractors hired for the role displayed little relevant background for the task in hand. In 2005 the US military took over responsibility for training the police. It found that the service was incapable of carrying out its internal security responsibilities as a result of illiterate recruits, poor leadership and pervasive corruption.

Counter-narcotic efforts in Iran and Pakistan as well as the economic destruction resulting from the war against the Soviets meant that Afghanistan had become the world's largest producer of the opium poppy. The British effort to lead the counter-narcotics effort also ran into the sand. A plan to offer financial incentives to farmers to switch from poppy to other crops failed. An attempt by British intelligence to create a paramilitary counter-narcotics unit and dedicated court comprising vetted personnel had some success, but its effects were a drop in the ocean.[6]

ISAF had for its first six months been led by the British. After the lead nation became Turkey, the force represented an ad hoc task force that represented a coalition of the willing. As time went on, it was increasingly difficult to find nations to take over the force leadership role. These essentially ad hoc arrangements were sub-optimal. In August 2003 NATO assumed responsibility for ISAF. The Iraq war had been very controversial in Europe, with only the UK, Poland and Australia joining the US-led invasion (although Italy, Denmark, Holland, the Czech Republic and Poland subsequently joined the coalition for stabilizing Iraq). Stabilizing Afghanistan, however, could be directly linked to the 9/11 attacks, in which hundreds of Europeans had died. For European countries looking to retain military influence with the US, Afghanistan looked like an ideal opportunity, particularly as it appeared much less dangerous than Iraq. There were many European and NATO politicians, and senior military officers, who feared that if NATO did not demonstrate a wider utility to both the US and Europe, it might become irrelevant and fade away. And the Pentagon was happy for NATO to be shouldering more of the burden in Afghanistan, to allow US troops to be shifted to the increasingly difficult mission in Iraq.

A plan was made for NATO to assume security responsibility for the whole of Afghanistan. The country was divided into four sectors and it was agreed that NATO would take them over in a counter-clockwise fashion. NATO took over northern Afghanistan in October 2004 and western Afghanistan in May 2005. Germany and the Netherlands took the lead in setting up PRTs. These sectors appeared to be relatively stable and secure. The areas did not pose demanding security challenges. So many of the troop-contributing countries did not need to have awkward conversations with their parliaments, media and electorates about potential risk, the mission being peacekeeping or stabilization along the lines of the missions in Bosnia and Kosovo. Germany and other European countries wished to draw a line between the US-led counter-terrorism mission, which was becoming unpopular domestically, and peacekeeping and reconstruction.

THE TALIBAN RETURN

In Afghanistan a few Taliban fighters and leaders had melted back into rural communities. Initially those former Taliban fighters and leaders who had fled to Pakistan had concentrated on survival and staying off the radar of the Pakistani security forces. Pakistan's Federally Administered Tribal Areas provided an environment in which the writ of Islamabad and its security forces was limited, and the areas' Pashtun population had long ties with the Taliban.

By 2003 a leadership council had established itself in the Baluchistan city of Quetta. It became known as the Quetta Shura, *shura* being a Pashtun term for an informal council of elders. Pro-Taliban mullahs were preaching in mosques and madrassas, exhorting young men to fight with the Taliban against infidels. From 2003 the Taliban infiltrated back into Afghanistan. The Taliban exploited widespread discontent with Afghan government officials' extortion and corruption, as well as a sense of humiliation resulting from the presence of infidels on Muslim soil. These discontents were reinforced by the Afghan civilian deaths and collateral damage resulting from US and Coalition operations and the actions of private military companies employed by the US and other nations, as well as by the threat to farmers' livelihoods posed by the counter-narcotics programme. Attacks against the Coalition, Afghan forces and government targets gradually increased. By 2004 previous Taliban fighters and commanders that had stayed in southern Afghanistan were travelling to Quetta to seek aid and Taliban 'vanguard teams' had begun returning to southern Afghanistan.

Numbers of Taliban infiltrating into Afghanistan continued to grow. As a result, US troops in eastern Afghanistan began to move into the key valleys of the mountain fastness across the border from Pakistan. There was a gradual increase of US forces in Nuristan and Kunar provinces, particularly the remote Pech, Korengal, and Chawkay Valleys.

In 2005 a US Marine Corps unit sought to better integrate its operations with those of US SOF. In June 2005 it launched Operation *Red Wings*. This began when a reconnaissance mission by a US Navy SEAL team seeking Ahmad Shah, the area's Taliban commander, landed by helicopter on Sawarto Sar, a mountain dominating the Korengal Valley. By chance an Afghan goat herder discovered the patrol. It was subject to heavy attack by Taliban fighters. All but one of the Navy

SEALs were killed and a Chinook helicopter carrying an SOF team intending to rescue the SEALs was shot down by a rocket-propelled grenade (RPG) fired by the Taliban, with the death of 16 US SOF troops. The commander of the destroyed SEAL team was posthumously awarded the Medal of Honor, the first time the medal had been awarded for action in Afghanistan.

PAKISTAN'S ROLE

The Pakistani military and its intelligence agency, ISI, had the dominant influence over Islamabad's foreign and defence policy. Both institutions saw an existential threat from India. They harboured considerable resentment over the outcome of the 1971 war between the two countries. Not only had they been militarily defeated by India, but also East Pakistan had become the independent state of Bangladesh. Many Pakistani officers would compare this to a traumatic amputation. There was a strain of Pakistan Army and ISI thinking that saw Afghanistan as a platform for India to strategically encircle Pakistan.

After 9/11 Pakistan sought to build a positive relationship with Afghanistan, but repeated Afghan and US allegations of active support to the insurgents by Islamabad increasingly created a considerable trust deficit between Pakistan on one side and Afghanistan and the US on the other. Karzai and the Afghan intelligence agency, the National Directorate of Security (NDS), increasingly claimed that Pakistan was actively supporting the Pakistan Taliban. And US forces deployed along the border between the two countries reported that Taliban fighters crossing the border were evading the Pakistani Frontier Corps, who were sometimes observed waving Taliban across.

This was vehemently denied by President Musharraf and Pakistani officials, who pointed to the direct Pakistani co-operation with the US against Al Qaida, as well as the difficulties of the mountainous terrain and the many cross-border ties between Pashtuns in both countries. But the Pakistani state's writ did not run in much of the Federally Administered Tribal Areas and Musharraf was reluctant to provoke a military confrontation in these tribal Badlands.

Key Taliban leaders and their families appeared to live openly in Pakistan, unconstrained either by law enforcement or by the powerful ISI. Whether this reflected the weaknesses of the Pakistani state, the unpopularity of the US-led NATO presence in Afghanistan or a secret policy of active support to the Taliban was hotly debated by the US military, State Department and CIA, although much of that agency's effort in Pakistan was directed against Al Qaida.

Pakistan was prepared to take some action against insurgents and exhibit some co-operation with the US. For example, an Al Qaida attack on President Musharraf in December 2003 resulted in Pakistani troops moving into South Waziristan. In 2004 there was considerable intelligence co-operation between the CIA and ISI against Al Qaida. As part of this Musharraf agreed that the CIA could operate armed predator drones over Pakistan's tribal areas, while denying in public that such authorization had been granted. This co-operation resulted in a Hellfire missile launched from a Predator, killing Nek Mohammed, a senior Al Qaida leader. He was in the process of making a satellite telephone call on a device the Americans had identified as his. Even so, relations between Washington DC and Kabul and Islamabad remained clouded with mistrust.

THE AUDIT OF WAR

When NATO agreed to take command of ISAF from the ad hoc coalition of nations that had previously run the force, and to expand its footprint in Afghanistan, both NATO and the US fielded provincial reconstruction teams, an innovation that applied interagency development and supplied political and reconstruction teams in order both to extend the writ of the Kabul government and to increase support for the presence of international forces.

As CENTCOM's attention increasingly became focused on planning for the attack on Iraq, Afghanistan became an 'economy of force' theatre of operations. This had considerable opportunity cost as the Iraq war would increasingly consume political attention, resources and leadership bandwidth of the military, foreign ministries and development agencies of the US and its allies.

Despite the efforts of US General David Barno to implement a strategy to support reconstruction, counter growing Taliban strength and reduce civilian casualties resulting from Coalition action, the lack of interest at CENTCOM and in Washington DC meant that opportunities for a more coherent and better resourced approach to

Afghan development and security were forfeit. This was exacerbated by the US-led international forces' support of predatory Afghan warlords who manipulated international forces into attacking rival warlords and their supporters, as well as civilian casualties and collateral damage arising from SOF raids and air attacks. These actions all created the conditions for a revival of the Taliban, who benefited from the relative security of their base areas in Pakistan. Throughout the period Taliban presence and influence in rural Afghanistan slowly increased.

4

Operation *Cobra II*

The invasion of Iraq

Iraq had always been a multi-ethnic state. The majority of the population were Shia Muslim Arabs mostly living in central and southern Iraq. The second largest group were Sunni Muslim Arabs, mostly living in western Iraq, particularly in Anbar Province. Northern Iraq was dominated by ethnic Kurds, many living in Iraqi Kurdistan in an autonomous mini-state under the protection of US and UK airpower enforcing the post-1991 no-fly zone. Some cities were largely ethnically homogenous, such as Basra in the Shia south and Fallujah in Anbar Province. But Baghdad was a mixture of largely Sunni and Shia communities.

The country had been run since 1979 by Saddam Hussein, a Sunni Arab. Sunnis dominated the organs of the state through the Baath Party. Saddam had consciously modelled his rule and the party on successful approaches by previous dictators including Hitler and Stalin. The party's tentacles extended to low levels in Iraqi society, for example schoolteachers and university lecturers were expected to be party members. The country had multiple intelligence agencies and Saddam acted with brutal ruthlessness against any challenges to his authority.

In the immediate aftermath of Operation *Desert Storm* Iraqi Shias and Kurds revolted against the Iraqi regime. Saddam moved rapidly to crush these rebellions. A brutal campaign of repression by government forces was unleashed on the Shias, concentrating on southern Iraq, where they were in a majority. The US declined to intervene in their support. This would contribute to subsequent resentment of the US amongst Iraq's Shias.

The Kurds are a distinct ethnic group. They lacked a state of their own, but significant Kurdish minorities are found in south-east Turkey, north-west Iran and northern Iraq, an area often named Kurdistan by its Kurdish inhabitants, who harboured a long-held desire to carve out an independent homeland of their own across the mountainous boundaries between Turkey, Iraq and Iran.

After Operation _Desert Storm_ Iraqi Kurds rose in revolt and seized many urban areas. But the Republican Guard moved north and forced the Kurds out of the towns and cities. Kurdish civilians fled. Those that could not make it to Iran or Turkey headed into the mountains. Without food or shelter the death toll rose. US, UK and other allied forces intervened to protect the Kurdish refugees, creating a safe zone, making it clear that Iraqi movement into that zone would be met with force. Saddam chose not to test this.

Subsequently the US, British and French established two no-fly zones over northern and southern Iraq, to reduce Saddam's ability to repress the Kurds in the north and Shia in the south. Under the air umbrella, the Iraqi Kurds established the Kurdish Autonomous Zone. Control of the zone was split between the Kurdistan Democratic Party (KDP) in the west and the Patriotic Union of Kurdistan (PUK) in the east of the zone. Both groups were politically opposed to each other but prepared to co-operate against Iraq. Turkey faced an insurgency amongst its Kurds, regularly attacked terrorist bases in Iraqi Kurdistan and opposed any measures or initiatives that would have put the Iraqi Kurds on the road to statehood.

By now Saddam Hussein had increased his already paranoid concern about his security and that of the Iraqi regime. A self-confessed admirer of Josef Stalin, he went even further than the Soviet dictator in creating a range of organizations dedicated to his personal protection. He re-organized his security forces to better protect against further insurrections or potential coups. The elite regime-loyalist formations of the Republican Guard increased in importance. Saddam already had direct control over Military Intelligence, the Iraqi Special Security Service and the General Security Service. In 1992 three more security forces were created. All the security organizations competed against each other and answered separately to Saddam. Saddam had centralized power over the armed forces, Republican Guard and plethora of intelligence and security agencies. All his principal subordinates were expected to display total loyalty and those who displayed any signs of initiative that might be taken as disloyalty could not expect to survive.

A new Military Security Service was formed to identify and suppress any dissent in the armed forces. Saddam's son Uday formed the Fedayeen Saddam, or Saddam's Martyrs, to directly protect Saddam and conduct anti-smuggling operations. The Special Republican Guard was a 15,000 strong force, distinct from the Republican Guard, recruited from tribes and areas that were especially loyal to Saddam. Commanded by Saddam's son Qusay, it was the only military force allowed in Baghdad. Qusay also commanded the existing Republican Guard and Special Security Service. The latter increasingly acquired the authority to investigate the loyalty of the other security services.

In the 1990s the Iraqi security apparatus thwarted several coup attempts. But the effectiveness of the Republican Guard was reduced by repeated purges of its officers. The Iraqi conventional forces, principally the army, remained the lowest priority.

The UN Security Council imposed economic and trade sanctions and an inspection regime on Iraq. This was to constrain Iraq's ability to develop ballistic missiles and weapons of mass destruction and to compel it to comply with Security Council resolutions requiring the cessation of Iraqi programmes to produce ballistic missiles and weapons of mass destruction (WMD).

The UN Special Commission (UNSCOM) succeeded in destroying tons of chemical agents and thousands of chemical warheads, as well as ballistic missiles and launchers. It also found and destroyed a previously undetected nuclear weapons programme. But it could not guarantee that Iraqi WMD capability had been eliminated.

In the 1990s, as UN sanctions shrank the Iraqi economy, regime members and supporters were prioritized for receipt of food and medicine. These factors, together with damage to infrastructure caused by Operation *Desert Storm*, resulted in many Iraqis suffering from hunger, lack of medical treatment and inadequate sanitation.

In 1996 some relief of the sanctions was granted. A UN 'oil for food' programme was meant to allow the sale of Iraqi oil on international markets to fund import of food. Food distribution arrangements favoured Baath Party loyalists, being used by the regime to strengthen its hold over the Iraqi people. Throughout these years Saddam sought to place the blame for the sufferings of the Iraqi people on the US and the UN. Many Iraqis found this argument persuasive. And amongst Iraqi Shias, trust in the US had been eroded by the US's failure to assist those Shias in southern Iraq who rose up in 1991 against Saddam, only to be brutally crushed by his remaining forces. The chances of a warm welcome from the majority of Iraqi Shias were low, much lower than the US assumed.

The regime made ever-increasing efforts to smuggle oil out of Iraq. The US and UK used their civilian and military intelligence capabilities to detect this smuggling and attempted to interdict it. They succeeded in intercepting a proportion of the traffic, but Iraq oil increasingly found its way onto international black markets.

THE CONTAINMENT OF IRAQ

Throughout the 1990s the US sought to contain Iraq by supporting UN sanctions, encouraging other states to do the same and deterring Iraqi aggression against the Kurds in northern Iraq and neighbouring states. US military strategy was for containment of Iraq, including enforcement of the no-fly zones. In this it was supported by the UK and France. Based in Turkey and Saudi Arabia, US, British and French jets flew long patrols over Iraq. These were contested by Iraq which attempted to shoot down the aircraft with surface to air missiles. As the decade continued the US maintained considerable numbers of land, sea and air forces in the Gulf.

Demonstrations of force were used in 1994 and 1996 to support this approach. In December 1998 Iraq's obstruction of UN weapons inspectors, meddling in Kurdish politics and threatening troop movements resulted in the US and British mounting Operation *Desert Fox,* four days of strikes by cruise missiles and jets. It subsequently emerged that these attacks had considerable effect on Iraq's remaining WMD capability.

Since 1991 the US had covertly supported efforts to remove Saddam from power. All had failed. At the end of 1998 the US publicly added support for regime change to its Iraq policy. The Iraq Liberation Act provided for financial support to Iraqi opposition groups. But by now Saddam's hold on power was even greater and the chances of any armed opposition groups establishing a foothold in the country appeared extremely low.

Since Operation *Desert Storm* the US had retained a considerable military presence in the Gulf. A brigade-sized force was continuously deployed in Kuwait, drawing on pre-positioned equipment, vehicles, weapons and ammunition. By 9/11 the size of this stockpile was doubled. This was used by battalions and later brigades on rotational deployments. Ranges and five large camps were built in the Kuwaiti desert.

IRAQI MILITARY CAPABILITY

CENTCOM's intelligence staff estimated that the Iraqi armed forces had a total strength of over 350,000 troops. The army had 17 divisions, of which three were armoured and three mechanized.

At the end of Operation *Desert Storm*, the Iraqi Navy had largely been destroyed, while many of the ground forces that had occupied Kuwait and southern Iraq had been destroyed or had fled. An arms embargo imposed as part of the UN- and US-led efforts to counter Iraqi oil smuggling had successfully interfered with efforts to reconstitute Iraq's conventional military capability. But about half of the elite Republican Guard had survived, with their armoured vehicles. This included about 700 of its most up-to-date tanks, the Soviet T72s.

After the 2003 war, the US put considerable effort into gaining a retrospective understanding of the Iraqi military plans and how they were defeated. These were complemented by journalists' reports. As with journalists' interviews of senior Nazi officials and German officers after World War II, a degree of caution must be applied, but a consistent picture emerges of Saddam's military strategy.[1]

Saddam gave every appearance that he believed that the US would not attack. A diplomatic campaign was mounted to reduce the chance of an invasion and to gain support in the UN Security Council, by emphasizing that Iraq no longer had WMD. Saddam appears to have thought that if the US did attack, air and missile strikes would be more likely than a ground invasion; and that, in the unlikely event of a US ground attack being launched, such an attack would be defeated by well-motivated and effective Iraqi forces who would conduct an effective defence. They would be joined by Iraqi civilians who would rise up to fight the invaders.

Almost half of Iraqi land forces, I, II and V Corps, were deployed in northern Iraq facing Kurdistan. III and IV Corps were deployed in southern Iraq, most of their divisions facing the Iranian border. Four divisions of the Republican Guard were deployed around Baghdad, but outside the city. Only one division was deployed in the lower Euphrates Valley, at Nasiriyah.

This deployment seemed to be orientated against Saddam's previous enemies, the Kurds and Iran. He seems to have decided to keep the Iraqi Army and Republican Guard out of Iraq's cities, probably because he still feared both forces' ability to mount coups. In mid-March Saddam set up new command arrangements. Four regional commands were established, each headed by a senior official of proven political loyalty, but of little military expertise. This did nothing to improve the effectiveness of command and control.

As the probability of a US attack increased, the Iraqi forces were augmented by foreign jihadists. It appears that up to 5,000 foreign fighters made their way to Iraq before the invasion. There is evidence of their being provided with small arms and training in Iraqi camps.

US PLANNING AFTER 9/11

On 27 November 2001, as the battle of Tora Bora was at its height, Rumsfeld tasked Franks to present his initial ideas for an attack on Iraq. To maintain operational security, planning was for many months confined to a small circle of commanders and staff officers in CENTCOM and its subordinate HQs. Over 15 months, the military plan to attack Iraq was subject to continual development by CENTCOM through multiple iterations. It received intense scrutiny by Bush, Rumsfeld, the National Security Council and Pentagon.

Rumsfeld was a difficult man to work with. Since taking over the Defense Department he had made no secret of his ambitions to modernize and transform the US armed forces, making them more agile and faster to act. Despite his publicly confident persona, there is abundant evidence that within the Pentagon, he acted differently, constantly bombarding his principal subordinates with short memos, christened 'snowflakes'. He often seemed to avoid making hard decisions or giving firm directions, apparently preferring to constantly 'nudge', by incessantly questioning his subordinates. Often, he would ask questions like 'Do you need that?' or 'Are there other ways of doing this?'

Franks would eventually establish a working, but strained relationship with Rumsfeld. But considerable friction developed between Rumsfeld and Franks on one side and the Joint Chiefs of Staff, the leaders of the four US services, on the other. Part of this was the result of Rumsfeld's insistence on a very high level of operational security, which deliberately sought to keep the circle of knowledge of Iraq planning as small as possible. Part of it was the result of leaks which, understandably, greatly irritated Rumsfeld and Franks. Part of the friction was Rumsfeld's perfectly legal insistence on working directly with Franks, excluding the Joint Chiefs from planning. Franks saw the chiefs as parochial, narrow minded and offering no value to him at CENTCOM. It was widely reported that Franks had, in private, referred to the service chiefs as 'Title 10 motherfuckers' – Title 10 being the constitution provision that allocate funds direct to the four services.

Arriving at the Pentagon in late 2002 then-Major General Stan McChrystal found the atmosphere in the Pentagon tentative and sometimes anxious, exacerbated by Rumsfeld's famously abrasive style. As the Defense Secretary was legally required to authorize all US troop deployments, he would scrutinize the Pentagon's proposals in great detail. He had every right to do so, but McChrystal observed that:

> operational commanders were left concerned they might not have what they needed if and when fighting broke out. Logisticians became terrified they'd not be able to make such an ad hoc approach work.
>
> It was an almost classic struggle of cultures and will. Both the secretary and the military were making their best efforts to accomplish the mission. Both were right on a number of points. All were good people. Without question the secretary's intractability forced the military to be more flexible. But in the process, we also experienced a painful period of uncertainty and doubt ...[2]

CENTCOM had an existing plan, Operations Plan (OPPLAN) 1003, for another war with Iraq. This envisaged a large force of 340,000 troops assembling over time. Franks thought that assembling the forces required by the existing concept of operations would take far too much time. He felt that the existing plan reflected old-fashioned thinking. It did not incorporate the lessons of the unexpectedly rapid success of SOF and precision air strikes in Afghanistan. The surprisingly swift victory was thought to be pointing to a way of war that would exploit the technological and tactical advances the US had made since 1991. A new plan was required that could be launched and executed much more rapidly.

All the planning for Iraq shared some core assumptions. These provided the basis for both the CENTCOM and subordinate plans, so it is worth understanding them. The first two were given to General Franks by Rumsfeld and his close associates. The first was that Iraq would use chemical weapons against US forces, most probably as they neared Baghdad. The second was that most of the Iraqi people would treat any US invasion as a liberation, not an occupation, displaying eagerness for a new democratic government. This assumption was reinforced by Iraqi expatriate leaders in exile.

General Franks also provided strategic assumptions of his own. These included an assumption that a large US or Coalition force of division or corps size would be able to attack from the north, moving from Turkey to do so. CENTCOM also assessed that the majority of the Iraqi Army would not fight, and once the fighting began, Iraqi troops would surrender or desert.

At a 28 December briefing for the President, Franks briefed his commander's concept. The operation envisaged in the new OPPLAN 1003V would have four major phases:

- Phase 1 would include creating the sea and air lines of communication necessary for forces to flow into the operational theatre. It would also be essential to gain and sustain international political support.
- Phase 2 would 'shape the battlespace', to make it more difficult for the Iraqis to mount an effective defence.
- Phase 3 would see the defeat or capitulation of regime forces and the regime leadership 'dead, apprehended or marginalized'.
- Phase 4 would be 'post-hostility operations'. Franks thought that this might take 'years, not months'.

In 2002 and early 2003 there were least a dozen such briefings for President Bush. He and Rumsfeld wanted the war to be seen not as a conquest, but as a liberation. They repeatedly showed concern about the overall size of the force, how quickly it could deploy to the operational theatre and how long it would take to succeed in defeating Iraqi forces. They were especially concerned to minimize avoidable civilian casualties and collateral damage.

The small number of staff officers at CENTCOM who were used to plan the campaign worked to the point of exhaustion. It was not until 21 March 2002 that Franks and his planners briefed CENTCOM's component commanders and small cells of their staff on the plan and their likely roles. The main effort would be a land advance north from Kuwait to Baghdad. To confront Saddam's forces with multiple simultaneous problems, SOF and a smaller land force would advance from south-eastern Turkey into Kurdistan and push south. SOF would advance into the deserts of western Iraq to prevent them being used for launching ballistic missiles at Israel, Jordan or Saudi Arabia, and to simulate a major conventional land advance from the west towards Baghdad. A wide range of measures would be taken to counter Iraqi use of WMD.

An iteration of the plan briefed to the President and National Security Council envisaged that:

- Two days would be allowed for intensified air strikes in the no-fly zones and for SOF to begin infiltrating into Iraq.
- On A-Day five days of air attacks would begin.
- On G-Day the ground offensive would begin. This was expected to take up to 90 days.
- For Phase 4, post-hostilities operations, Franks envisaged a maximum of 250,000 Coalition troops.

Throughout 2002 as US forces in the Gulf increased in strength CENTCOM sought to reduce the size of the ground force required at the start of the attack, to reduce the time needed to assemble the force in Kuwait and the Gulf. Rather than beginning the war with the long air campaigns that US-led forces had employed in Operation *Desert Storm*, the ground and air offensives would start at the same time. There would be a significant effort to persuade Iraqi troops and commanders not to fight. This would include a wide range of information operations including air drops of leaflets, radio broadcasts and contacting individual Iraqi military commanders by telephone.

The plan was constantly being adjusted. In part this was to be expected as the intelligence picture of Iraqi forces developed. And it was natural to expect the plan for such a large operation to be constantly refined. But an extra dimension was the role of Donald Rumsfeld. Brimming with confidence, he immersed himself in planning. As Defense Secretary he was entitled to do this, but many US officers found his constant probing challenges of General Franks and the staff hectoring and redolent of micromanagement. Franks briefed Rumsfeld several times between February and April 2002. After each briefing the planned size of the US force would reduce.

THE TURKISH OPTION

In the north of Iraq, 13 divisions of the Iraqi Army were guarding the 'Green Line', the boundary between Iraqi government-controlled territory and Kurdistan. If Saddam realized that the main US effort was coming from the south and moved formations from the north to the south to assist in defending Baghdad, it would make the advance of land forces from southern Iraq to Baghdad much more difficult. It was essential to prevent this. Initially it was planned to deploy a corps to advance into Kurdistan from Turkey. This would attack the Iraqi troops deployed along the 'Green Line'. The formation would consist of the US Army's 4th Infantry Division and 173rd Airborne Brigade. The British were asked to provide a division and a corps HQ. This would be based on the British-led Allied Command Europe Rapid Reaction Corps HQ, normally assigned to NATO. These forces would need to travel to south-east Turkey along a lengthy line of communications, for which the US would deploy the command and control elements of its 1st Armored Division. And the British would need to mobilize most of their regular and reserve logistic forces to sustain themselves.

Taking advantage of the control of Kurdistan by a Kurdish militia, the Peshmerga, the force would attack Iraqi forces facing north on the 'Green Line' and advance south. This would prevent any Iraqi formations from being redeployed southwards. With luck it might draw off Iraqi reserves that might otherwise be used to hinder the US land forces' main effort – an advance from Kuwait, north to Baghdad. Should the Iraqi commanders eventually establish that the main effort was heading from Kuwait to Baghdad, the advancing land forces would seek to mislead the Iraqis as to the strength and direction of their main advances. They would do this by advancing more rapidly than the Iraqis could respond.

All this would depend on the consent of the Turkish government and assistance from the Turkish military. Difficult negotiations took place, but by the end of 2002, it was clear that the Turkish parliament would not agree to the deployment of at least 50,000 US and UK ground troops into the country. Indeed, the Turkish general staff would not even consent to aircraft carrying Coalition troops to Kurdistan entering Turkish air space. Following an early January 2003 visit to Turkey to discuss the passage of British troops only, Geoff Hoon, the UK defence minister, concluded that the Turks would not consent to British forces moving through the country. The British division was re-assigned to deploy to Kuwait, to attack southern Iraq.

Despite this British decision, CENTCOM remained much more confident that the Turks would eventually consent to the US plans. So the vehicles, helicopters and equipment of the 4th Infantry Division (despite its title, the most modern heavy armoured division in the US Army) was loaded onto civilian ships and sailed towards Turkey. It was not until late March 2003 that the US concluded that the Turkish government would not allow US ground forces to attack from Turkey. Franks decided that rather than send the 4th Infantry Division straight to Kuwait, the 37 ships carrying the division's weapons, vehicles, equipment and supplies would remain afloat in the eastern Mediterranean to reinforce the deception plan.

DECEPTION

Early on, Franks and the CENTCOM planners decided that the main land force would assemble in Kuwait and advance north-west to Baghdad. For this to have maximum chance of success, Saddam and his military leadership had to think that major advances would come elsewhere. This required strategic-level deception to provide evidence that the major thrusts would come from the north and west, combined with operational security measures to conceal the strength and intentions of Coalition forces that would be assembled in Kuwait.

The previous autumn in a conversation with President Saleh of Yemen, Franks had deliberately over-emphasized the likelihood of a US advance from Turkey. Saleh was thought to be close to Saddam and likely to pass on this misleading insight. This was complemented by a highly secret deception operation that attempted to feed false information to Iraqi political and military decision makers. One of the channels used was a US officer who had been approached by Iraqi intelligence. He had agreed to co-operate, but was, in fact, being used by CENTCOM as a conduit for false information. The Iraqis were fed a false plan that the US main effort would be the 4th Infantry Division attacking south from Turkey. This impression would be reinforced by parachute landings in Iraqi Kurdistan, and near Kirkuk and Tikrit.

PLANNING TURBULENCE

Although the US military has a deserved reputation for its ability to thoroughly plan its operations, the capacity of all HQs is limited, by the numbers of people in its planning staff and by the commitments and capabilities of its commanders. Generally, the size of planning staffs reduces as the command chain is descended. CENTCOM, its component HQs and many of the subordinate HQs would increasingly be consumed by planning as the attack on Iraq drew nearer.

Leaving aside the question of the attack from Turkey, the CENTCOM plan was subject to constant revision between February 2002 and March 2003. From the US Army's official history of the invasion of Iraq it is possible to discern at least three significant versions of the plan, each requiring different land force packages and different tactical plans.[3] For the land forces a particularly disruptive factor was the development of a CENTCOM contingency plan to cater for the collapse of the Iraqi regime before the main US attack was launched. It was judged that this only required SOF and the two full divisions.

Rumsfeld added extra turbulence to planning by forbidding the US Army to use its previous planning process which carefully matched deployment of combat formations with the necessary 'enablers' of combat support and logistic troops. Instead he insisted on a new 'request for forces' process that allowed him much greater control of the units that were deployed. This, combined with his confidence that he knew better than the services, led to a disconnect between the forces deployed and their essential enablers, particularly logistic units. This adversely impacted not only US Army units but also Marine and SOF units that also needed US Army 'enablers' to support them.

This planning turbulence had considerable impact on the Army and Marine formations that had been warned by their chain of command that they might or might not be employed in the attack. For example, the US Army's V Corps in Germany was warned for the attack on Iraq. It was certain to be committed but the plans for its role and the forces assigned to it kept changing. As an instance, in October 2002 the land component plan envisaged the initial main effort being made by the Marines. After secret wargames in December 2002 and January 2003 the plan was changed to make V Corps the main effort from the outset. At the time this would require the corps to have two heavy armoured division: the 1st Armoured and 3rd Infantry divisions. Rumsfeld and Franks would subsequently decide that the corps should initially attack only with the 3rd Infantry Division; and Major General Ricardo Sanchez, commanding one of the corps' main formations, the 1st Armoured Division, in Germany, found that orders from V Corps to the division constantly changed. The division was initially told that it would accompany the corps to Iraq. Next it was told that it would not take part in the initial attack but that it would be a follow-on force. It was then warned it would not go to Iraq at all, only for its role to be changed to post-conflict operations.

Each change of mission required an adjustment to plans for the preparation and training of the division. Sanchez found these constant changes sapped the energy of commanders and their supporting staffs, increasing frustration. Sanchez decided to focus the division's planning and training on the most demanding potential role – that of the corps' reserve division. This did not require any training for stabilization operations, or for countering an insurgency.

PLANNING FOR THE DAY AFTER

Throughout 2002, it seemed to many in the US military establishment that the rapid defeat of the Taliban had demonstrated a new way of war in which airborne surveillance and precision attack would achieve rapid US dominance of a land battlefield. The 'inconvenient truths' of the failures at Tora Bora and during Operation *Anaconda*, which highlighted the limitations of airborne surveillance and the practical difficulties of attacking elusive enemies, appeared to be ignored. And the post-conflict US operations in Afghanistan were seen both as successful and as vindicating a 'light footprint' approach.

The interests of Rumsfeld, Franks and the CENTCOM staffs were almost entirely focused on the military defeat of Saddam's regime forces. Much less attention was paid to what might happen afterwards. There was an assumption at the White House, Pentagon and in CENTCOM that US troops would be welcomed. The post-conflict operation was assumed to be relatively undemanding. But planning for the civilian aspects of post-conflict stabilization and reconstruction lagged far behind military planning.

Even with the optimistic attitude prevailing, post-conflict planning was far from complete. The State Department had done considerable analysis of Iraq. But it was only in early 2003 that the US government decided to assign responsibility for post-conflict stabilization to the Defense Department. The Pentagon set up the Office for Reconstruction and Humanitarian Assistance (ORHA). Its prime role would be humanitarian assistance. It would also assign international advisors to Iraqi government ministries. CENTCOM planned to recall the surviving units of the Iraqi Army to maintain order.

ORHA and CENTCOM were not the only organizations planning post-conflict stabilization. Teams were working at the State Department, the US Agency for International Aid and within the office of the Secretary of Defense, and there was a 50-strong team in the Pentagon. Perhaps the most advanced post-conflict plan was that developed by the land component HQ. But these were all disparate, overlapping and unco-ordinated efforts. They could have been co-ordinated and unified, but it would have required the authority of President Bush to insist on a level of integration that Rumsfeld and Franks would not or could not provide.

Planning for post-conflict operations was not helped by the late February 2003 eruption of a public disagreement between General Shinseki, the US Army chief, and Rumsfeld. When testifying to the Senate Armed Services Committee Shinseki had been asked how many US troops would be required for a post-conflict occupation. Shinseki replied 'something of the order of several hundred thousand soldiers'.[4] Shinseki later explained to Rumsfeld that he based this figure on the size of the NATO force in Bosnia in 1997, multiplying it to reflect the greater population and size of Iraq. Two days later the Army Secretary, Thomas White, endorsed Shinseki's assessment.

These statements provoked a media and political firestorm. Rumsfeld fired White and Deputy Defense Secretary Paul Wolfowitz publicly contradicted Shinseki's statements, saying that they were 'wildly off the mark'. History would make a different judgement.

CONCEPT OF OPERATIONS

The final version of the CENTCOM plan emphasized surprise and speed of manoeuvre, reducing the number of troops required. The operation would use about 170,000 troops. It was US-led with the UK, Australia and Poland contributing combat forces. Of this the UK contribution was much larger than those of Australia and Poland. Some other nations contributed medical and chemical defence units. After the invasion, Franks described the concept of operations:

> Our ground offensive would proceed along two main avenues of advance from the south, each route having several axes. Army forces, led by the 3rd Infantry Division, would attack up lines of march west of the Euphrates River in a long arc that curved from lines of departure in Kuwait to reach Baghdad. The 1st Marine Expeditionary Force – divided into reinforced Regimental combat teams – would follow the road network along the Tigris River, farther east. The Army and Marines would link up and destroy any surviving Republican Guard units south of the capital ... A division-plus-size British ground force would pivot northeast out of Kuwait and isolate Basra, forming a protective cordon around the southern oil fields. And US, Brit, and Australian Special Operations Forces would control Iraq's western desert, preventing the regime freedom of action to launch long-range missiles toward Jordan and Israel.
>
> On paper it looked like an attack against a numerically superior enemy with a relatively small offensive force. Was I tempting fate by defying the war college maxim that an attacking force should have a 3-to-1 numerical advantage over an entrenched defender? 'Not a

bit of it,' as my Brit friends would say. On the twenty-first century battlefield, strength would derive from the mass of effective firepower, not simply the number of boots or tank tracks on the ground.

Our ground forces, supported by overwhelming airpower, would move so fast and deep into the Iraqi rear that time-and-distance factors would preclude the enemy's defensive manoeuvre. And this slow-reacting enemy would be fixed in place by the combined effect of artillery, air support, and attack helicopters.

Without question, our lines of communication would be long and exposed in places, stretching more than three hundred miles from the border of Kuwait to the outskirts of Baghdad. But the object was to destroy the Iraqi military's will to fight. A larger, slower, methodical, attrition-based attack model could defeat the enemy in detail, and our lines of communication could be better protected with such a force. But the time it would take to stage and launch such a juggernaut would leave Saddam too many strategic options: He could use the time to destroy Iraq's water or oil infrastructure, launch his missiles against his neighbours, or use WMD against our troops – and his track record suggested he wouldn't think twice about any of those options.

No, manoeuvre speed would be our most important asset. If high-balling armour units could sustain that speed for days and nights on end, they would own the initiative, and our momentum would overwhelm Iraq's ability to react – tactically and strategically. We would not apply overwhelming force. Rather, we would apply the overwhelming 'mass of effect' of a smaller force. Speed would represent a mass all its own.[5]

Operation *Desert Storm* and the NATO attack on Kosovo had both featured lengthy air campaigns before the introduction of ground forces. CENTCOM originally proposed that the war begin with 16 days of air and missile strikes. As the plan evolved, it was increasingly thought that the Iraqis would be expecting the US to employ the same approach as they did in 1991. By March 2003 the gap between the start of the air and land campaigns was reduced to 15 hours. Although it was impossible for the US to achieve strategic surprise, beginning the ground operation shortly after the air attacks started would create operational and tactical surprise.

Franks also intended to attack before the ground force build-up was complete. This carried with it the risk from reduced combat power, from not having the full number of brigades. It would also mean that the land component would attack before it had its full complement of supporting logistic and communications units.

THE ROLE OF SPECIAL OPERATIONS FORCES (SOF)

The west and north of Iraq would be assigned to Special Operations Forces (SOF). This would be another departure from the approach used in Operation *Desert Storm.*

In 1991 the then-CENTCOM commander, General Norman Schwarzkopf, had little time for SOF. Stanley McChrystal, then a mid-ranking officer in the US Army Rangers, observed the operation from the US SOF HQ. He saw how the command was initially only afforded the most limited of roles in Operations *Desert Shield* and *Desert Storm.* He attributes this to 'the challenges of incorporating its specialist skills into a huge conventional effort. Additionally, some leaders were uncomfortable with the force.'[6]

Shortly after Operation *Desert Storm* began, Iraqi Scud missiles began landing in Israel. These were fired from mobile launchers operating in western Iraq. The Israelis threatened to respond by sending aircraft and commandos into the area. Even without any US assistance, this would have resulted in many of the US's Arab allies withdrawing from the coalition. So, the British SAS and the US Joint Special Operations Command (JSOC) were hurriedly assigned the role of interdicting the Scud launchers in western Iraq. It was not clear that these operations had any significant effect on the Iraqi forces. McChrystal later concluded that the very short notice of JSOC's deployment and other problems meant that:

> our intelligence simply could not generate enough clarity on Iraqi Scud operations to support an effective campaign to cripple the system. As a result, our efforts relied on thoughtful guesswork by intelligence teams and risky operations by the forces on the ground. We were largely dependent on luck. It was a position I never wanted to be in again ... I doubt our operations ever had much direct effect on Iraqi Scud operations.[7]

Twelve years on the extensive employment of US SOF in a wide variety of operations and the success of SOF in Afghanistan meant that Franks assigned them major roles in Iraq. Denying Iraq the ability to launch missiles from western Iraq would be the responsibility of the Joint Special Operations Task Force – West (JSOTF-W), formed around the US Army's 5th Special Forces Group together with British and Australian special forces. The problem of finding and destroying mobile missile launchers had received considerable study by the air forces and SOF of the US and UK. In 2002 an extensive combined joint US–UK exercise in the western US tested plans for 'Scud hunting' by air forces and SOF.

The SOF would also seek to deny the area to Iraqi conventional forces and stop senior Iraqi government and military officials fleeing Iraq into Jordan. They were also to work with Iraqis who were opposed to Saddam Hussein.

Based in Saudi Arabia was Task Force 20, part of the secretive JSOC. It comprised a squadron of Delta Force, Rangers, USAF MC130 Hercules, US Army helicopters and a parachute infantry battalion from the 82nd Airborne Division. The force prepared to seize Baghdad airport by an air assault, then to clear the runway of debris and obstacles to allow the 2nd Brigade Combat Team (BCT) of the 82nd Airborne Division to be flown in. The plan had been rehearsed twice in the US.

Unable to attack with conventional forces from Turkey, CENTCOM considered it even more important to press Iraqi troops facing the Kurds. In Kurdistan there were almost 70,000 Kurdish Peshmerga militia fighters, who would be reinforced by the US 10th Special Forces Group. The group would be used as the core around which the Joint Special Operations Task Force – North (JSOTF-N) would form. Many of its soldiers knew Kurdistan well having previously operated there.

COALITION AIR AND LAND FORCES

Almost 800 combat jets stood ready for the operation. About 90 per cent of these were from the US Air Force, US Navy and Marine Corps. Most were based in the Gulf, either on land or on US Navy aircraft carriers. But B1 and B2 bombers would fly from outside the theatre, from the Indian Ocean island of Diego Garcia or the continental US.

The remaining combat aircraft were British, with Australia contributing a squadron of F18 Hornet fighters.

These were complemented by an array of reconnaissance and surveillance aircraft. These included the US Air Force's signals intelligence aircraft, the RC135 Rivet Joint, that was used to intercept Iraqi radars and military communications, as well as the E-8 Joint Surveillance Target Attack Radar System (JSTARS), an enormous airborne radar. This had been procured in the Cold War to locate and track Soviet armoured columns. Both of these aircraft were amongst the few airborne sensors that could locate enemy units through all weathers and through dust storms. Also arrayed around air bases throughout CENTCOM were large numbers of tanker aircraft.

In June 2002, the US air operation in the southern no-fly zone, Operation *Southern Watch*, assumed a more aggressive character, becoming Operation *Southern Focus*. Without any publicity US aircraft began engaging a much wider range of Iraqi targets including missile sites, communications systems and radars. By the time of the invasion, Iraqi air defences in the south of the country would be neutralized.

By mid-March 2003, Kuwait was full of US troops. Assembled in austere camps in the desert was the US Army's V Corps. Its principal striking force was the 3rd Infantry Division. The use of a historic US Army title obscured the character of the division. It was a heavy armoured division, one of the most capable of such in the world. It had three armoured brigade combat teams, each comprising three heavy battalions. Tank battalions were equipped with the M1 Abrams tank, as powerful and well protected as any tank in the world. The infantry battalions had M2 Bradley armoured infantry fighting vehicles. These carried a squad of seven infantrymen and had a turret with a 25mm Bushmaster cannon and a pod of TOW anti-tank missiles. They were less well protected than the tanks, but their armour still offered greater protection than that found on any comparable Iraqi vehicle. The division had an aviation brigade of Apache attack helicopters and Black Hawk transport helicopters. Supporting firepower comprised four battalions of artillery, three battalions of self-propelled 155mm howitzers and a battalion with the Multiple Launch Rocket System (MLRS). It was also well provided with combat engineers.

The reason the division had this diversity of capabilities was that it intended to fight a 'combined arms' battle. The principle of combined arms is a core tenet of the doctrine of all credible modern armies. It reflects that all the capabilities used in war have strengths and weaknesses. No single arm of the land force can operate entirely independently of each other, so land forces need to conduct operations on a combined arms basis, where the sum of the parts is greater than the whole. It is a lethal version of scissors, papers, stone. Armies apply complementary capabilities to achieve their objectives.

For example, the firepower, mobility and protection of tanks make them the ideal weapon for fighting other armoured vehicles in open terrain. But tanks cannot make their way into buildings, bunkers and trench systems to evict a tenacious enemy, a task which only infantry can perform. In close country such as woods and urban areas, tanks have a very restricted field of view and are vulnerable to infantry with handheld anti-tank weapons. So tactical teams combining tanks and infantry are essential in these terrains.

Tanks and infantry can be greatly aided by artillery suppressing the enemy to allow them to manoeuvre. Engineers can assist by bridging obstacles such as rivers, canals and anti-tank ditches. Equally they can hinder enemy movement by improving the delaying power of natural obstacles and creating man-made ones such as anti-tank ditches or minefields.

The 3rd Infantry Division were trained to do this. The brigade combat teams habitually fought as battalion-sized 'task forces' which grouped tank and infantry companies under a single battalion HQ. The infantry and tanks were trained to operate together down to single tanks supporting an infantry platoon. The brigades could also support the task forces with engineers and artillery. Habitually the same supporting elements were grouped with the same tanks or infantry.

The division had practised at this at platoon, company, battalion, brigade and divisional level, doing so in simulators on training areas in the US using laser weapon effects simulators to allow units to fight each other. Over the preceding years, the division had also provided a battalion, later increased to a brigade, deployed forward in Kuwait. It was as well prepared for war as it was possible for a division to be.

V Corps' other division was the 101st Airborne Division. Again, the division's name was slightly misleading. Unlike most airborne formations, it did not descend into battle by parachute, but moved around the battle by helicopter. To do this the division had more organic helicopters than any other division in any army. Two aviation brigades had large numbers of Apache, Black Hawk and Chinook helicopters. These could lift any one of the division's three brigades of light infantry. These brigades were similarly organized to those of the 3rd Infantry Division but had no armoured vehicles. The division's fighting power was its nine infantry battalions, artillery and Apache helicopters.

Also in the corps were the 11th Attack Helicopter Regiment, a brigade-sized formation of Apache attack helicopters, an artillery brigade with more MLRS, an air defence brigade with Patriot missiles, an engineer brigade which included bridging units and a signals brigade. All these formations could be used by the corps commander to support his divisions, or independently. There were many logistic units and three medical brigades.

The 1st Marine Expeditionary Force (MEF) provided another corps level HQ. It too began the war with two divisions. The 1st Marine Division was lighter than the 3rd Infantry Division, but heavier than the 101st Airborne Division. Three regimental combat teams were centred on three marine infantry battalions. But these would be given a partial armoured warfare capability, by allocating marine tank battalions and light armoured reconnaissance units that fought from their eight wheeled light armoured vehicles. The Marines habitually conducted amphibious landings by swimming ashore in amphibious assault vehicles (AAVs). The need to float necessarily meant that these vehicles were both large and lightly armoured. But for the attack on Iraq they were fitted with additional external armour and used as armoured personnel carriers for some of the marine infantry. There was also an independent Marine expeditionary brigade, known as Task Force Tarawa, under direct command of the MEF. And the three brigades of the British 1st Armoured Division were arriving by sea and air.

Kuwait was crammed with troops, armoured vehicles, artillery, weapons of all kinds. US and Coalition aircraft were parked to maximum capacity around its airfields. A steady stream of transport aircraft, military and civilian, were delivering troops and priority cargo. As with its airfields, Kuwait's ports were being used to maximum capacity.

To protect the forces being assembled and Kuwait itself the US had deployed batteries of Patriot missiles. Originally designed as anti-aircraft missiles, these had been used in 1991 to intercept Iraqi Scud missiles. This capability had been subject to considerable research and development. Many missile batteries would advance into Iraq to protect the ground forces as they advanced, but others would remain in Kuwait for the duration of the war to protect US bases, airfields and Kuwait city.

An armada of naval vessels filled the northern Gulf. Some were protecting the stream of civilian shipping bringing endless streams of equipment vehicles, helicopters, ammunition, missiles and food into Kuwaiti ports. US and UK amphibious shipping was carrying a US Marine expeditionary unit, Royal Marines of 3 Commando Brigade and US Navy SEALS.

In Operation *Desert Storm* General Schwarzkopf had not used an overall land HQ, with the US Army and US Marine Corps commanders reporting directly to him, and a coalition of Arab land forces reporting to a Saudi prince. Many US Army officers viewed this arrangement as sub-optimal. Franks decided that to command the land campaign a Combined Forces Land Component Command (CFLCC) would be formed. This was based on the headquarters of the Third US Army, augmented by Marine Corps and British officers. The US Army decided to make the HQ as effective as possible and provided many highly experienced and effective staff officers to fill its ranks. The HQ acquired the nickname 'the Dream Team'.

The HQ developed its plan in parallel with CENTCOM's. V Corps would advance to Baghdad on the left, to the south of the Euphrates River. The 101st Division would help secure the long and vulnerable route from Kuwait to the capital. The MEF would advance to the west of the river. The capture of Baghdad was to be the main effort. The MEF tasked the British division to screen Basra, Iraq's second city. The city would need to be captured, but this must not divert airpower or other resources from the drive on Baghdad.

In mid-February the land component HQ conducted a mission rehearsal exercise. On a giant terrain model of Kuwait and Iraq the senior staff officers and the V Corps and MEF commanders explained how they saw the campaign unfold. This was the final chance for the land component commander, US Army General David McKiernan, to satisfy himself that the commanders and staff understood the plan for the land campaign and to identify any major problems.

There was much discussion of the potential use of Iraqi chemical weapons. Nasiriyah and Karbala might act as 'choke points' that would force US forces to bunch or slow down, providing potential targets for attack. But it was thought more likely that they would be used when the regime identified that US forces were closing to within artillery range of Baghdad crossing an imaginary 'red line'. However, there was also much optimism that once the war started, the Iraqi forces would surrender. Indeed, CIA teams and UK and US SOF operating in western and southern Iraq were tasked with contacting the commanders of Iraqi formations that US intelligence considered likely to surrender.

Even with the vast amount of planning that the Pentagon and the land component HQ conducted, in some areas direction to land forces was sketchy. General James Mattis of the US Marine Corps was to observe that:

> The ground forces received vague guidance. That meant I was planning without the answers to the most basic question. Were we going all the way to Baghdad? Or only deep enough into Iraq to force Saddam to allow UN inspectors back into the country? These and other gaps in our understanding required us to plan largely in a vacuum. We didn't know the ultimate political intent.[8]

THE ATTACK ON IRAQ BEGINS

On 17 March President Bush issued an ultimatum to Saddam Hussein and his sons, giving them 48 hours to leave Iraq. Two days later he ordered an attempt to kill him. The CIA had previously recruited an informant who worked at Dora Farms, a compound of buildings in a Baghdad suburb. On 19 March, the agent reported strong indications that the Iraqi leader would be visiting the compound. This was confirmed by another US agent. President Bush agreed to a pre-emptive attack. Killing Saddam Hussein, Bush and key advisors agreed, might shorten the war, or even make it unnecessary. The complex was attacked by cruise missiles and two F117 stealth fighters. After the strike the CIA was told that Saddam Hussein had been seriously injured and had been taken away on a stretcher.

As this operation was being planned and conducted CENTCOM received a letter from the British contingent stating that officials in London were unsure if the British role in the attack was legal. General Franks' response was to continue with the attack without the British, but the CENTCOM deputy commander, General Abizaid, advised that advancing without the British would be an unnecessary risk. Hours later the British told Franks that they would be able to take part.[9]

Three-quarters of an hour later President Bush broadcast that the attack on Iraq had begun. Within a few hours Saddam Hussein appeared on Iraqi television, condemning the attack. After the war, the US discovered that he had not been at Dora Farms since 1995. After the strike took place Saddam appeared at his personal secretary's home, where he wrote his short speech, which was recorded on video tape and delivered to the Ministry of Information for broadcast. This attack was the first of many air and missile strikes against key Iraqi leaders. None succeeded.

Originally CENTCOM had planned to begin the air campaign at least five days before the ground forces advanced into Iraq. As the plan evolved this delay between the air and land attacks was reduced. An important factor was Rumsfeld's and Franks' willingness to launch the ground attack before all the formations required were complete in Kuwait. The final version of the CENTCOM Plan was to start the air and land attacks at the same time on 21 March. But intelligence and aerial surveillance indicated that the Iraqis were starting to sabotage oil installations in southern Iraq. Preserving Iraqi oil infrastructure was one of the key tasks assigned to the land forces. So the decision was taken to advance the land attack to the night of 20/21 March. The highly complex plans for the air campaign, could not be altered at this short notice and A-Day, the start of the air campaign, remained 2100hrs on 21 March, 17 hours after the land campaign began. The first conventional group unit to enter Iraq was the 1st Battalion, 7th Marines at 0400hrs on 21 March.

This represented a calculated risk. Against the advantage of increasing the surprise imposed upon the Iraqi forces, only two Coalition divisions were completely ready to go; the 3rd Infantry and 1st Marine divisions. The single armoured brigade of the British 1st Armoured Division had only three of its four battlegroups at full readiness. The 101st Airborne Division was still arriving in Kuwait and would not be ready before 22 March, the 4th Infantry Division's equipment was at sea and the

1st US Armored Division was still preparing to deploy from Germany. Whilst Kuwait had many batteries of US Army Patriot missiles to protect the Coalition forces assembled there, the US Army and Marine Corps logistic troops and stockpiles of spare parts were incomplete. Franks considered that the benefits of advancing into Iraq straight away outweighed the risks.

Coalition troops including US and Polish SOF seized Iraqi offshore oil platforms and the oil manifolds at Faw. Iraqi efforts to damage the oil installations ashore and at sea had little success. But in a harbinger of future encounters with Iraqi infrastructure, the oil installations were found to be in a state of deep disrepair. Naval mine clearance parties, engineers and naval specialists worked to re-open Iraq's only port at Qasr.

Concurrently, 1st Marine Division advanced north from Kuwait, seeking to seize the Rumalia oil fields near Basra, before the Iraqis had a chance to demolish or sabotage them. In this they were largely successful, brushing away fragmented opposition from an Iraqi mechanized division that seemed not to have the stomach for a fight. Following the Marines was the British division. CENTCOM was expecting a proportion of the British force to advance towards Baghdad with the Marines. In the event the whole division remained in southern Iraq.[10]

The full pre-planned air offensive began with cruise missile strikes against Iraqi command centres and air defence sites. The Coalition air component had much to do. For the first days of the campaign the air component main effort consisted of attacks on strategic targets. The land component's main effort was V Corps' advance west of the Euphrates. Once past the Iraqi air base at Talil, few Iraqi troops stood between Kuwait and the key towns of Karbala and Najaf. But the many bridges and towns on both sides of the river would afford Iraqi formations plenty of opportunities to interfere with the advance, should they choose to do so.

The corps advance would be led by the three armoured brigade combat teams of the 3rd Infantry Division. Initially the division had three tasks:

- to destroy Iraqi forces south of Nasiriyah and capture the Iraqi military airfield at Talil
- to seize bridges that crossed the Euphrates
- to advance as fast as it could to the area west of Najaf.

A rapid advance to Najaf would potentially dislocate the Iraqi defence plan. The corps would also need a place for units to refuel and replenish before they advanced on Baghdad. And the corps had greater ambitions. The Apache attack helicopters of the 11th Aviation Regiment would be used to conduct deep attacks against Iraqi armoured and mechanized formations that potentially obstructed V Corps' advance towards Baghdad. An area to the south and west of Najaf, named Objective Rams, would act both as a logistic replenishment area and as a springboard from which the attack helicopters could launch their deep attacks.

The need to clear and then hold Rams against any Iraqi attacks became a key driver in V Corps plan. The other key factor was the long lines of communication from Kuwait to Rams. On the west of the route, there was largely uninhabited empty desert. But on the east were the towns on the banks of the Euphrates. These provided potential bases from which Iraqi forces could sally out to attack the many large convoys of vulnerable unarmoured supply vehicles. Such vehicles were protected only by some vehicle-mounted machine guns and grenade launchers and the small arms of their crews. Safely getting the necessary ammunition, food, spare parts and other essential supplies to Rams would require any Iraqi attacks from the Euphrates towns to be contained.

The V Corps attack from Kuwait began on 20 March with the 3rd Infantry Division crossing the extensive berm that Kuwait had built along its border with Iraq. It planned that its 3rd BCT would capture Talil airfield. The 2nd BCT would secure Objective Rams and the 1st BCT would move to the north of Najaf to isolate the city from Baghdad.

The 3rd BCT pushed aside the Iraqi 11th Infantry Division defending the southern approaches to Nasiriyah, seizing both Talil airfield and the Highway 1 bridge west of Nasiriyah over the Euphrates River. Preceded by its helicopter scouts, the 3rd Infantry Divison's armoured cavalry squadron, 3/7th Cavalry, raced across empty desert to Samawah. Reaching it on 22 March it linked up with a US SOF team who had entered the city some days before.

Over the next day the Abrams, Bradleys and armed helicopters of the squadron fought regular and irregular Iraqi forces, while the 2nd BCT of the 3rd Infantry Division bypassed the town to the south and west heading for Najaf. Task Force Tarawa moved from Kuwait to take over Talil airfield from the 3rd Infantry Division. The division's 3rd BCT left Talil airfield to drive north to take over responsibility for Samawah, relieving the 3/7th Cavalry to advance on Najaf.

The CIA and some military intelligence officers were sure that Iraqi units had little stomach for a fight. Elaborate plans had been made to reinforce this perceived Iraqi unwillingness to fight. Considerable efforts had been made by the CIA and the US military to persuade the Iraqi military not to fight. Large numbers of leaflets were dropped from the air urging Iraqi troops not to resist and explaining how Iraqi units could surrender. The US had obtained the mobile phone numbers for many Iraqi commanders and used these to talk to them. The idea was to have direct conversations to persuade the Iraqi officers to surrender themselves and their troops to advancing US units. But the Iraqi officers concerned thought this was a ruse by Saddam's security services and refused to enter a conversation about surrendering to the US.

Not knowing about the abortive telephone calls, the 3rd Infantry Division had been briefed to expect surrenders by Iraqi Army units. But in the division's advance to Baghdad things turned out differently. Often Iraqi Army troops were surprised by the unexpected appearance of US armour. Morale was often low and leadership by their officers conspicuous by its absence. Sometimes Iraqi units would use effective tactics, for example directing accurate and effective mortar or artillery fire at US forces. More often, their actions would appear poorly co-ordinated, sometimes even random.

But after these initial contacts with Iraqi conventional forces, US troops began to experience attacks by irregulars. Usually wearing civilian clothes and using civilian vehicles these would often swarm towards US units. Many could not shoot straight but could produce a terrifying volume of small arms and RPG fire. They would often display suicidal bravery, including driving cars and other vehicles straight at US troops. They were usually quickly overwhelmed by the firepower of the Abrams and Bradleys, as well as artillery, attack helicopters and fighter bombers. But the less well-protected amphibious assault vehicles (AAVs) used by the Marines and the long columns of army tracks and tankers making their way to Objective Rams would be more vulnerable.

FRICTION OF WAR: THE 507TH MAINTENANCE COMPANY,
TASK FORCE TARAWA AND THE BATTLE OF NASIRIYAH

Nasiriyah is a town that commands the southern Euphrates River and the Saddam canal which flows past the north of the town. The plan for the advance of the Marines depended on capturing the bridges over both waterways. Task Force Tarawa was a US Marine Expeditionary Brigade under direct command of the HQ of the MEF. It was tasked to secure two key targets, both bridges on the east side of the town, the Highway 8 bridge in the south-east of Nasiriyah, and the bridge on the north-east of the town that carried Highway 8 over the Saddam canal, to allow the 1st Marine Division's advance north.

As it attacked northwards towards the centre of the city, the brigade's leading battalion was astonished to see US Army trucks approaching them heading south from Nasiriyah. These were the survivors of the 507th Maintenance Company, part of a Patriot missile unit. It had originally been a convoy of 33 soldiers in 16 trucks and Humvees, one of the many logistic units heading to Objective Rams. It had set out as part of a convoy of 600 vehicles. During a cross-country move over the night of 21/22 March its heavier vehicles had become stuck in soft sand. The company commander continued with the lighter vehicles.

By now the troops had been travelling for 60 hours. They were exhausted. Looking for a traffic checkpoint, but finding none, the convoy missed a turning and headed north-east to Nasiriyah. Not realizing that they were now in Iraqi-held territory they travelled through two Iraqi security checkpoints without incident. Why the Iraqis failed to open fire is not known.

Eventually realizing the error, the commander turned the convoy round to head south. As they did this Iraqis opened fire. Manoeuvring the large trucks quickly in the streets was impossible. The convoy broke into three groups to head south, out of the town. The volume and effectiveness of Iraqi fire increased, while Iraqi fighters placed vehicles on the road south to slow the Americans down. Eleven soldiers were killed, seven were captured and nine were wounded. Only half the convoy's vehicles survived.

The incident was a practical demonstration of friction, the tendency of military plans to go wrong. In this case it was amplified by the fatigue of the convoy's members. Other frictions came from most of the convoy's vehicles not having radios. It also appears that the only vehicle-mounted machine gun jammed, as did many of the soldiers' rifles. This was an indicator of a logistic unit that was inadequately prepared for combat.

The survivors of the 507th were lucky that the Marines of Task Force Tarawa were so close to the town. The Marines did what they could to treat and evacuate the convoy's wounded. That there might be survivors of the convoy hiding in the town or held captive by the Iraqis added urgency to the task force's attack against Iraqi defenders, who now knew that US forces were in the area.

The attack on Nasiriyah's two eastern bridges by 1st Battalion, 2nd Marine Regiment (1/2nd Marines) ran into difficulties and frictions of its own. The battalion was mounted in AAVs that had far lower levels of protection than the Bradley fighting vehicles that carried the 3rd Infantry Division's infantry. As it approached the first, south-eastern, bridge the tanks supporting the battalion unexpectedly departed to refuel. As Company B crossed the bridge and entered the city it came under heavy fire from a mixture of Iraqi Army and Fedayeen fighters. Cobra helicopter gunships and Hornet fighters were called to assist the Marine infantry.

Attempting to approach the second bridge at the north-east corner of the city over the Saddam canal from an unexpected direction, Company B turned east, only for many of its vehicles to be bogged down in soft ground. It soon found itself surrounded by enemy fighters. It was followed across the south-eastern bridge by Company A, who stayed to secure the north side of the bridge. It too came under small arms and RPG fire. Marines found it difficult to distinguish between fighters wearing civilian clothes and uninvolved Iraqi civilians.

Company C followed, speeding up the road, by now christened 'Ambush Alley'. As Company B was unable to move, Company C would have to seize the Saddam canal bridge. As they drove north, Iraqi small arms and RPG fire grew ever more intense. Just south of the canal an AAV was hit by an RPG. Despite the additional armour fitted to the AAVs the vehicle caught fire. The resulting column of smoke provided a helpful marker to the Iraqi fighters making their way to join the fighting.

The company successfully crossed the Saddam canal bridge into flat open terrain. This triggered a fusillade of fire: small arms, RPGs, mortars and artillery. Marines were being killed. More became casualties as the company was bombed and strafed by a pair of USAF A10 Warthog attack aircraft. In error a tactical air controller with Company B had tasked them to attack the area of the Saddam canal bridge. Five AAVs heading south along Ambush Alley were attacked by the jets. Three were hit. Only two vehicles made it through.

Later two tanks joined Company C, their main guns silencing Iraqi firing positions. Company C lost 18 Marines killed and 36 wounded as well as seven of its 12 AAVs that day. The battalion had seized the two bridges crossing the Euphrates in eastern Nasiriyah, but Task Force Tarawa had control only of 'Ambush Alley' and a small part of the town.

Friction had again made operations more difficult than expected. The lack of tanks meant that 1/2nd Marines had less mobile protected fire support than they had planned. So Iraqi fire that would have been suppressed by tank guns was able to inflict more casualties and impose more delay than had the tanks been present. In particular, RPGs that might have been fired at the tanks and been defeated by the vehicles' advanced armour hit the larger, much less well-protected AAVs. Had Company B not got bogged in soft ground east of Nasiriyah the Marines would have had more combat power, improving the odds in their favour. And it would have been less likely that US aircraft would have attacked Company C.

The next day the task force attacked north from Nasiriyah. Its plan was to secure the routes that US troops needed to pass through the town, but not to occupy it. Otherwise Nasiriyah would be surrounded and isolated, the Iraqi forces being contained by air and artillery strikes and probing attacks. The level of fighting along 'Ambush Alley' reduced and 1st Marine Division began to pass along the road.

The Marines continued to advance northwards from Kuwait up Highways 1 and (after reaching Nasiriyah) 7, followed by British troops who secured the oilfield area for the rest of the war. The British advanced to isolate Basra, secure Qasr for the delivery of humanitarian aid by the Royal Navy and allow the naval forces to clear the Shatt al-Arab waterway that linked Basra to the Gulf.

THE ADVANCE NORTH BY V CORPS

The V Corps plan had called for early attacks by the Apache helicopters of the corps' 11th Attack Helicopter Regiment and those of the 101st

Airborne Division. In addition, both the 3rd and 101st divisions would be using helicopters for reconnaissance, command and control and movement of key personnel and supplies. The 101st Airborne Division had more organic helicopters than any other division in the US Army or any other army in the world. It would use its many Black Hawk and Chinook helicopters to move its infantry and artillery. Lacking any tanks, the division would use its Apaches as 'flying tanks', not only conducting attacks in their own right, but also providing intimate fire support to the division's infantry.

This required the creation of two Forward Arming and Refuelling Points (FARPs). FARP Exxon would be in the desert 100 miles north of Kuwait. FARP Shell would be close to Objective Rams. Both would be secured by the 3rd BCT of the 101st. Provisioning the fuel required large numbers of heavy fuel tankers to get across the Iraqi desert and road network in sufficient time to be ready for the helicopters' arrival.

Meanwhile the 3rd Infantry Division advanced to the north-west of Objective Rams, Samawah, and the outskirts of Najaf a day later. Both towns were screened. It found the Euphrates river valley towns to not only be garrisoned by Iraqi Army troops but also to be swarming with irregular fighters, a mixture of Iraqi Fedayeen paramilitaries and jihadists who had come from Syria. These fought with suicidal determination and it became necessary to commit substantial numbers of troops to prevent these fighters moving west from Samawah and Najaf to attack the V Corps lines of communications.

DEEP ATTACK

V Corps tasked the 11th Attack Helicopter Regiment to launch a deep attack against Iraqi formations to the south of Karbala. This was to be executed over the night 23/24 March, with the regiment's helicopters staging through forward arming and refuelling points established at Objective Rams. There were great expectations invested in the attack. Deep attacks by battalion- or brigade-sized groups of Apache helicopters had been a feature of US Army doctrine and plans since the aircraft entered service and the regiment had undergone extensive training for such a task, including a demanding exercise in Poland the previous autumn. In the event the helicopters were surprised to encounter much heavier anti-aircraft fire than they expected. There was little damage inflicted on the targets, an Apache was shot down and 31 others were damaged, many seriously. The attack was a failure. Why was this?

The mission had its share of friction. There was little up-to-date intelligence of the targets and no intelligence on the location of Iraqi air defences. Not all fuel tankers had made it to Rams in time. The areas used for fuelling and arming were unexpectedly bisected by irrigation ditches and very dusty. As helicopters landed or took off, they threw up vast clouds of dust obscuring visibility to the aircraft's crews and troops on the ground alike. The resulting 'brownout' conditions and disorientation could be very dangerous, with a high risk of collisions and accidents to aircraft and troops and vehicles on the ground.

So, take off was delayed for a couple of hours. The plan had been that over 30 Army Tactical Missiles (ATACMS) would be fired at likely Iraqi air defence sites just before the Apaches arrived. This went ahead at the time originally planned, giving any Iraqi troops attacked by the missiles time to recover.

Of the 60 Apaches in the regiment, only 31 lifted off from Rams to take part in the attack. Heading north, they ran into considerable small arms fire. Much of it appeared inaccurate, but the volume of fire was so high that all the helicopters were hit. Of the two helicopter battalions launched, one reached its target area, but was forced to abort its attack, while the other engaged only a few vehicles at its target area. The Apache was the best protected helicopter in the world, so although one aircraft was shot down and its crew taken prisoner, the rest made it back to Objective Rams. But the damage to the helicopters meant that two of the regiment's three helicopter battalions had been rendered inoperable. The mission had failed.

That day, 23 March, would come to be seen as the darkest day of the US campaign so far. The destruction of the 507th Maintenance Company, the casualties resulting from the subsequent confused fighting in Nasiriyah and the expensive failure of the attack helicopter raid were forceful reminders of the uncertainty, friction and cost of war. They were also an illustration of how over confidence and a failure to anticipate the operational environment that US forces would encounter in Iraq would frustrate their plans. The attack and its failure were harbingers of factors that would bedevil the first years of the war.

MAP 5: COALITION ATTACK ON IRAQ,
20 MARCH–9 APRIL 2003

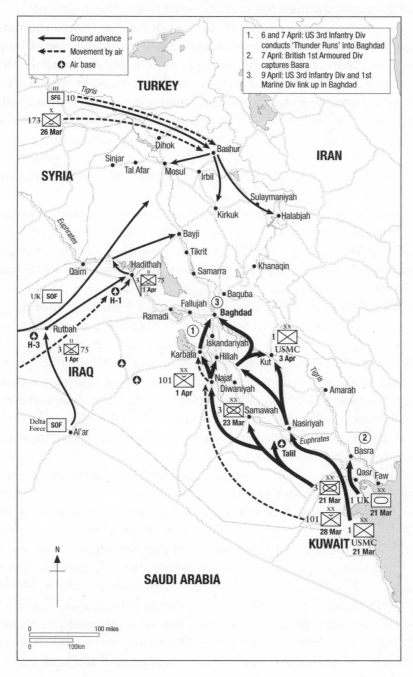

Ground advance
Movement by air
Air base

1. 6 and 7 April: US 3rd Infantry Div conducts 'Thunder Runs' into Baghdad
2. 7 April: British 1st Armoured Div captures Basra
3. 9 April: US 3rd Infantry Div and 1st Marine Div link up in Baghdad

The ground advance continued. The 3rd BCT reached Samawah on 23 March. Running fights developed. The brigade combat team did not seek to occupy the town but moved quickly to isolate it, to prevent Iraqi forces interfering with forces moving to the west of the town. The SOF team that had infiltrated Samawah provided useful intelligence that the town had been reinforced by hundreds of Republican Guard troops, as well as paramilitary fighters. These were brave and persistent, but tactically weak. The brigade combat team's commander, Colonel Dan Allyn, ordered probing attacks to distract the Iraqis, to better contain the threat.

THE WAR IN KURDISTAN

Meanwhile, increasing numbers of US troops were entering Kurdistan. These were SOF from the Joint SOF Task Force North. Led by a joint HQ formed by the US Army's 10th Special Forces Group and 352nd Special Operations Group of USAF, the Task Force had originally planned to fly from its base in Rumania over Turkey and into Kurdistan from the north. But closure of Turkish airspace made that option impossible. The alternative was to fly from a base in Jordan across Iraq.

On the night of 20 March, six MC130 Combat Talon aircraft were flown across Iraq at low level, carrying SOF troops. In the course of the four and a half hour flights, three aircraft were hit by Iraqi air defences, one being so badly damaged that it had to make an emergency landing at an airfield in Turkey. But the insertion of the leading elements of the SOF task force was successful.

The first target for the US SOF was not Iraqi government forces, but was Ansar al-Islam, an Al Qaida splinter group that the US suspected was experimenting with chemical and biological weapons. It had fought Kurdish forces to establish a safe haven in a wild, inaccessible mountain fastness close to the border between Kurdistan and Iran.

The terrorist mountain base was struck with Tomahawk cruise missile strikes on 23 March. Five days later an attack was mounted by some 10,000 Kurdish fighters accompanied by US SOF. Together with Peshmerga fighters with vehicle-mounted anti-aircraft cannons and mortars, the SOF used machine guns and grenade launchers on Humvees to provide fire support to the Peshmerga infantry, as well as call in US air strikes. The defending jihadists put up heavy fire from small arms, cannons, and rockets. It took 48 hours to defeat them.

The SOF and an accompanying chemical reconnaissance detachment recovered chemical defence equipment and evidence that the jihadists were developing chemical weapons. The battle demonstrated to the Kurdish fighters that small detachments of US SOF were able to accompany the Peshmerga into the heat of the fighting and that they had the know-how, organic firepower and access to US airpower to greatly multiply the effectiveness of the Kurdish forces. This created mutual trust and gave the Peshmerga leadership confidence to advance against numerically superior Iraqi government forces.

Concurrently the SOF Task Force was being reinforced. On 26 March the 173rd Airborne Brigade was delivered by parachute into Kurdistan. The brigade was augmented by the air landing from USAF C17 transports onto a captured air strip of the 1st Battalion, 63rd Armor Regiment. This had a company of Abrams tanks and Bradley fighting vehicles and a mechanized infantry company in M113s. All of these were logistically sustained by air, except for Turkish contractors providing fuel. The capabilities of the SOF, paratroopers, heavy armour and Marines acted both as a force multiplier for the Kurds and also as a restraint on any actions that the Kurds might take that could prompt Turkish intervention.

THE ISOLATION OF NAJAF

To allow Objective Rams to be turned into the logistic base for the attack on Baghdad it was essential to stop Iraqi forces getting into or out of the nearby town of Najaf. This mission was assigned to the 1st BCT of the 3rd Infantry Division, commanded by Colonel Will Grimsley. The brigade combat team also had to secure two large bridges over the Euphrates River to the east of Najaf, one south-east of the town, designated Objective Floyd, and the other to the north, Objective Jenkins.

On 28 March the 3/7th Cavalry was tasked to seize Objective Floyd and move east of the town. It found the bridge at Abu Sakhair was not wired for demolition. The cavalry squadron rolled straight over. The sandstorm was at its height and soldiers could see no further than 25 yards. But the thermal sights of the Abrams and Bradleys could see further through the gloom.

As the squadron moved north along the eastern bank of the Euphrates it fought off repeated attacks by paramilitary fighters approaching on foot and in civilian vehicles. The intensity of the dust storm by now meant that they were being seen and engaged only at very close range. Increasing numbers of vehicles, including a bus and a fuel tanker, attempted to ram the US vehicles. The drivers were invariably killed by close-range fire, but often the momentum of the vehicles meant that they still collided with the US armoured vehicles. And RPGs scored lucky hits on two tanks' ammunition storage at the rear of the turret, forcing the crews to abandon them.

The cavalry squadron fought its way north around the east of the city. The 1st BCT still had troops spread between Najaf and Samawah so had no spare battalion task forces. An ad hoc task force was assembled to skirt round the north-west of Najaf and attack Objective Jenkins, the bridge at Kifl. This was based on the brigade combat team's air defence battery. It was equipped with the Linebacker anti-aircraft vehicle, a variant of the Bradley fighting vehicle that had its TOW anti-tank missiles replaced by Stinger anti-aircraft missiles. The vehicles retained their machine guns, 25mm cannon and night sights.

The battery, commanded by Captain Charley Branson, was augmented with some of the brigade combat team's scouts and a laser designation team. Setting off in the early hours of 25 March, it had a long fight against paramilitary troops. These were cleared from the west bank of the Euphrates, but Branson asked for assistance to get across the bridge. He was joined by the executive officer of Task Force 3-69 Armor, Major Mike Oliver, a tank company and a platoon of Bradleys. At 1100hrs the fourth tank of the leading tank platoon was crossing the bridge when the Iraqis detonated explosives along the bridge's spine.

The bridge was relatively undamaged and the arriving commander of Task Force 3-69 Armor, Lieutenant Colonel Ernest 'Rock' Marcone, was unimpressed by what he described as a 'small indentation'. Marcone led his own tank across the bridge and then joined the close-quarter fighting against Iraqi paramilitaries, shooting one and wrestling a rifle away from another. US armoured vehicles were charged by pickup trucks and vans. As US infantry with Bradleys consolidated their positions on the east bank, Iraqi mortar rounds landed amongst them. The blasts concussed Marcone who remained unconscious for 45 minutes. Iraqi paramilitary fighters in pickup trucks streamed towards the bridgehead from the north. Most of the vehicles were destroyed by Bradleys, using their thermal sights, but surviving fighters used buildings and the cover of sandstorm to work their way forward, sometimes close as 30 feet.

All the US troops on the east bank of the Euphrates continued to be attacked from all directions. On 26 March, the air defence battery at Objective Jenkins was relieved by Task Force 2-69 Armor, and then moved south to reinforce the cavalry squadron. The next day fighting began to taper off.

UNSUCCESSFUL AND SUCCESSFUL APPLICATIONS OF AIRPOWER

During the night of 28 March the Apache helicopters of the Aviation Brigade of the 101st Division launched a deep attack against Republican Guard formations that US thought were based north of Karbala. The brigade sought to learn from the failure of the previous deep attack five nights earlier. The routes taken by the helicopters avoided populated areas. ATACMS missiles would be fired to suppress likely Iraqi air defences four minutes before the helicopters arrived and the manoeuvre was co-ordinated with attacks by Hornet fighters. But when the Apache helicopters arrived at their objectives the intended targets could not be found and only a few Iraqi armoured vehicles were engaged.

In Afghanistan the ability of US Army and Marines attack helicopters to provide close air support had proved invaluable. For example, without them, casualties during Operation *Anaconda* would probably have been much higher. And elsewhere in Iraq both Apaches and Cobras would prove themselves invaluable in this role, integrated into tactical manoeuvre of the companies, battalions, brigades and regiments on the ground. But the ease with which helicopters flying over built-up areas could be seen at night, their vulnerability to ground fire and the difficulties of providing sufficiently accurate and timely intelligence made the independent deep attacks in Iraq much less effective than the US Army had hoped. The 101st Airborne's deep attack would be the last such operation in Iraq.

Bombers and fighters flying above the effective range of small arms fire were proving much more effective at attacking Iraqi armour. They were succeeding in reducing the effectiveness of the Republican Guard forces between the US troops and Baghdad.

THE SANDSTORM AND US OPERATIONAL PAUSE

On 24 March a huge sandstorm developed. It would last over two days.

It enveloped much of the country from Baghdad southwards. Thunder and lightning combined with strong gusts of wind to fling sand everywhere. To many US troops 'the whole world went orange'. The Army and Marine battalions advancing north found their progressed slowed. Helicopters found the conditions varied from very difficult to impossible, and the laser-guided bombs carried by many Coalition aircraft could not be used. But the huge clouds of dust could be penetrated by radars, both those with US ground units and the powerful airborne radars carried by the JSTARS aircraft. And Coalition signals intelligence units on the ground and air could still listen in to Iraqi radio communications. Artillery and mortars could still be used to engage targets identified by ground troops and their radars, and the GPS-guided JDAM bombs could still be used through the dust. From 25 March, the Coalition air forces increasingly attacked Iraqi ground forces, especially the Republican Guard south of Baghdad and any armoured units that were seen to be moving towards Coalition troops on the ground.

In western Iraq, SOF seized two Iraqi airfields, developing them into forward operating bases. But the Land Component HQ had always envisaged that an operational pause might be required, to allow the forces approaching Baghdad to top up their logistic supplies and to prepare to resist the anticipated Iraqi chemical attacks.

As there was heavy fighting going on in the Euphrates Valley, the land component commander Lieutenant General McKiernan decided that the time was right for such a short pause in the advance, to 'take time to clean up and make sure we have the right stance in our battlespace before we commit into the Baghdad fight, because once we commit to the Baghdad fight, we can't stop'.

But there was considerable disagreement between Franks and McKiernan. Franks saw the pause as unnecessary, whereas McKiernan reasoned that the wholly unexpected resistance from irregular Iraqi forces in and around the Euphrates Valley towns posed a real threat to the huge convoys of logistic vehicles that would need to move north-west to sustain the advance with ammunition and fuel. There needed to be a pause to allow the tanks and other armoured vehicles to be refuelled and replenished. And the ability of the Iraqi irregulars to sortie from the Euphrates Valley towns would need to be countered by moving up 101st and 82nd Airborne divisions to defend against such sorties and to clear the major towns of enemy. Franks reluctantly accepted that the land advance pause from 27 to 29 March.

The 1st Marine Division had been rapidly advancing east of the Euphrates to attack Baghdad from the east, greatly aided by continuous attacks by the aircraft of the 1st Marine Air Wing. To Major General Mattis, the divisional commander, the pause seemed wholly unnecessary. His division's logistic convoys had encountered Fedayeen snipers but had quickly dealt with them. Mattis reluctantly halted the division, withdrawing the leading regimental combat team and mounting probing attacks across his front to keep the Iraqis off balance.

In training and operations Mattis had emphasized the need for speed, to wrest the initiative from the enemy and deny the Iraqis the ability to concentrate forces, either in defensive positions or to conduct counter-attacks.

Mattis had planned, trained and organized the division to optimize its ability to move so rapidly that Iraqi forces would not be able to adjust their plans in time. Mattis was an avid reader of military history and had extensively studied historic campaigns where rapid advances had got inside the decision cycle of the enemy. To achieve this Mattis had sought to reduce 'logistic drag', the way logistic demands could slow down an advancing force. For example he deliberately took a risk by reducing the amount of artillery ammunition that the division carried in its logistic vehicles, reasoning that the accuracy of precision bombs and missiles recently demonstrated in Afghanistan meant that Coalition aircraft could supply much of the fire support traditionally provided by the Marines' artillery. That the Marine Corps was the most highly integrated air–land force in the world gave him and the whole division great confidence that the risk was worth taking.

A high priority would be given to the capture of Iraqi airfields so that the Marines' C130 Hercules could deliver fuel and ammunition to Marine spearheads. Their vehicles would carry as much fuel and ammunition as they could. Troops would eat two, rather than three, meals each day and to free up space in vehicles, camp beds would only be used for casualties. The whole division, including Mattis, would sleep on the ground.

Since the division had crossed the Euphrates, the Marines had not been delayed by Iraqi regular or irregular forces. So Mattis found the application of the halt order both frustrating and confusing. He halted the division's advance but determined to keep the Iraqis off balance by mounting probing attacks all along his front.

The advance had shown Mattis that one of the division's regiments was not advancing as aggressively or as fast as the other regiments. Mattis met the regiment's commander. He assessed that he was being over-cautious and was excessively worried about the risk of Marine casualties. Judging that the commander was unlikely to overcome this ingrained caution, Mattis fired him.

On 28 March the land component commander Lieutenant General McKiernan met with the commanders of V Corps and MEF. He wanted to hear his commanders' assessment of the situation and their concerns for the impending attack on Baghdad.

Baghdad had always been identified as the Iraqi centre of gravity, but for the moment the unexpectedly heavy resistance offered by the irregular Fedayeen, paramilitary forces and jihadists was a major factor delaying V Corps' advance. Regular Iraqi Army forces were offering less resistance. Some had disintegrated and disappeared. But the efforts made before the war by the CIA to arrange negotiated surrenders of Iraqi units were proving unsuccessful. Until the towns of the Euphrates Valley were cleared, the 3rd Infantry Division would be unable to concentrate to mass the full divisional combat power that would be required to attack Baghdad. V Corps wanted to improve their position before they crossed the assessed 'Red Line' around Baghdad that might trigger Iraqi chemical attacks.

US commanders wanted to minimize the strength of Iraqi forces in Baghdad. Iraqi units that could interfere with the advance from Karbala or reinforce the capital and the city would be subject to relentless attack from the air, both to reduce their combat power and to prevent them moving.

It had not been originally intended to use the 82nd and 101st Airborne divisions to secure the line of communication. During planning, there had been some discussion of using them in the attack on Baghdad, to assault from the air. The 82nd had already rigged its fighting equipment to be dropped by parachute. Instead, by clearing the urban conglomerations of the Euphrates, both divisions would protect the convoys loaded with fuel, ammunition and spare parts flowing from Kuwait to Objective Rams and beyond and the empty trucks and tankers returning. They would also release the armoured brigade combat teams of 3rd Infantry Division to concentrate on the advance to Baghdad. This would turn out to be as important a contribution to victory as any risky descent on Baghdad by helicopter or parachute.

The HQ and a brigade combat team of the 82nd Airborne Division had been assigned to V Corps on 26 March. The corps commander, Lieutenant General Scott Wallace, sent a short message to the 82nd Airborne's commander: 'message from Gen Wallace to MG Swannack as follows: get your ass up here.'[11] So a brigade combat team of the 82nd Airborne Division was flown into the recently captured Talil air base near Nasiriyah, moving north-west to replace the armoured brigade combat team at Samawah by 29 March. The paratroopers cleared the town.

Simultaneously, the 101st Air Assault Division relieved 3rd Infantry Division of responsibility for Najaf. While its 2nd Brigade Combat Team isolated the town, the 1st Brigade Combat Team cleared the city. Meanwhile Task Force Tarawa had been chipping away at Iraqi resistance in Nasiriyah, by mounting ground, artillery and air attacks.

FIVE ATTACKS AND THE ADVANCE TO BAGHDAD

The 3rd Infantry Division had spent several days at Rams, replenishing fuel and ammunition and giving its vehicles much-needed maintenance. With the division concentrated, refuelled and re-armed, and the 101st and 82nd Airborne divisions securing the long line of communication to Kuwait, V Corps was ready to move on Baghdad. The main attack would be made north of Karbala, between the town and the Bahr al-Milh lake, moving towards Baghdad from the south-west to north-east. So the corps sought to deceive the Iraqis that the main attack to Baghdad would come south of this through Najaf and Hillah.

To achieve this, the corps mounted five simultaneous attacks to prevent the Iraqi command from re-deploying forces to interfere with the main advance towards Baghdad. In the north, an Apache attack helicopter battalion of the 101st Airborne would attack Iraqi forces south of the Bahr al-Milh lake. The 2nd BCT of 3rd Infantry Division would conduct an attack to destroy Iraqi forces defending Hindiyah. The 101st Airborne would conduct a feint attack towards Hillah and continue to attack Najaf to contain the town's Iraqi defenders. The fifth and final attack would see the 2nd BCT of the 82nd Airborne Division continue to attack the Iraqi defenders of Samawah.

On 1 April, the 3rd Infantry Division moved through the Karbala Gap, heading north-east towards Baghdad. Republican Guard forces opposing it had suffered greatly from air attacks. They and Fedayeen fighters often resisted the division's armour, but their defensive battles and the brave but suicidal attacks by the irregulars were piecemeal and unco-ordinated. Comprehensively overmatched by the division, they did little to slow down its advance. Iraqi howitzer and rocket artillery fire was defeated by the division's artillery, which used radar to target it, and by close air support.

THE SOF CAMPAIGN FOR WESTERN IRAQ

As the war began JSOTF-W left its forward base in Jordan. The British SOF advanced in the north, paralleling the Iraqi–Syrian border, the Australians in the centre and the US SOF in the south. In the event JSOTF-W failed to find any operational Iraqi ballistic missile launchers.

A Delta Force squadron mounted in soft-skinned all-terrain vehicles crossed into Iraq, checking for suspected WMD storage sites. Iraqi forces encountered were attacked or ambushed at night, with the troops making maximum use of the plentiful air support they had been allocated. Captured Iraqi troops were briefly interrogated and then released. These actions were designed to create and reinforce the impression that major US conventional forces were advancing from Jordan towards Baghdad.

A second Delta Force squadron with its vehicles was loaded into C17 transports and flown to an airstrip in western Iraq that had been captured by the US commandos. Rangers descended by parachute on the H1 airfield in central Iraq. Engineers rendered the airstrip operational. A company of tanks from 3rd Infantry Division were re-assigned to the

Map 6: US forces in Iraq, 9–30 April 2003

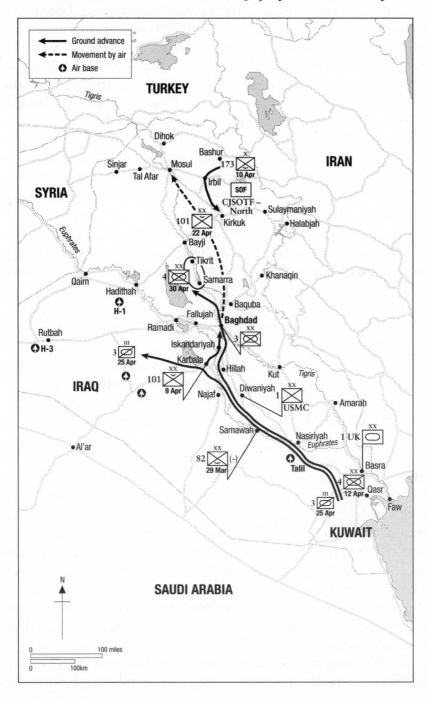

US SOF. Flown in C17 transports from Talil airfield to H1, they would not only add much needed protection and firepower to support the light soft-skinned vehicles used by the SOF but would also reinforce the impression that the SOF sought to create – of US armoured forces heading to Baghdad from the west.

But a British SOF detachment got into more trouble than it could cope with. This was a squadron of the Royal Marines' Special Boat Service, the maritime British SOF equivalent to the US Navy's SEALS. Operating on the edge of the Sunni triangle they were attacked by Iraqi fighters and forced to scatter. Most were eventually picked up by Coalition helicopters. Others exfiltrated into Syria. Abandoned British vehicles, weapons and radios were jubilantly displayed on Iraqi television.

On the night of 1 April Rangers landed from helicopters to seize control of the Hadithah Dam. Releasing the flood gates of this structure on the Euphrates River 125 miles north-west of Karbala would probably have caused catastrophic flooding. Potentially disastrous, such a flood had the power to slow down the US advance on Baghdad. Although the attackers achieved surprise, rapidly overwhelming Iraqi defenders, the next three weeks saw major Iraqi counter-attacks, which the Rangers used attack helicopters and airpower to defeat. But there was no evidence that the Iraqis had ever planned to open or demolish the dam.

SEIZING THE BRIDGE AT OBJECTIVE PEACH

Military history is replete with examples of attempts to 'bounce' a river crossing by capturing bridges intact. These more usually fail than they succeed. Defenders will often rig the bridge with demolition charges, so as to destroy it once all friendly troops have withdrawn across the river. Should they fail to capture an intact bridge, attackers will have no alternative to conducting an assault river crossing requiring infantry to cross the river in boats to secure a bridgehead, after which combat engineers can construct a military bridge. Such operations are invariably risky and can impose much delay on an advancing force.

The last physical obstacle between the 3rd Infantry Division and Baghdad was the Euphrates River. There was an intact bridge at Kaed.

On 2 April a battalion task force based on the 3/69th Armor was ordered to seize the crossing, named by the division as Objective Peach. The fighting saw the largest battle of the campaign between US and Iraqi conventional forces.

TF 3/69th contained two tank companies and two infantry companies with Bradleys, an armoured engineer company and a smoke platoon, and had an artillery battalion in direct support. It had already fought over a bridge over the Euphrates, the 25 March capture of Objective Jenkins at Kifl. Its commander, Lieutenant Colonel 'Rock' Marcone, drew on lessons from that action, planning to use artillery and airstrikes on the places where Iraqi engineers might be waiting to fire any explosive charges they had placed on the bridge. The ground attack would begin by seizing ground on the west side of the bridge from which defenders on the east side could be suppressed. A smoke screen and close support from artillery and attack helicopters would allow the rest of the task force to cross. Marcone anticipated that once it was across the river, it would be counter-attacked by the Iraqi Republican Guard Medina Division to the east.

The advance was led by the battalion scouts, whose forward movement was stopped by an Iraqi infantry battalion west of the bridge. Supported by mortars and by artillery firing high-explosive and smoke shells, a tank company attacked the Iraqi forces from the south, while an electronic warfare unit sought to jam the radio frequencies used by the Iraqi defenders. Three Apache helicopters joined this attack but quickly came under intense small arms fire from Iraqi soldiers in well-concealed fighting positions. The damage inflicted forced all three aircraft to conduct emergency landings.

A following infantry company in Bradleys occupied the west bank next to the bridge. Combat engineers checked the bridge for Iraqi demolitions and removed any explosive that they found. Infantry and engineers crossed the river in rubber boats to check the eastern half of the structure. Some of the boats were swept downstream and landed hundreds of yards south of their planned landfall. As this hazardous crossing was going on, the Iraqis fired the demolition charges. The bridge had two spans side by side. The northern span was damaged, but the southern remained usable. The American infantry rushed the bridge, followed over the next 30 minutes by the remaining tank and infantry companies.

At the same time a barrage of Iraqi artillery shells and mortar bombs struck the company team on the west bank. Their explosive force uprooted palm trees. The Abrams and Bradleys were battered by shrapnel and some received direct hits from the mortar bombs. Apart from minor scarring on their armour, the vehicles were unscathed and none of their crews became casualties. After this initial salvo the artillery fire continued for an hour, but its accuracy decreased.

Having got the task force across the bridge Marcone arranged his two tank and infantry companies in defensive positions. Soldiers also found a map which was marked with the Iraqi commander's assessment of the situation. This seemed to show that the US main attack was anticipated to be heading north along the east bank of the Euphrates.

Shortly before 2100hrs the task force was told that signals intelligence indicated that infantry of the Special Republican Guard was advancing towards its positions. Soon afterwards Iraqi infantry began an attack from the north, supported by mortar fire. This continued intermittently during the night. Many of these attacks were broken up, but in places the ground allowed enemy infantry to approach within 200 yards of the Americans. Two Bradley platoons were overrun by Iraqi infantry, which were only seen off by neighbouring Abrams tanks using their machine guns to sweep the enemy away from the Bradleys.

In the early hours of the next morning, an Iraqi armoured force attacked from the east, a T72 tank company leading, followed by a mechanized infantry battalion in M113 armoured personnel carriers. But the thermal sights on the US fighting vehicles gave the task force a decisive advantage. The leading tanks were destroyed, and the Iraqi unit withdrew, harassed by US artillery and close air support as it retreated.

As the fighting continued, combat engineers consulted over an electronic link with experts in the US – a capability named 'tele engineering'. This allowed them to immediately begin repairing the road bridge. At the same time engineers built a floating bridge across the Euphrates, giving the 3rd Infantry Division three crossings over the river.

In the light of day, the task force counted approximately 600 dead Iraqi fighters, 14 tanks, six light armoured vehicles and ten trucks destroyed. Next to a burned-out Iraqi tank, soldiers found the body of the commander of the 10th Brigade of the Medina Division, with documents showing the layout of the division. The papers showed that the brigade had begun the previous day at 80 per cent of its strength. Now it was no longer capable of combat. The task force had a few soldiers wounded and none killed. The superior leadership, training, tactics and combat capabilities of the task force contributed to a stunning success. A major factor was that it had much greater combat power and better protection than the Marine battalion of Task Force Tarawa that had sought to 'bounce' the river crossing at Nasiriyah.

But there were still risks to the task force. Of these, the greatest was the lack of intelligence. The attack on Objective Peach was the main effort of the brigade combat team, the division and the corps. The Coalition had a large amount of airborne intelligence, surveillance and reconnaissance systems. But the only intelligence or information that the task force received was a few minutes warning of the first enemy attacks and some reports received from a JSTARS aircraft that had detected vehicle movement on its radar.

This apparent inability to get timely intelligence or information to brigades or battalions would be a persistent complaint of US land tactical commanders during the invasion. Often the first they knew about enemy locations was when their helicopters, scouts, tanks or Bradleys saw them, if the Iraqis had not opened fire first.

One reason for this was the lack of a unified Iraqi military command, with little or no co-ordination between the different armed state actors. And an Iraqi tendency to pass decisions and orders by word of mouth or civilian telephone made it difficult for US signals intelligence to detect orders being passed over military radio networks. All of this presented considerable challenges to US intelligence staffs, who could often detect conventional units or formations, but were unable to assess their intentions.

It was not that the intelligence did not exist. Indeed, it had been available to units in their staging areas in Kuwait. Rather the problem was a result of the speed of advance and the extended distances that formations were operating over. Often battalions and brigade and regimental combat teams were operating beyond the range of their organic radios. And the US Army's higher formation communications network, the Mobile Subscriber Equipment, was equally stretched, operating over far greater distances than envisaged in the Cold War scenarios for which the equipment was purchased. So once V Corps moved forward from Kuwait it proved extremely difficult to provide high-capacity bandwidth to brigade combat teams and units.

Instead units and formations made extensive use of a few tactical satellite (TACSAT) radios. And they also had an innovative new system, the Blue Force Tracker. Installed in key company and battalion vehicles it transmitted its location to a satellite, which retransmitted the data. All Coalition vehicles and HQs with the device could see the locations and identities of all units so equipped on a digital map. The system also showed identified enemy ground units. It included a simple email system. This gave commanders much better situational awareness of their own forces than ever before. With this went a reduction of the chances of accidental friendly fire incidents and greater tactical confidence.

The Blue Force Tracker system was available to all levels of command from company HQ to CENTCOM. This was invaluable to all tactical commanders. For example, it helped avert friendly fire between US battalions. But the land component HQ and V Corps both experienced friction with General Franks at CENTCOM. He appeared to constantly monitor the icons on the tracker. As the red icons excluded the many groups of irregular fighters that emerged during the battle, he did not share the same understanding of the threat the jihadists and guerrillas posed to V Corps, both to its advancing divisions and to its vulnerable logistic convoys. This was to cause considerable friction between Franks and McKiernan, Franks making plain his frustration at the delay in the land forces' advance.

The 2nd BCT began crossing the bridge in the early hours of the next morning. As they crossed an MLRS battery drew up alongside and added its firepower. At first light 400 Iraqi soldiers went forward to surrender to the Americans. They had spent the night watching and hearing a brigade of armour moving through the bridgehead. The brigade combat team was to lead in isolating Baghdad from the south and west. Speed was of the essence to prevent the Iraqi defence from quickly reacting to the approaching threat. As they did this the combat engineers constructed another bridge across the Euphrates close to Objective Peach. This was a so-called 'ribbon bridge', modelled on Cold War-era Soviet pontoon bridges. As the original bridge at Peach had been damaged, this reduced the risk at the crossing and greatly increased the rate at which US vehicles could cross the river.

CLOSING ON BAGHDAD

It was a shared understanding amongst the Coalition's three invading armies that urban areas tended to favour defenders over attackers and non-state armed groups over state forces. The complex terrain, shorter fields of fire and presence of civilian population limited effectiveness of longer-ranged weapons and made leadership, command and control more difficult. Despite the likely US predominance in airpower and artillery, the need to keep civilian casualties and collateral damage to a minimum would greatly constrain the US forces' ability to use these weapons. So attacks into towns and cities would be particularly difficult.

Senior commanders and staff from V Corps had assembled in Germany the previous autumn to study the problems posed by urban warfare. This included computer-assisted war games simulating US attacks on the city. These had shown that whilst US infantry armoured vehicles would have great utility, unarmoured vehicles would easily become casualties to Iraqi fire.

An operational concept for the attack on Baghdad had been developed. This envisaged an encirclement and isolation of the city beginning with the capture of five bases around the edge of the capital. These would allow the city to be isolated from reinforcing Iraqi forces. Supplies would be built up, units would re-arm and refuel, while the Army and Marines would mount probing attacks and raids into the city. These would be complemented by precision air strikes. The plan to isolate Baghdad had identified three base areas to be seized and then used to project power into Baghdad: Objective Saints to the south of the city, Objective Lions (Baghdad International Airport) to the west of the city, and Objective Titans on the city's north-west edge. All were named after famous American football teams.

US planners accepted that it would be impossible to predict the exact situation when the US forces arrived at the edges of the capital. So, whilst there was a general concept of operations, there was no detailed plan. Baghdad had been studied in detail and it had been a priority for intelligence gathering. There had been detailed analysis of potential targets. But there was little up-to-date intelligence on the actual Iraqi forces in the capital. The US anticipated that the international airport and the complex of palaces in the centre of the city would be most heavily defended.

V Corps had also developed contingency plans to seize Baghdad airport from the air. These included proposals for SOF and a brigade of the 101st Airborne Division to air assault by helicopter and the 82nd Airborne Division to land by parachute. After the failure of the first US helicopter deep attacks, it was judged that any descent on the airport by parachute or helicopter would be likely to suffer heavy casualties. The idea was abandoned.

When 3rd Infantry Division crossed the Euphrates, it was at the end of very long supply lines. Ammunition, food, fuel and spare parts had to travel by truck from the US supply dumps and warehouses in Kuwait, a journey of almost 375 miles. These were stretched almost to breaking point. Truck drivers were exhausted. Stocks of high-explosive shells for the division's artillery and tanks were dangerously low. The system for supplying spare parts to V Corps had collapsed. For example, one artillery battalion was only able to obtain spares for its Paladin howitzers by taking parts from an M109 howitzer that the Iraqi Army had captured from the Iranian Army in the 1960s. These difficulties were in part a result of the speed of the advance to Baghdad, all part of the ambition of the land component's plan. But they were exacerbated by Rumsfeld's insistence that the US Army's normal planning process be discarded. This had resulted in fewer logistic units arriving in Kuwait than V Corps needed.

The division's logistic situation argued for a pause to replenish its supplies. But its commander, Major General Buford 'Buff' Blount, judged that it was even more important to maintain momentum and keep the Iraqis off balance. And he needed to know more about the strength, layout and will to fight of the Iraqi forces in the city. So, raids on the city would start immediately.

On 3 April Blunt radioed General Wallace, the V Corps commander, to ask permission to begin the attack on Baghdad airport that day. He told Wallace 'Sir, we trained for this ... we prepared for this ... we're ready for this. We need to go now.' After a pause Wallace signalled his agreement: 'Have a good fight.'[12]

SEIZING BAGHDAD AIRPORT

Leading the divisions' advance on Baghdad would be the 1st BCT. With only two bridges available, it took some time for its units to cross the Euphrates at Objective Peach. But to maintain speed, the brigade combat team's commander, Colonel Grimsley, decided not to wait to concentrate the brigade but to send the battalions to Baghdad separately. The lead battalion sped north to Objective Lions, Baghdad airport, directly west of the city.

As the division crossed the Euphrates, the terrain changed. There were more fields and irrigation ditches. In areas roads ran above the fields and the ground alongside was boggy, miring any heavy vehicles that attempted to traverse it. In these areas a competent defence could have delayed the US advance for hours or even days. This had happened in September 1944 to the British spearheads advancing into Holland to link up with British and US airborne divisions, resulting in the failure of Operation *Market-Garden*. But here the Iraqi opposition was scattered, disorganized and unco-ordinated. As night fell, Task Force 2-7 Infantry found that the constricted terrain caused much friction that slowed their advance. For example, in darkness a Humvee carrying an American journalist fell into an irrigation canal. The journalist and a soldier were trapped and drowned. The task force was subsequently to describe their move through darkness to the airport:

> An intricate series of irrigation canals that created a waffle-like pattern on maps and satellite imagery stood between the task force and the nearest high-speed avenue of approach. In the darkness TF 2-7 Infantry pushed down small farming roads. The Bradleys hung over the elevated roads in some places. Under the heavy traffic, a key unsupported bridge crumbled into the canal road. Water flooded into these areas making them all but impassable.

The commander and about a quarter of his battalion were already past the bridge that had collapsed. They moved as quickly as they could to the airport. But the rest of the battalion had to take an even more difficult route:

> Turning the large tracked vehicles around was not even remotely possible, pivot steering would result in further damage to the road.

Backing the vehicles down the route was the only alternative. Adding to the frustration, most task force mortar and engineer vehicles pulled trailers. Mired vehicles further blocked the route. Only a sliver of moon provided light as the rear three quarters of the task force slowly worked its way to LIONS, ultimately arriving too late to participate in the initial stages of the attack.[13]

Simply achieving the move in darkness and without using vehicle headlights, with troops who were exhausted from days of continual movement and combat, was testament to a high standard of small unit leadership and a determination to overcome the considerable friction and join the battle at the airport. It was lucky for the task force that the Iraqi defenders were not able to locate the column of vehicles slowly winding its way through this constricting terrain and attack it. An accurate artillery or rocket strike would have inflicted US casualties and imposed additional delay.

A brigade of Iraqi Special Republican Guard and some Iraqi special forces had been assigned to protect Baghdad's Saddam International Airport. Obstacles and fortifications had been prepared. These included efforts to prevent aircraft landing on the runways by blowing up civilian airliners. Trenches and bunkers were constructed. Iraqi troops had also been positioned in the airport's many buildings, which in total size was equivalent to a small town. That the rest of the airfield was flat and open terrain ought to have given well-led defenders the ability to fire on US troops at considerable range.

The brigade's leading battalion task force was Task Force 3-69, which had played such a key role in capturing the bridge over the Euphrates River at Objective Peach. On the evening of 3 April it breached the 10-foot-high concrete wall around the airport and rapidly moved to seize the eastern part of the airfield. By 0200hrs infantry were dismounting to clear trenches and bunkers. The battalion was struck by Iraqi artillery but the tanks and Bradleys proved invulnerable to the resulting shrapnel. As the sun came up on the morning of 4 April, embedded media teams from CNN and Sky News broadcast the news of the airport's capture. Simultaneously the 3/7th Cavalry moved to block any reinforcement of Baghdad from the north.

The size of the airfield meant that there was no clear front or rear; Iraqi fire and small unco-ordinated counter-attacks came from all directions. For example, at the airport access road a shell from an Iraqi T72 tank struck the side of a Bradley. The force of the impact catapulted the Bradley's commander out of the vehicle's turret and onto the front of the vehicle. Although soldiers' rucksacks hung on the outside of the armoured vehicle were set on fire, the driver was able to reverse the Bradley out of danger. Infantry brought up Javelin anti-tank missiles to fire at the tank and three other T72s spotted nearby. The missiles flew over the top of the battalion tactical operations centre (TOC) to destroy the Iraqi tanks. The TOC was then attacked by Iraqi mortar fire, the mortars subsequently being destroyed by cannon fire from a Bradley. At this time an Abrams tank, towing a disabled Abrams, arrived at the TOC. Looking to assist with the fight it detected and destroyed two more Iraqi tanks approaching from the south. Iraqi troops kept attacking the Americans at the access road for another two hours.

Concurrent with these attacks, Iraqi troops attacked a nearby company of the 11th Engineer Battalion that had begun building a prisoner of war holding area amongst some abandoned buildings. When they were unexpectedly attacked by Iraqi troops in at least company strength, the sappers fought as infantry. When an M113 armoured vehicle was hit Sergeant Smith braved Iraqi fire, taking command of the vehicle to evacuate three seriously injured crew. He then returned to use the vehicle's heavy machine gun to suppress the Iraqi attack. Smith was killed. The citation for his posthumous Medal of Honor, the first awarded in Operation *Iraqi Freedom,* assessed that Smith killed up to 50 of the Iraqi attackers.

It took another two days for the airfield and its buildings and surrounding bunkers and trenches to be completely cleared. The US infantry used artillery, mortars and A10 close support aircraft to clear Iraqi troops from the airport's many buildings. It would take a week for the brigade to recover and bury all the bodies of Iraqi troops killed in the battle for the airport. Even while the fighting to secure the installation continued, the division's engineers were surveying the airport's infrastructure and utilities, none of which were working. They began clearing the obstacles and airliners from the runways and started to bring the airport back into operation.[14]

The division's 3rd BCT had been screening Karbala. It was relieved of this task by the 101st Airborne Division and fought its way through yet more unco-ordinated Iraqi forces. By 6 April it had fought its way to Objective Titans to the north-west of Baghdad. In its advance to Baghdad the division had destroyed most of the combat power of three Republican Guard divisions and killed many paramilitary fighters. In this it had been greatly aided by Coalition airpower that had imposed considerable attrition and delay on the Iraqi Republican Guard divisions. The US Air Force had begun to operate A10 Warthog attack aircraft out of Talil airfield in southern Iraq. They would play a leading role in providing close air support to US troops in Baghdad. The Coalition's total control of the air meant that there was as much close air support as the SOF and ground forces needed.

While V Corps armour had reached the outskirts of Baghdad, the two SOF task forces were successfully fixing Iraqi forces to the west and north of the country. To the south the 101st Airborne was clearing Najaf, without damaging the Shia sacred sites in the city, and the 82nd Airborne was pressing the enemy in Samawah. It was being reinforced by the armoured Humvees of the 2nd Armored Cavalry Regiment (Light). The leading ships carrying the 4th Infantry Division's equipment had begun unloading in Kuwait.

The MEF had advanced towards Baghdad to the west of the Euphrates River. The 1st Marine Division had advanced north on Highway 1. This was to give the impression that this was the main attack, directly towards Baghdad from south to north. Later it changed direction, moving east to cross the Tigris River near Numaniyah. The division then executed a right-angle turn advancing towards the capital from the south-east. Brushing aside a greatly weakened Baghdad Republican Guard division and Fedayeen irregulars, it reached the edge of Baghdad on 5 April. Task Force Tarawa had completed clearing enemy forces out of Nasiriyah and moved to attack Iraqi units that could threaten the 1st Marine Division's lines of communication. And the British were patiently reducing the Iraqi forces in Basra.

THE FIRST THUNDER RUN

While aircraft and artillery attacked identified Iraq positions in Objective Saints the 2nd BCT fought its way there. The brigade also took the opportunity to clear the area to its south. Opposition was relatively light and continued to be a mixture of conventional and irregular forces. If the Iraqis had any co-ordinated plan it was not apparent to the commander of the division's 2nd BCT, Colonel David Perkins. He planned that Task Force 1/62nd Armor was to conduct a raid into western Baghdad. Christened a 'Thunder Run', it was to drive north along Highway 8 from Objective Saints to the edge of the city centre and then turn west to Objective Lions, the airport.[15]

That task force had spent the previous day attacking Iraqi Republican Guard forces south of Objective Saints. It was expecting that it would have the next day to refuel, replenish its stocks and resume attacking south the next day. Its commander, Lieutenant Colonel Rick Schwartz, arrived at the brigade TOC to receive orders. Perkins told him that Task Force 1-62 Armour was instead to attack north into Baghdad at dawn the next morning. He showed the route into the city on a map.

Schwartz was clearly taken aback. He knew that there was no detailed intelligence of Iraqi forces in the city, into which US forces were yet to enter. He said, 'You must be fucking crazy, Sir'. Perkins replied, 'I don't think so and I am coming with you.'

His confidence restored, Schwartz returned to his task force, giving brief orders to his commanders at 2200hrs on 4 April. The mission was to 'conduct a movement to contact north along Highway 8 to determine the enemy's disposition, strength, and will to fight.'[16] Some of his subordinates were worried, but Schwartz reassured them that the division was not sending them in to fail, telling his men that 'Somebody at the HQ has done the analysis. They are not going to send us in to fail'.

Like the other battalion task forces in the division, 1/62nd Armor had three companies with Abrams and Bradleys. They had 28 tanks and 14 Bradleys and many of the more lightly armoured M113 APCs as support vehicles. Schwartz decided to leave his vulnerable unarmoured vehicles such as HUMVs and logistic trucks out of the battle. He ordered that from dawn the advancing column would keep moving at a steady 9 miles per hour. Any attacking Iraqi forces would be engaged from the move, any undestroyed targets being handed over from vehicle to vehicle. The combat engineers travelled in M113s, with an unarmoured heavy machine gun being the vehicles' only organic weapon. But they would contribute to the battle by standing upright in the vehicles' large roof hatch. Their rifle and machine-gun fire would be invaluable against any close assault by Iraqi infantry and could also fire at the upper floors of high buildings, which the limited elevation of the tank and Bradley guns prevented them from doing.

True to his word Colonel Perkins accompanied the task force. An embedded media team from Fox news travelling in Perkins' M113 would broadcast the battle live to the news channel in the US.

The advance began at 0630hrs on 5 April, US vehicles moving forward 50 yards apart. V Corps had allocated their single unmanned aerial vehicle to the division and US aircraft were overhead, reporting enemy movement.

Almost immediately Iraqi resistance began with the columns of US vehicles receiving sporadic RPG and small arms fire from both uniformed Special Republican Guard soldiers and paramilitary fighters in civilian clothes and vehicles. Twenty minutes into the operation Iraqi fire had become very heavy. 1/62nd responded with tank guns, cannons on the Bradleys and the heavy machine guns mounted on the M113s. The US troops fired pistols, carbines, rifles, machine guns from open hatches. These allowed them to fire at a higher elevation than the turret guns of the tanks and Bradleys, to engage enemy above them in multi-storey buildings and on overpasses. Iraqi cars, buses and lorries attempted to ram US vehicles. Some got very close to the US troops before they were stopped by fire.

Many of the tanks and Bradleys were struck by RPGs, but the vehicles' advanced armour meant that most RPG strikes had little or no effect. There were two exceptions. A Bradley was disabled by an RPG warhead, the driver being blown out of his seat. The damaged vehicle was towed for the rest of the advance.

A tank was hit from behind by an RPG or recoilless rifle. A fire resulted, which the crew attempted to fight. The advance was halted. This stranded vehicle became a magnet for Iraqi fighters, who arrived in cars, trucks and buses. At one stage over 200 were estimated to be attacking the position. After 20 minutes, efforts to put out the fire and recover the tank were abandoned, two crewmen having been wounded in the process. Grenades were dropped into the Abrams as the US troops left and it was later attacked by the US Air Force.

An Abrams tank commander standing up in his cupola firing his carbine at Iraqi infantry too close for the tank to engage with its gun was shot and killed. Perkins, in his M113, was as much in the thick

The Manhattan skyline following the terrorist attacks on the World Trade Centre, September 2001. (Universal History Archive/Universal Images Group via Getty Images)

A US Air Force combat controller watches as another airstrike hits Taliban positions. Note the 'green beret' in the Afghan pakol hat to the right using the laser designator. In the foreground is a satellite radio antenna. (US Army)

US Army SOF travelling on horses to support General Dostum's militia, Afghanistan, 2001. (USASOC)

Commander CENTCOM General Tommy Franks (right) meets with US SOF in Afghanistan. (USASOC)

A British paratrooper with ISAF outside Kabul's Darulaman Palace, February 2002. (Paula Bronstein/ Getty Images)

US troops searching for jihadist fighters in the Shah-i Kowt mountains after Operation *Anaconda* (pages 86–9). The troops are not in contact with the enemy. (Pool Photo/Getty Images)

The British island airfield at Diego Garcia acted as a major base for US strategic bombers operating over Afghanistan and Iraq. Here a B2 Spirit stealth bomber flies over B52 bombers and KC135 tanker aircraft. (TSgt Richard Freeland)

Lieutenant General James T. Conway (left), Commanding General 1st Marine Expeditionary Force and Major General James N. Mattis, Commanding General 1st Marine Division. (Sgt Joseph R. Chenelly/ USMC)

A soldier of 1st Battalion, 2nd Marine Regiment inspects the burned-out hulk of C211, the first AMTRAC hit in Ambush Alley. The battle is described on pages 133–4. (David Dunfee/USMC)

An M1 Abrams tank being used by a fighter pilot acting as a Forward Air Controller (FAC) with 2nd Battalion, 5th Marine Regiment in Iraq. US Marine Corps regiments would have three FACs allocated to each battalion, demonstrating a very high level of air/land integration. (USMC)

A US M1 Abrams tank takes part in the capture of Baghdad Airport, April 2003. The battle is described on pages 156–7. (Scott Nelson/Getty Images)

Mechanized infantry with their Bradley infantry fighting vehicle patrol in Baghdad, April 2003. The 3rd Infantry Division's battle for the city is described on pages 158–65. The Bradley has a turret with a 25mm cannon and a pod of two TOW anti-tank missiles. (Scott Nelson/Getty Images)

A Warrior fighting vehicle and soldier of the Irish Guards cover British combat engineers attempting to extinguish an oil fire outside Basra, April 2003. (WO2 Giles Penfound/Crown Copyright 2020)

Secretary of Defense Rumsfeld with Lieutenant General Wallace, Commanding General, V Corps, and Lieutenant General McKiernan, Combined Forces Land Component Commander at Baghdad International Airport, April 2003. (Staff Sgt Cherie A. Thurlby/DoD)

A peaceful demonstration in Kut, monitored by US troops and a TV network cameraman. As 2003 went on, demonstrations would become less peaceful. (Kevin Ellicot/USMC)

An Iraqi mother and children raise their hands as US troops search their home in Tikrit, December 2003. (JEWEL SAMAD/AFP via Getty Images)

CPA head Paul Bremer and CJTF-7 commander Lieutenant General Ricardo Sanchez in Baghdad, April 2004. (CRIS BOURONCLE/AFP via Getty Images)

US Marines take cover in front of an HMMWV during the first battle of Fallujah, April 2004, described on pages 205–10. (Cpl Matthew J. Apprendi/USMC)

US Army infantry in Fallujah. All are wearing body armour and night vision sight attachment brackets on their helmets. The second battle of Fallujah is described on pages 224–8. (Sgt 1st Class Johancharles Van Boers/US Army)

Abu Musab al-Zarqawi, self-proclaimed leader of Al Qaida in Iraq. (DOD via Getty Images)

Shia militia fighters loyal to radical Iraqi cleric Muqtada al-Sadr in Najaf, August 2004. (SAEED KHAN/AFP via Getty Images)

A US Army Stryker wheeled armoured personnel carrier with two of its infantry crew in Mosul, 2005. The soldier on the left is carrying an M249 squad machine gun. (Spc Jeremy D. Crisp/US Army)

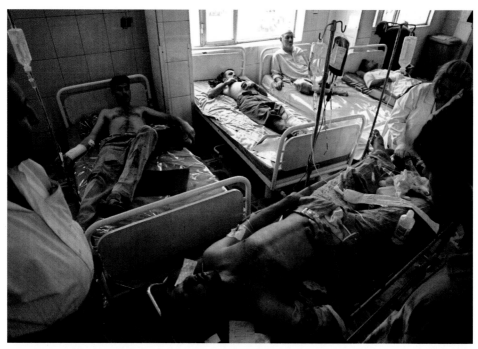

Wounded Iraqis rest in the emergency room of a hospital in Baghdad, July 2005 after a suicide bomber blew himself up at the entrance of an Iraqi Security Forces recruiting centre. At least 17 people were killed and 41 wounded. Most of the casualties were young men waiting to enlist. (KARIM SAHIB/AFP via Getty Images)

A British soldier prepares to jump from a burning Warrior infantry fighting vehicle during the September 2005 incident at the Jameat police station in Basra. The confrontation is described on pages 315–16. (Atef Hassan/Reuters)

General George Casey hands control of the Iraqi armed forces to Prime Minister Nouri al-Maliki, September 2006. (Daniel Berehulak/Getty Images)

Rangers conduct a night operation in Mosul, Iraq, December 2006. (75th Ranger Regiment)

Fully constructed Explosively Formed Projectile (EFP) roadside bombs in Husseiniyah, Iraq, 2007. When emplaced they would be disguised as rocks or hidden amongst rubbish. (Staff Sgt Russell Bassett/ US Army)

UK Prime Minister Tony Blair talks to British troops at divisional HQ in Basra, May 2007. (STEFAN ROUSSEAU/AFP via Getty Images)

Protected Mobility (1). The British Bulldog was a simple FV 432 tracked APC with several tons of reactive armour added to protect against RPGs and EFP roadside bombs. (Cpl Andy Benson/Crown Copyright 2020)

Protected Mobility (2). The US fielded thousands of Mine Resistant Ambush Protected (MRAP) personnel carriers. These employed very thick armour and a V-shaped hull to protect against roadside bomb attacks. (Master Sgt Paul Tuttle/US Army)

Iraqi police and paratroopers from 2nd BCT, 82nd Airborne Division patrol Adhamiyah in Baghdad as the US surge begins in early 2007. (Staff Sgt Michael Pryor/US Army)

Left to right: General David Petraeus, Secretary of Defense Robert Gates and US Ambassador to Iraq Ryan Crocker at a press conference in Baghdad, June 2007. (Cherie Thurlby/DoD)

of it as any of the task force's solders. A staff officer in the vehicle was firing both the .5-inch heavy machine gun and his rifle. At one stage while reloading the officer saw an Iraqi close to the vehicle about to fire his rifle. Instinctively he threw the empty ammunition box at the Iraqi, Perkins rapidly following up by shooting the man with his pistol.

Both Highway 8 and Airport Road were four-lane highways with access roads for vehicles leaving and joining. Many civilians heading for work found themselves driving into the midst of the US columns. Troops found it very difficult to distinguish which vehicles contained civilians and which had Iraqi fighters. Soldiers fired warning shots but avoiding firing on innocent vehicles or causing accidental casualties was impossible in practice. For example, an Iraqi family were badly hurt by secondary explosions from a technical vehicle that was destroyed by US fire. In another example, a Bradley blocking an access ramp was hit by a civilian car. A following car halted and an Iraqi colonel making his way to work was captured.

As the leading tanks approached the airport Iraqi opposition increased. These may well have been fighters preparing to attack other US troops defending Objective Lions. They encountered an improvised barrier of slabs of concrete. But it was rammed by an Abrams tank which broke through the obstacle. Almost two and a half hours and 10 miles after beginning the Thunder Run, the task force passed into a secure area. It had lost an abandoned tank, one soldier killed and eight wounded.

Protected by the US troops securing the airport 1/62nd reorganized and refitted. Casualties were evacuated and fires were extinguished in two armoured vehicles. Many others required minor repairs. Much ammunition had been fired and the vehicles were full of the brass cartridge cases Emotions were high – a mixture of elation of survival and success, but also sadness at casualties. This was described by Schwartz:

> There was a tremendous feeling of loss; there was a feeling of mission success, which was a great feeling. There was everyone looking at their vehicles and wondering how we were able to survive. Bradleys had gotten hit with multiple RPGs and kept rolling ... I don't think any of us had a dry eye.[17]

1/62nd later returned to Objective Saints by a rural route to the south of the city. Whilst there was strong Iraqi opposition to the first Thunder Run, it appeared random and tactically unco-ordinated. The Iraqi colonel captured in the Thunder Run told his captors that he had no idea that US forces had been so close to the centre of the city. The raid succeeded at a much lower cost than many had anticipated.

THE BATTLE FOR THE NARRATIVE IN BAGHDAD — THE UNANTICIPATED EFFECTS OF 'COMICAL ALI'

Since hostilities began, the Iraqi information minister, Mohammed Saeed al-Sahhaf had provided daily briefings to the Iraqi and international media in Baghdad. As time went on these had become increasingly divorced from reality. Americans nicknamed him 'Baghdad Bob', others called him 'Comical Ali' after 'Chemical Ali' the nickname of Ali Hassan Abd al-Majid al-Tikriti, a cousin of Saddam's who was infamous for repression of the Iraqi Kurds and Shias.

After the Thunder Run, Sahhaf appeared oblivious of the strength of the US forces around Baghdad. He claimed that 'They fled. The American louts fled. Indeed, concerning the fighting waged by the heroes of the Arab Socialist Ba'ath Party yesterday, one amazing thing really is the cowardice of the American soldiers. We had not anticipated this.'

This was reinforced by Iraqi television showing images of the burnt-out and abandoned US tank. Colonel Perkins watched the statement on satellite TV. He was concerned that the success of the raid was being successfully countered by Iraqi propaganda. There was a danger that this might stimulate Iraqi troops, Fedayeen and jihadists to continue to fight. He reasoned the US needed to counter Iraqi fabrications by demonstrating that US armour was attacking Baghdad. It was decided that 2nd BCT would conduct another Thunder Run on 7 April, this time in brigade strength. Again, they would strike into western Baghdad and leave.

Perkins planned to conduct the raid as directed, but he did not want to keep repeating such missions. He thought that, should the circumstances allow, it would be just as easy to go into the city centre and stay there. This more ambitious idea was not a short-term impulse but was a result of Perkins' assessing the key factors and examining possible scenarios and options. For example, if Iraqi resistance was more coherent and better led than earlier, it might not only be more difficult to fight into Baghdad, but it also could be even more difficult to get out of the city. Perkins identified four criteria that would need to be met for the brigade combat team to stay in Baghdad:

- the 2nd BCT successfully fighting its way into Baghdad
- seizing defensible, important, and symbolic terrain in Baghdad
- opening and maintaining a line of communication into Baghdad
- resupplying the brigade combat team sufficiently to remain overnight.[18]

Despite intelligence reports of Iraqi preparation of defensive positions, Perkins was confident that the enemy could be handled by similar tactics to those used in the first attack into the city. Once the advance began it was likely that Iraqi fighters and foreign jihadists would use 'swarm' tactics, rapidly making their way to any US troops they could find to attack them. The brigade combat team would need to keep moving, engaging targets as they passed. But key overpasses would need to be denied to the enemy by being held by US troops. As the brigade combat team advanced air bust artillery fire would be used to neutralize any defenders. One of the brigade's task forces would then be used to secure these features.

The order of march would be Task Force 1-64 Armor, Task Force 4-64 Armor, with Task Force 3-51 Infantry at the rear. If Perkins decided to go to the city centre Task Force 1-64 Armor would seize Objective Diane, the Tomb of the Unknowns, and the park and zoo next to it. Task Force 4-64 Armor would capture two of Saddam's palaces: Objectives Woody East and Woody West. The BCT's third task force, 3-51 Infantry, would secure Objective Saints and three major highway intersections and overpasses. Running from north to south these were designated Objectives Moe, Larry and Curley.

THE SECOND THUNDER RUN

In preparation for the attack, crews removed all the bags, fuel and ammunition that had been strapped to the outside of the vehicles. The previous Thunder Run had shown that these were easily set alight by tracer bullets or exploding RPG warheads.

The operation began with breaching a minefield that the Iraqis had laid on Highway 8, just north of Objective Saints. It was not covered by any organized defensive fire, so the engineers were able to remove the mines by hand. As it began its advance, the brigade started receiving small arms, RPG and mortar fire. It encountered some improvised obstacles of overturned lorries and construction equipment. Although there were some defenders in trenches and bunkers, neither their fire nor the obstacles delayed the brigade. But as the brigade moved north up Highway 8, Iraqi fire increased in intensity. Most of the fighting was at ranges of 100 yards or less. Fighters often swarmed at the vehicles, requiring American crewman fire down at them with their rifles and carbines.

As the brigade passed through Objective Moe, it headed east into the centre of Baghdad. Little more than an hour after it had begun the operation, it drove under the iconic crossed-swords monument and across the massive parade ground. The troops established hasty defence positions amongst the palaces and memorials of the city centre, taking advantages of the long fields of fire offered by the parks and parade grounds. Quickly Iraq fighters and jihadists began attacking the US positions. The brigade used all the weapons at hand, from infantry rifles and machine guns through the cannon of the Bradleys and Abrams to artillery, to defeat these attacks.

Colonel Perkins commanded the brigade from the armoured vehicles of his small forward HQ amongst the battalions. The essential co-ordination and control was provided by the TOC. This larger HQ was in an empty Iraqi military compound. At 0700hrs it was busy co-ordinating air and artillery support. A brief whining sound was heard by some soldiers. An instant later all heard and felt the explosion of an Iraqi missile. It exploded between the tent, from which staff officers were running the battle, and parked US vehicles, producing a crater 10 feet deep and 8 feet wide. The area was full of burning debris, smoke and wounded, burned and dazed soldiers. Many of those involved described a sensation of moving in slow motion. It took 15 minutes to find all the dead and wounded. Three soldiers and two embedded civilian journalists were killed, another 17 soldiers wounded and 22 vehicles destroyed. After cannibalizing surviving radios, vehicles and equipment, an ad hoc TOC was functioning three-quarters of an hour after the strike.

The time was approaching when Perkins had to decide if the brigade was to remain in the city centre. If the two task forces stayed downtown they would need resupplying with fuel and ammunition. These would need to be carried forward in unarmoured trucks. The line of communication from Objective Saints was far from secure. The brigade's Abrams tanks' gas turbine engines consumed vast quantities of fuel. The tanks were ordered to switch off their engines, to save fuel.

To the south, battles were raging around the three highway intersections secured by Task Force 3-15 Infantry. There was a constant stream of counter-attacks by Iraqi and Syrian fighters. Some attacked on foot. Others drove towards the US troops in cars or vans, wildly firing through the windows. Other attacks were made by Iraqi tanks and light armoured vehicles. All these attacks were stopped, but they came at such pace and speed that Iraqis often got very close to the US positions. When hit by US fire, some civilian vehicles exploded, indicating that they had been rigged as suicide bombs.

The US troops rapidly used up the ammunition they had brought with them. Some of the supply trucks moving to replenish the brigade were hit and set on fire. Agreeing that the 2nd BCT should stay downtown, General Blount reinforced it with another battalion task force. Iraqi counter-attacks continued throughout the next day, 8 April, both against the US troops in the city centre and against the 3rd BCT, which by then was in control of Objective Titans. These were all defeated.

Meanwhile, having crossed the Euphrates west of Nasiriyah, the MEF, now east of the river, was making progress pushing north up Highway 1. On 7 April, Task Force Tarawa attacked towards Amarah to defeat remnants of the Iraqi 10th Armoured Division. In the south, the British 1st Armoured Division had encircled Basra surrounding and isolating the city. Under orders not to draw resources away from the Marines' advance towards Baghdad they used patrols, raids, SOF, Phoenix unmanned aerial vehicles and other sources to develop an increasingly detailed understanding of the city, choosing to attack when they thought the defenders' capability and morale were folding. In this the protection of Challenger and Warrior armoured vehicles was key.

On 6 April, the British attacked into Basra, destroying the Fedayeen forces and clearing the city. By now the 1st Marine Division had reached the eastern edges of the capital. On 9 April the 3rd BCT attacked south from Objective Titans into Baghdad and the Army and Marine columns linked up, completing the encirclement of the city. The Marines pushed rapidly westwards into the city centre, taking care to avoid any accidental clashes with the 3rd Infantry Division.

Although the Marine Division had an intense firefight in north-east Baghdad, organized Iraqi resistance throughout the country was rapidly disintegrating. The Marines detached their reconnaissance battalions from the division. Formed into Task Force Tripoli they moved to capture Tikrit, Saddam's hometown. In this they were assisted by the SOF that had advanced across western Iraq. In early April Delta Force had established a base west of Tikrit. Together with their supporting tanks they mounted raids into Tikrit and attempted to interdict Iraqi officials attempting to escape towards Syria along Highways 1 and 12.

In early April the Peshmerga supported by SOF began to advance southwards, supported by US aircraft including B52 bombers. At times fighting was heavy, with SOF having to join Kurdish infantry in dismounted assaults, supported by their vehicle mounted cannon, machine guns and Javelin anti-tank weapons. On 8 April the Iraqi defences began collapsing and the Kurdish forces began a general advance southwards. The 26th MEU was flown from Cyprus to reinforce JSOTF-N. Landing at Irbil airfield on C130 Hercules transports the unit was flown in SOF helicopters to Mosul, securing the city until relieved by the 101st Airborne Division.

Organized Iraqi resistance had collapsed.

THE BRITISH ROLE IN THE INVASION

Since the 1980s the Royal Navy had sustained a small naval force in the Gulf. And since 1991 British aircraft had been taking part in US-led air operations to enforce no-fly zones over southern and northern Iraq. In 2002 a small number of British officers became involved in planning with CENTCOM for the potential involvement of British forces in regime change in Iraq. This was conducted under conditions of great secrecy.

Throughout the middle part of 2002 Prime Minister Tony Blair and his Defence Secretary Geoff Hoon resisted any assumption that the UK would provide a division. In September 2002 air and maritime forces were offered to CENTCOM. The British government was attempting to balance supporting a diplomatic solution to the issue of Iraqi weapons of mass destruction, with making essential military preparations. The Ministry of Defence (MoD) was reluctant to be seen to be conducting overt preparations to deploy troops, including approaching British industry for additional equipment and supplies. The policy changed in September 2002. However, this was too late to complete all the necessary logistic and equipment preparations.

The US wanted a UK ground force to join the campaign to avoid the image that the attack on Iraq would represent unilateral US action. It also asked for access to British bases and for UK SOF to be involved. The MoD assessed that the US could defeat the Iraqi forces on their own, but it wanted to contribute not only SOF but a balanced force with maritime and air components and a division of three brigades. This large force package was seen as a way of influencing US planning and decisions, as well as reducing 'the UK's vulnerability to US requests to provide a substantial and costly contribution to post-conflict operations'.[19]

In the second half of 2002 the UK planned on providing a small division, to take part in the proposed UK–US ground attack from Turkey into northern Iraq. By early January it was clear that the Turkish government was not going to agree to this, so the US formally asked for UK land forces to fight in southern Iraq.

In early 2003, most of the British public were in favour of the intervention. This was reflected in a parliamentary vote in February which endorsed a British role in the attack. But the size of public opposition to the war was reflected by the estimated 750,000 protestors who marched against it. Prime Minister Tony Blair did not want to be seen to be deploying ground forces to the war until all diplomatic options had been exhausted. A further complication was that the UK armed forces were heavily committed to operating as temporary firemen while the British fire service was on strike. These factors meant that UK government refused to commit UK troops until almost the last safe moment.

The British Army assigned the HQ of its 1st Armoured Division to the operation. The British planning assumptions for a large-scale ground-intervention division-sized operation required the army to mobilize three armoured brigades at 30, 60 days and 90 days' notice. But this would not meet the likely deadlines for participation in the US operation. In peacetime it had three armoured brigades, but there was only time to deploy a single British armoured brigade, the 7th. So this was the only British armoured brigade sent.

The 7th Armoured Brigade's peacetime complement consisted of two battalions (called regiments for British armour) of Challenger 2 tanks and two armoured infantry battalions with the Warrior armoured infantry fighting vehicle. These were equivalent in firepower, mobility and protection to the US Army's Abrams and Bradleys, except that the Warrior lacked an organic anti-tank missile. The brigade also had regiments of self-propelled artillery and armoured engineers. The army had long-standing plans that armoured brigades would deploy to war with four major units, two armoured infantry battalions and two armoured regiments. To achieve this, the brigade required much reinforcement. The brigade's existing units (the Royal Scots Dragoon Guards, the 1st Royal Tank Regiment, 1st Battalion the Black Watch and 1st Battalion the Royal Regiment of Fusiliers) were reinforced by additional tanks from the Queen's Royal Lancers and armoured infantry companies from the Irish Guards and Light Infantry. These reinforcements made it the largest and most lethal armoured brigade the British Army had ever sent to war.

The division took under its command the UK's two high-readiness intervention brigades, the Royal Marines 3 Commando Brigade, the UK's specialist amphibious landing force, and the 16 Air Assault Brigade. Both formations could be deployed at 30 days' notice.

These additional British brigades were much lighter than the armoured brigade. The 16 Air Assault Brigade consisted of two parachute infantry battalions and an air assault infantry battalion. The 3 Commando Brigade had two marine commandos, equivalent to a US Marine infantry battalion. Apart from some armoured reconnaissance vehicles and lightly armoured Viking all-terrain vehicles, the air assault and commando brigades had no armour and less organic artillery and engineers.

Meanwhile, British air units were assigned to the air component and a naval task force joined the maritime component. Both were seamlessly integrated into US-led operations, which the RAF and Royal Navy had been taking part in since 1990.

A combination of sea and air movement meant that the vehicles and troops required arrived in time. But provision of logistic support found it difficult to fully match the shortened timelines. An example was body armour. Since the 1980s troops in Northern Ireland and the Balkans had been equipped with body armour that comprised a Kevlar vest and ceramic plates. There was a stockpile of this armour for intervention operations, but insufficient quantities had been procured for the whole of the British division. Its HQ determined that the priority for the full armour should be the infantry as they were most likely to be exposed to enemy small arms fire. Many supporting personnel and tank crews would have to use standard issue body armour without the ceramic plates.

The 1st (UK) Armoured Division was assigned to the MEF, where it more than doubled the MEF's strength in tanks and heavy armour. It also increased the number of armoured brigades in the land component from three to four. Whilst the British Army and US Marines had little previous experience of working together, the British division made great efforts to integrate themselves into the MEF. They were welcomed by the Marines as they would be able to protect the Marines' advance north from Iraqi forces sallying out from Basra, thus allowing 1st Marine Division and Task Force Tarawa to concentrate on the advance to Baghdad. The British were given great freedom of action to accomplish this task, but they were also constrained. Whatever the British did in southern Iraq, the Marines ordered that they were not draw airpower or other resources away from the Marines advancing northwards, the MEF main effort.

The Faw peninsula provided a site from which Iraqi missiles and rocket artillery could be fired into Kuwait. It also controlled access from the sea to Qasr, Iraq's only port. Seizing the peninsula and capturing the port was assigned to 3 Commando Brigade. Its two commandos (the British term for battalions of Royal Marines) were augmented by the US 15th MEU.

As the 1st Marine Division advanced across the border berm into southern Iraq to capture the oil infrastructure, 3 Commando Brigade attacked to seize Qasr. A plan to land a commando by US Marine helicopters was aborted after a fatal mid-air collision between two US helicopters. After six hours delay the operation was re-mounted using British aircraft. There was some heavy urban combat, but the Royal Marines prevailed. The US Marines destroyed most of the Iraqi forces to the west of Basra.

On 21 March, 16 Air Assault Brigade moved north to relieve the US Marines of responsibility for the Rumalia oil fields and for protecting the British forces' northern flank.

The 7th Armoured Brigade advanced next, relieving the US Marines securing oil installations around the town of Zubayr. The US Marines had also seized the western bank of the Basra canal. They were relieved by 7th Armoured Brigade, whose armoured battlegroups forcibly seized the four bridges carrying roads into Basra. These were each defended by Iraqi infantry and armoured vehicles. But attacking with Challenger tanks and Warrior infantry fighting vehicles and artillery, the brigade quickly destroyed the Iraqi defenders, although the British troops that controlled the bridges were subjected to subsequent Iraqi artillery and rocket attacks. Local counter-attacks by Iraqi infantry and tanks were quickly defeated.

Although the British division had the firepower to flatten large parts of both Zubayr and Basra, it sought not to do this. Major General Robin Brims, the divisional commander, did not want to fight a battle like Stalingrad. Instead 7th Armoured Brigade mounted a loose cordon around both places. The British sought to avoid unnecessarily antagonizing Iraqi civilians, who were allowed to pass through the British checkpoints; but they would exploit the protected mobility of their tanks and infantry fighting vehicles to mount raids into urban areas.

The brigade also surrounded the smaller town of Zubayr. This was held by large numbers of irregular fighters, who fired wildly at the British troops that approached the town. Over the next week, patrols and armoured raids were used to test the Iraqi defences and develop a better understand of Iraqi dispositions, plans and morale. Initially these met fierce resistance with large numbers of irregular fighters putting up a high level of small arms and RPG fire. The British got the best of all these engagements and became increasingly bold, including sending an armoured column through the centre of the town and establishing a forward patrol base in the town's prison. After UK special forces located a Fedayeen stronghold in the town, it was attacked by a precision bomb. A counter-attack by Fedayeen was defeated. After this, resistance crumbled and the British took control of the town.

During this fighting, in an incident at a checkpoint on the edge of Zubayr the first British soldier was killed in Iraq. Sergeant Roberts was commanding a Challenger tank deployed outside Zubayr. While attempting to stop and search vehicles for weapons and militia he was attacked by an Iraqi civilian. His tank gunner attempted to fire warning shots, but Roberts was hit and killed.

Subsequent investigations showed that there were two factors that contributed to his death. Firstly, at short ranges, the tank machine-gun sight was not accurate. Secondly, although Roberts had previously had a set of enhanced body armour with ceramic plates, it had been withdrawn. If Roberts had been wearing the enhanced armour the bullet that killed him would have been stopped by the armour's ceramic plate. In the overall conduct of the war in general and the British attack into Basra, this incident, tragic as it was, would initially seem small. But it was later to become much more significant, as over time it stoked increasing sentiment that the British Army was being insufficiently supported by the government.

The channel to Qasr port was swiftly cleared of mines. On 28 March a British logistic ship delivered a cargo of humanitarian aid to the port.

BASRA — A MODERN SIEGE

Basra itself was a city of over a million people. Information and intelligence on the city was sketchy. The predominantly Shia Baswaris were thought to have no love for Saddam or his regime. But Saddam Hussein's cousin Ali Hassan al-Majid had been given authority over both army and paramilitary units in the city. Nicknamed 'Chemical Ali' for his role in attacking the Iraqi Kurds in 1988, he was thought to rule Basra using fear.

The British assessed that likely Iraqi tactics would be to attempt to draw them into battles inside the city, where the resulting civilian casualties and collateral damage could be exploited by Iraqi government propaganda. Over the winter of 1994/95 Russian troops had attacked the Chechen capital, Grozny, to clear it of nationalist insurgents. The attackers had used heavy, ruthless and indiscriminate firepower, resulting in much destruction and many civilian casualties. The British command wanted to avoid any such outcome, none more so than the division's commander, General Robin Brims. As it was likely that the British would take the lead for post-conflict stabilization of southern Iraq, their commanders wanted to minimize destruction of civilian infrastructure.

Having isolated Basra by seizing the bridges to the west of the city, the British applied a more developed version of the model they had developed for the capture of Zubayar. Deep operations would both identify and attack key targets with artillery and air strikes. Close operations would seek to crumble away Iraqi forward defences that would oppose any British move into the city. At the same time information operations would seek to reduce the will of Iraqi forces to resist. These included leaflets, radio broadcasts and mobile telephone calls to Iraqi officials.

The British sought to better understand the city, the morale of the Iraqi Army and irregulars, and the degree of Iraqi government control of civilians, as well as to identify military positions, especially command and control nodes. Ways of doing this included reconnaissance patrols by British infantry and carefully limited ground attacks by tanks and armoured infantry. British SOF had some success in infiltrating into the city, while military human intelligence and signals intelligence teams all helped refine the picture of the civilian and military groups in the city.

The British had an artillery regiment operating the Phoenix drone. Originally procured for the Cold War to find targets for attack by artillery, it provided real-time video to British commanders. Over a hundred Phoenix sorties would be flown over Basra, with six aircraft being shot down by Iraqi fire. It proved particularly useful as a method of controlling artillery fire. The division had the authority to engage enemy mortars and artillery units detected by radar, but chose not to, as the radar could give no indication of how close the Iraqi artillery was to civilians. Phoenix could do this.

As time went on and the British operations increased in strength and accuracy, Iraqi civilians increasingly shared information with them. The division's commander, Major General Robin Brims, was to summarize the British approach as follows: 'Launching of a plan is top down, but becomes bottom up as troops in contact find out what is really happening as opposed to what you think is happening or the intelligence picture tells you is happening'.[20]

At the same time, the Iraqis established defensive strongpoints on the western edge of Basra opposite the four bridges that had been captured by the British. Over a week there was a contest for the control of the flat no-man's land between the two front lines. The British sought to dominate the Iraqis by exchanging direct and indirect fire and by mounting raids on the Iraqi positions. A sortie from Basra by 14 Iraqi tanks ran into a British armoured squadron of Challenger II tanks. All were quickly destroyed. In some respects, this was similar to the battles between static defence lines that had characterized the Western Front in 1914–18, the 1943–45 Italian Campaign and the static phase of the Korean War. But in 2003 the British had Challenger and Warriors that were effectively invulnerable to enemy anti-tank fire, support from US and British drones, superior artillery and armed helicopters.

While 7th Armoured Brigade probed into Basra, 16 Air Assault Brigade continued to secure the oil fields. Its northern flank saw a battle between it and an Iraqi division. Here the brigade's armoured reconnaissance squadron and artillery traded fired with Iraqi artillery, whose South African-made 155mm artillery guns out-ranged the smaller 105mm light guns of the British brigade. But aided by artillery locating radars and airpower, the British kept the Iraqi division away from Basra.

To the south of Basra, 3 Commando Brigade, supported by British tanks and armed helicopters, engaged in hard fighting to clear the towns south of Basra and block any Iraqi fighters fleeing south from the city. Up to now the British had not tightly cordoned the north of Basra. A parachute battalion supported by tanks sealed off the north of the city and blocked the potential escape along the main road to Baghdad.

Meanwhile the fighting around the bridges, British raids, special forces using civilian vehicles, electronic warfare and the Phoenix drone were all helping the British gain an increasingly detailed picture of the Iraqi defenders of Basra. The Iraqi Fedayeen militia, Baath Party members and the Iraqi intelligence services seemed to be making ever-increasing efforts to prevent an uprising by Basra's civilians. And Iraqi government-controlled media was reporting that British efforts to advance into the city were being repulsed by Iraqi forces. In fact, this was British armoured columns successfully withdrawing from the city at the end of raids.

On 5 April the British thought they had located Chemical Ali and US smart bombs were used to attack the target. The British believed the attack had succeeded. In fact, it had not, but the British sensed that Iraqi resistance was crumbling. On 6 April, 7th Armoured Brigade's armoured battlegroups began advancing into the city. As they did so, they overcame sporadic and unco-ordinated resistance. The exception was Basra's College of Literature, where Arab foreign fighters from Egypt, Morocco and Tunisia required armoured infantry from the Irish Guards to fight room to room to evict them. The next day the British planned to complete the clearance of the city with an attack on its oldest part, the souk. But the paratroops and tanks assigned to this role met nothing but cheering crowds.

The division had succeeded in its tactic of combining intelligence gathering with raiding. It had avoided destroying Basra and had struck as Iraqi resistance was faltering. It had been a successful siege, waged with 21st-century equipment and an attitude that was the antithesis of traditional sieges. The British operation around Basra conformed to the concept of the 'three-block war', defined in 1999 by US Marine Corps General Charles Krulak as 'Contingencies in which Marines may be confronted by the entire spectrum of tactical challenges in the span of a few hours and within the space of three contiguous city blocks.'[21]

For a week in March, the British had isolated Basra city and were attacking it with airstrikes, indirect fire and raids by ground troops, while simultaneously conducting stabilization operations in the town of Zubayr, as well as unloading humanitarian supplies brought in by amphibious shipping and managing its distribution.

By the end of 6 April, the British were in control of the city. The four armoured battlegroups, parachute battalion and a Royal Marine commando occupying Basra comprised about 5,000 troops. This would be largest British military presence in the city throughout the whole war.

Between the start of the war and 7 April, 31 British ground troops had been killed. Only six were killed by Iraqi fire, the remaining deaths resulting from a variety of causes including friendly fire incidents and traffic accidents.

Once the fighting in Basra ceased, looting began. BBC journalist Caroline Wyatt watched 'looters carrying school desks, baby incubators, wires cables – all the things that would be very useful to get the city going again'.[22] Iraqi civilians told her that the looting was letting off steam. Like the US forces, the British had not anticipated this. Like the US, they were reluctant to use lethal force to contest the looting. The commander of 7th Armoured Brigade later stated that:

'We reached the conclusion that the best way to stop looting was just to get to a point where there was nothing left to loot ... we could either try and stop the looting, in which case we would have to shoot people, or we could try and prevent it but knowing that we weren't going to prevent it and take a pragmatic view ... and then when we are ready we will restock it and guard it. But actually, trying to interpose ourselves was difficult.[23]

THE AUDIT OF WAR

In Operation *Desert Storm* in 1991 over 85,000 Iraqi troops had been taken prisoner and many Iraqi divisions, including a significant proportion of the Republican Guard, remained intact. By the time that Iraqi resistance ceased in April 2003, only 7,000 Iraqis had been captured. But all Iraqi units and formations that had not been destroyed had 'self-demobilized', with many of their personnel simply heading home.

Twelve years after *Desert Storm*, the US and UK forces displayed an impressive degree of air–land synergy, where precision attack and rapid manoeuvre by well-equipped and well-trained SOF, land and air forces led to an even more decisive defeat of the Iraqi military than in 1991. The plan was very bold and succeeded in destroying Iraqi conventional forces. But a more determined, capable, motivated and better trained enemy would not have been so forgiving.

As the exhausted troops of 3rd Infantry Division, 101st Airborne Division, the 1st Marine Division, the British 1st Armoured Division and the SOF task forces welcomed the collapse of the regime, a mixture of elation and self-confidence was felt in CENTCOM, the Pentagon and the UK Ministry of Defence. In less than a month a force with a total strength of fewer than 800 aircraft and five divisions, with only four heavy armoured brigades, had destroyed 14 infantry, three mechanized and six armoured divisions.

Similar examples of such an overwhelming defeat of a numerically superior force are rare. Such as exist include the German defeat of the French Army in 1940 and Israel's defeat of the Egyptian Army in 1967. But in 2003 the attacking forces were much smaller in proportion than the defenders. And the advance of V Corps and the MEF from Kuwait to Baghdad was even more breath-taking than the 1940 advance of the German Panzer divisions through the Ardennes and northern France. Moreover, the mystification of Saddam and his key commanders was even greater than that of the French High Command in 1940.

HOW IS THIS DECISIVE SUCCESS TO BE EXPLAINED?

One factor was superior military technology. Since 1991, the US and British had comprehensively modernized their forces. Many of the same platforms were in service: Abrams, Bradley, Patriot, Black Hawk and Apache, the F15, F16 and F117 fighters. But they had all been modernized, unlike Iraqi forces, which had not received any significant modernization. For example, precision weapons could be carried by all the Coalition fighters and bombers deployed. As well as the laser-guided bombs used in 1991, US aircraft could now use Joint Direct Attack Munitions (JDAMs) with GPS guidance that allowed them to be employed through cloud cover and even the late March sandstorm.

Important technological advantages for the land forces included the advanced armour fitted to Abrams and Challenger 2 tanks and Bradley and Warrior infantry fighting vehicles, which conferred a very high degree of immunity to rocket-propelled grenades. So, US and UK armoured columns were able to outmanoeuvre Iraqi defenders, even in urban areas.

Secondly, most of the Iraqi land forces displayed a much lower standard of training than the US and British land forces. This was most starkly exhibited in the accuracy of their shooting, the vast majority of which was extremely poor. In contrast, the British and US infantry, marines, armoured vehicle gunners and artillery crews hit many more of their targets, much more often. This reflected organizational cultures that saw hitting the target as a central to combat effectiveness and which were prepared to devote long uncomfortable hours to firing their weapons, day after day and week after week, on infantry, tank and artillery ranges in the US, UK, Canada and Germany. All three armies, US Army, US Marines and British, insisted on regular demanding training with live ammunition in simulated battle conditions.

Thirdly, Iraqi tactics were often poor. Although there were instances of hard fighting by Iraqi troops and the Fedayeen and jihadists fighters often displayed suicidal bravery in their attacks, much of the Iraqi fighting appeared unco-ordinated. Even though Iraqi forces lacked the high standard of leadership and training of the Coalition forces and Iraqi weapons and equipment had not been modernized since Operation *Desert Storm*, they missed many opportunities to inflict greater delay and casualties on the advancing US Army and Marine Corps divisions. For example, if the Euphrates bridges had been properly prepared for demolition and destroyed before the US could capture them, the advance by both the MEF and V Corps would have been slower and more difficult. And if the Iraqis had achieved unity of command between Republican Guard, Army formations and irregulars, the US forces would have faced greater difficulties. As well as this almost complete lack of integration between regular forces and the Fedayeen irregular fighters, large numbers of elementary tactical mistakes were made, such as often failing to cover minefields and elementary obstacles with fire.

Neither the Iraqi Air Force nor the Iraqi Navy sought to challenge Coalition control of the sea or air. And Iraqi missile attacks against Kuwait inflicted no meaningful damage on Coalition military capability.

In southern Iraq Saddam's forces failed both to block the port of Qasr by sinking ships and demolishing port infrastructure and also to destroy the oil fields and facilities. The many water obstacles that stood between Kuwait and Baghdad were not exploited by demolishing bridges and there was no effort to flood the Tigris and Euphrates river valleys. The considerable potential of land mines to enhance defensive positions was largely unexploited. Those land mines that the Iraqi Army laid were very rarely covered by fire.

Urban terrain should have provided many more opportunities to hide from Coalition surveillance, which would have neutralized the advantages conferred by many UK and US long-range weapons and provided many more opportunities to delay Coalition ground troops and to inflict additional casualties and delay. By positioning much of the Iraqi Army and Republican Guard in the open Saddam made it much easier for them to be found and attacked by Coalition aircraft. And Iraqi commanders appeared not to appreciate that concealment measures that they employed in rural areas were inadequate against the thermal sights on Coalition aircraft and armoured vehicles. The considerable defensive potential of Iraqi cities went unexploited, with there being neither serious preparation of urban obstacles nor deployment of Army and Republican Guard formations into Baghdad, Basra and the other cities and large towns.

The build-up of Coalition forces in Kuwait was widely covered by international media, which was watched and read by the Iraqis. But once the war began the Iraqi military from battalion level to Saddam himself had much less situational awareness and understanding. Often the first Iraqi commanders knew of the Coalition advance was when US forces arrived and began attacking. This meant that the speed and scale of the US advance up the Euphrates valley was not appreciated until too late.

There were many reasons for this fatal lack of Iraqi situational awareness and understanding. Total US air superiority effectively grounded the Iraqi air force. Iraqi military commanders were often unwilling to report bad news. And Saddam's personal security measures of constantly moving and concealing his location from all but his most trusted subordinates added friction and delay to already dysfunctional Iraqi command and control.

It was not that the Coalition had perfect situational awareness. Indeed, there were many instances of intelligence not arriving at brigade level in sufficient time for it to be used. But the US had much better understanding of the battlefield than did the Iraqis. And their land and air forces were well equipped with advanced thermal imagers that enabled them to detect and attack Iraqi forces from considerably greater ranges than the Iraqis could.

The Euphrates valley towns posed unanticipated problems for V Corps, slowing the advance of the 3rd Infantry Division, and necessitating commitment of the 101st and 82nd Airborne divisions. And this was against relatively unco-ordinated sallies by irregulars. If the Iraqis had organized an effective defence for the towns and used them as springboards for properly organized counter-attacks, the V Corps' supply lines would have been much less secure. This would have made it unlikely that Baghdad could be captured as quickly as it was.

A co-ordinated defence of Baghdad would have combined Iraqi Army and Republican Guard forces in properly sited urban strongpoints, with counter-attacks by Iraqi armour, Fedayeen and foreign jihadists. Such a defence of the city would have made it much more difficult for the US to mount the two Thunder Runs that brought US troops into the city centre. The US would have had little alternative to mounting a more prolonged siege of Baghdad.

This would have resulted in more delay to the US plan and in more US casualties. There would also have been more Iraqi civilian casualties and collateral damage. The delays would have encouraged jihadists to continue to travel to Iraq through Syria and would have been exploited by both the Iraqi government and Al Qaida propaganda, as would have been the increasing number of civilian casualties. All of this would have reduced the international legitimacy of the invasion and of the US and UK.

So why were the Iraqi military strategy, operational design and tactics so ineffectual? Much of the responsibility was Saddam's. Most military decision making was centralized, with him and his two sons having absolute authority over the many security forces. A combination of absolute authority, tendency to micromanage, and avoidance of consultation with experts were important ingredients. Megalomania manifested itself by consistent over-optimism and the deliberate creation of a climate of fear. Saddam exhibited considerable ignorance of international affairs and military matters, but his advisors were too afraid to offer independent advice.

Iraqi military leadership was often poor. The centralization of power by Saddam and his sons meant that the necessary co-operation between the different forces was almost completely absent. For example, Iraqi corps commanders lacked the authority to move units or demolish bridges without permission from Saddam. Sometimes Baghdad ordered Iraqi units to move without informing the commanders of their parent corps.

In the aftermath of the war the US Army assessed that it had been very difficult to discern a clear shape or design to many Iraqi operational and tactical actions. Sometimes Iraqi Army and/or Republican Guard forces conducted defensive operations or counter-attacks. These would sometimes be joined by various militias, irregular forces and foreign fighters. Sometimes these actors would take the initiative on their own. This was in stark contrast to the high degree of co-operation between land, air, sea and SOF exhibited by the Coalition. For example, the three different armies in the Coalition land component, the US Army, US Marine Corps and British Army, exhibited a considerable degree of internal and external co-operation. And their commanders had much more devolved authority and independence than any Iraqi commanders.

There was also a considerable difference in morale. Most US troops were convinced that after 9/11 the rules of the game had changed and that this would be a just war. They were supremely confident in themselves, their weapons and equipment and the teams they belonged to. The majority were extremely well trained, which itself was a source of confidence. The same applied to the Australian and British forces, although the British troops were less confident that Saddam represented a clear and present danger.

Iraqi forces exhibited much lower morale. The majority were conscripts, whose pay and rations were poor. There was a vast gap between officers and soldiers. Administration and logistics were permeated with corruption. For example, bribes were often required from soldiers seeking to take their leave.

There is some evidence that Iraqi troops' morale was eroded by US psychological operations. Particularly unsettling were intrusions into Iraqi radio nets by Arabic-speaking Americans. Since discipline in the Iraqi Army was largely based on fear, once a threat that was even more fearful materialized, morale discipline was rapidly eroded. A major factor was the effectiveness of Coalition air attacks, against which the Iraqi ground troops had no effective defence. As the Coalition attacks proceeded, there was a steady stream of desertions by both soldiers and officers. If officers deserted, their subordinates would rapidly head for home.

A minority of Iraqi units displayed fighting spirit, for example the counter-attacks mounted during the night of 10/11 April to push the

US forces back across the Euphrates at Objective Peach. Iraqi artillery barrages against the British north of Basra were accurate and effective. This showed that some Iraqi units were willing to fight. The Fedayeen and foreign jihadist fighters showed greater fighting spirit, presumably because of their loyalty to the regime (though even these groups were to fall apart after the collapse of the regime). Thousands of foreign jihadists had travelled to Iraq to repel the invasion and kill Americans. Their suicidal tactics meant that many were killed. This and the regime collapse caused a lull in their activity.

But they would return with a vengeance ...

Descent into Chaos

Iraq 2003–04

CATASTROPHIC SUCCESS

The Pentagon, CENTCOM and many US and British commanders seemed to have originally expected that, as had happened in Kosovo, US and international troops would be welcomed as liberators. It appears that only light armed opposition to the Coalition was anticipated. Such planning as had been made for post-conflict operations sought to first stabilize, then develop a secure country and finally to transition Iraq from Coalition control to a peaceful, self-governing Iraq. But matters did not turn out that way. The Iraqi regime at national, regional and local levels rapidly disintegrated and the Iraqi people embarked on an outbreak of looting. Government and Baath Party buildings were ransacked and stripped of their contents and fittings. Many police stations and hospitals were looted. The surviving Iraqi armed forces and many of the Iraqi Police had demobilized themselves, while those police who remained at their posts were unwilling to challenge the looters.

US troops initially did little to suppress the looting. Neither the Pentagon, CENTCOM nor the land component HQ had anticipated this mass outbreak of public disorder, nor did they offer any timely instructions to V Corps and the MEF as to how they should tackle this unforeseen challenge. Failure of US forces to rapidly provide security in the towns and cities they occupied not only allowed mass looting of government institutions, but also created a climate of lawlessness. As British expert on Iraq Toby Dodge put it:

> What began in April 2003 as a lawless celebration of the demise of Saddam's regime grew into three weeks of uncontrolled looting and violence. To Baghdad's residents, coalition forces appeared unable or unwilling to curtail the violence that swept across the city. The growing perception among Iraqis that US troops were not in full control of the situation helped turn criminal violence and looting into an organised and politically motivated insurgency[1]

On 11 April, the land component HQ ordered units to step up patrols around key governance buildings and hospitals. This was actioned, but by then much damage had been done. For example, many pharmaceuticals and much medical equipment had been stolen from Iraqi hospitals. So heavy was the looting of the Iraqi National Museum in Baghdad that the stolen artefacts quickly appeared in the regional black markets. At an 11 April Pentagon press conference Donald Rumsfeld publicly proclaimed that this was clear evidence of liberation into freedom:

> Think what's happened in our cities when we've had riots, and problems, and looting. Stuff happens! But in terms of what's going on in that country, it is a fundamental misunderstanding to see those images over, and over, and over again of some boy walking out with a vase and say, 'Oh, my goodness, you didn't have a plan.' That's nonsense. They know what they're doing, and they're doing a terrific job. And it's untidy, and freedom's untidy, and free people are free to make mistakes and commit crimes and do bad things. They're also free to live their lives and do wonderful things, and that's what's going to happen here.[2]

By mid-April some remaining Iraqi police were conducting joint patrols with US and British troops. This seemed to have some effect in reducing the level of looting, but by then much that could be looted, had been. By the end of April anti-Coalition demonstrations were regularly occurring.

It was very easy for people to arm themselves. Large numbers of Iraqi weapons and ammunition storage sites lay all over the country.

The Coalition could only secure a very small proportion of these places. And as the Iraqi forces demobilized themselves, they simply abandoned their heavy weapons and ammunition stockpiles, many of them taking rifles and pistols home.

RAPID COMMAND CHANGES

The CENTCOM land component HQ remained in Kuwait, never deploying to Baghdad. On a 16 April visit to Baghdad, General Franks told his CENTCOM component commanders that they should be prepared to remove most of their forces from Iraq by September 2003. Heavily influenced by public statements by Donald Rumsfeld, Franks decided that the US 1st Cavalry Division, then preparing to move its equipment to Iraq, was not needed in the country.[3]

By the beginning of May, the CENTCOM forward HQ in Qatar had closed. On 16 May it was announced that the land component HQ was to rapidly leave Kuwait, to take charge of land operations elsewhere in CENTCOM. It was to be replaced by HQ V Corps, designated CJTF-7, as the Coalition military HQ for Iraq, to be based in Baghdad. This would act as a theatre HQ, operating at the strategic and operational levels, and would continue to fulfil the tactical command role of a corps HQ in commanding and controlling its subordinate divisions. These decisions had not been part of any previous plan. Gone was the 'Dream Team' with its highly experienced staff, effective teamwork, considerable understanding of Iraq, institutional memory and well-developed intelligence architecture that integrated tactical, operational and strategic intelligence. This greatly reduced the effectiveness of US command and control in Iraq.

Throughout April, May and June there was considerable deployment and redeployment of US and Coalition forces, as some formations were withdrawn from the country and others moved to new areas of responsibility. The British would lead Multinational Division South East including British and Italian brigades and Danish and Dutch battalions. This division took over Basra and the three other southern provinces; and US Army divisions became responsible for Baghdad and the rest of the country. The MEF departed Iraq but were subsequently to return to take responsibility for Anbar Province.

A Polish-led multinational division took responsibility for provinces south of Baghdad. Called Multinational Division Centre South, it contained substantial contingents of Polish, Ukrainian and Spanish troops. Countries providing smaller contingents included Albania, Bulgaria, the Czech Republic, the Dominican Republic, Georgia, Honduras, Hungary, Kazakhstan, Latvia, Lithuania, New Zealand, Nicaragua, Norway, Portugal, the Philippines, Slovakia, Spain and Thailand, and a small number of Canadian military personnel on attachment to US and UK forces were secretly allowed by Ottawa to accompany their host units to Iraq. The US attached great diplomatic importance to these contributions, as increasing the international legitimacy of the Coalition. But many of the national governments were highly conscious of the war's diminishing legitimacy and popularity, including in their own countries. Most reassured their own publics and parliaments that the troops were in Iraq for stabilization and reconstruction missions. So most of these contingents were deployed under considerable national restrictions, including an unwillingness to allow combat missions. A high proportion of such contingents were found in the Polish-led multinational division.

Concurrently the complex of palaces and government buildings in central Baghdad that had been seized in the second Thunder Run into Baghdad became a major US base. It was christened 'the Green Zone'. The rest of Baghdad became known to US troops as the 'Red Zone'.

V Corps and its divisions were not idle. All were responsible for large areas of Iraq, in which lived millions of people. Without waiting for orders or support from ORHA they attempted to get schools, colleges and universities re-opened. In many places they attempted to re-establish town, city and provincial councils. V Corps began work on a comprehensive plan.

THE 'MISSION ACCOMPLISHED' SPEECH

It was probably a sense of success and optimism about the future of Iraq and Afghanistan that informed President Bush's speech of 1 May 2003. An aircraft carrier that was returning from the Middle East to its home port in California hosted the event. The crew had rigged a giant banner across the superstructure of the vessel's central tower. It bore the slogan 'Mission Accomplished'. Strictly speaking this applied to the warship and its crew. But the arresting image meant that the speech became known as the Mission Accomplished Speech. The text of Bush's speech was not as triumphal as the slogan on the banner. He said that:

> We have difficult work to do in Iraq. We're bringing order to parts of that country that remain dangerous. We're pursuing and finding leaders of the old regime, who will be held to account for their crimes. We've begun the search for hidden chemical and biological weapons and already know of hundreds of sites that will be investigated. We're helping to rebuild Iraq, where the dictator built palaces for himself, instead of hospitals and schools. And we will stand with the new leaders of Iraq as they establish a government of, by, and for the Iraqi people.
>
> The transition from dictatorship to democracy will take time, but it is worth every effort. Our coalition will stay until our work is done. Then we will leave, and we will leave behind a free Iraq.[4]

By seeking to portray the regime change operation as successful and ignoring the looting and deteriorating security, the speech was designed to encourage US allies to contribute troop contingents to the Coalition. But an unexpected consequence may have been that the 'mission accomplished' message may have reduced any sense of priority and urgency in US government departments, including the Pentagon.

THE COALITION PROVISION AUTHORITY AND ITS DECREES

In the immediate lawlessness, insecurity and collapse of most of the state apparatus of Iraq, ORHA had been unable to achieve much. At the end of April 2003, three weeks after ORHA had arrived in Baghdad, it was unexpectedly and rapidly replaced by the Coalition Provisional Authority (CPA). By mid-June all its staff had left the country.

Head of the CPA and Special Presidential Envoy to Iraq J. Paul Bremer was an experienced diplomat, but he had little background in the Middle East or Iraq, or in reconstruction and development. Bremer took over on 11 May. On paper he answered to the Department of Defense in the form of Rumsfeld, but in practice Bremer often seemed to behave as if he were personally responsible to the President.

Bremer rapidly antagonized US military commanders. An early meeting with Lieutenant General Wallace, the V corps staff, and senior US military leaders went badly. By all accounts Bremer bluntly stated that he was in charge and the corps HQ was to collocate with the CPA in the Green Zone. The many US officers who had served in Bosnia and Kosovo were taken aback. This was not the partnership with the international civilian authorities that had worked so well in the Balkans but appeared to be direction by arrogant diktat. Many left the meeting wondering 'who the hell is this guy?'

CPA Order Number 1, 'De-Baathification of Iraqi Society', issued on 16 May removed from their posts any Iraqis who were members of the top four levels of the Baath Party. Those with lower ranks but who held public office would be subject to review. This measure removed from office most public officials in the country. These were the people whom ORHA had planned would assist in running the country from the Iraqi government ministries.

This was followed a week later by CPA Order Number 2, 'Dissolution of Entities'. This disbanded all Iraqi armed forces and intelligence agencies. This made hundreds of thousands of Iraqi officers, soldiers and intelligence officials jobless. It also made it even more difficult for the Coalition military to implement the pre-war plan to employ surviving Iraqi Army units to assist with security and reconstruction.

Some kind of de-Baathification was always going to be necessary. Indeed, it was inevitable that sooner or later the Shia majority would have insisted on it. But neither Coalition military commanders nor the CIA had ever envisaged so maximalist a policy. Nor do the US forces, the British or the CIA appear to have been consulted by Bremer.

These decrees disbanding the Iraqi Army and removing senior and middle-ranking Baath Party members from public life immediately removed from public office most of the people managing Iraq's state apparatus: government ministries, provincial and local government, education, transport, the many state-owned industries, and all the security and intelligence agencies. This made reconstruction much more difficult by destroying any residual Iraqi governance and law and order capability. The rapidly deteriorating security situation made it much more difficult to interact with such Iraqi officials as remained.

Nine days later the CPA created an Iraqi de-Baathification council. This reported solely to Bremer. It was chaired by the former Iraqi émigré

Ahmed Chalabi. Neither he nor the members of the council were in any mood to be sympathetic to appeals made by former Baath Party members.

Bremer was repeatedly told by the US military that de-Baathification was not working and that no appeals were being processed. Bremer in turn objected to the military engaging former Baathists. In this and many other areas, there was considerable friction between the CJTF-7 and the CPA. General Sanchez thought that the CPA were treating the issues 'like they were issuing an academic theoretical paper. They simply released the order and declared success. But there was no vision, no concept and no experience.'[5]

ORHA had planned that sovereignty be transferred back to the Iraqis as early as possible. In mid-May Bremer indefinitely postponed this. The CPA and Coalition forces would continue as the political and military authorities for the foreseeable future. UN Security Council Resolution 1483 recognized that the US and UK were Iraq's 'occupying powers'. This and Bremer's July announcement of a multi-year programme to develop a new Iraqi constitution and government further increased Iraqi negative perceptions of the Coalition.

During the very brief life of ORHA, an Iraqi Senior Leadership Council had been appointed. They had seen themselves as an Iraqi government in waiting. Bremer told the council that this no longer applied and that CPA was in charge. In Washington the Pentagon had been placed in charge of Iraq. CENTCOM was told that it was to directly support the CPA.

To the hard-pressed US troops in Iraq, the CPA seemed to add little value, creating more problems than it solved. For example, in the area south of Baghdad, the 1st Marine Division worked with the remnants of the Iraqi Army in the area, with the commander, General Mattis, hosting former Iraqi generals to discussions over coffee. In conjunction with a US Army civil affairs unit they paid stipends to former Iraqi officers and soldiers. The Marines judged that they had the capability to re-mobilize Iraqi forces in three days. But this was not to be. Mattis observed that:

> We could have weeded out the oppressors and die-hard Baathists without slicing off the sinews of governance, public services and security. Demobilising the Iraqi Army, instead of depoliticising it set the most capable group of men in the country on an adversarial course against us.

As an example of the disarray, we were methodically building the process for local elections when, again against our advice, CPA told me to press for local elections. Swallowing our misgivings, we publicly engaged with tribal and local leaders to urge rapid elections, and then the CPA suddenly reversed course, leaving us with egg or our face as we had to explain why we were now delaying elections we had been extolling.[6]

CJTF-7: AN OVERSTRETCHED HQ

On 15 June 2003, command of US and Coalition ground forces in Iraq passed to an ad hoc HQ based on US Army V Corps HQ. It was commanded by the newly promoted Lieutenant General Ricardo Sanchez, who had only just finished his term as a divisional commander.

Whilst US Corps HQ were designed as higher tactical-level formations, CJTF-7 would have to assume strategic, operational, joint, combined and civil–military responsibilities. The HQ had not had time for meaningful preparations for its post-conflict theatre-level role and the high level of civil-military responsibilities it would exercise. Lieutenant General Wallace, the outgoing V Corps commander, was later to observe that:

You can't take a tactical headquarters [V Corps] and change it into an operational [level] headquarters at the snap of your fingers. It just doesn't happen. Your focus changes completely, and you are either going to take your eye off the tactical fight in order to deal with the operational issues, or you are going to ignore the operational issues and stay involved in the tactical fight.[7]

As the HQ was setting itself up a high proportion of staff left on routine postings to new units and professional courses. They were replaced by new personnel. Although Sanchez had designed the new CJTF HQ and identified the additional staff required from all four US services, the HQ never received more than a small proportion of the reinforcing staff it required. This unforeseen, unco-ordinated and ill-supported deployment of an unprepared tactical land HQ into a theatre-strategic role was a considerable challenge. It would have overfaced even the most capable military commander and staff. Unsurprisingly the HQ struggled and was rapidly overwhelmed.

Sanchez honoured Bremer's direction that the task force HQ should collocate with the CPA in the Green Zone. It split into two parts. A theatre-strategic HQ moved to the Green Zone to deal with strategic issues and support the CPA. A tactical HQ to command the divisions was set up at Baghdad airport. Both HQs reported to Sanchez; both were inadequately manned, the tactical HQ especially so.

Sanchez identified five lines of operation: security, governance, economy, essential services and information operations. He allowed a great diversity of approaches amongst his subordinate formations: a reflection of the load on his HQ, which with its strategic and operational responsibilities had little spare bandwidth for tactical direction or co-ordination. He gave the following mission to his divisions:

> Conduct offensive operations to defeat remaining noncompliant forces and neutralize destabilizing influences in the AO in order to create a secure environment in direct support of the CPA. Concurrently conduct stability operations to support the establishment of government and economic development in order to set the conditions for a transfer of operations to designated follow-on military or civilian authorities.[8]

There was considerable civil–military friction. Relations between General Sanchez and Paul Bremer, the head of the CPA, often appeared strained. The CPA itself had far too few quality staff and many were on much shorter tours of duty than the US military. The CPA focused on Baghdad. Given that the capital was the country's political centre of gravity this was inevitable. But it meant that the CPA HQ added little value to the efforts of CPA staff and reconstruction efforts elsewhere in Iraq. And the directives and reconstruction plans of the CPA usually seemed to add equally little value to hard-pressed tactical commanders. Having just departed the Pentagon to assume command of the Joint Special Operations Command in October 2003, General Stan McChrystal observed that:

> I arrived with some prejudice about the uneven and often unserious national resolve to make hard decisions in the months after the invasion. Many agencies were at fault for that, but the atmosphere in the palace added to my doubts about the CPA. Certainly, many smart

people worked hard to overcome great odds that summer and fall. But seven months of spotty progress had left many cynical. Policies kept them cloistered behind the palace walls, where they often worked alongside unqualified volunteers whose tour lengths were far too short to gain adequate, let alone advanced understanding of the complexities of Iraq. The CPA ordered fundamental challenges – that would affect the lives of Americans and the Iraqis fighting among them – to be tackled by spectacularly unqualified people, like a 25-year-old with no financial credentials responsible for rebuilding the stock market. I left the palace that day thinking Holy Shit.[9]

Initially US troops found it difficult to obtain funds for reconstruction. A June 2003 initiative that was to bear fruit in both Iraq and Afghanistan was the Commander's Emergency Response Program, universally known as CERP. This came from a chance discovery by soldiers of the 3rd Infantry Division. In one of Saddam's palaces they found $700 million in cash. Once CJTF-7 had confirmed that the money was not counterfeit, it persuaded Bremer that $178 million could be used by Coalition units for local reconstruction. Relatively simple and speedy approvals processes meant that this money was easy for units and formations to access. This visible success was reinforced by Congress supporting and extending the CERP programme.

From the outset of the occupation the US military wanted to recall Iraqi troops to service to assist them and to re-establish the Iraqi Ministry of Defence. Bremer opposed this, insisting that Iraqi units be built from the bottom up and vetoing the creation of any command and leadership structures above battalion level.

Bremer brought in Walter Slocombe, a former Undersecretary of Defense, to take charge of rebuilding the military. They envisaged an effort from three to five years in length, with training delivered by contractors. This plan was agreed in Washington and presented to the military in Iraq as a fait accompli.

SINEWS OF WAR – LOGISTICS, BASES AND CONTRACTORS IN IRAQ

All deployed military forces depend on logistics – the supply of food, water, ammunition, spare parts, spare equipment to replace that damaged and destroyed during operations. The initial attacks on Afghanistan and Iraq carried with them considerable logistic risk. For the US Army's V Corps advancing towards Baghdad this risk was exacerbated by Donald Rumsfeld's impatience and micromanagement. But as the US-led stabilization operations developed, the forces of the US and its allies enjoyed unprecedented logistic abundance. The international forces' sea and air lines of communication from the US, Europe and Australia were not interfered with. This allowed troops to move freely in and out of Iraq by air and prodigious amounts of equipment to move to and from Iraq via Kuwait.

The main US bases, known as Forward Operating Bases, or FOB, outside the major towns and cities were often huge. Many of the functions necessary to support them including engineering, security guards and catering were provided by contractors. Troops based on them ate very well, lobster and fresh ice-cream being unexceptional items on the menu. At the base shop, known as the Post Exchange or PX, it was possible to buy a wide variety of goods, including televisions and games consoles. In previous wars US troops had referred to support and logistic troops based well behind the front line as 'rear echelon mother fuckers', or REMFs. In both wars this term was still used, but was complemented by the nickname 'fobbits', reflecting the popularity of the diminutive heroes of the recent epic films of the *Lord of the Rings* trilogy.

These nicknames were not entirely fair. For example, logistic troops in the vast convoys that flowed from Kuwait to Baghdad and the enormous logistic base at Balad were at considerable risk from sniping, rocket attacks, roadside bombs or combinations of these, often integrated into well-planned ambushes. These convoys could be huge, hundreds of vehicles long. The US was later to conclude that in both Iraq and Afghanistan a quarter of all convoys saw a soldier killed or seriously injured.

The US made extensive use of contractors to provide security for civilian officials. Whilst this reduced the numbers of troops that were needed, their aggressive behaviour and apparently minimal rules of engagement resulted in both Iraqi civilian casualties and increased humiliation. This greatly damaged the legitimacy of international forces. Other Coalition nations were reluctant to use private security companies to assist with armed guarding.

For the 2003 attack on Iraq, the US and its allies made extensive use of ports and airports in Kuwait where previously existing US bases were used for logistics and for both the reception of forces moving into Iraq and the recovery of those departing. These bases were shared with the British and other Coalition forces. After the invasion, this extensive network of bases provided an invaluable foundation for the rotation of troops in and out of the country. As US troop levels reduced from 2008 onwards these bases greatly assisted with the reduction and withdrawal of Coalition forces.

At even the most austere forward base in Iraq, international forces had an enormous appetite for fuel: for helicopters, manned and unmanned aircraft, vehicles, for generators that provided electrical power to radios and computers and to recharge the numerous batteries required for the plethora of radios, jammers and night sights carried by dismounted troops. And the many US armoured vehicles had a prodigious ability to consume diesel. The US Army's numerous helicopters and the US Air Force and Marine Corps fighter jets and transport aircraft based in Iraq all needed aviation fuel. As did the Abrams tanks, and their gas turbine engines consumed more than twice as much fuel by volume as other nations' tanks. So, fuel became the single greatest commodity carried by logistic convoys.

This fuel, as well as most of the ammunition, spare parts and food, was delivered by merchant ships to ports in Kuwait. At the US logistic bases in Kuwait the supplies would be loaded onto trucks and assembled into large convoys that would head into Iraq and then northwards. Many would travel to Balad, where around an airfield the US had constructed a logistic base that held large quantities of spare supplies.

Whilst equipment and vehicles were rotated in and out of theatres by sea and road, troops flew in and out. This was a huge operation, often requiring civilian airliners to fly into secure air bases in the Gulf. Troops were then cross-loaded into US Air Force transports fitted with defensive aid suites to deflect any insurgent man portable anti-aircraft missiles before being flown further forward to Balad, Baghdad or other major bases with their own airfields.

SUNNI INSURGENTS

Increasingly Sunnis came to see that regime change and CPA decrees had not only removed Saddam's control of the country and but had also destroyed the privileged position of the Sunni minority. Now the majority Shia would have political and economic dominance, reversing the political and economic polarity of the country. This was amplified by frequent US proclamations of a democratic future for Iraq. Much of the leadership of the Iraqi Army, the Republican Guard and the Iraqi intelligence and security agencies was made up of Sunnis. Now that their former status, privileges, salaries and pensions had been arbitrarily removed by decree of a foreign plenipotentiary, they had nothing to lose and much to gain from taking up arms against the occupiers.

It appears that although Saddam had no pre-war plan to create an armed resistance to a US-led occupation, his actions had helped create the conditions for an insurgency. These included the arming of Baathist and Sunni tribal loyalists. The Fedayeen Saddam militia had taken many casualties but there were many surviving members who had gone home. Moreover, despite a heavy death toll, some foreign jihadist fighters had survived. And more continued to enter Iraq from Syria.

In the immediate aftermath of 9/11, the Syrian government of President Bashar al-Assad had co-operated with the US effort to neutralize Al Qaida's regional networks. But after President Bush's 2002 'Axis of Evil' speech, which named Damascus as a member of this grouping, Assad changed direction, seeking to deter any US efforts to change his regime. Once the US attack on Iraq succeeded, Damascus had every interest in helping the US-led occupation to fail, as a deterrent against Syria being subject to attack by the US. Disrupting the US attack and increasing the costs to the Coalition occupying Iraq would make it more difficult for the US to attack Syria.

Jihadists in Syrian jails were released to fight the Americans in Iraq. Simultaneously international jihadists were encouraged to travel to Syria, where they were given false passports and taken to the border with Iraq and assisted across it. The Syrian government made no effort to hide this activity, with the buses carrying would-be fighters from Damascus airport to the Syrian passport office driving past the British and US embassies.

As the Iraqi military fell apart, one of Saddam's key henchmen, Izzat Ibrahim al-Douri, fled to Damascus taking with him a considerable sum of money. From here he activated an extensive network of contacts of former Baathists remaining in Iraq. Many of these had links to profitable smuggling networks that moved contraband across the long border between Syria and the Iraqi provinces of Anbar and Nineveh. These networks were re-purposed to help the insurgents. He also arranged support from the Syrian government that allowed anti-Coalition fighters to freely move across the Syrian–Iraqi border and to purchase supplies there. He and other Baathist leaders helped organize resistance groups in Nineveh and Anbar provinces.

Saddam loyalists, former Baathists, Sunni members of the Iraqi forces and other disaffected Sunnis rapidly started attacking Coalition troops with ever-increasing frequency and effect. The same was true of jihadists and Al Qaida fighters. These flocked across the unguarded Syrian border, creating Al Qaida in Iraq. The exact total of jihadists that entered the country by these means will never be known, but by March 2004 Coalition intelligence in Baghdad held over 10,000 Syrian passports that had been seized from killed or captured jihadist fighters, most of whom were clearly from nations other than Syria.[10] This was clear evidence that the Syrian government of President Bashar al-Assad was seeking to frustrate the US-led Coalition.

During the summer of 2003 many resistance groups of former Baathists and Sunnis emerged. There were two major groups based on Baathist networks: Jaysh Muhammad and Jaysh al-Islami. They and other smaller groups operated separately, but all made increasing use of Islamic rhetoric. Jaysh Muhammad had conducted an effective and multifaceted information operation. It drew on a magazine, a satellite TV channel run by the mayor of Mosul and sympathetic editors in other Arab media. And Sunni mullahs increasingly used Friday prayers as a platform to criticize the Coalition and Iraqis working with the Americans.

Although Ansar al-Islam had been evicted from its camp in Kurdistan, it rebuilt and then expanded its networks, recruiting foreign fighters, including many who had survived the Coalition invasion and Iraqi veterans of the Afghan and Chechen wars. The organization planned to make major use of suicide bombers.

The extremely violent Jordanian militant Abu Musab al-Zarqawi led the terrorist group Tawhid wal-Jihad and rapidly developed a network across Syria, Jordan and northern Iraq. He hated the UN for supporting Israel and not stopping the US attack on Iraq. He had a visceral, virulent hatred of Shia Muslims. As the Iraqi regime collapsed,

Zarqawi formulated a strategy to attack the Coalition and prevent the Iraqi Shia from controlling the country. This required fomenting a civil war between Shia and Sunni, absorbing many surviving foreign fighters, including Syrians and Saudis. The principle means to achieving this would be suicide bombings to cause mass casualties.

Al Qaida also sought to attack the Coalition and its Iraqi allies. It declared a jihad in Iraq, established an HQ in Fallujah and sought to recruit both Iraqi and foreign fighters into its ranks.

During 2003 the Coalition had only partial visibility of the development of these networks. The inadequate manning and insufficient background knowledge that applied to HQ CJTF-7 also applied to its intelligence staff. Much detail would emerge during 2003 and 2004 and later, from captured documents, computers and prisoner interrogation, but the full extent of the efforts made by Baathists, Sunnis, Zarqawi and Al Qaida to exploit Sunni resentment was not initially clear to the US.

IRAN'S STRATEGY FOR IRAQ

There were two events that greatly influenced Iranian attitudes to Iraq. The first was the impact of Iraq's September 1980 attack on the fledgling Islamic Republic which led to the long and very bloody Iran–Iraq war (1980–88). As well as widespread and diverse conventional conflict, both Tehran and Baghdad had sought to use proxies to conduct guerrilla and terrorist operations on each other's soil. The second was the conflict between Iran and the US which began with the seizure of the US hostages. It flared again in the late 1980s 'tanker war', during which the US sank most of Iran's navy and accidentally shot down an Iranian airliner. This became linked to Iran's antipathy to the US' regional allies: the kingdoms of the Gulf and Israel. In early 2003 as it became increasingly clear that the US would attack Iraq, Iran prepared to further its interests in Iraq. It sought to deter a US attack to change the regime in Tehran by increasing the costs of post-war US occupation. It also wanted to prevent a Sunni regime hostile to Iran from ever again coming to power in Baghdad. It was keen to avoid any new Shia-dominated Iraqi government becoming a military ally of the US that would allow Iraqi territory to be used for any attack on Iraq. So Iran would seek to influence any post-war Shia-dominated regime to be as closely aligned to Tehran as possible. Militarily, this required driving up the cost of the Coalition occupation by attacking its troops. Politically, it would require directly and indirectly supporting as wide a variety of Shia political actors as possible. Since many of the Shia political groups were linked to militias, politics and armed action were intertwined. And this would be supported by diplomacy and propaganda, seeking to blame the chaos and suffering on the US occupation. Iranian support for groups attacking the Coalition would be clandestine and deniable, to minimize the chance of US reprisal attacks on Iran.

Since the 1980s Iran had played host to several anti-Saddam Iraqi groups. The most prominent of these was the Supreme Council for the Islamic Revolution in Iraq (SCIRI). This was an Iranian-backed political party, strongly linked to the Badr Corps, an Iranian-sponsored militia. Both had been previously formed from Iraqi prisoners of war and anti-Saddam exiles in Iran. By March 2004 Iran had moved the Badr Corps' units to its border with Iraq. The group assembled lists of former Iraqi government and Baath Party officials and Shias that they assessed had collaborated with Saddam's regime. These people were to be targets in a programme of systematic targeted killings.

Iranian strategy for Iraq would be led by the Iranian Revolutionary Guards Quds Force, an organization that combined support to terrorism, unconventional warfare, special forces, diplomacy and political roles. Within the Iranian government Quds Force had the policy lead on Lebanon, Syria and Iraq, often providing the Iranian ambassadors to those countries. It would conduct a multi-faceted strategy to influence both Shia politicians and armed groups, including providing funding, training and logistic support, both in Iran and by Quds Forces personnel working covertly in Iraq.

As the US invasion turned into occupation, Badr Corps death squads began hunting for Saddam-era senior Sunni and Baath officials, as well as Shias who had collaborated with Saddam's government, to execute them. The Coalition saw evidence that weapons and equipment were being brought across the Iranian Border for the Badr Corps, which rapidly established footholds in Basra Province and throughout southern Iraq. It also saw mullahs who were sympathetic to Iran increasingly criticizing the Coalition as occupiers.

Badr Corps personnel sought to join and influence the emerging Iraqi security forces, often retaining their previous ranks. These people often achieved rapid promotion owing to their political connections. Badr Corps members came to dominate the Federal Police, the Interior Ministry Emergency Response Division and at least two Iraqi Army divisions. At the same time it developed its militia units.

SHIA POLITICS AND MILITIAS

New political and military actors were emerging amongst the Iraqi Shia. Throughout Baghdad and also central and southern Iraq, powerful Shia political parties and armed groups rapidly emerged. Each had its own objectives. Not all were intent on overthrowing the nascent Iraqi government, as they saw it as an opportunity to gain political power. But the various Shia groups were united in wanting to permanently replace Sunni dominance of Iraq with a Shia ascendancy. They wanted to seize the levers of state power in Baghdad as soon as possible and did not want the Coalition to get in their way.

The most prominent Shia Ayatollah was Grand Ayatollah Sistani, who commanded enormous religious authority and prestige. He and his followers seemed to espouse the 'quietest' Shia tradition and reacted cautiously to the regime change and resulting political and security turmoil.

Iraqi exiles who had based themselves in the US and West, such as Ahmed Chalabi, also attempted to gain political influence. However, Saddam's ruthless security machine had successfully constrained the growth of any support networks within Iraq. They also lacked the credibility of Iraqi Shias who had remained in Iraq throughout the Saddam years. And they did not have the extensive support that Iran was providing to SCIRI.

A major grouping was headed up by Muqtada al-Sadr, son of a prominent Shia cleric who had been murdered by Saddam's forces. Sadr was strongly nationalistic and initially avoided aligning himself with Iran. He formed a Shia militia, the Jaysh al-Mahdi (JAM). Initially he and his followers were little known to the Coalition. But the Coalition soon encountered his militia, which rapidly grew in strength, as did Sadr's increasingly bellicose rhetoric. Sadr was strongly implicated in the 10 April murder of Shia Ayatollah Abdul Majid al-Khoei in Najaf. The JAM matched Sadr's increasingly incendiary anti-Coalition rhetoric by displaying increasing aggression towards US forces in Shia areas.

Both the Badr Corps and the JAM were able to rapidly build up stocks of arms, ammunition and explosives by looting unguarded Iraqi military logistic installations, where the Coalition had very few resources to dedicate to guarding the large stockpiles of military ordnance. The CPA and emerging Iraqi authorities struggled to counter the Shia militia. Although CJTF-7 proposed arresting Sadr, the CPA vetoed this, seeking to either co-opt or discredit him as a political actor.

Overall, the early months after the US invasion saw an intra-Shia contest for political influence, in which propaganda, politics and formation of militias and armed action all featured. And Tehran deployed its agents to support SCIRI and the Badr Corps and gain better understanding of the Shia political dynamics.

SECURITY CHALLENGES

By now the planning assumptions for the subsequent stabilization operation had been overtaken by events. Iraq's civilian infrastructure was in a far worse state than expected. The Coalition force, designed for and successful in the combat phase of the campaign, proved to be too small for post-conflict stabilization. To make things worse, the Coalition had insufficient positive impact on Iraqi citizens, and the impact that it did have came insufficiently quickly. This rapidly eroded any support that might have been given by the Iraqi people.

The security vacuum was filled by criminals, insurgents and sectarian militias, making use of abandoned and unsecured Iraq Army weapons, munitions and explosives to further their interests using force and intimidation. For example, when the US 1st Armoured Division arrived in Baghdad to relieve the 3rd Infantry Division on 8 May it found that conditions in the city were chaotic. Media reporting of looting and burning resulted in great pressure on the division to rapidly stabilize the city.

All the Coalition multinational divisions sought to both counter insurgents and militias, as well as support the stabilization of Iraq. They all attempted to identify local Iraqi leaders that they could work with and did what they could to promote local reconstruction. But for the

US forces, their own protection from attacks became the top priority. And specialist US civil–military co-operation units, military police and engineers were in short supply. The Iraqis had great expectations that the US would rapidly reconstruct Iraq's already crumbling public infrastructure. Even without the security challenges posed by ever more active Sunni insurgents and Shia militias, this would have been very difficult. That the security challenge was much greater than the US had anticipated made rapid reconstruction of the country much more difficult than the US had planned.

Early Iraq support for the Coalition presence evaporated and criminal, ethnic and sectarian groups resorted to violence to advance their various interests. In the political and security vacuum of the months which followed the invasion, armed groups emerged to oppose the Coalition and to secure their own position and interests.

By mid-April suicide bombers began to attack US troops. At the end of May, the first US soldier was killed by insurgents. In June a helicopter was shot down and insurgents were mounting occasional ambushes on US troops. Insurgents began attacking Iraqis working with the Coalition. For example, in early July seven Iraqi police recruits were killed by a bomb at a US-run training centre in Ramadi.

As the hot summer wore on, in Sunni areas, particularly Anbar Province, the Sunni and Al Qaida insurgencies quickly gained strength. Initially the attacks were largely small-scale shooting, rocket, mortar and roadside bomb attacks against Coalition patrols, convoys and bases. But the frequency and effect of the attacks rapidly escalated, to include the use of cars and trucks filled with explosives and driven by suicide bombers using improvised explosive devices (IEDs). Attacks against US forces became increasingly sophisticated, co-ordinated and effective. There was also an increase in kidnappings, but the Coalition did not know the extent to which this was simple criminality or fundraising for Sunni and Shia militants.

Insurgents displayed an increasing resolve and willingness to fight. By July 2003 insurgent groups were offering payments to Iraqis who attacked the Coalition: $100 for the killing of a US soldier, $500 for the destruction of an armoured vehicle. Insurgents increasingly used IEDs, constructed from the abundant supplies of explosives, land mines, mortar bombs, and artillery and tank shells that littered the country's abundant military installations, most of which had not been secured by Coalition troops. Roadside bomb attacks increased in frequency, effectiveness and resulting US casualties.

By the end of June attacks were running at about 500 a month. In August 2004, there were over 600 insurgent attacks. Most took place in Baghdad and areas of western Iraq with Sunni majorities. In the 'Sunni Triangle' of western Iraq, the newly arrived 4th Infantry Division, commanded by Major General Ray Odierno, was faced by more intense armed opposition, the majority of which came from former Baathists. The division mounted many offensive operations or 'sweeps' and made considerable use of artillery. Countering the insurgency became the Coalition's main effort, albeit often executed by 'sweeps' as there were insufficient forces to secure the whole country.

By now General John Abizaid had been promoted from deputy commander to succeed Franks as CENTCOM commander. Born to a Lebanese American family he had earned a master's degree at Harvard studying Saudi Arabian defence policy and had learned Arabic. He displayed expert understanding of the Middle East, which earned his views great respect in the US military, the Pentagon and beyond.

At a 16 July press conference, Abizaid characterized the conflict as a 'classical guerrilla-type campaign' conducted by former Baathists, including some from Saddam's intelligence service and loyalist paramilitaries. Defense Secretary Rumsfeld was uncomfortable with this terminology and told Abizaid so. In two subsequent memoranda to Rumsfeld Abizaid attempted to explain his thinking, for example that both former Baathists and radical Islamists had found an abundant source of manpower amongst the newly disenfranchised Sunni communities.

For much of this period, there was little co-ordination between SOF and conventional forces. Conduct of operations was largely devolved to the multinational divisions. Many US commanders applied the conventional doctrinal principle of 'focusing on the enemy'. This led them to conduct offensive operations, such as raids or 'cordon and search' operations focused on the burgeoning insurgency. In many cases, the lack of accurate intelligence and inadequate language and cultural awareness meant that these operations antagonized and humiliated ordinary Iraqis, further undermining the legitimacy of the Coalition.

For example, the 101st Airborne Division was operating in and around Mosul where initially the threat was lower. The commanding general, David Petraeus, had recently served at the NATO HQ in Bosnia. He had seen that on behalf of the International High Representative, the NATO HQ in Sarajevo had designed a 'multi-year road map' that was an interagency plan to co-ordinate security, reconstruction and political activity. This formed the basis of his approach, which emphasized short-term reconstruction and efforts to boost local employment, as well as organizing local elections.

The effectiveness of insurgent attacks increased. Initially they were often at short ranges. The fighters rapidly learned that extending the ranges at which they attacked US troops by making more use of rockets, mortars and roadside bombs made them less vulnerable and numbers killed or captured by the Coalition reduced. As attacks increased, US formations increased their force protection. This slowed the upward trend in US casualties but came at the expense of the troops' ability to interact with Iraqi civilians. But insurgents adapted by increasing the proportion of their attacks on Iraqi targets, including journalists, judges, public officials and translators.

On 7 August, a vehicle bomb killed 11 people at the Jordanian Embassy. This was followed on 19 August by an Al Qaida suicide truck bombing of the UN HQ in Baghdad which killed 24, including the UN chief of mission, Sergio Vieira de Mello. The UN withdrew its mission from the country. This greatly reduced the UN's ability to use its good offices and negotiating powers to contribute to the political progress. Many in the Coalition military who had served in Kosovo had hoped that the UN would be able contribute to the post-conflict stabilization of Iraq. By greatly reducing UN engagement in the country, the suicide bombing of its HQ had strategic effect.

Later that month the main Shiite mosque in Najaf was bombed, with 95 people killed including an influential cleric. The level of violence increased from 10–15 attacks on the Coalition a day during the summer to 20–35 a day in the autumn. US and Iraqi casualties increased proportionally. Car bombings in Baghdad increased. Two US helicopters were shot down in early November, resulting in 22 US deaths. By the end of the month the number of attacks per month was over a thousand.

As well as attacking foreign troops, workers on reconstruction projects, public officials and Iraqis working with the Coalition, insurgents attacked infrastructure including the power grid and oil pipelines. CJTF-7 had only enough troops to protect a small proportion of these installations. Not only did this make restoring the Iraqi economy more difficult, but the resulting frequent outages of electrical power shut down air conditioning. In the sweltering summer heat this made the Iraqi people increasingly angry and much less likely to give the Coalition the benefit of the doubt.

Iraqis and the Arab media, such as the increasingly influential Al Jazeera network, frequently asked why the most powerful nation in the world, that had been able to put men on the moon, seemed incapable of providing basic services to Iraq, including electrical power and running water. The US' inability to answer the question convincingly reinforced conspiracy theories that the invasion was a US or even Israeli plot to turn Iraq into a vassal state.

What had been seen by many Coalition leaders as a Balkan-style stabilization operation had become a bloody war in a broken country against enemies who, unlike the Balkan factions, stood their ground, fought and died. US and Coalition forces struggled to adapt quickly enough. Iraqis saw conditions of endemic lawlessness. This starkly demonstrated the political and military weaknesses of the Coalition, especially limited numbers of troops with which to contain and control the security situation and the absence of an Iraq government capable of implementing a national development and security plan.

The attacks by insurgents reduced many of the military advantages that US forces had displayed in regime change. The Revolution in Military Affairs seemed to offer little help to the hard-pressed Coalition forces grappling with insurgency. The advanced surveillance systems that had worked so well against Iraqi conventional forces were of little use against irregulars who blended into the civilian population.

Organized crime prospered, gangs often overmatching both the firepower and will of the Iraqi police. Iraqi citizens continued to see many negative consequences of the Coalition impact, not least insecurity and deterioration of public services, especially electricity supply. Iraqis saw few positive outcomes. Coalition forces had insufficient strength to impose security but had sufficient troops to be seen as occupiers, an image reinforced by lack of understanding, cultural insensitivity, civilian casualties and detentions.

Iraqi politicians had been strongly arguing for a rapid transition of sovereignty. The highly respected Shia Grand Ayatollah al-Sistani issued a fatwa supporting rapid elections. In October, the CPA's plan for a lengthy transition to Iraqi sovereignty was overruled by President Bush. It was rapidly agreed that the Coalition would transfer power back to the Iraqis on 30 June 2004.

In winter 2003 there was a reduction in insurgent attacks, which dropped to 600 per month in December. Many Coalition officials attributed this to the capture of Saddam Hussein. In December 2003, as a result of patient intelligence work by SOF and the 4th Infantry Division, Saddam Hussein was found in a gloomy underground hide. It was hoped by the Coalition that former Baathist fighters would be discouraged by this. They were not.

CJTF-7 used the rotation of US forces over the turn of 2003/04 to begin to reposition into fewer larger bases on the edges of Iraqi towns and cities. As Coalition troops took ever greater measures to protect themselves, insurgents increasingly attacked political and religious rivals and Iraqis who worked for the emerging state institutions. Assassinations and intimidation increased. By the end of January numbers of attacks had reached new highs. Political negotiations continued apace, however, and a Transitional Administrative Law was agreed in March 2004. This would serve as a working constitution for the country until elections in January 2005.

In Shia areas the JAM was increasing in strength and influence. There were also increasing numbers of sectarian attacks by Sunni insurgents and jihadists against the Shias. These included car bomb attacks in March 2004 against Shia pilgrims in Baghdad and Karbala that killed almost 300 people. A week later jihadists bombed commuter trains in Madrid, killing almost 200 people. Even though police investigations were in an early stage the Spanish electorate seemed to link the bombings to Prime Minister Pedro Aznar's support for the invasion of Iraq. Shortly afterwards a newly elected Socialist Party government honoured its election pledge to withdraw Spanish troops from Iraq.

PRESIDENT BUSH ANNOUNCES THE TRANSITION STRATEGY

In a March 2004 speech at the US Army War College, President Bush set out US national strategy. He summarized this as placing:

> the Iraqi people in charge of Iraq for the first time in generations, to give strength to a friend – a free, representative government that serves its people and fights on their behalf …
>
> There are five steps in our plan to help Iraq achieve democracy and freedom. We will hand over authority to a sovereign Iraqi government, help establish security, continue rebuilding Iraq's infrastructure, encourage more international support, and move toward a national election that will bring forward new leaders empowered by the Iraqi people.[11]

The UN Security Council Resolution set an 18-month timetable for political transition. It directed the Coalition to form the sovereign Interim Iraqi Government (IIG) that would assume governing responsibility and authority by 30 June 2004, Democratic elections were to be held by 31 December 2004 if possible, and in no case later than 31 January 2005, for a Transitional National Assembly, which would have responsibility for forming an Iraqi Transitional Government (ITG) and drafting a permanent constitution for Iraq. This would lead to a constitutionally elected government by 31 December 2005.

THE FIRST BATTLE OF FALLUJAH

Fallujah, a large town in Anbar Province with a Sunni population, lay about 50 miles west of Baghdad on the Euphrates. US operations in Fallujah had started badly. After Saddam's regime collapsed the town became the responsibility of a brigade of the 82nd Airborne Division. An April 2003 confrontation between the paratroops and a crowd of angry demonstrators resulted in US troops opening fire, leading to 17 deaths. There was little support for the Iraqi government or for the US troops. After Saddam Hussein's arrest in December 2003, there had been a demonstration supporting the former Iraqi president. By then

Fallujah had a very high level of violence, but the town ranked very low in the priorities of the CPA.

Anbar Province subsequently became the responsibility of the Marine Expeditionary Force (MEF). Commanded by Lieutenant General James Conway, the force included an aviation wing and the 1st Marine Division, still commanded by Major General James Mattis, who had led it to war the previous year. The Marines found that of Fallujah's population of about 250,000, some 70,000 were unemployed Iraqi men. On 31 March 2004 four American contractors driving through Fallujah were lynched by a hostile mob and their corpses strung up from a bridge. These images were beamed around the world by satellite. To many viewers in Iraq, the Middle East and throughout the world they symbolized the violent anger of Iraqi Sunnis and the apparent descent into chaos of Iraq and impotence of the Coalition.

Immediately after the disturbing images of the hanging bodies were shown around the world, Mattis gathered his key staff to consider how the Marines should react. Conscious that defilement of human bodies affronted the US people's sense of dignity, he considered that the military response should be guided by moral power. So, he sought to kill those:

> who had violated our common humanity whilst maintaining our moral compass.
>
> It did not take us more than fifteen minutes to decide on a low key three step approach.
>
> First, we would avoid sparking further outburst ... Second, we had to hold to a steady course. Across Anbar, our commanders would continue their patrols to provide security. Third we would deliver justice by discriminate use of force. We would learn the identities and locations of the ringleaders, using pictures of the murderers who had posed among the bodies and overhead photos of their homes. We would respond with raids at times of our choosing. I would employ, to quote Napoleon, 'an iron fist in a velvet glove'.[12]

But Bush, Rumsfeld, Bremer and Sanchez saw the lynching as a challenge that required a forceful response. Bush was reported to have said that the US response had to be 'tougher than hell'. They may well have recalled the 'Black Hawk Down' incident of just over ten years earlier where bodies of US servicemen were dragged through the streets of Mogadishu. That had been not only a tactical defeat: when President Clinton withdrew US forces from Somalia, it also became a strategic defeat.

Bremer ordered that the town be recaptured, and that the murderers be apprehended. Sanchez passed the order to the Marines. Mattis argued against a rapid direct attack on the city. Neither of them thought it was a good idea to act out of emotion, favouring continuing with the counter-insurgency approach. An immediate attack would probably result in a high level of civilian casualties and it would be extremely difficult to capture the people who had murdered the contractors. Mattis was later to argue that:

> Great nations don't get angry; military action should be undertaken only to achieve specific strategic effects. In this case we were in an extremely violent campaign over ideas, and we were trying to treat the problem of Fallujah like a conventional war. I believed we had a more effective sustainable approach for the situation we faced, but that was the order: attack.[13]

Their objections were overruled by Bremer. The Marines had no alternative but to comply. But their already shaken confidence in the leadership above them was further eroded by the failure of the operation order issued by Sanchez's HQ to articulate the military and political strategic objective that the operation was designed to accomplish.

On 2 April the Marines threw a cordon around Fallujah and set up checkpoints, while bulldozers created a berm. There was little time for more preparatory or shaping operations. An ultimatum was issued to the town's leaders to hand the lynching's ringleaders over to the Coalition. On 5 April the US Marines launched Operation *Vigilant Resolve*, initially attacking with two marine infantry battalions of the 1st Regimental Combat Team. A third Marine battalion joined the attack on 8 April. Fighting made slow, but steady progress. In the urban terrain of Fallujah, the jihadists put up enough resistance to slow down but not to stop the Marine advance. Bing West described the advance of Kilo Company of 3/4th Marines:

> With three platoons on line, Kilo began searching the rows of sand coloured houses. There were about twenty to thirty houses on each

block, most enclosed by courtyard walls. One or two squads took each block, posting a four-man fire team for outside security, while another team used a loop of det-cord to blow the locks on the gates. A half-dozen Marines with the assault element would rush inside a courtyard and stack themselves against the wall of the house. If there was no shooting, they broke down the door and swarmed in, covering each other as they searched the rooms for weapons. If there were outside stairs, or if they could jump from roof to roof, they would clear down floor by floor. In about every fifth house, the Marines found a family, generally huddled together in the centre room. The Marines warned them to stay inside and moved on …

The Marines were quickly engaged by gangs of insurgents who knew the back streets and fell back before they were trapped. The insurgents darted into houses and fired from open windows, staying well back so the muzzle flashes would not be seen. Many wore black warm-up suits with AK47 magazine chest pouches, sneakers and red-and-white checked kaffiyehs. From alleys several blocks away, rocket propelled grenades arced in and exploded randomly. The insurgents fired from one row of houses for a few seconds, then ran out to the back of another position, never pausing for long, or getting too close to the advancing Marines.[14]

The insurgents threw up a high volume of small arms and RPG fire, but often their tactics were amateur in the extreme, rushing at the Marines and being quickly cut down by more accurate fire from Marine rifles and machine guns. At night the Marines were joined by an AC130 Spectre gunship with the radio call sign 'Slayer'. It could easily spot parties of insurgents taking advantage of the darkness, and just as easily employ its devastating firepower.

Two more Marine battalions joined the operation. The new Iraqi Army's 2nd Battalion was despatched to Fallujah. On the road to Fallujah the battalion was confronted by both protesting civilians and Sunni and Shia gunmen. It refused to proceed and many of its soldiers deserted.

As the MEF had anticipated there was collateral damage and civilian casualties. Except for US journalists embedded with the Marines, the international media coverage was universally critical of the operation. By now many Iraqis were watching satellite TV, with the Qatar-based

Arab news channel Al Jazeera having gained the lion's share of the Iraqi audience. It too was hostile to the US attack.

Within Iraq there was a storm of protest. The Iraqi Governing Council threatened to resign, and some key members did. Many US allies, including the UK, brought diplomatic pressure to bear on Washington, DC. Throughout Iraq, in both Shia and Sunni communities, there was outrage and sympathy for the population of Fallujah. Sunni politicians used public criticism of the US to bolster their credibility. This resulted in immense political pressure being brought to bear by the Iraqi Governing Council. It almost collapsed under the strain.

On 9 April, the CENTCOM commander, General John Abizaid, visited the Marines' HQ just outside Fallujah. The MEF argued that the Marines already controlled a third of the city and that the insurgents were running out of ammunition. Their forces were growing in size, so it would only be a few days before Fallujah was cleared. But Abizaid was clear that, in his judgement, the political risk of continuing the attack outweighed the military benefits.

The Marines were overruled and General Abizaid and Bremer agreed that the attack be suspended. Sanchez ordered that a unilateral ceasefire be declared by the Coalition. This was a source of much frustration to the 1st Marine Division. They felt that only a couple of days' more fighting would be necessary to destroy the remaining insurgents.

General Mattis arrived late. He usually travelled by road, with a small mobile HQ including two light armoured vehicles (LAVs). On the trip to Fallujah he found a Marine patrol fighting off an ambush. He added the firepower of his LAVs to the fight, allowing a counter-attack. This concluded, his small convoy raced to Fallujah, Mattis arriving late, sweaty and dishevelled. Abizaid interrupted the meeting, asking for Mattis' input. Mattis told him:

'First we're ordered to attack, and now we're ordered to halt' I said. 'if you're going to take Vienna, take fucking Vienna.'

I was repeating Napoleon's outburst to his field marshal who had hesitated to seize that city. I expected my frontline commanders to speak frankly to me, and I did the same to my seniors.

Silence followed. The several dozen officers and senior NCOs in the room were all looking at the floor or gazing into space. All recognized that no one in the room, regardless of rank could change the political decision. There wasn't anything more to say. Although we were on the brink of a tactical success, we were stopped dead in our tracks.[15]

The Marines complied with orders and ceased their ground offensive. It was assessed that deaths in the battle included 36 US troops, about 200 insurgents and 600 Iraqi civilians. An ad hoc Iraqi Army 'Fallujah Brigade' was rapidly improvised from largely Sunni ex-soldiers and a former Iraqi Army general found to command it. The formation assumed responsibility for the security of Fallujah and the Marines withdrew from the town. The brigade was seen to quickly reach an accommodation with insurgent leaders and it was not long before many members of the formation had switched their loyalties towards the insurgents. But as this happened central and southern Iraq were convulsed by an even more widespread and dangerous security challenge.

THE SHIA UPRISING

The first part of 2004 saw increasingly incendiary anti-Coalition pronouncements by Muqtada al-Sadr and increasingly assertive behaviour by the JAM, his militia. In March, Sadr's rhetoric became even more violently opposed to the Coalition. On 5 April, the CPA ordered his newspaper to be shut down, it was announced that a warrant for Sadr's arrest had been issued in connection with the murder a year earlier of a rival Shia leader, and US Navy SEALs arrested one of his key lieutenants, Maustaf al-Yacoubi.

Coalition intelligence had suggested that this action might cause protests and riots, but that any Sadrist reaction could be contained. Instead televised images of Yacoubi after capture wearing a bright orange detainee overall were redolent of Guantanamo Bay and incensed Sadr and his many supporters. The Shia saw this as a direct challenge and responded with widespread armed rebellion. On 6 April, Shia fighters rapidly moved to violently confront the Coalition.

An early taste of this was an attack in Sadr City in north-east Baghdad, Sadr's greatest stronghold. A platoon of the 1st Cavalry Division was escorting waste disposal trucks through Sadr City. Driving past a Sadrist office, the platoon was ambushed by heavy small arms and RPG fire, took casualties and was forced to take up defensive positions in a nearby house. The parent battalion attempted to mount a rescue, but troops advancing into Sadr City were also ambushed. So heavy was the militants' fire that these efforts were abandoned. After dark a column of Abrams tanks forced its way to the besieged platoon and helped it withdraw to base. By the end of the evening seven US soldiers had been killed and over 60 wounded.[16]

Fighting erupted with uprisings in towns and cities in southern and central Iraq, including Basra, Nasiriyah, Najaf and Karbala. Many public buildings were occupied by militia fighters. The southern half of the country, which up to now had been relatively secure, became a battleground.

The Iraqi police proved unwilling to stand against the JAM. The sophistication, co-ordination, and aggressiveness of JAM attacks on other US and international forces and supply routes increased sharply. Previously supply convoys had only suffered occasional attacks, usually from a single roadside bomb. Now they were subject to well-planned and co-ordinated ambushes by both Sunni insurgents and Shia militias. These could involve groups of between 50 and 100 fighters who would combine small arms, RPGs and roadside bombs and land mines. For example, on 9 April Sunni insurgents ambushed a US vehicle supply convoy, killing seven US troops and wounding 14. A US soldier and civilian contractor were captured.

These attacks included the destruction of key bridges on the main supply routes used by the US to move troop and supply convoys from Kuwait to Baghdad. Particularly targeted were big bridges capable of bearing the weight of armoured vehicles. Many of the attacks succeeded in placing the bridges beyond use and displayed expertise that suggested that former Iraqi Army combat engineers were conducting the attacks. US forces started drawing on their stockpiles of emergency supplies.

These attacks had two effects: making it more difficult for US troops to move south to counter-attack the Shia uprising, and challenging US logistics. They also demonstrated that insurgents and militias could think and act at the operational level. An entire US brigade had to be taken away from stabilization operations to escort US convoys.

The attacks caused panic in the CPA staff. After particularly alarming reports that the CPA compound in Najaf was about to fall, General Sanchez flew down to see the situation for himself. What he found was that the threat from an angry mob had passed, that the compound was under light sniper fire, which was being dealt with, and that the Spanish defenders had the defence of the installation well in hand. Exaggerated reporting of the threat by an inexperienced reserve officer was reinforced by panicked reporting from CPA staff and some private security contractors.

There was political and military friction between the British-led Multinational Division South East and CJTF-7. Like many other Coalition members, the British felt that the Shia uprising was an avoidable strategic error that had been needlessly provoked by Bremer. The British divisional commander in Basra, Major General Andrew Stewart, refused to accept Bremer's direction that Shia militants who had seized public buildings and bridges in Nasiriyah and Basra be immediately attacked. Stewart preferred to play a longer game to neutralize the Shia rebels, and over succeeding days the British and Italian troops used a combination of offensive action and negotiation to achieve this.

Elsewhere in Iraq some contingents from US allies retreated to their bases and refused to take part in any counter-attacks. This reflected the fact that, of the Coalition forces, only the US and UK troops had national authority to conduct combat operations. This was an especial weakness in the area of responsibility of Multinational Division Centre South. The formation contained 10,000 troops from 19 different countries. Poland led the division's HQ and together with Ukraine and Spain provided a small brigade. It proved difficult, however, to integrate the division and its national contingents into the Coalition. This particularly applied to operations: many national capitals clearly expected that operations in Iraq would be benign peacekeeping missions, rather than combat, and insisted that national capitals retain tight control over tactical operations.

The division was to be severely challenged by the uprising. Its limited combat capability would result in its being overfaced by the Shia militias. It was necessary to bring up US troops from other areas to neutralize the militias. For example, in Kut, the arrest of a prominent Sadr supporter resulted in the JAM seizing local radio and TV stations, government, police stations and key bridges. The Ukrainian troops withdrew to their bases and refused to take part in any counter-attacks. The CPA office in the town came under attack but was defended by aerial fire support from an AC130 gunship and a vigorous defence by contractors from Triple Canopy, a US private security company. Other national military contingents in Multinational Division Centre South refused to attack the Shia militias, hunkering down in their camps. By incorporating an ad hoc division composed of contingents whose governments would not allow them to fight, the US had taken a considerable military risk, for which events were holding them to account.

It quickly became clear that there was a degree of political and military co-operation between Sunni and Shia fighters. In Baghdad, communications intercepts and leaflets distributed by activists indicated Sunni–Shia co-operation against US troops, while in the areas south of Baghdad both were attacking Coalition forces. Heavy fighting took place in Shia areas of Baghdad, especially Sadr City.

The uprising posed multiple challenges. If unchecked it promised to accelerate a disintegration of Iraq into Shia, Kurdish and Sunni mini-states. It would also establish a political threat to US-led efforts to establish a democratic model of governance. And control of the sacred sites and pilgrimage towns and cities would both burnish Sadr's religious credentials and act as a lucrative source of revenue.

The decision to arrest Sadr at the same time as the Marines were attacking Fallujah had created great difficulties for the Coalition military. It meant that the thinly spread US and Coalition troops and small outposts of the CPA were in real danger of being overwhelmed. Analysts had long warned that if the insurgency spread from Iraq's Sunni to its majority Shiite community, the Coalition would be in an untenable position. Sanchez was later to write that:

> Coalition forces were fighting Sunnis, Shias and Saddam's insurgents all at the same time. The insurgents were fanning the flames by attacking both Shia and Sunni tribes and blaming it on the Coalition. Sunni and Shia tribes were fighting each other. Shia-on-Shia infighting was just below the surface .... And in the area south of Baghdad Sunnis and Shia were actually fighting *together* against Coalition forces. We were now in the middle of a civil war. And what's more, we had created these conditions ourselves.[17]

Sanchez decided that there were enough US forces to defeat the Sadrist fighters in Baghdad and that the British and Italians in southern Iraq would have to deal with the uprisings themselves. But the inability of most of the national contingents in Multinational Division Centre South to use force to do anything more than defend themselves would mean that would mean that actively countering the Shia uprising in that area required US troops to be redeployed.

The uprising had come at a time when many of the US Army divisions and brigades were being relieved by new formations entering the country from the US and Germany. Even without the relief in place, US troops elsewhere in the country were already heavily committed to stabilization operations and attempting to keep the lid on the Sunnis, Al Qaida and now the Shias. Sanchez decided that he urgently needed to create a strike force to counter the Shia uprising in central Iraq. A brigade combat team equipped with Stryker wheeled armoured vehicles was withdrawn from northern Iraq and sent south of Baghdad.

THE 1ST ARMORED DIVISION'S EXTENSION CAMPAIGN

But even these measures would not be enough. So, the withdrawal of the 1st Armored Division was reversed. The division was at the end of a year's tour of duty in Baghdad, in the middle of its relief in place by the 1st Cavalry Division. Over half the formation's combat power had already left Baghdad. Much of its personnel equipment, weapons, vehicles and helicopters were on the move, with much material already in the vast US logistic bases in Kuwait and some of the division's soldiers already back at their barracks in Germany. The division was told that its year's tour of duty in Iraq would be extended. In an extraordinary display of command and logistic agility, movement of equipment and troops on their way from Baghdad to Kuwait and thence to Germany was stopped and turned around, to return to Iraq as quickly as possible.

In what became known as 'the extension campaign', 1st Armored Division was deployed to the Shia towns and cities south of Baghdad. The extended supply lines from US logistic bases in Baghdad and Kuwait were under considerable threat of militia attack. The division used the considerable number of Chinook and Black Hawk helicopters in its aviation brigade to create a logistic air bridge, the 'Iron Eagle Express'.

To reduce logistic and maintenance burdens Abrams tanks and Bradleys would be carried by tank transporters. To be able to counter ambushes crews would travel inside the armoured vehicles. On one occasion such a convoy was attacked by militia; the vehicle crews not only returned tank gun and cannon fire, but also drove off the trailers to counter-attack, breaking the heavy chains that bound them to the transporter trailers

The division's 2nd BCT had already deployed from Baghdad to Najaf. Moving in the early hours of 8 April to Kut, it attacked that night. This began with attacks by Apache helicopters and an AC130 gunship on the Sadr Bureau, the militia's HQ in the town centre. Two of the town's three bridges were easily recaptured, but militia resistance to efforts by tanks and Bradleys to recapture the third bridge were so stiff as to require further support from an AC130 gunship before it could be seized. By 10 April the militia in Kut had been defeated.

Najaf was a city of about half a million people. A Shia spiritual centre and pilgrimage destination, it was home to the Imam Ali Mosque. The division's 3rd BCT was assigned the task of evicting the militia. This began on 9 April with road moves south of Baghdad. The various units that made up the brigade combat team had to overcome ambushes and roadside bombs and find a route that took them around the bridges across the Tigris and Euphrates that had been demolished by vehicle bombs.

The brigade combat team surrounded the city and skirmished with the militias. This fighting was concurrent with political negotiations and the US were very reluctant to mount a ground attack into the centre of Najaf, considering that damage to the sacred sites would be counter-productive. The crisis in Najaf was resolved through political negotiations and the BCT withdrew.

Like Najaf, Karbala was sacred to Shias. The JAM had seized control of the Old City, although the two shrines were controlled by militiamen of the Badr Corps pro-Iranian militia. The town was officially the responsibility of a Polish-led multinational brigade. It had a Thai engineer battalion that was only allowed to conduct humanitarian operations and a Polish battalion that was not allowed to conduct offensive operations.

The brigade was joined by a US armoured task force. They gradually pushed the militia out of all but the Old City. Although the Polish troops were forbidden to conduct direct attacks, they could secure terrain captured by the American forces, the US troops 'clearing' while the Polish troops 'held'. The US and Polish troops were joined by the Iraqi Counter Terrorist Force, an elite group of Iraqis that had been raised by US SOF. On 11 May the operation began with the capture of the Mukayem Mosque by US armour and the Iraqi SOF forcing the JAM to retreat into the Old City.

The Poles were joined by the rest of the 1st BCT of the 1st Armored Division. A full brigade attack to clear the Old City and the shrines was developed and rehearsed. But on 20 May, the US decided that the risk of damage to the shrines was too great. A stalemate between the JAM and Collation troops was developing. That night, to restore the initiative, Colonel Pete Mansoor, the brigade combat team commander, and Brigadier Gruszka, the local Polish commander, chose to attack the JAM commander in Najaf and his HQ. The building was only a short distance from the Husayn Shrine. Mansoor described his radio conversation with the aircraft's commander:

> 'This is Ready 6, the senior American ground commander in Karbala. I want to talk through this mission, so we all understand the stakes. We cannot damage the shrine – even its outer wall. If you do not think you can conduct the attack without collateral damage, then I need to know now.' The pilot responded that he was sure of the target, the angle of fire and the shell-fuse combinations to be used and he believed that the target could be struck without damage to the shrine.[18]

After firing a single shell to confirm that the target could be hit as planned, the gunship spent 15 minutes firing delay-fused 105mm shells into the building, which was destroyed. This had the required effect and the remaining JAM fighters disappeared.

The air strike was a decisive moment. Mansoor had acted boldly against the key leader of JAM in the city. But had even one of the shells from the AC130 hit the Husayn Shrine, the resulting Shia backlash could have revitalized what was by then a failing Shia insurgency. This was a decisive tactical action that dealt a death knell to the Shia uprising. It depended on Mansoor's judgement, born of a career in the US Army and almost a year's experience commanding his brigade combat team in Baghdad. It also depended on the training and confidence of the commander and crew of the AC130. Political negotiations eventually resulted in a ceasefire and on 20 April the brigade combat team pulled out from Najaf. The Iraqi police took control of the city. In late June Sadr ordered a unilateral ceasefire.

The operation also illustrated the advantages that command of the air and a high standard of training of soldiers and airmen gave the US military. The militia were brave and determined. For example, a 14 April encounter between US Army infantry and jihadists outside the town of Kufa lasted five hours and it was only after the best part of 400 mortar rounds were dropped on the militia that they withdrew.

The Shia militias often chose to fight in a way that optimized the effectiveness of US combat capability. Sometimes their tactics were of a high standard, but more often they were disorganized and ill co-ordinated. Their small arms and RPGs were overmatched by the heavier weapons available to the US. And their RPGs usually had little or no significant effect against the advanced armour on the US Abrams tanks and Bradley fighting vehicles. Also, they had little capability to fight at night, whilst US soldiers, fighting vehicles, helicopters and aircraft were lavishly equipped with night-fighting equipment.

The fighting in Fallujah and its abrupt end had weakened the military credibility of the Coalition, but the suppression of the Shia uprising had gone some way to restore credibility. The very success of the US forces, however, may have obscured CJTF-7's lack of a coherent operational concept, the political weaknesses of the CPA and the threat to Iraqi stability posed by Sadr and his militia.

The fighting against the JAM in Baghdad and central Iraq had resulted in 27 US deaths. The US estimated that up to 3,000 militia men were killed but had no estimate for the number of Iraqi civilians who died. Although the JAM had suffered many casualties, the political and religious foundations of the movement were not challenged. And Fallujah was rapidly becoming a stronghold for jihadists and Sunni insurgents. Neither the Iraqi Governing Council nor the Bush Administration had the political appetite for further heavy fighting before Iraq achieved its sovereignty or before the autumn 2004 US presidential election. So, confronting both these sets of malign actors was deferred.

'SOME ASSHOLES HAVE JUST LOST THE WAR FOR US' – PRISONER ABUSE AT ABU GHRAIB

As these two parallel operations were taking place, the US and the Coalition were to inflict a blow on themselves that would greatly weaken their credibility in Iraq, in Afghanistan, across the Muslim World and globally. This was the effect of the late April 2004 reports of abuse of Iraqi prisoners by US military police (MPs) at the Abu Ghraib prison. Photographs taken by US MP guards showed revolting sexual abuse of male Iraqi prisoners and of them being threatened with dogs.

The images were deeply humiliating to the Iraqi victims, their friends and families, to Iraqis of all faiths and to many Arabs and Muslims. The pictures caused great damage to US claims that the removal of Saddam's evil dictatorship had been an act of global moral leadership. They instantly gave the impression that the Coalition's regime in Iraq was an illegitimate occupation that continued to abuse prisoners as Saddam's henchmen had done, but deliberately did so at the same notorious prison complex where the Baathists had incarcerated their opponents. The abuses became a recruitment tool for militias and insurgents. This was probably the single greatest blow to the legitimacy of the US and its operations in Iraq and Afghanistan.

Several different, but comprehensive, investigations concluded that the units involved had insufficient training for handling prisoners and that there was too little guidance on policy and procedures. In addition, the chain of command for both prisoner handling and interrogation was unclear, and leadership was often poor. Lieutenant General Anthony Jones was to conclude that:

> Clearly abuses occurred at the prison at Abu Ghraib. There is no single, simple explanation for why this abuse at Abu Ghraib happened. The primary causes are misconduct (ranging from inhumane to sadistic) by a small group of morally corrupt soldiers and civilians, a lack of discipline on the part of the leaders and soldiers of the 205th Military Intelligence Brigade and a failure or lack of leadership by multiple echelons within CJTF-7.[19]

The investigations provided ample evidence that the US Army appeared to have collectively forgotten the potential intelligence value of properly and humanely handling prisoners. In addition, there had been inadequate planning both for detaining prisoners and for their interrogation. This may in part have been a result of over-optimism in the run up to the war. It was certainly the case that as US forces found themselves under pressure from insurgent and militia attacks, they detained far more Iraqis than had been anticipated. By January 2004 the Coalition were holding nearly 10,000 prisoners and were detaining around 80 Iraqis a day. There was immense pressure on wholly inadequate numbers of military interrogators to produce results.

In mid-May 2004, Donald Rumsfeld, testifying to Congress, accepted full responsibility 'for the terrible activities that took place at Abu Ghraib.' He apologized to the abused Iraqis stating that their maltreatment 'was un-American and … inconsistent with the values of our nation.'[20]

The commander of the military police brigade responsible for Abu Ghraib was relieved of her command in 2005 and a private and a corporal were court-martialled. Both were found guilty and dishonourably discharged, the private being sentenced to three years in prison. The lieutenant colonel commanding the interrogation centre was court-martialled in 2007 but was acquitted of mistreatment of detainees. By then the damage had been done. As the story broke in the US media, Major General James Mattis, the commander of 1st Marine Division, asked a group of off-duty Marines what was on the television they were watching. A lance corporal told him: 'Some assholes have just lost the war for us'.[21]

The prisoner abuse was widely reported by Iraqi media and media throughout the Muslim world. This coverage lasted for months. By now many Iraqis had purchased satellite TV receivers. The Qatar-based Arab language news channel Al Jazeera and the Saudi-owned Al Arabiya news channel were trusted by ordinary Iraqis much more than the US-funded Al Iraqiya news channel. The images not only greatly inflamed tensions in Iraq but also served to de-legitimize the Coalition's authority there and eroded its standing in Arab and Muslim nations. Arab commentators linked the US occupation of Iraq with Israel's action in Palestine. The prisoner abuses reinforced anti-war sentiments in the nations that were providing troops to the Coalition. Abu Ghraib acted as a powerful inducement to those recruiting anti-Coalition fighters. General Stanley McChrystal observed that of the first-time jihadists captured by US SOF in Iraq, nearly all told US interrogators that Abu Ghraib had been a major inducement to fight.

The US initiated remedial action. It was necessary to greatly increase the resources allocated to detention facilities. Just as important were the appointment of a senior officer to command detainee operations and measures taken to increase the number of properly trained interrogators. This was a slow process, but as the quantity and quality of interrogators increased in both countries, so did the flow of actionable intelligence.

On 28 June Bremer transferred sovereignty back to the Iraqis and departed the country.

THE AUDIT OF WAR

US strategic, operational and tactical errors in the first year of the war after the fall of Saddam Hussein strengthened the Shia militias, Sunni insurgents and Al Qaida in Iraq. The humanitarian crisis that the US military had expected to follow regime change did not happen. Instead, there was a security crisis, where mass looting of government buildings and infrastructure by Iraqi civilians went unchallenged by the Coalition. This set the conditions for the resulting collapse of law and order, severe challenges for reconstruction and rapid loss of confidence in the Coalition by Iraqi civilians. This was exacerbated by poor intelligence, inadequate understanding and sub-optimal tactics. The disgraceful abuse of prisoners at Abu Ghraib inflicted near-fatal damage on the legitimacy of the US, in Iraq, the Muslim world and further afield. These factors accelerated the development and growth of Sunni insurgents and Shia militias. Capitalizing on these factors, Al Qaida established a presence in Iraq.

Despite Bush, Rumsfeld and Cheney having declared that nation building would not be done by the Bush Administration, nation building was precisely what Bremer and the CPA set out to do, envisaging a multi-year plan for the country. This decision was a reasonable reaction to the unanticipated conditions that prevailed in Iraq after regime change.

But the CPA often failed to meet the requirements placed on it. One key factor in this strategic failure was that the Department of Defense and CENTCOM had conducted inadequate planning for post-conflict operations and deliberately rejected the State Department's pre-war analysis of Iraq and its expertise in post-conflict stabilization. And the personality of Paul Bremer, the CPA administrator, together with the manifest failure of the Pentagon to provide enough qualified and effective personnel for the organization, both put civil–military relations under tension. But CJTF-7, the US military HQ, was equally crippled by having insufficient staff.

Although Sadr's uprising had been militarily defeated, the aggregate effects of the battle of Fallujah, the Shia uprising and the Abu Ghraib abuses had greatly damaged the Coalition's reputation in Iraq and the Middle East.

6

'As the Iraqis stand up, we will stand down'

The Transition Strategy 2004–06

THE TRANSITION STRATEGY

In June 2004, political authority was handed over to an interim Iraqi government. The CPA was disbanded. Those US civilian responsibilities that were not passed back to the Iraqi administration were transferred to the newly formed US Embassy.

The US military command arrangements changed. The chronically overstretched and understaffed HQ CJT-F7 was expanded and split into three HQs. A theatre HQ, HQ Multinational Forces – Iraq (MNF-I), was formed together with two subordinate HQs. The Multinational Corps – Iraq (MNC-I) would be responsible for tactical operations. This would be based on an existing US Army corps' HQ that would rotate through Baghdad on one-year tours. Building the new Iraqi military and police forces would be the responsibility of Multinational Security Transition Command – Iraq (MNSTC-I).

These arrangements greatly improved the effectiveness of military command and control. Both HQs were predominantly manned by US Army officers and personnel, joined by officers from the US Marines, Navy and Air Force. There were sizeable contingents of British officers, including generals as deputy commanders of MNF-I and MNC-I. Most of the key staff branches in the HQ would be headed by US officers, but would usually have British, or some Australian, deputies.

At the beginning of July General Sanchez departed, to be succeeded by General George Casey. Casey also sought to maximize the co-ordination of MNF-I's efforts with those of the US embassy. Casey was given clear direction by Rumsfeld that by trying to do too much for the Iraqis, the US troops would create a culture of dependency and would slow the necessary Iraqi efforts to solve problems for themselves. He frequently used the analogy of teaching a child to ride a bicycle, arguing that for a child to ride a bicycle, the parent has to take their hand off the seat. It was essential that the Iraqis rapidly take charge of their own government and security.

This view was shared by the CENTCOM commander, General John Abizaid, Casey's immediate superior. He had served in Bosnia as an assistant divisional commander, where he had formed the view that US troops there had attempted to do too much, thus inhibiting action that the Bosnians should have taken for themselves and creating a dependency culture.

Abizaid considered that Coalition troops were seen by Iraqis as occupiers and were thus aggravating the security situation. He described the presence of large numbers of US forces in Iraq as an infection that would eventually create antibodies. These would manifest themselves as ever-increasing Iraqi opposition to the US presence. Abizaid instructed Casey to set conditions for successful Iraqi elections, protect key Iraqi leaders and build loyal and capable Iraqi security forces.

Casey ordered a new joint campaign plan to be written over the summer of 2004. The US adopted a transition strategy. Politically this would restore legitimacy to the Iraqi government through the holding of elections. The military strategy would seek to rapidly develop the Iraq security forces in order to hand security over to the Iraqi authorities as soon as could be achieved. This was to be implemented by building Iraqi security forces as fast as possible.

Published that August, the campaign plan followed four broad lines of operation: security, governance, economic development and essential services. At six-months afterwards intervals, the campaign would be reviewed.

Casey told his command that the creation of new Iraqi security forces was the US military's exit strategy, that would allow US forces to draw down. He also directed the withdrawal of US forces from Iraqi cities to a few large forward operating bases. This would intentionally result in closure of US bases inside towns and cities, thus reducing the frequency of US patrolling.

The campaign plan explained how this would happen:

- 'Iraqi local control' would be when Iraqi forces could handle local security incidents without Coalition oversight and support.
- 'Iraqi regional control' would be when the Iraqi security forces could operate under Iraqi civil control in a province and could maintain local security.
- 'Strategic overwatch' would be when Iraq forces could handle internal and external threats on their own. At this stage Coalition forces would largely have left Iraq.

The terminology used in subsequent plans would change and evolve, but the Transition Strategy would continue to use a similar approach.

THE SECOND BATTLE OF FALLUJAH[1]

Since the abandonment of the April offensive to clear Fallujah, the US Marines had largely remained outside the town. With the rapid disintegration of the hastily formed Fallujah Brigade it became an insurgent stronghold. For the first time insurgents had achieved control of a major Iraqi town. The self-proclaimed leader of Al Qaida in Iraq, Abu Musab al-Zarqawi, set up his HQ there. Hostages captured by Al Qaida were held in improvised prisons. Many were tortured. Some were beheaded, sometimes by Zarqawi himself. The gruesome executions were recorded by video camera and subsequently uploaded to the internet.

The Marines anticipated that sooner or later the town would need to be cleared of insurgents. In July 2004 preparation began. The city was again cordoned to control civilian and insurgent movement. Large amounts of military supplies, particularly ammunition and fuel, were stockpiled. Information operations were mounted to persuade civilians to leave the city, to reduce chances of civilian casualties or their being used as human shields by insurgents. By the end of October Marines assessed that the town contained 3,000–5000 insurgents, but very few civilians.

The Marines set about collecting information and intelligence. They had an ever-increasing allocation of drones. They put pressure on the insurgents through air strikes and raids by both marine infantry and SOF. Both helped generate further intelligence, including more raid or air strike targets. The layout of the town was surveyed in detail. Maps were produced that that gave every building a unique reference number. These would be supplied to all the Army and Marine commanders for the forthcoming attack, to increase co-ordination and reduce the risk of fratricidal 'blue on blue' fire.

After the autumn 2004 US election, Casey was given permission to clear Fallujah of insurgents. A large division-sized force was assembled. At its core would be two Marine regimental combat teams. Each regiment would have two Marine infantry battalions, each with tanks attached, and an Army heavy armoured battalion task force with Abrams tanks and mechanized infantry in Bradleys. A British armoured infantry battalion would take over responsibility for the area of North Babil, south of Fallujah, releasing Marines for Fallujah. A large amount of airpower was made available, the Marines' own attack and transport helicopters, US fighters and the AC130 gunships.

Preceded by nights of intense raids by SOF, the attack began on the night of 8 November with co-ordinated air and artillery attacks. US Army sergeant David Bellavia described the final preparations of the battalion task force he served with:

Task Force 2-2's soldiers scramble to their feet. Cigarettes are stomped out. Last words are exchanged. We throw on our full battle rattle, which includes: ballistic-proof eye protection, smoke grenades for concealment, reinforced knee pads any skateboarder would envy, a five-quart CamelBak reservoir of water that can be accessed by a mouthpiece, thirty-five pound Interceptor Ballistic Armor fully loaded two-and-a-half-pound Kevlar helmet, night vision, grenades, weapon, and ammunition. It's about sixty-five pounds of gear, but we're so jacked up we scarcely notice the load. We saddle up for the ride to the attack position'.[2]

Army and Marine forces moved to seize a hospital and road bridges to the west of Fallujah and captured an electricity substation to cut off power to the town. The main effort was the attacks by two regimental combat teams into Fallujah from the north. First, they had to breach the large berm that the Marines had earlier constructed to seal off Fallujah.

In rain and darkness this would be a difficult manoeuvre. Under fire the difficulty was amplified. Some units breached the berm relatively quickly, others took up to five hours to do so.

The plan was for the two US Army units to disrupt the insurgents' defences by exploiting their armoured vehicles to push faster and further south than the Marine battalions. This they did, reaching their objectives in the middle of the town by the end of the first day's fighting. With fewer armoured vehicles, the Marines followed behind, deliberately clearing every single building. All the US forces had to deal with IEDs, snipers and rocket and mortar attacks. Some buildings were rigged to explode.

As they advanced, the troops discovered ever-increasing numbers of fortified defensive positions in buildings. And the character of the insurgents changed from Iraqis to foreign jihadists. The fighters had high morale, were well motivated and appeared determined to fight to the death. The complexity of the urban environment made it more difficult for units to move as a body. David Bellavia summarized the tactical effects of combat inside the town: 'Urban warfare is not like fighting out in the countryside where each platoon and company can support one another. Each platoon must fight in isolation, supported only by the assets attached to it.'[3]

Fighting tended to break down into a series of small, intense battles between small groups of jihadist fighters and Army and Marine platoons supported by fire from Abrams tanks and Bradley fighting vehicles. Artillery and air strikes were sometimes used in direct support of infantry, but this required a very high degree of co-ordination to avoid mis-directing firepower onto friendly forces.

The further south the troops pushed into Fallujah, the stronger the resistance and the greater the numbers of US casualties. Most of these were Marines and soldiers moving through Fallujah's dangerous streets or attacking buildings. There were far fewer casualties amongst Army troops in armoured vehicles.

By the night of 12 November, the two Marine regimental combat teams had reached the southern edge of Fallujah. This was not the same as having secured the whole town as many determined jihadist fighters would lie low, hiding from the leading US units, to attack troops following on. US units had to clear and often clear again buildings of insurgent fighters. It was necessary to ensure that every building was

MAP 7: SECOND BATTLE OF FALLUJAH,
NOVEMBER 2004

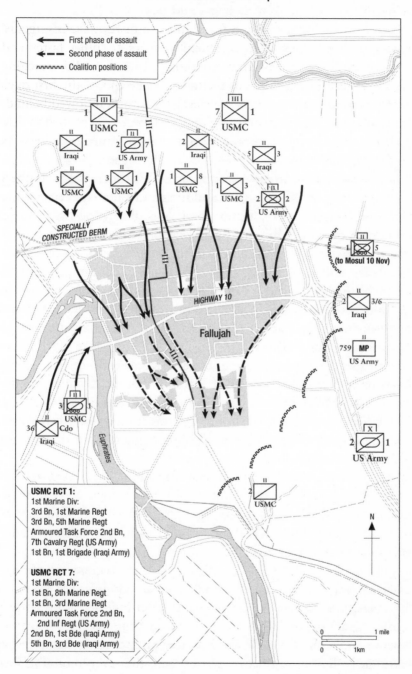

First phase of assault
Second phase of assault
Coalition positions

USMC RCT 1:
1st Marine Div:
3rd Bn, 1st Marine Regt
3rd Bn, 5th Marine Regt
Armoured Task Force 2nd Bn,
7th Cavalry Regt (US Army)
1st Bn, 1st Brigade (Iraqi Army)

USMC RCT 7:
1st Marine Div:
1st Bn, 8th Marine Regt
1st Bn, 3rd Marine Regt
Armoured Task Force 2nd Bn,
2nd Inf Regt (US Army)
2nd Bn, 1st Bde (Iraqi Army)
5th Bn, 3rd Bde (Iraqi Army)

cleared and that all insurgents were captured or killed. By now surviving enemy fighters were determined to sell themselves dearly and fought to the death. Many exhibited high levels of tactical skills, discipline and the ability to fight as small teams. For example, they knocked holes in walls and floors and excavated shallow tunnels to better fight the Americans.

Initially Marine platoons had cleared buildings by entering them and fighting room to room to evict any insurgents they encountered. This resulted in heavy casualties. As the battle wore on, both Army and Marines increasingly made more use of firepower from armoured vehicles. On finding that a house or building was defended US troops would withdraw and use all firepower they could. Where they were available this would include the guns of the Abrams and Bradleys. Other tactics were used to similar effect, including calling in JDAM precision-guided bombs or employing armoured bulldozers to demolish the building.

By 15 November organized insurgent resistance had been broken. There were still sniper and rocket attacks and occasional firefights, but these gradually died away. The battle did not have a clear-cut 'end' but operations slowly shifted from combat to stabilization and reconstruction. There appears to be no single definitive assessment of US casualties, but it seems that over 90 US troops were killed. There was considerable damage to the town. It has been said that General Casey found his visit to Fallujah after the battle a mournful experience. This was probably reinforced by the first campaign review at the end of 2004, which assessed that 'the insurgency was intensifying'. This formed an inauspicious background to establishing democratic government in a country unused to it.

BUILDING NEW IRAQI SECURITY FORCES

As the CPA had disbanded the Iraqi security forces, passing security leadership to the Iraqi authorities would require international forces to build up Iraqi security forces. The plainly inadequate numbers of Coalition troops between 2003 and 2006 would also need boosting. The Transition Strategy in Iraq depended on building the country's security capability.

Before 9/11, the US experience of 'foreign internal defence' largely resided in SOF. The majority of US SOF units were 'green berets'. Their role was to support indigenous forces. They were organized, selected and trained to support and assist resistance movements and insurgents, working behind enemy lines to provide advice, leadership and bring in US air strikes and supply drops. In this role they had been decisive in the overthrow of the Taliban. Of course, in peacetime there were few resistance movements to support. So, the SOF would perform the role of foreign internal defence, providing training, advice and assistance to armies of US allies.

This contrasted with the approach used by the British, where special forces would be used to train other special forces. Most of the training assistance given to other units would be done by conventional army units. The US Army approach whereby most of the foreign army training was conducted by SOF meant that there was much less understanding of training other armies than in the British Army. And US SOF in Iraq had their hands full conducting counter-terrorism strikes against Al Qaida and in training up Iraqi SOF. So, in attempting to train the new Iraqi Army, the US Army was handicapped by a lack of knowledge and experience.

Many Coalition and NATO nations had considerable experience of security-sector reform in the Balkans, Africa, Latin America and Asia. They had learned that this was an inherently multi-agency activity that required not only the training and equipping of armies, police forces and intelligence services, but also the rebuilding and reforming of judicial systems and security ministries, as well as establishing top-level mechanisms for managing security, such as national-security councils.

Thus many US allies knew what they needed to do, but in Iraq doing this proved much more difficult than anticipated. Initial efforts to create new Iraqi security forces received insufficient resources and inadequate leadership. Initial capacity-building efforts concentrated on volume at the expense of quality, to be able get Iraqi forces on operations as quickly as possible. Capacity-building in relevant ministries (defence for the armed forces, interior for the police) and necessary logistics and training infrastructure began later.

Iraqi SOF, supported by US SOF mentors and intelligence, surveillance, target acquisition and reconnaissance (ISTAR), became increasingly capable as the war continued, but US SOF had no spare capacity to assist with building Iraqi conventional forces. Initial

US efforts to provide military trainers were not given priority, and were further inhibited by a lack of US Army experience of capacity building. With the 2004 formation of MNSTC-I, command focus, and resources, improved. The enterprise was conducted on a huge scale: it involved the creation of recruit-training organizations; schools for all branches of the Iraqi armed forces; basic and advanced officer schools; a staff college; and a massive US-led equipment programme. All this required co-ordination and synchronization to ensure that new units and formations were based on properly trained personnel with the right equipment.

This sequencing was understandable, but the risks it involved were exposed during Iraqi Army operations in which weaknesses in high-level Iraqi command, control and logistics constrained the effectiveness of Iraqi forces. The US recognized the risk that too rapid an expansion of Iraqi forces risked producing quantity with inadequate quality. Indeed, by September 2005 only one Iraqi battalion was assessed as fully capable of planning and conducting counter-insurgency (COIN) operations. But with security appearing to constantly deteriorate, the need for increasing the size of the Iraqi forces became the priority. Initial efforts to raise local security forces were tested in the 2004 Shia uprising and the operations to stabilize Fallujah, exposing considerable limitations and weaknesses resulting from a shortage of time, resources and command priorities. This suggests that full-spectrum security-sector reform requires such higher management and supporting capacities to be generated in parallel with combat capability rather than as an afterthought.

The US embarked on a $5.7 billion plan to train 270,000 Iraqi security forces by summer 2006. The US divisions were ordered to partner with Iraqi Army formations. Iraqi divisions, brigades and battalions were assigned small detachments of US troops, known as military transition teams (MiTTs), that would be embedded with them and would advise and accompany them not only in training, but also as the Iraqi forces deployed on operations, helping develop the Iraqi Army's capability and confidence. The MiTTs would also help co-ordinate the operations of the Iraqi units with those of US units, including by being able to call on US logistics, medical capabilities, artillery, helicopters, drones and airpower. In this role they had significant effect.

The US recognized that these small parties of US troops working alongside Iraqi units would be at greater risk than if they were working with battalions. So each team would be within reach of a US quick reaction force, either mounted in armoured vehicles or able to rapidly deploy by helicopter. This helped the Iraqis climb the very steep learning curve resulting from learning how to fight while engaged in operations, with the goal of making them capable of conducting operations independent of US support. The teams also provided the Coalition with accurate information on the Iraqi forces' operations and capabilities.

As Iraqi Police and Army units were formed and deployed on operations, evidence of politicization was revealed. For example, the most competent Iraqi officers would be not necessarily appointed to top leadership positions, their places being taken by less competent officers with stronger political connections. And the Shia authorities tended to discriminate against former Sunni officers, despite their proven competence.

The effectiveness of the Iraqi forces was further reduced by corruption. This not only diminished the morale and cohesion of the Iraqi soldiers, but also degraded logistics, as military supplies, including fuel and food, were stolen or sold on the black market. When Coalition mentor teams observed corruption in Iraq, they brought it to the attention of the senior Iraqi commander of the unit or formation. Although this sometimes addressed the problem, there was evidence that the more militarily effective an Iraqi unit, the more willing Coalition mentors were to tolerate corruption within it. On several occasions, Iraqi units were withdrawn from operations for periods of retraining, providing an opportunity to dismiss corrupt and ineffective commanders.

2005 – FROM INSURGENCY TO CIVIL WAR

In January 2005 the Iraqis went to the polls to form a Transitional National Assembly to draft a constitution. The election was boycotted by the Sunni. Forming a government afterwards proved slow and problematic, with a new Iraqi government, under Prime Minister Ibrahim al-Jaafari, eventually taking office in May 2005. The new government was a weak coalition. The new constitution was ratified in an October 2005 referendum. Subsequent Iraqi parliamentary elections held in December 2005 were successful, in part because all major Shia actors saw them as an opportunity. They were again boycotted by many Sunni. It took months of negotiations before a coalition government could be formed – a coalition led by Nouri al-Maliki of the Dawa Party. This had been formed as an Islamic party in the 1950s but had been banned by Saddam and fled into exile, returning to Iraq in 2003. Maliki was chosen as a compromise candidate for prime minister, as he was seen not to threaten any of the better-established Iraqi parties.

Two years after regime change, security was poor across much of Iraq and organized crime was endemic. This allowed Shia militias, Al Qaida and Sunni insurgents to fill the considerable vacuum in governance and local delivery of security and basic services. This in turn increased their legitimacy and support. Often the insurgents and militias had the initiative. They quickly organized themselves and rapidly learned roadside bomb technology, an adaptation that was accelerated by exploiting the internet. They ruthlessly exploited the internet and satellite television to get their message over, using the 'propaganda of the deed' as an integral part of their tactics and strategy.

SHIA MILITIAS AND FIGHTING GROUPS

Government ministries assigned to the control of Shia politicians mostly became fiefdoms of their political party and aligned with its associated militia. Despite the military defeat of the JAM in 2004, Shia militias were growing in size and influence, as well as infiltrating the new Iraqi Security Forces. The Shia militias all sought first and foremost to secure and maintain their position of influence. Some were linked directly with Iraqi ministries or with provincial councils. All had members in the emergent Iraqi Security Forces. The Shia militias were deeply implicated in corruption and organized crime.

JAM military leaders assessed that similar open rebellions to those attempted in 2004 would be defeated. Instead they sought external assistance from Iran. Qais al-Khazali, one of JAM's top leaders, asked General Qassim Soleimani, commander of the Iranian Revolutionary Guards Quds Force, to provide, training, advice and weapons. The Iranians were assisted by trainers from Lebanese Hizbullah. JAM acquired the explosively formed projectile, or penetrator, (EFP) roadside bombs that could defeat all existing Coalition armoured vehicles. The militants also re-organized on a cellular structure. These cells would become known as 'special groups'. The programme of training in Iran took about a year, reducing JAM attacks in Iraq in 2005. Concurrently SCIRI sought to influence the Coalition that it was a moderate party and a force for stability. But the Badr Corps continued its programme of covertly assassinating Sunni leaders.

Qais al-Khazali subsequently set up his own fighting group, Asaib Ahl al-Haqq, which inflicted many Coalition casualties. In 2007 he was arrested by British SOF. He proved a very co-operative prisoner. The notes the US took from his interrogation provided a detailed picture of how Iran supported his group and other Shia militants who were attacking the Coalition.[4] Khazali explained how from 2003 Iran's strategy was to use Shia militants to attack Coalition forces. From 2005 his militant group received weapons, supplies and money from Iran's Quds Force. These came from existing weapons depots in Iran. They were smuggled through the porous Iran–Iraq border, particularly by using smuggling networks to take ordnance through the marshlands of Maysan Province. The militants' covert logistic chain was designed on 'just in time' principles, seeking to reduce the need for fighting groups to have to hide and manage large caches of arms, ammunition and explosives in Iraq.

Those recruited as fighters would use smuggling networks to enter Iran, mainly through Maysan Province. At cross-border training camps the Iranian Quds Force provided a month's basic training in weapons, IEDs and basic military tactics, while Lebanese Hizbullah taught guerrilla warfare and insurgent tactics. Recruits that showed especial aptitude would receive extra training in Iran. Khazali's group was but one of many anti-Coalition fighting groups.

Command of the various groups was necessarily decentralized and covert. Iran had a clandestine command and control network, in which operational security was improved by applying the 'need to know' principle. But subsequent capture of militant groups' records suggested that some groups had to account to Iran for how they had spent money they had been given and the use that had been made of supplied weapons, including rockets and explosively formed projectile roadside bombs.

SUNNI AND AL QAIDA INSURGENTS

Many Sunni and Al Qaida fighters had been killed or captured in Fallujah, especially former officers of Saddam's forces. Collateral damage from fighting in Fallujah and other Sunni towns in western Iraq could not rapidly be rectified owing to the slowness of Iraqi government bureaucracy and sectarianism, which resulted in increased Sunni disaffection. This and the large numbers of Sunnis who had served in Saddam's security forces provided ample recruits for Zarqawi's branch of Al Qaida, which pledged allegiance to Osama Bin Laden, Bin Laden in turn passing additional funds to Zarqawi.

Al Qaida also had income from wealthy Iraqi Sunnis and raised additional revenue through smuggling, protection rackets and kidnappings. This meant that Zarqawi could pay better wages to its fighters than Iraqi forces. For example, an Iraqi soldier was paid about $150 a month, Al Qaida paid between $100 and $200 to a fighter taking part in a single attack. Sunni civilians were offered $10 a day for conducting surveillance on US and Iraqi government forces. In early 2005 there was a significant increase in use by Sunni and Al Qaida insurgents of large suicide car bombs to target Coalition forces, the Iraqi government and Shia civilians. Zarqawi was seeking to trigger a Sunni–Shia civil war.

THE WESTERN EUPHRATES RIVER VALLEY OFFENSIVE

Given the political significance of Baghdad, the capital was the main military effort. That most of the residents of Anbar Province were Sunnis reduced its political priority to the Iraqi government. After the re-capture of Fallujah, in Anbar Province, Anbar was not the Coalition's main concern either. The MEF was deployed in a more dispersed fashion, partly because the province was too large to allow large forward operating bases to be effective, but partly through a desire to patrol the area as vigorously as possible. Even so it lacked enough troops to hold all urban areas.

By early 2005 car bombs, usually delivered by foreign jihadist suicide bombers, were causing increasing numbers of civilian casualties in Baghdad and elsewhere. In May there were more than 60 suicide bombings. Increasingly large bombs could kill tens of people at once and demolish whole buildings. The repeated bombing of Shias in Baghdad greatly inflamed sectarian tensions. Concerned that the increasing Sunni–Shia tension could undermine the political progress necessary for the forthcoming constitutional referendum and December elections, General Casey sought to reduce these attacks.

Al Qaida and the Sunni insurgents were united in their opposition to the Coalition and new Iraqi forces and government. Intelligence suggested that the great majority of suicide bombers were not Iraqis, but foreign fighters. By now Al Qaida had become an international brand that motivated young Muslims to think it their duty to come to Iraq to fight and kill the crusader infidels. They came from North Africa, Saudi Arabia, Central Asia and Europe to Syria. With the active support of the Assad government, smugglers were paid to guide them across the ill-secured Syrian border into Iraq. Insurgent networks moved them through the Euphrates Valley or the corridor down the Tigris River Valley from Mosul to Tal Afar. Much terrain in both routes was effectively controlled by insurgents and Al Qaida. Volunteers with science or engineering qualifications would be talent spotted and sent to join bomb-making teams. Those who had volunteered for suicide missions would be passed from safe house to safe house, isolated from ordinary Iraqis and subject to constant indoctrination, so as to sustain their motivation to kill themselves.

By now much of western Iraq was controlled by jihadists and Sunni insurgents. All were highly motivated with many being well equipped, including wearing body armour. Although the US controlled Fallujah, the key towns of Hadithah, Hit and Rawah were under insurgent control. The insurgents and jihadists could move around Anbar Province with little hindrance from the Coalition. They were able to mount large-scale attacks, such as the April 2005 attack against a US Marine base. Here three successive large vehicle-borne IEDS were used to attack the Marines' compound, rapidly followed by a massed attack by a hundred fighters.

The Coalition assessed that between 100 and 150 such jihadists were entering Iraq every month. As the US would not conduct attacks into Syria, Casey ordered a major effort to secure Iraq's western border and reduce the Sunni–Al Qaida insurgency and its threat to central Iraq.

The operational justification for the offensive was disputed by Casey's principal subordinate, US Army Lieutenant General John Vines, commander of Multinational Corps – Iraq. Vines thought Baghdad was the centre of gravity of the war. Deploying additional forces to western Anbar would, he considered, make less of a difference to the security of Baghdad than employing them in and around the capital. So concerned was Vines that he insisted in receiving orders from Casey in writing.

The Marines in Anbar were to shift forces to the border, clearing the western town of Qaim. And General McChrystal's SOF would attack insurgent nodes along the two routes. The Marines in western Anbar were reinforced by US Army battalions, increasing troop numbers from about 3,000 to almost 8,000.

McChrystal brought more Delta Force, Rangers and SEALS into Iraq. Many veteran special operators had considerable misgivings about their role in the campaign. It would require them to operate at much greater distance from their bases, quick reaction forces and the bases of medevac helicopters.

As his SOF began to operate in the Euphrates the nature of the facilitation networks was uncovered. Al Qaida had used cash to purchase safe houses, but also relied on a network of guest houses run by sympathizers. McChrystal's troops encountered, tough well-trained and well-equipped enemy fighters. For example, some fighters had modern night vision devices. Houses occupied by insurgent fighters were well prepared for both defence and rapid escape. The commandos often encountered defenders at high readiness – for example sleeping in suicide vests, constructing fortifications inside some buildings and rigging other buildings for instant demolition. In central Iraq, Delta Force had often conducted surprise raids from helicopters with troops landing or descending by rope onto roofs, exploiting surprise. In the Euphrates Valley in 2005, these tactics were often too risky, with the US commandos having to land away from the target site and to march to their objective.

The fighting was fierce, much fiercer than the commandos had encountered before. Some SOF raids ran into such heavy opposition that the attacks could not proceed, the commandos having to abandon the raid and withdraw. Casualties mounted and the SEALS, Delta Force operators and Rangers became more fatigued, while morale was dented by a steady stream of troops killed in close-quarter battle with fighters who stood their ground and fought to the death, as well as in

IED blasts. It was increasingly necessary to use conventional forces to support the special forces. Indeed, a SOF force based in Rawah was assigned Army forces in direct support, including an infantry battalion, Apache attack helicopters and an artillery rocket battery.

Many of McChrystal's special operators had reservations about this redeployment. Feeling that defeat in Iraq was increasingly possible, McChrystal had to use all his powers of persuasion to explain the mission and overcome the doubts of his commanders.

At the end of August, McChrystal flew to Qaim to visit a squadron of Delta Force that had been particularly hard hit. That day it had lost a particularly popular sergeant to an IED attack. Meeting with the squadron, McChrystal told them, 'Listen, this really hurts. But let me tell you what would make this hurt even more: if it is all in vain. Now I am not fucking around. I am here with you, not just physically here, but I am completely committed to this thing. We can beat these bastards, and we we're going to.' In his memoir, McChrystal concluded that, 'Victory could not offset the terrible price already paid – a price that would increase as the fight expanded. But losing would make the pain unbearable.'[5]

Both the Marines and the SOF found themselves making considerable use of airpower to overcome jihadist and insurgent fighters. But whenever the jihadist and Sunni fighters were ejected or chose to withdraw from an area, they would usually not have to wait long for the US troops to withdraw. On return they would exact lethal retribution from Iraqis who were suspected of collaborating with the US forces.

While these battles were going on, Al Qaida was faced with a rebellion by Sunnis. In the parts of Anbar Province that it controlled and influenced, Al Qaida sought to impose a severe Islamic way of life. By Iraqi standards this was extremely brutal and harsh. For example, the enforced marriage of local women to Al Qaida leaders was extremely unpopular. As early as 2005 Sunni tribes near the Syrian border had started to resent the influx of Al Qaida into their area, and the resultant competition in their lucrative smuggling operations. They decided to resist.

Al Qaida retaliated with a campaign of murder and coercion against them, and the tribes turned to the Coalition for help. Offers of providing Sunni recruits to the Iraqi Security Forces, on condition that they stay in Anbar, were rejected by both the Coalition and Iraqi Army as the policy was that the Army should be a non-sectarian national institution. By September 2005, Al Qaida had defeated tribal resistance against it.

The SOF offensive was complemented by US Marines. They mounted numerous clearance operations to eject insurgents and jihadists and to disrupt the infiltration of car bombs and suicide bombers. They also attempted to increase security along Anbar's long border with Syria. This also saw heavy fighting.

The main road from central Syria to Iraq ran through the irrigated Euphrates valley. Much legal and illegal traffic crossed the Syrian–Iraqi border at the border crossing between the Syrian town of Abu Kamal and the Iraqi town of Qaim that dominated the northernmost part of the Euphrates Valley and the roads into Iraq. In September 2005, the 3rd Battalion, 6th Marine Regiment assumed responsibility for Qaim. The commander, Lieutenant Colonel Dale Alford, told the battalion its objective was 'to make the people choose us over the bad guys'.[6]

After initial conventional operations he dispersed the battalion amongst the sprawling town, in a total of 16 small outposts. Combined action platoons that incorporated both Marines and Iraqi troops were based there. Platoons were directed to patrol on foot, rather than by vehicle, and as many patrols as possible incorporated Iraqi forces. In parallel with the raising of an Iraqi Army battalion from Sunni tribes, the battalion increased efforts to recruit policemen and engage local tribes. The security situation improved, allowing more reconstruction to be delivered.

In spring 2006, 3/6th Marines left Iraq and were replaced by 1st Battalion, 7th Marine Regiment, commanded by Lieutenant Colonel Nick Marrano. They continued the approach begun by the previous battalion. They sought to better gather intelligence using the platoons dispersed throughout Qaim to improve their understanding of the small areas that their outposts were situated in. The battalion also conducted a census of the townspeople and their vehicles. This allowed the creation of a town database. Using this in conjunction with locally gathered intelligence, the battalion was able to build up an increasingly accurate understanding of the town, its people and the insurgents and jihadists that threatened it. The combined effect of both battalions' work meant that security in Qaim improved and continued to improve.

TAL AFAR

Concurrent with the SOF and Marine offensives in the Euphrates Valley and on the Syrian border, a US Army regiment was deployed to clear Tal Afar in Nineveh Province. Sitting aside a major staging area for foreign fighters moving into Iraq from Syria, by mid-2005 the town had become an Al Qaida stronghold. The Iraqi government was demanding that it be cleared and the Shia population relieved. British Lieutenant General Robin Brims, then deputy commander of MNF-I, takes up the story:

> We resisted this and the 3rd Armored Cavalry Regiment conducted a very well-planned operation which took into account the very mixed population of Tal Afar (Arab Sunni, Arab Shia, Turcomen, Kurd, and Turk). The operation was planned and conducted by US forces, but we persuaded the Iraqi Government to lead on the presentation of the operation and the negotiation with the City Council. A deal was struck between the Government and City Council: this was all arranged by the Coalition. The US Ambassador forced the pace in making the Iraqi Government take responsibility. So, this was a successful operation in itself but it also was a start of Iraqis taking ownership of their country.[7]

This operation to clear Tal Afar took place between August 2005 and May 2006. It was conducted by 3rd Armored Cavalry Regiment, commanded by Colonel H.R. McMaster. He believed that it was a core responsibility of professional officers to prepare themselves and their organization for combat through the study of military history; accordingly he and his regiment studied previous counter-insurgency campaigns. The regiment's pre-deployment training emphasized cultural awareness and Arabic language skills. One out of every ten soldiers received a three-week course in conversational Arabic, so that each small unit would have someone capable of basic exchanges with Iraqis. McMaster distributed a lengthy reading list to his officers that included studies of Arab and Iraqi history and most of the classic texts on counter-insurgency. He also quietly relieved a battalion commander who failed to understand the approach that he was advocating.

The regiment surrounded Tal Afar, isolated it and took time to better understand the military, social and political dynamics of the population. Interdiction operations on the Syrian border disrupted insurgent movements into and out of Tal Afar. A preliminary clearance operation in a nearby town helped McMaster to refine his plan, gain the confidence of his superiors and secure the additional forces and equipment needed. A berm was constructed around the city. Much of the city's population moved into a specially built camp outside the berm. Many insurgents were detained as they tried to leave the city.

The operation was an early example of successfully using the 'clear, hold and build' approach to stabilize an insurgent-controlled area. Tal Afar was systematically cleared by the regiment in a sequenced operation. Fighting was intense but use of heavy weapons was carefully controlled. Having cleared the city, the regiment then built 29 patrol bases to dominate all the main urban routes. They recruited and trained 1,400 Iraqi police to build legitimacy and partnered with Iraqi Army and Police units. Civil development projects were started. The Iraqi government led on the public presentation of the operation and in negotiations with the city council. This allowed popular consent to be built by re-establishing essential services and targeted reconstruction efforts. Popular support for US and Iraqi forces increased, generating additional intelligence that was exploited to attack remaining insurgents.

During this period, direction to US formations and units and US strategic messages appeared contradictory. CENTCOM and MNF-I considered the US presence an 'antibody' and sought to minimize the irritation it was causing to Iraqis by the implementing the Transition Strategy and handing security leadership to the Iraqis as soon as possible. But General Casey was also telling US commanders that the campaign was counter-insurgency. This was reinforced by his establishing a counter-insurgency school. Here incoming US commanders at battalion level and above were required to attend a two-week course before assuming command. However, the MNF-I plan was for 'transition' not counter-insurgency. A significant number of US battalion and brigade commanders saw these lines of direction as mutually contradictory.

In her October 2005 testimony to Congress, US Secretary of State Condoleezza Rice described the US strategy as 'clear, hold and build'.[8] It is worth quoting from the November 2005 US 'National Strategy for Victory in Iraq'. Its executive summary began with three clear statements:

Victory in Iraq is Defined in Stages

- **Short term**, Iraq is making steady progress in fighting terrorists, meeting political milestones, building democratic institutions, and standing up security forces.
- **Medium term**, Iraq is in the lead defeating terrorists and providing its own security, with a fully constitutional government in place, and on its way to achieving its economic potential.
- **Longer term**, Iraq is peaceful, united, stable, and secure, well integrated into the international community, and a full partner in the global war on terrorism.

Victory in Iraq is a Vital U.S. Interest

- Iraq is the central front in the global war on terror. Failure in Iraq will embolden terrorists and expand their reach; success in Iraq will deal them a decisive and crippling blow.
- The fate of the greater Middle East – which will have a profound and lasting impact on American security – hangs in the balance.

Failure is Not an Option

- Iraq would become a safe haven from which terrorists could plan attacks against America, American interests abroad, and our allies.
- Middle East reformers would never again fully trust American assurances of support for democracy and human rights in the region – a historic opportunity lost.
- The resultant tribal and sectarian chaos would have major consequences for American security and interests in the region.[9]

It also repeated that this would be accomplished by the 'clear, hold and build' approach. But President Bush contradicted this policy in subsequent speeches stating that 'US troops will stand down as Iraqi troops stand up'. US military commanders could be forgiven for being confused.

The December 2005 elections in Iraq saw a significant turnout of 76 per cent to elect a new parliament and government. Both elections were largely boycotted by Sunnis. But the overall success of both of these elections and the role that the Iraqi security forces and Iraqi civil society played in them gave many Coalition commanders, as well as Washington and London, a sense of guarded optimism that the corner had been turned.

This sense of optimism was, in part, a result of the successes in western Iraq: the killing of many insurgents and jihadists and the successful clearances of Qaim and Tal Afar. But the resources switched from Baghdad and central Iraq had meant that the security of Baghdad was, of necessity, reduced. And Baghdad was the centre of gravity of the escalating Shia–Sunni conflict.

2006 – DESCENT INTO CIVIL WAR

Security in Baghdad had greatly deteriorated throughout 2005. Apart from Kurdistan, most of the country remained in the grip of violence. Organized crime was endemic. Militias of all types proliferated from simple neighbourhood self-defence groups to large-well organized groups such as the Badr Corps and the JAM.

Shia militias had extensively infiltrated the Iraqi security forces and Shia-controlled ministries, particularly the Interior Ministry, where thousands of members of the JAM and Badr Corps served in various police and paramilitary units. Both were complicit in the large-scale kidnapping, torture and murder of Sunnis. In a notorious case in late 2005, US troops discovered a bunker in a Ministry of Interior building holding 166 Sunni prisoners in poor conditions, many of whom showed signs of torture. The prisoners were awaiting ransom, execution or trial.

Sectarian violence became increasingly common, with Al Qaida suicide bombers targeting Sunni areas and self-defence forces springing up all over Baghdad. Increasing ethno-sectarian cleansing would see extremists intimidate civilians of one sect into moving out of mixed areas. Increasing numbers of bodies were found floating in the Tigris River and canals every morning. It became increasingly risky for Sunni civilians to leave their neighbourhood, for fear of running into checkpoints manned by Shia militias or Shia-controlled security forces.

US and Coalition strategy remained premised on the return of security responsibility to Iraqi forces as soon as possible. Transition was the main effort. By now the US Army contingent in Iraq was led by V Corps, commanded by Lieutenant General Peter Chiarelli. Initial direction from General Casey to the corps was to reduce the US footprint, both in troop numbers and in numbers of bases. Forward operating bases were to be reduced from 110 to 50. But progress stalled and sectarian violence significantly increased after 22 February 2006 when Al Qaida bombed the Golden Mosque in Sammara, one of Shia Islam's great shrines.

This was a decisive point in the campaign. It triggered a Shia–Sunni civil war of murder and sectarian cleansing. The level of violence increased dramatically. Shia death squads stepped up their efforts against Sunni communities, supported by rogue elements of the Iraqi security forces, particularly the police, and by Shia-controlled ministries which denied their services to Sunnis.

Al Qaida staged mass casualty attacks using suicide bombers primarily against Iraqi government and Shia civilian targets. This in turn triggered mass kidnapping, torture and murder of Sunnis by Shia death squads mostly from the Jaysh al-Mahdi, which itself reinforced the credibility of Sunni and Al Qaida insurgencies and the foreign jihadists.

Iraq was increasingly caught in a self-reinforcing cycle of atrocity and counter-atrocity which triggered significant population movements within the country and a flow of refugees to surrounding states. In Baghdad, Shias and Sunnis retreated into controlled districts directed by militias of their own ethnicity, using existing or improvised obstacles to deny access to death squads and car bombs. Some areas that had previously been stabilized by Coalition forces fell under militia control.

The Coalition and Iraqi forces struggled to counter this upsurge in violence. It was not possible to concentrate enough US and competent Iraqi forces to clear and then hold the key areas of Baghdad. Indeed, the shifting of the best part of a division's worth of US combat power to western Iraq in 2005 had drawn forces away from the Baghdad area, thus reducing security there.

At Prime Minister Maliki's insistence, an Iraqi-led operation was planned and quickly put into action to try to re-establish security in Baghdad. Operation *Together Forward* and its sequel Operation *Together Forward II* saw the deployment of 7,000 extra US troops into Baghdad. The Iraqi government pledged 4,000 troops but, in the event, the Iraqi forces were only able to find a quarter of the troops offered. Despite some limited success by US forces in clearing parts of Baghdad, there were insufficient US and Iraqi troops to hold the areas cleared.

Both operations failed because the numbers of US and Iraqi forces were insufficient, as was the overall effectiveness of the Iraqi forces. There was sustained interference in the conduct of operations from Shia politicians and clear evidence of complicity in Shia ethnic cleansing amongst the Iraq security forces.

By mid-2006, it was clear that the Coalition's focus on supporting the elected Iraqi government was adding to the problem rather than solving it. Supporting the Shia-led government only fuelled continued violence from and disengagement by the Sunni minority. In turn, the Iraqi government was unable to provide basic services, to lead the counter-insurgency effort and to take any serious steps to reconcile the country politically.

The Coalition's efforts to stabilize Iraq were being frustrated by multiple destabilizing factors. These included the insurgencies; communal power struggles; weak and divided institutions; destabilizing aims and fears of the participants, and regional interference which verged on being a foreign-fuelled proxy war.

Without a strong, impartial and effective government, the militant ethno-sectarian factions used violence and subversion to oppress and intimidate sections of the population. It was a blood-soaked 'zero-sum game' where factions fought to secure their political and economic power; a struggle for the division of power and resources among and within ethnic and sectarian communities. In response, the Iraqi population returned to its foundations of tribe, sect or ethnic group and society, polarized under the Baathist regime, fractured along ethnic and sectarian lines. Sectarian intimidation and killings spiralled out of control in Baghdad and central Iraq. The Transition Strategy was close to defeat.

INSTRUMENTS OF DARKNESS — THE DEVELOPMENT
OF SPECIAL OPERATIONS FORCES (SOF)

Conventional military operations in Afghanistan and Iraq were the responsibility of US Central Command. The Pentagon assigned the global lead for operations against Al Qaida to US Special Operations Command (SOCOM), answering directly to the US Defense Secretary.

In some respects, SOCOM resembled a fifth US armed service. The Army provided 'green berets', the elite Delta Force and a regiment of bespoke helicopters. The SEALS were supplied by the US Navy as were small boats. The Air Force provided a range of modified transport aircraft and long-range helicopters. But there were never enough SOF to fulfil the requirements of the US commanders in Iraq and Afghanistan, let alone missions outside those countries.

Within SOCOM the lead for counter-terrorism was with the Joint Special Operations Command (JSOC). General McChrystal had taken command of JSOC in October 2003. He found brave and dedicated SEAL and Delta Force teams mounting raids against suspected Al Qaida networks. They were supported by a dedicated force of helicopters and elite light infantry from the US Army Rangers. They were joined by a British SAS contingent.

Travelling by vehicle or helicopters the troops would rapidly surround the target house or compound, force entry by breaking down the door or using explosives and rush into the building, each soldier covered by their comrades. Entering each room would be a moment of high tension – would the troops be met by an armed terrorist or by only women and children? Remarkably few innocent bystanders were killed. Living terrorists were much more valuable than dead ones. The buildings would need to be searched for documents, computers, arms and explosives.

No matter how fast and stealthy the approach to the target, once the raid began the location of the target would be impossible to conceal. Hostile insurgents or militias would attempt to counter-attack the raiders. So SOF commanders emphasized speed of action. The SOF soldiers conducting the raid would spend much of their spare time training, honing the drills for assaulting buildings, testing their weapons to ensure accuracy and reliability and working out to keep themselves fit.

But despite the highly trained operators and their relentless training regime, the effectiveness of the operation was limited by the fact that its various parts were insufficiently connected with each other and the whole force itself was insufficiently connected to the conventional US military force and the US government's intelligence agencies. Independently the CIA was also countering Al Qaida, with its own intelligence-gathering and direct-action assets, including armed drones and paramilitary militias.

McChrystal described attending a 2005 National Security Council meeting at the White House to discuss countering Al Qaida:

> Notably absent were any members of the National Security Council Staff with the Iraq portfolio. The meeting, like those leading up to it, excluded these Iraq officials, drawing a line between the counterterrorist fight and the war in Iraq. This was a division of labour at odds with my thinking about Al Qaida's ascendant role in Iraq.[10]

McChrystal spent much time working to overcome this sub-optimal strategic command and control by personally co-ordinating JSOC's activities with CENTCOM's conventional forces and with the CIA and other US intelligence agencies.

He set out to rectify the evident weaknesses by acquiring more communications bandwidth, intelligence analysts and interrogators. Just as importantly he sought to better integrate JSOC with the US conventional forces. And he reached out to the rest of the US intelligence agencies, particularly the CIA, to increase the force's ability to develop targeting intelligence. At the same time, he was making ever-increasing use of airborne surveillance, both from drones and from manned aircraft, as well as of US 'special reconnaissance' operators conducting plain-clothes surveillance.

JSOC were allowed to detain and interrogate terrorist suspects. Shortly after his arrival, McChrystal also revised the approach to detention of prisoners which caused, among others, the Abu Ghraib scandal of April 2004. Once JSOC's interrogation operation was placed on a proper footing it often produced intelligence that could not be obtained in any other way. This was combined with the full range of JSOC's other intelligence and surveillance capabilities, including the ability to rapidly analyse captured documents, computers and telephones. This allowed

JSOC to greatly increase its decision making and tempo to better attack Al Qaida's networks.

For the first part of both Afghan and Iraq wars, there was insufficient co-ordination between conventional forces and SOF. The ground forces who had responsibility for ground areas of operation often received little or no warning of SOF raids and were usually left managing the consequences, not least collateral damage, civilian casualties and antagonized local populations. Ground force commanders often complained about the apparently lavish allocation of scarce intelligence, surveillance and reconnaissance (ISR) resources, in particular of scarce drones, to SOF. Over time co-ordination improved, not least through the efforts of McChrystal and other SOF commanders to reach out to the conventional force commanders. This allowed joint intelligence and target development by the two different forces. An increased effort was made by US and British to integrate SOF into pre-deployment briefings and training.[11]

These and a host of other initiatives were led by McChrystal and his subordinates to catalyse the energy of the whole command: 'I tried to set a climate in which we prized entrepreneurship and free thinking, leaned hard on complacency and did not punish ideas that failed.' He set out to delegate decision making to the lowest possible level: 'we pushed authority down until it made us uneasy ... But I thought of the alternative – corseted centralization – and that squelched my inclination to grab control.'[12]

The US chose to grow the size of its SOF, while maintaining the demanding selection and training requirements. Given the tempo of operations and numbers of casualties this was no easy task. At one stage in the middle of both wars Delta Force was reported as having suffered 50 per cent killed and wounded since 9/11. Between 9/11 and the end of 2008 US SOF grew by 30 per cent to an overall strength of 55,000 troops.[13]

SOF MANHUNTING – THE DEATH OF ZARQAWI

A high-priority target for JSOC was Abu Musab al-Zarqawi, the bloodthirsty leader of Al Qaida in Iraq. It took JSOC a year-long intelligence and surveillance operation to track down their target – a sequence of events as gripping as any fictional manhunt.

The hunt began with an early false start when one of the main leads to Zarqawi, his lieutenant Abu Zar, ran cold. Unexpectedly, Abu Zar was later captured by Iraqi forces. Once handed over to JSOC he was patiently interrogated, resulting in the identification of some buildings in Yusufiyah outside Baghdad that were periodically used for meetings by Al Qaida.

An intelligence warrant officer organized occasional aerial surveillance of this complex. After three months, a drone operator spotted an unusual convoy of civilian vehicles in the area, suggesting that an Al Qaida operation was about to be mounted. An immediate helicopter-borne raid by Delta Force resulted in the killing of five insurgents and the capture of a vast quantity of terrorist equipment. Concurrently, the drone showed another suspicious convoy of vehicles outside a house close by. This became a second target, raided two hours later, which captured 12 men who appeared to have leadership roles.

Exploiting captured documents, computers and mobile phones allowed the patient and lengthy interrogation of these men. One was cultivated by the interrogators over two weeks. He was eventually persuaded to give up the name of Zarqawi's spiritual advisor, Abu al-Rahman, who regularly met him. Drones and JSOC special reconnaissance operators in civilian clothes watched Rahman for over three weeks. They finally saw him travel out of Baghdad to a compound at Hibhib where he was met by someone who fitted Zarqawi's description. McChrystal's preference was to launch a helicopter-borne force to attempt to capture the people there, but there was insufficient time. The building was bombed and Zarqawi fatally injured.

The US had hoped that this would deal a body blow to Al Qaida in Iraq. But the organization was more resilient than expected and Zarqawi's death was no more than a temporary setback to the jihadist network.

RAMADI – A TIPPING POINT IN ANBAR

By summer 2005 Ramadi had become the centre of resistance to the Coalition and a centre for criminals and outlaws. Much of the city had been abandoned to the insurgents with the police barricaded into a single remaining police station under a state of siege. Coalition activity in Ramadi consisted largely of sustaining that station and carrying out raids from outside the town.

In mid-2005 the US Army National Guard's 2nd Brigade, 28th Division began to tackle Ramadi systematically. With a strength of five National Guard battalions, a US airborne battalion and a US Marine Corps battalion, they constructed six new combined police stations and company outposts in the city. These became the bases from which successful operations to unearth arms caches were conducted.

There was heavy fighting requiring the use of tanks and Bradleys. This were complemented by key leader engagement and information operations. The brigade adopted the philosophy of 'first do no harm', as it attempted to minimize friction with the locals – for example in ceasing random searches of vehicles and houses. It also stopped using artillery for terrain denial and counter-battery fire. It used feedback from local sheikhs to help understand what tactics were working and which were not.

Successful conduct of elections in December 2005 coincided with successful efforts to recruit Sunnis for the Iraqi police. Al Qaida struck back with an effective suicide bombing and assassination campaign.

The brigade was also responsible for security of a large area outside of Anbar. This meant that it could not bring any more forces to bear on the city. When the brigade rotated back to the US the insurgents remained in charge of most of the city. Attacks in the town averaged over 30 per day. Fewer than 100 police out of a total of 4,000 were present and few left the safety of their stations.

The National Guard formation was succeeded in June 2006 by the 1st 'Ready First' Brigade, 1st Armored Division. The brigade had already served for four months in Tal Afar, where it had seen how tactical success could be achieved. As it took over the city the MEF HQ reduced the size of its area of operations to allow it to concentrate on Ramadi city. The MEF also gave the brigade two more battalions.

The brigade disregarded the theatre strategy of withdrawing to large forward operating bases. It deliberately continued its predecessors' approach by pushing its forces out into the city to build company combat outposts in the worst insurgent areas. These were to act as bases for US and Iraqi forces and to restrict insurgent movement.

The brigade was prepared to stay in Ramadi and fight it out with the insurgents. Fighting was often heavy, with insurgent groups of platoon size attacking US outposts. US troops gradually gained the upper hand over the insurgents. Tactical census patrols improved intelligence. The 1/1st sought to minimize use of air strikes, artillery and tank guns inside the city. Colonel Sean MacFarland, the brigade commander, described the approach:

> With new outposts established in an ever-tightening circle around the inner city, we wrested control from the insurgents. As areas became manageable, we handed them over to newly trained Iraqi police (whom we kept a watchful eye on) and used the relieved US forces elsewhere to continue tightening the noose.[14]

The brigade used an information operations campaign to discredit Al Qaida. Iraqi and US troops took control of the city's large hospital, freeing access to medical care. Micro and macro-economic development projects started in co-operative areas, providing much-needed local jobs and alternative, legitimate sources of income.

THE ANBAR AWAKENING

Concurrently the brigade engaged with those tribal leaders who remained, offering protection and economic development in exchange for police recruits to clear the city. In this a decisive role was played by Captain Travis Patriquin. He was one of the few US Army officers who spoke fluent Arabic and whose previous service in the Middle East had immersed him in Arabic and Iraqi culture. Able to speak Arabic with an Iraqi accent and phrases, he was designated by Colonel MacFarland to reach out to the Ramadi tribal leaders. He was uniquely suited to do so and made rapid progress, exploiting many local leaders' increasing opposition to Al Qaida.

This outreach was central to the 'Anbar Awakening', the backlash against Al Qaida by the Sunni population of Anbar. As in 2005, this was a result of Al Qaida's harsh rule. It is also likely that Al Qaida posed a threat to a lucrative smuggling business controlled by Sunni tribes.

In mid-2006 the rebellion against Al Qaida centred on Sheikh Sattar abu Risa of the Dulaimi tribal federation. Although himself a relatively minor sheikh, Sattar provided a focus for tribal opposition to Al Qaida. Prime Minister Maliki and Shia allies in the Iraqi government were extremely reluctant to countenance the recruitment of Sunnis. But the

MEF went ahead and supported the Sunni militia. Sattar's tribesmen were co-opted in large numbers into the Iraqi police.

A blind eye was turned to his extra-legal streams of revenue generation. Sattar's success in resisting, surviving and making money proved exemplary; more sheikhs brought more men, and by the end of 2007 the forces ranged against Al Qaida had doubled in size.

Retaliation by Al Qaida, killing tribal leaders and their supporters, was not enough to deflect this movement. Sattar's eventual assassination by Al Qaida caused a temporary hiatus, but the momentum was maintained by his brother, who inclined it further towards mainstream politics. The movement was now called the 'Anbar Awakening'. The previously dormant Anbar Provincial Council (PC) was re-established and slowly links were restored between Anbar and Baghdad.

Over 4,000 recruits were provided to police Ramadi during the following six months. Tribal councils selected mayors and local leaders to rebuild the human infrastructure of the city. The friendly tribes were often much better at identifying Al Qaida insurgents than US troops. This led to raids which further demoralized Al Qaida. By February 2007, violence had decreased by nearly 70 per cent. By summer 2007, attacks had practically ceased in Ramadi.

Sensing diminishing support and legitimacy among the population, Al Qaida attempted to retaliate against co-operating tribes through a murder and intimidation campaign. The brigade provided the tribes with air and artillery support and US troops to defend against insurgent attacks when required. This demonstration of unity solidified the tribal rebellion, which expanded exponentially.

The Anbar Awakening was a result of three incremental realizations by tribal sheikhs: first that the political process might confer more benefit than continued fighting, second that Al Qaida's transnational and fundamentalist goals were at odds with their own local or national objectives, and third and most importantly, that Al Qaida was competing for control of revenue sources, such as banditry and smuggling, which had previously been the exclusive province of the tribes. But it was also a response to conditions created by the US operations, by means of dynamic security operations and engagement with tribal leaders, all underpinned by risk-taking by the US commanders in Anbar. In retrospect the clearance of Ramadi and the Anbar Awakening were decisive points in the campaign.

Two US Army officers had played a decisive role in the Anbar Awakening. Firstly, Colonel Sean MacFarland. By using his brigade to conduct a counter-insurgency operation in Ramadi, he successfully degraded Al Qaida's hold over a town that had been a sanctuary for the jihadists. Secondly, Captain Travis Patriquin. By using his language and cultural skills, he was able to engage with Sheikh Sattar and other Sunni leaders in a way that helped persuade them to side with the Americans.

Patriquin had also worked with a US Marine Corps officer, Major Meghan McClung, to bring groups of US and international journalists to Ramadi to see the progress that was being made against Al Qaida and the early stages of the Anbar Awakening. Neither Patriquin nor McClung would see the fruition of both developments. They were both killed in a roadside bomb attack on 6 December.

McClung was the highest-ranked female in the Coalition to be killed in the war, the most senior female Marine to die in Iraq and the first female graduate of the US Naval Academy to have been killed in combat. Her death symbolized that in Iraq, female personnel of the forces of the US and its allies were just as much as risk as males. The same was true of the conflict in Afghanistan.

Before 9/11 the US Army and Marine Corps excluded women from serving in infantry, armour, artillery, combat engineers, air defence artillery, special forces and any support units that 'collocated' with these units. This policy was based on an assumption that future battlefields would be 'linear', with a distinction between forward areas and rear areas. But the campaigns in Iraq and Afghanistan saw no clear distinction between front line and rear echelons, with personnel serving in bases or travelling in logistic convoys subject to a 360-degree threat of mortar and rocket attack, ambushes and roadside bombs. And women were increasingly employed with combat units, for example as frontline medics, to search women and as specialist 'female engagement teams'. Between 9/11 and January 2013, 152 US servicewomen were killed in action in Iraq and Afghanistan. By then women made up almost 15 per cent of US military personnel. In both the US and British forces women won awards for gallantry. Notable amongst these were bravery awards to helicopter pilots and medical personnel.

As a result, the Pentagon abandoned its previous policy. In January 2013 Secretary of Defense Leon Panetta and Chairman of the Joint Chiefs of Staff General Martin Dempsey announced that 'we are eliminating the direct ground combat exclusion rule for women and we are moving forward with a plan to eliminate all unnecessary gender-based barriers to service.'[15] The British followed suit.

THE AUDIT OF WAR

The success of the first Iraqi elections in 2005 created a mood of cautious optimism in Washington DC and in London. But security deteriorated after that. With the February 2006 bombing of the Sammara shrine, there was a collapse of security and the sectarian conflict between the Shia and the Sunni was precipitated into a civil war that the Coalition was unable to suppress. The inability of the Iraqi government and security forces to play the role that the Transition Strategy required of them was cruelly exposed that summer with the failures of Operations *Together Forward I* and *II* in Baghdad.

In Baghdad and central Iraq, the Transition Strategy had neither built up Iraqi security capability sufficiently, nor neutralized the Sunni–Al Qaida insurgency. The US and British governments failed to appreciate that the situation had changed and that transition as envisaged was very unlikely to succeed and highly likely to fail.

But in Qaim, Tal Afar and Ramadi US Army and Marine Corps formations successfully stabilized key towns by conducting counter-insurgency operations. Although the fights for the three towns were conducted by different commanders and formations, they shared common principles. These including isolating the urban areas and achieving large enough numbers of troops on the ground by combining their forces with relatively competent and trustworthy Iraqi forces.

Each operation deployed US troops into relatively small combat outposts in the heart of the urban areas controlled by insurgents. These provoked heavy insurgent counter-attacks, which required the full spectrum of combined arms firepower to defeat, albeit under tight rules of engagement to minimize unintended civilian casualties. The operations achieved an adequate force ratio, for example one US soldier to every 22 residents of Tal Afar. They also integrated reconstruction and development, increasingly as the balance of security shifted away from the insurgents.

The same 'clear, hold and build' approach and concentration of force that had been used in Tal Afar was applied in Ramadi. It was combined with non-military and political measures, as well as efforts to build the strength and capability of local Iraqi security forces. The additional ingredient in Ramadi was reconciliation with Sunni tribes who were so fed up with Al Qaida that they were prepared to join with US forces to fight the jihadists.

By summer 2006, the balance of power in Anbar Province had changed in favour of the Coalition. This proved to be a tipping point in the campaign, although it was not widely recognized as such. But these positive developments had not reversed the deterioration of security in Baghdad.

7

The Iraq Surge

Regaining the initiative

THE REDISCOVERY OF COUNTER-INSURGENCY BY THE US ARMY AND MARINE CORPS

There were many factors that contributed to the Coalition's difficulties in Iraq. A key factor that made the US military less effective than it might have been was that the US Army had for the previous 30 years walked away from thinking about counter-insurgency. Most US land forces that served in Iraq and Afghanistan between 2002 and 2005 had little preparation for post-conflict stabilization and equally little understanding of Iraqi or Afghan culture. Most were unfamiliar with the military's role in counter-insurgency.

After the Vietnam War the US Marines had retained interest in counter-insurgency, not least because they considered some of their stability operations in Vietnam to have succeeded. SOF retained an understanding of insurgency and counter-insurgency, partly because some of their clandestine operations required them to assist US allies with countering insurgency. But as an institution, the US Army had deliberately turned away from training and education in these topics. And the US Navy and Air Force were optimized for war against states. So, most Pentagon staff and leaders in the Army, Navy and Air Force were in a state of self-inflicted institutional ignorance.

This was reinforced by the determination of President Bush and Defense Secretary Rumsfeld that the US military should not be involved in nation-building. They wanted a more flexible and agile US military. So the armed forces would withdraw from the many nation-building missions assigned to them by President Clinton's government.

The US Army's experience in Bosnia and Kosovo since 1995 and 1999 respectively had clearly shown that stabilization operations had a long tail that made rapidly withdrawing US forces difficult. Despite all the frustrations of these operations, including the all too obvious weaknesses of the UN, more perceptive US officers had seen that the narrow military role of stabilization had to be complemented by political, reconstruction, economic and development progress. The US military capabilities in these areas were extremely limited, so the best had to be made of a bad job by supporting the UN administration in Kosovo and the High Representative in Bosnia. And many diplomats and State Department officials also understood this. But any efforts to point this out to new Bush government officials in 2001 would have been unwelcome.

Nevertheless, by the middle of 2003 some US Army and Marine officers had concluded that both the Afghan and Iraq wars were insurgencies. This was initially manifested by General Abizaid's declaration that US forces in Iraq were facing guerrillas and insurgents. His view was concurrent with General David Barno's adoption of a counter-insurgency (COIN) approach to Afghanistan in 2003.

What is COIN? When faced with an insurgency, a government requires a national strategy to counter the insurgents. This should blend political, economic, psychological, and civic actions to erode support for the insurgents. Since the insurgent campaign will be based on violent means, security, police, military and intelligence must be integrated into the strategy. Military forces conducting counter-insurgency after 1945 often identified common strategic, operational and tactical principles that led to success. There was a rich literature of such analysis, drawing on French and British colonial conflicts and the Vietnam War. There was no global shortage of applicable analysis of COIN from outside the US Army available for US officers who wanted to study it for themselves. Some, like US Army General David Barno, Colonel H.R. McMaster and US Marine Lieutenant Colonel Julian Alford, did so. But these officers made up a small proportion of US commanders and senior staff who deployed to Iraq or Afghanistan, particularly in the early years of both wars. The US Army's previous deliberate neglect of the study of insurgency and COIN meant that it lacked an adequate intellectual foundation on which to build a foundation of understanding of the topic. Indeed a 2005 survey conducted by General Casey's close advisors had identified that only 20 per cent of US brigades in Iraq understood COIN.[1]

In 2004–05, some US Army and US Marine Corps commanders in Iraq began to see the opportunities to be gained by employing a counter-insurgency approach. This was seen in the Marines operations to clear Qaim and in the stabilization of Tal Afar by Colonel H.R. McMaster's 3rd Armoured Cavalry Regiment.

US thinking about COIN reached critical mass in 2006 when US Army Lieutenant General David Petraeus and Marine General James Mattis both applied their considerable operational experience and intellectual energy to develop new doctrine for COIN. Field Manual 3-24 'Counterinsurgency', published at the end of 2006, drew not only on the emerging lessons from Iraq, including the clearance of Qaim and Tal Afar, and from Afghanistan, but also on a historical analysis of successful and unsuccessful COIN campaigns. The manual's key points were that:

Military efforts are necessary and important to COIN efforts, but they are only effective when integrated into a comprehensive strategy employing all instruments of national power. A successful COIN operation meets the contested population's needs to the extent needed to win popular support while protecting the population from the insurgents.

The integration of civilian and military efforts is crucial to successful COIN operations. All efforts focus on supporting the local populace and host nation government. Political, social, and economic programs are usually more valuable than conventional military operations in addressing the root causes of conflict and undermining an insurgency ...

An essential COIN task for military forces is fighting insurgents; however, these forces can and should use their capabilities to meet the local populace's fundamental needs as well. Regaining the populace's active and continued support for the host nation government is essential to deprive an insurgency of its power and appeal. The military forces' primary function in COIN is protecting that populace. However, employing military force is not the only way to provide civil security or defeat insurgents. Indeed, excessive use of military force can frequently undermine policy objectives at the expense of achieving the overarching political goals that define success. This dilemma places tremendous importance on the measured application of force.

Durable policy success requires balancing the measured use of force with an emphasis on non-military programs. Political, social, and economic programs are most commonly and appropriately associated with civilian organizations and expertise; however, effective implementation of these programs is more important than who performs the tasks. If adequate civilian capacity is not available, military forces fill the gap.

COIN is also a battle of ideas. Insurgents seek to further their cause by creating misperceptions of COIN efforts. Comprehensive information programs are necessary to amplify the messages of positive deeds and to counter insurgent propaganda.[2]

The manual also recommended the 'clear, hold and build' approach applied in Qaim and Tal Afar. It became an extremely influential document, greatly informing the training and approach of US forces in Iraq and Afghanistan from 2007 onwards and those of their allies in both theatres.

FRESH THINKING IN THE WHITE HOUSE

November 2006 was a bloody month, with the highest number of monthly Iraqi civilian casualties: almost 3,100 people killed. Almost a hundred thousand Iraqis a month were leaving the country, many of them relatively wealthy members of the middle class, the people who were needed to run the country and energize its economy. Over a hundred US troops were killed and nearly 800 were wounded.

In all the countries providing troops to Iraq, the war was becoming increasingly unpopular. Of all the Coalition nations the unpopularity of the war was probably least in the US. The country had developed a profound strain of support to its armed forces. There were many who still thought that the removal of Saddam Hussein had been a just cause. And the key role played in the insurgency by Al Qaida demonstrated a link with the 9/11 attacks. But despite these factors, the apparent intractability of the war and increasing chaos meant that the unpopularity of the war steadily increased. Increasing numbers of US citizens judged the Iraq war to be unwinnable.

This was reflected in US politics, with opposition Democrats using the war as a political stick with which to beat President Bush and his administration. In the 7 November mid-term congressional elections, the Democrats won a majority in Congress. The next day President Bush announced that he and Defense Secretary Rumsfeld had agreed that 'the timing is right for new leadership at the Pentagon'. Robert Gates would take over the job. A former career CIA officer, who had risen to become the Agency's top leader, Gates would leave the university in Texas that he was running and take over at the Pentagon.

Meanwhile, from mid-2006, a small group of serving and retired military officers and civilian strategists concluded that the US strategy of transition in Iraq was flawed. Force reductions, while politically attractive in terms of reducing the casualty rate, were adding to the problem, not solving it. The principal protagonists were retired US Army general Jack Keane who had recently retired from the post of Vice Chief of Staff of the US Army and Fred Kagan, a former West Point history professor who worked at the American Enterprise Institute think tank.

Kagan used the Institute as a public platform to offer his advice. Keane used his position as an influential, credible retired officer to challenge the accepted view of US policy, with its leading proponents in the Department of Defense. In discussions with the advocates of the Transition Strategy in the Pentagon, Keane and Kagan argued persuasively enough to prompt a Pentagon internal analysis of the concept of a surge, and this, in turn, gave them the opportunity to influence President Bush personally.[3]

A late 2006 internal assessment in HQ MNF-I had concluded that 'we are failing to achieve our objectives in economic development, governance, communicating and the security lines of operation'.[4] The prerequisite to success, the MNF-I report identified, 'will be protecting the Iraqi population from the violence spurred on by Al Qaida in Iraq and extremist organizations such as JAM.' The key to making political progress was to reduce sectarian violence. This meant having to 'retain the cleared areas to guarantee a sustained security,' which in turn meant there was 'a need for and a mission for a surge of forces.'[5]

At the beginning of December 2006, Keane and Kagan presented their case at the Pentagon and then to the President. They argued that the campaign in Iraq remained vital to US security, but it was at a critical point. Widespread sectarian violence threatened the whole campaign and US political strategy had failed. Of the strategic options available to the US, Iraq's neighbours could not be persuaded to change their unhelpful behaviour. And US withdrawal from the country would remove all constraints on Al Qaida, Sunnis fighters and Shia militia. This would rapidly engulf the country in a bloody civil war, with untold consequences for the people of Iraq, the region and US international standing. It would also encourage Al Qaida, offering the opportunity to establish a caliphate in Anbar.

Instead they proposed that security be restored by a rapid and decisive change in US policy. The development of new Iraqi security forces needed to be complemented by a determined effort to secure the Iraqi population and contain the rising violence. The security of the Iraqi population had to become the main priority. This required sending more, not fewer US troops.

Baghdad was the decisive point. The city required clearing and holding to create the conditions for building on economic development, political development, reconciliation, and the development of the Iraqi Security Forces to provide permanent security. Kagan proposed that:

American forces, partnered with Iraqi units, will clear high-violence Sunni and mixed Sunni-Shi'a neighbourhoods, primarily on the west side of the city. After those neighbourhoods are cleared, US soldiers and Marines, again partnered with Iraqis, will remain behind to maintain security, reconstitute police forces, and integrate police and Iraqi Army efforts to maintain the population's security. As security is established, reconstruction aid will help to re-establish normal life, bolster employment, and, working through Iraqi officials, strengthen Iraqi local government. Securing the population strengthens the ability of Iraq's central government to exercise its sovereign powers'.[6]

This advice was not supported by the Joint Chiefs of Staff, the commander of CENTCOM, nor the majority of the US national security establishment. But it was accepted by President Bush. In January 2007 Bush halted the Transition Strategy. He announced a 'New Way

Forward' strategy of surging extra troops to protect the population, to create enough security and the space for reconciliation and politics.[7] The withdrawal of US troops from Iraq was halted. Instead five additional brigades would be sent to the country. A new US commander would be appointed: General David Petraeus; as would a new US ambassador to Iraq: Ryan Crocker.

PETRAEUS TAKES COMMAND

With planning for the Surge underway, General David Petraeus was appointed to command MNF-I in February 2007. During his Senate confirmation hearing, Petraeus affirmed that 'making security of the population, particularly in Baghdad, and in partnership with Iraqi forces, [was to be] the focus of the military effort.'[8]

Petraeus suspended the transfer of security from the US to Iraqi forces, but the fielding of new Iraqi security forces continued apace. Petraeus and Ambassador Crocker and their staffs worked together to quickly develop a joint campaign plan. This was but one example of the considerable effort that both made to promote military and civilian collaboration. Their joint leadership fostered much greater military and civilian integration. It was the antithesis of the dysfunctional relationship between Sanchez and Bremer.

'Clear, hold and build' counter-insurgency operations were conducted to protect the Iraqi people. These would become the campaign's centre of gravity. The aim was to secure the broad support of the Iraqi people for the Iraqi government. All military, political and reconstruction activities were to be focused towards the goal of established legitimate national and regional governance. These actions had to take place in partnership with the Iraqi government and the 'transition of security responsibility had to take place at a responsible rate based on conditions and the Government of Iraq's capacity.'[9]

The US would encourage local political accommodations and economic development. This would create enough political space for the Iraqi government to make progress towards the long-term political goals which insurgent violence had prevented. There were to be major cross-cutting initiatives to engage with disenfranchised but reconcilable actors – principally Sunni – to move them away from violence and to reintegrate them into Iraqi political, economic and social development.

Map 8: US forces in central Iraq, early 2007

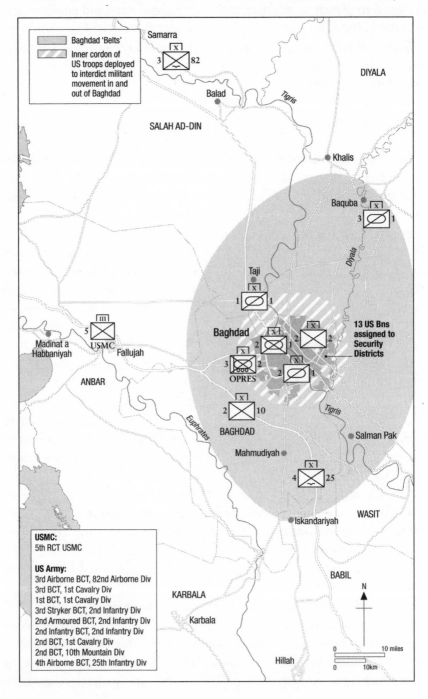

And there was to be renewed emphasis on regional diplomatic initiatives designed to secure an international and regional environment in which Iraq could flourish.

These themes were reflected in a revised mission, developed personally by Petraeus in discussion with President Bush: 'The coalition, in partnership with the government of Iraq, employs integrated political, security, economic and diplomatic means, to help the people of Iraq achieve sustainable security by the summer of 2009.'[10]

Shortly after arriving in Baghdad Petraeus commissioned an independent review of the campaign, forming a Joint Strategic Assessment Team, a multi-disciplinary group of military and civilian experts. The team assessed that there was reducing Iraqi support for the Coalition presence. And that the Iraqi government was increasingly assertive, thus reducing US political and military freedoms. But sectarianism and corruption meant that the government and its ministries were considerably less effective than they needed to be. Enduring success would not be possible without accommodation and reconciliation among the competing sects, factions and parties. Achieving political progress had to be the main effort.

The team identified the key objectives to be achieved: protect the Iraqi population from criminal and extremist organizations; break the cycle of sectarian violence; establish representative and responsive government; ensure effective application of the rule of law; and create sustained economic development. Petraeus had the Joint Campaign Plan adjusted to link the creation of short-term, localized security across Iraq, through sustained Iraq-led security in the mid-term, to longer-term Iraqi national development.

US units were partnered with Iraqi units, constructing Joint Security Stations on key urban terrain. Once the insurgent and militia activity had been reduced and the area broadly stabilized it became possible for the increasingly capable and confident Iraqi forces, supported by embedded US mentors to assume security responsibility for these areas, allowing US units to be redeployed for further clearance operations.

The US threw its political and military weight behind Prime Minister Maliki, President Bush instituting weekly video conferences with him.

NEW CAMPAIGN DESIGN

As the US and multinational commander in Iraq, Petraeus, like Sanchez and Casey carried great responsibilities. Much of his energy was absorbed in dealing with high-level political and military issues with the Iraqi authorities and synchronizing military, political and diplomatic efforts with the US Ambassador. Direction and command of Multinational Corps – Iraq (MNC-I) was the responsibility of the commander of the US Army's III corps, Lieutenant General Ray Odierno, and his HQ.

Odierno had hired Emma Sky, a British development expert, as political advisor. He particularly sought her contrarian viewpoint. Also contributing to Petraeus' and Odierno's thinking was David Kilcullen, a retired Australian Army officer turned counter-insurgency expert.

As the reinforcing US brigades arrived in Iraq, their command groups went through a five-day package at the COIN Centre in Taji, where Kilcullen led seminars and gave presentations on counter-insurgency doctrine and best practice from across Iraq. The divisional commander and MNC-I principal planning and operational staff presented their concept of operations and laid out their expectations in terms of approach. Petraeus gave the closing address to each course.

A key influence of Odierno's thinking was the yield of a 19 December 2006 raid on an Al Qaida safe house.[11] This included the files stored on several computer hard drives. There was also a sketch map, thought to have been produced by Abu Ayyub al-Masri, the new head of Al Qaida in Iraq. The map showed the Al Qaida command structure in Baghdad, with the city divided into sectors, each under a different leader. It also showed that the area that surrounded Baghdad comprised support zones, in which relative sanctuary Al Qaida prepared its car bombs and assembled IEDs, ammunition, weapons and fighters to be sent into Baghdad. This ring of Al Qaida base areas around Baghdad was christened 'the Belts' by the US.

The five additional brigades arrived over the first six months of 2007. Odierno drew up a campaign plan seeking to employ the US forces to best effect, in order to break the cycle of sectarian violence in Baghdad. This involved both the protection of the Iraqi population and defeating firstly Al Qaida and Sunni extremists and then the Shia death squads and special groups.

MAP 9: US FORCES IN CENTRAL IRAQ, JUNE 2007

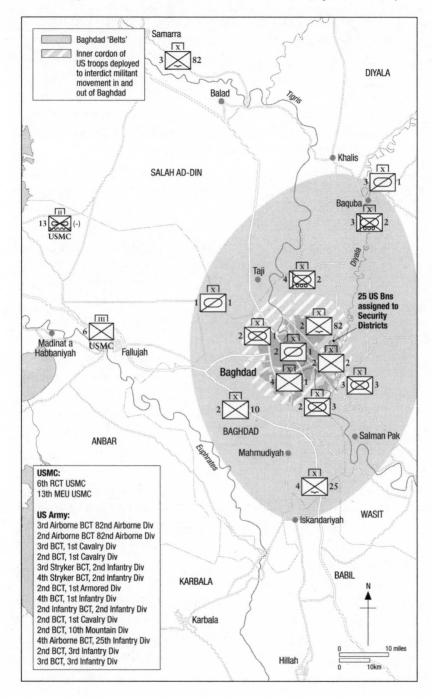

Baghdad 'Belts'

Inner cordon of US troops deployed to interdict militant movement in and out of Baghdad

Samarra

Balad

SALAH AD-DIN

DIYALA

Tigris

Khalis

Baquba

Divala

Taji

25 US Bns assigned to Security Districts

Baghdad

Madinat a Habbaniyah

Fallujah

USMC

ANBAR

BAGHDAD

Salman Pak

Mahmudiyah

WASIT

Iskandariyah

BABIL

KARBALA

N

Karbala

USMC:
6th RCT USMC
13th MEU USMC

US Army:
3rd Airborne BCT 82nd Airborne Div
2nd Airborne BCT 82nd Airborne Div
3rd BCT, 1st Cavalry Div
2nd BCT, 1st Cavalry Div
3rd Stryker BCT, 2nd Infantry Div
4th Stryker BCT, 2nd Infantry Div
2nd BCT, 1st Armored Div
4th BCT, 1st Infantry Div
2nd Infantry BCT, 2nd Infantry Div
2nd BCT, 1st Cavalry Div
2nd BCT, 10th Mountain Div
4th Airborne BCT, 25th Infantry Div
2nd BCT, 3rd Infantry Div
3rd BCT, 3rd Infantry Div

0   10 miles

0   10km

Hillah

First Baghdad would be stabilized. At the same time the Al Qaida and Sunni insurgents in the Belts around Baghdad would be kept off balance by raids. Once Baghdad had been secured, the farmland and Belts around Baghdad would be cleared of insurgents. That having been achieved, the corps would aim to re-establish stability in Diyala Province and its capital Baquba. Subsequent operations would aim to stabilize Mosul.

THE PROBLEM OF SHIA MILITANTS

During 2006 and 2007 there was a bloody contest for influence between Shia political parties, the majority of which had armed militias. Iran played a central role in training, arming and supporting the militias. For this it used the Iranian Revolutionary Guards Corps Quds Force. This is an elite force that conducts extra-territorial warfare around the world. Quds Force is a major security actor, its leader sitting on the Iranian National Security Council. It also appears to have the policy lead for Iran's activity in Lebanon, Syria, Afghanistan and Iraq. In early 2008 an SMS message was sent through a Kurdish intermediary to the US commander in Iraq: 'General Petraeus, you should know that I, Qassim Soleimani, control policy for Iran with respect to Iraq, Lebanon, Gaza, and Afghanistan. The ambassador in Baghdad is a Quds force member. The individual who's going to replace him is a Quds force member.'[12]

Quds Force ran training camps for Shia militants in Iran. It supplied them with money, arms, explosives. Its officers also covertly deployed into Iraq to provide advice with planning and preparation of operations. This had two objectives: both to strengthen the political position of Iraqi Shia groups that were affiliated with Iran and to inflict casualties on the forces of the US and its allies. By the end of 2006, the main weapon used against Coalition forces by Shia militants was the explosively formed projectile/penetrator (EFP). These bombs matched a highly engineered warhead with civilian infrared control technology, optimized against armoured vehicles. The highly machined devices were smuggled across the Iran–Iraq border, taking advantage of the relative lack of Coalition strength on the international boundary, particularly in Maysan Province, which the British had abandoned in 2006.

In early 2007 as US troops focused on Sunni and Al Qaida insurgents, the Shia militants stepped up their attacks. Two groups were particularly vigorous and effective in their attacks on Coalition forces. The first, Kat'aib Hizbullah, was headed by Abu Mahdi al-Muhandis, an Iraqi parliamentarian, who had been indicted for the 1983 bombings of the French and US embassies in Iraq. The other was Asaib Ahl al-Haqq, headed by Qais al-Khazali. Both were closely supported by Quds Force.

Several Quds Force senior officers were seized by US SOF in a January 2007 raid in Kurdistan. Nine days later there was an audacious attack which the US attributed to Asaib Ahl al-Haqq. The target was the Karbala Provincial Joint Co-ordination Centre where 30 US soldiers worked alongside Iraqi police officers. Arriving in a convoy of black sports utility vehicles and wearing US military uniforms, Shia fighters assaulted with small arms and grenades, killing a US soldier, wounding others and taking four soldiers prisoners. Although there was much evidence that many of the Iraqi police at the centre were complicit in the raid, an Iraqi police squad manning a checkpoint between Karbala and the Iranian border became suspicious when the hostage takers sped through the checkpoint. The police set off in hot pursuit. The militants headed for the Iranian border, abandoning their vehicles, US uniforms and the bodies of their four captives who had been shot. It may be that the aim of the operation had been to seize hostages to exchange for the Quds Force officers seized earlier.

As SOF raids continued to target Asaib Ahl al-Haqq, a March 2007 raid captured Qais al-Khazali and his brother Laith al-Khazali, along with a senior officer of Lebanese Hizbullah and several laptops full of documentary evidence, including an after-action report of the Karbala attack. The commander of Quds Force told the Iraqi National Security Advisor that he was willing to order a reduction in Shia militant attacks on US forces, if Qais al-Khazali were released. General Petraeus declined the offer.

Apart from SOF raids, US forces were not contesting JAM-held areas in Baghdad, MNF-I intending to address Shia extremism only after the Sunni–Al Qaida insurgencies were neutralized. Shia strongholds such as Sadr City were not at this stage contested. For most of the Surge, US and Iraqi forces would concentrate on the Sunni–Al Qaida insurgencies, seeing the Shia as a less serious problem, to be dealt with once the Sunni insurgency was neutralized. And the links between Shia political parties, government members and militias with death squads inhibited action against the Shia.

At the beginning of 2007 there were neither the Coalition force levels, nor the Iraqi government will to attack the JAM. So, the main body of the JAM in exclusively Shia areas such as Sadr City were largely left alone. Only after Mosul had been secured would US forces turn their attention to countering the Shia militias in Baghdad, Basra and elsewhere.

In April 2007 Sadrist support for the Maliki government evaporated and Sadr withdrew his ministers from the government, criticising Maliki openly. In August 2007, Maliki agreed a new political coalition with Iranian-backed Shia parties and with the two Kurdish parties, and that significantly strengthened his position and removed his reliance on the Sadrists.

THE BAGHDAD SECURITY PLAN – OPERATION
FARDH AL QANOON (ENFORCING THE LAW)

Lieutenant General Odierno, the commander of MNC-I, had been developing a plan for Baghdad since the end of 2006. It was designed explicitly to make use of the Surge troops to secure the population.[13]

The Baghdad Security Plan's objectives were to secure Baghdad and to clear what were referred to as insurgent 'belts' surrounding the city. These were suburbs and outlying towns which were being used by Sunni insurgents and Al Qaida as base areas, particularly for the projection of suicide car bombs into Baghdad.

Tactical plans began by clearing insurgents from key neighbourhoods. These were then held and secured by Iraqi and Coalition forces at the same time as political and economic development programmes got underway. Unlike many previous US operations, security forces were to remain in the areas they had secured and to work to reduce the threat of violence and intimidation which sat over so much of Iraq since 2003.

This required construction of Joint Security Stations on key urban terrain. These usually contained a company of US troops and were in the middle of Iraqi neighbourhoods. They would be designed from the outset to be shared with Iraqi forces. That this made them more vulnerable was accepted. At times this risk was considerable, and insurgents mounted heavy attacks, attempting to overrun and capture outposts. Many of these attacks saw heavy fighting, but none of them succeeded.

It was necessary to reduce the freedom of movement of both jihadists and Shia death squads. Use was made of natural obstacles including canals. But US forces created their own obstacles. They used great numbers of concrete walls, known to the construction industry as Jersey barriers, to protect Iraqi neighbourhoods from suicide bombs and attacks by death squads. Many long walls of Jersey barriers were built to create 'gated communities', where the only entrances for vehicles and pedestrians were through checkpoints controlled by US and Iraqi troops. This constrained vehicle movement, increasing traffic jams, but also reducing successful car bombings. Even though Prime Minister Maliki was unwilling to allow US forces to directly attack Shia death squads, the building of barriers and checkpoints and higher density of US troops all served to reduce the number of Shia extremist attacks on Sunni neighbourhoods.

US journalist Bing West described the operation as follows:

Inside Baghdad there was a steady rhythm. Everyone could see it coming. Every few weeks the concrete caterpillars advanced across the city, walling people in – or out. You could walk between many openings in the Jersey barriers, but cars were blocked or canalised. While traffic jams increased, car bombings dropped. Every few weeks bulldozers and cranes constructed another joint security station or combat outpost. US and Iraqi forces moved in. At first nothing seemed to change. Then little by little, the residents and the soldiers got to know one another. Cell phone numbers were exchanged. Tips started to come in. Worried about betrayal, insurgents and high-profile criminals moved out. The one hundred odd combat outposts and joint security stations in Baghdad blanketed the city, with the major exceptions of Sadr City, Kadhimiyah and Shula. These were the strongholds of the JAM.[14]

The increase in force levels meant that, for the first time in the city, areas that were cleared by US forces were subsequently held by Iraqi forces. This gained the trust of the population, resulting in improved flow of intelligence from civilians and the Iraqi forces. The increased coalition presence along the Sunni–Shia interfaces in Baghdad helped protect the Sunni population against Shia death squads.

Petraeus also directed US troops to embrace the Anbar Awakening, not only in that province but also in Baghdad. Many Sunni fighters switched sides to join the US attacks on Al Qaida. Groups that the US named Concerned Local Citizens (CLC) manned checkpoints and conducted static guards and 'neighbourhood watch' type tasks, with similar success to that achieved in Anbar. Over 2007 and 2008 US forces recruited, paid, trained and equipped some 103,000 Iraqis, over 80 per cent Sunni, many of whom were former insurgents.

By mid-2007 the US force level had increased significantly. Not only were five additional US brigades, an aviation brigade and a divisional HQ available to III Corps, but the capability of the Iraqi Army had improved considerably. Combined with the increasing capability of the Iraqi Army and increasing numbers of Sunnis changing sides to fight alongside the US, Petraeus and Odierno had the ability not only to manoeuvre at the tactical level but also to implement an operational level design – an offensive campaign plan. For the first time, US forces in Iraq had enough strength to wrest the initiative from their enemies and put them under widespread, as opposed to local pressure. Every former Sunni insurgent who changed sides represented not only a gain for the coalition, but also a loss for the enemy.

The Surge had reversed the process of transition. Initially it was highly controversial in the US, particularly as casualties rose when US forces deployed into contested areas and continued to rise as jihadists and insurgents fought back, resulting in increased US casualties. But the approach worked. American military efforts, fighting alongside the Iraqi security forces, and using money from the Commander's Emergency Response Program, started to win round the people. Sunni insurgents continued to switch from fighting against US troops to fighting alongside the GIs. By the end of the summer, the Baghdad Security Plan was achieving significant effect and US casualties in the city dropped dramatically.

BOOTS ON THE GROUND IN BAGHDAD

In March 2007, 1st Squadron/4th Cavalry Regiment of the 4th Infantry Brigade Combat Team, 1st Infantry Division, a battalion-sized US Army unit, deployed as part of the Surge into Doura, a Sunni neighbourhood in Rashid, at that time the most violent part of Baghdad. The squadron's mission was to conduct 'combat, stability, and support operations in co-ordination with the Iraqi Security Forces to defeat Al Qaeda and irreconcilable extremists, neutralize insurgent and militia groups, and gain the support of the people in order to reduce violence, protect the population in its area of operations'[15]

Lieutenant Colonel James Crider, the commanding officer, faced two types of insurgent fighters: Al Qaida and disgruntled Iraqis. Al Qaida hid among the population and intimidated it, trying to separate US and Iraqi forces from the public by fostering the belief that Doura's desperate economic and social conditions were in some way the fault of the US. The jihadists' message was that without Al Qaida, Shia militias would come into the district to kill innocent Sunnis. As it did elsewhere in Iraq, Al Qaida recruited the young and uneducated and used money from criminal activity to turn insurgency into employment for young men with no prospects.

The Iraqi government reinforced the jihadists' message by failing to provide any essential services, or a functioning legal system, and by doing nothing to counter the perception among Sunnis that it was subject to Iranian influence on all its decisions. With no effective Iraqi governance in the district, Crider was the de facto government.

In its first 30 days in Doura, the squadron was subjected to more than 52 attacks, over 70 per cent of which were IED attacks. Sunni insurgents had unrestricted freedom of movement to place IEDs almost wherever they wanted. Crider soon realized that the enemy was hiding in plain view and that his unit could not detain or kill its way to victory. It was, instead, about the people. He readjusted his plan so that he could re-establish authority over the population and physically isolate the insurgents from the people. The approach was to make contact with the population, protect it and win its support, while seeking to break its connections with the insurgents.

This meant, first and foremost, providing a continuous presence on the streets, so the squadron deployed two platoons on the streets 24 hours a day. Crider notes that this had an immediate effect: 'In the 10 days following this tactic, IED attacks dropped to four – with two of those found prior to detonation – and civilian murders dropped to only one.' The troops began to realize that the longer they were out, the safer they were, not least because their permanent presence meant that it was difficult for the insurgents to plant IEDs.

Initially the squadron had virtually no intelligence to work with. So, it put considerable effort into developing understanding and intelligence from the bottom up. Crider fostered a very active interest in intelligence gathering, encouraging his soldiers to be curious and to speak to everyone that they could. The squadron took photographs of everyone they met. Platoon commanders visited every house, where the people were generally much more open and informative. By the end of June, the squadron had built up almost 40 human intelligence sources, who were willing to talk to US human intelligence teams. Its members gradually gained the confidence of the population. For example, since they knew where people lived, there was no need to mount large arrest operations. Platoons simply went to the target house and detained the suspect.

As with other troubled areas in Baghdad, Jersey barriers were used, with checkpoints for people entering or leaving the area. This restricted the ability of insurgents to move into or through the district, and increased the protection of the people of Doura from attacks by sectarian death squads.

The squadron also set about improving essential services. This included attempting to repair the dilapidated electricity supply, clearing and disposing of rubbish, running clinics and providing micro-loans to stimulate the local economy. They brought fuel into the neighbourhood, thus avoiding insurgent-run price rackets, hired trusted and proven contractors and employed local workers.

Attacks against the squadron reached their height in June but violence quickly reduced in the second half of the year. This was as the final US surge brigade moved into Baghdad, the construction of concrete walls got underway, the small-scale, local development projects started to improve the economic situation and the squadron's approach started to have effect.

The success of the Anbar Awakening was reinforced by the US recruiting Sunni men into the 'Sons of Iraq' US-sponsored militia. Many of those recruited were former Sunni insurgents. A detachment was enlisted in Doura. This directly contributed to a further marked reduction in violence, to the point where in November and December there were no attacks at all.

Also responsible for security of Doura was a detachment of Iraqi National Police. This largely Shia force was thoroughly distrusted by the Sunnis of Doura who saw them as under the influence of Iran. This reinforced Al Qaida's narrative. The squadron ceased its joint patrols of the district with the National Police, assigning them to checkpoints on the edge of Doura. They also assigned Sons of Iraq to the same checkpoints. A degree of grudging accommodation between these former opponents was achieved under US mentorship.

PETRAEUS TAKES STOCK

In the last six months of the squadron's deployment to Doura there were no attacks on the unit. In January 2008, most remarkably, given the security situation less than nine months before, displaced Shia families started to return to Doura, although there was a small increase in violence as a result.

In June 2007, based on his experiences in the first four months of the Surge, Petraeus gave additional direction to his command. Taking the offensive against the insurgents to secure the population would require not only applying tried and tested counter-insurgency principles but also adopting new mindsets. To promote this, he published new guidance:

> As you read, think through, talk about, and ultimately operationalize these points, always remember that in this environment, 'business as usual' will not be good enough. Complacency will kill us; we must *visibly* improve security. A sense of urgency and good situational awareness will also be critical. Troopers on the spot, and their immediate instinctive reactions, will win or lose the perception battle at the local level. Everything we do supports and enables this battle of perceptions, locally here in Iraq and also in the global audience.[16]

He listed ten requirements for the conduct of operations:

a. Secure the people where they sleep. Population security is our primary mission. And achieving population security promises to be an extremely long-term endeavour – a marathon, not a sprint – so focusing on this mission now is essential. This protection must be kept up until the area can be effectively garrisoned and controlled by Iraqi police.

b. Give the people justice and honor. Second only to security, bringing justice to the people and restoring their honor is the key task.

c. Integrate civilian/military efforts — this is an inter-agency, combined arms fight. Close working relationships, mutual respect, and personal interaction between Brigade Combat Team/ Regimental Combat Team commanders and PRT Team Leaders are critical to achieving 'interagency combined arms'.

d. Get out and walk — move mounted, work dismounted. Stop by, don't drive by. Patrol on foot to gain and maintain contact with the population and the enemy.

e. We are in a fight for intelligence — all the time. Intelligence is not a 'product' given to commanders by higher headquarters, but rather something we gather ourselves, through our own operations. Most actionable intelligence will [be] locally produced. Work with what you have.

f. Every unit must advise their Iraqi Security Force partners. Joint Security Stations and Combat Outposts have put coalition and Iraqi forces shoulder-to-shoulder throughout the battlespace. Regardless of mission, any coalition unit operating alongside ISF [Iraqi Security Forces] is performing a mentoring, training, and example-setting role.

g. Include Iraqi Security Forces in your operations at the lowest possible level. Units should build a genuine, field-based partnership with local ISF units: move, live, work, and fight together.

h. Look beyond the IED — get the network that placed it. Over time, units that adopt a pro-active approach to IEDs will degrade enemy networks and push back the IED threat in their area. This will ultimately save more lives than a purely reactive approach.

i. Be first with the truth. Tell the truth, stay in your lane, and get the message out fast. Be forthright and never allow an enemy lie to stand unchallenged.

j. Make the people choose. People in Iraq exercise choice collectively, not just individually; win over local leaders to encourage the community to shift to the side of the new Iraq.[17]

OPERATION *PHANTOM THUNDER* IN BAGHDAD
AND THE BELTS

By now the US Army had four large divisions in Iraq, with the Marine Expeditionary Force responsible for Anbar being equivalent in strength to another division. Although called 'multinational divisions', they were largely multinational in name only, with all their brigades coming from the US Army.

As US troop strength in Iraq increased, Lieutenant General Odierno sought to complement success in Baghdad with clearance of the ring of towns around the city, the so-called 'Belts'. These had been used by Al Qaida and insurgents as base areas, from which attacks were launched into Baghdad, particularly the large vehicle borne suicide bombs that were particularly effective at causing mass civilian casualties.

Launched in June 2007 Operation *Phantom Thunder* sought to exploit the impact of successes in Baghdad and disrupt the Al Qaida–Sunni insurgency both in the Baghdad Belts and in greater depth. It consisted of simultaneous offensives by US forces throughout central Iraq. Multinational Division North cleared the troublesome city of Baquba north-east of Baghdad. Multinational Division Centre cleared the areas east and south-east of Baghdad, including the Al Qaida stronghold in Arab Jabour, south of the capital. The division also disrupted al Qaeda's movement of weapons and fighters by boat along the Tigris River. Multinational Division West cleared Al Qaida sanctuaries west of Baghdad.

As Operation *Phantom Thunder* ended in mid-August, a follow-on III Corps offensive operation, Operation *Phantom Strike,* was launched immediately. It aimed to prevent Al Qaida, Sunni and Shia forces from reconstituting their forces in Baghdad, the Belts, or elsewhere, seeking to destroy the remnants of enemy groups, eliminate any new safe havens and prevent Shia militias from taking over territory once controlled by Al Qaida.

To the effects of the conventional forces of III Corps were added the ever-increasing numbers of raids by SOF on key individuals in Al Qaida's networks. SOF were responsible for most of the deaths or arrests of leaders of both Al Qaida and Shia fighters. Together with the 2007 US troop surge and the rise in the numbers of Sunni fighters changing sides to fight alongside the US forces, the balance shifted in favour of the US and Iraqi forces. This allowed US SOF to devote an increasing proportion of its efforts to countering the danger of armed Shia extremists. Ever closer tactical co-ordination between SOF and US conventional formations paid dividends. This was complemented by a political and military effort to counter Iranian influence and support for these groups.

Concurrently with III Corps offensives, Petraeus and Crocker sought to persuade Maliki and his government to act on behalf of the whole of Iraq, not just their Shia supporters. A major part of this was persuading Maliki to understand the threat that Shia militias, particularly the JAM, posed to the prosperity and stability of the country. The longer the JAM was left to itself, the deeper the roots it put down and the more its racketeering disrupted the legitimate economy. So once Al Qaida had been defeated it would be necessary to confront Shia extremists and militias, politically and militarily. Although MNF-I had identified the eventual need for this, no concrete plans were made.

It was also necessary to influence Maliki to use the Iraqi Army impartially, using the Iraqi Ministry of Defence, rather than Maliki's office, to direct operations. A decisive point was reached in August 2007 when a JAM group in Karbala attacked mosque security guards. The Iraqi Army fought back, and Maliki flew to Karbala and took charge of the security operation, including personally arresting a JAM leader. This action was widely supported by the Iraqi media. Sadr declared a largely meaningless ceasefire, and the Coalition maintained the pressure of SOF operations against the Shia 'special groups' targeting the Coalition.

STATEMENT TO CONGRESS: A DECISIVE POINT

As Petraeus had forecast, the early part of 2007 saw US casualties rise. And many of the initial successes of the surge in summer 2007 were not widely reported by the US media. There was still intense political pressure in Washington, DC, for the US to cut its losses, hand over security leadership to the Iraqis and withdraw.

Admiral William Fallon had taken over from General Abizaid as the commander of CENTCOM in March 2007. Acting on his own initiative against President Bush's strategy, Fallon set about an effort to build the case for ending the surge early. This baffled and exasperated

Petraeus. An increasingly acrimonious dialogue resulted in Petraeus telling Fallon that if the Admiral wanted to change the Presidentially mandated US strategy in Iraq, he should discuss it with the president himself. Fallon backed down.

Over the summer Petraeus, Odierno and the staff in Baghdad began intensive planning for the next stage of the campaign. They had to recommend to the Secretary of Defense and the President when to begin reducing US forces levels and what the pace of reductions should be. Gates was to receive the recommendations at the end of August. Petraeus and Crocker would testify before Congress on 10 September.

Petraeus' assessment was that the surge was working, and it would be wrong to begin to reduce US troop levels too soon. This was challenged by the Joint Chiefs of Staff. At a 27 August briefing by Petraeus they called for an early reduction of forces, to reduce strain on the US military and to allow reconstruction of a strategic reserve. After several difficult conversations, the joint chiefs accepted Petraeus' proposals.

The governance of the US separates powers between the executive, the President and his appointed officials, the judiciary who preside over the courts and the legislature – the two houses of Congress. Congressional powers to approve budgets and appointment of senior officials are normally exercised by Congressional committees. Together with the way committee testimony is covered by the media, testimony in front of them is often a decisive act in US politics.

On 10th September Petraeus appeared before a joint hearing by the House of Representatives Armed Services and Foreign Affairs Committees. It is worth quoting from his testimony:

this is my testimony. Although I have briefed my assessment and recommendations to my chain of command, I wrote this myself, and did not clear it with anyone in the Pentagon, the White House, or Congress ...

As a bottom line up front, the military objectives of the surge are, in large measure, being met. In recent months, in the face of tough enemies in the brutal summer heat of Iraq, coalition and Iraqi security forces have achieved progress in the security arena. Though improvements have been uneven across Iraq, the overall number of security incidents in Iraq, for example, has declined in eight of the past 12 weeks. During this time, ethno-sectarian violence has also been reduced, and the number of overall civilian deaths has declined, though both are clearly still at troubling levels.

The progress is a result of many factors. Coalition and Iraqi forces have dealt significant blows to al-Qaeda-Iraq, and have disrupted Shia militia extremists. Additionally, in a very significant development, we and our Iraqi partners are being assisted by tribes and local citizens who are rejecting extremism and choosing to help secure Iraq. Iraqi security forces have also continued to grow and to shoulder more of the load, albeit slowly and amid continuing concerns about the sectarian tendencies of some elements in their ranks.

Based on all this and on the further progress we believe we can achieve over the next few months, I believe that we will be able to reduce our forces to the pre-surge level of Brigade Combat Teams by next summer, withdrawing one-quarter of our combat brigades by that time, without jeopardizing the security gains that we have fought so hard to achieve.

Beyond that, while noting that the situation in Iraq remains complex, difficult, and sometimes downright frustrating, I also believe that it is possible for us to achieve our objectives in Iraq over time, though doing so will be neither quick nor easy.[18]

Petraeus and Crocker were asked a wide variety of questions. Those from Democrat committee members were often hostile and sometimes very challenging. Under great pressure both witnesses remained calm and sought to carefully explain both their recommendations and the reasoning behind them. The session lasted over six hours.

The next day the Senate Armed Services and Foreign Relations Committees held similar hearings. Senator John Kerry pointed out that this was the first time that a US military commander had come from a war zone to testify since General William Westmoreland, the US commander in Vietnam, had testified in 1967. Many of the questions asked were as uncompromising and tough as those posed the previous day.

Although Petraeus and Crocker had not convinced any of the members of Congress who were opposed to the war to change their minds, they had projected patience, expertise and confidence, tempered with realism. The sessions in both Houses and subsequent engagements with the media tilted the media and political balance sufficiently that President Bush acquired enough political capital to implement Petraeus' recommendations. The testimony was a decisive point in the campaign. Had Petraeus and Crocker been less persuasive, the war would have become even more unpopular and politically toxic and President Bush would have come under even greater pressure to end the Surge early.

By the end of 2007, the results of the Surge were clear. Fragile security, which had been so lacking in Iraq since the invasion of 2003, had returned to Baghdad. By the end of 2007 Baghdad saw a 90 per cent reduction in murders, an 80 per cent fall in attacks on citizens, and a 70 per cent decline in vehicle-borne IEDs. In Anbar the Marines were able to report ten straight months of decreasing incidents and a fall in attacks of some 90 per cent. Iraqi police numbers had more than doubled, from 10,600 to 25,800, with thousands more candidates keen to join. Al Qaida strength was estimated to have fallen from some 12,000 in mid-2007 to 3,500 by December.

As the Surge visibly reduced the threat to the Shias and Iraqi government from Sunni and Al Qaida fighters, so the tectonic plates of Iraqi politics shifted. Muqtada al-Sadr withdrew from the governing coalition in February 2008. Maliki responded by removing restrictions on targeting of active JAM fighters by US SOF and the fledgling Iraqi SOF. But the Iraqi government, Army and Police were reluctant to directly confront the JAM, so US battalion and brigade commanders were limited in the effect they could have against it. The areas around some Shia mosques and shrines were treated as exclusion zones to US troops. Most mainstream JAM chose not to shoot at US troops, but EFPs continued to be emplaced.

THE AUDIT OF WAR

A year after the start of the Surge, transition was in progress on the battlefield, albeit in a different way to that envisaged by the original US strategy. By concentrating enough ground troops, armoured vehicles, attack helicopters and armed drones and visibly putting the increasingly effective Iraqi forces to the fore, the Surge reversed the deteriorating security situation. It restored and reinforced the growing capability and confidence of the Iraqi forces and the confidence of key Iraqi political leaders. It took advantage of the Anbar Awakening and other reconciliation efforts to persuade Sunni insurgents to change sides and become US paid auxiliaries. All these measures greatly improved relations between the Iraqi population, the Iraqi forces and the US military.

The Surge also illustrated the value of a corps HQ to synchronize a multi-divisional land operation. The sequence of MNC-I offensive operations from Operation *Fardh Al Qanoon* in Baghdad, through Operations *Phantom Thunder* and *Phantom Strike*, required tactical synchronization, not only of US and Iraqi ground troops, but also of intelligence, surveillance and all types of air, as well as tactical reconstruction and influence operations. These operations increased in effectiveness as US and Iraqi forces learned from their experience. They were orchestrated by the corps HQ to keep Al Qaida off balance and succeeded in this. At the next level down US division commanders shaped the battle for their brigades, tactically co-ordinated with the Iraqi Security Forces and civilian agencies and reinforced their efforts with assets held at divisional level, not least their powerful combat aviation brigades.

The Surge had seen US forces develop a highly effective approach to clearing areas of insurgents and militias. They combined infantry, armour and engineers to attack insurgent strongholds, complemented by surveillance and precision attack using artillery, missiles, helicopters, fighters and unmanned aerial vehicles, as well as reconstruction, development and information operations. Tanks and other armoured vehicles supported and protected infantry, combat engineers and explosive ordnance disposal (EOD) teams. Firepower from armoured vehicles was invaluable, as was intimate tactical co-operation between armoured vehicles and dismounted infantry.

The more the operation involved Iraqi forces, giving an 'Iraqi face' to build empathy with the civil population, the better. The clearance of Baghdad showed the value of physical barriers in urban areas and permanent checkpoints. US forces also sought to protect the population around them by minimizing collateral damage and civilian casualties. This required restrictive rules of engagement, complemented by precision weapons with relatively low-explosive yields including Hellfire missiles and guided artillery rockets. Bombs dropped from fighter aircraft were still used in extremis, but in ever smaller numbers.

8

Learning under Fire

The struggle to adapt to the unexpected character of the conflicts

Most wars unfold in ways different to those anticipated by the combatants before the hostilities begin. This requires them to adjust their techniques, tactics and capabilities during the war. In his definitive analysis *Military Adaptation, with Fear of Change*, Professor Williamson Murray explains that:

> War is a contest, a complex, interactive duel between two opponents ... which presents the opportunity for the contestants to adapt to their enemy's strategy, operations, and tactical approach. But because it is interactive, both sides have the potential to adapt to the conflict at every level, from the tactical to the strategic. Thus, the problems posed by the battle space do not remain constant; in fact, more often than not, they change with startling rapidity.[1]

Even if the leaders identify that their plans are not working and can then formulate an appropriate response, the financial, organizational, political, cultural and personal costs of adapting can be considerable. Critically re-examining pre-war assumptions seems particularly difficult.

For the much of the war in Iraq the insurgents often seemed to adapt more quickly than Coalition forces. For example, the Iraqi Sunni insurgency was unencumbered by bureaucracy, with the insurgents rapidly developing their capability to deploy IEDs, an adaptation that was accelerated by the transfer of technical knowledge from Lebanese militia Hizbullah and the exploitation of the internet. In this and in many other areas, the US military often seemed to struggle to adapt quickly enough to the unforeseen character of post-conflict stabilization. Adaptations were eventually made, but at a cost in time, money, avoidable casualties and political and military credibility.

This chapter comes in the middle of the narrative of the book, between US operations in Iraq in 2007 and 2008. Of necessity it not only covers developments before 2007, but some activities afterwards. As many of the problems of military adaptation were similar in both Iraq and Afghanistan, it considers both wars together.

PREPARATION AND TRAINING

Unlike World War II, when armies had continuously deployed to operational theatres 'for the duration', Coalition troops were rotated in and out of Iraq. US Army units deployed to Iraq for a year, with British units spending six months in the country. The US and their allies usually granted their troops leave in the middle of their tour of duty. This allowed front-line personnel respite from the danger and challenges of the hostile and austere environment, as well as providing an opportunity to renew links with friends and family.

Each new rotation required incoming troops to be as well prepared for the operation as possible. All the armies deploying to Iraq knew that success in combat engagements depended on thorough training in warfighting and confident and experienced commanders and HQs. These needed to be refreshed before each deployment. And the constant turnover of personnel joining and departing from units meant that teams had to be formed afresh, get to know each other and train together. Not doing so would reduce cohesion and effectiveness, inevitably increasing risks.

Units from most troop-contributing nations therefore underwent a period of preparatory training. As the wars went on this became better organized. For example, the major land warfare training centres in the US and UK were adapted to replicate the Iraq environments, with increasing numbers of simulated small towns and villages. Growing numbers of civilians would be portrayed on these exercises.

Commanders would deploy to the operational area before their troops, spending up to a week learning from the outgoing commanders. Even so new units inevitably had a steep learning curve after they relieved outgoing units. A common problem was training on new equipment. Understandably military and political leaders sought to deploy the maximum capability on operations. But unless equipment was available for pre-tour preparation, troops would not reach full effectiveness in using it before deployment but would have to learn how to do so while on operations. For example, British commanders reported that until a full suite of counter-IED equipment was fielded for pre-tour training, the early period of unit tours saw additional casualties.

GETTING 'LEFT OF BOOM' – ADAPTATION IN THE BATTLE AGAINST IEDS

A vivid illustration of the dynamics of adaptation was the contest between international forces and insurgent bomb makers. In the 20th century's wars between states most army casualties were inflicted by mortars and artillery. Insurgents, guerrillas and terrorists came increasingly to use Improvised Explosive Devices (IEDs), including roadside bombs, suicide devices and improvised rockets and mortars as part of their asymmetric approach. So, security forces sought to counter IEDs. For example, the Northern Ireland conflict between the IRA and the British government from 1970 to 1997 saw ever-increasing sophistication of both terrorist IEDs and army counter-IED capabilities. Even so, half of all British casualties in Northern Ireland were inflicted by just 12 IRA bombs.

These weapons had been almost completely ignored by the proponents of the Revolution in Military Affairs. But in Iraq and Afghanistan insurgents, militias and jihadists found IEDs to be cheap, simple to use and effective. In Iraq in 2003 large amounts of ammunition and explosives were left abandoned by the disbanded Iraqi Army. The vast majority of these stockpiles were not secured by over-stretched Coalition troops. This made it very easy for insurgents to acquire the necessary ingredients for IEDs. Insurgent bomb-making capabilities improved rapidly as information and expertise was rapidly shared over the internet. British explosive ordnance disposal (EOD) experts assessed that Iraqi militias and insurgents learned to make and employ IEDs much faster than did the IRA in the previous century.

By August 2003, US casualties in Iraq from IEDs had overtaken those from small arms and rocket-propelled grenades. By the end of the year, two-thirds of US deaths were caused by IEDs. They were extensively used to cause casualties, reinforce perceptions of instability and erode national political will.

In southern Iraq, the British forces had the advantage of extensive experience countering IEDs in Northern Ireland, and were able to use their existing capabilities, such as EOD teams and specialist intelligence units as a basis for their approach. This included a critical mass of engineer search teams, specifically trained for high-risk environments, and a cadre of very experienced EOD operators. They had also applied considerable resources to jamming the radio command links that the Irish Republican Army (IRA) had used to set off roadside bombs and had a base of radio jammers, with scientific and industrial support. For many years this had been a well-concealed British equivalent of a US 'black programme', where the British had established a global lead. It had been one of the UK's most closely guarded military technology secrets.

US forces did not have the benefit of this experience, but the problem was quickly recognized by their commanders in Iraq. At the end of 2003, CENTCOM commander General John Abizaid wrote to Rumsfeld to ask him to commission a major cross-governmental response to the IED threat, of a similar scale to the World War II Manhattan Project to develop the atomic bomb. But the Pentagon's initial response was slow and under-resourced. Efforts conspicuously failed to match the scale of effort that Abizaid had requested.

Across both wars, approximately 70 per cent of US, Coalition and NATO casualties were inflicted by IEDs. This had the strategic effect of helping to erode public support for these wars. By the end of the decade senior US officers were calling the IED threat 'the new artillery'. So, protection against IEDs became of ever-increasing importance. Billions of dollars were spent on efforts to detect and neutralize IEDs and in procuring protected vehicles.

Initially US and Coalition forces struggled to match the threat. In the absence of more effective measures, great effort was put into detecting the devices before they were initiated. This ranged from handheld detectors through sniffer dogs to sophisticated searching techniques and equipment. And tactics were adjusted to make it more difficult for insurgents to fire their bombs. But unless there were enough troops to dominate the ground and deter emplacement of IEDs, the initiative remained with the insurgents. Between 2003 and 2007, these conditions usually did not apply. US troops in Iraq resorted to desperate expedients. Most prominent of these was the addition of metal plates, some of which were obtained from scrap yards and by cannibalizing the carcasses of vehicles damaged or destroyed in previous attacks. In other cases, Kevlar material expropriated from spare body was fixed to the outside of the cabs of trucks, adding protection to soft-skinned trucks and Humvees.

From the outset of post-conflict operations in Iraq, Donald Rumsfeld displayed great reluctance to accept that that security in Iraq was rapidly becoming much worse than he had anticipated. The protection of US Humvees and trucks came to symbolize this. Whilst the front-line units of US heavy divisions and brigades had large numbers of armoured vehicles, these were absent from the 82nd and 101st Airborne divisions and from the great majority of combat service support and logistic units. All their vehicles were 'soft skinned', that is without any armoured protection at all. As roadside bomb attacks increased throughout 2003, these units suffered far greater casualties from bomb attacks than did units with armoured vehicles. Since the outbreak of the insurgency in mid-2003, many logistic and supporting units that had no armoured vehicles had improvised armour for their Humvees and trucks by welding additional metal onto the sides and bellies of the vehicles. Some logistic units had even re-purposed their supply trucks as 'gun-trucks', where additional armour was complemented by machine-gun positions. These vehicles were not used in their primary functions, but as improvised armoured vehicle escorts.

An incident that was captured by a television crew and broadcast worldwide rapidly acquired notoriety. 8 December 2004 saw Rumsfeld visit Camp Buhring, a US staging area in Kuwait. Here incoming US Army National Guard units were preparing to deploy into Iraq. At a 'town hall meeting' with the troops, Specialist Thomas Wilson told Rumsfeld that soldiers in his unit had been scavenging local landfills and scrap yards for scrap metal to weld to their vehicles for additional protection. 'Why don't we have those resources readily available to us?' he asked, supported by cheers and clapping from his comrades. Rumsfeld's reply that the military was providing additional armour as soon as possible clearly failed to convince the troops. A subsequent question asked what Rumsfeld and the Army were doing 'to address shortages and antiquated equipment'.

The troops murmured their support. 'Now settle down, settle down,' Rumsfeld said. 'Hell, I'm an old man, it's early in the morning and I'm gathering my thoughts here.' He went on to say that all organizations had equipment, materials and spare parts of different vintages, but he expressed confidence that Army leaders were assigning the newest and best equipment to the troops headed for combat who needed it most. But he warned that equipment shortages would probably continue to bedevil some American forces entering combat zones like Iraq: 'You go to war with the army you have, not the army you might want or wish to have at a later time'. He went on to say that adding more armour to vehicles did not make them impervious to enemy attack. 'If you think about it, you can have all the armour in the world on a tank and a tank can be blown up,' he said. 'And you can have an up-armoured Humvee and it can be blown up.'[2]

Rumsfeld was perfectly correct to explain that for short notice operations such as the invasions of Afghanistan and Iraq the US forces had to employ the weapons and equipment they had previously acquired. But most of the US troops serving in Iraq, or preparing to go there, found his response deeply unconvincing, especially the mobilized citizen soldiers of the National Guard and Army and Marine Corps reserves. This incident was a major blow to Rumsfeld's credibility with the US military.

Although many armoured HMMWVs were fielded by US forces in 2004, they were in turn quickly overmatched by improved insurgent IEDs and it was not until November 2006 that the requirement was identified for the more heavily armoured mine-resistant ambush protected (MRAP) vehicle.

By the end of 2005 a common counter-IED approach was being applied across Iraq. This had three 'lines of operation': defeat the device, attack the network and train the force. All three needed to be integrated by rapid information exchange across the force, initiating counter-action and passing direction and information back down the chain of command. As the British had learned in Northern Ireland, this could not be delegated to specialists, but had to be core business of commanders at all levels.

By 2006, a 12-strong US Joint IED Defeat Task Force had evolved into the Joint IED Defeat Organization (JIEDDO) with several thousand dedicated government, military and contract personnel. Between 2006 and 2010 the organization spent $16.6 billion. Countering the new threats not only required an array of armoured vehicles, electronic jammers and remote-controlled robots; it also required close co-operation between intelligence and operations staff, industry and scientists (both at research establishments and forward deployed into operational HQs). This placed considerable demands on the flexibility and agility of armies, military procurement bodies and defence ministries of all the coalition nations. Not all rose to the challenge quickly enough.

The large number of potential ways of initiating bombs Iraq meant that it could often take six to 12 months between emergence of a new bomb technology threat and the point where enough technical countermeasures were being fielded by properly trained troops. In the interim, the deployed force had to adjust their tactics as best they could in the meantime.

So, an enormous effort was put into physical protection. Greatly improved personal body armour was fielded, albeit of increased weight, thus reducing the agility and endurance of infantry on the ground. Armoured vehicles were fitted with additional armour and electronic counter-measures to jam radio command links to roadside bombs. This increased size and weight: for example the UK Warrior fighting vehicle increased from 27 to 40 tons.

Moving troops and supplies by air partially circumvented the threat, although some helicopters and transport aircraft struck IEDs that insurgents had placed on field landing sites. Many countries bought more helicopters and in Afghanistan and on Iraq's borders there was a revival in the supply of isolated units by parachute, but not even the US forces had enough helicopters to move more than a proportion of troops and supplies by air. So previously 'soft skinned' logistic vehicles also had armour and jammers added.

Considerable effort was also devoted to neutralizing devices that were detected before detonation or seized in search operations. Although devices could be often simply destroyed with explosives, recovering them for forensic analysis improved intelligence. Much effort was put into developing the specialist equipment used by EOD operators.

Defensive measures were complemented by intelligence gathering to identify insurgents involved in IED construction and supply, as well as those planning, emplacing and operating the devices. These were then attacked, to disrupt the network. Airborne surveillance, particularly from long endurance manned and unmanned aircraft, proved particularly useful in identifying insurgent teams planting devices. These could then be attacked or, in the case of those making or moving bombs, followed.

Although precision weapons could be used to attack bomb makers or people emplacing the devices, it was preferable to detain insurgents and seize bomb-making material and other evidence that could be exploited to better develop further intelligence. Such operations were often, but not exclusively, conducted by special forces, but depended on having enough intelligence surveillance and reconnaissance capabilities.

No less important was training and preparing troops before they deployed. This relied on rapid passage of information between the operational theatre and those training at home. It also required troops to be able to train on the specialist counter-IED equipment they would employ in theatre. Often there was insufficient equipment for pre-operational training, resulting in troops learning on the job.

BETTER UNDERSTANDING AND INTELLIGENCE

Before it disintegrated in the early 1990s, Yugoslavia been a modern state with a largely European outlook, and this reduced the cultural gap between NATO forces and the civilian population of Bosnia and Kosovo. There was a much greater cultural gap between US and NATO forces and the populations of Iraq and Afghanistan. Both states had complex ethno-sectarian frictions, volatile political dynamics and troubled relations with neighbouring states. In both countries it took too long for international actors to understand this.

This had implications from grand strategic to tactical level. An example was the US and UK forces' use of sniffer dogs for searching Iraqi homes. This had worked in Bosnia and Kosovo, but Iraqi Muslims considered that bringing such unclean beasts into their homes was deeply humiliating. This aggravated resentment. International forces in Iraq and Afghanistan were not only less culturally aware than they should have been, but also inadvertently increased humiliation and resentment amongst the populations of both countries.

Initially, international forces had insufficient linguists and translators. Hiring local Iraqis who spoke English was a practical expedient, but such people could not be security vetted and were highly vulnerable to intimidation. It took some years before enough vetted national military and civilian personnel were recruited and trained. The US, UK and other armies gradually incorporated cultural factors into their pre-tour preparation and training. Specialist cultural advisors were deployed, in some cases down to battalion level and the UK formed a specialist unit of such experts.[3]

The US Army identified a need for divisions and brigades to achieve a better, more granular understanding of the Iraqi people in their areas and their power structures, key relationships, customs and attitudes. Specialist human terrain teams were formed to achieve this, with anthropologists and social scientists recruited to provide their expert skills. These were also successfully employed in Afghanistan.

Well before 2001 many western forces had recognized that fully exploiting new technology required integrating the previous separate capabilities of intelligence, surveillance, target acquisition and reconnaissance, to reduce the time between detecting targets and engaging them. All this was to be enabled by high-technology communications systems and was at the core of the arguments put forward by the advocates of the Revolution in Military Affairs (RMA).

There was nothing new about this. These principles had been at the core of the British air defence system that won the Battle of Britain in 1940. The Iraq and Afghan wars showed that whilst the Revolution in Military Affairs advocates had been correct about the centrality of Intelligence, Surveillance, Target Acquisition and Reconnaissance, stabilization operations required considerable adaptation, especially the re-learning of intelligence lessons from previous COIN campaigns.

In September 2001 the US and its allies had insufficient accurate intelligence on Afghanistan, the Taliban and Al Qaida. This was a reflection in reductions in national strategic intelligence capability over the decade since the end of the Cold War. For example, between 1990 and 2001 both the US CIA and UK Secret Intelligence Service (SIS) reduced personnel numbers by 25 per cent.[4]

This gap was alleviated by assistance from Russia and near-total concentration of US civilian and military intelligence assets on the country. But it was only when CIA and SOF teams linked up with warlords and their militias on the ground that sufficient understanding of the Northern Alliance was achieved to allow co-ordination of US air strikes with attacks by opposition ground troops. And the difficulties experienced in Operation *Anaconda*, in early 2002, highlighted the ease with which fighters who know their business could conceal themselves from aerial observation

In 2002, most US, UK and Australian national intelligence capabilities were switched from Afghanistan, to support the planning of the attack on Iraq. Planners were also able to take advantage of the information about Iraqi air defences gathered during the previous 12 years of US and UK air operations policing the no-fly zones over northern and southern Iraq. An adequate high-level intelligence picture of Iraqi conventional forces was assembled. But human intelligence (HUMINT) was less well developed, in part because of the ever-present fear that Saddam Hussein's police state imposed on Iraqi officials and military officers.

Unsurprisingly, intelligence for the air campaign over Iraq was generally adequate and contributed to reduction of civilian casualties and collateral damage. There were some notable tactical intelligence successes, such as the British identification of the location and time of a Baath Party meeting in Basra. This was successfully attacked by a precision bomb, resulting in the Iraqi defences of the city losing their cohesion.[5] But US ground troops advancing towards Baghdad were often surprised by undetected Iraqi conventional ground troops.[6] And unexpectedly heavy Iraqi air defences contributed to the failure of a deep strike attack by a US Army aviation brigade. Attacks by Fedayeen Saddam irregular forces in civilian vehicles and clothes came as a complete surprise to the US military from the Pentagon downwards.

Initially Coalition forces conducting stabilization operations found acquiring intelligence more difficult. The expensive high-technology ISTAR systems that had worked so well against Iraqi conventional forces were of little use against irregulars who blended into the civilian population.

Previous counter-insurgency campaigns had shown that a major source of intelligence was the local population – provided that security forces gained their trust and confidence. This required expanding and decentralizing intelligence staff. As this lesson was rediscovered and applied, intelligence staffs greatly increased at all levels from corps to company and even platoon level. The British found that developing adequate ISTAR capability for their forces in Afghanistan not only required the acquisition of more collection systems, analysts and the bandwidth to connect them, but also needed a change of approach. Previously British ISTAR capability had tended to be acquired and directed in a top down fashion. To maximize ISTAR support to COIN, this approach had to be changed by 'inverting the pyramid', prioritising tactical support to tactical forces.[7]

This was accompanied by the use of opinion polling. When conducted by Afghan civilian companies, polling could reveal attitudes and opinions that Afghans would not easily share with international troops. Combined with sophisticated analytical tools developed by the international polling industry, these could provide useful indicators of the attitudes of Afghan civilians.

Throughout both wars, global usage of the internet and social media was of rapidly increasing importance. The information carried, and opinions expressed, could provide useful insight into the thinking of the civilian population. And monitoring traffic on media such as Twitter could provide near-real-time information about security incidents. By mid-2013 the ISAF Joint Command HQ in Kabul was doing this.[8]

There were considerable improvements in intelligence collection and analysis. This included a massive expansion in intelligence gathering from airborne systems. Both manned and unmanned aircraft played a role in this as did airborne radar.

This was complemented by fitting surveillance systems to masts and balloons above bases. Commanders and their intelligence staffs became increasingly connected to secure networks, consuming ever-greater amounts of bandwidth. Increasing amounts of computer processing power allowed new ways of analysing intelligence and surveillance data. Examples included the use of civilian law enforcement software to map insurgent networks and more sophisticated ways of fusing data, to offer greater insights in new ways.[9]

As the intelligence architecture in both theatres became better developed and more mature, its ability to understand insurgent networks and generate intelligence sufficient to attack key individuals greatly improved. There was ever-increasing integration of tactical intelligence with national strategic intelligence capabilities. For example, by 2008 US divisions in Iraq had intelligence fusion centres, where the tactical intelligence they had developed was combined with US national signals intelligence. And the British in Basra and Helmand developed the concept of the Operational Intelligence Support Group which provided tactical HQs with national strategic intelligence. All this depended on the highest degree of co-operation between deployed forces and the full range of military and civilian intelligence agencies.

As well as exploiting captured or detained personnel, it was necessary to exploit material seized from insurgents. This had always included documents, but now included mobile phones, video recordings, computers and hard drives. So, the forensic investigative skills that had become part of modern police investigations became essential to military intelligence. This included the US rapidly deploying biometric systems into the field to provide rapid identification of civilians for patrols, checkpoints and arrest operations.

None of this adaptation was smooth and easy. Whilst US and UK SOF had been applying these principles to find war criminals in the Balkans and terrorists elsewhere, US Army conventional forces had little background in counter-insurgency and even less in the necessary intelligence capabilities. And whilst the British had relevant experience from colonial campaigns and Northern Ireland, the teaching of the necessary skills had ceased some years before. In a number of important intelligence and surveillance capabilities they were slower than the US to adapt, for example fielding unmanned aerial vehicles more slowly and not managing to field an adequate tactical intelligence database before they withdrew from Iraq.

PRISONERS AND DETAINEES – PARTIAL RECOVERY FROM SELF-INFLICTED DISASTER

In previous counter-insurgency campaigns prisoners and detainees had provided valuable intelligence. US General Stanley McChrystal explained that:

> detainees can explain the meaning of what we see from other intelligence sources and can let us step into the mechanics, mind-set and weaknesses of the enemy organisations. Detainees, whether they talk out of fear, because they think it's pointless not to, or because their egos can be manipulated and played, can reveal

not just what the enemy thinks, but how he thinks and why he fights ... Detainee operations were as difficult and sensitive as they were vital.[10]

Detaining suspected insurgents was also an important way of reducing threats without killing people. But in the early years of both wars US and UK troops abused Iraqis and Afghans that they had detained. Some were murdered. Images of these abuses were quickly propagated by global media, causing immense damage to the perceived legitimacy of US and British forces, not only in Iraq and the Muslim world, but globally. The abuses acted as a recruiting sergeant for jihadists. Investigations revealed that the abuses committed by US troops at Abu Ghraib and by British troops in southern Iraq had been committed by inadequately trained and supervised guards. They were the result of insufficient resources, insufficient training, poor planning, neglect of basic principles and poor leadership. In both armies there had been insufficient attention by senior leadership. This cascaded down the chain of command, resulting in inadequate resources and attention being dedicated to detention. Weaknesses in strategic leadership had led to tactical failures, that rebounded to negative strategic effect.

An independent inquiry into the mistreatment of detainees by British troops in 2013 concluded that 'historic failures to maintain adequate prisoner of war handling and interrogation doctrine led directly to inadequate prisoner of war handling guidance being issued in the lead up to the warfighting phase'.[11] British planning for prisoner handling had begun too late.

Why had the US and British Armies failed to adequately prepare for this? Their negligence may have partly resulted from there being little requirement to take and handle prisoners between 1991 and 2003. For example, Iraqi prisoners taken in Operation *Desert Storm* had been quickly released. During UN and NATO operations in Bosnia and Kosovo international forces were never at war with the local forces, so few prisoners were detained. Those taken were rapidly released. Indicted war criminals detained by NATO troops were quickly passed to the detention facility at the International War Crimes Tribunal in the Hague. So, the requirement for US, UK and NATO forces to hold prisoners had been minimal.

Both armies and their senior leadership appeared to have had collectively forgotten the potential intelligence value of prisoners – provided they were properly and humanely handled.

General McChrystal recognized that 'detainee operations were as difficult and sensitive as they were vital,' but:

> the US had not institutionalised the policies or devoted the resources required to professionalize detention operations … I was one of the leaders who lacked experience in detainee custody and exploitation. I had studied history and understood the theory but had never done anything remotely like running a prison. My peers and subordinates were similarly positioned.[12]

Even before the Abu Ghraib revelation, McChrystal began taking measures to improve the detention facility, its leadership and the mindset of the force, particularly in using 'mature seasoned leaders' rather than augmentation personnel from outside JSOC, to run the detention operation.

Once these incidents came to light both countries rapidly initiated remedial action. For example, the US in both Iraq and Afghanistan found it necessary to greatly increase the resources allocated to detention facilities. As important was appointing a senior officer to command 'detainee operations' and measures taken to increase the number of properly trained interrogators. This could not be done quickly, but as the quantity and quality of interrogators increased in both countries, so did the flow of actionable intelligence.

Contrary to images portrayed by most film and television dramas, getting information from detainees depends on properly trained and qualified interrogators and expert linguists. And prisoner guard forces must be properly trained and led. Greatly increased leadership and management effort was required to ensure that the Coalition detention facilities and regime met the higher standards required by understandably nervous governments.

The vast majority of those detained by international forces in Iraq and Afghanistan were held in US detention facilities. By mid-2007, the US was detaining over 27,000 people in Iraq alone. There were regular releases of prisoners, but these were largely based on a 'first in, first out' principle. This resulted in Coalition forces arresting some insurgents on multiple occasions, christened 'catch and release' by the troops.

An active Al Qaida insurgency in Camp Bucca, the main US detention facility, saw ever-increasing attacks on US guards and other violent non-co-operation. After a riot by 10,000 detainees nearly succeeded in becoming a mass breakout, the US decided that this needed to be tackled by 'counter-insurgency operations inside the wire'.

Although the minimum legal requirements were being met at Camp Bucca, the facilities had become recruiting grounds for the insurgents. The additional arrests of Al Qaida operatives being made by the Surge and increasing SOF operations meant that greater numbers of hard-core Al Qaida insurgents were being detained. There was no segregation of hard-core activists from the general body of detainees. This allowed insurgents to impose their will on other prisoners by violence, including murders. Al Qaida were actively recruiting from the detainee population and conducting indoctrination and training.

This required not only an improved guard force, but also separating out the hard-core irreconcilable insurgents from the rest of the prison population. Complementary efforts were made to develop a robust and transparent process to allow release of prisoners who were assessed to no longer pose a threat. A rehabilitation and re-integration scheme was introduced. It included paid work for 'reconcilable prisoners' and literacy programmes. Graduates of the rehabilitation programme at Camp Bucca had a recidivism rate of less than one per cent.

ROBERT GATES' WAR ON THE PENTAGON[13]

Donald Rumsfeld's replacement as US Defense Secretary, Robert Gates, was sworn into office on 18 December 2006. Gates came with considerable national security experience, having been Director of the CIA. He also came from running a large university, Texas Agricultural and Mechanical University.

Before he assumed the post, he had formed the view that the US Army and US Marine Corps were over-stretched by the war and would need to increase in size. These objectives he was able to achieve relatively quickly.

Gates brought a fresh mind to the Pentagon. When he arrived, the strategic decision to mount the Iraq Surge had already been made by

President Bush. Gates saw an important role for himself in helping
to sustain political support for the US efforts in Iraq and Afghanistan
and devoted much time and effort into handling Congress. He
also determined to do everything he could to improve the military
capabilities that the US was deploying to both wars. He quickly
formed the view that not enough progress was being made. During
the first half of both wars US commanders clearly saw the need to
improve their counter-IED and aerial surveillance capabilities. But
despite repeated requests technical adaptations were not reaching US
troops in Iraq and Afghanistan quickly enough. Gates saw considerable
institutional resistance in some parts of the Pentagon, as was reflected
in an initial reluctance to buy additional protected vehicles for land
operations. But within a short time of his arrival, he assessed that
success in Iraq:

> would require a sense of total commitment in the Department of
> Defense that I was staggered to learn did not exist ....
>
> Even though the nation was waging two wars, neither of which we
> were winning, life in the Pentagon was largely business as usual when
> I arrived ... there was no one of high rank in Defense whose specific
> job it was to ensure that the commanders and troops in the field had
> what they needed.
>
> There never was intentional neglect of the troops and their well-
> being. There was however, a toxic mix of flawed assumptions about
> the wars themselves; a risk-averse bureaucracy; budgetary decisions
> made in isolation from the battlefield; Army, Navy and Air Force
> focus in Washington on the routine budget process and protecting
> dollars for future programmes; a White House unaware of the needs
> of the troops and disinclined to pay much attention to the handful
> of members of Congress who pointed to these needs; and a Congress
> by and large so focused on the politics of the war in Iraq that it was
> asleep at the wheel or simply too pusillanimous when it came to the
> needs of the troops.[14]

Gates decided that the size, complexity and cultural inertia of the
Pentagon bureaucracy meant that it would only exhibit the necessary
speed and drive if it was given firm top-down direction and leadership
by the Secretary of Defense, the service chiefs and top civilian

officials. A major reason for this institutional friction and inertia was an apparent reluctance of the Pentagon and some service chiefs to shift US armed forces' funding and management effort away from acquiring the weapons and equipment planned for future conventional state versus state conflicts. The mechanisms for funding the US armed forces, where Congress and the four individual services, rather than the Pentagon, controlled equipment budgets, provided opportunities for those officials who preferred business as usual to create friction and delays.

Gates decided that he needed to apply personal leadership and energy to accelerate the development, production and deployment of the necessary capabilities. To achieve this, Gates had to overcome entrenched interests and the Pentagon bureaucracy. He had to act to personally inject greater urgency into the Pentagon to get it to prioritize fielding the capabilities that were so urgently needed in Iraq and Afghanistan in order to increase tactical success and reduce avoidable casualties. He told the senior military and civilian leaders working for him that business as usual was not meeting the urgent needs of operational commanders and troops in the field and that the leadership of the Pentagon and US armed forces would need to apply a sense of urgency and a 'willingness to break china'.

Gates initially focused on the MRAP vehicle, discovering that although some MRAPs had been funded and were being delivered to the US Army and Marine Corps, numbers ordered were limited, as neither service wanted to divert funds from its future vehicle programme. To create greater momentum and set up a crash programme to buy as many vehicles as were needed, Gates had to issue a directive to the Pentagon making the MRAP the US military's highest priority. He also set up a special task force in the Pentagon that reported to him every two weeks. This had the required effect. By 2011 over 20,000 of these MRAP-type vehicles had been acquired by US forces at an estimated cost of $35 billion.

As the MRAPs were fielded, American casualties from roadside bombs significantly reduced. In Afghanistan the Taliban responded by increasing the size of their bombs. And MRAPs offered no protection for the increasing number of US soldiers on foot patrol. These included quadruple amputees who had lost all their limbs in IED attacks. Gates visited the first two of these in hospital. He determined that the US forces needed to do better at countering IEDs. Whilst a wide range of new equipment was being developed, the effort was insufficiently co-ordinated, with no master integrator of counter-IED capabilities; intelligence collection was insufficiently focused on the IED threat; and information and intelligence was not being shared effectively enough between the different US military commands in Afghanistan.

Gates thought this showed that the Pentagon was not properly structured to support a constantly changing battlefield or to fight an agile enemy. He set up a special Pentagon task force to produce a comprehensive plan to improve counter-IED capability. It did precisely this, spending $3.5 million on countering the IED threat in Iraq.

Gates found himself similarly frustrated with the US Air Force's attitude to improving airborne ISR capabilities. There appeared to be unhelpful cultural attitudes in the service. For example, it exhibited considerable institutional unwillingness to shift resources and pilots from manned aircraft to unmanned aerial vehicles (UAVs). Whilst it was extremely capable of using its extensive air transport fleet to rapidly deploy troops to operations and it was delighted to be providing close air support whenever asked, it was not doing all it could to grow its fleet of Predator and Reaper drones, nor to support and grow the specialist crews so necessary to operate the aircraft. Gates had to compel the US Air Force to increase its fleet of Predator and Reaper drones. Again, he had to resort to setting up a special task force reporting direct to him. Gates approved initiatives costing $2.6 billion to improve airborne capability. These included not only growing drone capabilities, but also fielding 50 manned intelligence, surveillance and reconnaissance (ISR) aircraft, the MC12 Liberty. These were to prove extremely useful in detecting insurgent IEDs and the networks that supported them.

In October 2008, President Bush paid his final visit to the Pentagon, to meet Gates and the Joint Chiefs of Staff. They took stock of how the US forces had changed in the seven years since 9/11. The Army chief, General Casey, explained that the Army had moved from having eight UAVs in 2003 to a fleet of 1,700 in Iraq alone. Meanwhile the US Air Force was *planning* to move from 300 UAV pilots to 1,100.[15] This was a vivid illustration of how it had displayed less institutional momentum to embrace the UAV than the Army.

Gates later observed that these and other initiatives that that he personally championed were required:

> because people were stuck in the old way of doing business, it's been like pulling teeth ....
>
> People at lower levels had good ideas, but they had an impossible task in breaking through the Bureaucracy, being heard and taken seriously. The military too often stifled younger officers and sometimes more senior ones who challenged current practices.
>
> Secretary Rumsfeld once famously told a soldier that you go to the war with the army you have, which is absolutely true. But I would add that you damn well should move as fast as possible to get the army you need. That was the crux of my war with the Pentagon.

THE AUDIT OF WAR

Robert Gates proved much more successful than Donald Rumsfeld in forcing the Pentagon and its bureaucracy to adapt to the Iraq and Afghan wars. He had to firmly insist that 'business as usual approaches' were too slow and force powerful organizations, like the US Air Force, to move outside its comfort zones by prioritizing new capabilities at the expense of traditional ones. His example and the other examples in this chapter show that adaptation in war requires senior political and military leaders to provide energy, encouragement and enthusiasm to implement necessary changes. Bottom-up adaptations could not succeed without the engagement, encouragement and enthusiasm of unit leaders. Top-down adaptation worked best when it was driven by the most senior leaders. Although technology can assist with adaptation, the key challenges for adaptation are leadership, culture, and mental and organizational agility.

9

The Battles for Basra

Britain's near-defeat in southern Iraq

The British Army that entered Iraq in 2003 had a 30-year record of operational successes. This included its role in the Northern Ireland conflict, leading the 1979–80 Commonwealth monitoring mission that played a key role in helping a peaceful transition from war-torn Rhodesia to a peaceful Zimbabwe, the Falklands War, Operation *Desert Storm*, Bosnia, Kosovo, East Timor, Sierra Leone, Macedonia and setting up ISAF in Kabul in 2001–02. All these operations were supported by Parliament, the public and the media.

At the end of 2003 the British Army, other armed forces and the Ministry of Defence (MoD) were basking in the warm glow of recent success. But British military leaders were conveniently ignoring that in all these cases enemy ground troops were usually of lower quality than the British, mostly unwilling to stand and fight and overmatched by NATO and British all-arms and joint warfighting capabilities. In retrospect, operational success had become the mother of complacency.

But by 2009, as British troops withdrew from Iraq, their reputation and that of the MoD were damaged with the British people and media and with the US military. And their self-confidence was dented. This reflected the increasing unpopularity of the war. It also reflected the shock of fighting opponents who stood and fought and who at the tactical level inflicted more casualties than enemies in previous campaigns. It was a long time since the British had conducted stabilization or counter-insurgency operations where the bulk of the host country's elected politicians had opposed their presence. And it was the first time since the 1956 Suez campaign that a war had been so controversial in the UK. With every British casualty its unpopularity increased, and the credibility of Prime Minister Blair decreased.

The war had proved much more challenging than any the British Army had taken part in since the Korean War, 50 years earlier. There were many in the UK and US media and in the British Army itself who considered that the British had failed in Basra and from a position of weakness had been forced to negotiate a humiliating 'accommodation' with Shia militia who had forced the British out of Basra. And when the Iraqi Army counter-attacked to regain control of the city, it was American troops, not British forces, who played the greater role in turning early tactical defeat into a decisive victory. British military credibility was damaged both with the US and with Iraqi Prime Minister Maliki and British military self-confidence was greatly diminished.

How had this occurred? There is copious evidence. Two internal British Army reports on the war were leaked and the third, written by this author, was eventually declassified, as was an internal UK MoD report on its role in the war.

An independent inquiry into Britain's role in the war was commissioned by Blair's successor, Gordon Brown.[1] The Iraq Inquiry was an exhaustive analysis of high-level government decision making, comprehensively tracking the paper and email trail of advice and assessments flowing into the Prime Minister's office at Number 10 Downing Street and to the Cabinet Office, the central co-ordinating machinery of British government. It studied the relevant decisions made in Number 10 and the extent to which the decisions were implemented. The resulting report also provides analyses of decision making in the key government departments: the Foreign and Commonwealth Office (FCO), the Ministry of Defence (MoD) and the Department for International Development (DfID).

Chaired by former senior civil servant Sir John Chilcot, the inquiry reported almost seven years after it was commissioned. Chilcot never adequately explained why the inquiry lasted a year longer than the British war in Iraq. This was a source of considerable frustration to many British anti-war activists. Some parents of British servicemen killed were very disappointed that the inquiry neither declared the war illegal nor recommended the arrest of Tony Blair on war crimes charges.

The inquiry identified that prior to the invasion, the British government had an 'ingrained belief' that Iraq possessed some weapons of mass destruction. This gave rise to flawed assessments that were never adequately tested, challenged or probed. It particularly criticized both the chairman of the Joint Intelligence Committee and the head of the British Secret Intelligence Service for presenting weak intelligence concerning Iraq's weapons of mass destruction with excessive certainty. It assesses that 'the circumstances in which it was decided that there was a legal basis for UK military action were far from satisfactory'.[2]

In the run-up to the war Blair had committed the UK to help the Iraqi people build a new united Iraq at peace with itself and its neighbours, in which its people should enjoy security, freedom, prosperity and equality with a government that would uphold human rights and the rule of law as cornerstones of democracy. The British government failed to achieve the strategic objectives it had set for itself both for Iraq as a whole and particularly for the four provinces of southern Iraq that it occupied.

The Iraq Inquiry assessed that this was because the scale of UK effort in post-conflict-Iraq:

> failed to take account of the magnitude of the task of stabilising, administering and reconstructing Iraq, and of the responsibilities which were likely to fall to the UK.

This was because Prime Minister Blair:

> did not establish clear Ministerial oversight of UK planning and preparation. He did not ensure that there was a flexible, realistic and fully resourced plan that integrated UK military and civilian contributions.

The inquiry concluded that:

> by 2007 militia dominance in Basra, which UK military commanders were unable to challenge, led to the UK exchanging detainee releases for an end to the targeting of its forces. It was humiliating that the UK reached a position in which an agreement with a militia group

which had been actively targeting UK forces was considered the best option available. The UK military role in Iraq ended a very long way from success.[3]

FROM OCCUPYING POWER TO THE JANUARY 2005 ELECTIONS

After the invasion, the British offered to take responsibility for Basra City and the four southern provinces: Basra, Maysan, Dhi Qar and Muthanna. Designated as Multinational Division South East, the formation was considered by the military HQ and CPA in Baghdad to be conducting an 'economy of force' mission, whilst the Coalition main effort was in Baghdad.

The British attempted to find local interlocutors to help with administering their sector. The divisional commander's efforts to use Iraqi tribal structures were initially successful:

> We had to put somebody in charge, and we had to try and get Iraqis in charge and I would assist. So I on 7 April [2003] met Sheikh Musaheem in a tent in the middle of the desert. He sat me on the ground for about an hour. He gave me a lecture on the law of Armed Conflict and the rights and responsibilities of an occupying power. He had been a brigadier in the Iraqi navy, but in real life he was a lawyer. After the lecture I said: will you assist me in my rights and responsibilities, and can we get together a council that will run Basra Province through the difficult days ahead. He said yes and we worked together for some time, until the end of May 2003, when the de-Baathification lines were drawn and he was thrown out of office.'[4]

UK force levels declined after May 2003. The British rapidly reduced their footprint, downsizing from the large invasion force of a division of three brigades and full combat support capabilities to a much smaller force with a single British brigade. A divisional HQ would command British- and Italian-led multinational brigades, which would be joined by Dutch and Danish battalions. Having provided one of the three divisions that initially crossed into Iraq, increasing by one third the number of armoured brigades taking part in the invasion, the British force reduced to about 10 per cent of the Coalition forces occupying

Iraq. This was a much greater proportionate reduction than that made by the US forces. It was an early indicator that the UK was going to make a lower strategic commitment to Iraq than the US would.

The British military expected that this reduction in military strength would be accompanied by a significant increase in UK civilian capabilities, reconstruction and development. This expectation would not be met.

The UK, like the US, was taken by surprise by the extensive looting and rapid deterioration of security. But the UK had little influence on the US-led CPA that administered Iraq. It had no influence over the CPA's decisions to disband the Iraqi security services and exclude Baath Party members from public service.

Basra had a history of detachment from Baghdad, based on its distinct economy, demography and geography, and a record of autonomous and secessionist ambitions. The southern Shia people initially welcomed Coalition forces but restoring governance and public services was handicapped by the CPA's abrupt removal of Iraqi middle-class administrators. The combination of the parlous state of southern Iraq's infrastructure, the expectations of the population for a rapid improvement in their living conditions, and a significant failure to meet these expectations resulted in bewilderment and rapidly growing disaffection with the Coalition.

British forces represented the only coherent form of security authority in the city, law and order, the police and the judicial system having collapsed. Riots were common and armed attacks on the troops were increasing. Immediately after the defeat of the Iraqi forces and collapse of Saddam's regime it had been possible for troops to move around the city with relative ease. But British forces moving into Basra quickly became very vulnerable to attacks by small arms, rockets and roadside bombs. The environment was becoming increasingly hostile and unpredictable.

The Sunni–Al Qaida insurgency hardly featured in southern Iraq. The intensity of violence was initially low, but throughout the long hot summer of 2003 frustrations of the civilian population escalated, as did attacks by Shia militants. Whilst Basra City and Nasiriyah had been captured by UK and US troops during the invasion, much of the rest of southern Iraq had liberated itself. As with the rest of the country, apparently inexhaustible stocks of arms and ammunition were there for the taking. An early harbinger of growing Shia discontent with the British was the 24 June murder by an armed mob of six military policemen in Majar al-Kabir.

By the second half of 2003 the Basrawi population was increasingly resorting to violence. Increasing numbers joined the Shia militias. Iraqi Security Force capability could not be grown fast enough. The limited Coalition and British funds available for reconstruction made little practical difference to the population and the combination of looting, lawlessness, tattered infrastructure, and electrical power shortages exacerbated discontent. In mid-August there were serious riots in Basra.

British units were required to conduct operations that covered security, governance, economy and essential services, and tasks included the re-establishment of freedom of movement and the rule of law. The range of activities required soldiers to conduct security operations as well as acting as diplomats, local administration advisors, infrastructure consultants and economic development advisors, all through an interpreter. The need to maintain and build the consent of the local population remained a central British military aim, but one that became increasingly difficult to achieve.

For example, before 2003, Basra received electricity about 20 hours a day. By August 2003 it was receiving half that amount. This was a consequence of the damage inflicted by looting on the electrical infrastructure and the CPA having prioritized the distribution of electric power to Baghdad.[5] With summer heat in Basra often reaching 50 degrees Centigrade and a very high degree of unemployment, it was unsurprising that riots ensued.

The summer heat also affected British troops. Most front-line soldiers had no access to air conditioning and unlike the citizens of Basra had to deploy wearing helmets, body armour and other fighting equipment. It was only their high standard of physical fitness that reduced the number of casualties from heat exhaustion.

INADEQUATE BRITISH STRATEGIC LEADERSHIP OF POST-CONFLICT OPERATIONS

In late 2002 and early 2003 planning in Whitehall had identified that post-conflict operations would be decisive and that a major reconstruction effort would be necessary. The risks of Sunni–Shia conflict, external interference by Iran and intervention by Al Qaida activity in Iraq, were all identified. Reports from British military officers engaged with US military planners assessed that the US plans for post-conflict activity were weak. And there was a deep sense of foreboding that the rapidly improvised US Office of Reconstruction and Humanitarian Assistance (ORHA) would be overfaced by the task.

However, when the British forces launched their attack there were no contingency plans to deploy more than a handful of UK civilians to Iraq. It seems that no effective plans had been made to fulfil the UK's obligations as an occupying power, for example in providing essential services and reconstruction in the south. No British government money had been allocated for post-conflict reconstruction. Moreover, Prime Minister Blair placed no one person or government department in charge of pre-war planning of reconstruction. Leadership of the UK reconstruction effort was eventually given to the FCO in late March 2003. An ad hoc committee was established to consider reconstruction plans, but it played no effective role in leading the implementation of reconstruction.

Despite agreement by Clare Short and Foreign Secretary Jack Straw that the UK should do more to support ORHA, her development department effectively opted out of doing so. Why was this? Short was deeply troubled by US actions. To the military, Short and her department seemed to be waging a campaign of institutional resistance to British participation in the war. The Iraq Inquiry assessed that Short displayed: 'reluctance to engage in post-conflict activity other than for the immediate humanitarian response to conflict, until it was confirmed that the UN would lead the reconstruction effort'.[6]

This appears to have been tolerated by Prime Minister Blair. After Short's resignation in May 2003, DfID assumed leadership for reconstruction, but by then the UK reconstruction effort had fallen well behind the requirement in Basra and far behind Blair's public and private rhetoric. Relations between DfID and the British military were badly damaged and took years to recover.

It very quickly became apparent to British commanders in Basra that the situation had significantly changed from that which was envisaged by London. The inquiry identified that there were several occasions from August 2003 onwards when changes in the situation in Iraq were sufficiently great to have prompted a strategic reassessment by the British government. No such action occurred. The Iraq Inquiry assessed that the military leadership, specifically the Chief of Joint Operations and Chief of Defence Staff, should have pressed for this. It is unclear why the top British military leadership did not press for such action. This is but one of many examples identified by the inquiry of sub-optimal performance by politicians, government departments, and intelligence staff, senior military officers and civilian officials.

For example, following a June 2003 visit to Iraq, Blair told his ministers that the British government should return to 'a war footing' to avoid 'losing the peace in Iraq'. The inquiry concluded that there were 'no indications that Mr Blair's direction led to any substantive changes in the UK's reconstruction effort.'[7]

At a July 2003 Cabinet meeting, Blair concluded that the UK should make the CPA regional office in Basra, CPA (South), 'a model'. In a subsequent video conference Blair told President Bush and other US strategic leaders that the UK would do its 'level best to meet any demand for additional resources.'[8] A senior diplomat, Sir Hilary Synnott, was called out of retirement to head the team.

But the CPA in the south was neither staffed adequately nor capable of resourcing the required degree of reconstruction. The initial lack of an effective civilian organization and civilian leadership, expertise or financial assistance forced additional responsibilities onto the shoulders of military officers, who found themselves involved with a wide variety of essentially civilian projects and tasks that meant they were often operating well beyond their training and experience.

The Iraq Inquiry identified that the FCO, the department responsible, 'did not provide adequate practical support to Sir Hilary Synnott as Head of CPA (South)',[9] going on to identify that the FCO's Permanent Secretary failed to ensure that the FCO provided the support. What the inquiry did not explain is why inadequate implementation of a Cabinet decision, which had been declared to the US government, was tolerated by the central co-ordinating machinery of government, the Foreign Secretary or by the Prime Minister. In his memoir Synnott offered his assessment that:

> there was little evidence that the British Government as a whole saw itself as being at war. Management and oversight at ministerial and senior official level was essentially ad hoc and bore little resemblance

to the highly organised arrangements for post-conflict reconstruction which had been put in place, for instance, some four years before the end of the Second World War. Blair put a constant public emphasis on the importance and urgency of making progress in Iraq. But seemingly little interested in the processes within Government by which this might be brought about, he proved unable to mobilise Government departments to produce the necessary results.[10]

ABUSE OF DETAINEES – ANOTHER LEADERSHIP FAILURE

It was in this environment that troops of 1st Battalion, The Queen's Lancashire Regiment raided a hotel in Basra. Suspects detained at the hotel were transferred to the battalion's detention facility. Over the next 36 hours they were physically abused. One, Baha Mousa, died of his injuries.

This self-inflicted wound on British legitimacy was wholly avoidable. A court martial held four years later acquitted many of the perpetrators. But a subsequent independent public inquiry showed that throughout the British chain of command there had been a top-to-bottom lack of understanding of the provisions of the Geneva Conventions, as well as a lack of British doctrine for prisoner handling and adequate resourcing for prisoner handling and interrogation. In addition, government policy and rules for detainee handling had been comprehensively forgotten by the MoD, the British Army and both joint and army intelligence organizations.

By taking their eyes off their responsibilities, key actors in the British chain of command not only failed in their duty, but also created conditions that made it more likely that prisoners would be abused and thus contributed to a significant erosion of the legitimacy of British operations in Iraq.[11]

The Baha Mousa Inquiry provided unequivocal evidence that the British Army's leadership had been negligent of its responsibilities for the army's implementation of the law of armed conflict. Compliance with the laws of war is not optional, but the army leadership had decided it was a low priority. As apparently had the Air Marshal Sir Joe French, UK Chief of Defence Intelligence (CDI), the UK military 'process owner' for intelligence, who was also responsible for intelligence training. The chair of the inquiry judged the then-CDI's evidence unconvincing, rejecting some of it out of hand, stating that the CDI did not have a proper understanding of what policy and doctrinal guidance applied to interrogation and tactical questioning. That the failures of policy and doctrine had built up gradually over several years did not absolve CDI of his responsibilities. But neither he nor the British Army's senior leadership were ever held accountable for these personal failings.

BRITISH STABILIZATION OPERATIONS 2004–05

The war had quickly become unpopular in UK. The failure to find weapons of mass destruction, and the suicide of Dr David Kelly, an MoD weapons scientist who had told the BBC that the government's dossier that assessed that Iraq posed an active weapons of mass destruction had been 'sexed up', led to a sense that Prime Minister Blair and his inner circle had deliberately exaggerated the Iraqi threat. The descent of Iraq into apparent chaos amplified the increasing discontent in Parliament, the media and the public.

From mid-2003 onwards the national strategic direction given by London to the British general commanding in Basra was unambiguous and uncompromising: a timetabled withdrawal from Iraq measured by troop numbers. Over time British staff officers came to refer to this as 'strategy by spreadsheet'.

The dilemma for the UK tactical commander was two-fold. First, he had to manage the imbalance in expectation between the British policy of disengaging from southern Iraq and often contradictory US campaign direction.

Secondly, he had to manage his own troops' morale. For the first time in the careers of all the troops deployed to Iraq, they were fighting a war that was unpopular in the UK. This was reflected in direction to reduce numbers of avoidable British casualties. But for highly trained professionals, especially the military commanders, there was an expectation that by positive action, they ought to be making a difference to the situation.

The Shia uprising had considerable impact in southern Iraq. On the early morning of 6 April the JAM mounted 35 attacks on British troops in Basra and occupied the Iraqi governorate building. There was a full-scale insurrection in Amarah. Militants took over the bridges in Nasiriyah. The town was the responsibility of the Italian brigade.

For about six days the British divisional commander in Basra, Major General Andrew Stewart, was unable to persuade the Italians to use force to remove the militias, any offensive action being blocked by Rome. At that point, Stewart told the Italians he would send British troops to clear the militants. Rome then authorized offensive action, which was successful.

In Basra the British employed a dual-track approach of threats to storm the buildings seized by the militia combined with negotiations with key political figures; this eventually led to the withdrawal of the militants from the buildings they had seized. But this was not before Ambassador Bremer had issued a diplomatic *demarche* to the British demanding that force be used more robustly to defeat the Shia. He required the replacement of Major General Stewart. London supported Stewart and declined to replace him. This was the first significant military divergence between the UK and US. It would not be the last.

Force was being used very robustly in Maysan Province, especially in its capital Amarah where the single UK battlegroup experienced intense fighting. A small British base in a fortified house in Amarah was under siege from Shia militants and was only secured through a determined defence by British infantry and use of airpower, including AC130 gunships. A ceasefire was eventually negotiated with local leaders but not before the battlegroup had earned a high number of gallantry awards, the most earned by any British battalion in Iraq. The highest of British military gallantry awards, the Victoria Cross was awarded to the driver of a Warrior infantry fighting vehicle. At the time the British Army claimed that the fighting in Amarah was the most intense that any British battalion had experienced since the Korean War over 50 years earlier. This claim was correct, but unbeknownst at that time, over the next ten years other British battalions in Afghanistan would experience combat at equal or even greater levels of intensity.

The March 2004 departure of the Spanish brigade from Multinational Division Centre South following jihadist bombings in Madrid caused a significant reduction of that division's strength. The US asked the UK to assist by deploying British troops to fill the gap. They also requested that the British deploy the NATO-assigned HQ of the Allied Command Europe Rapid Reaction Corps, to assume control of the whole of Iraq south of Baghdad. This request was supported by the British Army, but it was eventually declined by the British government, in part because the Ministry of Defence was planning to deploy the HQ and additional troops to Afghanistan in 2006.

The Shia uprising in the summer again saw significant fighting between Shia militias and Coalition forces across the country and in Multinational Division South East in Basra, Maysan, Nasiriyah and Amarah. These uprisings were thwarted, as much through political as through military means. After this the security situation in southern Iraq gradually improved. The Iraqi election of January 2005 saw a significant contribution by the Iraqi security forces. This gave some cause for guarded optimism in the British government.

In late 2004 the British government decided to commit a major British force to NATO operations in Afghanistan in 2006. This decision assumed that British troop levels in Iraq would have significantly reduced by then.

By the January 2005 Iraqi elections, the UK forces had sustained 86 fatalities in Iraq. To the public and media some of these appeared to result from poor leadership and management of the war. The most prominent was the death of Sergeant Roberts in the initial invasion. This incident became a *cause celèbre*. An army board of inquiry and the hearings by the civilian coroner made it clear that the failure to procure enough enhanced body amour directly contributed to his death. Explanations offered by Defence Minister Geoff Hoon failed to convince his highly articulate young widow, who was much better at engaging the press and media than was Hoon.

The second incident was the death of Fusilier Gentle in a roadside bomb attack. A subsequent investigation showed that protective equipment that might have prevented the attack had not been fitted to the vehicle in which he travelled but was sitting on a shelf in a store.

Increasing numbers of British casualties, the failure to find weapons of mass destruction and the lack of Coalition success all meant that the Iraq war was becoming increasingly unpopular with the UK media and public.

Between 2003 and 2007 the UK strategic and Coalition operational direction to Multinational Division South East were broadly complementary: a transition of responsibility to the Iraqi forces by generating and training Iraqi units, while simultaneously supporting the development of Iraqi governance and economy. The main effort was to be 'security sector reform'.

Much of the British effort to build the capacity of the Iraqi security forces was similar to that mounted by the US. Training camps and training teams were established, and Iraqi soldiers and police were trained. But there was one important difference between the UK and US approach. The British chose not to form and deploy military transition teams with the Iraqi units that they had trained. It appears that the decision was influenced by concerns about force protection. With a much lower density of troops in southern Iraq, providing the same level of quick reaction forces that the US had assigned to their transition teams would have been very difficult.[12]

Instead of advisors and trainers embedded down to battalion level, Iraqi units in southern Iraq were visited by British advisors. This meant that the Iraqi forces were receiving much less supervision, advice and mentorship than if they were operating in the rest of Iraq. It also meant that compared with the Americans, the British were far less able to understand both the strengths and weaknesses of the Iraqi units and the security situation in their area of responsibility. But at the time the British HQ in Northwood and MoD in London seemed oblivious of this greatly reduced level of situational awareness.

Tensions were starting to show between the US and UK. British officers working in Baghdad in 2004 and 2005 noted an increasing US irritation that the British did not seem to fully appreciate the scale of the American commitment, and the scale of effort and intensity of operations being conducted. The biggest area of friction came from an apparent British arrogance over the American approach to operations, the British sometimes being seen to display an attitude of 'we know better and we can do it better'.[13] Some misunderstandings and tensions inevitably followed from attempts made to highlight the strengths of the so-called British way to American allies. Thomas Mockaitis noted that:

> American officers [were] barraged with ungenerous, over-simplified, and often glib comparisons between their supposedly ineffectual methods in Vietnam and the allegedly superior British approach employed in Malaya. Similar comparisons between the British army's handling of Basra and the U.S. military's alleged mishandling of the far more challenging Sunni triangle [made] American officers understandably resistant to what they [saw] as 'more British tripe'.[14]

BLOODY BASRA

Before the January 2005 Iraqi elections, the UK expected that there would be political and security progress in southern Iraq. Instead, the Sadrists declined to stand, excluding themselves from mainstream politics. And all the local politicians elected strongly opposed the British presence.

The victorious Islamic coalition failed to agree on a governor, allowing the election by default of Muhammad al-Wa'ili, whose Fadhila Party had gained only 13 of the 41 seats. For the next four years, Wa'ili deftly circumvented all political and legal attempts to unseat him, consolidating his position at the heart of a black economy based on oil-smuggling, overseen by his militia within the Facilities Protection Service. Other militias – notably the JAM – carved out similar fiefdoms in electricity generation and the ports. There was ever-growing influence of Shia militias, including over the fledgling Iraqi security forces. Shia militias and their Iranian-sponsored 'special groups' increasingly sought to gain political capital by attacking the British.

A weak Iraqi government could do little to stop them. Before 2008, preoccupied with the plethora of more serious threats to its existence, it showed little sustained interest in Basra. The effect was to turn Basra Province into a kleptocracy, where armed political–criminal groups excluded both the central government and the Iraqi people from power.

That elected local politicians opposed the British presence and that consent to the British footprint in southern Iraq was declining created an unprecedented problem for the British. Stabilization operations in Malaya, Northern Ireland, Bosnia, Kosovo and Sierra Leone and in Kabul in 2002 had all featured a high degree of consent by most of the local population. Now the Iraqi electorate had spoken, and it was telling the British that their troops should leave southern Iraq. This was a strategic shock, although it does not seem to have been widely recognized as such by London.

The conflict in Basra was fundamentally different to that in Anbar and Baghdad where Al Qaida was essentially nihilistic; in other words, escalation was open-ended, with total collapse of the Iraqi secular state the desired objective. Conflict in the Shia South was not nihilistic. Even at the height of the violence in 2006–07 the oil and energy infrastructure remained largely undisturbed. None of the militias wanted to bring the south to the point of collapse; they simply wanted as large a slice of the cake as possible. They were parasites that wanted to keep the host alive.

The British priority was to build the capacity of the Iraqi forces. The British felt that the Iraqi Army was being successfully developed. By many metrics progress was real. But corruption remained debilitating. British troops were also increasingly frustrated that because of the financial rules imposed from Whitehall, relatively inexpensive yet important reconstruction tasks were not funded properly, a major drawback given the value placed on 'buying consent'. There was not a British equivalent to the US Commander's Emergency Response Program.

For the first half of 2005, the level of violence against Coalition Forces was markedly less than experienced in 2004. But the JAM fielded EFP roadside bombs that could penetrate all British vehicles then in service, including Challenger tanks and Warrior infantry fighting vehicles. Drawing on expertise provided by Lebanese Hizbullah and a supply of EFP components by Iran, Shia militias used EFP devices to great effect against British vehicles. This increased UK casualties. There was nothing new about EFP technology, which used explosive to form a high energy metal slug, capable of punching through even tank armour to lethal effect. Indeed, during the Cold War, the British had a stockpile of French manufactured EFP mines for use against attacking Warsaw Pact armour.

Many British lightly armoured 'Snatch' Land Rover 4x4 patrol vehicles were destroyed by EFPs, causing well-publicized casualties. This produced considerable media criticism of the government, MoD and army for too slow a reaction.

Initially the British had no technical counter-measures and could only reduce the threat by adapting tactics. This included rigorous control of road movement and devoting considerable resources to force protection. This so reduced the available combat power of the British brigade, that not only was its operational effect reduced, but also it had to reduce the troops available to train the Iraqi forces. It took months before additional armour and other counter-measures to protect against EFPs were fielded. It was only in the aftermath of the 2008 Iraqi forces' surge in Basra, Operation *Charge of the Knights*, that the level of security forces on the streets in Basra City was sufficient to disrupt the emplacement of EFPs by Shia fighters.

While efforts were made to devise technological counter-measures, British tactics and procedures were adjusted. The then British commander Major General Jonathon Riley was to later observe that:

It was borne in on me very strongly how much the collective experience of the Army of dealing with the IED threat had wasted out during the long period of ceasefire in Northern Ireland. We had forgotten institutionally how to deal with this ... not just as a series of devices but as a system and how to attack the device and attack the system behind it. So as well as asking for upgrades in protection, we also began to refocus the Intelligence-gathering effort on to people who were likely to be initiating and running the networks to try and break the thing up ...

The armour on the Warrior and Challenger main battle tanks was upgraded very rapidly. The Snatch Land Rover was also up armoured and I began to see the introduction of a new series of vehicles which were more effective, but these devices were of such power that there was ... no technological silver bullet in this. So, we were doing what we could within the constraints of the available technology. There was nothing else around. The responses to it were therefore not just about protection against the device. They had to be about breaking the networks.[15]

This greatly reduced movement by road. In the absence of enough helicopters, the ability of the British to train and support the Iraqi forces in the second half of 2005 was reduced.

THE JAMEAT INCIDENT

The image that British efforts with the Iraqi security forces were succeeding was rudely shattered on 19 September 2005. At a checkpoint the Iraqi police arrested two British SOF soldiers in civilian clothes who had been carrying out a surveillance operation. They were detained at the Jameat police station in Basra. This was an Iraqi police unit notorious for sectarianism and human rights abuses. The Iraqi media were told that two Israeli spies had been captured. The British HQ feared that the men would be tortured and quite possibly killed.

A British team was despatched to the police station to negotiate the men's release. This team was also taken hostage. A quick reaction force of armoured infantry in Warrior vehicles positioned itself outside. Angry Iraqi civilians rapidly gathered to confront the British and heavy rioting resulted. Petrol bombs were used, a Warrior armoured vehicle was set on fire and its commander, his uniform aflame, had to evacuate his position in the turret.

The British decided to act. The police station was forcibly entered by British armour crashing through its perimeter. The negotiating team were secured, but the captured British SOF were nowhere to be found. A Royal Navy helicopter over the Jameat had spotted the prisoners being spirited away to another building. By now British SOF had arrived from central Iraq and rescued their comrades.

Images of the soldier escaping from the Warrior, his uniform ablaze, appeared widely in the international and UK media. Reports of the incident contributed to increasing political, media and public perceptions that the British mission was failing.

The incident was a strategic shock to the British. It raised serious doubts over the Iraqi Police, especially the extent to which it had been infiltrated by Shia militias. On the Iraqi side, the Basra provincial governor broke off relations with the British. The Basra Provincial Council announced a policy of non-co-operation and disengagement with the British. It became much more difficult for the British to engage the Iraqi forces. The Basra authorities broke off relations with the British, refusing to meet British officers. It looked as if the British would not make any more progress with the Iraqi police. The UK response was to concentrate effort on implementing transition in Muthanna and Maysan provinces to get the Iraqi Security Forces ready for Provincial Iraqi Control. The British also stepped up intelligence-led detention operations.

An independent review of Basra's police force was conducted. It was decided that responsibility for training police in southern Iraq should pass from the Foreign Office to the military. The British, who had been arguing with Baghdad for an overarching strategy for the Iraqi Police, changed track and increasingly concentrated on getting Iraqi police capacity in Basra 'good enough' for security transition from British to Iraqi leadership.

The Iraqi National Referendum took place on 15 Oct 2005 without incident. A jointly run Iraqi–Coalition security operation was seen to be a success. But internal power struggles and malign criminal and political influences were largely hidden from Coalition sight.

OPERATION *SINBAD*

The war was becoming increasingly unpopular in the UK. The British government agreed in January 2006 that Iraq was Britain's top overseas security priority. But it also announced plans to increase the UK role and troop numbers in Afghanistan. This commitment increasingly placed Iraq as a lower priority. In March 2006, plans to reduce UK force levels in Iraq from 8,000 to approximately 7,200 were announced. The British continued to implement the Transition Strategy. This envisaged that as Iraqi forces became increasingly effective, Coalition troops would reduce their footprint. Once Iraqi forces were sufficiently capable, they would assume the lead for security and the Coalition would declare a state of Provincial Iraqi Control. At this stage Coalition forces in that province would assume 'operational overwatch' with their forces being able to return to support the Iraqi forces should they become overfaced.

Transition to Iraqi control of provincial security remained the British main effort. But by 2006 the Transition Strategy was failing in southern Iraq. Local politicians and Iraqi forces were unwilling to confront Shia militias, which sought to gain political capital by attacking the British. Roadside bomb attacks by Shia militants sharply increased British casualties. The commander of the British 1st Armoured Division, Major General John Cooper, took steps to recast the campaign as one of counter-insurgency (COIN):

> I encouraged my subordinate commanders to think things through against the COIN principles, and so we used them always ... If you consider 1st (UK) Armoured Division on warfighting operations, it consists of infantry, armour, guns, aviation, artillery, engineers and logistics. Which do you consider to be the most important element? None of them; it is the sum of the parts that is important; the synergy they create. It is the same with COIN; everyone is part of it; it is the sum of military operations offensive and defensive, Iraqi leadership engagement and development, the training of the ISF in SSR, reconstruction operations and,

just as with conventional operations, it is the synergy that comes from the sum of all of the component parts that will make the difference.[16]

Security continued to deteriorate. The threat to Coalition Forces from an increasingly confident enemy was rising. Basra Provincial Council's disengagement with British forces continued to stall the momentum gained through earlier efforts. Local government officials had started to show increasing independence and less interest in working with the Coalition. It was clear that corruption was a widespread problem. The Sunni minority was leaving the south in response to a campaign of sectarian intimidation and murder.

Over the summer months, through careful work from military commanders and British diplomats, Basra's Provincial Council started to re-engage with the British. A joint British–Iraqi command and control system was established through the creation of a Provincial Joint Coordination Centre. The British declared Provincial Iraqi Control to have been achieved in Muthanna Province in July, and in Dhi Qar Province in September. Both provinces were relatively stable, probably because there was a balance amongst the various local political forces.

Camp Abu Naji, the main British base in Amarah, was handed back to the Iraqi Army in August 2006. It was immediately looted by the local population. Iraqi troops did nothing to stop this, an indicator that they shared the anti-British attitude. The ransacking of the camp was widely publicized. All subsequent withdrawals from British-held bases were meticulously planned to avoid a repeat of the Abu Naji fiasco.

By now the British divisional HQ in Basra was the HQ of the 3rd UK Division commanded by Major General Richard Shirreff. He assessed that the British had lost the initiative in the city:

there continues to be a belief that we are carrying out some form of Peace Support Operation and that the remedies that applied to Bosnia, apply equally to Iraq. This is not the case, and the way in which hard and soft effects are balanced in a theatre like Iraq needs to be vested in one person. In Iraq, there were several uncoordinated agencies involved in the process, including the FCO, DFID and the PRT, there was no supremo; and the consequent effect was dissipated.[17]

The security situation limited freedom of movement for both Coalition Forces and British officials, with the result that no momentum could be generated. The principal task was, therefore, to restore security and Shirreff prepared an operation, *Salamanca,* to conduct counter-insurgency in Basra to achieve this. Shirreff assessed that this would require forces to be concentrated on Basra, and for economic effort to be similarly concentrated so that consent could be bought in the short term. To conduct *Salamanca,* Shirreff realized that he needed more forces, in spite of the ongoing troop withdrawals. He also required support of the British development agency, but they would not support the concept of short-term economic effect because it was believed 'it would foster a dependency culture ... indeed they believed it to be counter-productive.'[18]

So Shirreff resolved to conduct the operation with whatever resources he could get. Even though Prime Minister Maliki had vetoed *Salamanca* and significant UK reinforcements were not available, he and Brigadier James Everard, commanding the 20th Armoured Brigade, set out to restore security. The division managed to secure $87 million of US Commanders' Emergency Response Programme money.

Operation *Salamanca* was replaced by Operation *Sinbad.* This would attempt to improve security in Basra area by area. Firstly a 48-hour security 'pulse' would take control of an area of Basra to establish a secure environment, during which British troops were to deliver immediate-impact improvements. During a 28-day 'pause', a high level of Iraqi Army military presence would be maintained in the area, during which effort would be focused on improving the Iraqi Police.[19] Longer-term reconstruction projects were to be delivered by Iraqi contractors, employing local people to lay electrical distribution cables, water pipelines or repair roads. At the end of the 'pause', the Iraqi Army would depart, and the Iraqi Police would take over responsibility for the area.

In early September, as Operation *Sinbad* was being prepared, the British Army chief, General Sir Richard Dannatt, was interviewed by the *Daily Mail* newspaper. Discussing Iraq, he described the British Army as 'part of the problem in Basra'. He said that the army was involved in two wars and it was important to ensure that the combined commitment did not break the army. Whilst Dannatt's remarks were fully in keeping with the government and MoD policy at the time, they were seized upon by the UK media as a further argument in favour of UK withdrawal from the increasingly unpopular war.

The operation began at the end of September. An estimated 2,300 Iraqi Army troops and 1,000 British soldiers took part. As British and Iraqi troops focused on sequenced pulses into the district of Basra, they continued to mount intelligence-led strike operations against JAM targets. These included cells of Shia fighters, their commanders and arms caches, with the EFP roadside bombs being a priority.

By now the British had refined their approach to such operations. Intelligence would be collected and fused at brigade HQ. Ideally this would be from multiple sources, including national strategic intelligence. Once the intelligence was sufficiently refined to produce an address, the target would be surrounded and forcibly entered. The troops doing this had been trained in tactics by British SOF.

The Shia militants would react rapidly to movements of British troops. Once it was clear where the British were striking, the Shia fighters would move quickly to attack the troops forming a protective cordon around the targets. They would also seek to attack the British columns as they withdrew. The urban geography of the city meant that once the British forces closed on their targets it was easy for the JAM to work out the limited number of British withdrawal routes. This allowed them to arrange hasty ambushes on British columns. These used small arms, RPGs and rapidly emplaced roadside bombs.

Strike operations in Basra turned into company and battalion level raids, in which the longer the operation went on, the greater the fighting. So armoured vehicles, particularly the Warrior infantry fighting vehicles, were essential for these operations, although commanders would sometimes use the smaller, lightly armoured Snatch Land Rovers to achieve speed and surprise, particularly in congested narrow streets.

In its six-month deployment to Basra in 2006, 20th Armoured Brigade conducted almost 70 such raids. A typical strike operation was described by Major Wilson of 4th Battalion, the Rifles:

Our first operation was a real baptism of fire. We had 30 minutes planning time prior to leaving camp. The powers that be had decided that on this occasion it would be worth striking in daylight, something that was routinely considered too dangerous. On route to the first of two houses that we were to strike, the target house changed and therefore some hasty re-planning took place, limited by the very poor communications fit in Snatch. We eventually hit the first house but soon came under small arms attack.

Having arrested four young men, we remounted our vehicles and made our way to the second target house. Just short of the target, the lead Snatch of 1 Platoon was hit by an IED that disabled the vehicle but caused no casualties. It managed to limp around the corner before becoming immobilised. At this point we came under heavy small arms fire and took two casualties, Corporal Graham with a gunshot wound to the leg and Sergeant Buckle with a shrapnel wound to the ankle. To add to our challenges, a Snatch that was trying to manoeuvre into a position to hook up the damaged vehicle got stuck in a ditch. We had two casualties, two stuck vehicles and a decent firefight raging all around us.

Eventually everything was hooked up and we got moving, having decided that we had had enough for our first operation. Rifleman Gormley guided the damaged Snatch that was now hooked up to a Warrior Recovery variant through the streets looking through the back doors, because it could only be towed rearwards and very slowly.

Unfortunately, it was now around 0700 and we had been on the ground for some time and the enemy had set up a well-coordinated ambush on our route out. As we were being led out by Warrior, the lead vehicle was hit by an RPG, injuring the driver and blocking the route. What followed is what riflemen now describe as the 'Mogadishu Mile'. We were hemmed in front and rear and took a large amount of small arms and RPG fire. One of the RPGs hit a 2 Platoon Snatch and caused two injuries. Amazingly it hit just behind the driver's door; the tail fin forced its way through the door, cutting the driver across the chin before coming to rest on the dashboard, still smouldering, in front of a rather surprised vehicle commander. Eventually the Warrior was dragged out of the way and we got moving once again.[20]

Operation *Sinbad* had some local tactical success. But the operation had been insufficiently resourced. There were not enough British troops to create enough military impact to significantly change the political situation. Iraqi troops did not want to be seen to be closely co-operating with British forces, for fear that as well as attacking the British, the militias would attack Iraqi forces working with them. The lack of political support from Prime Minister Maliki, who was still unwilling to confront Shia militias, along with Iraqi security forces that were either infiltrated by militants or had insufficient numbers and confidence to hold areas that the British cleared, meant that the operation only achieved transient effect. It did not change the Basra political dynamic, particularly the unwillingness of the Iraqi authorities and forces to take on the militias.

On Christmas Day 2006 British troops conducted a raid on the notorious Jameat police station, where British SOF had been held hostage in 2005. The police there had continued their malign sectarian activity. British engineers rigged the building with explosives and demolished it. But the operation was taken badly by the Basra Provincial Council who stopped contact with UK forces in protest.

BRITISH FAILURES TO ADAPT QUICKLY ENOUGH

The British Army that deployed to Afghanistan in 2001 and Iraq in 2003 felt confident that it would be the equal of whatever challenges the conflicts presented. It thought that it had adapted well to the conflict in Northern Ireland, the Falklands War and Operation *Desert Storm*. From 1992 it rapidly adapted to the more challenging environment of Bosnia. Not only did it play a leading role in UN and subsequent NATO operations, but it also quickly developed new doctrine of 'wider peacekeeping' which was influential and rapidly adopted by many armies. It coped equally well with the unforeseen challenges of Kosovo, as well as the intervention in Sierra Leone. In all these campaigns, the successful adaptation had greater positive effect than the negative impacts of any failures to adapt. But by the third anniversary of the start of the war in Iraq March 2006 the British were struggling to adapt quickly enough.

In the later years of the Iraq and Afghan wars senior British officers often claimed that the British Army had 'transformed in contact'. This was partly true: for example the fielding of new equipment resulted in considerable improvements in capability. In Iraq and Afghanistan there was much hard fighting and good tactical adaptation and learning by British troops in contact with the enemy. And there was a revolution in British battlefield medicine. But the evidence suggests that for every positive example of British military adaptation, there were at least as many examples of failures to adapt. By the later stages of both wars the middle and senior management of the army shared a general sense of 'we could and should have done better'. And there was much evidence that in both wars US forces often learned and adapted faster than the British did.

The British Army had considerable experience of succeeding, and sometimes failing, in counter-insurgency from post-war colonial campaigns and from Northern Ireland. In Sir Robert Thompson and General Sir Frank Kitson, the British had produced two soldier-scholars who had written authoritative books on the topic. But in the late 1990s they had stopped the teaching of insurgency and counter-insurgency at their staff college, in favour of studying peace support operations. Although the army had relevant COIN doctrine published in 2001, it had not been widely read. The British Army was slower than the US to produce up-to-date COIN doctrine, their equivalent of Field Manual 3-24 only being published in 2009, after the British had left Iraq.

They also failed to grow tactical intelligence capabilities quickly enough. It appears that in this and many other areas, they had failed to institutionalize the hard-won lessons of Northern Ireland. For example, in Northern Ireland airborne surveillance by helicopters and fixed-wing aircraft had provided decisive advantage over the IRA for force protection and intelligence gathering and in supporting ground operations. The US forces were quickly discovering that unmanned aircraft could be used to similar effect and were rapidly fielding ever-increasing numbers of drones. The British Army had made extensive use of the Phoenix drone in March and April 2003, but having been designed for operations in Europe, the aircraft could not fly in the warmest six months of the Iraqi summer.

Although some small Desert Hawk drones were procured, a 2004 RAF initiative to join the US Air Force's Predator force did not entitle the British force in southern Iraq to any support from Predator. Priorities for Predator were set by the HQs in CENTCOM and Baghdad. Since southern Iraq was not a high priority UK troops rarely saw Predators operate in their area. In 2007 the UK leased Hermes 450 drones, but for the first four years of the war, airborne surveillance over southern Iraq was inadequate. It was particularly galling to British commanders that Italian and Australian troops in southern Iraq acquired drone capabilities more quickly than the British did.

The UK applied many of the counter-IED capabilities developed in Northern Ireland to the campaigns in Iraq and Afghanistan. The Warrior armoured infantry fighting vehicle had additional armour fitted to provide better protection against RPGs and EFPs. The Warrior became the armoured vehicle of choice to send in harm's way in Iraq. But between 2003 and 2006 the British were unable to deploy enough armoured vehicles with adequate protection against IEDS to Iraq.

It was only when a June 2006 intervention by Defence Secretary Des Browne and Procurement Minister Lord Drayson imparted much needed urgency, that a new vehicle, the Mastiff, entered service in December 2006. This was based on a protected patrol vehicle being produced for the US Marine Corps. The British also adapted their existing tracked armoured personnel carrier, the FV432, by upgrading it into the Bulldog. This added an outer shell of additional armour, optimized against RPG and EFP attacks, giving it a much higher level of protection.

A major factor in this failure to adapt quickly enough was that the complex structure of the MoD diffused responsibility and accountability. For the first three years of the war, it was not clear where responsibility and accountability lay for additional or improved equipment for British forces in Iraq and Afghanistan, especially the critical needs to improve airborne surveillance and protected mobility. The Iraq Inquiry assessed that:

> The Ministry of Defence was slow in responding to the threat from Improvised Explosive Devices and delays in providing adequate medium weight protected patrol vehicles should not have been tolerated. It was not clear which person or department within the Ministry of Defence was responsible for identifying and articulating such capability gaps. But it should have been.[21]

It was only public, media and political pressure that forced the MoD to move with the speed the situation demanded. It streamlined its diffuse bureaucracy and aligned responsibility, authority and accountability, thus reducing friction and streamlining and accelerating both decision making and implementation.[22] Overall it seems to have taken the MoD too long to develop the sense of urgency that Robert Gates imparted to the Pentagon. A contributing factor may have been the rapid turnover of UK defence secretaries, the UK having five between 2001 and 2009, one of whom was also Minister for Scotland. During the same period the US had only two defense secretaries: Rumsfeld and Gates. None of the British defence ministers seem to have exhibited the same effectiveness at energizing adaptation as that displayed by Robert Gates.

The UK MoD's own in-house study of the Iraq war identified that 'In comparison with the US, the UK military was complacent and slow in recognising and adapting to changed circumstances. It took us too long to update our thinking on how to counter the type of insurgency encountered in Iraq.'[23]

There was an ingrained assumption that UK force levels in Iraq would quickly reduce. Combined with the increasing unpopularity of the war, this meant that many in the MoD and the army struggled to find enthusiasm for the campaign. This reticence increased considerably once British troops in Helmand became engaged in heavy fighting. There is also evidence that the army's key leadership was worried that the effect of fighting two unpopular wars at the same time might so greatly damage the army to the extent that after the wars ended, it might not be able to recover its capability and its reputation.[24]

These factors inhibited some people and organizations in the British Army and UK Defence from making a psychological commitment to success in Iraq, acting as a disincentive against changing organization, process or capability. This is not saying that units and formations who served in Iraq were not committed to the operation. The opposite is true, as demonstrated by the fighting spirit exhibited by units in the war against the JAM. But there is a powerful sense that the further away from the front line some parts of the army and defence organizations were, the less likely they were to suggest or support adaptations or resources necessary for success in Iraq.

It is likely that British military adaptability was constrained by the MoD not being on a war footing. Even after 2006 when the Air Chief Marshal Sir Jock Stirrup, the new UK Chief of Defence Staff, gave clear direction that 'we are in two wars and we have got to win them both' there were UK defence organizations where there was little sense of urgency.[25] Stirrup's successor as UK Chief of Defence, General Lord David Richards, assessed that in Iraq:

> Critics say that our long experience in Ulster made us complacent about tackling insurgency elsewhere, a case of 'we've done this in Northern Ireland, so we know what to expect and how to deal with it.' As a result of our experience in Ulster, we certainly had a feel for the requirement to keep people with us and work within a political environment.
>
> But I think in Iraq, for example, too many British officers would, without realising what they were doing, slip into a Northern Ireland mind-set. Very early on that was an appropriate response when the efficient administration of law and order along the Northern Ireland pattern was required. But once things escalated, we needed to think in new and innovative ways, in order to deal with a complex and unique insurgency and the collapse of Iraqi society. That did happen, but maybe it took longer than it should have done.[26]

Many British officers observed that the US military considered themselves 'at war' whilst the British were 'on operations'. Some people and organizations in the British Army and the UK Ministry of Defence seemed to demonstrate a lack of commitment to the war in Iraq. There is clear evidence that some parts of the British Army tried hard not to bend themselves out of shape. For example, retaining previous campaigns' default settings for individual operational tours at six months may have enhanced resilience, but it led to sub-optimal campaign continuity. The MoD centralized management of many important areas of the army's capability. These included setting and funding equipment requirements, commanding the Iraqi campaign and managing the UK media. But there were many areas where the army could make its own decisions for itself. These included training, personnel policy, allocation of responsibilities and changing its structure. Like some parts of the MoD, not all the army treated the Iraq and Afghan wars with the urgency they deserved. Even allowing for the unpopularity of the war and time-consuming inflexibility and centralization imposed by the MoD, between 2003 and 2008 the British Army could have been more flexible and agile.

THE WAR AGAINST THE JAM

From mid-2006 British troops were fighting a war with the Shia militias and heavy fighting took place, as Shia fighters vigorously attacked British strike operations and convoys into Basra. This 'war against the JAM' saw fighting as intense as that anywhere else in Iraq and a high number of UK casualties, both from the intense battles in Basra and from mortar and rocket attacks on British bases. The lack of organic airborne surveillance and ever-reducing troop numbers meant that it was not until the arrival of the Hermes 450 drone in Basra in 2007 that British forces could seize the initiative against both threats. The British took care to avoid collateral damage and civilian casualties, but at times considerable use was made of the full range of joint fires from mortars and artillery and airstrikes.

The few remaining British bases in Basra were often under increasing rocket, mortar and small arms attacks, resulting in significant casualties. Convoys carrying supplies into the British bases in the city were almost continuously attacked. An example of the fighting around a British convoy in Basra is described by Corporal Smith of 4th Battalion, the Rifles based in Basra Palace at the height of the fighting. It was June 2007, on his first day of a six-month tour:

> After a long and hot wait in the small base we rolled out into the busy streets of Basra. Almost immediately we came under small arms fire from a very well sited ambush. A civilian fuel tanker driver was killed, and a large crowd began to develop around the tanker which was almost immediately set alight. We broke contact and continued to the Palace but a second civilian vehicle in the convoy, a low loader, collapsed on the bridge at Red 10 – it had been badly shot up in the ambush. Also, in the initial ambush Corporal Jex Brookes the other section commander in my platoon had been hit by small arms.
>
> The task for the rest of the small convoy was to evacuate him back to Basra Palace. My Bulldog and our lead element of Warriors were tasked with the protection of the low loader. This was my first major contact! We were now fixed by the low loader – we had to protect – all we could do was hard target the Bulldog like a dismounted Rifleman. This is where our driver Rifleman

McColl really came into his own, moving us about without any command so we, the top cover and Scotty could concentrate on our arcs.

I was positioned with my head and shoulders out of the mortar hatches using the Bulldog as a firing platform. I was observing my arcs when I noticed the streets were emptying and the vehicle traffic decreased – an attack was imminent. I was relaying this to Scotty, when the first mortar rounds landed. They resulted in civilian casualties; I had never expected to take indirect fire on the city streets. For the next few hours we fought a 360-degree battle to protect the disabled low loader.

I found it really hard to locate the enemy. This was a city street with corners, walls, cars, windows and rooftops. Added to that the smoke, crack and thump of small arms, RPGs and rounds banging off your vehicle all confused the situation.

We were engaging targets from as close as 25 metres away and up to 100 metres away snap shooting and rapid fire popping up and down like jacks-in-the-box, although there was not much Scotty could do about hard targeting, waist up in his cupola as he was. I don't think we ever won the firefight; once one position was suppressed another would engage from a new or previous position. To combat this, we started to fire into likely enemy and previous positions as warning shots. The situation was getting worse. We were now taking fire from an Iraqi Police Station, which we were using as cover. Our driver 'Mac' was now showing signs of stress. He'd already fired all his pistol ammo and was shouting over the speakers that we needed to get out of here. I don't blame 'Mac' for stressing out. He was on his own in his hatch, isolated from the rest of us, gunfire all around him so I pushed through to his hatch and gave him a shake and told him to just drive. Immediately he snapped out of it.

We finally got back to the Palace after more than 11 hours on the ground. The low loader was eventually denied to the enemy by Warrior 30mm fire. As we were extracting, the Bulldog commanded by my platoon commander was hit by an IED, forcing another recovery. It had been an extraordinary first day in Basra. Men killed, other serious casualties, vehicles destroyed and recovered and a real test for troops on the ground.[27]

Intelligence-led precision urban strike and detention operations played an important role in sustaining morale and in detaining suspects for protection. These could be very demanding. For example, a typical 2007 raid into Basra required a company at the target area and the rest of a battalion to get the force to and from its objectives, a total force of three armoured infantry companies in Warrior vehicles and a squadron of tanks. One such operation encountered 14 roadside bombs along a 2-mile stretch of road. Vehicle columns were in almost continuous firefights.

Between November 2006 and May 2007 the 19th Light Brigade conducted almost 130 strike operations. Many of these were mounted against militia rocket and mortar teams. By now the British had Hermes 450 unmanned aerial vehicles and their ability to conduct intelligence-fusion had increased. And British rules of engagement were changed to allow 'hostile intent' to be targeted. The brigade sought to strike early, disrupt the enemy, exploit any intelligence leads and create opportunities in order to ensure that the militia could not gain the upper hand.

After Operation *Sinbad*, MoD officials in London argued that Basra's Shia majority made the city different from the rest of the country, and that previous efforts to stabilize it had failed to change its political dynamic. They assessed that the conflict in Basra was Shia internal competition for power and influence, rather than an insurgency against the Iraqi state. The British felt that, as they were losing legitimacy in Basra, it was now up to the Iraqi government and security forces to take the lead. As the UK had agreed to build up forces in Afghanistan, at US request, no British reinforcement of Basra was possible. Instead troop levels would continue to reduce in Iraq to reinforce their contingent in Afghanistan who were fighting unexpectedly bloody and difficult battles.

The announcement of the US Surge did not increase optimism or strategic confidence in London. As UK public support for the war was decreasing with every casualty, the British declined to match the 2007 US Surge. Although evidence of the success of the Surge was reported by senior British officers in Baghdad, it seems that the UK Chiefs of Staff and the British government probably considered that the US Surge would fail.

So UK and US strategic, operational and tactical approaches diverged. The British could no longer militarily 'win' in Basra. The best that could be hoped for in Basra was building up the Iraqi forces' capability and encouraging Iraqi political leaders to tackle the Shia militants. Within the MoD and army this outcome was given a sporting nickname: 'score draw'.[28] Air Chief Marshal Stirrup stated:

> we needed to break the political logjam. We needed to change the dynamic. Clearly, though, the fact that we had people sitting at locations in Basra City being rocketed and mortared, the fact that we were having to run resupply convoys to those locations that were being attacked and on which we were suffering casualties, and, politically, our forces were not being allowed to do the job for which we were in the city, that's not a sustainable position.
>
> It is a sad fact that on military operations one sustains casualties. That's the nature of the business. But those casualties must be producing something of strategic benefit if they are to be justifiable, and they certainly weren't in the case of Basra City. But the principal rationale -- was actually to find a way forward politically in Basra.'[29]

THE ACCOMMODATION WITH SHIA MILITANTS

Operation *Zenith* was the British national plan for Basra in 2007. It intended to reposition British forces, withdrawing from the few remaining outposts in Basra to a single remaining base at Basra airport. This was to allow further British force reductions in Iraq, so as to enable increases in British forces in Afghanistan.

The continuing reductions in the size of British forces in Iraq meant that they increasingly lacked the strength to eject Shia militias from Basra. And many of the scarce intelligence and surveillance capabilities being used in or over Basra were being redeployed to Afghanistan. So as the year went on, the British understanding of events in Basra reduced, as did their ability to influence events in the city.

The new British commander, Major General Jonathan Shaw, thought it worth attempting to find an interlocutor with whom the British might be able to negotiate. Shaw discovered that Ahmed al-Fatusi had considerable influence over the Basra JAM. At the time Fatusi was incarcerated in the British detention centre in Basra, having been arrested in 2005 by British troops.

Shaw began negotiating with him. These discussions led to an 'accommodation' between the British and the Basra JAM. The militants would cease attacks on the British and not oppose their withdrawal from Basra Palace, while the British would suspend their strike operations against the JAM and progressively release 120 internees, including, at the end of the process, Fatusi himself. Although not explicitly stated, there appears to have been an underlying understanding that UK forces, once redeployed outside the city, would have little reason routinely to return to Basra; security responsibilities within the city would be discharged by the Iraqi security forces. It was hoped that this would encourage more responsible JAM elements to move towards legitimate politics and away from Iranian influence.

As well as releasing prisoners, the British sought to reduce inadvertent friction with the militia. They largely stayed out of Basra city and convoy movement through Basra was notified in advance to the militia. The benefits of this were felt immediately. Mortar and rocket attacks dropped from a campaign peak in the preceding months to minimal levels, total attacks on UK forces fell by some 90 per cent, and the rest of 2007 saw no further UK deaths from mortar or rocket attacks. The British battalion was able to transfer Basra Palace to the Iraqi forces and relocate to its remaining base at Basra airport – potentially a highly complex and hazardous operation – without a shot being fired. The British then refocused their priorities from force protection onto training the Iraqi Army. With indirect fire attacks greatly reduced, re-development work at the airport was able to resume, paving the way for its handover to the Iraqi authorities, and local politicians were content to resume their visits to the British base to engage with British consular staff. The building of the Basra Children's Hospital – suspended over access difficulties for Coalition staff and contractors – was able to resume, and with British forces no longer in the city, the people of Basra were less likely to be caught up in any crossfire.

But the Iraqi Army lacked the confidence, capability and political support to impose any effective authority on the city. And the Basra Police had been thoroughly corrupted, infiltrated and intimidated by the militia. The unintended consequence of the accommodation was to consolidate the Shia militia takeover of the city. A hard-line Islamist regime was imposed. Corruption and organized crime flourished. The extent of militia depredations is difficult to judge objectively, but there is overwhelming evidence that they ranged from widespread dress restrictions, through the forced closure of alcohol outlets and music shops, to ethnic cleansing, brutality and murder. Basra police chief Major General Jalil later claimed that in the last three months of December, some 40 women were killed in Basra for wearing make-up, not veiling, or otherwise failing to observe the narrow rulings of the hard-line local militias. All these had been occurring before the accommodation, but the British withdrawal removed the one remaining constraint on the militias.

This greatly increased divergence between the UK and US strategies and tactics. MNF-I was orchestrating a re-engagement with the Iraqi people by surging US troops into contested areas in partnership with the Iraqi Security Forces, while the British had disengaged from the Iraqi people on a timetabled drawdown plan. This was reluctantly accepted by General Petraeus, as the British sector was an economy of force mission of lower priority than Baghdad and the Belts. There was a lack of appetite in Baghdad for a military confrontation with the main body of the Shia militias until the Sunni–Al Qaida insurgency had been defeated. Many senior US commanders and officials were still scarred by the experience of 2004 when they had to simultaneously confront the Shia uprisings, at the same time as confronting the Sunni and Al Qaida insurgencies.

It now appears that the British overestimated the Shia militias' perceived legitimacy and public support in the eyes of Basra's civilians. In retrospect, the British view of JAM in 2007 appears rose-tinted: in seeing its prime motivation as criminal and self-interested, they neglected its religious leanings, and thus underestimated its potential antipathy towards those secular and progressive elements of Basra's population that refused to conform to their strictures. The British also underestimated the importance of Basra as a source of revenue for JAM in Iraq as a whole. For example, many of the roadside bombs and rockets used against Coalition forces in Baghdad had either been smuggled through Basra and Maysan provinces or purchased with funds raised in Basra, or both.

But as far as the British government was concerned the Transition Strategy was working in Iraq. In October 2007 it had announced that British force levels would reduce from 5,000 to approximately 2,500 by spring 2008. Provincial Iraqi Control of Basra Province was declared on 16 December 2007. British forces assumed operational overwatch.

The accommodation initially brought a temporary end to attacks on the Basra airport, the last remaining British base, the so-called

'Contingency Operating Base' (COB). But the British had ceded control of the city to JAM. Once Fatusi was released from detention in December 2007 the JAM gradually abandoned restraints on attacking the British. This was unsurprising as the British now lacked any leverage over the militia. They could have applied coercion by resuming strike operations against JAM networks. But the British now had far fewer troops than in 2006 and the withdrawal of British troops from the city had greatly reduced situational awareness. And London insisted that the British stuck to their side of the deal, even as the JAM steadily abandoned their side. This restriction reinforced the weakness of the accommodation with Fatusi.

Mortar and rocket attacks on the remaining British base at Basra airport increased. For example, on 31 January 92 rockets were fired at the base. The defences of the airport had already been increased. Troops who had previously lived in unprotected tents were now protected by improvised concrete shelters – designated Operation *Stonehenge*. These survived strikes by 107mm rockets and close impacts from 122mm rockets. Warning radars were deployed to Basra, as were Phalanx guns. Originally procured by the Royal Navy for shooting down anti-ship missiles, these and the radars were integrated into a defence system to detect and destroy incoming mortars and rockets.

A battery of AS 90 self-propelled guns with heavy 155mm howitzers was deployed to conduct counter-battery fire, but the guns were constrained because many of the firing points were in or close to urban areas. In conditions of great secrecy, the British rushed into service an Israeli missile: Spike NLOS. With NLOS standing for 'non-line of sight', this was an anti-tank missile with an optical sensor in the nose, allowing an operator to fly the missile to the target. Named *Exactor*, what if any use the British made of this new weapon in Iraq is unclear.

Unable to take the fight to the enemy, many British officers and soldiers felt intensely frustrated. And they all knew that popular support for the war was draining away. This factor and the rain of rockets onto the remaining British base unsurprisingly acted to depress morale. BBC reporter Caroline Wyatt noted that:

> For the country, every single death was one too many as it was a war that by then very few people supported. It was very hard for the soldiers, sailors and airmen who contributed to that campaign

to come back to the UK and to feel that people didn't understand what they were doing. Some troops felt the deal and withdrawal from Basra Palace was humiliating. With troops confined to Basra air base with nothing to do, being shelled was frustrating and depressing. And they saw Afghanistan as real soldiering and real fighting. The UK people developed a huge mistrust of politicians, because the public felt they had been lied to about reasons for war.[30]

The British continued to train Iraqi Army units outside the city. They and the local Iraqi commander, General Mohan al-Furayji, developed a plan for a deliberate operation by the Iraqi Army, to clear Basra. This envisaged that once Iraqi troops were sufficiently trained there would be an information operation that would seek sow the seeds of doubt in the militia's mind that they would not be able to resist the Iraqi Army for ever. This would be combined with a six-week long weapons hand-back programme, to allow fighters to disarm themselves with honour. Finally, there would be Iraqi Army operations against any non-compliant militia. Preliminary operations were to take six months. The earliest that the operation could be mounted would be summer 2008.

The plan was briefed to US commanders in Baghdad. They agreed the concept of operations but wished to first complete their campaign to counter Al Qaida in Mosul and northern Iraq, before turning to Basra. General Petraeus and the Iraqi National Security Advisor briefed the plan to Prime Minister Maliki on 22 March. At the end of the meeting Maliki announced that he had his own plan to clear the militia out of Basra. An Iraqi force would deploy to Basra the next day and Maliki would go to Basra the day after.

OPERATION *CHARGE OF THE KNIGHTS*

The operation was given the Iraqi name *Charge of the Knights*. Despite the inspiring title, the operation started without any effective planning or co-ordination by the Iraqi military. It began on 25 March with a brigade of the Iraqi Army's 14th Division being ordered to attack into Basra. The formation was only partially trained. Unsurprisingly its attack was routed by the militia and most of its surviving soldiers deserted. With no shortage of weapons and ammunition, the militias struck back by raining mortars and rockets on Basra Palace, the Iraqi

HQ for the operation. They also attacked Iraqi Army checkpoints and bases in Basra, overrunning many of the installations. The cohesion of many of the Iraqi troops in Basra disintegrated.

General Petraeus was greatly concerned that Prime Minister Maliki had bitten off too much and there was a real prospect of the Shia militants defeating government forces. He directed the Coalition to make Operation *Charge of the Knights* the theatre's main effort.

The remnants of the in-place and partially trained Iraqi 14th Division were rapidly reinforced by an Iraqi divisional HQ, two additional brigades and a National Police brigade, all with their attached US mentoring teams. None of these formations had had any prior notice of the operation; they arrived in Basra without notice to the British and deployed straight into action. Iraqi logistic planning was conspicuous by its absence. Iraqi units were arriving short of water, fuel, rations and ammunition. British logistics units helped overcome the logistic challenge, but the battle quickly posed serious tactical and reputation challenges to the British.

The British tried to influence the conduct of the operation with General Furayji, but there was no doubt that it was Prime Minister Maliki who was directing operations personally, basing himself at Basra Palace with the Minister of Defence. An immediate point of friction was the Iraqi forces' calls for artillery, helicopter and air attacks on militia positions that resisted the Iraqi troops. Iraqi calls for fire would be initiated on a mobile telephone and then had to pass through several nodes before guns or aircraft could even begin to acquire the target location. Often, by the time the target had been acquired, either the moment had passed or the target had moved on. The British did not have the ability to attack the targets being requested by the Iraqi forces. They had no mentoring teams deployed with Iraqi troops. There were no British attack helicopters in Basra, and all the British drones were unarmed. So, the British could not rapidly engage targets of opportunity. In addition, many of the Iraqi requests for fire were vague exhortations for strikes on neighbourhoods of Basra, rather than specific observed targets. These requests were well outside the scope of UK and Coalition rules of engagement.

These factors gave rise to bitter Iraqi accusations that the British were neither willing nor able to support the Iraqi forces in contact with the enemy. They also created similar doubts in the mind of many US officers

Map 10: Battle for Basra, March–April 2008

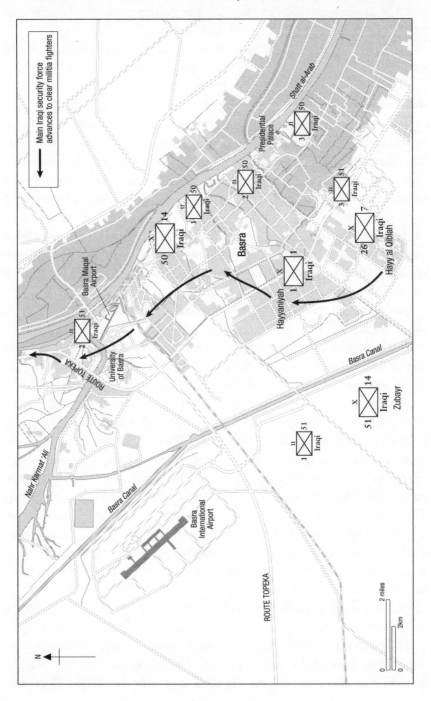

in Baghdad. The start of the operation had exposed the British lack of situational awareness and resources to take the fight to the militias. This led to the Iraqis and the Americans doubting the British commitment to the fight. The British military reputation with the US and Iraqis was rapidly and seriously dented.

The British major general commanding in Basra was away on leave. In his place was Brigadier Julian Free, the commander of 4th Mechanised Brigade. His initial efforts to support the Iraqi operation were rebuffed by Maliki. But by then General Petraeus had designated the operation the main effort. The new US corps HQ, from XVIII Airborne Corps, deployed its tactical operations centre, led by the corps deputy commanding general, US Marine Major General Flynn. Flynn explained to the British that the corps HQ had been deployed to ensure that the operation did not fail. He considered that the British HQ had not had the necessary situational awareness to prevent a crisis from occurring, and that needed restoring.

The US rapidly surged fighter bombers, armed Predator drones and Apache helicopter gunships to the skies above Basra. The Iraqi formations sent south to Basra came with their embedded US mentoring teams. These included US tactical air control parties. Fighting alongside the Iraqis, these were quickly in position to observe, identify and engage targets by speaking directly to the attack helicopters, Predator drones and fast jets flying over Basra. They could receive camera images beamed directly from armed Predator drones. They were quickly able to begin striking militia teams firing rockets and mortars. As the operation developed, US air controllers also co-ordinated attacks on militia teams laying roadside bombs and intimate close air support to advancing Iraqi units.

The British were surprised to see the Iraqi troops and their attached US mentoring teams being welcomed by the people of Basra. Without waiting for orders from the UK, Brigadier Free ordered his troops to form similar mentoring teams to support the Iraqi 14th Division deployed in Basra. This worked and quickly started adding value to the battle.

By March 30, Iraqi forces in the city had been fully reinforced, as had Iraqi SOF. These immediately began to conduct aggressive raids into the city, supported by the Warrior armoured vehicles and Challenger tanks of the Scots Guards. By now the British had reorganized their other forces to provide mentoring teams to the Iraqi Army that accompanied Iraqi battalions and companies into Basra.

Once coerced into direct action by Prime Minister Maliki, General Furayji's initial impulse was to launch everything he had into the Hiyyaniyah district of Basra, a notorious militia stronghold. He was dissuaded from this and took a more measured approach, first securing the access routes into the city and cordoning off the Hiyyaniyah. He was then persuaded to tackle other smaller areas of resistance while simultaneously pouring humanitarian aid into the Hiyyaniyah. This enabled the soldiers of the Iraqi Army to chalk up some successes, which increased their confidence and bought consent for their actions.

With the US having surged attack helicopters and armed Predator drones to Basra the main Iraqi Army offensive was launched on 2 April. Colonel Richard Iron, the British advisor to General Furayji, takes up the story:

> For the first time we had access to plentiful Coalition airpower with seemingly endless attack helicopters and armed Predators over Basra. The militia fought bravely, but not intelligently, they defended in the open against Iraqi Security Force attacks to clear their roadblocks. We found it easy to identify them with drones and then destroy them one by one with Hellfire missiles.
>
> For example, in the al-Latif area of northern Basra, the militia attempted to block the northward movement of the National Police brigade by establishing roadblocks and fighting positions around Qarmat Ali Bridge on the main north-south route into Basra. We quickly identified their headquarters and resupply centre in al-Latif school and that they used a taxi to carry ammunition to their various defensive positions. We simply followed the taxi on the drone camera until we had identified all the positions, and then destroyed them with missiles.[31]

The US also sent a US Civil Military Operations Centre. Its officers were able to follow immediately behind the Iraqi troops and fund clean-up operations, and other employment-generating work. This too reinforced local support for the Iraqi Army, as people saw well-known criminals, murderers and thugs being taken off the street and their neighbourhoods being rapidly cleaned up. By the time the Iraqi forces deployed into the Hiyyaniyah, Iraqis were coming forward to point out weapons caches, criminals and hard-line militia members. Very little resistance was encountered.

While the operation was going on, a self-appointed delegation of Iraqi parliamentarians flew to Iran. General Qassim Soleimani, the commander of Iran's Quds force, brokered a ceasefire between the Iraqi government forces and Sadr's supporters, which took effect from 31 March. This political agreement, the increasing effectives of the Iraqi forces and the welcome given to the Iraqi troops by the people of Basra combined to reduce the level of resistance to the operation. It produced a remarkable change in the operational situation.

Despite its initial reverses, some of which directly sprang from weaknesses of the previous British approach to the city, Operation *Charge of The Knights* created the opportunity for the Iraqi Army to conduct operations that both the Coalition and the people of Basra wanted them to conduct. By redefining the militia and Iranian-supported 'special groups' as enemies, Prime Minister Maliki had changed the political dynamic in southern Iraq. Air Chief Marshal Stirrup subsequently testified to the Iraq Inquiry that:

I had a number of conversations on the telephone with General Petraeus about this. They were taken by surprise as much as we were. They were as nervous as we were, but General Petraeus described this to me as an express train that just couldn't be stopped. Our concern was the lack of planning. It wasn't the Iraqi capability. It was just going down there with no plan; and just doing it is a recipe for confusion at best and disaster at worst. As it turned out, we got the best, which was confusion, but then eventually some order out of the chaos ....

We were cautious about reintroducing an overt UK presence on the streets, and the other very significant factor was that the Iraqis were very reluctant to have us with them because they felt we attracted fire. So we were slower than we should have been, I think, in hindsight, in getting that mentoring going ...'[32]

AFTER OPERATION *CHARGE OF THE KNIGHTS*

The Anbar Awakening and the US Surge had created the security and political conditions to allow Prime Minister Maliki to take on the Shia extremists and their militias. By ordering Operation *Charge of The Knights*, Maliki redefined the JAM and its Iranian supported 'special groups' as insurgents. Without these, the whole US campaign would almost certainly have failed, as would have the UK approach in Basra. So, Operation *Charge of The Knights* was another decisive point. If it had failed it is difficult to see how either Maliki's or the UK's strategy would have survived. It could also have fatally derailed US strategy.

Having cleared Basra, the Iraqi Army went on in April and May to clear and hold the town of Amarah in Maysan Province. Multinational Corps Iraq then switched its main effort away from southern Iraq to the next step in its original operation design, clearance of Al Qaida from northern Iraq. Although Basra reduced in the Coalition's operational priority, the British played an essential role in reinforcing the successes in security, not least by continuing to build Iraqi Army capability. And Iraqi Police capacity was improved by a US police-mentoring task force. A highly successful British mentoring mission throughout 2008 and the first half of 2009 partially restored some of the UK's military reputation with the US and Iraqi Army. But not with Prime Minister Maliki.

At the height of the war with the JAM, the British provincial reconstruction team (PRT) had, out of concern about the safety of its civilian staff, been withdrawn from Iraq to Kuwait, greatly reducing its effectiveness. After Operation *Charge of the Knights* it returned to Basra. This meant that the British HQ could encourage and energize the comprehensive approach – effectively acting in support of the PRT, UK Consul General and US Regional Embassy Office. As the British continued to slowly reduce their troop numbers, they continued to train the Iraqi security forces in southern Iraq, who were seen to grow in confidence and capability. In June 2009, the British handed over to the US 10th Mountain Division and left Iraq.

THE AUDIT OF WAR

Between 2003 and early 2009 the British government consistently failed to produce a properly integrated interagency strategy for southern Iraq.

From mid-2006, the concurrent operation in Afghanistan competed with Iraq for resources and intellectual horsepower. When the US decided to surge additional troops into Iraq in early 2007, the British declined and UK and US strategies diverged. From a position of increasing weakness, the British made an 'accommodation' with Shia militias that conceded control of Basra to their malign rule.

This saved British lives but led to the subsequent near-failure of British strategy. Its weaknesses were brutally exposed by the initial failures of Operation *Charge of the Knights*. This damaged the reputation of British forces with the US and the Iraqis and inflicted major dents in British military self-confidence.

Before Operation *Charge of the Knights*, US commanders and their staff in Baghdad had assumed that the British were sustaining the required level of operational overwatch over Basra. In fact, the level of capability that the US expected was considerably greater than the British actually possessed, and their increasingly defensive operational posture and failure to embed British mentors in Iraqi forces contributed to insufficient awareness of the true situation in Basra.

Discovering this for the first time in the early part of Operation *Charge of the Knights*, many US officers were disappointed. Some were shocked. This disappointment was reinforced by exposure of gaps in situational awareness, military capability and integration with the Iraqi forces. These factors were reinforced by the impression that while US troops had been fighting hard in the Surge, Britain had cut a deal with JAM and had hung up its boots, as well as by an almost complete lack of US knowledge of the hard and bloody fighting in Basra that had preceded the accommodation.

All this resulted in a significant erosion in trust between many US commanders and staff officers and the British Army. Both the US HQs in Baghdad and the British in Basra had drifted by mutual consent into a situation where each HQ paid insufficient attention to the other's operations. This was exacerbated by the fact that the British in Multinational Division South East tended to look towards London, rather than Baghdad. All of these factors combined to create mistrust between the US and British military. They were rapidly amplified by reporting and commentary in the US and British media. In this the London press were reinforcing a long-standing narrative of an illegitimate and failing war.

The rapid British tactical response to the shock inflicted by the opening phase of Operation *Charge of the Knights*, namely the rapid formation and deployment of mentoring teams, had some limited effect in countering this. Subsequent successful UK operations in Basra also restored a degree of confidence in US commanders. But there is little doubt that between 2008 and 2014 British military credibility with the US never reached the peak established in the immediate aftermath of the overthrow of Saddam Hussein.

Unsurprisingly, the British Army's confidence was damaged. The 'abandonment' of Basra to the JAM is the aspect of the deal which subsequently has probably caused most unease, including within the British Army. For example, troops who served in Basra before the accommodation who returned after Operation *Charge of the Knights* found that many Iraqi civilians that they had previously interacted with were no longer in Basra. Some had fled Iraq; others had been murdered. This created a sense that the British had abandoned the ordinary decent people of Basra. And by 2008 it was abundantly clear that in many ways the British military rate of adaptation to the Iraq war had been slower than that of the US Army and Marine Corps.

LIMITS TO BRITISH INFLUENCE

The shock administered by Operation *Charge of the Knights* also forced the British to realize that their influence with the US in Iraq was less than they had previously assessed. The balance of evidence strongly suggests that from 2003 onwards the British government and military had very little influence over the US civilian and military direction of the war. For example, the Iraq Inquiry concluded that the UK had little positive impact on the US-led CPA. And it had no influence over the CPA's decisions to disband the Iraqi security services and exclude Baath Party members from public service.

Daniel Marston, a Sandhurst academic, played an important role the COIN Centre for Excellence that the US set up in Iraq. But the UK's failure to provide any military staff to the Centre and reluctance to send incoming UK commanders and staffs to the short courses there was an influence opportunity that was missed. A British civilian, Emma Sky, had great influence, particularly as a political advisor to Lieutenant

General Ray Odierno, the Commander of III US Corps. But her work seems to have had little impact on thinking in London.

Apart from Lieutenant General Graeme Lamb, US journalists and commentators have not identified any UK officer who achieved the influence of Emma Sky or David Kilcullen, the Australian COIN expert. Lamb himself played a decisive role in leading the reconciliation negotiations with Sunni insurgents in 2007. Both Petraeus and McChrystal have cited the influence of his work and the value of his perspective.

British influence was also reduced by the national command and control. The British national commander was not the British lieutenant general in Baghdad, but the major general commanding in Basra. Usually he saw his main responsibility as being to the British joint HQ in Northwood, rather than the US-led HQs in Baghdad. It also seems that neither the UK joint HQ nor the MoD paid enough attention to the Iraq campaign as a whole. This shows that to maximize campaign coherence and multinational unity of effort, there is a clear requirement for a single campaign plan, owned by the in-theatre operational headquarters. British military influence in Iraq should have been focused at influencing the campaign plan and establishing clear and unambiguous situational awareness at the theatre level. It was not.

An aggravating factor was that the tours in Iraq by British units and officers were usually shorter than the tours of US units and individuals. This disrupted continuity of command and understanding, compared with the US Army who deployed units and individuals on 12-month tours. Peacetime process often seemed to trump the operational need. For example, even though they were only on six-month tours, British unit and brigade commanders and key staff officers were allowed to change over in mid-tour. There was an 18-month period in 2004–05 when this policy meant that the British brigade in Basra was commanded by no fewer than five different officers. In the same period US brigade sectors would have seen only two different brigade commanders.

Many British generals commanding southern Iraq asked that 'continuity personnel' on longer accompanied tours be based in Kuwait. Despite this model having been successfully applied by the British Army in Northern Ireland these requests were denied. This apparent 'business as usual' approach to manning undermined effectiveness and credibility of the British with the Iraqis and with the US.

PRIME MINISTER BLAIR'S FAILURE AS STRATEGIC LEADER

Between 2003 and 2009 Britain's war in Iraq became increasingly unpopular with the British people, politicians and media. This greatly damaged the domestic political credibility of Prime Minister Tony Blair. Also eroded were the reputations for competence of the British government, its defence, foreign and development ministries and the UK's intelligence services and armed forces.

For example, from mid-2003 onwards British military commanders in Basra all sensed a profound lack of civil–military co-ordination in London, a lack of top-down leadership, and a government approach to Iraq that was under-resourced and inadequately led and co-ordinated.[33] This is but one of many examples of sub-optimal performance by politicians, government, departments and intelligence staff, senior military officers and civilian officials identified by the Iraq Inquiry. There is overwhelming evidence that Blair's leadership and management of post-conflict stabilization of Iraq was insufficiently effective. Whilst there is abundant evidence of decisions being made in Number 10, there is equally abundant evidence of follow-up action being either absent or being poorly co-ordinated. There was consistent failure to adequately monitor progress. And on many occasions politicians, government departments and senior officials not only ignored direction given by Blair, but were allowed to do so.[34] The Inquiry could not:

> identify alternative approaches that would have guaranteed greater success in the circumstances of March 2003. What can be said is that a number of opportunities for the sort of candid reappraisal of policies that would have better aligned objectives and resources did not take place. There was no serious consideration of more radical options, such as an early withdrawal or else a substantial increase in effort. The Inquiry has identified a number of moments, especially during the first year of the Occupation, when it would have been possible to conduct a substantial reappraisal. None took place'.[35]

Moreover:

> Better planning and preparation for a post-Saddam Hussein Iraq would not necessarily have prevented the events that unfolded

in Iraq between 2003 and 2009. It would not have been possible for the UK to prepare for every eventuality. Better plans and preparation could have mitigated some of the risks to which the UK and Iraq were exposed between 2003 and 2009 and increased the likelihood of achieving the outcomes desired by the UK and the Iraqi people'.[36]

Prime Ministers David Lloyd George and Winston Churchill had both used war cabinets to exercise strategic leadership, both for decision making and for overseeing the implementation of these decisions. The 1940–45 war cabinet bound together political, military and civil service decision making, planning and delivery. It had a permanent secretariat that recorded decisions, assigned responsibilities for implementation and monitored progress, providing essential management and discipline that Blair appeared content to ignore. The same principles were applied by Prime Minister Margaret Thatcher in 1982. In all these examples the war cabinet was a key vehicle for effective strategic leadership. Indeed, the evidence paints a comprehensive picture of strategic leadership and management of the Iraq and Afghan wars that fell below the standards achieved by Churchill and Thatcher.

The implications are clear. After the successful regime change operation, the British government failed to adequately align strategic ends with the ways and means it chose to apply. A consistent failure was inadequate implementation of decisions made. Although many organizations, officials, military officers and ministers in the Foreign and Commonwealth Office, MoD and Department for International Development contributed to this display of inadequate strategic competence, the single most important factor was probably the inability of Prime Minister Blair to make the decisions he had taken stick.

The Iraq Inquiry pulled its punches. It should have been much more critical of Blair. By inadequately leading and resourcing British stabilization operations in Iraq, Blair was directly responsible for the military weaknesses that led to the accommodation. This not only resulted in the imposition of malign militia rule over Basra, with its resulting civilian deaths, but also the near-failure of the first part of Operation *Charge of the Knights*.

There is a sad irony that one of Blair's main motives for assisting with US-led regime change was to gain and sustain influence with the US.

But he was responsible for a net reduction in British influence over the US and for the loss of British influence over Prime Minister Maliki.

As war leader Blair should be judged a failure. It is very difficult to have any sympathy for the considerable damage that the war inflicted on Blair's domestic political credibility. Other reputations were badly damaged, including those of key UK government departments including defence, foreign and development ministries and the UK intelligence services and armed forces. Whilst many other politicians, senior officers and officials must shoulder their share of the blame for British strategic failures in Iraq, the ultimate responsibility is Blair's.

Endgame in Iraq

Success turns to failure

THE BATTLE OF SADR CITY

Sadr City was a vast housing project in north-eastern Baghdad occupied by 2.4 million people. It mainly consisted of two- or three-storey buildings laid out in rectangular grids of flat streets and narrow alleyways. Its people were impoverished, disenfranchised, and subjected to sectarian violence, rampant criminality, and corruption. The Sadrist JAM militia controlled the area, administering justice, and providing services, using its own brand of violence and crime to control the streets and intimidate the district's inhabitants. During the Surge US and Iraqi forces had largely left the neighbourhood alone, the exception being some SOF raids against 'special groups'.

As Operation *Charge of the Knights* began in Basra, the Sadr City JAM reacted strongly. The militia overran Iraqi security checkpoints on the edge of Sadr City and fired salvos of rockets and mortars into the International Zone, the so-called Green Zone, home to the US HQ, Iraqi government offices and foreign embassies. On 25 March Prime Minister Maliki authorized US and Iraqi forces to stop the rocket attacks and defeat the militants in Sadr City.

The 3rd BCT, 4th Infantry Division was assigned the task, along with troops from the Iraqi Army's 11th Division. The brigade developed a plan for a combined arms manoeuvre operation that would employ its Stryker-equipped mechanized infantry, supported by a wide range of surveillance and strike capabilities. The Green Zone was at the maximum range of the JAM's weapons. Pushing back the JAM to the north-east would therefore significantly reduce the effectiveness of their attacks. The US brigade would set up a forward defence in the southern quarter of Sadr City as part of Operation *Striker Denial* to stop mortar and rocket fire on the Green Zone further south.

On 15 April the brigade began to build a 12-foot concrete barrier along Al Qods Street ('Route Gold'), cutting off the southern route into Sadr City. The aim was to deny JAM forces the ability to access the population and the lucrative markets to the south of the district and to push the rocket teams beyond the range at which they could fire rockets at the Green Zone.

It soon became apparent that the JAM viewed the market areas and the zone from which it could fire rockets at the Green Zone as key terrain. Its fighters came out of hiding to attack the soldiers and combat engineers building the wall. The brigade initially used Stryker vehicles to defend the wall and the engineers building it. But these vehicles suffered attrition from RPG attacks and roadside bombs. The city's small, cluttered alleys also significantly restricted the movement of the Stryker vehicles, which had a wide turning radius. Six Strykers were destroyed in the first week of fighting.

The brigade brought in Abrams tanks and Bradley fighting vehicles. These were considerably better protected and could turn on the spot. This greatly reduced US vehicle and personnel casualties. Most Strykers were armed with a single heavy machine gun. The 120mm guns of the Abrams tanks and 25mm cannon of the Bradley together with both vehicles' thermal sights greatly improved the firepower that could be brought to bear against the militia fighters.

The construction of the wall required soldiers on the ground to build it and armour to protect it. The armoured vehicles and concrete wall segments provided some protection for the engineers and their unarmoured cranes. But after the cranes had set the wall segments in place a US sapper had to clamber atop the wall to unhook the chains that lifted the concrete slabs from the crane hook. This required no little courage.

As the wall grew, the JAM found itself cut off from key launching positions and critical sources of revenue. The wall's construction drew out the enemy, enabling US forces to fight from a position of advantage. The barrier created a dilemma for the militia. If they allowed it to be

MAP 11: BATTLE FOR SADR CITY, MARCH–MAY 2008

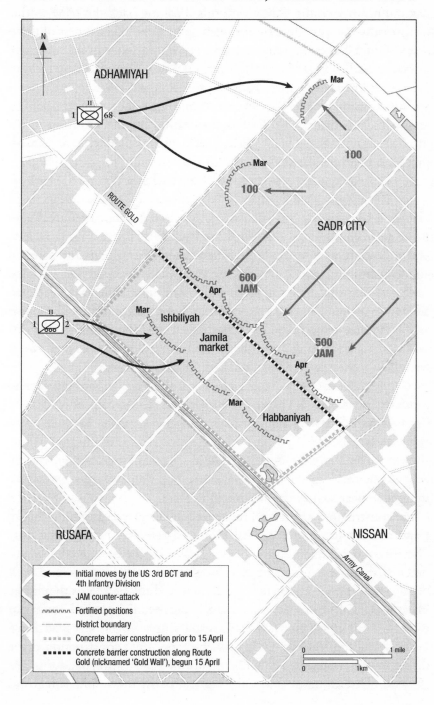

N

ADHAMIYAH

II
1 ⊠ 68

ROUTE GOLD

Mar

100

Mar

100

SADR CITY

600
JAM
Apr

II
1 ⊘ 2

Mar Ishbiliyah

Jamila
market

500
JAM
Apr

Mar

Habbaniyah

RUSAFA

NISSAN

Army Canal

Initial moves by the US 3rd BCT and
4th Infantry Division

JAM counter-attack

Fortified positions

District boundary

Concrete barrier construction prior to 15 April

Concrete barrier construction along Route
Gold (nicknamed 'Gold Wall'), begun 15 April

0   1 mile

0   1km

built they could not bring their rockets into range to attack the Green Zone. But if the militia fighters attacked the wall and its builders, they had to fight Abrams tanks and Bradley fighting vehicles, at considerable risk of being detected and attacked by the armoured vehicles.

As the battle unfolded the JAM rocket and mortar teams attempted to set up and launch their rockets as quickly as possible. And JAM groups attacking the wall attempted to minimize the time they spent in the open. This made them fleeting targets. But as well as fire from US infantry and armoured vehicles the militia fighters had to contend with precision fire from the sky above Sadr City.

To complement the construction of the wall and to reduce the threat from JAM fighters, the brigade was allocated round-the-clock access to pervasive intelligence, surveillance, and reconnaissance and precision-strike capabilities. These included the P3 Orion, a US Navy maritime patrol aircraft and at least one Predator drone constantly orbiting above Sadr City as well as smaller US Army Shadow and Raven drones. Aerostats, tethered balloons with high-resolution cameras, were flown above US combat outposts to watch into the neighbourhood. As well as the Hellfire-armed Predators, there were continuous patrols by jets armed with laser-guided bombs as well as Apache attack helicopters with cannon and Hellfire missiles. Counter-battery radars were used to locate the rocket-firing points and the brigade had on-demand access to the Guided Multiple Launch Rocket System, which could use rockets fitted with GPS guidance to strike targets to the nearest cubic metre.

Before the Iraq war, many of these capabilities would have been held at division, corps or even theatre level. But for this operation, they were all placed under the control of the brigade. This allowed the brigade to achieve previously unprecedented levels of integration of ground combat, airborne surveillance and precision strike capabilities These gave the brigade the ability to fight a highly integrated air–land battle that made it much more difficult for rocket teams to fire their missiles and survive and which greatly reduced the effectiveness of JAM fighters attempting to attack the wall. Neither the ground force nor the airborne surveillance and strike capabilities would have succeeded in defeating the JAM on their own, but together they accelerated the defeat of the militants. As with Operation *Charge of the Knights*, the tactic of concentrating sufficient ground troops, attack helicopters and armed unmanned aerial vehicles over the city defeated the JAM in Sadr City months earlier than had been planned.

By mid-May, the pressure had taken its toll on JAM fighters, and rocket attacks both on the US troops and on the Green Zone greatly reduced. The Iraqi Army's 44th Brigade took the lead in pushing north of the wall to take control of the whole of Sadr City. It was welcomed by many of Sadr City's residents, who had visibly seen the JAM's ability to control their neighbourhoods destroyed. On 11 May 2008, Sadr requested a ceasefire, but not before an estimated 1,000 fighters had lost their lives.

THE SURGE ENDS AND US WITHDRAWAL BEGINS

The defeat of the JAM in Basra and Sadr City allowed US forces to return to the original campaign plan. US forces switched their attention and efforts back to the towns around the capital, known to the US military as the Baghdad 'Belts', and into Diyala Province. There was heavy fighting around Baquba. But by 2009 Iraqi forces were competently and confidently holding the areas cleared during the Surge, large numbers of Sunni insurgents had switched sides and Al Qaida was reeling from precision attacks on their leaders and networks by US and Iraqi SOF. Al Qaida's networks that funnelled fighters, fake documents, suicide bombers, arms and explosives into Iraq from Syria were disrupted by an October 2008 US SOF raid across the Iraqi border into eastern Syria. This killed Abu Ghadiya, reportedly Al Qaida in Iraq's organizer of cross-border networks.

Popular support for the Iraqi Army increased and it was able to play an increasingly confident role in operations. By mid-2008 some 80,000 Sunni and 20,000 Shia irregulars had been taken on the US government payroll as 'Sons of Iraq', putting four times as many additional 'boots on the ground' as had been sent to Iraq by the US Surge. The US had developed the Iraqi Security Forces into an effective counter-insurgency and internal security force that commanded a degree of national respect.

By mid-2008, the US ended the Surge and began to reduce troop numbers, resuming the Transition Strategy. General Odierno, corps commander during the Surge, replaced Petraeus in September 2008, the latter moving to command CENTCOM. Security in Iraq continued to improve as did the capability and confidence of the Iraqi security forces. By the end of 2008 the improvement in security was, by Iraqi standards, dramatic. At the peak of the violence in 2006 attacks recorded by US forces had averaged over 140 per day. By the turn of 2008 there was an increasing number of days in which no attacks were recorded by US forces.

Despite the improvement in security the war in Iraq was still extremely complex. For example, in 2008 US forces in Iraq were conducting the following lines of activity:

- attacking Sunni and Al Qaida insurgents in the Baghdad 'Belts'
- countering Shia 'special groups' in Baghdad and Basra
- growing, training and equipping the Iraqi Security Forces
- administering the Sons of Iraq militias
- mentoring the Iraqi Ministry of Defence and Interior
- seeking to persuade the Iraqi prime minister to employ his forces in ways that reinforced political progress, rather than inhibited it.
- attempting to reduce friction between Iraqi Security Forces and Kurdish Peshmerga units by deploying US forces in a peacekeeping role between the two
- seeking to avoid Kurdistan being destabilized by Turkish strikes against PKK guerrillas in Iraq. This involved sharing intelligence and drone imagery with Ankara.

The UN Security Council Resolution that authorized the US military presence in Iraq was due to expire at the end of 2008. Throughout that year the US sought to negotiate a security agreement for US forces to remain from 2009 onwards. Negotiations were prolonged and difficult. A deal was eventually agreed. After approval by the Iraqi cabinet and parliament the Iraqi presidential council approved the security pact on 4 December 2008.

The agreement required that US troops withdrew from Iraqi cities by July 2009. It also stipulated that US forces would co-ordinate their operations through Iraqi military and police commanders. These would take the lead in obtaining the necessary warrants from Iraqi judges. US military operations had to be co-ordinated with the Iraqi forces. This meant that that the Iraqi authorities now had an effective veto over operations by US forces, other than US operations in self-defence and to counter immediate threats, which the agreement allowed.

During the 2008 US presidential election campaign, candidate Barrack Obama had called for an end to the US military presence in Iraq, while endorsing the war in Afghanistan. After his January 2009 inauguration Obama made it clear that the US government was to implement his pledge to 'responsibly end the war in Iraq'. He directed that US troop numbers were to reduce from 142,000 in February 2009 to about 50,000 at the end of summer 2010.

Elections for provincial governments were held in January 2009, with the Iraqi forces to the fore in providing security. With a total of 750,000 Iraqi security forces and US troops deployed attacks on election day were low. Many Sunnis voted, and many politicians elected were on Iraqi nationalist platforms.

The large US military HQ had reduced from 7,000 staff at the height of the Surge to about 2,000. Ambassador Ryan Crocker had ably partnered Generals Petraeus and Odierno. He departed in mid-2009, replaced by Ambassador Christopher Hill. Hill saw Iraq and the role of the US military very differently from Odierno, appearing to believe that his mission was to civilianize the US presence in Iraq and turn the US Embassy into a normal diplomatic outpost. The US military HQ felt that neither the security situation nor the capabilities of the fledgling Iraqi government allowed for this approach, which they considered carried great risk. Hill and his staff often appeared to be unwilling to engage with the US military.

In 2009 the vast new US embassy complex opened. As diplomats and civilians moved into this huge fortified compound, Hill's staff sought to restrict access by US military officers. US civil–military relations in Baghdad rapidly deteriorated back to the level of friction that had been such a feature of the CPA's tenure in 2003–04.

In spring 2009, US and Iraqi forces mounted attacks to push Al Qaida out of its remaining base areas in Diyala Province, northern Iraq, seeking to disrupt its ability to mount further attacks before the July deadline for the US withdrawal from Iraqi cities. Concurrently a combined US–Iraqi operation sought to attack Al Qaida in the city of Mosul. These forces were vigorously attacked by jihadist suicide bombers who killed a US battalion commander and his security team and destroyed a US outpost, killing five US and three Iraqi soldiers.

The US and Iraqi troops made some progress in gaining the confidence of Mosul's citizens, resulting in increased amounts of intelligence being provided by civilians living in the city. Whilst considerable attrition was inflicted on the jihadists, they retained significant networks in Mosul. Extensive corruption in Mosul's courts meant that hundreds of captured insurgents were able to bribe or intimidate police, judges and court officials to release Al Qaida fighters from detention.

The defeat of the JAM in summer 2008 had resulted in a considerable reduction of armed attacks by Shia militants. But Iran continued to train Shia fighters and in 2009 attacks on US troops by Iranian-supported 'special groups' resumed, with increasing numbers of attacks by roadside bombs, as did rocket attacks against US bases. All US detainees had been handed over to the Iraqi authorities at the end of 2008, reducing US leverage over the Shia groups. The US military were particularly concerned by the Shia militant group Asaib Ahl al-Haqq. There was ample evidence that the group had been at the forefront of those supported by Iran in its attacks on Coalition troops. But for political reasons Prime Minister Maliki was keen to negotiate with Qais al-Khazali, the leader of the group. He insisted that the US military conform with this initiative, although once the negotiations broke down US operations against this group resumed.

As US troops withdrew from Iraqi cities in June 2009 their ability to gather intelligence against both Al Qaida and Shia militants reduced. And the handover of responsibility for southern Iraq from British to US forces had not seen the US successfully take over UK human intelligence networks, further reducing situational understanding of Shia militants. Shia fighters stepped up their attacks on US forces, to portray a message that it was their fighters that were forcing the US from urban areas.

On 31 August 2009 President Obama announced that the US combat mission would end in September 2010. It would be replaced by Operation *New Dawn*, a 'train, advise and assist' mission.

The withdrawal of US forces from Iraqi cities created opportunities that Al Qaida exploited. In mid-August Al Qaida conducted four near-simultaneous suicide car bombs in Baghdad, killing 75 Iraqis and wounding almost ten times as many. But intelligence-led operations by US SOF and Iraqi Police were able to shut down key nodes in the network that generated the suicide vest attacks and an Al Qaida attempt to resume attacks on Baghdad by suicide car bombs only partially succeeded.

The US assessed the successes of the bombings as due to the complacency of the Iraqi security forces, but Prime Minister Maliki used the bombings as an excuse to blame a network of former Baathists operating from Syria. A subsequent wave of suicide car bombings on 25 October caused even more casualties. The Iraqi government sacked some incompetent security commanders and increased physical security in Baghdad, although its checkpoints were dangerously reliant on fake bomb detectors purchased by corrupt Iraqi officials from an unscrupulous British businessman.

Another series of suicide attacks in mid-December killed 50 Iraqis and wounded another 200. These series of attacks greatly reduced the credibility of the Maliki government with the Iraqi people. It came close to collapse.

In the meantime, the Sons of Iraq transferred from US to Iraqi government control. In 2010 they came under pressure from offensive actions by Al Qaida and the disfavour with which they were viewed by the Maliki government. Increasingly Maliki seemed to view them as a threat to his regime. An indicator of this in 2010 was ever-increasing delays in paying their wages.

THE COUNTER-ATTACK AGAINST AL QAIDA

Intelligence about Al Qaida gathered during US and Iraqi SOF raids in Mosul the previous year as well as investigations of the autumn 2009 bombings in Baghdad provided a great deal of intelligence that was exploited as the springboard for offensive action against Al Qaida in early 2010. This began with raids by US and Iraqi SOF on 16 targets in Mosul on 4 January 2010. Several Al Qaida leaders were killed, with others captured including its 'border wali' who organized the flow of foreign jihadists into northern Iraq. Raids in Baghdad disrupted Al Qaida's advanced plans for another car bomb offensive into Baghdad.

Al Qaida's commander for Baghdad was captured by Iraqi forces. Prime Minister Maliki was initially reluctant to allow him to be interrogated by the US, but after a wave of car bombings on 4 April against foreign embassies in Baghdad he allowed the US to question him. This disclosed plots to attack the 2010 football world cup tournament in South Africa, as well as a plan to hijack airliners and crash them onto Iraq's main Shia shrines to inflame another sectarian civil war. In response, the Iraqi government rushed to account for all non-US aircraft and Iraqi airliners and US anti-aircraft defences were deployed to protect the shrines.

Arrested senior Al Qaida leaders provided extensive information under interrogation that was rapidly exploited to allow further raids, which yielded important documents, including letters, documents, CDs and computer data. The US and Iraqi forces were able to unravel the clandestine management network of Al Qaida. Yet more raids yielded more documentary evidence and detainees. Particularly decisive was the capture of Zarqawi's successor as leader of Al Qaida in Iraq, Abu Ayyub al-Masri, and the group's head of operations, as well as another cache of documents and over six terabytes of computer data.

This was rapidly exploited over the next month, with another 19 Al Qaida leaders being killed or captured in subsequent raids. By mid-May General Odierno assessed that three-quarters of the senior leadership of Al Qaida in Iraq had been neutralized.

Analysis of intelligence gained showed that Al Qaida had established a stranglehold over the illicit trade in black market petrol across northern Iraq and Syria. Iraqi and US action to disrupt this network, including simultaneous raids on all of 117 black market petrol stations, greatly damaged Al Qaida's finances. These actions had a huge impact on Al Qaida, the former Al Qaida commander in Baghdad detained by the Iraqi authorities telling CNN in May 2010 that 'it is 80 to 100 per cent harder to operate for Al Qaida these days'. Documents captured by US forces in their 2011 raid on Osama Bin Laden's compound in Pakistan showed that his communications with Al Qaida in Iraq had become much more difficult.[1]

PEACEKEEPING IN NORTHERN IRAQ

As US forces withdrew from northern Iraq, tensions between the Kurdish authorities and the Baghdad government rapidly increased. A previous flashpoint in 2008 had been defused by US commanders, but in early 2010 multiple frictions developed across the Green Line – the de facto southern boundary of autonomous Kurdistan. This friction was also exploited by Al Qaida insurgents. US forces sought to reduce tensions by establishing Combined Co-ordination Centres manned by Iraqi, Kurdish and US troops. A combined security force of Iraqi, Kurdish and US troops was formed to man checkpoints and patrol the territory disrupted between Arabs and Kurds. But without resolution of the underlying political tension between Kurdistan and Baghdad these arrangements could only be a stop-gap measure, as shown by a February 2010 confrontation between Kurdish and Iraqi forces that resulted in both sides taking hostages. It took US officials and the Iraqi deputy prime minister to negotiate their release.

MALIKI STEALS THE 2010 ELECTION

In the run-up to the March 2010 Iraqi parliamentary elections, another indicator of increasingly partisan behaviour by Maliki was the efforts by the Iraqi de-Baathification committee to cancel the candidacy of over 500 allegedly Baathist electoral candidates, including some who already held public office. This was a naked and successful effort to manipulate the poll.

The provision of security for the March 2010 parliamentary elections was successful. Former prime minister Ayad Allawi formed the Iraqiya coalition of mainly Kurdish and Sunni groups, while Prime Minister Maliki had formed a Shia coalition called State of Law. Iraqiya won the election by 91 seats to State of Law's 89 seats.

The Iraqi constitution clearly implied that Iraqiya should have had the first opportunity to form the new government. But Maliki was determined to frustrate this. He used a variety of methods, including securing a questionable ruling from the flagrantly sectarian Shia Chief Justice, threatening members of Iraq's Electoral Commission, and inducing further candidate disqualifications by the de-Baathification Commission (formerly Council). Malaki tenaciously clung on to power. Despite considerable reservations expressed by General Odierno, the formation of Maliki's government was supported by the US ambassador and Vice President Joe Biden. Ironically, Maliki's retention of power was also supported by Tehran. By now it was a major actor in Shia politics. It had the funds, political influence and support from Shia militias to enable General Qassim Soleimani, the commander of Quds Force, to use a mixture of incentives and threats to persuade Iraqi Shia politicians to acquiesce in Maliki's continued rule. Maliki's retention of power had a polarizing effect that increased the disenchantment of Iraq's Sunnis.

THE END OF THE US MISSION IN IRAQ

From August 2010 US forces conducted an advise and assist mission. A key objective would be to make the Iraqi Security Forces as self-sufficient as possible. This would be enabled by the US combat brigades being replaced by specially organized US Army advise and assist brigades to operate 'by through and with' the Iraqi forces. These formations were explicitly designed to provide Iraqi units with training, advice and mentoring. They contained stability transition teams for the army, police and border security forces, essentially the previous military transition teams under a new name. The brigades also had a civil affairs company, psychological operations teams, contracting officers and lawyers. They also provided security for the remaining US PRTs. These were shifting their effort from funding reconstruction to achieve Iraqi popular consent to the presence of US troops to assisting the Iraqi authorities in developing their provinces.

President Obama directed that the US military hand over lead responsibility for Iraq to the State Department by September 2010. The security assistance mission and support to Iraqi Security Forces became the responsibility of the US Embassy's Office of Security Co-operation and was conducted by contractors. Ambassador Hill decided that the US embassy should greatly reduce its engagement with Iraqi government ministries. Reports reaching the embassy were of a relatively low level of violence. It is now clear that these were not accurate. Two factors may account for this. First, the lack of US troops deployed with Iraqi forces throughout the country to provide 'ground truth'. Secondly, one of Iraq's two intelligence agencies that had proven itself effective against Sunni and Al Qaida targets was purged and politicized by Maliki, greatly reducing its effectiveness.

AS US TROOPS WITHDRAW, MALIKI BECOMES THE MIDWIFE OF ISIS

Remaining US advisors had assessed that the Iraqi Forces had considerable weakness. They were capable of manning security cordons of checkpoints and conducting simple infantry and police tasks, but co-operation between the Iraqi Army and Police was poor, as was co-operation between Iraqi federal and local police forces. Indiscipline and corruption provided opportunities for Al Qaida bombers to pass through the security cordons.[2] Iraqi forces were reluctant to hold Sunni neighbourhoods that had been cleared by US forces, preferring to ring the areas with checkpoints and to conduct raids. Iraq commanders were increasingly being appointed for Shia sectarian political reasons, rather than non-sectarian professional merit.

Whilst the Iraqi Army was capable of simple infantry platoon-level operations, Iraq struggled to field more advanced capabilities. The army had difficulty introducing into service US M1 Abrams tanks and the Iraqi Air Force's capabilities were even less well developed than those of the Iraqi Army. Plans to train Iraqi pilots to fly F16 fighters progressed very slowly and whilst the Iraqi Air Force had an operations centre capable of controlling 350 air sorties, its ability to provide the necessary overall control over Iraqi air space was lacking. A partial exception to these weaknesses was the Iraqi Navy and its marines who had benefited from British training and assistance, but by the end of 2009 the Iraqi government had suspended this re-arming mission.

An example of the Iraqi forces' weaknesses was a September 2010 battle in Diyala Province where a very small force of Sunni insurgents held off no fewer than seven attacks by different Iraqi units, before the Iraqi forces requested US assistance. The so-called 'battle of the Palm Grove' exposed many command and leadership failings, including considerable weaknesses in infantry tactics and mistreatment of detainees and local civilians.[3]

In addition, Iraqi forces lacked a systematic approach to training. They refused to set up an operational rotation system that would allow units an opportunity to withdraw from operations for rest and refresher training.

Throughout 2010 the US military had been proposing that a small US force remain in the country after 2011. This was not accepted by the Iraqi government. Washington had asked Baghdad for a Strategic Framework Agreement and Status of Forces Agreement (SOFA) to cover long-term support to Iraq by the US government and US forces respectively. However, the SOFA negotiations failed, mainly because of overwhelming opposition in the Iraqi parliament to the US requirement that their troops be granted immunity from prosecution in Iraqi courts. Iran made it clear to many Shia politicians that it strongly opposed a residual US force in the country and that Tehran expected Shia politicians to support this line.

The 2011 Arab Spring wave of popular protests throughout the Middle East was reflected in Iraq. Much Iraqi public dissatisfaction with the Maliki government was expressed in a late February 'Day of Rage', but in Baghdad demonstrators were killed by heavy-handed security operations.

Over the next three years, Maliki greatly consolidated his sectarian power base.[4] Appointing himself as Minister of Defence and Minister of the Interior, he marginalized and persecuted key Sunni and Kurd politicians. A toxic combination of discrimination, deliberate neglect and increasingly heavy-handed repression increasingly disenfranchised and alienated the Sunni minority.

Maliki also centralized control of security by directly assuming ministerial authority for the armed forces, police and intelligence agencies. Tried and tested police and army commanders were replaced by less capable, but politically loyal proxies. The Iraqi SOF were increasingly used to target Sunnis and Maliki's political opponents. The forces became increasingly flagrant in their sectarian alignment with the Shias. For example, the Iraqi SOF leadership changed the uniform of the elite Counter-Terrorism Service Brigade from camouflaged fatigues to an all-black uniform. This appeared a deliberate effort to intimidate Sunnis, the JAM Shia militia having often worn all-black uniforms. A fall in the price of oil led to cuts to the Iraqi defence budget. This became an excuse to greatly reduce the budget, including for the Iraqi Security Forces. Maliki and his government's aims and actions were increasingly diverging from those of US.

These developments greatly reduced the effectiveness of the Iraqi security forces as well as their impartiality, eroding their authority with the Iraqi Sunnis. Despite possessing large amounts of US military equipment, endemic corruption further reduced the effectiveness of the army and police, particularly by reducing their logistic capability, thus eroding the credibility of many senior officers.

During 2011, Al Qaida rebuilt capabilities, including recruiting former Iraqi Army officers and increased its attacks against Iraq government institutions and forces.

From mid-2011, Iranian-supported Shia fighters stepped up attacks on remaining US forces, using rockets, mortars and EFP roadside bombs. They sought to reinforce the narrative that they had forced the US from Iraq and to gain political credibility they could exploit. The Shia militants refrained from attacking Iraqi forces. This made Iraqi forces reluctant to support the US in countering these attacks, particularly in the Shia-dominated southern Iraq. Shia militia members routinely infiltrated the Iraqi security forces. In one notorious example a mortar was fired from the Iraqi forces area of a shared security force base. This attack at Forward Operating Base Loyalty in Baghdad killed seven US troops and wounded 30.

Over a period of seven weeks in late 2011 all remaining US troops departed Iraq. To withdraw some 40,000 troops and 36,000 contractors out of the country over such a short period of time was a massive logistic and movement task, complicated by the need to guard against attacks by Iranian-supported Shia fighters. Some 500–800 US troops left Iraq each day by road or air. As the conventional forces withdrew, US SOF acting as a covering force attacked Shia militant networks, both unilaterally and with remaining trustworthy Iraqi SOF. All US troops were withdrawn by mid-December 2011. The last US troops left Iraq in a convoy of 110 vehicles carrying 500 soldiers, one of whom was an Iraqi who had immigrated to the US in 2009 and had joined the US Army in 2010.

THE RISE OF ISIS AND IRAN'S INFLUENCE IN IRAQ

Meanwhile the remnants of Al Qaida in Iraq took up arms against the Assad regime in Syria. Rebranding itself as the Islamic State of Syria and al Sham (ISIS), it carved out territory from the central town of Raqqa to the Iraqi border. As well as imposing its brutal version of sharia law it sought to achieve stability in the towns it controlled, generating revenue, raising taxes, and carrying out kidnappings and black-market trading of oil and looted antiquities.

It rebuilt networks in the increasingly discontented Sunni communities across western and central Iraq. It conducted bombings, assassinations and attacks on Iraqi security forces. It mounted sophisticated propaganda, including well-edited videos on YouTube and a highly effective Twitter operation to garner international jihadist volunteers, financial donations and support from Syrian and Iraqi Sunnis.

In early 2014 Sunni insurgents seized Fallujah, from which they were not dislodged. The town rapidly became an ISIS base. Over the following months, ISIS gained an increasing advantage over the Iraqi government forces around Mosul. Iraqi senior commanders' precipitate self-evacuation from the city seems to have triggered a widespread rout, resulting in the disintegration of the Iraqi 2nd Division and badly damaging three other divisions. Tikrit quickly fell afterwards as did Tal Afar and key border crossings from Iraq to Syria and Jordan. There was a large flight of terrified refugees. It seemed that ISIS was unstoppable, its spearheads advancing towards to Kurdish enclaves in northern Iraq and towards Baghdad. From the group's bases in Iraq and Syria it used propaganda to radicalize citizens of Europe to mount terrorist attacks at home.

The US deployed SOF and advisors to Baghdad and Mosul and conducted limited air strikes to protect Irbil and Baghdad. Following a *fatwa* by Grand Ayatollah Sistani, militias were mobilized to fight ISIS, with Iran providing much support, material and advice to the groups, which became known as popular mobilization units. Most of these were composed of Shias and the majority were strongly influenced by Iran.

In September 2014 US President Obama invited nations to join an international coalition against ISIS and began a US-led campaign of air and missile strikes against ISIS in both Iraq and Syria. By the end of 2014, ISIS's expansion in Iraq had been halted and Prime Minister Maliki had been deposed. As Iran was building the capabilities of the popular mobilization units, US advisors were helping the Iraqi government build the capability of selected Iraqi Army and police formations for a counter-offensive against ISIS. But it was not until September 2017 that operations by the US-backed Iraqi Army and Police units and the Iranian-supported Popular Mobilization Units drove ISIS out of all the Iraq towns that it had occupied in 2014.

The human suffering inflicted in Iraq by ISIS's nihilistic death cult was immense. There were significant political consequences in Iraq, where Iran's influence was greatly strengthened, not least because of the political impact of the Iranian-supported militias. From 2018, as President Trump withdrew from the Joint Comprehensive Plan of

Action deal to limit Iran's nuclear capabilities that had been negotiated by President Obama's administration between the US, EU and Iran, he applied a policy of 'maximum pressure' to persuade Iran to stop supporting proxy actors in Iraq, Syria and the Lebanon. In the second half of 2019, Iran shot down a US Navy drone, and was widely considered to have sponsored a combined drone and cruise missile attack on a major oil refinery in Saudi Arabia. In the same period, tensions between the US, Iran and Iraqi Shia militias increased, as did militia attacks on US bases. In late December 2019 the US accused an Iraqi Iranian-supported Shia militia of responsibility for rocket attacks on US bases in Iraq that killed a US civilian contractor. In early January 2020 the US bombed several of that militia's bases. A 3 January 2020 US missile attack killed Iranian Revolutionary Guards Quds Force commander Qassim Soleimani and Abu Mahdi al-Muhandis, the commander of Kat'aib Hizbullah.

The US authorities claimed to be acting in self-defence as Soleimani was posing an imminent threat by organizing further attacks on US forces. But the attack clearly violated both Iraqi sovereignty and the agreement between Washington and Baghdad that set out the legal basis for US operations against ISIS in Iraq. Iran vowed to avenge Soleimani's death and the Iraqi parliament passed a resolution requiring US forces to depart the country. A mass protest was organized by Iraqi politicians and militias outside the US embassy. A subsequent Iranian ballistic missile attack against a US base in Iraq saw no US deaths, but this was due more to luck than any other factor. Shortly after the attack Tehran stated that it considered the missile attacks a proportionate retaliation for the death of Soleimani, resulting in an uneasy, fragile truce between the US and Iran.

Iraq itself had been undergoing a domestic political crisis. Widespread popular protests had taken place against corruption and Iraqi politicians' inability to deliver essential services and jobs. These had been brutally suppressed by the Iraqi security forces, with the active support of Iran.

Iraq was also greatly threatened by the COVID-19 pandemic, particularly from infected Shia pilgrims returning from Iran's holy city, Qom. The government of Iran had demonstrated considerable strategic incompetence; by keeping the holy city of Qom open to pilgrims, it provided a perfect epicentre that enabled the rapid spread of the virus in Iran, Iraq and Shia communities further afield. The fragility of Iraq's health services, large amount of urban poverty and presence of hundreds of thousands of internally displaced people most living in overcrowded camps all meant the country was likely to struggle to manage the impact of the coronavirus.

THE AUDIT OF WAR

By summer 2008, the security balance had shifted in Iraq. The Surge had succeeded. Taking advantage of Prime Minister Maliki's turning against the Sadrists, the US, UK and the Iraqi forces defeated the JAM and Iranian-sponsored 'special groups' in both Basra and Sadr City. This considerable improvement in security allowed the safe conduct of the 2009 provincial elections. A subsequent Al Qaida bombing offensive was counter-attacked effectively by US and Iraqi SOF raids. Intelligence seized pushed Al Qaida in Iraq back onto the ropes. But it retained sufficient presence in Iraq to exploit Prime Minister Maliki's subsequent repression of Iraq's Sunnis.

The British and other multinational contingents withdrew, as US forces reduced and transitioned to a train, advise and assist mission.

Once the Iraqi government was established there always was a danger that Iraqi forces could become excessively politicized. This was a major problem in Iraq from 2007 onwards, as Prime Minister Maliki exerted ever-increasing control of Iraqi forces. US commanders expressed concern that this would allow him to use Iraqi forces to further a narrowly political and sectarian agenda rather than to meet the full security needs of Iraq. There were 'robust discussions' between Petraeus, his successors and Maliki, but the US had only limited leverage, which decreased further after its 2011 withdrawal. Maliki's assumption of direct ministerial authority for the armed forces, police and intelligence agencies saw the replacement of tried and tested police and army commanders with less capable but politically loyal proxies. This greatly reduced the effectiveness and impartiality of the Iraqi security forces.

Through political manoeuvre and intimidation Prime Minister Maliki stole the 2010 parliamentary elections. It is not clear if the US could have prevented this, but the acceptance by the State Department and Vice President of Maliki's seizure of power helped entrench his dominant political position.

The US military had reservations about Maliki. These were borne out by his nakedly sectarian behaviour. The Pentagon had hoped that they could negotiate a follow-on force but in the light of the accumulated resentment against the US occupation and influence of Iran, it is unsurprising that Maliki and many Iraqi Shia politicians were unwilling to support a long-term US presence. Given the humiliations and enormous resentment that the Coalition's occupation of Iraq had generated, the nationalism of the Sadrist politicians, Maliki's increased assertiveness and his dependence on Shia political support, there was probably little that the US could have done to shift the political balance in Iraq in favour of a long-term US presence.

Whilst the Iraqi security force capabilities had been sufficient for the operations of 2007–10, as US troops drew down, the limitations of the Iraqi forces became increasingly apparent. The opportunities created by the successful counter-offensive against Al Qaida in 2010 had been squandered by Maliki's creating the conditions for Al Qaida's resurgence while meanwhile eroding the capability of the Iraqi Security Forces, so that they were incapable of countering ISIS' 2014 offensive. This failure of the Iraqi Security Forces gave rise to the popular mobilization units that greatly increased Iran's influence in Iraq.

This illustrates how important it is to build supporting and institutional capability in parallel to front-line capability. This was cruelly exposed by the collapse of four Iraqi divisions in the face of the 2014 ISIS offensives. But the principal reasons for their military defeat were the way that the Iraqi Army's military capability had been hollowed out through the replacement of competent leaders by Shia political appointees and the growth of institutional corruption, as well as the generation of support for ISIS by Maliki's repression of Sunni politicians and communities.

The Enemy Gets a Vote

Afghanistan 2006–09

By the end of 2005, NATO had taken over security leadership in northern and western Afghanistan, the most stable parts of the country. Washington considered that despite an increase in Taliban attacks, the time was right to reduce US forces in Afghanistan, in order to reinforce Iraq. NATO agreed that in autumn 2006 the alliance would deploy a multinational brigade to southern Afghanistan. Initially the brigade would be under command of the US HQ, then in late summer a NATO HQ would assuming security leadership for the whole of Afghanistan, including command of US forces already in eastern Afghanistan. Counter-terrorist operations by US SOF against Al Qaida would remain under US national command, as part of Operation *Enduring Freedom*.

Many senior US officers had reservations over the NATO nations' political will to take military risk. Apart from the British and French, most European armies lacked recent combat experience. But the Pentagon and CENTCOM both intended that the increase in NATO strength in Afghanistan would allow US troops to be reduced, so these reservations were overruled.

British Prime Minister Tony Blair, his Chiefs of Staff and the British Army and were keen to play a leading role in this. There were several factors that influenced this judgement. It was thought that the US and British Transition Strategy for Iraq would succeed, allowing the British footprint in Basra to reduce significantly from 2006. The strategic planning assumption was that considerable reductions of British troops in Iraq would allow rapid growth of the British contingent in Afghanistan. Within the MoD there appeared to be another school of thought – that the Iraq war's problematic character, combined with its ever-increasing unpopularity in the UK, made it imperative to shift military efforts from Iraq. British military operations in Afghanistan, in contrast, could be directly linked to 9/11 and to the flow of narcotics into the UK. The Iraq war was losing legitimacy with the public and media in the UK, but Afghanistan could be portrayed as a legitimate war. These arguments were often combined.[1]

The British would deploy the British-led NATO Allied Command Europe Rapid Reaction Corps (ARRC) HQ to Kabul to take command over ISAF. NATO deployments in northern and western Afghanistan would not change. Southern Afghanistan had only a few US troops present. The Canadians, British and Dutch agreed to fill this gap by deploying a multinational brigade and three national PRTs. Each nation would take responsibility for a province; the British would go to Helmand, the Canadians to Kandahar and the Dutch to Uruzgan. They would secure key areas for reconstruction and development. The plan was that Canada would provide the commander and core of the brigade HQ, with the Dutch and British following on in turn to lead the brigade.

General David Richards, the new ISAF commander, drew on extensive analysis of both COIN and development to formulate a campaign plan that deliberately sought to support and empower the Afghan authorities. He intended to:

> reinforce the people of Afghanistan's belief that long term peace and growing economic prosperity from which everyone can benefit is possible if they continue to give their government and its international partners their support and encouragement ... My main effort is to extend and deepen the areas in which the Government of Afghanistan can safely operate in the interests of the people of Afghanistan, enabling the ANSF [Afghan National Security Forces] to increasingly take the lead in in achieving the aim ... I will seize the initiative against those who oppose the Government of Afghanistan through violent means, by using appropriate and well considered measures – including robust use of force should it be necessary - at times and places of my choosing thereby forcing them to respond to my design.[2]

A Policy Action Group was developed to better co-ordinate Afghan and international efforts. This was a top-level committee, chaired by President Karzai, where the key military and civilian actors formulated military and civilian policy for security and development and oversaw its execution. It was intended to give the president and his national security advisor the tools necessary to synchronize Afghan and international efforts. Rural operations were to secure Afghan Development Zones, areas selected for concentrated international and Afghan efforts to improve local governance and prosperity. PRTs would play a leading role in delivering these non-military objectives. ISAF troops would provide security for these zones.

This approach worked in the relatively benign areas of northern and eastern Afghanistan where the threat from the Taliban was low, but in Helmand, Kandahar and Uruzgan provinces, the UK, Canadian and Dutch forces found the Taliban much stronger than had been anticipated, resulting in much heavier fighting than they had expected.

This was in part a function of an inadequate understanding of the insurgents. It was clear that there were two major groupings of insurgents, drawing on higher command, logistics and support networks across Afghanistan's porous borders. One of these was the Peshawar Shura, a group of Taliban commanders that drew on the authority of Mullah Omar. Another was the Haqqani network, which based itself in the north-western Pakistani city of Peshawar. As the war went on a Taliban *shura* based in the eastern Iranian city of Marshad became increasingly important, especially as the Iranian Revolutionary Guards Corps Quds Force stepped up its support to the Taliban. This Iranian support was, however, much less significant than support that the Taliban received in Pakistan. The Pakistani government repeatedly denied that it provided direct support to the insurgents, but US and Afghan officials publicly insisted that the insurgents received considerable support from the ISI, the Pakistani intelligence agency.

This much was known to US and NATO intelligence. But there was precious little detail available about the Taliban in southern Afghanistan. There was equally little known about the complex dynamics between corrupt Afghan government officials, local warlords, drug barons and a wide range of tribal leaders. And the British, Canadian and Dutch commanders and their staffs had insufficient understanding of how in

Sons of Iraq staff a checkpoint in Himbus, Iraq, March 2008. (Staff Sgt Russell Bassett/US Army)

Shia militia celebrate the destruction of an Iraqi Army vehicle at the beginning of Operation *Charge of the Knights*, Baghdad, March 2008. The initial defeat of the Iraq Army's attack on Basra is described on pages 334–5. (Khaldoon Zubeir /Getty Images)

A British mentoring team deploys on Operation *Charge of the Knights* in the new Mastiff protected mobility vehicle. The rapid deployment of these teams is described on page 337. (Cpl Rob Knight/ Crown Copyright 2020)

Combat engineers prepare to use a crane to lift a section of the concrete barrier along Route Gold (known as Gold Wall) during the battle of Sadr City. They are protected by an M2 Bradley infantry fighting vehicle and an M1 Abrams tank. (Sgt Joseph Rivera Rebolledo/US Army)

Iraqi Army troops cross the Gold Wall to clear the rest of Sadr City, May 2008. The battle is described on pages 347–51. (Robert Nickelsberg/Getty Images)

Canadian and Afghan troops in Panjwai District, Kandahar Province after Operation *Medusa*, Autumn 2006. The operation is described on pages 375–82. (JOHN D. MCHUGH/AFP via Getty Images)

US paratroops fight off a Taliban ambush in August 2007 during a halt to repair a disabled vehicle near the village of Allah Say, Afghanistan. (Sgt Michael L. Casteel/US Army)

A British bomb disposal robot disrupts a suspected IED in Afghanistan. (Cpl Phil Ryan RAF/Crown Copyright 2020)

British troops disembark from a Chinook helicopter in Helmand Province, May 2009. (Cpl Rupert Frere RLC/Crown Copyright 2020)

British troops rush a casualty to a US Air Force 'Pedro' casualty evacuation helicopter during Operation *Panther's Claw* in Helmand, summer 2009. The operation is described on pages 398–401. (Cpl Dan Bardsley RLC/Crown Copyright 2020)

An Afghan Army commando with a US SOF advisor searches for IEDs in Marjah during Operation *Moshtarak*, June 2009. The operation is described on pages 413–15. (Spc Audfred LaboyCruz/ US Army)

A US Army soldier watches as F-15 fighter jets destroy insurgent positions after a 20-minute gun battle in the Korengal Valley, Kunar Province, in August 2009. (Sgt Matthew Moeller/US Army)

US Army Staff Sergeant Clinton Romesha patrols near Combat Outpost Keating in Kamdesh, Nuristan Province, Afghanistan. He was awarded the Medal of Honor for actions during the battle at COP Keating on 3 Oct, 2009, described on pages 402–4. (US Army)

A US soldier cleans his machine gun at an observation post in Paktika Province, November 2009. (Staff Sgt Andrew Smith/US Army)

Afghan soldiers use hand-held mine detectors to search a track for IEDs in Helmand Province, December 2010. (Sgt Rupert Frere RLC/ Crown Copyright 2020)

British mentors advise an Afghan Army officer prior to entering a village near Gereshk, Afghanistan, October 2010. (Cpl Mark Webster/Crown Copyright 2020)

ISAF Commander General Stanley McChrystal briefs Afghan President Hamid Karzai at ISAF HQ in Kabul, April 2010. (OMAR SOBHANI/AFP via Getty Images)

US Army Rangers clear a room in Kandahar Province. (Spc Justin Young/DoD)

US soldiers of 327th Infantry Regiment, 101st Airborne Division during a firefight with Taliban forces in Kunar Province, Afghanistan, March 2011. (Pfc Cameron Boyd/US Army)

A US Army counter-IED team blows up a roadside bomb in Panjwai district, Kandahar Province, January 2012. (US Army)

Carter Malkasian, State Department representative in Garmser, Afghanistan (left) with Garmser police chief Omar Jan. Malkasian's work as a US political officer is described on pages 401–2. (Rajiv Chandrasekaran/The Washington Post via Getty Images)

An M1 tank of the US Marines' 2nd Tank Battalion overlooking the Helmand River, September 2013. (Cpl Trent A. Randolph/USMC)

A Reaper UAV armed with Hellfire missiles lands at Kandahar airfield. (Sgt Corinne Buxton RAF/ Crown Copyright 2020)

The US military increasingly deployed aerostat balloons above their bases in Afghanistan. Known as the Persistent Threat Detection System, they carried advanced surveillance technology to detect any threats to the base. (US Army)

During both wars, female US, UK and NATO soldiers played increasingly significant roles. Here two female US Army Military Police with the 3rd Brigade Combat Team maintain security for a Female Engagement Team chief during a consultation at a clinic in Zabul Province, Afghanistan, in September 2013. (Sgt Kandi Huggins/US Army)

A USAF A10 attack aircraft supporting an Afghan Army operation in Nangarhar Province in March 2014. The pick-up trucks are Afghan Army vehicles, the armoured vehicles belong to US advisors assisting the Afghan Army's 201 Corps. (ROBERTO SCHMIDT/AFP via Getty Images)

A British Apache helicopter being loaded into a C17 Globemaster transport aircraft as the British leave Helmand Province, July 2014. (Cpl Daniel Wiepen/Crown Copyright 2020)

Afghan Army soldiers, Taliban fighters and local civilians gather in Maiwand, Kandahar Province, during the June 2018 ceasefire for the festival of Eid. (JAVED TANVEER/AFP via Getty Images)

the previous four years, tension had been amplified by SOF raids and air strikes on targets offered by 'friendly' warlords, who were portraying their enemies as Taliban. Nor did they anticipate that their interventions in these southern provinces might enmesh them in local disputes, with considerable danger of inadequate understanding making the situation worse by exacerbating local rivalries and extant conflicts.

THE UNANTICIPATED BATTLES FOR SOUTHERN AFGHANISTAN

Since the end of 2001 there had been a major US and Coalition base at Kandahar airfield. So, the US and NATO had some understanding of the province and its human terrain. It was clear that its size, political and economic significance as the country's second city made it a key area to protect from the Taliban.

The British and Canadian planners were unaware that the Taliban in southern Afghanistan had been expending considerable effort to build up their influence and forces. They exploited several years of grievances arising from the way in which local warlords had returned to power in 2002, as allies of President Karzai.

One of these local warlords, Mir Wali, was heavily involved in the narcotics business. But he persuaded US SOF to build a base, Camp Price, adjacent to his compound near Gereshk. For a fee his militia guarded the camp and accompanied US SOF on patrol, thus reinforcing his malign and corrupt patronage network.

The US offered up to $2,000 for information leading to the successful capture of Taliban or Al Qaida fighters. This allowed warlords to manipulate their activities to generate revenue, dispose of rivals and gain advantage in long-standing feuds. Many Afghans detained in this way were sent to the US detention facility at Bagram, which was gaining notoriety for harsh conditions and prisoner abuse. A proportion were subsequently sent for detention at secret CIA 'black sites' overseas or to Guantanamo Bay.

The Afghan National Police and the National Directorate of Security (NDS), the national intelligence agency, were often suborned by warlords to turn a blind eye to oppressive, predatory and corrupt behaviour. The Afghan forces also engaged in these practices themselves. These factors often aggravated existing frictions, fault lines and disputes amongst tribal groupings. This reinforced a sense of injustice and oppression amongst the rural population in all three southern provinces.

Garmser, a district in southern Helmand, illustrates this. After the 2001 fall of the Taliban, Garmser's various tribes achieved a working accommodation that balanced their competing interests and antagonisms. These governance arrangements collapsed when, in 2004, a popular district governor was replaced by a less capable official, who failed to maintain the balance between the tribes. Combined with increasingly predatory behaviour by the Afghan National Police and ever more Taliban attacks, this failing local governance meant that a growing number of tribal elders and local people switched allegiance to the Taliban.

During 2004 and 2005 previous Taliban networks rebuilt themselves throughout southern Afghanistan. They were increasingly joined by fighters from Pakistan. Initially cautious, they used intimidation and murder to remove those who opposed them and began small-scale attacks against Afghan government forces and institutions such as district centres. Taliban-supporting mullahs came from Quetta and Peshawar, using intimidation to displace moderate mullahs.

In Helmand the US eventually insisted that Mir Wali's private militia, the so-called 93rd Division, be disbanded. Turning against him they raided his compound, twice. Mir Wali's top commander formed an alliance with the Taliban, taking most of the former militia members with him.

Meanwhile in London, the early failures in Baghdad and Basra to properly integrate military action with adequately resourced and delivered reconstruction and development had been a wakeup call to the British government, particularly to the three ministries involved, Defence, International Development and the Foreign and Commonwealth Office. A doctrine of the Comprehensive Approach to better integrate civil and military action was developed and an interagency Post Conflict Reconstruction Unit had been set up.

Military and civilian planners deployed to Kabul and Kandahar at the end of 2005, to produce an interagency plan for Helmand. This was duly done, but the very process of planning revealed that, apart from recognizing its significant contribution to Afghanistan's drug economy, the British did not know much about the province. And the commander and HQ of the brigade that would provide most of the troops for Helmand were not part of planning team.

The US had largely left Helmand to its own devices, apart from a PRT in Lashkar Gar, the provincial capital, and some SOF. There had been some British reconnaissance of Helmand by British SOF who found the province to be largely at peace. This was mainly the result of the significant revenue being generated from opium to the benefit of drug barons, warlords and the Taliban. The provincial governor's personal militia enforced a brutal rule. The SAS had been operating in Helmand and their commanding officer advised that removing the governor and deploying British troops had the potential to destabilize the province, resulting in increased violence.

British reconnaissance missions in 2005 and 2006 only scratched the surface of the complex tribal, political and economic dynamics of the province. But it was clear that 70 per cent of the population were illiterate, such provincial and district government as existed was in thrall to tribal and patronage networks and the police were highly corrupt, behaving in a predatory fashion towards the civilian population.[3]

In London the defence, foreign and development ministries all displayed considerable optimism about the venture. The Defence Secretary, John Reid, told the media that this was a dangerous mission because 'terrorists will want to destroy the economy and the legitimate trade and the government that we are helping to build up'. To emphasize the importance of stabilization and reconstruction he also stated that 'we would be perfectly happy to leave in three years and without firing one shot because our job is to protect the reconstruction'.[4] These words were quickly overtaken by events and would return to haunt successive British defence ministers.

The British Task Force Helmand would come from the 16 Air Assault Brigade. The formation would provide its HQ and a parachute battalion to secure for development the area around the provincial capital Lashkar Gar and the town of Gereshk. The battalion would be supported by a light armoured reconnaissance squadron, combat engineers, a squadron of Apache attack helicopters and a few 105mm artillery guns. This would be complemented by a PRT. British SOF in southern Afghanistan would also increase in strength.

Command and control arrangements were complicated. Regional Command South would be the responsibility of a multinational brigade HQ based on the existing HQ of Canadian Brigadier David Fraser. It was envisaged that leadership of the multinational brigade would rotate from Canadian to Dutch and then British command. The British decided that to place the commander of its air assault brigade, Brigadier Ed Butler, under another brigadier would not work. Instead Butler would become the UK national contingent commander based in Kabul. He would answer to the UK joint HQ in north London and held the national 'red card', the power to veto direction and orders given by NATO. Butler, who had personally prepared and trained the British combat troops from his brigade, found this very frustrating, particularly as the British effort in Helmand, named Task Force Helmand, would be commanded by a colonel from outside the brigade, who had not been involved with its training and preparation.

The British prevailed upon Hamid Karzai to replace Helmand's provincial governor, Sher Mohammed Akhundzada, whom they saw as irredeemably corrupt and the leader of a notorious private militia. Akhundzada was a close political associate of Karzai, but the President reluctantly complied with the British demands. Many former members of Akhundzada's militias now had nothing to stop them siding with the Taliban and did so.

The British slowly deployed to southern Afghanistan, their speed of arrival limited by the need to simultaneously build up supplies and the main British base, named Camp Bastion. Although the British force had over 3,000 troops, the necessary deployment of engineers, logistic, maintenance and medical personnel meant that its fighting elements were only a third of this number; both Mohammed Daoud, the former Afghan government national security advisor newly appointed provincial governor of Helmand, and President Hamid Karzai were shocked to discover how little combat power the British had brought to Helmand.

The arrival of the British force coincided with increasing Taliban attacks. Many of these targeted the government's district centres throughout Helmand. As the British deployed, a request from the new provincial governor led to the British deploying small groups of infantry to isolated district centres in Helmand's key towns: Sangin, Now Zad and Musa Qala.

Given the lack of British combat power, this meant that not only had protection of the planned Afghan Development Zone became more difficult, but the parachute battalion became fixed in these locations in small bases, often called 'platoon houses'. These were repeatedly subject to close assaults by large numbers of Taliban. Casualty levels were much higher than anticipated and some bases came close to falling, but considerable use of machine guns, anti-tank missiles, mortars, precision air strikes and cannon attacks from AC130 gunships meant that they survived.

By mid-July the base at Sangin was besieged. Although its helicopter landing zone was inside its perimeter, the intensity of Taliban small arms, rocket and mortar fire meant that helicopters could only land during the hours of darkness. This not only limited efforts to resupply the base with food and ammunition but also meant that any soldiers wounded during the day had to wait until night before they could be evacuated. But even at night the intensity of Taliban fire made such missions extremely difficult, helicopters often having to abort their landings for fear of being shot down. After an attempt to drop food supplies by parachute failed, the base was only successfully replenished by a Canadian mechanized infantry company bringing the ammunition and food to Sangin inside their armoured vehicles.

Initially the Taliban attacks appeared poorly executed, with waves of brave fighters attempting to assault the British bases. Often these got dangerously close to British positions, so close that hand grenades would be thrown by both sides. Repelling such Taliban assaults required mortars, artillery and air strikes to be called in 'danger close', that is so near to friendly troops that they themselves were within the radius of lethal effects.[5] But the considerable use of infantry weapons, mortars, artillery, attack helicopters and fighter bombers caused inevitable civilian casualties and collateral damage around the bases, generating more recruits for the Taliban. This, coupled with an inadequate understanding of local cultural and tribal dynamics, resulted in security in Helmand further deteriorating. Unexpectedly heavy British casualties also reduced the domestic popularity of the Afghan war in UK.

In Sangin the British found themselves amid a dispute between two tribes. The Alikozi were using control of government appointments to gain advantage in a struggle over land and narcotics. Their opponents, the Ishaqzai, were siding with the Taliban. The British deployment of a parachute infantry company in support of a notoriously abusive district police chief in Sangin, an Alikozi, made matters worse. Sangin was to achieve notoriety as the district where the greatest number of British casualties occurred in Afghanistan. In the four years in which the British occupied the district centre, 106 troops would be killed in the district.

The British Army was later to claim that the 2006 fighting in northern Helmand was the most intense fighting it had experienced since the Korean War. This claim had been made previously about fighting in the 2004 Shia uprising in Iraq. But in Afghanistan the infantry had far less recourse to heavy armoured vehicles and were in a more precarious logistic and medical situation. Without the use of satellite communications and air-ground radios, as well as the precision firepower that attack helicopters and fighter bombers could deploy, some or all of the British bases might well have fallen to Taliban attacks.

In the long term such a defeat would probably have entered British military mythology as another glorious defeat alongside the mythical character of the siege of Rorke's Drift, the evacuation from Dunkirk and the battle of Arnhem. But such an event would have had immediate catastrophic political effects on ISAF, NATO, the British government and the credibility of the British military. Too few analysts and commentators have pointed out this 'inconvenient truth', nor have the British commanders in Helmand during this period been given the credit they deserve for preventing such a strategic shock.

These first four months of British operations in Helmand featured considerable friction between the British, the Canadian-led multinational brigade HQ in Kandahar, the US-led Operation *Enduring Freedom* HQ in Bagram and ISAF in Kabul.

As in Basra, the UK national contingent commander, Brigadier Ed Butler, saw his primary loyalty as to the UK, rather than the Canadian-led brigade HQ. This meant that Butler, the US Army general Ben Freakley initially commanding land forces in southern and eastern Afghanistan and subsequently General David Richards all saw the command and direction of the campaign from very different perspectives. This was exacerbated by the very different personalities of the three commanders, all of which grated upon each other, with both Richards and Freakley finding Butler particularly difficult to deal with. In the summer and autumn of 2006 there was much friction between Butler and the various higher HQs that sought to direct operations in southern Afghanistan.

The original British design for command and control reinforced these frictions rather than smoothed them out. Only in autumn 2006 was the UK chain of command eventually rationalized. Butler remained national contingent commander but was moved from Kabul to Helmand to take command of all British forces there. He was given orders from the UK that he was to subordinate Task Force Helmand to the direction of Brigadier Fraser.

The British, Canadians and Dutch also realized that both the unexpectedly heavy fighting and the complexity of the civilian and military missions in southern Afghanistan meant that a single multinational brigade HQ was overfaced with the challenges posed by its span of command over southern Afghanistan. And more command capacity was necessary at the Kandahar HQ of Regional Command South. This was increased in size and upgraded to a multinational divisional HQ, a major general's command, still to be led in rotation by Dutch, Canadian and British major generals.

CANADA IN KANDAHAR – OPERATION *MEDUSA*

The 9/11 attacks had shaken Canada. Not only were 24 Canadian citizens killed, but the US imposed security checks on the border between the two countries. These disrupted previously frictionless trade. Ottawa realized that it was in Canada's national interest to be seen by Washington, DC, as a reliable security partner to the US. But French political opposition to the Iraq war was reflected in the French-speaking province Quebec and made it politically impossible for Canada to join Operation *Iraqi Freedom*, although a few Canadian military personnel serving with the US military were initially allowed to take part.

The Canadian military had also come to the view that several decades of peacekeeping operations had limited the Canadian military's political impact with the US. Canadian forces needed to show themselves as militarily useful to the US, including by being capable of demanding combat operations. And the Canadian military, diplomats and development agency had developed a '3D' doctrine to integrate the three lines of effort. Both Canadian government and military were keen to prove themselves and their new thinking.

A Canadian brigade HQ assumed the role of commanding ISAF's Regional Command South. The Canadian task force and PRT deployed to Kandahar Province were broadly similar in composition to the British force in Helmand. But their fighting troops were a mechanized battalion. They had similar combat support but lacked their own attack helicopters. Unlike the British they sought not to use this battalion in a 'ground holding' role. The Canadian battalion was employed throughout southern Afghanistan assisting the British and Dutch contingents to deploy to their operational locations. It had some bruising encounters with the Taliban. The armour and 25mm cannon of the Canadian light armoured vehicles gave them protection, mobility and firepower that the British airborne infantry lacked.

During the summer increasing numbers of Taliban fighters were detected forming up in Panjwai district to the west of Kandahar City, apparently preparing for an attempt to recapture the city. They were capable fighters. For example, a Canadian foray into Panjwai in early August saw an armoured vehicle hit by an IED. Previously the Taliban would have seen this as sufficient destruction, but on this occasion, they brought effective fire on to the vehicle and troops around it. Four Canadians were killed. This was the first time they had seen the Taliban fighters using conventional infantry tactics, covering a land mine with effective fire. This was common practice in NATO armies, a tactic designed to make it more difficult for enemy troops to get out of minefields and to inflict additional casualties and delay, but previously the Taliban in Kandahar had not applied these tactics. Now they had learned to do so, greatly increasing the effectiveness of their ambushes.

Throughout the summer of 2006, the build-up of Taliban insurgent strength so close to Kandahar increasingly alarmed many Afghan civilian leaders in the city. It was considered such a threat that countering it became the ISAF main effort. On 2 September, the Canadian-led brigade HQ began Operation *Medusa*, a multinational attack to clear the Taliban concentration in Panjwai. The main ground force was Canadian, but it was assisted by Dutch, US and Afghan forces. It was the designated main effort for intelligence surveillance and reconnaissance and Coalition airpower in Afghanistan, but only for two weeks, after which the theatre's priorities would switch to eastern Afghanistan. The brigade HQ and its commander, Brigadier David Fraser, were under considerable pressure: from NATO to eliminate the Taliban force, from the Afghan government to minimize civilian casualties and from Ottawa both to minimize Canadian casualties and to re-establish Canada's military reputation.

The operation was thoroughly planned. This included an extensive effort to collect intelligence on the Taliban in Panjwai. A wide range of surveillance and reconnaissance systems, including signals intelligence, human intelligence gathered from friendly Afghans and manned and unmanned surveillance and reconnaissance aircraft, were used to gather information.

Based on this the brigade HQ assessed that insurgent strengths included high levels of morale and motivation, as well as a much better understanding of Afghan human terrain than NATO had. They had proven their guerrilla tactics against the Soviets and were refining them against NATO and US troops. They could easily merge into the Afghan population and the agricultural terrain of Panjwai was ideally suited to the defence, particularly the way hard-baked mud walls divided the farms into small grape orchards. These walls and those of agricultural buildings could withstand small arms fire and even defeated the high-velocity 25mm cannon round fired from the Canadian armoured vehicles.

Intelligence also suggested that the Taliban had weaknesses. These included an inability to withstand the considerable aerial firepower that NATO had available. Any serious Taliban attack on NATO troops would see airpower start to come to the aid of NATO soldiers within half an hour. This inhibited the Taliban's options. And unlike the lavish issue of night-fighting equipment to western troops, vehicles and manned and unmanned aircraft, the Taliban at that time had no meaningful night vision devices

Compared to US and NATO forces, Taliban command and control could be very centralized – dependent on a small number of experienced leaders. They made extensive use of communications that could be intercepted by NATO and US signals intelligence: VHF radios, handheld walkie-talkie radios and mobile phones. Their logistics was dependent on pre-stocked caches of weapons ammunition and equipment, limiting their flexibility. And their medical system depended on civilian paramedics who supported the Taliban being pre-positioned at pharmacies in towns – a capability that NATO could disrupt. These strengths and weaknesses were factored into the plan.

Assembling this intelligence was but one part of the work of the brigade HQ. David Fraser, its commander, gave a vivid picture of the tactical operations centre at Kandahar airfield:

> The TOC was dominated by a wall of knowledge: a broad sweep of oversized computer monitors displaying Predator feeds, live charts tracking the locations of every unit and incident, dynamic checklists

that kept us on track, and a seemingly endless stream of intelligence from other sources. Beneath this array of information stood two rows of desks at which men and women referenced computer screens as they interacted with troops in the field, our higher HQs in Kabul and Canada and the operations staff of other organizations. There were our liaison officers from all subordinate units, such as 1st Battalion the Royal Canadian Regiment, or flanking formations and aviation, medical, logistics, legal, artillery, ISR (intelligence, surveillance and reconnaissance) and so on. We had people connected to every unit and enabler we controlled, co-operated with or reported to. And we needed every bit of it to maintain a high situational awareness and be able to respond to any event ...

There I had everyone I needed to give me the right information to make informed decisions and coordinate the fight. This was the location from which we pushed assets to any affected 'call sign' (our jargon for a unit or individual with whom we were in contact).[6]

Fraser did not spend all his time at his Kandahar HQ. Instead, he spent much time away from it, visiting his subordinate units and meeting Afghans, as well as trips to Kabul. For Operation *Medusa* he would spend much time visiting the units conducting the operation.

Starting 2 September, the main effort was to be made by a Canadian mechanized battalion battle group, based on the 1st Battalion, the Royal Canadian Regiment. The Canadians asked the British to contribute troops from Helmand. They declined, citing the difficulty they were having defending the platoon houses spread through Helmand. But British SOF did join the operation, deploying in depth to interdict any Taliban reinforcements from moving to Panjwai.

The start of the battle was marked by an avoidable tragedy in the skies above Kandahar, visible to all: Taliban, Coalition troops and Afghan civilians alike. A British Nimrod surveillance aircraft caught fire. Like a malevolent comet it streaked earthwards over the battlefield, increasingly consumed by flames. None of its 14-strong British crew survived the crash. Later investigation showed the accident to be the product of design flaws and inadequate management of the safety of the aircraft.[7]

A Canadian mechanized infantry company forded the Arghandab River on 3 September. It ran into an ambush. Much heavier Taliban

fire than had been expected killed four Canadian troops, wounding 11
more. The company was forced to withdraw under fire, taking its dead
and wounded with it.

The Taliban defensive positions were well prepared. Their fighters
were difficult to dislodge; for example the 25mm cannon shells fired
by the Canadian light armoured vehicles often had little or no effect
against Taliban bunkers.

The Canadian brigade HQ was shocked to find out that an earlier
logistic oversight meant that they were about to run out of ammunition
for their armoured vehicle cannons. And artillery ammunition had
been expended at twice the rate they had expected. If these unexpected
shortages were not resolved, it would be impossible to provide essential
fire support and Operation *Medusa* would have to be paused. Stocks
elsewhere in both Afghanistan, Canada and NATO were insufficient to
fully resupply the Canadians. Fortunately for them, the New Zealand
Army was able to help. One Canadian officer observed that at times
Taliban bomb makers found it easier to get explosives than Canadian
troops found it to get ammunition resupply.

On 4 September, as the Canadian battalion was preparing to resume
the advance, the same company and the battalion HQ were mistakenly
struck by US A10 attack aircraft. A soldier was killed and 30 were
wounded. This rendered the company ineffective. The axis of the attack
was shifted.

To assist with the operation, US SOF assembled an ad hoc task force
of several SOF detachments. Afghan soldiers, a US infantry company
and two howitzers. Task Force 31, as it was designated, was able to
attack to the west of the Canadians and gradually push the Taliban
back. In doing so, it met increasing Taliban resistance, but Apache
helicopters, A10 jets and AC130 gunships were used to devastating
effect. The task force discovered that Sperwan Ghar, the hill around
which these pitched battles took place, was both a Taliban command
post and an insurgent training facility.[8] To maintain the momentum
of the attack, the deputy commander of the multinational brigade, US
Army National Guard Colonel Steve Williams led another ad hoc unit,
Task Force Grizzly, to deceive the Taliban as to the direction of the
main Canadian attack. It vigorously engaged the Taliban, not only by
fire but with loudspeakers on William's personal Humvee pumping out
heavy metal music at maximum volume.

It appeared that the Taliban had used up much of their combat power defending Sperwan Ghar and steady pressure slowly pushed them back from their network of fortified fighting positions and bunkers. By now the insurgents were fighting less as guerrillas, more as conventional infantry. This made them more vulnerable to Coalition artillery and airpower. From 11 September, Taliban resistance faded away, those that had not been killed or wounded withdrawing from the area.

Operation *Medusa* had seen unexpected setbacks and the friction of war resulting in accidental and avoidable British and Canadian casualties in the Nimrod crash and friendly fire incident. But its eventual success undoubtedly demonstrated not only that after decades of peacekeeping operations Canadian troops could close with a tough, resilient enemy, but also that they were capable of commanding and co-ordinating complex and difficult operations. Like the British in Helmand, Canadian forces had undergone their heaviest combat since the Korean War.

In the heavy fighting the Canadians had seen the strength and weakness of multinational operations. The US support to the brigade in terms of helicopters, air strikes and Predator drones had been freely offered, without any restrictions. But the support from other national contingents was far less certain. Fraser was later to reflect that for Coalition operations to succeed:

> they need reasonable give and take negotiated through tremendous amounts of dialogue. The uneven distribution of resources among coalition partners and the willingness (or lack thereof) to share capabilities needed by others made figuring out how to deliver any one effect even more complex. During Operation Enduring Freedom we had seen the US provide a reasonable balance of support across each province and contingent, but under ISAF each province was the responsibility of one nation alone tasked with coordinating all the activities related to security, diplomacy and development. With such a broad mandate, nations tended to be less willing to share assets such as aircraft, vehicles and even their own troops ...

> During Operation Medusa many nations simply would not show up to fight at all. Planning was agony. Even when the operation was only days away, we weren't certain who would support us at H-Hour. Many of the caveats exercised had never been put down in writing:

instead they were decisions of the moment, presumably made in national capitals by people with no idea of the stakes. NATO's mission in Afghanistan had been touted as a coalition of the willing, however in practice we all found it to be a coalition of arbitrary limitation.[9]

After Operation *Medusa* tactical reconstruction and development operations were conducted, although the lasting impact on Panjwai was insufficient to prevent the Taliban regaining control of the district over the next three years.

The Taliban in Helmand and Kandahar had shown themselves to be brave and determined fighters, often suicidally so. At times they had displayed battlefield learning and adaptability, for example in their efforts to get as close as possible to NATO troops, to make it difficult for the international forces to safely bring mortars, artillery and airpower to bear. Canadian troops also showed themselves capable of learning under fire and institutional adaptation. Nothing illustrated this better than the way they rushed tanks to join their troops in Kandahar.

Prior to 2006 the Canadian Army had decided to retire their Leopard tanks. They planned that all armoured vehicles were to be wheeled and lightweight. So, the tanks were to be replaced by wheeled Stryker Mobile Gun Systems. Shortly after Operation *Medusa* began, it became clear that the protection and 25mm cannons of the Canadian light armoured vehicles was insufficient to overmatch determined Taliban defences. And ISAF wanted to see less use made of aircraft bombs, to reduce civilian casualties and collateral damage. Brigadier Fraser identified an urgent need for improved precision firepower, protection and mobility.

This was met by the loan of 20 Leopard 2 tanks from Germany. These were rapidly flown to Kandahar to be rushed into service in the province. Whilst the tanks arrived after the end of Operation *Medusa*, they had a decisive effect on the morale and confidence of the Canadian troops in Afghanistan. This was followed by purchasing of 80 Leopard 2s from Holland.

It would be at least at least three more years before British troops in Helmand would receive enough protected mobility vehicles. Despite many British commanders wanting to deploy some of their Challenger 2 tanks to Helmand, requests to do so were turned down. Ironically for many British commanders, the Danes deployed a battlegroup to Helmand with their own Leopard tanks. To many British officers it seemed as if the militarily sensible requirement for tanks was being institutionally rejected for fear of the media seeing deployment of British tanks as further evidence that the British mission was failing.

THE BRITISH GET BOGGED DOWN IN HELMAND

The British parachute battalion was spread out in Helmand amongst company- and platoon-sized bases. The latter were particularly vulnerable to Taliban attack. So, British participation in Operation *Medusa* had been limited to SOF operating in depth in the desert to interdict any Taliban reinforcements. So far, Taliban assaults on the isolated British bases had been brave, but usually conducted with unsophisticated tactics. These had been defeated by accurate small arms fire from the defending troops and heavy use of mortars, artillery, attack helicopters and NATO attack aircraft. All these attacks had been defeated, the Taliban often suffering heavy casualties. Without this ability to call in firepower from outside, the Taliban might well have succeeded in defeating the numerically inferior defenders of the small British bases. If this had happened, with Taliban propaganda making maximum use of images of dead and captured British troops, the Taliban would have been seen to have inflicted a strategic defeat on the British and NATO.

The price paid to avoid such a defeat was the massive use of airborne and indirect firepower, with resulting civilian casualties and destruction of homes and livelihoods by collateral damage. These consequences of British action directly increased Taliban recruiting in Helmand, particularly as friends and family members were killed.

As the summer faded into autumn, British commanders in Helmand noticed that Taliban tactics and marksmanship had improved, including the accuracy of their fire. The insurgents also sought to evade aircraft and artillery fire by getting as close as they could to British positions, knowing that the defenders would be reluctant to bring in friendly fire so close as to pose a threat to themselves. But many such 'danger close' strikes were called in by British commanders who thought the risk to their own troops was outweighed by the need to stop Taliban attacks overwhelming their defences.

Although the British contingent in Helmand had been reinforced by some 800 additional troops, with only a squadron of light armoured reconnaissance vehicles the force still lacked protected ground mobility.

Troop movement, resupply and casualty evacuation was totally dependent on a small force of six Chinook helicopters. The Taliban knew where all the landing zones at the British bases were and were making credible attempts to shoot them down. Helicopter flights into the British bases had become even more hazardous. Many British officers considered it a miracle that at least one of the huge helicopters had not already been shot down.

The British base at Musa Qala was at greatest risk. The district centre buildings that British troops occupied were less well constructed and offered less protection than other bases in Helmand. Its helicopter landing zone was also outside its low walls. The Taliban attackers created a formidable volume of small arms fire. Fortunately for the ad hoc infantry company of British defenders, the Taliban fire was far less accurate than the marksmanship of the British. On 6 September an attempt to evacuate casualties by Chinook helicopter had to be abandoned when the helicopter was repeatedly hit by Taliban fire. A fresh aircraft was used for a later attempt, this time supported by fire from an artillery battery, two A10 close support aircraft, an AC130 gunship and two Apache helicopters. This time the evacuation mission succeeded.[10] The British decided they had to withdraw from Musa Qala. This caused more tension with ISAF, who saw that the Taliban would claim that they had forced a British retreat. Some local elders proposed a ceasefire deal that would see the British and Taliban both withdrawing from the town, which would be policed by local men enrolled as auxiliary police. This was agreed by both the British and Taliban. The British troops left the town in local Afghan civilian trucks.

The deal lasted until early the next year, when changing tribal dynamics, the sacking by Karzai of the British-supported governor and an increasing lack of trust among the three parties to the agreement all led to its collapse. Undoubtedly British, Afghan civilian and Taliban lives had been saved, but the deal painfully illustrated that the British had bitten off more than they could chew in Helmand.

Overall, it was clear that the British had blunted the Taliban offensive in Helmand. Both sides had fought each other to a standstill. The Taliban had failed to gain control of northern Helmand, the British holding out in the district centres, but at the cost of major collateral damage in the towns around them. This and civilian casualties had turned many Helmand civilians against the British, stoking the grievances that were driving the insurgency. The security situation had greatly inhibited the ability of the British PRT to achieve more than a small proportion of its planned work. This was exacerbated by lack of secure communications to interface with the British military. Far less British funded development had been done than planned.

In October 2006 the British air assault brigade rotated out of Helmand, to be replaced by the Royal Marines 3 Commando Brigade. The troops deployed were slightly greater in number than the previous brigade.

ATTRITION 2007–09

In early 2007 the ARRC HQ left Afghanistan. For the rest of the campaign, US officers would command the theatre of operations. HQ ISAF could not be based on a US corps HQ as all three existing HQs were either preparing to command US troops in Iraq, in Iraq, or recovering from a year's deployment. And US contingency plans for any war against Iran or North Korea also required at least one corps HQ. So, ISAF became a US-led multinational HQ with officers rotating through their appointments. Through 2007–09, ISAF continued to follow the broad outlines of the ARRC campaign plan. ISAF and the Afghan forces achieved some stability in Kabul. Force levels in northern and western Afghanistan were generally adequate to meet the lower threats in those areas. In the south and east of the country in that period, force levels were insufficient to regain the initiative over the Taliban. This meant that ISAF could only control small areas.

For example, in Helmand Province, repeated British offensive operations were mounted, which usually succeeded in clearing insurgents from the targeted areas, but there would be insufficient troops to hold the area for any length of time. So sooner or later the British forces and Afghan forces would have to withdraw. The British greatly relied on firepower to make up for the lack of troops on the ground. As well as creating unnecessary civilian casualties and collateral damage, these operations exposed to Taliban retaliation any Afghan civilians that had supported the Afghan government, or the British. Commanders came to call this approach 'mowing the lawn'.

As the British slowly reduced their troop levels in Iraq, troop numbers in Afghanistan gradually increased, as did awareness of counter-insurgency doctrine being used by US forces. Despite the lack of any up-to-date British doctrine in this area, the British sought to apply the concept of 'clear, build and hold'. The problem was that the very gradual rate of increase in size of both Task Force Helmand and the Afghan security forces meant that the additional capacity that the British had to hold newly cleared terrain was very small. This not only applied to the infantry and cavalry units needed on the ground, but also to the essential combat support and logistics, including EOD specialists, electronic warfare, intelligence analysts and the small force of British helicopters in Helmand.

The problem of the resource constraints imposed by fighting two wars with a single pool of forces and insufficient specialized capabilities also applied with equal force to the US contingent in Afghanistan. But an important difference in the way the two countries handled both wars persisted: the different length of operational tours. As in Iraq, the British brigades rotated through Helmand on six-month deployments. Some of the civilians in the PRTs were on longer tours, but with this came more frequent breaks from Afghanistan. Only a few officers were on longer tours. As in Iraq, this reduced continuity and corporate knowledge and promoted the short term over the long term.

Over the autumn of 2006 the Royal Marine 3 Commando Brigade replaced the exhausted air assault brigade. The Marines brought a larger force, including a Marine commando (battalion equivalent) dedicated to mentoring the Afghan Army. They also brought with them a group of Viking armoured vehicles. These were lightly protected all-terrain amphibious vehicles organic to the brigade. They were used alongside armed Land Rover 4x4 vehicles as the basis of Manoeuvre Outreach Groups (MOGs), which would be used to manoeuvre through the desert to raid Taliban-controlled areas. As they arrived, local elders and the governor of Helmand negotiated additional ceasefires in Sangin and Now Zad. Both deals later collapsed, requiring a brigade operation using Royal Marines which sent MOGs into the desert to attack Taliban positions on the edges of the lush irrigated 'Green Zone' surrounding the Helmand River. Once the Taliban woke up to these British manoeuvres, they would fight back, allowing the brigade's attack helicopters, artillery and full weight of air support to be to be applied. This approach was nicknamed 'advance to ambush'.

From April 2007 the third British brigade in Helmand, 12th Mechanized Brigade, benefited from the first Afghan deployments of the heavy Mastiff vehicle. Able to defeat small arms fire, RPG rockets and all but the largest roadside bombs, the vehicle had the same protection as a tank. But it would not be until after the 2009 end of the British mission in Iraq that Task Force Helmand had enough of these vehicles.

The brigade now had three infantry battalions and a reconnaissance regiment mounted in Scimitar lightly armed reconnaissance vehicles. With their 30mm cannon these would often be used by the British as light tanks. The Vikings and Scimitars were extremely useful. Not only were their weapons extremely effective, but also their small size and relatively low weight meant that they could easily move along the narrow roads and tracks of the irrigated Helmand River Valley. However, operational experience confirmed that their low level of armour made them very vulnerable to rocket propelled grenades, land mines (of which there were many left from previous conflicts) and roadside bombs. The Mastiff in contrast was bigger, far less manoeuvrable and much heavier, but was much better protected against mines, roadside bombs and RPGs.

The brigade sought to secure the terrain around Lashkar Gar, the provincial capital, with a network of company bases, but in practice the infantry spent much time patrolling in depth or carrying out operations to strike Taliban concentrations. Fighting could often be heavy. For example, soldiers from one of the brigade's battalions, the Royal Anglians, sometimes had to fix bayonets as they fought the Taliban at close quarters. By the end of its six-month tour of duty the battalion had used over 20,000 mortar and artillery rounds. Death, wounds, illness and injuries had reduced the battalion's strength by 20 per cent.

Despite this attrition, the overall British force level in Helmand had risen, as had the number of British outposts. Holding the network of bases and cleared terrain in Helmand depended not only on the British troops, but also on the Afghan security forces. For most of the British responsibility of Helmand, they partnered with the 3rd Brigade of the 215th Corps of the Afghan Army. This was organized along similar lines to a NATO army's infantry brigade, with three *kandaks*, equivalent to light infantry battalions. Each of these had four *tolays*, equivalent to companies. A fourth *kandak* provided combat support: engineers, artillery, reconnaissance and counter IED *tolays*.

The British found that the Afghan Police were often corrupt and displaying predatory behaviour such as shaking down civilians for bribes at check points and abducting and sexually abusing boys. They attempted to counter this by deploying mentors to the police. This had some limited effect.

But by now the British had developed a plan for building the size and capabilities of the Afghan Army in Helmand. They constructed a base, Camp Shorabak, next to their main base at Camp Bastion and helped the Afghans set up a training depot there. To the Afghan brigade in Helmand was attached an operational mentoring and liaison team (OMLT). This was based on a British infantry battalion, with the commanding officer responsible for mentoring and advising the brigade commander and infantry companies providing mentoring teams to Afghan battalions and companies.

The Afghan Army's way of war was very different to the British Army's approach. They were often very aggressive but would frequently disregard detailed planning and logistic preparation. But they valued the embedded British teams for the artillery and airborne firepower that they could summon, as well as their ability to bring in helicopters to evacuate casualties and bodies of dead Afghan soldiers. During summer 2007, the OMLT was provided by the Grenadier Guards, operating in Land Rover 4x4 vehicles with only a modicum of land mine protection. Many of the guardsmen and officers found this an extraordinary adventure.[11]

But since 2005 increasing numbers of Afghan civilians throughout the country were being killed. This increasingly irritated Karzai, not only because of the political damage it did to him and his government, but also because in practice he had no authority over ISAF. For example, in late June 2007, an air strike on a village near Gereshk killed 25 civilians. Karzai bitterly criticized ISAF in public. Less than a week later another air attack killed at least 25 civilians in Helmand. Investigation showed that the strikes were not conducted by NATO, but by US SOF, operating outside of NATO command, as part of the US Operation *Enduring Freedom*. The rules of engagement applied to British troops were subsequently changed to constrain pre-emptive British use of artillery and airpower.

Arriving in November 2007, the next British formation, the 52nd Infantry Brigade, was the first to assign units to remain in the same area of operations during their tour. This had been standard practice for most of the British campaigns in Northern Ireland, the Balkans and Iraq, but since 2006, the brigades rotating through Helmand had moved battalions and companies around as required. Indeed it was only after 18 months in Helmand that the British had the resources and motivation to apply this approach. The brigade commander, Andrew Mackay, had been greatly influenced by the new US counter-insurgency doctrine. Copies of Field Manual 3-24 'Counterinsurgency' were widely circulated within the British Army, made easier by the posting of the manual on the internet, from which it could easily be downloaded. The brigade also sought to better influence the civilian population in Helmand. They found that within the UK MoD and joint HQ there was very little understanding of the social dynamics of Helmand as a whole, let alone its districts, towns and tribes. The brigade had to turn elsewhere to understand the province's human terrain. Assisted by the UK Defence Academy, it developed a more detailed picture of the population of Helmand, as well as a concept of 'behavioural conflict' with which it sought to develop more dynamic ways of achieving influence at the tactical level. The brigade fielded 'non kinetic effects teams' to assist commanders from battalion to company level and below to act in ways that maximized influence over the population.

Mackay sought to reduce Taliban influence by physically ejecting them from the town of Musa Qala, which the insurgents had controlled since the 2006 ceasefire deal with the British collapsed. After the town was encircled with British armour, a battalion of US paratroops landed by helicopter outside it. With overwhelming air support, the Taliban were pushed out. Three days later the British escorted an Afghan Army brigade into the town. The British troops and vehicles were positioned out of view and the Afghan troops were filmed and photographed liberating the town and raising the Afghan flag. This was propaganda of the deed to give the Afghan and international media the impression that the Afghan forces had played the leading role in the recapture of the town.

The British allocated £3 million to be spent on reconstruction to repair roads and renovate the district medical centre and school. A new district governor was installed, He was a former Taliban leader who had changed sides, or 'reconciled'. Initially he made progress. But as time went on, he quarrelled with the district police chief, a member of a rival tribal grouping. And his personal militia engaged in increasingly predatory behaviour towards local Afghans. This was reinforced by the way that wealth, land and power were channelled through family, tribal and criminal structures that often co-opted the flimsy formal government power structures at provincial and district levels. What appeared on paper to be a formal mechanism to national, provincial and local government, was in practice more like arrangements made in Europe during feudal times. This illustrated how Musa Qala, like much of Helmand, was embroiled in a perfect storm of Taliban resistance that fed off local grievances, reinforced by civilian casualties and collateral damage caused by the fighting.

Earlier that year, Michael Semple, an Irish expert on Afghanistan, working for the EU, had used contacts with Taliban to persuade a group of insurgents to change sides. Elsewhere in Helmand, a scheme to persuade a Taliban group to change sides and act as part of the Gereshk police succeeded. The former Taliban were allocated a sector to patrol, the British finding them more professional than the Afghan Police. Semple had also persuaded several Taliban armed groups not to oppose the capture of Musa Qala, with a view to their subsequent reintegration being supported by the British.

These initiatives had been approved by the Helmand governor, Asadullah Wafa, and by the Afghan security authorities in Kabul. But Governor Wafa then had Semple arrested and persuaded President Karzai to expel him from Afghanistan. The governor had been fully informed about Semple's work, as had many of Karzai's officials, but it appears that none of them had shared this with the president. It is likely that when Wafa realized that the considerable sums of money involved did not include a percentage for him, he acted to double cross Semple.

Over the winter Taliban attacks in Helmand increased in frequency and effectiveness. The Danish deployed Leopard tanks to reinforce their battalion attached to the British brigade. Local attitudes were conditioned by a widespread belief that the British intended to eradicate poppy production. This was reinforced by US-funded efforts to eradicate poppy-growing in Helmand, which to the British seemed to work in isolation from the military campaign.

In both Helmand and Kandahar provinces the Taliban retained considerable freedom of movement outside areas that were controlled by ISAF. In these places there was an insurgent 'shadow government'. The evidence suggests that in many areas it was no more effective than Afghan local government; often it was worse. But unlike in many government-controlled areas it had an effective shadow judicial system. This provided a harsh but effective way to resolve local disputes, particularly over land and water. The beneficiaries of rulings by Taliban judges had even more incentive to support the insurgency.[12]

Militarily, the Taliban had learned lessons from their battles with US and NATO troops. They sought to make more effective use of their small arms and RPGs. Despite these improvements, whenever the Taliban stood and fought for more than a quarter of an hour, NATO would add extra firepower. This would include mortars, artillery, attack helicopters and fighters. These would inevitably inflict Taliban casualties, as did the ever-increasing number of raids by SOF. Apart from some heavy machine guns, the Taliban had very few dedicated anti-aircraft weapons. Although the insurgents were able to occasionally ambush low flying helicopters with machine guns and rocket propelled grenades, they were never able to seriously contest NATO's control of the air. This placed the Taliban at a considerable disadvantage, and gave the US and its allies the ability to make extensive use of manned and unmanned aircraft for intelligence gathering, for bomb and missile strikes and to move troops and supplies around Afghanistan.[13]

As a result, the Taliban made increasing use of IEDs to attack NATO troops and vehicles. As NATO fielded increasingly well-protected vehicles, the size of Taliban roadside bombs increased, often producing devices of between 400 and 1,600 pounds in weight.

In Helmand, there had been considerable friction between the British brigade and the civilian-led PRT. A formal review of the British operation resulted in an uplift of the number of civilians. Integration between the brigade HQ would be improved by co-locating both organizations next door to each other in the same compound at Lashkar Gar, the provincial capital, with some of the brigade military planners and its deputy commander working within the PRT. It was also decided to deploy civilian stabilization advisors forward, to co-locate with the HQs of the battalions. These would be assisted by military stabilization support teams, soldiers assigned to the role, who could deploy into more dangerous environments than civilians to act as the eyes and ears of the stabilization advisors.[14]

Relations between Afghanistan and Pakistan continued to worsen, with the already considerable level of mutual mistrust continuing to grow and the US becoming increasingly convinced that the Pakistani intelligence agency, the ISI, was actively supporting the insurgents. Bilateral relations reached a new low in 2008 when Karzai threatened to launch the Afghan Army south into Pakistani territory to neutralize Afghan Taliban bases. After General Musharraf was succeeded by an elected civilian president, Asif Ali Zadari, relations thawed sufficiently for Kabul to allow Islamabad to expand its diplomatic footprint in Afghanistan.

By then large amounts of military supplies for the Afghan forces, the US and its allies were being delivered to the bustling Pakistani port of Karachi. Civilian contractors would haul these as cargo along Pakistan's road network, crossing the border at Spin Baldak in the south and the Khyber Pass in the north. They would use the garishly decorated 'jingly' trucks (the name coming from the sound of bells fitted on them) for this. It was widely suspected that a proportion of the fees paid by the US and its allies was spent by the contractors on 'protection', that is buying off the Pakistani and Afghan Taliban. As US and NATO contingents in Afghanistan and the Afghan Army increased in size, so the volume of logistic traffic from Karachi across Pakistan increased, thus creating a dependency on the good will of Islamabad.

THE UNFORGIVING MOUNTAINS OF EASTERN AFGHANISTAN

In eastern Afghanistan from 2003 to 2006 the Taliban also sought to extend its networks and to attack US and Afghan forces. There were few US troops deployed in the region, the great majority of US activity being raids by helicopter-borne SOF. In 2006, at the same time as the British and Canadians were moving into southern Afghanistan, US forces increased their strength in the mountainous terrain of eastern Afghanistan. Here the folded jagged mountains of the Hindu Kush sheltered small agricultural communities of fiercely independent Afghans. Across the Durand Line in Pakistan were networks of Taliban in the equally forbidding and harsh mountains of Pakistan's Federally

Administered Tribal Areas. Here, the writ of the Pakistan government and the capabilities of the Pakistan Army were limited at best. The area provided cross-border bases for the Taliban from which they were able to send both fighters and supplies northwards into Afghanistan.

In late 2006 the 3rd Brigade, 10th Mountain Division, commanded by Colonel John Nicholson, assumed responsibility for the mountainous eastern Afghanistan provinces of Kunar and Nuristan, meeting increasing Taliban opposition as they did so. In the Korengal Valley Nicholson sought to separate the Afghan civilians from the insurgents. This required deploying combat outposts deep into the network of steep twisting valleys. For example, the 1st Battalion, 32nd Infantry deployed its 1,200 troops in a dozen outposts in an area covering some 1200 square miles. Most of these positions were occupied by platoon-sized forces of 30–40 US troops.

Getting the troops into the valleys was not especially difficult, but the local Afghan contractors hired by US Army engineers to help build their bases were often subject to attacks and intimidation by the Taliban. The bases were usually next to villages that had been constructed on the small proportion of flat land in the valley, overlooked by steep and vegetation-covered ridges of up to 10,000 feet. This meant that they were easily observed by insurgents and very vulnerable to sniping and stand-off attacks by rockets and mortars. Fortifying the bases was difficult, often limited to trenches, bunkers and earthen walls. And the large area over which the US troops were spread limited the number of helicopters that could be spared for resupply sorties, making them reliant on convoys of supply trucks slowly making their way along the twisting roads in the winding valleys that led to the bases. These were very vulnerable to ambush and attack.

The Korengal Valley was to be an area of significant resistance to US forces. The mountainous nature of much of eastern Afghanistan had resulted in a very complex human terrain, with isolated valleys occupied by a wide variety of tribes, with different customs, cultures and sometimes different languages. The factors that divided most tribes were greater than those which united them, other than a strong dislike of outsiders. Different provinces posed different challenges. For example, a US battalion in Nuristan Province sought to actively engage tribal elders and use development money to strengthen the authority of those who opposed the Taliban. Months of patient negotiation resulted in a truce between the elders, Taliban and US troops, allowing the battalion to advance deep into Nuristan without any armed opposition.

But advantage could rapidly switch between both sides. Khost Province in 2006 was one of Afghanistan's most violent. But in 2007 a US battalion achieved a high degree of partnership and integration with the US PRT and with US SOF operating in the province. They worked very closely with the provincial governor and set out to boost both the capability and confidence of the Afghan Army and Police. By the end of 2007 security had greatly improved.

But in 2008, the battalion rotated out of the province and the PRT leadership changed. Integration and co-ordination between both units and the US SOF decreased and the highly regarded provincial governor resigned – probably because of Taliban death threats. As insurgent attacks increased, security in the province deteriorated.

THE BATTLE OF WANAT

A persistent low-level conflict developed in the valleys, with attacks on US bases, patrols, helicopters and convoys. The insurgents appeared to be both local fighters and Taliban moving into the area from Pakistan. Inevitably there were civilian casualties and collateral damage.

This was illustrated by the battle of Wanat in the Waygal Valley on 13 July 2008. The US 101st Airborne Division was responsible for eastern Afghanistan. As well as its own troops, it had attached the 173rd Airborne Brigade. The brigade had a small base, Combat Outpost (COP) Kahler, at the village of Wanat in Nuristan Province. This contained 49 US troops, mostly paratroopers, and 24 Afghan soldiers with a few US Marines acting as mentors. It was surrounded by mountain ridges that reached up to 10,000 feet. These not only offered many opportunities for the Taliban to covertly observe the base, but also constrained the utility of the Raven and Shadow drones that by now were organic to US divisions. USAF Predator and Reaper drones still had considerable utility in providing observation and as signals intelligence platforms, but there were not enough of them available to fly over eastern Afghanistan and conducting surveillance around Wanat was not a high priority.[15]

Just after sunrise on 13 June 2008 the base was attacked by hundreds of Taliban fighters. Their firepower was intense enough to suppress key parts of the US defensive plan, including the base's single 120mm heavy mortar and TOW missile launcher. A signaller found that microphones of his radios were quickly riddled with bullet holes. Under this covering fire the attackers rapidly approached. Some got so close that the US troops could make them out as individuals wearing a mixture of camouflage uniforms and traditional Afghan clothing. Some wore face masks. The GIs managed to keep the Taliban outside the perimeter of the base, but only just. At times the Taliban fighters were so close that the defenders had to use hand grenades against the attackers.

US artillery was quickly brought to bear. The US and Afghan troops held on with grim determination. After an hour of fighting, two Apache attack helicopters arrived from the US aviation quick reaction force based at Jalalabad. Using their thermal sights, they were able to pick up Taliban fighters hiding in scrub and undergrowth around the base. Their very first attack was to use cannon 'danger close' against Taliban only 10 yards away from the US troops. By now nine US troops had been killed. A platoon drove in Humvees to reinforce the outpost, every spare space in the vehicles crammed with additional ammunition. They had to fight their way through Wanat's bazaar to reach the base.

By now many US aircraft had gathered in the sky above Wanat, including A10s, F15s and drones armed with Hellfire missiles. They bombed observed insurgent positions and likely movement routes. The balance of firepower gradually turned in favour of the US. Wounded soldiers were picked up by Black Hawk casualty evacuation helicopters, while Apaches conducted strafing ruins to suppress Taliban fire. A total of 16 wounded Americans and four wounded Afghan soldiers would be evacuated by air that day.

The next day a company of Afghan commandos and their US SOF advisors searched Wanat. Whilst Afghan soldiers at the US base had joined in the fighting by wildly firing from their positions, a squad of Afghan Police in Wanat village had not participated. Indeed, there were plenty of discarded Taliban weapons in the police compound, as well as bloodied items of clothing and many brass cases signifying that the attackers had fired at the US base from there. The police had probably been bribed or intimidated to stay out of the fight. This is likely to have reflected the general attitude of the Afghans living in the town.

With a total of nine Americans killed and 27 wounded this was the bloodiest US battle in Afghanistan so far. The Taliban had achieved surprise by stealthily approaching the US position and taking advantage of dead ground that could not be observed from COP Kahler to approach to within a short distance of the base's defences. The operation had been well planned and executed with bravery, aggression and discipline.

Although not apparent at the time, post-conflict analysis indicated that whilst the Taliban initially produced a very high volume of fire, much of it was inaccurate. Had the Taliban been better trained to shoot their RPGs and small arms, displaying the same levels of marksmanship found in US or British infantry, they would have killed more US troops more quickly, increasing the chances of overrunning COP Kahler in that first hour before the Apache helicopters arrived.[16]

Were it not for the determined defence of the base that made skilful use of existing US fortifications and barbed wire, the use of over a hundred rounds of artillery and the rapid deployment of Apache attack helicopters and formidable quantities of US fixed-wing airpower, the base would certainly have been overrun by the Taliban attackers. After the battle the 101st Airborne Division decided that the costs of sustaining the combat outpost in such hostile human and physical terrain outweighed the benefits. Even with the greatest numbers of organic helicopters of any division of any army in the world, they could not be everywhere at once. Shortly afterwards the base was closed.

THE BRITISH BECOME INCREASINGLY STRETCHED IN HELMAND PROVINCE

From March 2008 until March 2009, Helmand would see again the first two British brigades to serve there: 16 Air Assault Brigade and 3 Commando Brigade Royal Marines. With the considerable reduction of British troops in Iraq, both brigades that previously had deployed little more than a battalion's worth of infantry now had a Danish battalion and five British battalions, one of which provided the OMLT. The British were receiving ever-increasing numbers of the heavily armoured Mastiff patrol vehicle. In addition, they had also acquired a brigade-level drone capability for Afghanistan, the Hermes 450. They also had a company of Estonian infantry. Tallinn wanted to demonstrate its country's utility to NATO. The Estonian contingent deployed to Helmand with no national restrictions on their employment.

Much of the additional British infantry was now disbursed across the irrigated area of the Helmand River Valley in forward operating bases, the British having embraced General Petraeus' exhortations that the main effort of countering insurgency should be protecting the people and that this required basing of troops in the midst of their areas of operations. This reduced the spare combat power available to be used in a more mobile role.

And the British could not be everywhere. In the south of Helmand, they had no forces south of Garmser. This area, known as the 'Snake's Head', was a staging area for Taliban moving north from Pakistan. There was evidence that newly trained Taliban would hone their combat skills by attacking the British base at Garmser.

In April 2008 ISAF ordered that the area south of Garmser be cleared by a US Marine expeditionary unit. The Marines had 600 infantrymen, the Taliban having about the same number of fighters, including Pakistanis, Arabs, Uzbeks and Chechens. A long hard battle resulted, the Taliban fighting from well-prepared bunkers that were often resilient to attack by all but a direct hit from a precision bomb. Marine infantry and helicopters were often on the receiving end of volleys of RPG rockets. Those Taliban that stood and fought were killed or captured. After several weeks of fighting the surviving Taliban abandoned Garmser district, which was then held by British and Afghan forces.

In October 2008 the Taliban sought to regain the initiative by attempting to mount a surprise attack on Lashkar Gar, the Helmand provincial capital. This was discovered at almost the last minute by the National Directorate of Security as about 400 Taliban fighters were advancing to capture the town. These reports were quickly confirmed by intercepted Taliban communications suggesting that the Taliban planned to attack the governor's compound and storm the prison to release jailed comrades. Mortars and rockets struck the town. As drones and Apache helicopters were flown over Lashkar Gar they detected a group of Taliban advancing 'in a disciplined fashion'. As staff officers left their desks to defend the brigade HQ, Apaches strafed Taliban detected by drones, but not before Afghan police on the edge of the town were attacked by a company-sized group of Taliban. Throughout the night Taliban were attacked by Apache helicopters, breaking off the attack only at 0400hrs. Rather than kill all the retreating insurgents outright, drones were used to follow some back to their homes – yielding invaluable intelligence.

After the Lashkar Gar attack, the British realized there was more Taliban presence in central Helmand than they had initially assessed. They decided to clear part of the Nad-e Ali district of central Helmand. A battlegroup of Royal Marines, Estonian and Danish mechanized infantry and a troop of Danish Leopard tanks was given the mission to secure three walled villages, called *kalays* by the Afghans. To achieve it took 18 days of hard fighting in agricultural terrain crossed by ditches.

The first village captured was Khushhal Kalay, which turned out to be defended by militia from the Kharoti tribe, who chose to stand down rather than face destruction of the village. The British later discovered that the principal role of the militia had been to contest control of narcotics with the Noorzai tribe, who controlled the Afghan police in the district. This was after the British had introduced the same police into the village. Without the British realising it, the battle had turned into another round of a tribal dispute.

The village of Zarghun Kalay in contrast supported the Taliban and commanders mobilized their fighters to join the defence. It took two days of fighting to capture the village, in which the British used artillery, Apache helicopters and Harrier jets. This resulted in both Taliban and civilian casualties. The Estonian company deployed to Zarghun Kalay, discovering that some Afghan police were already present in the village. As the NATO troops' understanding of local tribal dynamics and politics improved, they began to understand that that the Aghezai clan in the village had strong links of kinship with both the local police and the Taliban district *shura*. All three groups had strong interests in avoiding armed conflict.

After the attack, a new district governor was introduced and the British set about consolidating their control. During the initial British attacks, the Taliban had laid relatively few IEDs. But as the British troops moved into static patrol bases the Taliban were able to plant IEDs in large numbers, ringing the bases with the bombs and restricting, complicating and slowing down British movement as well as causing almost two-thirds of British casualties. By early 2009, there had been a 40 per cent increase in IEDS detected by the British in Helmand.

But for all their hard fighting and the slowly increasing commitment of resources the British were only making slow progress in clearing the Taliban from Helmand. Although the deployment had been sold to the

British public as a 'necessary war', the violence of the Taliban response, the resulting heavy fighting and ever-increasing British casualties had come as another strategic shock to the British government and people. The contentious character of the Iraq war, especially a prevailing sense that, even if they had not been lied to, Prime Minister Tony Blair and his spin doctors had greatly exaggerated the threat of Iraqi weapons of mass destruction was reinforced by the country's apparent descent into intractable chaos. The British public's confidence in the case for the fighting in Afghanistan was fatally undermined by the Iraq war.

CRUEL SUMMER – OPERATION *PANTHER'S CLAW*

In late June 2009 the British launched a major offensive, Operation *Panther's Claw*, to secure terrain between Helmand's two most important towns, Lashkar Gar and Gereshk, by clearing Taliban from the central Helmand districts of Babaji and Nawa. This would be the last major operation mounted by the British while they still had troops in Iraq. Despite government statements to the contrary, the British force had insufficient helicopters, surveillance drones armoured vehicles and equipment for countering roadside bombs. By now, the IED was the Taliban's principal weapon in Helmand. Large numbers were laid around the British bases. There were insufficient British helicopters to meet the logistic requirements of the troops in the bases by air delivery of the essential food, fuel, ammunition and medical supplies, so almost all of the material necessary to sustain the British battalions in the field had to be delivered by convoys of trucks. And the lack of British helicopters also meant that the great majority of patrols had to walk in and out of the British bases on necessarily predictable routes, increasing their vulnerability to Taliban bombs.

In Northern Ireland, the IRA insurgents had used roadside bombs to lethal effect in South Armagh, a stronghold of militants and their supporters. By the later 1970s British troops had abandoned routine vehicle movement by road in the area. Patrols were largely deployed by helicopter and routine resupply of the network of half a dozen bases was entirely conducted by helicopter. To achieve this the British battalion responsible had three or four dedicated helicopters and an allocation of at least 300 helicopters hours a month.[17] This was sufficient for both operations and logistic resupply. In 2009 British battalions in Helmand had far less support from helicopters than their forefathers had received in South Armagh in the preceding 40 years of the Northern Ireland conflict. For example, a British infantry battalion in South Armagh had a Gazelle and two Puma helicopters permanently deployed at its main base. No British battalion in Afghanistan was ever to receive such levels of dedicated helicopter support.

The British had adapted by making widespread use of handheld mine detectors and devising drills to use these to sweep the ground ahead of them for Taliban bombs. These drills were given the official code name of '*Barma*'. Using these procedures greatly reduced movement to the pace of a cautious soldier, and movement stopped completely when a bomb was found, to allow it to be dealt with by specially trained explosive ordnance disposal experts. This meant that movement by logistic convoys in most of central Helmand was often very slow, with accumulating risks to the infantry protecting the resupply routes from Taliban shooting attacks and the laying of yet more IEDs.

For both vehicle crews and infantry, the IED threat was an ever-present danger. It required real courage to keep driving on threatened roads and tracks and for infantrymen patrolling the bomb-strewn fields of Helmand. This was a considerable challenge to the young leaders of the troops, the corporals, sergeants, lieutenants and captains. That the British Army, US Marines and US Army managed to sustain operations in such a hostile environment was testimony to very high standards of leadership and morale.

Between May and December 2009, the British brigade in Helmand was 19th Light Brigade. Its commander, Brigadier Tim Radford, had to limit the ambition and tempo of the operation to match the less than optimal level of the resources available to his brigade. Several months of intelligence gathering preceded the launch of *Panther's Claw*, which began on the night of 18/19 June with the launching of helicopter-borne British SOF raids against identified Taliban commanders, while a dozen Chinook helicopters delivered the 3rd Battalion, the Royal Regiment of Scotland (the Black Watch) into Babaji.

The Welsh Guards advanced from the south, a push that was held up by large numbers of Taliban IEDs. The Welsh Guards' commanding officer hitched a lift with a convoy bringing supplies to his leading troops and was killed when the lightly armoured Viking vehicle in which he was riding struck a roadside bomb. Lieutenant Colonel Rupert Thorneloe was the first British battalion commander to be killed in action since the 1982 Falklands War. The next day, the helicopter carrying Radford, the brigade commander, ran into heavy insurgent fire and came close to being shot down.

The next phase of the attack saw the main advance carried out by the Light Dragoons. Normally a battalion-sized armoured cavalry regiment equipped with light armoured vehicles for scouting and reconnaissance, they had been reinforced by infantry from the Mercian Regiment to become in effect an infantry battalion.

The Light Dragoons' advance towards Babaji was as hard fought as any other of the British attacks in Helmand since 2006. Large numbers of IEDs and tenacious resistance from Taliban fighters firing small arms and RPGs both slowed the British advance and inflicted casualties. The first two days of the operations saw the Light Dragoons advance 2 miles, deal with over 50 IEDs and incur 30 casualties. The Black Watch were added to the advance, as was an infantry company from the British battalion in Sangin. This was sufficient to overmatch the Taliban and allow the advance to resume and reach Babaji.

Operation *Panther's Claw* had of necessity been the British priority in Helmand for helicopters, drones and other intelligence systems. These were not available elsewhere in Helmand and so the Taliban found it comparatively easy to sew large numbers of IEDs in Sangin, resulting in further casualties. In total, the British battlegroup in Sangin, based on 2nd Battalion, the Rifles, had lost 15 killed in as many days.

These caused great political difficulties for Prime Minister Gordon Brown. By now the unpopularity of the Iraq war had migrated to the Afghan war. Efforts to promote the legitimacy of the conflict had been undermined by the avoidable failures of the Iraq war, including slow fielding of armoured vehicles and inadequate care and support for wounded troops and their families.

These were all exploited by the media and opposition parties. A totemic issue was whether British troops in Afghanistan had sufficient helicopters. All the evidence was that they did not, and government attempts to persuade the media and public otherwise lacked credibility.

By now there was a breakdown in civilian–military relations. Gordon Brown had previously been Chancellor of the Exchequer, the UK finance minister, and was widely seen by the service chiefs as having insisted on defence cuts that led to reductions in capability. The reductions in defence spending required by Brown in 2004 had resulted in funding for new helicopters being cut. If these had not been made, the UK would have had more helicopter capability in Helmand by 2009. The helicopter crews knew this, the MoD knew it, the services chiefs knew it, but Brown persisted in denying it.

The service chiefs and Brown made several efforts to explain the rationale behind the Afghan war to the British public. But by then the UK media were so unsympathetic that these efforts failed. Fighting a second unpopular war was becoming increasingly difficult.

ARMED POLITICS IN GARMSER

As *Panther's Claw* was begun, US Marines replaced the Light Dragoons in Garmser district. Carter Malkasian, a US State Department official, has provided a detailed account of the relation between war and politics in a single district of Afghanistan in *War Comes to Garmser*.[18] He shows how between 2004 and 2006, the Taliban exploited grievances with predatory Afghan government officials, using these factors to evict the few remaining pro-government tribal militia, soldiers and police and all presence of the Afghan government, apart from a small outpost of British and Afghan troops in the district centre.

From mid-2006 to mid-2008 Garmser remained largely under Taliban control until a 2008 offensive by US Marines recaptured key territory from the Taliban. This was successfully held by British and Afghan troops, but most of the district remained under Taliban control. The smaller area under Afghan government control received British funded development projects, mediated by a community council that sought to involve tribal elders and local stakeholders in these.

With the 2009 reinforcement of Helmand by US Marines, a sustained operation was conducted to extend Afghan government control over the rest of Garmser district. Offensive operations cleared Taliban from key areas of the district holding them with combat outposts of Marines and ever-increasing numbers of Afghan forces. But local politics was just as important a factor in determining the character of the conflict. For example, each offensive operation by the Marines was accompanied by efforts to find an Afghan tribal elder with political influence in that particular area, the US funding a limited number of tribal militias to protect the elder and funding quick impact development projects to reinforce the Afghan government's, district governor's and local elder's authority.

Malkasian, a US civilian acting as a political advisor, was able to use his authority to conduct 'armed politics', combining political action, development money and armed action by the Marines to promote political progress in parallel with security operations. Over a year, this combination of offensive operations by the Marines and the district governor's expansion of his political influence and development projects, together with the arrival of ever-greater numbers of relatively capable new Afghan troops and police resulted in the near-complete eviction of the Taliban from the whole district. In COIN terms, these operations were a demonstration of military 'clear', followed by 'hold' and 'build' being a combination of security, local politics and development.

But political difficulties were also multiplying for the US and its allies in Afghanistan. One of the key drivers leading to the British offensive in Helmand had been the August 2009 Afghan presidential elections. Previous Afghan elections had been supervised by the UN, but these would be run by the Afghan Electoral Commission. The UN and international diplomats saw overwhelming evidence of efforts to fix the election, including blatant stuffing of ballot boxes by President Karzai's supporters. At the same time Karzai saw a plot by the US to unseat him, led by veteran US diplomat Richard Holbrooke, Special Representative for Afghanistan and Pakistan. Although Karzai was proclaimed winner of the election, these two factors greatly worsened relations between President Karzai and the US.

THE BATTLE FOR COMBAT OUTPOST KEATING

Meanwhile in eastern Afghanistan, the US-led Regional Command East was continuing to attempt to stabilize the mountainous districts that abutted Pakistan's Federally Administered Tribal Areas. US troops in the area had sought to apply counter-insurgency doctrine to protect the Afghan population. This resulted in many of them being dispersed in small bases, close to key towns and villages. There was an extensive programme of road and bridge construction and improvement. This sought to better connect the agricultural communities with bigger towns where produce could be sold at markets. US PRTs funded these and other development projects. But the mountainous terrain meant that the US outposts were distributed over a wide area. Although the US Army had more helicopter support for its troops than any other army in Afghanistan, it still had insufficient rotary-wing aircraft to provide all the support that ground commanders in eastern Afghanistan wanted. US vehicle movement along the narrow roads that ran through the mountainous valleys was very vulnerable to insurgent roadside bombs. This meant that most of the logistic resupply of US bases was conducted by helicopters, reducing the US forces' capability for offensive operations. The insurgents had a strong presence in eastern Afghanistan, but US troops found it difficult to find them. Many of the Afghan communities in the region, like isolated mountain communities the world over, were intensely suspicious of outsiders. Although the intelligence and surveillance systems fielded by US forces had greatly improved, Iraq remained the US strategic priority. And the high altitude, complexity of the terrain and frequent clouds and mist meant that the utility of drones was greatly reduced. All of these factors meant that many of the small US bases in the mountains would, like the British outposts in Helmand in 2006, be very vulnerable to insurgent attacks.

These vulnerabilities and difficulties would be cruelly exposed by an October 2009 insurgent attack on a US base at Kamdesh in Nuristan, known as Combat Outpost Keating, which came close to defeating the Americans. When originally occupied by US troops the base had been intended as the location for a PRT. But this never deployed. By mid-2009 US commanders assessed that the isolated base was having little positive effect and was of limited utility as a platform from which to engage local Afghans. It had originally been intended to close the base in July and August. But this was delayed by the need for the brigade to support the Afghan forces. And surveillance capabilities such as drones were diverted away from the brigade to assist with the search for a US soldier who had gone missing from their base.

The Talban had spotted the base's increased vulnerability. Over the previous months they had mounted increasing numbers of probing attacks, seeking to better understand the base defences and the reactions of the US troops. Although numbers of attacks had risen threefold, the US chain of command had become desensitized to the increasing threat.

Just before 0600hrs on 3 October 2009 the Taliban awoke the US soldiers of Bravo Troop of the 3rd Squadron, 61st Cavalry Regiment with an unprecedented volume of fire. Casualties were inflicted and many of the defenders and the outpost's mortars were rapidly suppressed while the generator serving the command post was knocked out. Afghan soldiers failed to hold their defensive positions and Taliban fighters penetrated inside the base's outer perimeter, forcing the surviving US soldiers into a tighter inner perimeter.

As at the previous year's battle of Wanat, the rapid firing of artillery, arrival of Apache helicopter gunships and close air support stopped the Taliban assault in its tracks. Of value to the hard-pressed defenders was a B1B *Lancer* bomber. Based in Qatar, the aircraft had been on patrol over Afghanistan for almost eight hours, before it was vectored to Kamdesh. It turned on its engine afterburners and broke the speed of sound to get to the outpost as quickly as it could. Arriving over the base, the crew were alarmed to see that most of it appeared to be on fire. As the bomber topped up on fuel from a nearby tanker aircraft, the US troops frantically planned to use the aircraft's 20 guided bombs to attack Taliban-held positions, including some about 100 yards from the base. As soon as the bomber had laid down its barrage the defenders opened with all the weapons they had. Once the B1 bomber had expended its ordnance, Apache helicopters, A10 Warthog attack aircraft and artillery were all used to attack known and suspected Taliban positions.

Through a long afternoon of hard fighting the surviving defenders evicted Taliban fighters from the base and re-established the outer perimeter. Eight US soldiers were killed. The battle came even closer to a US defeat than the narrow margin by which the defenders of Wanat had prevailed. No fewer than two Medals of Honour were awarded to the defenders.[19] After the battle it was decided to rapidly proceed with closing the base. A subsequent US Army inquiry determined that prior to the attack US commanders displayed 'a mindset of imminent closure that served to impede improvements in force protection on the COP. There were inadequate measures taken by the chain of command, resulting in an attractive target for enemy fighters.'[20]

Four officers in the chain of command above COP Keating were formally reprimanded. These reprimands were rescinded on appeal.

The battles at COP Keating illustrated the difficulties that US troops were facing in eastern Afghanistan. To apply 'protecting the population' the priority had to be the largest towns, such as Jalalabad. Extending the US and Afghan forces footprint up the valleys was going to increase the population protected and it would constrain the insurgents. But with a finite force in a large mountainous area and insurgents who had bases a short march away in the tribal badlands of Pakistan, the US outposts and the limit of the network of bases were going to be vulnerable to a concentrated insurgent attack.

As the British had found in 2006 in Helmand, platoon- or company-sized outposts that in previous wars would have been overrun by attackers with the same numbers, firepower and determination as possessed by the Taliban could in the 21st century be held; but this was possible only when the US and British were able to rapidly concentrate the firepower of large quantities of rotary- and fixed-wing aircraft in defence of the outpost. They were lucky that the satellite communications and ground to air radios with which they had equipped their armies and air forces were never seriously subjected to electronic attack by the Taliban.

THE AUDIT OF WAR

Between 2006 and 2009 security slowly deteriorated and numbers of NATO and US troops gradually increased. Numbers of US and NATO troops reached 65,000 at the end of 2008. In 2008 Admiral Mullen, Chairman of the US Joint Chiefs of Staff told Congress that 'I'm not convinced we are winning in Afghanistan', a view shared in many NATO capitals.

Between 2006 and 2009 the war in Iraq was the top priority for the US, UK and many of their allies. ISAF and the Taliban fought each other to dominate southern and eastern Afghanistan. As the strength of NATO forces increased, so did that of the Taliban.

On taking command of all US and Coalition troops in Afghanistan ISAF sought to implement a counter-insurgency approach that combined security and development, as well as better engaging President Karzai and his government. This often required infantry to be dispersed in company or even platoon-sized bases. In both Helmand and eastern Afghanistan, sustained Taliban attacks on these positions were only beaten off with extensive use of artillery, attack helicopters and ground attack aircraft.

Some major brigade-level offensive operations to clear concentrations of Taliban from key terrain were mounted. These included Operation *Medusa*, the first ever brigade attack by NATO, in which Canadian, US and Afghan troops attacked Taliban fighters assembling in Panjwai for an attack on Kandahar City. This not only showed that Taliban fighters could be dogged defenders requiring aggressive use of combined arms capabilities in which infantry were supported by armoured vehicles and artillery. It also illustrated the considerable advantages that control of the air bestowed upon NATO, including manned and unmanned surveillance aircraft, precision bombing and close air support by fighters and attack helicopters. Were it not for Coalition command of the air many of these Taliban attacks would probably have resulted in insurgent victories.

Despite the considerable destruction inflicted on the Taliban, the small Canadian brigade in Kandahar lacked the required number of troops to hold the area for any length of time, and the Taliban regained control. The British in Helmand Province suffered from similar problems. Operations that cleared Taliban-controlled areas became known as 'mowing the lawn', achieving temporary positive effect, but having a resulting cost in NATO and civilian casualties and collateral damage that did nothing for NATO's credibility in Afghanistan or troop-contributing nations. It did not have the sufficient troops or aircraft to adequately dominate its area of responsibility and protect itself, let alone sustain enough pressure on insurgent networks. As a consequence, many of its key bases came to be surrounded by belts of insurgent IEDs. As the British also lacked helicopters, supplies had to be largely delivered by road, requiring major operations to clear IEDs. Both the convoys and the clearance operations led to British casualties. The British were failing to wrest the initiative from the insurgents and the steady stream of casualties was undermining UK popular support for the war.

In Helmand, the British attempted to apply McChrystal's new approaches but were increasingly constrained by lack of infantry, armoured vehicles, helicopters and airborne surveillance, as well as ever-increasing numbers of Taliban IEDs. Operation *Panther's Claw*, their 2009 offensive in central Helmand, saw fighting as intense as that experienced in World War II and consequently heavy British casualties. These resulted in damage to the political and military credibility of the government of Prime Minister Gordon Brown, illustrating the difficulty of simultaneously fighting unpopular wars while reducing defence spending and military capability. It was only after a US Marine expeditionary force reinforced Helmand in the second half of 2009 that a sufficient force density was achieved to gain the initiative over the Taliban.

The Afghan Surge

2009–12

In the 2008 US presidential campaign candidate Barrack Obama had repeatedly emphasized that the US needed to finish its military engagement in Iraq, but that he supported the war in Afghanistan. Obama initiated the first of several reviews of US strategy for Afghanistan. This review linked eliminating threats to the US from Afghanistan and Pakistan as key US goals. It did not explicitly call for the defeat of the Taliban but stated that 'the Taliban's momentum must be reversed'. The priority missions of US forces were to secure the south and east of Afghanistan to prevent the return of Al Qaida and allow the Afghan government to control these areas. US forces would also develop and mentor the Afghan security forces, so they could take the lead for security operations, allowing foreign forces to withdraw. Whilst there would be other strategy reviews, these principles would remain at the core of US plans until 2014.

In February 2009 the newly elected Obama agreed to a request from the US commander in Kabul for more US troops to reverse Taliban gains and better support the impending summer 2009 Afghan presidential elections. He despatched an additional 17,000 troops to Afghanistan to reinforce the 36,000 US troops already there and initiated a review of US strategy for Afghanistan. He announced that the core US goal 'must be to disrupt, dismantle and defeat Al Qaida and its safe havens in Pakistan'.[1]

It was decided that a high proportion of these reinforcements would be US Marines. They would deploy to south-west Afghanistan, reinforcing the relatively over-stretched British forces in Helmand Province. The British would concentrate on central Helmand, including its capital Lashkar Gar, while the Marines would take over districts outside the periphery of British-controlled areas.

In June 2009, US General Stan McChrystal was appointed as the new ISAF commander and commander of US troops in Afghanistan. Previously commander of the joint SOF task force hunting Al Qaida, McChrystal found that many NATO contingents in Afghanistan reflected the original focus of ISAF on peace enforcement, rather than counter-insurgency. And ISAF's various regional command HQs were fighting their own different wars rather than executing a centrally planned and co-ordinated campaign plan. National restrictions on operations, the so-called 'caveats', high levels of personnel turnover and inadequate numbers of helicopters further reduced the effectiveness of many national contingents.

Afghan president Hamid Karzai had few resources to apply to governing Afghanistan and little direct political power. Whilst there was the architecture of an Afghan government in Kabul, including ministers and ministries, provincial government capabilities were much more rudimentary and those at district level were even less capable. This lack of Afghan government capability was to considerably frustrate the ability of NATO commanders to sustain the consent of Afghans. But the Afghan president did have the power of patronage, appointing government ministers and other public officials including provincial and district governors. He had to balance out the competing factions in Afghanistan and placate actual or potential warlords. This was a constant challenge.

By the time McChrystal arrived, Karzai was deeply troubled by what he saw as a high level of avoidable Afghan civilian casualties from NATO and US forces. McChrystal shared Karzai's concerns. Many Afghans thought that the successful precision bombing of the Northern Alliance in 2001 demonstrated that US aircraft were all-seeing and omnipotent. So any civilian casualties could not be seen as accidental, but were deliberate acts. Dark conspiracy theories of US malevolent action proliferated. And civilian casualties were easily exploited by the Taliban to reinforce grievances against international forces.

Soon after McChrystal arrived at the HQ, at an ISAF morning update, with regional commands linked in by video conference, he was told of an incident where ISAF had inflicted civilian casualties. McChrystal was incensed and banged the table:

'What is it that we don't understand? We're going to lose this fucking war if we don't stop killing civilians' I said, looking at the staff and at the commanders on the screen. It was uncharacteristic of me to swear during the morning update. I took a second and began again. 'I apologise for losing my temper, but we cannot continue to do this'[2]

McChrystal gave clear guidance to ISAF that the centre of gravity was the Afghan population. This was to be protected from the insurgents and from excessive use of ISAF's considerable firepower. This policy was implemented by more restrictive rules of engagement and was christened 'courageous restraint'. Behaviour by ISAF was to become less intimidating and threatening to Afghan citizens. For example, NATO convoys often forced Afghan drivers off the road and intimidated civilians. This was but one example of the considerable emphasis on force protection creating equally considerable gaps and barriers between Afghan civilians and international forces. This had to stop.

McChrystal also sought to improve co-ordination, both within NATO and between ISAF and the Afghan government. To better concentrate on high level political–military issues the single ISAF HQ was split in two, forming an Intermediate Joint Command to conduct tactical operations, exercising many of the functions of a corps HQ. McChrystal also advocated the concept of 'embedded partnering' between ISAF and the Afghan forces. This aimed to combine the two forces into a single team, exploiting ISAF's combat power and technology and the Afghan Forces' situational awareness. The concept applied at every echelon, from government ministries to patrols and checkpoints.

THE AFGHAN SURGE

McChrystal had been tasked by US Defense Secretary Gates to conduct a strategic assessment in his first 60 days in command.

McChrystal drew on a wide variety of military and civilian experts and recommended that a comprehensive COIN campaign be mounted, applying relevant lessons from Iraq, especially the need to protect the population. McChrystal subsequently requested that an extra 40,000 US troops be sent to Afghanistan to implement this strategy. Completed in August 2009 this report was leaked, sparking intense political and media speculation and damaging civil–military relations in Washington.

The autumn of 2009 saw Obama use the US National Security Council to conduct a further strategy review over a three-month period. By all accounts this was a protracted activity, over the course of about ten meetings of his national security staff, which Obama used to immerse himself in the topic, test assumptions and explore options. He made a considerable effort to see if there was a feasible alternative to McChrystal and the Pentagon's proposals for a troop-intensive COIN strategy. This included allowing Vice President Joe Biden to propose an alternative 'counter-terrorism plus' approach, which required far fewer US troops on the ground. But the US military, including Defense Secretary Robert Gates, General David Petraeus, who had led the Surge in Iraq and McChrystal, all strongly advocated a surge of troops, as did Hillary Clinton, the Secretary of State.

In December 2009 Obama announced that 30,000 US troops would be sent, NATO being invited to make up the difference. Obama declared that:

> As Commander-in-Chief, I have determined that it is in our vital national interest to send an additional 30,000 U.S. troops to Afghanistan. After 18 months, our troops will begin to come home. These are the resources that we need to seize the initiative, while building the Afghan capacity that can allow for a responsible transition of our forces out of Afghanistan ….
>
> Our overarching goal remains the same: to disrupt, dismantle, and defeat al Qaeda in Afghanistan and Pakistan, and to prevent its capacity to threaten America and our allies in the future.
>
> To meet that goal, we will pursue the following objectives within Afghanistan. We must deny al Qaeda a safe haven. We must reverse the Taliban's momentum and deny it the ability to overthrow the

government. And we must strengthen the capacity of Afghanistan's security forces and government so that they can take lead responsibility for Afghanistan's future.

We will meet these objectives in three ways. First, we will pursue a military strategy that will break the Taliban's momentum and increase Afghanistan's capacity over the next 18 months.

The 30,000 additional troops that I'm announcing tonight will deploy in the first part of 2010 – the fastest possible pace – so that they can target the insurgency and secure key population centres. They'll increase our ability to train competent Afghan security forces, and to partner with them so that more Afghans can get into the fight. And they will help create the conditions for the United States to transfer responsibility to the Afghans.[3]

Obama also announced that the military strategy would be complemented by a surge in civilian experts and a renewed US partnership with Pakistan. US troop numbers would begin to reduce from mid-2011, Obama stating that 'These are the resources we need to seize the initiative, while building the Afghan capacity that can allow for a responsible transition of our forces out of Afghanistan'. Obama's announcement was followed by similar announcements by other NATO nations.

McChrystal had also requested a US and NATO 'civilian surge' of diplomats, development staff and other experts to better develop Afghan governance, economic development and policing. By September 2010 numbers of US civilians had increased to over a thousand. But security requirements and bureaucratic factors meant that many of these people deployed to Kabul and major US bases such as Kandahar airfield, rather than into Afghan districts.

Obama's announcement meant that for NATO and the Afghan government, the campaign would be a race against the clock: to improve security, grow the Afghan security forces, develop the capacity of the Afghan state, reduce corruption and persuade 'reconcilable' Taliban to lay down their arms, all in time to meet the objective. The Afghan security forces would take the lead in conducting security operations in all provinces by the end of 2014. This timetable was widely known to Afghans of all persuasions: the Taliban, for their part, intended to frustrate these objectives, exploiting many Afghans' belief that insufficient enduring improvement in security and governance would be made before NATO left. The Taliban coined a slogan: that whilst the US and its allies had the watches, the Taliban had the time.

Based on the lessons of historic counter-insurgency campaigns and the Iraq war, ISAF planned to separate the insurgents from the Afghan people, improve their security, governance and economic prospects and degrade insurgent capabilities. The military roles targeted raids to capture or kill insurgent leaders, developing the Afghan forces and supporting the development of Afghan governance. Offensive operations were to be preceded by a programme of media announcements, to allow insurgents to withdraw from the area, thus reducing civilian casualties.

But where in Afghanistan should the reinforcing troops be employed? Two factors, apparently contradictory, guided this key decision. ISAF could not be strong everywhere, and any territory that was cleared of insurgents had to be subsequently held until it could be transferred to capable Afghan forces. The forbidding terrain of eastern Afghanistan made it likely that reinforcing US forces there would not have decisive effect. But analysis commissioned by McChrystal showed that most Taliban attacks were in the contested districts of Helmand and Kandahar provinces. He decided that given the earlier decision to reinforce Helmand with US Marines and the political importance of Kandahar as the historic heartland of the Taliban, these two provinces would be where most of the US surge reinforcements would be employed to clear the main populated areas of provinces of insurgents.

By now the US government, the Pentagon, the State Department and USAID had a shared understanding of the need for stabilization and how it would be conducted. They all agreed that the US had to deny Al Qaida the use of Afghan territory, from which to mount attacks on the US, its allies and interests. Because the Taliban had allowed Al Qaida to do this in the past and had not renounced its support for Al Qaida, the Taliban would need to be rendered incapable of doing so. This required the US and NATO forces to 'clear' by pushing the Taliban out of the key terrain they controlled and, with the assistance of the Afghan security forces, 'hold' the areas thus cleared. Because in the Taliban-controlled areas the insurgents provided services to Afghans, it was felt that provision of development and services by the Afghan authorities was an essential ingredient to 'build' popular support for the government by providing services to the populations in these areas. This meant that:

> the coalition needed to 'stabilize' those communities by extending the reach of the government, building up the capacity of local officials and institutions, and convincing the population that legitimate government was preferable to having the Taliban return. U.S. policy makers believed that only after such a paradigm shift occurred could the coalition withdraw and have the confidence the Taliban would be consistently repelled by the population, with its newfound appreciation for the continuous services and protection of the Afghan government.'4

ISAF's main effort was to tackle the heartland of Afghan support for the Quetta Shura Taliban in southern Afghanistan, by extending Afghan government control over the most heavily populated areas in Helmand and Kandahar provinces. Territory that was cleared was to be subsequently held for stabilization. Most reinforcing US forces were deployed there, as well as increasing numbers of Afghan forces. US forces in eastern Afghanistan were therefore not to disperse amongst remote villages but were to concentrate their forces on the most important areas.

OPERATION *MOSHTARAK* – THE BATTLE FOR MARJAH

McChrystal's first opportunity to use surge forces to mount clearance operations was Operation *Moshtarak*, by US, UK and Afghan forces in Helmand Province. This sought to expand the British-controlled footprint in central Helmand, but its main effort was to clear the insurgent stronghold of Marjah. The plan for the launch of the operation was developed by the US Marines brigade and the HQ of Regional Command South.

Marjah was an irrigated area to the west side of the main 'Green Zone' of agricultural terrain. It had fallen to the Taliban in 2008. The British lacked the forces necessary to clear and hold the district and had limited themselves to occasional raids. But as long as the district remained in Taliban hands it posed a major threat to the security of Helmand.

The plan to clear Marjah of Taliban had several novel features. The first was a deliberate information operation begun well before the ISAF attack, explaining that ISAF would move into Marjah. Since 2008, there had been several NATO attacks on the district. All had eventually withdrawn. The leaflets dropped on Marjah from the air and media operations all sought to explain that this time, NATO troops would remain in Marjah.

Secondly ISAF sought to minimize the use of the heavy firepower available to it, particularly artillery and air strikes. This was in accordance with McChrystal's doctrine of 'courageous restraint'. Not only would use of artillery and airpower be very tightly controlled, but the plan for the operation sought to reduce the necessity for using these weapons by achieving both surprise and concentration of force.

The scheme of manoeuvre sought to avoid an advance from the perimeter of Marjah towards the centre of the district, which it was expected that the Taliban would anticipate. Rather, night helicopter assaults would simultaneously deliver two battalions of US Marines and a battalion of Afghan commandos into the centre of the district, bypassing the IEDs and defensive positions that the Taliban had prepared on the likely routes that ISAF troops would have used for ground attacks.

The night air assault by 60 blacked-out US, British and Canadian helicopters, the pilots flying by night vision goggles, successfully leapfrogged over the main Taliban defences. There were no preparatory artillery or air attacks. Two companies of Marines accompanied by Afghan troops landed just outside the town of Marjah itself.

Tactical surprise was achieved, with the Taliban clearly wrong footed by the night-time descent from the sky of a brigade's worth of US and Afghan troops. But they quickly recovered and, correctly divining the routes that the air-landed troops would need to use, insurgents began to contest their advances over the complex terrain of fields and agricultural ditches and canals with sniping, ambushes and IEDs. A steady trickle of casualties resulted – US, Afghan military and civilians.

The next phase of the operation was to extend Afghan government influence in the cleared areas. In the British sector, around Nad-e Ali, the subsequent stabilization operation, and the restoration of Afghan governance, was relatively successful.

Before the operation McChrystal had expected that between the Marines, the US civilian stabilization effort led by the US Embassy in Kabul and the Afghan government, Marjah would benefit from 'government in a box'. This term was then being used by the US and ISAF to describe a package of measures to be taken by the Afghan authorities to promote rapid stabilization of an area cleared of Taliban.

Efforts to achieve this in Marjah were problematic. Neither the Marines nor the Afghan Forces initially had much understanding of the area's tribal and political dynamics. District governor appointments were made by the president and Karzai nominated an Afghan who had lived in Germany, had been imprisoned for assaulting his son and did not speak Pashto, the tongue of the Pashtuns who lived in Marjah. Worse still, before the attack on Marjah began, when Karzai attended a *shura* of local elders in Lashkar Gar, Helmand's capital, he brought with him Sher Mohammed Akhundzada, the former Helmand governor and Karzai loyalist that the British had in 2005 insisted be removed for narcotic trafficking, At the *shura*, Ahkundzada was positioned in front of Helmand's then governor Guleb Mangal, an efficient technocrat, highly regarded by the US and UK. Karzai nominated an associate of Ahkundzada's as police chief for Marjah and went on to greatly delay the nomination of other civilian officials. Karzai would later visit Marjah accompanied by both men, in his public remarks describing the US forces as 'invaders'.

The US Marines also found that, apart from Afghan commandos, many of the Afghan forces that they had partnered with were of limited military effectiveness. Clearance of Marjah proceeded more slowly than planned, with McChrystal widely reported in mid-2010 to have described it as a 'bleeding ulcer'. But by January 2011 the US had achieved a measure of stability in the district, with the centre of Marjah sufficiently stable to enjoy a thriving bazaar and resulting traffic congestion. The unexpected resilience of the insurgents who fought back after the initial assault indicated that, in 'clear, hold and build' operations, the 'hold' phase could be much more difficult than the 'clear'. These US and British operations eventually led to a significant improvement of security in central Helmand around the provincial capital of Lashkar Gar; for example Afghan officials routinely travelled by road, rather than by helicopter.

SOF IN AFGHANISTAN

Between 2002 and 2009 the main effort for US SOF was Iraq. With ISAF expansion in 2006 numbers of NATO SOF increased and grew again from 2009 as US SOF and supporting capabilities were transferred from Iraq to Afghanistan. Here their principal role was to attack Taliban and Al Qaida commanders, networks and key infrastructure such as bomb makers. To achieve this they applied the same approaches as had been employed in Iraq, particularly the development of actionable intelligence. By 2010 many raids were being mounted every night. As in Iraq they increasingly operated alongside Afghan SOF.

But in Afghanistan the increasing number of so-called 'night raids' became increasingly unpopular with the Afghan people, who saw this intrusion on their homes and families as humiliating. For example, an unsuccessful US–Afghan SOF raid in Garmser in January 2010 was exploited by the Taliban, who claimed that a Koran had been deliberately desecrated. Skilful Taliban propaganda and agitation triggered riots against the US and Afghan forces, resulting in the deaths of six Afghan civilians. It required extensive negotiations to defuse the situation and the district governor's political position was greatly damaged.

SOF raids thus became a totemic issue with President Karzai, who repeatedly criticized ISAF in public. There was no easy solution to this, other than to involve Afghan SOF in the raids and, from 2011 onwards, hand an increasing proportion of the SOF raids over to the Afghan forces to conduct for themselves. Afghan-led raids aroused far less criticism from Karzai.

SOF and conventional forces could mutually reinforce the success of each other's operations. In 2009–10 in southern Afghanistan, deliberate clearance operations by UK, US and Afghan forces saw pre-planned SOF attacks on insurgent leaders coincide with the start of conventional operations, to similar mutual benefit.[5]

Map 12: Aghanistan 2008–10

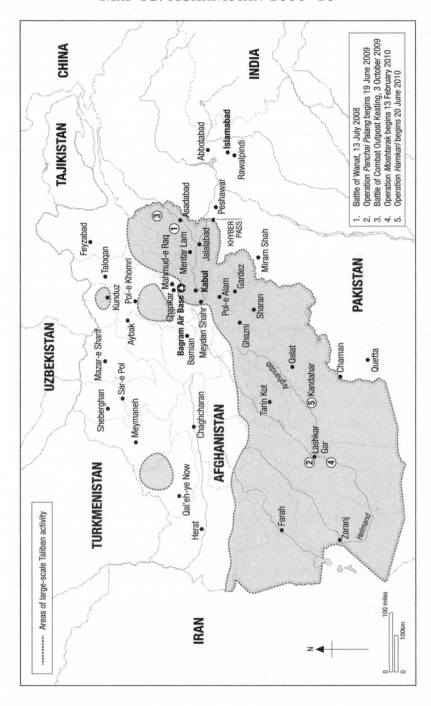

Areas of large-scale Taliban activity

1. Battle of Wanat, 13 July 2008
2. Operation *Panchai Palang* begins 19 June 2009
3. Battle of Combat Outpost Keating, 3 October 2009
4. Operation *Moshtarak* begins 13 February 2010
5. Operation *Hamkari* begins 20 June 2010

CHINA

TAJIKISTAN

INDIA

Abbotabad

Islamabad

Rawalpindi

Peshawar

KHYBER PASS

Asadabad

Mentar Lam

Jalalabad

Miram Shah

Feyzabad

Taloqan

Pol-e Khomri

Charikar

Mahmud-e Raq

Kabul

Kunduz

Bagram Air Base

Gardez

Pol-e Alam

Sharan

PAKISTAN

Aybak

Meydan Shahr

Bamian

Ghazni

Mazar-e Sharif

Sar-e Pol

Qalat

Chaman

Quetta

Sheberghan

Kandahar

Meymaneh

Tarin Kot

Arghandab

Chaghcharan

Lashkar Gar

AFGHANISTAN

Qal'eh-ye Now

Farah

Herat

Zaranj

Helmand

UZBEKISTAN

TURKMENISTAN

IRAN

N

100 miles

100km

A problem in Afghanistan was that for much of the conflict some US SOF were not under command of the senior US commander in the country. Up to this period SOF pursuing Al Qaida had been under command of the Joint Special Operations Command (JSOC). Between 2003 and 2009 its main effort had been in Iraq. Eventually the US chain of command was rationalized in 2010, and a single Combined Forces Special Operations Command for Afghanistan was created

OPERATION *HAMKARI* — THE CAMPAIGN FOR KANDAHAR PROVINCE

After Marjah had been stabilized, ISAF's main effort switched to stabilizing Kandahar Province. The centre of gravity of the province was Kandahar City, second only to Kabul in size and economic and political importance. It was the largest urban concentration of Pashtuns in the country. Whilst Operation *Medusa*, the Canadian-led 2006 attack on Panjwai, had disrupted insurgent plans to encircle and then capture Kandahar, the Canadian task force in the province had insufficient strength to inflict a lasting defeat on the insurgents. For the Taliban, contesting the city was important for their attempts to appear a viable rival to the Afghan government.

The commander of Regional Command South, British Major General Nick Carter, saw that that efforts in Kandahar Province could not simply comprise a physical effort to drive out the Taliban; there would also have to be a political effort to reconnect the people to the Afghan government. The preliminary requirement was to understand the physical, human and information aspects of the environment.

During 2009 and 2010 reinforcing US Army brigades flowed into Kandahar, including an airborne brigade, a brigade of mechanized infantry carried in Stryker wheeled armoured personnel carriers, an aviation brigade with a hundred US Army helicopters and an intelligence surveillance and reconnaissance brigade bristling with intelligence-gathering systems.

An early initiative was to assign the high-technology US Stryker brigade exclusively to securing the major roads in southern Afghanistan, to reduce Taliban attacks on the key roads in Kandahar, and to improve freedom of movement, in order to reduce a significant limitation to economic development.

The city of about half a million Afghans was not controlled by the Taliban, but insurgent influence was rising. The insurgents were mounting a successful operation to assassinate pro-government leaders in the city and mortar and rocket attacks were increasing. McChrystal and Carter determined that as the city was not controlled by the Taliban, there was no need for a sudden surprise assault, as had been conducted in Marjah. Instead, ISAF would conduct a limited reinforcement of Afghan security forces in the city. To the south of the city were agricultural districts: Panjwai, Zhari, Shah Wali Kot and Arghandab. Clearing Taliban from these districts, especially the Arghandab River Valley, would be the main effort.

The operation was called *Hamkari* (from the word 'co-operation' in Dari and Pashto). It would be that largest operation conducted in Afghanistan. At its height Regional Command South would lead over 60,000, US, British, Canadian and Afghan troops. It would be the US, NATO and Afghan main effort for 2010. Not for nothing did staff officers sometimes refer to it as 'the main effort of the world'. It was designed from the outset to be a combined effort by NATO and the Afghans. This began with McChrystal attempting to persuade President Karzai to engage with elders and significant figures from Kandahar, to get Karzai to sell the operation to the Afghans who would be impacted.

Since he had been appointed as CENTCOM commander in November 2008, General Petraeus had sought to improve the strategic framework for the campaign, which he has described as getting 'the inputs right'. Applying lessons learned in Iraq, this had led to the establishment of an improved civil–military machinery for co-ordinating operations with the Afghan government at all levels, from Kabul to province and district.

A *shura* was held at the Kandahar Convention Centre on 4 April. About 1,500 people filled the building to listen to Karzai. After a wide-ranging speech in which he urged the audience to send more of their sons to join the Afghan Army, he asked the audience if they were worried about the forthcoming NATO operation. They were. Karzai told the crowd that if they were not happy, there would be no operation. Many NATO officers took this as a rebuke. McChrystal took it as a challenge to better set the conditions for success by gaining support of the key Kandahari figures at the *shura*.

A second but much smaller *shura* was held on 21 July, this time with only a few hundred elders. The requirement for the operation and its plan were briefed to the audience, with considerable emphasis on the role that Afghan Army brigades would play. There were hard questions for Karzai, McChrystal and Mark Sedwill, the senior NATO civilian in Afghanistan, but the openly expressed sentiment of the meeting was supportive of the operation.

McChrystal was not able to preside over these attacks. In mid-summer 2010 he resigned, not for any lack of success, but because of an article published on 8 July in *Rolling Stone* magazine. A reporter had been embedded with McChrystal's command team and filed an article in which he reported critical and personalized attacks on US politicians and government officials. None were directly attributed to McChrystal, but the general resigned; he was replaced by General David Petraeus who moved from command of CENTCOM to Kabul.

Another command adjustment was a change to the control of operations in southern Afghanistan. The ever-increasing flow of US and NATO reinforcements created additional demands on the HQ of Regional Command South in Kandahar. To better manage the campaign, an additional regional command HQ was formed in July 2010, with the US Marines providing the core of the new Regional Command Southwest, responsible for NATO operations in Helmand Province.

ISAF's understanding of the complex Afghan environment had greatly improved since 2006, as had surveillance and intelligence-gathering capabilities. Large numbers of unmanned aerial vehicles and other surveillance assets were redeployed by the US from Iraq to Afghanistan. Human intelligence has been a decisive factor in all successful counter-insurgency campaigns, but always has taken several years to develop. By 2010 it was starting to produce significant operational results in Afghanistan. These capabilities were applied to build a better picture of Taliban networks in and around Kandahar. They also generated intelligence to allow increased numbers of SOF raids against Taliban leaders in the province.

Between July and October 2010 Operation *Hamkari* saw heavy fighting by US, Canadian and Afghan troops to clear and hold the

MAP 13: OPERATION *HAMKARI*

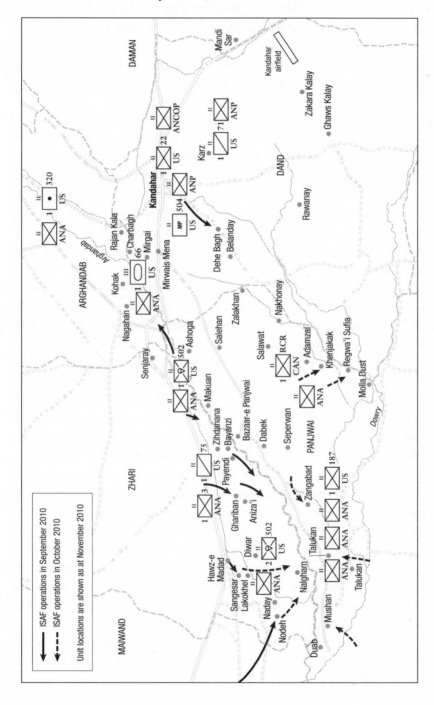

DAMAN

Mandi
Sar

Kandahar
airfield

Zakara Kalay

Ghaws Kalay

ANCOP
II 22 US

II 71 US
ANP

Karz
II 1 US

DAND

Rawanay

Kandahar
II 1 US ANP

504 US
MP

Dehe Bagh

Belanday

320 US

ANA

Rajan Kala
Charbagh
Mirgai

Arghandab

66 US

Kohak

ARGHANDAB

Nagahan
Ashoga

ANA

Mirwais Mena

Salehan

Zalakhan

Zalakhan

Salawat

RCR
II 1 CAN

Adamzai

Kherjakak

Regwa'i Sufia

Molla Dust

Dowry

Senjaray
502 US
II 1

ANA

Makuan

Zihdanana
Bayanzi

Bazaar-e Panjwai

Dabek

Seperwan

ANA

PANJWAI

Nakhonay

ZHARI

75 US
II

3 1 ANA
II 1

Payendi

Ghariban

Aniza'i

Zangabad

187 US
II 1

ANA ANA
II 1

Talukan

ANA ANA

Talukan

Talukan

MAIWAND

Hawz-e
Madad

Diwar

502 US
2

ANA

Sangesar
Lakokhel

Naday

Nalgham

Nodeh

Mushan

Duab

ISAF operations in September 2010

ISAF operations in October 2010

Unit locations are shown as at November 2010

districts of Arghandab, Panjwai and Zhari. Much of the terrain gave great advantage to the Taliban defenders. Heavily cultivated agricultural land was full of irrigation ditches and hard-packed mud walls. There were many vineyards where the vines were supported by such walls. These were difficult enough to move through in winter. By summer the vines had grown to make a leafy roof. Such terrain offered plenty of opportunities to the Taliban for ambushes and IED attacks against heavily laden NATO infantry. And the dense growth of vines and vegetation made it very difficult for pilots to see troops from the air, fear of attacking NATO troops by mistake greatly limiting the utility of close air support.

At the end of 2010, ISAF declared that Operation *Hamkari* had succeeded in evicting the Taliban from key districts. The final phase of the operation had been notable for being led by an Afghan Army corps HQ. This operation and the earlier Operation *Moshtarak* had depended both on patient tactical execution of the 'clear, hold and build' counter-insurgency approach championed by Petraeus, and on sufficient density of forces and co-ordination of military security with reconstruction and development tasks. Concurrently NATO made complementary efforts to improve the effectiveness of Afghan civil government in the province.

Unsurprisingly the number of US and international casualties suffered in 2010 was also the highest yet in the war. There was a reduction in civilian casualties counted by the UN, likely the result of the more restrictive use of artillery and airstrikes under ISAF's policy of 'courageous restraint'.

In December 2010 ISAF reached its peak strength of 131,000 troops, from 20 NATO and 28 non-NATO nations. Ninety thousand troops were US (with another 16,000 employed on US national operations, but under the command of COMISAF). And there were some 9,500 troops from the UK. Nations making substantial contributions of more than a thousand troops included Romania, Spain, Germany, France, Italy, Canada and Turkey. Apart from Turkey, the only Muslim nations represented in ISAF were Malaysia and the United Arab Emirates, which all had small contingents.

As the troop level in Iraq further reduced, key capabilities, such as counter-IED and SOF, were re-deployed to Afghanistan. ISAF increased 'night raids' by special forces against insurgent leaders. In 2010, a tripling in the number of raids resulted in the killing of more than 1,200, including some 300 thought to hold leadership roles, according to ISAF.

SINEWS OF THE AFGHAN WAR

All these troops generated a vast requirement for combat supplies: fuel, ammunition, food, water and spare parts. Many of these were sent by sea, arriving in the Pakistani port of Karachi. Pakistani contractors would load the freight onto their colourfully decorated 'jingly' trucks. These would wind their way through Pakistan, crossing into Afghanistan at the southern desert crossing point at Spin Baldak or the northern crossing point in the high Hindu Kush, the Khyber Pass. The trucks would then go on into Afghanistan.

Incoming troops and urgently required supplies including ammunition and scarce spare parts would be carried by military airlifters. At the height of the war, the British airfield at Camp Bastion in Helmand was counted as the fifth-busiest UK airport. Contracted civilian air freighters were used extensively and some use was made of contracted helicopters for supplying isolated bases.

The resupply needed by forward British bases in Afghanistan required several 'Combat Logistic Patrols' of a hundred or two hundred vehicles to leave Camp Bastion every week. These were mounted as combat operations, with sizeable escort forces, counter-IED teams and the full panoply of fire support.

The US Army had sufficient helicopter capacity to carry only a small proportion of the supplies required by forward units. Air dropping of supplies by parachute provided some relief to isolated bases in Afghanistan, but carried its own limitations of weather, mountainous terrain and security of drop zone, as well as the vulnerability of cargo aircraft making the drops, although these problems were reduced by the use of GPS guidance for parachute rigs. By later stages of the Afghan war US forces were seeking to reduce the logistic bill for deployed troops, experimenting with solar panels and other alternative energy sources. The British had deployed a 3D printer to allow spare part holdings to be reduced.

To reduce the numbers of troops deployed, extensive use was made of contractors to deliver supplies to military bases. As the wars progressed increasing numbers of civilian contractors filled other logistic roles 'behind the wire'. For example, the British base at Camp Bastion had contractors providing catering, repair and support of equipment and maintaining unmanned aerial vehicles, and Kraus Maffei Wegman deployed technicians to maintain German armoured vehicles in Mazar-e Sharif.

The US made extensive use of contractors to provide security for civilian officials. Whilst this reduced the total numbers of US troops on the ground, many contractors often displayed highly aggressive behaviour. Their use of lethal force often seemed unconstrained by any rules of engagement. In both Iraq and Afghanistan this resulted both in avoidable civilian casualties and in increased humiliation. This greatly damaged the legitimacy of international forces. Other nations were more reluctant to use private security companies to assist with armed guarding.

GROWING THE AFGHAN SECURITY FORCES

A keystone of NATO strategy was to develop the strength and effectiveness of the Afghan Security Forces, to prepare these forces for the transfer of security responsibility by the end of 2014. The greatest effort was to build the capacity of the Afghan National Army (ANA). Various disparate national efforts were brought together by the formation of the NATO Training Mission Afghanistan in November 2009 and numbers of NATO training staff were considerably increased. The mission was commanded by a US general, who also commanded US forces training the Afghans.

The Afghan National Army was a genuinely national institution, its ethnic composition reflecting the ethnic mix of Afghanistan as a whole. But this meant that most of the Afghan soldiers in the south – including Pashtuns – were not from that region. The ANA reached a strength of 134,000 in August 2010, two months ahead of schedule. The ANA's effectiveness as well as numerical strength had increased, while the better ANA units and formations proved themselves capable of taking the lead in operations against the Taliban. Overall performance across the force, though, remained variable.

By 2009, it was clear that the Afghan National Police (ANP) were almost as much a part of the security problem as of the solution, with endemic corruption and human rights abuses. In part this reflected the fact that, before 2009, police recruits had no formal training. Approaches to training the Afghan National Police varied greatly between international contingents, from non-existent to a British effort to set up a police training centre in Helmand.

A national paramilitary police force, the Afghan Civil Order Police (ANCOP), were often judged by NATO as relatively trustworthy and effective. For example, they often accompanied ISAF special-forces raids, liaising with civilians as the 'Afghan face'. NATO put considerable effort into mentoring and developing the ANCOP, especially as their attrition rates were high.

Shortly after his arrival McChrystal placed increased emphasis on building the capability of the Afghan National Security Forces (ANSF). This was continued by Petraeus. By 2010 all Afghan Army and Police units were supported by integrated NATO operational mentoring and liaison teams (OMLTs). These not only assisted ANA commanders with operational planning, but also helped the ANA units to obtain NATO support, including artillery, helicopters and air strikes. OMLTs have succeeded in this role since 2006, being typically deployed at every level of ANA command from corps to company.

During the Surge there was also a significant increase in similar teams working with the Afghan police. Over 300 police operational mentoring and liaison teams (POMLTs) were fielded, 90 per cent of them provided by US military police battalions specially trained for the role, using similar techniques to those applied in Iraq from 2008. Similar efforts were made with the Afghan Border Police, the Counter-Narcotics Police and the Afghan Air Force. Although little publicized, much UK and US effort was also applied to the Afghan security service, the NDS, helping it contribute to counter-Taliban intelligence efforts. In Helmand Province the US Marines engaged a private military company to field mentors to the Afghan intelligence staffs.

But despite the undoubted results accruing from the major US–ISAF effort to generate and sustain the ANSF, there were serious signs of weakness in the Afghan forces. Not only were there incidents of individual soldiers and police turning their weapons on their ISAF mentors, but it was also clear that considerable low-level corruption remained. High levels of illiteracy – and difficulties in identifying and developing sufficient commanders and leaders – were a powerful brake on achieving the necessary quality in the Afghan security forces.

AFGHAN GOVERNANCE

By the end of 2010 many NATO commanders had come to see that the greatest threat to the Transition Strategy and the military campaign was the continuing presence of poor governance and extensive corruption. ISAF had become particularly concerned by the impact of corruption on the campaign. By 2010 there was abundant evidence that letting of contracts by NATO and other international organizations had not only contributed to corruption, but had also helped fund warlords, drug barons and private militias. A particularly egregious example was the siphoning off of funds that had been allocated to the Afghan Army's military hospital in Kabul.

ISAF responded by establishing a multinational interagency task force: Combined Joint Interagency Task Force – *Shafafiyat* ('Transparency'), to better understand corruption in Afghanistan and plan and co-ordinate US and ISAF anti-corruption efforts. Its work resulted in ISAF requiring more rigour and formal assessment of the impact of contracts on the campaign. ISAF suspended operations by a major US contractor as a result of allegations of non-payment of Afghan sub-contractors. But these efforts only scratched the surface of the institutionalized corruption that permeated Afghanistan.

In his 2011 testimony to the Senate Armed Service Committee, Admiral Mike Mullen assessed that pervasive corruption, by criminal patronage networks that included government officials – at both national and local levels – impeded tactical successes throughout Afghanistan. Corruption made a mockery of the rule of law, hollowing out and reducing the legitimacy of the institutions to which the US and its allies would be transferring authority:

Few efforts to improve government capabilities and legitimacy over the past several years have borne fruit, and without a serious new approach, systematic change in next three years, before 2015, increasingly seems improbable. If we continue to draw down forces apace while such public and systemic corruption is left unchecked, we will risk leaving behind a government in which we cannot reasonably expect Afghans to have faith. At best this would lead to continued localized conflicts as neighbourhood strongmen angle for their cut, and the people for their survival; at worst it could lead to government collapse and civil war.'[6]

This assessment was prescient.

THE DEATH OF OSAMA BIN LADEN

In May 2011 US SOF flew from Afghanistan to raid Osama Bin Laden's compound in Pakistan. He was killed. This removed one of the main reasons for the US presence in Afghanistan. Seven weeks later, on June 2011, President Obama announced that the Surge had peaked and would reduce. Ten thousand US troops would depart by the end of the year with all the additional surge troops being withdrawn by summer 2012.

The US had chosen not to give Pakistan any warning of the raid, for fear that Bin Laden might be warned. The Bin Laden raid therefore considerably increased mutual suspicion between the US and Pakistan. Pakistani politicians were outraged that US helicopters had flown undetected so far into Pakistan and so close to a major army garrison at Abbottabad. That the US had deployed a hitherto secret variant of the Black Hawk helicopter widely thought to incorporate stealth technology was not a mitigating factor. The Pakistani security establishment had always worried that the US now had a proven capability to seize Islamabad's nuclear warheads. Now US forces had demonstrated the capabilities necessary to neutralize Pakistan's deterrent by finding, destroying or capturing nuclear warheads. The Pakistani media and political class were incensed.

The heads of the Pakistan Army, Air Force and ISI had uncomfortable experiences explaining themselves to closed sessions of Pakistan's parliament. A leaked copy of the report of Pakistan's independent Abbottabad Commission strongly criticized the Pakistani government, army and ISI for multiple missed opportunities and acts of negligence. The raid was another 'national humiliation' for the Pakistani military[7] and did nothing to dispose them to improve co-operation with Washington or Kabul.

THE AUDIT OF WAR

On taking command in 2009 US General Stanley McChrystal sought to improve ISAF's command and control by establishing a corps-level tactical HQ. He applied counter-insurgency doctrine to better protect the Afghan population, including from NATO firepower. He also stepped up NATO's efforts to partner with Afghan forces. But political difficulties for the US and NATO were increased by the 2009 Afghan election, which saw flagrant ballot stuffing by supporters of President Karzai, undermining the legitimacy of the war in NATO member states.

During 2009 President Obama considered future US options for Afghanistan using a thorough decision making process that involved the full US national security machinery. His announcement of an 18-month Afghan surge was a compromise between the ambitions of the US military and the greater scepticism of other US security actors. It also reflected increasing war-weariness in the US and the aftermath of the 2008 financial crisis. Obama stuck to his strategy of limiting the duration of the Surge. The killing of Osama Bin Laden reinforced the political justification for the US drawdown, but worsened relations with Pakistan.

By now key US capabilities, such as drones, counter-IED and SOF were being shifted from Iraq to Afghanistan. And the Iraq drawdown allowed more US and UK troops to reinforce Afghanistan. McChrystal decided that the reinforcing US troops should reinforce ISAF's main effort in the southern Afghanistan Taliban heartlands of Helmand and Kandahar provinces. Reinforcement of Helmand by US Marines increased NATO troop levels. The Marines cleared and held Garmser district through a combination of military action, political activity and development funding.

Operation *Moshtarak,* the early 2010 US Marine clearance of Marjah, began with a highly successful US Marine air assault into the heart of the contested district, but having 'cleared' the district, weaknesses in Afghan governance made the 'build' civil–military stabilization operations much slower than expected.

Lessons from Operation *Moshtarak* were applied to Operation *Hamkari* in Kandahar. This was NATO's largest operation in the Afghan war and was preceded by extensive intelligence gathering and a prolonged information operation. It was both NATO's and the US' main effort and the first NATO operation to fully engage President Karzai as commander in chief of the Afghan forces. Despite the operation's clear success in pushing the Taliban out of key districts in Kandahar Province, it revealed serious weaknesses in Afghan governance capability at district level.

The Failure of the Transition to Afghan Security Leadership

The reinforcement of Afghanistan by the additional US and NATO forces had been a major logistic operation. The withdrawal of the surge forces in 2011 and 2012, followed by the withdrawal of US and NATO combat forces in 2013 and 2014, was an even larger logistic operation. Large amounts of vehicles, ammunition and military equipment successfully departed Afghanistan the same way they had arrived, travelling by air, by land and sea through Pakistan to the port at Karachi and by rail along the Northern Distribution Network. Opened in 2008 this allowed NATO supplies and vehicles to travel to and from the Afghan border by rail through Central Asia and Russia to the Baltic.

The US and NATO logistic planners were successful in their objectives to successfully move large numbers of troops and equipment out over these routes. Despite the 2014 Russian annexation of Crimea and the eruption of a Russian-supported insurrection in eastern Ukraine, the Northern Distribution Network continued to function smoothly throughout 2014.

The additional 33,000 US surge troops deployed in 2010 withdrew by October 2012, leaving 68,000 US troops alongside 32,000 troops from other nations. The Afghan Army took an increasing lead for security, with 21 of 26 Afghan brigades operating independently of ISAF, or with ISAF support limited to advisors.

In spring 2012 the Taliban declared an offensive campaign to push back ISAF and Afghan forces. This failed, the combined capabilities and strength of the Afghan and NATO forces meaning that territory gained during the Afghan Surge was held against Taliban attacks. NATO statistics showed that insurgent attacks in 2012 remained at the same level as in 2011. Insurgent attacks by IEDs fell by 20 per cent. NATO claimed to be finding and clearing more IEDs than were successfully detonated by the Taliban. Whilst 42 per cent of the 315 NATO fatalities were from IEDs, over 80 per cent of Afghan Army fatalities were caused in this way, stark demonstration of their lower level of counter-IED capability. Most insurgent attacks were on the edges of territory under Afghan government control, some 80 per cent of attacks occurring in 20 per cent of Afghan districts. As a direct result of the ANSF taking the lead in many areas, ANA casualties doubled in 2012 to 1,056.

The Taliban became more active in western and northern areas. Kabul was the location of only 1 per cent of security incidents in the country in 2012. Concerted efforts by the Pakistan-based Haqqani network to launch spectacular attacks on the capital were successfully prevented by Afghan forces for most of the year.

In areas where the transition to Afghan responsibility had taken place, the United Nations detected that public perceptions of security had not improved. There had only been a slight reduction in civilian casualties: while ISAF was killing fewer civilians, insurgents were killing more – particularly with increasing numbers of indiscriminately laid IEDs that were accidentally triggered by civilians. Targeted killings of civilians, especially Afghan government officials, continued, with almost 700 killed in 2012, over double the number of such deaths in 2011.

Overall, the Afghan forces assumed an increasing responsibility for security as NATO troops withdrew. But it was far from clear that there would be enough improvement in Afghan governance and a reduction in corruption to neutralize the root causes of the insurgency. According to a September 2012 UN assessment:

little has changed in the underlying dynamics to mitigate a deep-seated cycle of conflict. Furthermore, a diminished international presence will have a significant financial impact in many areas that, at least in the short term, may even exacerbate predatory behavior, with a reduced flow of money encouraging criminality.[1]

INSIDER ATTACKS

Attacks on international forces by Afghan troops and police had occurred since at least 2006, but greatly increased in 2012, when 60 ISAF troops were killed in such 'insider attacks', a 40 per cent increase compared with 2011. Although attacks were invariably claimed by the Taliban, analysis by the Pentagon suggested that a significant proportion were instigated by Afghans who had unexpectedly 'snapped', often as a result of a minor grievance or provocation.

NATO and the Afghan authorities announced many initiatives to improve security against Taliban infiltration, including improved vetting and counter-intelligence. NATO troops were assigned to act as 'guardian angels' – providing armed guards for NATO troops who were training Afghans.

By the end of 2012 such attacks had greatly reduced, probably as a result of the additional security measures, though it is likely that war fatigue and accumulated Afghan resentment of the NATO presence were also major factors contributing to the motivation of attackers. But insider attacks were never totally eradicated, continuing at a lower level until the end of the decade.

THE ATTACK ON CAMP BASTION

In south-west Afghanistan NATO forces reduced by about 60 per cent during 2012, the numbers of US Marines reducing from 17,000 to 7,400 between March and September 2012. September saw the Taliban mount a well-planned and audacious surprise attack on the joint UK–US–Afghan army base in Helmand. A large squad of well-led and highly motivated Taliban fighters, dressed in US Army uniforms, infiltrated through a ravine, cut protective barbed wire, penetrated the base defences undetected and attacked the shelters containing US Marines' aircraft. They got close enough to these to attack them with hand grenades.

In confused close-quarter night fighting, an ad hoc force of US Marines maintenance personnel, USAF pararescue personnel and an RAF regiment quick reaction force fought with courage and determination against equally steadfast Taliban fighters. Two US Marines were killed, and 16 US and UK personnel were wounded. Two US Marines' AV8

Harrier jump jets were destroyed, two were badly damaged and six other aircraft were less seriously damaged. The US investigation into the attack resulted in the dismissal of two US Marine Corps generals, who were held accountable for the security breach.[2] Both the US investigation and an inquiry by the UK House of Commons Defence Committee illuminated with crystal clarity that the UK chain of command and the UK role in the security of the base was so complex, and accountability and responsibility so diffuse, that:

> Insufficient attention was given to the fundamental requirement of defending Camp Bastion from external assault. We believe that this was complacent. Given that the attack took place in the British sector of the camp, British commanders must bear a degree of responsibility for these systemic failures and associated reputational damage. We note the acknowledgement by the MoD that errors were made which, collectively, created the vulnerabilities which were so devastatingly exploited by the enemy.[3]

Despite this clear failure by the UK military chain of command, there is no evidence that any UK officer was ever held accountable for these weaknesses. This attack and successful suicide attacks on Afghan security bases in Kabul in January 2013 demonstrated the insurgents' continuing ability to launch well-planned attacks.

ARMED POLITICS AND DEVELOPMENT IN KANDAHAR PROVINCE, 2011–13

Douglas Grindle, a US civilian employed by USAID, the US aid and development agency, has produced an account of two years as a development advisor posted to a district support team, the small group of US civilians working at Dand District Centre, in Kandahar Province. It gives an informative picture of local governance, security and development in the second half of the Surge and afterwards.[4]

Grindle found his arrival at the huge NATO and US base at Kandahar airfield was a surreal experience. With its multiple civilian concessions, including cafes, restaurants, and large shops, it seemed disconnected from the war, as did the large number of American civilians working at the airfield.

The US Embassy's policy was that US resources were applied at the national level, the provincial level and to large cities, like Kandahar. The numbers of US civilian officials had greatly increased as a result of the US 'civilian surge'. To Grindle it seemed that their priority was managing the US bureaucracy that attended the distribution of aid money. It was not clear what value they were adding to the US and NATO effort in the rural districts of Kandahar Province.

Deployed first to Dand district south of Kandahar, Grindle found that the district had a competent and apparently honest governor. The district governor himself seemed incorruptible. But Afghan militias in the district would impose tolls of $150 on lorries bringing supplies to development projects funded by the US. The governor had built up a stable power base, using international development projects to build political stability by gaining the consent and support of local leaders. But this was despite, not because of, the Afghan government in Kabul or the Kandahar Province administration in Kandahar city. These proved incapable of disbursing money in a way that reached Dand. This was not just the effect of corruption; it was also a result of the Afghan authorities being unable to make their bureaucracy work.

The Afghan national and provincial authorities had delivered no services of any kind to Dand. The Kandahar provincial authorities were focusing the great majority of their attention on Kandahar City. For example, this was where all the provincial education budget was spent. Districts did not have their own budget and could not raise taxes. Any request for funding made by the Dand district governor to the provincial authorities was invariably turned down. A further frustration was that the Afghan government departments in Kabul were unable to make their own processes work to spend more than 75 per cent of the development money allocated to them. This appeared to be a result of old-fashioned Soviet-era decision making processes and the lack of enough educated, literate and numerate Afghan staff to work in provincial administration.

As US troops and funding reduced during 2011 and 2012, the district governor was able to retain political control of Dand, a reflection of the strength of political support the governor had built. But the flow of US aid money to Dand was rapidly reducing. When Grindle arrived, the district had been the responsibility of a US battalion. Between mid-2011 and early 2012 US troops reduced to company strength, in part to reinforce

Panjwai district. ISAF saw Panjwai as a route for Taliban movement and for drug smuggling, a greater security priority than Dand. By 2012, the US infantry was succeeded by a cavalry squadron whose priority was the security of Kandahar airfield. US spending on local development greatly reduced. As it did, security deteriorated.

The district governor predicted that as aid continued to reduce, the governance system of Dand would collapse. An effort supported by Grindle to use US Army funds get the district centre connected to the Afghan electrical grid failed, because the US Army brigadier at Kandahar with authority to approve funding was sent back to the US to face charges of sexual misconduct.

In mid-July the Dand district governor resigned. A major factor was his concerns for his security: he had been attacked 12 times by the Taliban. He had survived a recent Taliban suicide attack, owing to the armouring of his car, but the explosion had killed six nearby children. An aggravating factor was that a recent raid by US SOF had targeted the compound of one of his local allies, a tribal elder who actively supported his efforts to win over people to the government side. The provincial government had continued to refuse all requests for funding for Dand. The US-led PRT for Kandahar Province was asked to assist with funding. It declined, as its policy was to help the Kandahar provincial officials better manage their money; so that was where the district governor should get additional funds from. The replacement district governor chose not to work at the district centre, but to base himself in Kandahar. At the end of 2012, the district police chief was killed by a Taliban bomb.

In early 2012 Grindle was transferred from Dand district to Maiwand, another district in Kandahar Province. Here the district governor was less politically secure. His writ and that of the Afghan government extended only a few miles from the district centre and there was considerable mistrust between him and the US forces. This friction had begun in the 2001–03 period due to predatory behaviour by the then-governor of Kandahar, Gul Agha Sherzai. He persuaded US SOF to mount raids against his rivals. Ransoms would often be charged for the release of Afghans detained in these raids. Further US raids on villages in the district increased Afghan resentment over time.

Afghan police auxiliaries would routinely detain farmers travelling across the district. They would be required to pay ransoms of $100–$300 to secure their release, at a time when the average wage of Afghan farmers was $100 a month. The district education director was using a proportion of the meagre district education budget that had been allocated by Kandahar to pay the Taliban for protection.

The Maiwand district support team closed in mid-2013. The next year all US troops departed the district. Afterwards, district elders reported heavy fighting between the Afghan forces, Taliban and drug traffickers.

Grindle left Afghanistan. He assessed that although the US Surge had succeeded in pushing the Taliban away from Kandahar, it had also failed to prevent district-level government from falling apart after the American forces left. By 2013 very few districts had enough security force presence, money and local governance leadership capacity to do anything other than defend the immediate vicinity of the district centres. The Taliban would find these districts easy targets.

TRANSITION, 2013–14

At a January 2013 press conference with President Karzai in Kabul, President Obama had explained that after withdrawing from combat missions the US wished to conduct 'two long-term tasks, which will be very specific and very narrow – first, training and assisting Afghan forces and, second, targeting counterterrorism missions – targeted counterterrorism missions against al Qaeda and its affiliates'.[5]

The June 2013 announcement of 'Milestone 13' by President Karzai and NATO Secretary General Rasmussen saw Afghan forces assume country-wide leadership of security operations. Drawdown of international forces continued; for example British bases in Helmand Province reduced from 80 in April 2012 to five in October 2013. At the middle of the year ISAF comprised 87,000 troops, 60,000 of which were from the US. ISAF considered that plans for its combat mission to cease at the end of 2014 were on track. By now, the Afghan forces were in the front line against the Taliban, the majority of US and NATO troops having withdrawn from holding Afghan territory. NATO continued to advise Afghan forces, but the numbers of advisors and mentors had greatly reduced. At the height of the Afghan Surge advisory teams had deployed down to every Afghan infantry company. By now there were small advisory teams at battalion and brigade level. And these would withdraw as NATO troops withdrew from their combat role.

During the 2013 fighting season the Taliban failed to achieve their announced military objective of rolling back security gains made by NATO and Afghan forces since the start of the 2010 NATO Surge. Well-planned complex insurgent attacks continued against both isolated military bases and targets in Kabul. The Taliban attacked outlying Afghan Army and Police posts, some of which were temporarily overrun. All these attacks were successfully counter-attacked by the Afghan forces, usually operating with few if any NATO ground troops.

The Afghan security forces still relied on NATO for artillery and air strikes, airborne intelligence gathering, and for help in getting logistics and administration working properly. NATO's training mission concentrated on building these areas and medical, counter-IED, and intelligence capabilities.

By now over 80 per cent of operations were led by the Afghan forces, with less than 10 per cent conducted solely by ISAF. In many areas there were significant reductions in NATO footprint. After Washington and Kabul agreed that Afghans would assume the lead for special operations and would take over the US prison and detainees at Bagram, a US–Afghan strategic partnership agreement was signed and the US designated Afghanistan a major non-NATO ally.

NATO's training mission shifted effort from increasing the size of the Afghan Army to building logistic and support capabilities including medical, counter-IED, fire support and intelligence. Two new Afghan brigades were raised to form a 'mobile strike force' of infantry in wheeled armoured personnel carriers to provide much-needed reserves. NATO showed considerable confidence in the rapidly maturing capabilities of Afghan Army and Police special forces.

But despite earlier optimistic pronouncements by NATO, the Afghan security forces remained over 15,000 personnel short of their planned strength of 350,000. This was due to higher attrition than planned in the army, border police and civil order police. ISAF commander US General Joseph Dunford assessed that NATO was lagging some years behind in developing the police. And complementary improvements in the whole machinery of justice, including courts, lawyers and prisons, lagged further behind, as shown by NATO's refusal to send detainees to Afghan prisons betraying evidence of torture and human rights abuses.

The Afghan Local Police, village self-defence forces mentored by embedded teams of US SOF, reached a strength of 18,000 operating at

86 sites. Whilst these forces contributed to defending against Taliban incursions, concerns remained about issues of impunity, vetting, and the potential re-emergence of ethnically or politically biased militias. The spectre of a return of warlords' militias was raised by an October 2012 speech by Afghan government minister Ismail Khan, although this was widely criticized in both houses of the Afghan parliament.

President Karzai became more assertive with the US and NATO, particularly over issues he considered to be vital to Afghan sovereignty. For example, he made a surprise March 2013 decision to order US SOF to leave Wardak Province. And despite a specially convened Loya Jirga assembly endorsing the US presence after 2014, President Karzai refused to sign the required Afghan–US Bilateral Security Agreement (BSA), necessary to set out the legal status of international forces after the ISAF mission finished.

By April 2014 ISAF comprised 51,000 troops, of which 33,500 were US. In 2014 the ANSF largely reached their planned strength of 352,000, less a small shortfall in police manning. They still relied on NATO for airborne intelligence gathering, and for help in getting counter-IED, intelligence capabilities, medical, logistic and administrative systems working properly. The withdrawal of US and NATO troops was paralleled by withdrawal of development advisors and reduction in development aid.

The April 2014 Afghan presidential election saw security successfully provided by the Afghan forces. It featured determined and vigorous campaigns fought by the two main candidates, Ashraf Ghani and Abdullah Abdullah. Both sides accused the other of industrial scale vote-rigging. Neither achieved an outright majority, so a run-off was held in mid-June. Afghanistan's Independent Election Commission announced that Ghani had won. But Abdullah claimed that Ghani's supporters had conducted extensive vote-tampering. He and his supporters ceased co-operating with the election commission. Abdullah spoke of establishing a parallel competing government. This triggered a political crisis, with Abdullah's key supporters, who had been warlords in the Northern Alliance, talking openly of resorting to the use of force to install Abdullah.

Over the following months US Secretary of State John Kerry personally led negotiations in a highly charged atmosphere of wrangling, protests and threats of the use of force by former warlords.

He eventually brokered a deal that envisaged a power-sharing national unity government, with Ghani appointed president and his opponent Abdullah appointed to a newly created post, that of Chief Executive.

This took nearly six months. It took a further eight months before the composition of the cabinet was decided. This reflected considerable political disagreements between Ghani and Abdullah's supporters. The national unity government turned out to be highly disunited, with the whole amounting to much less than the sum of the parts.

Straight after his inauguration Ghani took a major initiative to defuse tension with Pakistan. In November 2014 he reached out to the government in Islamabad and the Pakistan Army and intelligence agency ISI in Rawalpindi, paying early visits to both cities, saying that he wanted to end the 'undeclared war' between the two nations. Ghani aimed to persuade Pakistan to bring the Afghan Taliban to the negotiating table.

Intelligence co-operation between the two countries was stepped up with Afghan forces acting to interdict Pakistani Taliban fighters and handing captured Pakistani insurgents over to ISI. But a planned intelligence co-operation agreement provoked considerable political protests in Afghanistan and was not implemented as Ghani had envisaged. Although Pakistani Prime Minister Nawaz Sharif proclaimed support for the Afghan government's struggle against the Taliban, it was unclear if the improved co-operation was creating any decisive advantages for Kabul.

Whilst politicians and the Pakistani military had long denied Pakistani sponsorship of the Afghan Taliban, attempts to hold this line were undermined by 2015 newspaper interviews given by former Pakistani president Musharraf, in which he stated that Pakistan had been waging a proxy war with India in Afghanistan, which required strong links between the Afghan Taliban and ISI, the Pakistani intelligence agency.

This outreach to Pakistan cost Ghani considerable political capital in Kabul, where most politicians were deeply suspicious of Pakistan, which, they felt, had consistently supported the Taliban and which, despite declarations to the contrary, continued to do so. Despite Ghani's efforts, the Afghan forces and intelligence agency the NDS saw Taliban infiltration from Pakistan as undiminished. Ghani's initiative collapsed and relations between Kabul and Islamabad rapidly deteriorated, returning to their previously distrustful state

All Afghan provinces transitioned to Afghan security leadership by June 2014. All the international PRTs and district support teams closed. International forces' casualties reduced, as Afghan security forces' casualties increased. Following the September 2014 signature of a US–Afghan–NATO Status of Forces Agreement, a US counter-terrorism force was based in Afghanistan to counter Al Qaida and other jihadist forces. In December 2014 ISAF was replaced by NATO's Operation *Resolute Support*, a 12,000 strong non-combat mission training, advising and assisting the Afghans, principally on improving the effectiveness of the defence and interior ministries, Afghan SOF, military intelligence and the Afghan Air Force. Other than Afghan SOF, US and NATO air forces were generally not available to support Afghan troops on the ground. The US plan was to gradually reduce troop numbers so that the by the end of 2016, the US military presence in Afghanistan would be no greater than a normal embassy presence in Kabul.

Whilst many personnel were based in Kabul, some US and NATO advisory teams were based at regional hubs such as Kandahar and Herat. It was initially planned that this mission should halve in strength by the end of 2015, reducing completely by the end of 2016.

THE AFGHAN AIR FORCE – TOO LITTLE TOO LATE

A complicating military factor was that the Afghan Air Force was struggling to achieve its full capability. A decision to create an Afghan air force and to provide international support to building the capability appears only to have been taken in 2007. A limited initial capability was fielded in 2010. In 2014 the Pentagon assessed that its development lagged that of all the other Afghan forces. This was due to shortages of educated personnel and the pernicious influence of corruption and infiltration by criminal patronage networks.

Developing an Afghan air force was always going to be difficult, as the service struggled to achieve the necessary critical mass of sufficiently educated personnel with adequate numeracy and English language skills to fill the many technical posts necessary to keep an air force flying safely and effectively.

The US Surge included increased efforts to build an Afghan air force optimized for counter-insurgency, employing modern US helicopters and light strike aircraft. Although this would not be the size of the considerable US and NATO air support at the height of the war, it was intended to be sufficient for the Afghans' long-term requirements, provided that the Afghan Army learned to make full use of its other sources of fire support, especially mortars and artillery. This the army failed to do, preferring to use mortars and artillery in the direct-fire role. By the end of 2018, the Afghan Air Force was providing about half the required capability.

2015 – AFGHAN FORCES UNDER PRESSURE

Following transition to Afghan security leadership at the end of 2014, US and NATO politicians and senior military officials expressed guarded confidence that the Afghan security forces would continue to defeat Taliban efforts to increase the area of Afghanistan that they controlled. International pledges of military, development and financial assistance after 2015 were designed to reassure Afghans that the country would continue to receive international support after 2014.

Over this period, successive Taliban campaigns sought to increase control over rural areas and to capture important rural district centres and key provincial capitals, while at the same time conducting high-profile attacks in Kabul and other important cities. The Afghan forces continued to display weaknesses in leadership, command, control and co-ordination. Taliban control over rural areas slowly increased.

Fighting in 2015 was heavy, with more Afghan military and civilian casualties than ever before. After July 2015, when the Taliban finally admitted the death of leader Mullah Omar, his successor, Mullah Mansoor, sought to cement his authority by intensifying attacks. He also reached out to Al Qaida and the Haqqani network. The latter kept up pressure in south-eastern Afghanistan and launched several high-profile attacks in Kabul.

Overall, whilst the ANSF still received close air support from the US, far less of this was provided during a fighting season in which Afghan troops saw more intense combat than ever before. Afghan forces' operational tempo was twice that of 2014. Casualties rose proportionately, reaching an all-time high. The US assessed in June that the Afghan Army was at 87 per cent of its funded strength, some 176,000 of 203,000 personnel. The Afghan Air Force had yet to reach full capability.

The 2015 fighting season saw Afghans and US counter-terrorism operations successfully maintain pressure on Al Qaida. But the Taliban sought to increase its operational tempo and apply more pressure to the ANSF. The group's stated objective was to seize and hold more territory, including at least one provincial capital. Offensives were mounted in the traditional Taliban heartlands of southern Afghanistan, including Helmand Province, while Taliban fighters increased their control of territory in the north, such as in Kunduz. In Helmand, the initial Afghan security forces' response was hasty and poorly co-ordinated, as key districts fell to the Taliban. After NATO and US advisors arrived, a better synchronized counter-offensive pushed back the insurgents.

THE BATTLE OF KUNDUZ, SEPTEMBER 2015

At the end of September 2015, the Afghan government and ISAF suffered an unforeseen strategic shock when the Taliban captured Kunduz City, the provincial capital of the northern province of the same name.[6] The defending Afghan Army and Police units were routed, survivors retreating to Kunduz airport. It took two weeks for the city to be cleared of Taliban fighters, at considerable cost to the Afghan forces and civilians, including from a misdirected US air strike on a hospital. The Taliban's successful capture of the town was a vivid example of the way the security situation had weakened since US and NATO troops had begun withdrawing after the peak of the Afghan Surge.

The province lay in northern Afghanistan. Its majority ethnic grouping were Pashtuns, an enclave geographically separated from the Pashtun heartlands of southern Afghanistan. The province also had significant numbers of minority Uzbeks and Tajiks. There was a long history of friction between these groups and the Pashtuns.

As ISAF expanded throughout Afghanistan, the northern sector was placed under German military leadership. Berlin was very reluctant to allow German troops to take risks that might result in casualties. The German contingent had very restrictive national caveats that greatly constrained the effectiveness of German operations in the province. US forces observed that Bundeswehr operations often consisted of 'presence patrols' where soldiers drove or walked around with little impact on the operational situation. Whilst the Germans were able to displace

Taliban fighters, they were unable to stay in cleared districts to hold them against returning Taliban.

In planning the Afghan Surge, most US reinforcements were sent to southern Afghanistan. So in 2010 the province was reinforced with a US infantry battalion. This was complemented by raids by US SOF against Taliban leaders. At the time these were judged by ISAF to have greatly degraded the insurgents' leadership. Detachments of the US-sponsored militia, the Afghan Local Police, were raised. But these were mostly composed of ethnic Tajiks and Uzbeks, which reinforced ethnic tension with the majority Pashtuns.

The insurgents countered with an assassination campaign against pro-government officials and stepped up use of IEDs. But as the relative success of ISAF operations in southern Afghanistan pushed Taliban fighters north towards Kunduz, numbers of insurgents in the province increased. As time progressed both German and US troops were increasingly constrained by Taliban IEDs on the edges of key districts. These were usually successfully cleared by ISAF but doing so usually took up to half a day. This loss of valuable time reduced the ability of German and US troops to spend significant time on the ground in the districts. They were wasting too much time 'commuting to work'. ISAF was again 'mowing the lawn', only disrupting rather than displacing the Taliban, whose position in the province was steadily improving. In February 2012 a violent demonstration against the accidental burning of Korans by US troops saw a successful grenade attack against Camp Warhorse, the major US rural base in the province. Several US troops were wounded, and the base was subsequently abandoned.

During 2013 and 2014 the Taliban and Afghan forces fought over control of the rural districts surrounding Kunduz City. In 2013 the Taliban assassinated the police chief of Imam Sahib district, greatly destabilizing the area. October 2013 saw the German PRT withdraw, the Germans handing its base over to Afghan forces. The PRT's protective detachment of German troops withdrew.

With the effective departure of NATO troops from the province, regular Afghan forces were used to clear areas of Taliban forces. But these had insufficient numbers to hold onto the areas from which insurgents had been displaced. So the Afghan authorities relied greatly on pro-government militias to subsequently hold these areas. These were known as *arbaki*, sponsored by the National Directorate of Security, the Afghan intelligence agency. Most of these had been raised by local warlords. These notionally pro-government groups often behaved in a predatory fashion, intimidating, extorting and taxing villagers in a way that strengthened support for the Taliban. Detachments of Afghan Local Police acted in the same way. There is evidence of both types of forces committing human rights abuses, which were ignored by the Afghan National Police. Meanwhile, the success of Pakistani operations against Taliban bases in Waziristan saw more fighters seeking refuge in Kunduz.

The Taliban were able to exploit these factors to extend their control and presence into the rural districts that surrounded Kunduz City. An effort to recapture the district centre of Chahrdara after it was seized by the Taliban in June failed. There was much infighting amongst supposedly loyal pro-government militias. This rivalry was accompanied by violent acts of revenge, which further reduced the credibility of the Afghan government with civilians living in the districts around Kunduz; as did the militias' predatory taxation of farmers, shop keepers and other rural businesses. The countryside was divided into fiefdoms, with local Afghan officials often complicit in these extortion rackets. The majority of Afghan Army and Police in Kunduz were deployed in static bases and securing checkpoints on the roads into the city. A so-called quick reaction force mainly conducted night raids and was not a capable reserve.

There was little effective co-operation between government forces, the army, police and NDS. At the same time political friction between Pashtuns, Tajiks and other ethnic groups, political parties and local warlords was increasing in Kunduz. To reduce the exacerbation of ethnic tension by the Afghan Local Police, President Ghani appointed a new provincial governor in December 2014, apparently without consulting Chief Executive Abdullah, a factor that created considerable political tension between Ghani and Abdullah's supporters within the provincial government.

During 2015 the Taliban mobilized to attack Kunduz. This included a major logistic effort to assemble the necessary supplies of arms and ammunition. The supplies were delivered by donkey caravans travelling from Pakistan through eastern and northern Afghanistan. The Taliban claim that at the height of the operations some 7,000 of their fighters were taking part.

By mid-April 2015, the Taliban had established a strong presence in all the rural districts surrounding Kunduz City. In late August they had boldly staged a rally in Chahrdara district, posting video on the internet of hundreds of fighters openly parading themselves. So, neither the late September Taliban attack nor the weak response by Afghan government forces should have surprised the government or NATO. But they did.

On the morning of 28 September, the Taliban attacked from three different directions, defeating Afghan forces holding checkpoints on the edges of Kunduz City. Afghan Local Police and local government officials fled. The simultaneous destruction of the ring of checkpoints around the city destroyed the confidence and morale of Afghan forces in Kunduz City. They collapsed into chaos with officials and commanders fleeing to Kunduz airport, rendering the remaining government forces in the city bereft of command and leadership. An isolated hilltop base lasted for two days but was eventually captured by the Taliban, giving them control of high ground that dominated the city.

Although the city was lost in little more than two days, it took two weeks for it to be recaptured by a combined force of formations from the Afghan Army, Afghan National Police and Afghan SOF commandos, the last of these supported by US military advisors and airpower.

The fall of Kunduz starkly illustrated the weaknesses of both Afghan governance and the local Afghan forces. These included local political divisions, poor intelligence and substandard co-ordination between the army and police. The battle also illustrated the Taliban's operational design, to increase their control of rural districts surrounding key towns and cities, in order to improve the chance of capturing politically significant urban areas.

During the fighting US advisors with Afghan SOF called in fire support from an AC130 gunship. It was night, the battle was both complex and chaotic. The US troops called for fire on a building occupied by Taliban fighters. In error, the crew of the gunship attacked a hospital operated by Médicins Sans Frontiers, an international medical charity also known as Doctors Without Borders. Forty-two people were killed in the attack: international medics, Afghan civilians and wounded fighters from both the Taliban and Afghan government forces.

A subsequent US official investigation showed that this resulted from an accumulation of factors: a fatigued crew that had been rapidly deployed to the battle with insufficient awareness of the situation on the ground, including the location of the hospital, a position that was also unknown to the US ground troops. The decision to strike had also breached the US rules of engagement in force in Kunduz at the time. To these human errors were added equipment failures. The attack was not intentional, but an example of friction where in war errors and misunderstandings multiply to produce unintended consequences. A US officer was removed from command, one of five US military personnel who were subject to disciplinary hearings.[7]

Subsequently the US forces acted to reduce the chances of similar mistakes. The utility and accuracy of a Central Command database of protected locations, the No Strike List, was improved, as were arrangements for Médicins Sans Frontiers to communicate with NATO HQ in Kabul HQ.

But these measures came too late for those killed and wounded in the strike. There was significant damage to the reputation of the US forces and the Pentagon paid over $7 million in compensation.

The people of Kunduz suffered greatly in the fighting. The UN estimated that over 800 civilians were killed and wounded in the fighting; homes were damaged and destroyed. Many children were traumatized. Those who had lived in Kunduz since the 1970s considered the fighting in the city to be the worst in living memory, including the war with the Soviets, the subsequent civil war and the overthrow of the Taliban government in 2001.

PRESIDENT OBAMA ADJUSTS US STRATEGY

It was no coincidence that on 15 October 2015 President Obama announced a change in US strategy. In announcing that he would keep the 9,800 American troops still in Afghanistan in place through most of 2016, he was responding to a request from Kabul, to press the pause button on the US drawdown, saying that doing so would:

> allow us to sustain our efforts to train and assist Afghan forces as they grow stronger – not only during this fighting season, but into the next one. By the end of 2016, we will maintain 5,500 troops at a small number of bases, including at Bagram, Jalalabad in the east, and Kandahar in the south.[8]

The rapid response to Kabul's call for assistance may have been influenced by greatly improved co-operation between the US-led Coalition and the Afghan national unity government of President Ghani and Chief Executive Abdullah Abdullah. The US considered them a much more capable strategic partner than the previous administration of former president Hamid Karzai. The US commander in Kabul, General John Campbell, described the difference as 'night and day'.

Following the defeat of the Kunduz offensive, the Taliban was unable to permanently evict the ANSF from key population centres. The insurgents made several attempts to encircle and then capture provincial capitals, but the momentum gained in initial successes would dissipate as US airpower would be brought to bear, inflicting significant levels of Taliban casualties, forcing the insurgents to break off their attacks.

The Afghan forces succeeded whenever they concentrated their forces and thoroughly planned and co-ordinated their operations. Their special forces appeared competent and capable of independently attacking insurgent networks. But the evidence was that Afghan forces still needed considerable external support in developing their leadership, administration and logistics, as well as their air force. Overall, the Afghan forces were neither able to evict the Taliban or ISIS from their heartlands, nor capable of applying enough military pressure to the Taliban to force them to a political settlement.

A further complication was that ISIS had established a foothold in the country. Helped by its global propaganda campaign, the jihadist group had success in recruiting Afghans. For example, one group of disgruntled Taliban members reportedly rebranded themselves as ISIS. Many of its fighters may well have marched to the ISIS banner from other groups, reflecting ISIS' strategic impact in the Middle East and its extensive and effective messaging to actual and would be jihadis.

Since 2014 the group had established a foothold in Nangarhar Province, in south-east Afghanistan, which it used as a base from which to project devastating suicide attacks to Kabul and other towns and cities. US forces and their Afghan allies sought to attack it. There was also some fighting between the Taliban and ISIS. At times, much of ISIS' military effort in Afghanistan was directed against the Taliban. In spring 2017 the Pentagon said that the Coalition had reduced the amount of Afghan territory controlled by ISIS by two-thirds and killed some 75 per cent of the group's fighters. But despite these attacks

ISIS proved resilient, expanding its footprint from its initial bases in Nangarhar Province to neighbouring Jawzjan and Nuristan provinces.

By mid-2017 the gains made in the 2010–11 Afghan Surge had largely been reversed by the Taliban. The great majority of rural areas from which the Taliban had been evicted in 2010 and 2011 had slowly fallen back under insurgent control. After the Kunduz battle the Afghan forces, with support from the US and NATO, prevented the Taliban from seizing control of further provincial capitals. NATO and the US reported statistics in 2017 that stated that 55.8 per cent of the country's 407 districts were under Afghan government control or influence. But the same statistics indicated that the percentage of districts under insurgent control or influence had doubled since 2015. The percentage of contested districts had risen by nearly 50 per cent in the period between 2015 and 2017. The percentage of districts under government control or influence had decreased by over 20 per cent in the same period. The Taliban were increasing their control of rural areas surrounding key provincial capitals, intending to recreate the circumstances that led to the capture of Kunduz in 2015.

After the 2014 withdrawal of US and NATO troops from combat roles, the Afghan government position also deteriorated in Helmand Province, which at the height of the Afghan Surge was controlled by 20,000 US Marines and 10,000 British troops. The Taliban's killing of the province's police chief in early 2015 resulted in a significant decrease in co-operation among the various Afghan government forces in the province. This greatly reduced the effectiveness of the Afghan government's efforts to counter the Taliban in Helmand. Over the next year the Taliban made significant advances. A major contributory factor was that the Afghan Army's 215th Corps' fighting strength was much lower than it should have been, owing to a 'ghost soldier' scam where corrupt commanders siphoned off salaries of non-existent soldiers.

In February 2016 a US Army battalion from the Resolute Support mission was deployed to the province to provide increased support to the Afghan forces. In May 2016 the Taliban mounted a major offensive. This included assassination teams targeting Afghan commanders in their homes. They made particular use of specially trained elite mobile strike groups to mount attacks, while local Taliban would secure captured ground. The Taliban had particular success at capturing Afghan Army and Police checkpoints. To disrupt this US airstrikes in Helmand greatly increased. But these did not break the Taliban advance, which came within a few miles of its target, the provincial capital Lashkar Gar. Many of the districts in Helmand Province had by now fallen under Taliban control, with the Afghan government having little influence beyond the immediate vicinity of the provincial capital.

In a blaze of publicity over 800 US personnel, Marines and contractors replaced the US infantry battalion. The Marines set about re-training Afghan battalions and helped the Afghan Army plan a series of counter-attacks. One was directed at the Taliban-controlled town of Sangin, where so many British and US casualties had been inflicted. These attacks benefited from air support, including the Afghan Army's recently introduced Scan Eagle short-range tactical drones. The US Marines also fired 240mm guided rockets to support the Afghan troops, who also benefited from US drones and copious US air strikes. This airpower prevented the Taliban defeating these attacks, but none of the attacks inflicted a decisive defeat on the Taliban. A popular Afghan general was killed by a roadside bomb. And there was evidence that following a late 2017 US media report of the way drones and airpower were being employed in Helmand, the Taliban adjusted their tactics to better conceal their forces from the air. This included ceasing the use of radio communications, to neutralize signals intelligence gathering.

By February 2020, when the Taliban and US signed their agreement in Qatar, 18 of the 20 districts in Helmand either were controlled by the Taliban or had major Taliban presence. These included the districts of Babaji, Marjah, Nad-e Ali and Sangin that had previously, at great effort and significant casualties, been cleared of Taliban by British troops and US Marines.[9]

PRESIDENT TRUMP'S NEW US STRATEGY, 2017–20

In 2017 the iconoclastic new US President Donald Trump assumed office displaying deep scepticism about the US contribution to the NATO alliance and the cost of US military commitments overseas. He commissioned a review of US policy to Afghanistan and Pakistan. It was masterminded by the then-National Security Advisor US Lieutenant General H.R. McMaster, the former commander of the 2nd Armoured

Cavalry Regiment, who had wrested control of Tal Afar from insurgent hands in Iraq.

The new US South Asia Strategy was announced by Trump in August 2017. The strategy re-assessed US and NATO support to Afghan forces. It concluded that the 2014 withdrawal of all US and NATO mentors away from Afghan Army forces had been akin to 'pulling the training wheels off too early'. It aimed to bring America's longest ever war to a close. Trump declared that 'conditions on the ground, not arbitrary timetables will guide our actions from now on', and that the US would 'fight to win'.[10] The strategy aimed 'to conclude the war in Afghanistan on terms favourable to Afghanistan and the United States'. This required convincing the Taliban that they could not win, in order to push the Taliban to negotiate a settlement with the Afghan government. It had three lines of action against the Taliban: military, financial and legitimacy. Pakistan would also be pressured to change its behaviour.

The military effort would seek to roll back gains the Taliban had made since 2014. By now the insurgents had recaptured much of the rural terrain cleared at such human and financial cost in the 2010–11 Surge. UJS military advisors were redeployed back to Afghan Army formations. These could use airpower much more freely to support Afghan security forces.

By early 2018, the Iraqi and Syrian government forces and the US-led coalition against ISIS had expelled the group from most of the territory it had controlled in Iraq and Syria, and many key towns and cities. With this, US Central Command's main effort shifted from Syria and Iraq back to Afghanistan. This made more airpower, intelligence-gathering systems and SOF available to US forces there. US air strikes in Afghanistan greatly increased. The US Air Force reported that more bombs were dropped on Taliban, Al Qaida and ISIS positions in August 2017 than in any month since 2012. The turn of 2017/18 saw deployment of 3,800 extra troops primarily to provide additional training for Afghan forces. This increased the *total* number of US troops in Afghanistan from 8,400 to around 14,000.

The second part of the strategy sought to attack the Taliban's finances. This manifested itself by intensive bombing of the Taliban's narcotics network, particularly heroin factories in Helmand Province, the epicentre of the Afghan narcotics industry. This was an option that had not been exercised by ISAF for fear of alienating rural communities.

The third line of action was to challenge the Taliban's legitimacy, increasing social and religious pressure on the insurgents. This involved convening meetings of Muslim religious scholars both in Afghanistan and elsewhere. These condemned the Taliban's violent acts, designating them as 'un-Islamic'.

Trump's speech that launched the new strategy included a blunt declaration that the US expected Pakistan to take decisive action against the Afghan Taliban and Haqqani network members on its territory: 'we have been paying Pakistan billions and billions of dollars at the same time they are housing the very terrorists that we are fighting. But that will have to change, and that will change immediately.'

The US would place greater pressure on Pakistan to end Islamabad's tolerance of and support for the Afghan Taliban. The speech was followed by a January 2018 Presidential Twitter message that Pakistan had 'given us nothing but lies & deceit'.[11] In his Senate testimony in early 2018 General Joseph Votel, CENTCOM Commander, commended Pakistan for its national counter-terrorism operations and noted an increase in positive Pakistani co-operation with the US, but stated that:

> ongoing national counter-terrorism efforts against anti-Pakistan militants throughout the country have not yet translated into the definitive actions we require Pakistan to take against Afghan Taliban or Haqqani leaders. This problem is compounded by increasing cross-border terrorist attacks and fires between Pakistan and Afghanistan, which hinders both countries' abilities to coordinate on border security.'[12]

US officials took a much harder line with Pakistan, both in private and in public. Military assistance to the country was suspended. At the end of 2018 it was not clear if Pakistan had decisively committed to constraining the Taliban and Haqqani network to coerce them to meaningful peace talks.

In May 2018, Taliban fighters breached the defences of the capital of Farah Province in western Afghanistan but were pushed out the next day by Afghan forces assisted by US SOF, drones and air strikes. Important provincial capitals including those of Ghazni, Kunduz, Helmand and Uruzgan provinces were threatened by the Taliban. In each case the insurgents had a strong foothold in key districts close to the edges of the province's capital.

The additional US forces authorized to support the new US Afghan strategy reached full strength in the middle of 2018. US air strikes further increased over the year, particularly the attacks on narcotic production and distribution networks. Official US figures showed that the number of bombs dropped in the first ten months of 2018 was greater than in any year since 2006.[13] Without these airstrikes and the forward deployment of US advisors to designate targets, the Afghan forces would have found it difficult to retain control over the remaining rural areas that they held. The Taliban and ISIS continued to conduct spectacular attacks in Kabul and other cities. Afghan police and special forces were well practised in containing and counter-attacking such attacks, but these incidents represented strategic messaging opportunities for the insurgents, reinforcing their narratives that the Afghan authorities were losing control.

The threat of insider attacks continued. This was vividly illustrated by an October 2018 insider attack on a meeting in the Kandahar provincial governor's house attended by the commander of US forces in Afghanistan, General Scott Miller. Miller was unharmed, but three US personnel were wounded. The Afghan police chief for Kandahar, General Abdul Raziq, was killed.

During 2019 the Pentagon ceased to publicly report key data, including the numbers of Afghan districts under Taliban control and casualty figures for Afghan forces. Many analysts saw this as an indicator that the Afghan government's control over the country was weakening. Credible media reports suggested that already high losses in Afghan forces due to casualties and desertion further increased in 2018. Media reports suggested a thousand Afghan soldiers and police were killed and wounded in August and September 2018 alone. These losses had operational effect. For example, US advisors assessed that the Afghan Army Corps in Helmand had only 40 per cent of its intended strength. Overall the Afghan forces had a personnel shortage of 12 per cent, and were struggling to retain key specialists including pilots, aircraft mechanics, technical specialists, and SOF. Although the modernization of the Afghan Air Force continued, maintenance difficulties reduced aircraft availability.

Overall, by the end of 2019, the additional troops and increased bombing had blunted the increasingly effective Taliban offensive, but since the announcement of the new US strategy, the increased US military effort had not increased the areas under Afghan government control. Despite persistent briefings by US military officials that the US military strategy was succeeding, officials privately conceded that the war was at a stalemate.[14]

The Pentagon's own assessment of the state of security in Afghanistan noted numerous weaknesses in the Afghan forces.[15] These included recruit training, with trainees arriving at their units malnourished and inadequately trained, command and leadership, logistics and pervasive weaknesses in management. Too many Afghan troops were inflexibly deployed to highly vulnerable static checkpoints. And the Afghan special forces, the most capable component of the Afghan military and police, were being persistently misused, to the extent that the US was fining the Afghan Ministry of Defence for mis-employing their special forces on tasks for which conventional forces would be more appropriate. Since the fall of Kunduz in autumn 2015, the Afghan forces, with copious US air support, had prevented the fall of any other provincial capitals to the Taliban. And it may have been that the casualties suffered by the Taliban in the Kunduz battles and later attempts to capture provincial capitals deterred the insurgents from all-out assaults on the other major towns and cities. But the Afghan forces lacked the combat power to clear territory held by the Taliban, who were slowly but gradually increasing their control over rural districts. That the Taliban did not press Kabul's forces harder in 2018 and 2019 may be due, not only to a fear of casualties, but also to a perception that they stood a good chance of achieving their objectives through direct negotiation with the US.

NEGOTIATION FROM A POSITION OF WEAKNESS

During 2018 both Kabul and Washington stepped up their efforts to negotiate with the Taliban. In June President Ghani unilaterally declared a cessation of hostilities against the Taliban for the holiday of Eid 2018. The US complied with this, although US and Afghan forces continued to attack ISIS and Al Qaida. The Taliban declared a parallel three-day ceasefire. Extraordinary sights were captured by the press, TV and social media, of armed Taliban fighters meeting and socializing with Afghan soldiers, police and civilians. Some Afghan government officials were able to visit their home villages deep in Taliban-held territory. But Kabul's efforts to extend the ceasefire were rebuffed by the Taliban.

The US government appointed former US ambassador to Afghanistan Zalmay Khalilzad as Special Representative for Afghan Reconciliation, authorized and empowered to talk to Taliban representatives. Despite the successful ceasefire for the festival of Eid and direct US talks with the Taliban by US officials, including Khalilzad, negotiations with the Taliban saw little real progress in 2018, the insurgents still refusing to deal with the Afghan government, insisting that it was a puppet of the Americans.

Negotiations continued in 2019, with President Trump being willing in principle to agree a ceasefire between the US and the Taliban. But with the autumn 2019 death of a US soldier in an insurgent attack, Trump abruptly suspended the talks, revealing that the Taliban and Afghan government had been on the verge of travelling to the presidential retreat at Camp David, presumably to seal the deal. Three months later, direct talks between the US and Taliban resumed, resulting in the signing in Qatar of the 29 February 2020 'Agreement for Bringing Peace to Afghanistan between the Islamic Emirate of Afghanistan which is not recognized by the United States as a state and is known as the Taliban and the United States of America'.[16]

This declared a bilateral ceasefire between the Taliban and US forces. The Taliban would 'prevent any group or individual in Afghanistan from threatening the security of the United States and its allies, and will prevent them from recruiting, training, and fundraising and will not host them.' All US and allied forces would withdraw from the country 14 months after the agreement. Over 135 days from the signing the US would reduce its forces to 8,600 troops, its allies reducing proportionately. The agreement envisaged 'the formation of the new post-settlement Afghan Islamic government as determined by the intra-Afghan dialogue and negotiations.' These negotiations would begin by 10 March 2020. By this date the Taliban were to release 1,000 prisoners that they held and 5,000 Taliban fighters held prisoner by the US and Afghan government would be released. The US also declared that it would begin diplomatic action to lift UN sanctions on the Taliban and that the US and its allies 'will refrain from the threat or the use of force against the territorial integrity or political independence of Afghanistan or intervening in its domestic affairs.' There is also evidence of at least one secret protocol to the agreement which, a US military spokesman implied, saw the Taliban commit to an 80% reduction in violence and to cease attacks in Afghan cities.

At the time of writing, May 2020, implementation of the deal had been imperfect. A week-long reduction in activity by the Taliban was not continued. The insurgents resumed attacks on Afghan government forces in rural areas but appeared to refrain from major attacks in urban areas. In early March the Taliban stepped up their attacks. In Helmand they mounted 43 attacks on Afghan forces' checkpoints on a single day in early March 2020. The US mounted an airstrike on the Helmand Taliban, their first since the Qatar agreement. ISIS continued to mount major rocket and suicide attacks in Kabul.

Concurrent with the US/Taliban negotiations, Afghan politics became increasingly dysfunctional. The 2019 presidential elections were much delayed and subject to many allegations of fraud and manipulation by the two contenders, incumbent President Ghani and Abdullah Abdullah. This resulted in several months' political impasse between the two. In early 2020, both held separate inauguration ceremonies in separate wings of the presidential palace. Many foreign diplomats attended Ghani's ceremony, but Abdullah's was attended by many former Northern Alliance powerbrokers. Although Ghani was recognized as president by the US and most of its allies, Russia and Iran withheld recognition. US Secretary of State Mike Pompeo withdrew $1 billion in US aid to incentivize political co-operation between Ghani and Abdullah. US diplomatic influence in Kabul was reducing, as the influence of Iran and Russia was increasing.

At the end of May 2020 the talks between the Afghan government and the Taliban had yet to start. The Taliban persistently complained that far fewer prisoners had been released by the government than had been agreed in Qatar. There was evidence that a significant number of important Taliban commanders had been very reluctant to support the Qatar deal. But the Taliban leadership had reassured their key commanders that there would be rapid release of Taliban prisoners held by the Kabul regime. Recovering prisoners appears to be a totemic issue to many Taliban leaders, fighters and supporters, who have comrades and family members in Afghan prisons. Indeed, the Taliban had handed over to Kabul a list of prisoners they believe were held by the Afghan government. Without rapid release of their prisoners, the Taliban leadership would find it much more difficult to enforce the ceasefire on their own fighting groups.

A particularly gruesome and ruthless attack took place in mid-May in Kabul. Gunmen stormed a Kabul hospital, attacking the maternity wing and killing 24 people including two new-born babies and a midwife. The Taliban denied the attack and many commentators attributed the atrocity to ISIS. As a response President Ghani ordered government forces to switch from their previous defensive posture to 'active defence'. All this was against a background of increasing numbers of infections of Afghans by COVID-19, amid much speculation that the virus would overwhelm the nation's fragile health capabilities. Although the Taliban publicly recognized the threat the disease posed, there were multiple reports of senior Taliban leaders succumbing to the disease.

But at the end of the month there were some encouraging signs. Ghani and Abdullah reached a power-sharing agreement, with Abdullah taking charge of negotiations with the Taliban. The insurgents unexpectedly declared another short ceasefire for the Muslim festival of Eid.

THE PROSPECTS FOR PEACE IN AFGHANISTAN

The deal contained neither implementation and enforcement mechanisms nor provisions for dispute resolution, although the existence of additional secret protocols cannot be ruled out. There was much media speculation that the US military would not completely withdraw but would leave a counter-terrorist force in the country. The US–Taliban ceasefire meant that the considerable weaknesses of the Afghan forces would only increase as any remaining US and NATO advisors withdrew. And if the US ceased to use its airpower to support Afghan forces, the Taliban would gain a considerable military advantage.

These factors meant that it was very unlikely that the Afghan forces would regain the military initiative sufficiently to improve Kabul's already weak bargaining position. The opposite was more likely: that the Taliban military position would continue to improve, increasing the strengthening of their negotiating position with the Kabul government. And removal of UN sanctions would improve the Taliban finances.

Apart from the Taliban's agreement not to allow international terrorists to threaten the US or its interests from Afghan soil, all other

US and NATO strategic objectives had been abandoned. All the evidence suggested that once the deal was signed, President Trump was willing to abandon the Afghan government, its forces and its supporters to work out an accommodation with the Taliban on their own. He had frequently pledged that he would end the 'foolish wars' begun by his predecessors. Being seen to do so would improve his chances of re-election in the 2020 presidential election.

The most likely scenario for Afghanistan is that as the US and NATO withdraw the Taliban will probably gain increasing advantage over the Kabul government, making the insurgents increasingly unlikely to make the compromises necessary for a balanced peace deal. But as this happens, the former Northern Alliance of non-Pashtun interests will feel increasingly threatened. There will probably come a point at which their former warlords will resort to force to protect their interests. Afghanistan will probably revert to a state of civil war. This will not only make it less likely that the Taliban will be able or willing to constrain international terrorist organizations on the soil they control. Even without the likely effects of the COVID-19 pandemic on the impoverished country Afghanistan's overall prospects look poor.

THE AUDIT OF WAR

Leadership of operations gradually passed to the Afghan forces as international forces withdrew. Between 2012 and the end of 2014, Taliban offensives were usually defeated. Following the withdrawal of US and NATO forces from combat roles and the considerable reduction in air support to the Afghan forces, the security situation slowly worsened. This was demonstrated by the Taliban's capture of Kunduz in September 2015, although the city was recaptured by Afghan forces with US support.

Despite the considerable resources, training and advice applied by the US and its allies to the Afghan security forces, at the end of 2018 the Afghan forces displayed considerable weakness. These probably reflected deep-rooted characteristics of Afghan governance, society and human capital. The situation also reflected that work to build a new Afghan air force began much later than work to create a new army. The fall of Kunduz was the product of weaknesses of the various Afghan forces, including predatory behaviour and inadequate co-ordination.

The Taliban had exploited these weaknesses and the grievances of Afghan civilians living in Kunduz's rural hinterland to encircle the city.

In mid-2020 the US-led efforts to stabilize Afghanistan appeared to have only partially succeeded, at best. The efforts made in the 2010–12 Afghan Surge to stabilize the country and expand Afghan government control must be judged as an overall failure. And this must be seen as part of a wider failure of the overall international effort to stabilize Afghanistan.

WHY DID THE INTERNATIONAL STABILIZATION EFFORT FAIL IN AFGHANISTAN?

Overall, the US and its allies set goals for Afghanistan that were unrealistic and over-ambitious. This was the product of over-optimism that followed the unexpectedly rapid 2001 defeat of the Taliban government, multiplied by inadequate understanding of Afghanistan at all levels, national, regional, provincial and district. The military and civilian strategies, campaign plans and tactics used were often inadequately adapted to the true conditions in Afghan districts and provinces.

The US and its allies usually described the war at the strategic, operational and tactical levels as an insurgency between the Taliban and the Kabul government. These assessments were often dangerous oversimplifications. In reality, it was a complex and multifaceted civil war. Local tribes, drug gangs, criminal networks, warlords, politicians at all levels and individuals holding Afghan government political and security appointments all sought to promote their interests by aligning with external actors including the US, NATO, the Afghan government and the Taliban. Force was often used to promote the armed actors' interests. This would often be in pursuit of local advantage, including over water, land, narcotic activity or long-lasting tribal grievances. At the national level, Presidents Karzai and Ghani had to sustain their political position by appointing powerful Afghan actors to national, regional and local political positions. This empowering of actual and potential malign actors further complicated the situation and reduced US and NATO freedom of action. The sponsoring and support of warlords and militias by the CIA and US SOF further complicated the situation and undermined unity of effort.

The Taliban's legitimacy with the Afghan people in the districts that the insurgents controlled comprised two capabilities: security and dispute resolution by Taliban sharia courts. The Taliban did not offer to improve agriculture, health, education or infrastructure in the way that international stabilization efforts did. In contrast, ISAF and national development agencies were setting out to help the Afghan government do many things, none of which they usually did well, whilst the Taliban were trying to do just two things, both of which they usually did well.

Stabilization was most successful when areas were under the physical control of sufficient numbers of security forces – provided that those forces did not behave in a predatory manner. An important factor was the presence of adequate local governance before stabilization began. International forces and development agencies, Afghan forces and government officials from district, provincial and national level all needed to co-operate.

The considerable weakness of Afghan government structures and officials at the province and district level were insufficiently improved during the Afghan Surge. The Surge was probably far too short an initiative to materially improve the considerable weaknesses in Afghan governance. When the districts that were prioritized by the international forces for clearance operations and development efforts transitioned to Afghan government control in 2014, the ability of the Afghan authorities to provide development and services at the district level and the Afghan security forces' ability to provide security were gradually overmatched by an emboldened and resurgent Taliban, whose control of rural areas inexorably grew.

14

COVID-19

A dark postscript

As this book was being finished the 2020 coronavirus pandemic swept the globe. It could have produced millions of deaths, but a combination of methods applied by wealthy nations greatly reduced mortality rates. Means of containing the virus included contact tracing and quarantining as well as reducing opportunities for the virus to spread from person to person by mass social distancing. In China, the US, UK, Europe and many Asian countries 'lockdowns' were used in an attempt to break the chain of infection. At one stage about half of the world's population was under some kind of lockdown. These measures greatly disrupted economic activity, against which Western governments massively increased public spending and borrowing. Whilst at the time of writing it is far too early to predict how the virus will be defeated, it is clear that for the US and many of its allies, there will be immense pressure on public spending. This is likely to result in large cuts to defence, diplomatic and development budgets.

In the case of the US and UK, there was considerable evidence of strategic incompetence that resulted in tens of thousands of avoidable deaths. In the US, much of this was due to the eccentric and unpredictable leadership of President Trump which provided a caricaturist's example of how not to lead a nation infected by a pandemic. Indeed, Trump's performance as national leader was far worse than the sub-optimal leadership of the Iraq war that President Bush displayed between 2003 and 2006. And unlike Presidents Bush and Obama, both of whom were able to energize and lead global coalitions, against Al Qaida and ISIS respectively, President Trump positively rejected such a role for the US, the only country that could have led a global coalition against the virus.

But in the case of the UK there was strong evidence of some of the same leadership pathologies that had led to strategic failures in Iraq in Afghanistan. This included complacency, paying insufficient evidence to early warning intelligence, government being insufficiently co-ordinated and a cabinet of government ministers whose principal qualification appeared to be political loyalty to the prime minister, rather than competence at strategic leadership and getting things done.

Both the US and UK suffered human and economic damage with considerably more deaths than those suffered by their troops in both wars. But by the end of April the virus looked set to wreak even greater damage on Iraq and Afghanistan. Both countries had fragile governments and very weak health systems. Their populations were going to pay a very high price for the damage that almost two decades of war had inflicted on the countries' economies, infrastructure and public services. And the greatly weakened legitimacy of national governments made measures to counter the disease more difficult to implement than in less fragile states. Overall, it seemed probable that the virus would increase suffering in Iraq and Afghanistan. In this very dark sky, one of the few shafts of sunlight was that the Taliban appeared to recognize the threat from the disease. This would be scant consolation for the citizens of Iraq and Afghanistan who were likely to succumb to this cruellest of diseases.

15

Bloody Lessons

OUTCOMES — WHO WON? WHO LOST?

Most of the great wars that the US and their allies had previously fought ended in a clear result. The infant United States had defeated the British Empire and prevailed over the Confederate States. It had helped Britain and France defeat Germany in 1918. It had led the defeat of Japan in 1945 and without US military and industrial might the UK and Soviet Union would have struggled to defeat Nazi Germany. The victories over Imperial Japan and Nazi Germany were clear cut and decisive.

But the US had faltered in Vietnam. That war not only helped tear US society apart, resulting in the resignation of President Johnson, but also ended in a military defeat when in 1975 North Vietnamese forces conquered South Vietnam and unified the country by force. This resulted in a period of strategic introspection and lack of confidence where the US was unable to promote its strategic interests as effectively as it needed to. Against this background, how are the outcomes of the US-led wars in Iraq and Afghanistan to be assessed?

The 2001 destruction of Afghanistan's Taliban government and its forces succeeded in evicting the majority of Al Qaida from Afghanistan. But the late 2001 failure to encircle and isolate the Al Qaida fighters in the Tora Bora mountains allowed the movement a better opportunity to reconstitute itself than if the US attack had been better planned and led.

The 2003 attack on Iraq succeeded in destroying Saddam Hussein's government. But the central justification for the attack, that Iraq had weapons of mass destruction and thus posed an imminent threat to the US, US interests and US allies, was false. And the perceived threat of Iraqi government support to international terrorist action against the US was eliminated, even though post-invasion analysis showed that this threat had been greatly exaggerated.

In 2003 there were those in the US government who had hoped that the destruction of Saddam's regime and his capture would discourage other states from acquiring weapons of mass destruction. It is true that in 2004 Libya's mercurial dictator Muhammar Ghaddafi unilaterally decommissioned his programme to develop nuclear weapons. But other countries that opposed the US and already had weapons of mass destruction programmes were not deterred from pursuing the necessary know how and industrial capabilities. These included North Korea, Iran and Syria. Indeed, their resolve to do so may have been incentivized by Saddam's failure to deter the US attack.

Iran is the only nation that can be judged to have succeeded in achieving its strategic aims in Iraq. By 2020, it had succeeded in greatly increasing its political influence in Iraq and the size of the US military footprint in Iraq was considerably less than at the height of the US Surge. This was because the war had created opportunities for Iran to greatly increase its influence in Iraq, opportunities that Tehran identified and adroitly exploited.

Comparing Iraq in May 2020 with the objectives set out in 2005 US National Strategy for Victory in Iraq that are quoted on page 241 is an instructive exercise. The US failed in its long-term aim of creating an Iraq that was 'peaceful, united, stable, and secure, well integrated into the international community, and a full partner in the global war on terrorism'. At the time of writing, these objectives had not been achieved. Iraq remained deeply unstable. Although ISIS had been physically evicted from the Iraqi towns and cities it had conquered in 2014, there was a large political gulf between minority Sunni and majority Shia. Apparent failure by the US in Iraq had emboldened global terrorists, particularly after the rise of ISIS in Iraq and Syria. The Iraq war had resulted in outcomes that were largely negative for the security of the US and its allies, not least the considerable rise in Iranian influence in the region. And the popular riots and protests of late 2019 showed that the Shia political elite was despised by many young Iraqis, who saw it as fundamentally corrupt. Politically Tehran dominated Shia politics and was unwilling to concede its dominant position.

The US and its allies had similarly ambitious goals for the stabilization and reconstruction of Afghanistan. By the beginning of 2020 Afghanistan had made progress. Many human development indices were improved including health, life expectancy and education, particularly women's education. But the country's economy remained almost completely dependent on international donors. The government remained heavily parasitized by corruption and its writ did not extend much further than Kabul and the major towns and cities. Throughout much of rural Afghanistan war with the Taliban had reached new heights, inflicting ever more civilian casualties. Afghan government forces and their US allies were in a mutually hurting stalemate with the Taliban, with a slow but inexorable shifting of the military balance in the war in favour of the Taliban.

At the beginning of 2020, the only unqualified strategic success of the two wars was the killing of Osama Bin Laden in 2011. Although the helicopter-borne force of SEAL commandos departed from a US base in Afghanistan, the evidence suggests that the necessary intelligence gathering did not depend on the presence of US forces then deployed in Afghanistan. Indeed, the intelligence was gathered by the CIA and other US intelligence agencies largely independently of US forces in Afghanistan.

It is true that after 9/11 there was no terrorist attack of similar magnitude on the US. That Al Qaida had been deprived of its bases in Afghanistan helped to contribute to this. But a much greater contribution was the assembly of an international coalition of intelligence agencies to identify and shut down jihadist networks. This was led by the CIA, with many of its close intelligence allies and partners in support. Against this success should be set the way that both wars were seen by many Muslims, both in the Middle East and further afield, as unjust, illegitimate and creating wholly avoidable civilian casualties. These factors helped motivate thousands of people to fight against the US and its allies in Iraq and Afghanistan and inspired much violent extremism further afield.

The US government's decision to invade Iraq must stand as the worst military decision of the 21st century. It was a military strategic folly on a level equal to that of Napoleon's 1812 attack on Russia and Hitler's

1941 attack on the Soviet Union. These are uncomfortable parallels. For example, all three attacks were launched in a mood of confident optimism that the campaigns would quickly yield decisive victory. The losses suffered in both the earlier invasions resulted in the Emperor and Hitler's combat power being so eroded that they proved unable to resist the converging attacks being mounted by the coalitions that were arrayed against them. Iraq administered no such massive attrition of the military capabilities on the US and its allies. But it had an effect of similar strategic magnitude – the significant loss of legitimacy.

Napoleon's attack on Russia and Hitler's attack on the Soviet Union had the effect of sucking up most of the bandwidth of the national leaders and their principal military and strategic leaders. This meant that inadequate government attention as devoted to the other wars their nations were involved in. The war in Iraq had the same effect on the US and UK strategic leadership. The deterioration of the US position in Iraq between 2003 and 2006 and the loss of legitimacy contaminated the legitimacy of the war in Afghanistan.

The February 2020 Qatar agreement between the US and the Taliban saw a Taliban ceasefire with the US and a guarantee that it would prevent Afghan territory from being used by international terrorists, traded for a US and NATO withdrawal from Afghanistan. The indications were that after this withdrawal the US would no longer support the Afghan government. So the great majority of the ambitious strategic objectives that the US and NATO articulated for Afghanistan would probably be forfeit. The Taliban had outlasted the US and its allies.

Before 9/11 the US had a confrontational relationship with Iran. But in the immediate aftermath of the attacks Tehran quietly co-operated with Washington over counter-terrorism and Afghanistan. This proved to be only an interlude, with Tehran unsurprisingly suspending co-operation after President Bush's early 2002 'Axis of Evil' speech which explicitly included Iran as a member of the malign grouping. Throughout the Iraq war Iran sought both to drive up the costs of the US occupation and to strengthen its influence in the country. It succeeded in achieving both objectives. By April 2020, it also had increased its influence in Afghanistan. It is an enduring irony of both wars that Iranian strategic competence and US strategic incompetence resulted in the US losing influence in both countries.

THE WARS' CONSEQUENCES

Hundreds of thousands of people were killed in both wars. Up to April 2019, the Iraq war is reported to have resulted in deaths of 4,496 US troops and at least 1,595 US contractors.[1] The Iraq Body Count website has produced a credible estimate that between March 2003 and April 2020 at least 288,000 people were killed in the war in Iraq, of which between 185,000 and 207,000 were civilians.[2]

Since 9/11 there have been 2,280 US military deaths in Afghanistan. There is no single official or unofficial estimate of numbers of civilian casualties. A credible estimate suggests that over 31,000 civilians were killed as a result of the Afghan war from 9/11 to the end of 2014.[3]

But as the war in Iraq descended into chaos, and the legitimacy of the US-led occupation was eroded, the ability of many countries' governments to openly associate themselves with US-led counter-terrorism efforts was reduced. And the perceptions of political blunders, an incompetent occupation and widespread human rights abuses came to contaminate the international legitimacy of the US-led war in Afghanistan. The widespread perception of intractability of the conflicts and difficulty in achieving strategic success resulted in the US and many of its allies losing confidence in the utility of force. The political and military credibility of the US and the UK was damaged. These consequences live with us today, with greatly reduced strategic confidence displayed by many key NATO and European countries, in contrast to greater strategic assertiveness displayed by Russia, China, Iran and North Korea. And the authority of the US in the Middle East has greatly reduced.

The increasing global opposition to the Iraq war made it much more difficult for many countries to co-operate with the US. And the reporting of both wars and the resulting civilian casualties throughout global Muslim communities created a sense of injustice and outrage. This fuelled radicalization, giving rise to new generations of violent extremists.

UNDERSTANDING THE OUTCOME OF THE WARS

The US-led regime change operation in Iraq had been thoroughly planned and drew upon the full range of US military capability. Well-trained and well-led modern, networked land forces and air forces defeated much less modern and poorly trained and led conventional forces. This exploited the considerable hollowing out of Iraqi military capability since 1991, their indifferent morale and lack of meaningful training, reinforced by the poor leadership of Saddam Hussain, his sons and their inner circle. The outcome of the US attack should have surprised no-one. The Iraqi armed forces struggled to understand what was going on and were unable to exploit Coalition forces weaknesses. But irregular forces including pro-government militias and foreign jihadists who flowed into Iraq from Syria were able to pose an unanticipated threat that slowed down the US advance on Baghdad. Had the Iraqis better co-ordinated their irregular forces' actions with those of their regular forces, they would have inflicted more delay and US casualties.

Regime change in Iraq had achieved the strategic effects of removing Saddam Hussein from power and removing any weapons of mass destruction threat his regime could pose, as well as ending a threat of Iraqi government support to international terrorists. The US had anticipated that its troops would be welcomed as liberators in Iraq and that in a matter of months they would be able to hand over to a functioning Iraqi administration, with a new Iraq becoming a strategic ally in the War on Terror and acting as a beacon for democracy in the region. Their failure to achieve this was but one symptom of the US government's and armed forces' wholly inadequate understanding of the country and their insufficient and unrealistic planning for post-conflict stabilization. Symptoms of this included allocating too few troops to rapidly re-establish security in the aftermath of regime change, and making inadequate provision for post-war civilian administration. These were compounded by the decision to disband the Iraqi police and security forces and the Baath Party, which both alienated the Sunni minority and made it much more difficult to raise enough competent new Iraqi security forces. Failure in these respects resulted in a self-imposed defeat.

The evidence suggests that initial stabilization operations in Afghanistan and Iraq were over-informed by preconceptions based on the previous success of US and NATO forces in Bosnia and Kosovo. This was probably reinforced by the apparent vindication of the Revolution in Military Affairs (RMA) concept by the rapid toppling of the Taliban and Iraqi regimes. By giving US Secretary of Defense Donald Rumsfeld and others undue confidence that Iraq and Afghanistan could be stabilized with minimal forces, RMA thinking probably contributed to strategic miscalculation.

Rumsfeld's and Bush's ingrained political aversion to nation building strengthened their attraction to the RMA, apparently making them reluctant to accept that the wars in Iraq and Afghanistan were different to those envisaged by the concept. This not only influenced the decisions they made about the conduct of both wars, but also predisposed them to persistently emphasize planning for long-term defence capabilities rather than fielding those urgently required in Iraq and Afghanistan. There is an overwhelming body of evidence that suggests that, between 2002 and 2006, the approach of the US and key allies was partly conditioned by the war that they would have liked to have fought rather than the war as it was.

In Iraq, Bush and Rumsfeld failed to identify that immediately after the deposition of Saddam Hussein the conditions were sufficiently changed beyond the pre-war planning to make it necessary to produce a fresh plan. Rumsfeld's insistence in 'off ramping' the 1st Cavalry Division from its planned role of joining V Corps at the earliest opportunity contributed to the post-invasion chaos, by making it even more difficult for US troops to establish post-war security. This was reinforced by his many public and private statements that post-conflict operations were going to plan. These were but the overture to his continued insistence that the Transition Strategy was working.

Rushed and inadequately informed US decision making continued throughout 2003–06, with Shia militias and Al Qaida exploiting legitimate grievances to further their political aims. In early 2006 the country descended into ethno-religious civil war which was increasingly beyond the capability of the US to suppress. The rapid descent into chaos, the failure to find any weapons of mass destruction, prisoner abuse and the lack of evidence of Saddam's support for terrorists all reduced the legitimacy of the US-led occupation of Iraq, in Iraq, the Arab world and globally. Iraq also provided a major opportunity for Al Qaida, thus undermining its near-destruction in Afghanistan.

The Coalition strategy was Transition: handing security over to the Iraqis as soon as possible. This neither built up Iraqi Security Forces capability sufficiently, nor neutralized the Sunni–Al Qaida insurgency. The exceptions were Qaim and Tal Afar in 2005 where 'clear, hold and build' counter-insurgency operations with sufficient US and Iraqi forces succeeded, and Ramadi in 2006 where a similar approach and the successful US embrace of tribes that were willing to fight Al Qaida created a potential campaign tipping point – although this was not widely recognized at the time.

In January 2007 the Transition Strategy was replaced by the US Surge: a strategy of surging additional troops to protect the population, to create enough security and the space for reconciliation and political progress. This succeeded in reversing the deteriorating security situation and, taking advantage of the Anbar Awakening where Sunni tribes deserted Al Qaida and joined forces with US troops, made significant inroads against the Sunni and Al Qaida in Iraq insurgencies.

The combination of improving security, changing Shia political dynamics and Prime Minister Maliki's authorising Iraqi and US action against Shia extremists restored a measure of security sufficient for the US to begin withdrawing its troops, although Iran continued to support attacks on Coalition forces. The US government had explicitly committed to the Surge to create the opportunity for political progress. But as security improved, US objectives for an inclusive political settlement in Iraq diverged from those evidenced by the behaviour of Prime Minister Maliki. The 2010 Iraqi election resulted in a narrow defeat for Maliki's coalition, but with tacit US support to the slow-motion constitutional coup that he staged, he was installed in power. He increasingly acted to marginalize the Sunni and to increase the political loyalty and Shia character of the Iraqi armed forces – at the expense of their effectiveness.

By 2011, the US lacked enough political legitimacy and influence with Iraqi parliamentarians to secure agreement for an enduring presence. And it also lacked the political will to prevent Prime Minister Maliki from stealing the 2010 election. That Maliki's behaviour directly led to the transformation of Al Qaida into ISIS and its near-defeat of the Iraqi security forces in 2014 demonstrated the failure of many of the US strategic ambitions so clearly announced by Bush and Rumsfeld in 2003. These actions drove the Iraqi Sunnis back into the arms of Al Qaida. Taking advantage of ungoverned space in Syria that resulted from that country's civil war, and rebranding itself as ISIS, the jihadist insurgency exploited the hollowing out of the Iraqi security forces to seize control of Mosul and much of Anbar and Nineveh provinces.

It was only the mobilization of Iraq militias, many supported by Iran, and US air strikes that stopped ISIS from reaching Baghdad. After ISIS imposed a savage regime over its territory and committed numerous sectarian atrocities, it took over three years to eject it from Iraq and two more years to destroy its physical control of Syrian territory. The hundreds of thousands of Iraqis and Syrians killed and wounded as a result were just as much casualties of the US attack on the country as those killed between 2003 and 2011.

It is therefore unsurprising that the US intervention against ISIS in 2014 eschewed any nation-building objectives.

The deep sectarian divisions in the country owed much to Saddam's decades of repressing the Iraqi Shia and Kurds. The resulting pressure release resulting from the removal of Saddam would always have exacerbated sectarian tensions. And this was made worst by the nakedly sectarian behaviour of many Iraqi politicians and officials. But many US decisions provided little incentive for the political co-operation necessary to move Iraqi politics beyond a zero-sum game.

Support for jihadists and proxy militias by Syria and Iran respectively was intended to help increase the cost of stabilizing Iraq for the US and its allies. These actions succeeded and had the additional effect of deterring the US from attempting to conduct regime change in both countries.

In 2001 the unforeseen requirement to remove the Taliban government from Afghanistan initially challenged US military capability. There were no contingency plans. The US' lack of intelligence and the landlocked position of Afghanistan posed formidable obstacles. But the plan that was rapidly improvised by the CIA and US military, using SOF and US airpower to support the anti-Taliban warlords and their militias, exploited these forces in being to defeat the Taliban more quickly than anyone anticipated. This was a major military achievement.

For Afghanistan the removal of the Taliban government, greatly reduced the threat from Al Qaida and was strongly supported by the international community, although Al Qaida was not totally defeated. In the immediate aftermath of the removal of the Taliban regime in late 2001 and throughout 2002, military operations in Afghanistan had great international legitimacy. The attacks of 9/11 had been widely seen as an outrage and unexpected, and the speed and decisiveness of the 2001 defeat of the Taliban was greeted with great relief. Many nations and international organizations shared a strong desire to assist reconstruction. Afghanistan was widely seen as a nation that had been victim of both external intervention and savage civil war.

The rapid deployment to Kabul of a UK-led multinational brigade over the winter of 2001–02 helped the fledgling Afghan authorities restore security to Kabul. But from early 2002 the attention of the US and British governments turned to Iraq. Afghanistan became an 'economy of force' theatre. In contrast to Iraq, which was a relatively modern country, Afghanistan was one of the least developed nations in the world. Its infrastructure had been badly damaged by decades of war, its human development indices were very low and many of its more educated people had fled.

The US and its allies initially planned to help the country develop itself beyond the self-imposed near-mediaeval level of the Taliban regime. Objectives included democracy, rule of law, eliminating the narcotics industry and improving the inferior status of women.

The reality was that the challenge of the resurgent Taliban insurgency meant that the war became the priority. And reforming Afghan governance had only limited effect in the rural areas that the Taliban contested.

The initial defeat of the Taliban was followed by efforts to build Afghan state capacity and counter residual Taliban insurgency that are now recognized as inadequately co-ordinated and resourced. International efforts to develop Afghan governance clashed with the county's deep-seated tradition of decentralization. This was reinforced by the political weakness of President Hamid Karzai, who had to govern through patronage, by making accommodations with local strongmen and warlords. Cultivation and empowerment of these warlords by the CIA and US SOF promoted predation on Afghan civilians. Malign behaviour by local Afghan officials, civilian casualties from Coalition attacks and inappropriate behaviour by international forces and private military companies all further alienated Afghan civilians and helped the Taliban re-establish themselves.

Between 2006 and 2009 the international intervention in Afghanistan came close to the brink of strategic failure. As NATO assumed security leadership in 2006, it met unexpectedly heavy opposition from the Taliban and fighting greatly intensified in southern and eastern Afghanistan, greatly increasing collateral damage and civilian and military casualties. But neither NATO nor the US were willing or able to commit enough forces to militarily defeat the Taliban.

For the US and those of its allies that contributed forces, the ever-deteriorating situation in Iraq between 2003 and 2008 also absorbed ever-increasing military, diplomatic and development resources and the bandwidth of strategic leaders and their government ministries. So, between 2003 and 2009 Afghanistan was of necessity a lower priority for the US, UK and some of their important allies. And other allies, including the key NATO states of France, Germany and Italy, would not or could not provide either the resources or the strategic leadership that the international effort in Afghanistan needed in order to provide sufficient development and security to give the country a greater chance of countering the growing Taliban threat.

It was only in 2010, with the improvement of security in Iraq, that adequate US, UK and NATO force levels were achieved, and that enough effort was allocated to building the capability of the Afghan forces. President Obama's Afghan Surge allowed a comprehensive counter-insurgency campaign to be mounted, applying relevant lessons from Iraq. 'Clear, hold and build' operations in southern Afghanistan's Helmand and Kandahar provinces pushed back the Taliban from key districts, which were then held by Afghan security forces. But Afghanistan was a much less developed country than Iraq and the political, ethnic and development challenges were even greater.

Given the ever-increasing civilian and military casualties in both wars as well as political pressures on the democratically elected governments of the US and its allies, it was inevitable that strategic ambitions would be scaled down. President Obama's 2011–12 surge was strictly time limited, with the key dates for its end announced simultaneously with Obama's declaration of the beginning of the Surge. Although US development efforts were intended to increase in line with the increase in troop strength, the 'civilian surge' was to reduce in a similar profile to the military force levels.

US and NATO forces gradually reduced after 2011, handing security leadership to the Afghan government in 2014. The 2015 capture of Kunduz by the Taliban demonstrated that there were still government and warlord forces that preyed on the local population. The Taliban took advantage of this and many other examples of poor Afghan governance to gradually encircle the city and then seize it. Although a government counter-attack evicted the Taliban, the insurgents continued to expand their control of rural areas.

US, UK and other efforts to build local Afghan government capability had been insufficient to create the necessary change, particularly cultural change, to produce enough improvement of Afghan local governance capability in order to create enduring political change at a local level. And the flow of insurgents from Pakistan had not significantly reduced. Indeed, the evidence in 2014 was that the Taliban were receiving support from both Iran and Russia. as well as from Pakistan.

Except for Afghan SOF, US advisors were removed from Afghan tactical units and US air support was greatly reduced. This reduced the Afghan Army's effectiveness and greatly increased casualties. So the gains made by the US and UK in the 2011–12 Surge were subsequently reversed by the Taliban.

For much of the war the Taliban enjoyed secure bases in Pakistan and could easily move fighters and supplies across the mountainous border with Afghanistan. The war had destabilizing effects on the country and many Pakistanis saw the Afghan Taliban as legitimate resistance fighters. From 2007 Pakistani Army counter-insurgency operations reduced their sanctuaries but did not eliminate them. There was credible evidence of Pakistani tolerance of some Taliban and of some active support to the insurgents, including the Haqqani network. This, US drone strikes in Pakistan and the location and killing of Osama Bin Laden in Pakistan led to an ever-increasing erosion of mutual trust between Islamabad on one side and Kabul and Washington on the other. This had the effect of greatly eroding practical co-operation across the Durand Line.

In 2017, President Trump announced a new US South Asia Strategy. This greatly increased bombing attacks on the Taliban and narcotic networks and redeployed US military advisors to the Afghan Army. It arrested the Taliban's gains but by 2019 the war was at a stalemate.

With the failure of the US–NATO 2010–2011 Surge the aims of the US and its allies became less ambitious. Many US and NATO officers and officials increasingly used the term 'Afghan Good Enough' to describe more limited strategic aims, recognizing that the idea of a European-style democratic state could not be achieved quickly, if at all. By 2019, US aims were to achieve a peace deal between the Kabul government and the Taliban, through diplomatic pressures on Kabul, Islamabad and negotiations with the Taliban, combined with increasing military pressure on the insurgents.

WHAT DO THESE WARS TELL US ABOUT WAR?

Given the length of the wars, the many casualties that resulted and the apparent strategic failures of the US and its allies, many have recoiled in horror at the wars' consequences. And the political and military establishments of the US and many of its allies have displayed great reluctance to get involved in similar wars again. But the world remains an unstable place with large numbers of armed conflicts occurring inside states. Many of these conflicts have deeply destabilizing consequences. The US and many of its allies are currently seeking to assist threatened states with training, advice assistance and air strikes, seeking to avoid another protracted war that puts 'boots on the ground'. And there are strategic flashpoints where frictions between states carry with them the risk of wars between states. Although current wars and possible future armed conflicts may have a different character from the Iraq and Afghan wars, many of the characteristics of the wars will probably still apply.

Success in war requires more than just strategy making. All those involved, particularly officials at the highest levels, need to understand how war is different from other human activities, including business and peaceful politics. Both wars show us some key aspects of war as a human activity. They remind us that war is an inherently unpredictable endeavour. No matter how well developed one side's plans and preparations, the other side will seek to frustrate their opponent's intentions.

Both wars were contests of willpower between political and military actors to achieve political aims. The will of political leaders and military commanders at all levels was a key determinant of the outcomes of these conflicts. Examples include the collapse of the Iraqi Army in March 2003 and of jihadists' readiness to fight to the death. Tactical leadership by US, Coalition and NATO commanders was often effective in combat. Commanders of Shia militia 'special groups' and Taliban fighters sometimes displayed equivalent powers of combat leadership.

In 2006–07, US President George W. Bush demonstrated a will to win in Iraq that had deserted many of his advisors. As commander of US Army Training and Doctrine Command, General David Petraeus played a crucial role in formulating US counter-insurgency (COIN) doctrine; he successfully applied the doctrine in Iraq, changing tactical, operational and strategic dynamics there. Both these efforts required great willpower – firstly, to achieve rapid change in the face of institutional inertia in the US Army and, secondly, to do so in the face of significant political and military friction in Iraq and Washington. It would be wrong to idolize Petraeus – especially as some US units and officers had already rediscovered the principles of COIN for themselves – but his inspirational and decisive leadership illustrates the enduring importance of the human factor in war.

The warring parties attempted to create all the advantages they could. The wars were replete with action–reaction cycles where an initiative by one side would be countered by the other, leading to a cycle of ever-increasing complexity. General Sir Rupert Smith's influential 2005 book *The Utility of Force* proposed that during armed conflict a key factor is the utility of force – its ability to achieve desired objectives.

At the start of the Afghanistan war US forces showed great utility by removing the Taliban regime, and doing so with fewer casualties and collateral damage than many commentators had anticipated. In 2003 US-led forces demonstrated high utility in rapidly destroying Iraqi President Saddam Hussein's army and regime. Subsequently the utility of US-led Coalition forces in Iraq was rapidly eroded by Iraq's rapid descent into chaos and the abuse of detainees. Washington's decision to rebuild Iraq on a new political model, but without the application of an effective strategy, further exacerbated the weaknesses of the US campaign. Throughout both wars force had great utility for the militias and insurgents that sought to disrupt reconstruction and security and further their political aims. Militia, insurgent and terrorist military operations and political activity threatened the survival of new governments and the success of missions conducted by international forces.

LINEAR, NON-LINEAR AND COMPLEX WAR

Much thinking about war, much commentary on armed conflict and much reporting in the media portrays the course of the wars as essentially a linear activity. The regime-change campaigns that opened both wars saw a linear sequence of events directly lead to the collapse of the enemy regime. But the following stabilization campaigns saw many variables interacting in a constantly changing fashion. This made the two wars much more complex and 'non-linear'. Complexity was also increased by the diversity and overlap between the armed actors. For example, in Iraq from mid-2003 onwards, there was a great deal of overlap between militias and organized criminal groups, as well as political and religious extremists and death squads. In both wars, smuggling, blackmail, protection rackets and organized crimes often funded malign political and military activity.

Within both wars there were multiple political, religious, ethnic and economic conflicts, resulting in increasing complexity. This became a key factor driving commanders' plans. At the height of the Iraq Surge General Petraeus told Congress that 'war is not a linear phenomenon; it's a calculus not arithmetic'.[4] Or, as British Lieutenant General Graeme Lamb, then deputy commander of MNF-I, put it in 2007, 'this is as complex as ... anything I've ever done ... this is three-dimensional chess in a dark room'.[5]

'NATION BUILDING UNDER FIRE'

Often characterized by British officers as 'nation-building under fire', the two wars featured prolonged and violent contests for the minds of the population, the insurgents and militias and their military political leaders. This meant that there was usually a political dimension to military operations, often right down to the tactical level. And the overlapping linkages of both narrative and politics at the local, national and international level meant that the military tactical, operational and strategic levels often overlapped. Twenty-first-century communications, particularly new opportunities provided by satellite television, the internet and social media, increased the interpenetration and interdependence of war and politics. Insurgents, terrorists and militias made the 'propaganda of the deed' an integral part of their operations. This meant that the "battle of the narrative" became increasingly important, often as important as the armed conflict, sometimes more so.

Some commentators have suggested that these two wars prove that counter-insurgency is impossible. This is disproved by the range of successful counter-insurgency campaigns, such as the Colombian government's defeat of the Fuerzas Armadas Revolucionarias de Colombia (FARC) Marxist guerrilla insurgents.

The Afghan and Iraq wars demonstrate the importance of having a properly framed strategy and adequate means. This is shown by the many decisions made by the US and its allies which made the Afghan and Iraq wars even more difficult to fight than they might have been. These problems resulted from multiple failures to adequately align the ends, ways and means of all instruments of national power, at every level from strategic to tactical.

Despite the international legal legitimacy conferred upon the US-led international forces by UN Security Council resolutions, US- and NATO-led operations in both countries often struggled to achieve moral legitimacy in the eyes of the world, particularly with Muslims. This was exacerbated by inadequate understanding, poor intelligence, abuse of detainees and counter-productive tactics, all of which reduced legitimacy with the local population and amongst Muslims the world over. As the wars went on, the US and its allies increasingly recognized that collateral damage and civilian casualties eroded legitimacy and aided the recruitment efforts of militias and insurgents. Therefore, they sought to use force with greater precision and discrimination, adopting highly restrictive rules of engagement and expanding their use of precision weapons.

Abuse of detainees at Abu Ghraib and Bagram starkly demonstrated the importance of operating in accordance with the law. Achieving legitimacy was of central importance to the actors in both conflicts. For example, the Taliban's claim that they were the legal government in exile of Afghanistan gave them legitimacy in the eyes of its supporters in Afghanistan and Pakistan.

Legitimacy was sometimes an issue for militias and anti-government forces as well. Taliban propaganda and statements increasingly stressed the importance of minimizing Afghan civilian casualties, although the conspicuous contradiction between these sentiments and the many civilian deaths from IEDs and suicide attacks rendered their message almost irrelevant.

COMBAT IS THE CORE MILITARY CAPABILITY

The wars were a bloody reminder that combat is the core military capability and that if they are to have utility, armed forces should be benchmarked against determined and capable enemies. The initial intervention in Afghanistan depended on the capabilities of US SOF and the CIA to operate in hostile battlespace to liaise with and advise Afghan indigenous forces. Money was an essential lubricant in this. The militias and warlords had their combat power greatly enhanced by US aircraft delivering precision bombs. US airpower was essential to provide surveillance, and to deliver and sustain the CIA and SOF parties.

The US-led Coalition attack on Iraq also exploited airpower to the maximum, benefiting from the previous 12 years of policing no-fly zones over northern and southern Iraq. The ground forces were a mixture of heavy armoured units and formations, such as US and British armoured brigades, mechanized forces such as the 1st Marine Division, and the light forces of the 82nd and 101st Airborne divisions. Of these, the decisive role was played by the heavy armour of the 3rd Infantry Division, without which the attack would have taken much longer and suffered far more US casualties. The deep attacks conducted by the two US Army attack helicopter formations both failed, but attack helicopters proved invaluable in providing close support to light forces, a function they would also perform in Afghanistan.

Both regime-change operations were conducted against enemy militaries that were far less modernized than attacking international forces. They were incapable of mounting effective challenge to US and Coalition attack aircraft. They also displayed considerable weaknesses in planning, leadership and morale.

All the US and British forces that attacked Iraq in 2003 were well prepared for combat operations and had the necessary culture to close with the enemy to fight. The same could not be said of many of the international contingents that deployed for stabilization operations in Iraq and Afghanistan. A significant proportion of Western armed forces had achieved results in the Balkans throughout much of the 1990s simply through their presence rather than by fighting. The governments, defence ministries and armed forces of the US and its allies entered both wars thinking that stabilization operations in Iraq and Afghanistan would be similar in character to those they had conducted in Bosnia and Kosovo, with a relatively low threat. The much higher level of violence generated by insurgent and militia fighters in both countries was a strategic shock to many governments, their forces and public opinion. Against opponents determined to fight, international forces who were unable to fight, or whose governments would not allow them to fight, were of little utility and often added military and political friction.

Post-conflict stabilization operations in both countries were challenged by more complex and much less transparent environments than had been foreseen by the advocates of the RMA. Understanding the situation and the myriad local military and political actors became as important as the simpler understanding of orders of battle and military hardware that had sufficed before 9/11. Before 9/11 US and NATO armed forces had prioritized intelligence gathering against hardware and conventional military targets. But successful development of intelligence for counter-insurgency saw intelligence collection optimized against people, their interactions and their intentions – intelligence targets that had been de-emphasized, if not ignored, by the advocates of the RMA. This applied to the full range of airpower and information, surveillance, target-acquisition and reconnaissance capabilities, as well as ground-combat forces. But unless stabilization operations saw sufficient security forces amongst the population, these technological advantages would count for little.

Fighting in both stabilization operations ranged in scale from low-level firefights, ambushes and roadside bomb attacks to corps operations featuring several divisions. Tactical ground combat was sometimes as intense as that experienced in World War II, Korea and Vietnam. Militias and insurgents sought to exploit international forces' weaknesses and sensitivity to casualties by using asymmetric approaches and tactics, particularly IEDs.

Many of the military capabilities developed during the wars are of wider applicability. For example, successful stabilization required concentration of troops to provide security for the people through a systematic 'clear, hold and build' approach, measures to control population movement and expanding and decentralizing tactical intelligence. Infantry, armour, artillery and combat engineers attacked insurgent strongholds, using combined-arms tactics, complemented by reconstruction, development and information operations. The more operations involving local forces, giving an indigenous face to build empathy with the civil population, the better. These are pointers for a wide range of future urban operations.

After the defeat of Saddam's regime, most combat in Iraq was in the towns and cities, reflecting the political importance of the settlements, where most of the Iraqi people lived. Afghanistan was a much less urbanized nation, but combat still revolved around towns, villages and farm compounds.

Infantry was the most important military capability for both urban operations and stabilization, but the firepower and protected mobility of armoured vehicles were invaluable, wherever terrain allowed. Tactical integration of fixed- and rotary-wing manned and unmanned airpower into land operations greatly increased, for example attack helicopters often providing intimate fire support.

The extraordinary efforts made to protect troops often reduced their utility. For example, in Afghanistan all infantry were equipped with handheld mine detectors and improved body armour. This additional weight meant that they could not move as fast as the less encumbered Taliban fighters. It also reduced the endurance of the infantry and increased casualties resulting from summer heat. Specially organized, sophisticated counter-IED task forces were fielded. Armoured vehicles increased in size, weight and cost. International forces' casualty levels were reduced by a revolution in battlefield medicine.

There was exponential growth in aerial surveillance, particularly by unmanned aerial vehicles, and greater integration of tactical intelligence with national strategic intelligence. Networking these capabilities allowed all-source intelligence analysis to lead the attack of enemy networks. SOF had an increasingly important, but not exclusive, role in this. The full potential of SOF was only realized when their operations were fully integrated with those of conventional forces.

WAR IS A MULTI-DISCIPLINARY ACTIVITY REQUIRING INTEGRATION OF ALL ACTIVITIES AT ALL LEVELS

A common theme across both wars at every level was the importance of integration. This applied not only to combined arms military tactics and the considerable improvements in integrating air and land forces and SOF and conventional forces, but also to fully integrating all levers of national power: military, intelligence, diplomatic and development. Institutionalizing future interagency co-operation is likely to be an enduring requirement for future conflicts. Doing so will require sustained effort by governments and strategic leaders.

Both wars illustrate the importance of achieving unity of effort. For example, in Afghanistan, the Taliban insurgency often achieved a greater political and military unity of effort than the Afghan government and various national contingents of the International Security

Assistance Force (ISAF). The US and its allies often had a problematic relationship with the Afghan president. During the US–NATO Surge, security operations gained unity of effort from the increasingly joint development of a unified NATO–Afghan military plan, and from a very high degree of co-operation between Coalition and Afghan forces. In Iraq and Afghanistan, 'partnering' Iraqi and Afghan units and formations, and embedding teams of advisors within them, promoted unity of effort at the tactical level.

The value of integrating both military and civilian capabilities and action was repeatedly shown at the tactical level. But the US and many of its allies conspicuously failed to achieve adequate levels of integration of military with civilian action, both before the invasion of Iraq and for much of the post-conflict stabilization period in both Iraq and Afghanistan.

This demonstrates that war and warfare are inherently interdisciplinary activities. Both military commanders and political leaders have key roles in integrating all the capabilities and activities at their disposal. Nations need to be able to fully integrate not just their military efforts, but also intelligence, diplomacy, development and information operations. Doing so is likely to be just as relevant to strategic, operational and tactical success in future conflicts as integrating combined arms and joint capabilities was for military success in the previous century.

MILITARY OPERATIONS TO LEARN FROM

Given the unpopularity of the wars and the apparent failure of international forces to achieve their strategic objectives, many military professionals, commentators and analysts in the US and its allies appear disinclined to study the battles in Afghanistan and Iraq. This is a mistake, as many of both wars' battles and operations are of considerable military interest. They have many lessons about the character of contemporary military operations. Military doctrine, training and educational establishments should be using these engagements to illustrate different approaches to war in the 21st century.

The air–land campaign where the CIA, US SOF and airpower were combined with indigenous anti-Taliban forces to destroy the Taliban regime is an excellent example of rapid development of a novel plan in response to an unforeseen challenge. The same applies to the deployment of the US Marines of Task Force 58 into southern Afghanistan. The battle of Tora Bora illustrates the dangers of over-reliance on indigenous forces and Operation *Anaconda* shows the dangers of over-optimistic planning.

Although Operation *Iraqi Freedom* must be regarded as a strategic failure, the regime-change campaign that began it contains many examples of modern joint, combined manoeuvre warfare. For example, the SOF-led operation in Iraqi Kurdistan demonstrated imaginative integration of SOF, airborne infantry and air-delivered armour both to fix Iraqi forces in place and to prevent political instability. The rapid advance of the 3rd Infantry Division and 1st Marine Division from Kuwait to Baghdad must rank as one of the best examples of deep manoeuvre in military history. And the 2nd BCT's Thunder Runs into Baghdad show how a city can be captured without destroying it. An alternative approach to attacking a city without turning it into Stalingrad was demonstrated by the 1st UK Armoured Division's approach to Basra – a 21st-century siege. And rapid reaction to unforeseen events, armoured manoeuvre and precision use of airpower were all demonstrated by 1st US Armoured Division in its 2004 'extension campaign' to counter Shia militia south of Baghdad, a campaign that would not have been needed had the Polish-led multinational division proved capable of resisting the Shia uprising.

The challenges of urban warfare were demonstrated by both 2004 battles of Fallujah. The first battle was mounted at short notice and showed that against an improvised defence a combined arms force could successfully advance, as well as demonstrating the perils of tasking a tactical force in an operation with inadequate and inconsistent strategic and operational direction.

In the second battle of Fallujah, the 1st Marine Division faced more numerous, more determined and better organized defenders, but using modern combined arms capabilities, including armoured vehicles, persistent surveillance and precision firepower, the US Marines and US Army were able to recapture the town. Most of the subsequent combat in Iraq was in urban areas, where the same success factors applied.

Increasingly US operations adopted a counter-insurgency approach. These included the clearance of Qaim and Tal Afar. The subsequent counter-insurgency operations in Ramadi were strategically decisive, as US engagement of Sunni tribes willing to fight Al Qaida triggered the Anbar Awakening. The success of this was multiplied by US forces being willing to support, fund and direct former enemies as they turned on their former allies.

All these factors came together in the tactical operations conducted during the Surge. By now there was an operational level dimension to the campaign, for example the way in which the HQ Multinational Corps – Iraq sequenced operations in Baghdad and amongst the surrounding 'Belts'.

Concurrently UK forces in Basra were engaged in pitched fighting with Shia militias. But the British 'Accommodation' ceasefire agreement with the militia was negotiated from a position of strategic and tactical weakness that led to UK forces increasingly losing the initiative. After Prime Minister Maliki redefined the JAM as enemies of the Iraqi government, two different operations showed alternative approaches to clearing cities of insurgents. Operation *Charge of the Knights*, in which Iraqi forces cleared Basra, had a chaotic opening round in which undertrained Iraqi forces were defeated, but the battle of Sadr City was a systematic clearance operation that exploited an artificial obstacle. Both attacks greatly benefited from control of the air and precision firepower.

In Afghanistan between 2006 and 2009 there were many battles around isolated British outposts in Helmand and remote US outposts in the mountains of eastern Afghanistan. The successful defence of these bases against numerically superior attacking forces of Taliban offers examples of the high degree of integration of artillery and a wide variety of attack helicopters and precision bombs and missiles. Without this highly developed degree of air–land integration some of these battles would have been won by the Taliban, allowing them to capture the bases and any surviving Coalition troops. In military terms these would have been tactical defeats, but the boost to Taliban propaganda that would have come from success in defeating US and UK forces would have had strategic impact in the battle of the narrative.

NATO conducted many deliberate operations to clear Taliban forces from agricultural terrain in southern Afghanistan. As in Iraq, these required a combined arms approach, integrating airpower and precision weapons, and were dependent on the close combat capability of infantry. The first of these, Operation *Medusa* in Arghandab in September 2006, showed the difficulty of evicting determined Taliban defenders from well-prepared defences. In 2010, Operation *Moshtarak* in Helmand and Operation *Hamkari* in Kandahar showed that British Army, US Army and US Marines had evolved a successful approach to clearing Taliban from rural areas, albeit depending on adequate force density.

After NATO withdrew from its combat role in 2014, the capture of Kunduz by the Taliban exposed the weaknesses of Afghan forces, particularly their co-ordination. The battle and subsequent Taliban efforts to capture important towns and cities showed that where US airpower could be brought to bear, the Taliban would suffer heavy casualties.

An overall theme in Iraq and Afghanistan was that combat increasingly occurred where people lived. This, along with the global mega-trend of urbanization, means that urban operations will increasingly become the 'new normal'. And that armed forces that are not competent in urban environments should be increasingly seen as incompetent.

LEADERSHIP OF THE WARS

Apart from the killing of Osama Bin Laden, why did the US and its allies fail to achieve so many of their strategic objectives? Why was it so often so difficult for tactical military and civilian activities to achieve the desired operational effects that would create progress towards both Coalition and national strategic objectives? How was it that the richest nation in the world, with the most powerful armed forces on the planet, was defeated by the Taliban, failed to stabilize Iraq and increased the strategic advantage of Iran, Washington's long-term bitter enemy?

In both countries the US and its allies initially had very ambitious strategic aims. But as the wars continued longer than expected and casualties rose, the level of ambition was reduced. Had strategic ambition not been adjusted downwards as both wars went on, current perceptions of strategic defeat would be even greater.[6] The simplest explanation is that the US government of President Bush displayed insufficient strategic competence between 2002 and 2007. This led to many complex failures, and multiple examples of sub-optimal decision making in Washington DC, CENTCOM, Kabul and Baghdad. Had the civilian and military planning for the post-conflict stabilization of

Iraq matched the intensity and volume of the thorough and extensive military planning for the invasion, there would have been a greater chance of successful post-conflict stabilization, reconstruction and political transition of Iraq. But with their deeply ingrained beliefs against practising 'nation building', whether Bush, Rumsfeld and other key members of their administration would have been capable of discarding their ideological baggage is unclear.

The major factor that contributed to the early failures in Iraq and Afghanistan was inadequate strategic leadership by President Bush and his government. Contributory factors included weaknesses in intelligence and inadequate understanding of Iraq and Afghanistan and inadequacies in reconstruction efforts, political strategies, military strategy, operational concepts, tactics and equipment. These, combined with failures across the government and armed forces to adapt quickly enough to unforeseen circumstances, provided opportunities that were exploited by insurgents and militias. In this period, some of Bush's key subordinates, particularly Defense Secretary Rumsfeld, displayed profound denial that Washington's plans were not working and that the US government and the Pentagon needed to improve their leadership and management of the wars.

It took several years for President Bush to recognize that the ends, ways and means being employed were inadequate. After 2006 Bush changed the US strategy to allow the US and allied forces to create enough security in Iraq for limited political progress. Subsequently, Bush provided effective strategic leadership for the new campaign. And the new US Defense Secretary Robert Gates provided the necessary realism and focused energy to compel the Pentagon to adapt to the Afghan wars as they were. His leadership was more realistic, better balanced and more successful than that provided by Donald Rumsfeld.

By articulating a strategy of ending the war in Iraq, President Obama reflected the US public's war weariness and frustration. To implement his pledge to do more in Afghanistan Obama made extensive use of the US National Security Council and a wide variety of expert opinions from the US Military, State Department and elsewhere. He thoroughly tested their advice and spent much time understanding Afghanistan and the strategic options available to the US. This was a competent approach to strategic decision making that stood in stark contrast to the Bush government's decision to attack Iraq. Even so, the strategic situation in Afghanistan in 2011–12 greatly limited the ability of the US and NATO to change the conflict dynamics sufficiently. In Afghanistan from 2010 no amount of military, development, political and intelligence resources could on their own make up for deficits of legitimacy of the central government, especially at local level.

As the nation that led both wars, the US had the deciding voice in the formulation and execution of strategy. This meant that the US' allies would always struggle to influence US decision making. The UK example is instructive. It thought that it had more influence over political and military decision makers than any other nation. But London had far less influence on Washington's decision making than UK leaders often claimed. And the accumulated evidence clearly shows that the British contributions to the first parts of the Iraq and Afghan wars were degraded by a lack of strategic competence in London. The British government of Tony Blair lacked the insight, determination and strategic leadership either to craft successful strategies for Basra or Helmand provinces or to influence the US to adopt winning strategies for both Iraq and Afghanistan. Together with the unwillingness of London to mobilize for both wars as fully as Washington had, the evident failure of the British 'accommodation' with Shia militia in Basra, and the difficulties of British stabilization operations in southern Afghanistan, all reduced the UK's military credibility with the US, as well as denting the British Army's self-confidence.

Between 2003 and 2008 British strategy in Iraq came within an inch of failure. This was demonstrated by the early failure of Operation *Charge of the Knights*, which exposed the considerable weakness of British strategy for Basra. The eventual success of the operation was due more to Iraqi and US efforts than those of the British. The Iraq Inquiry clearly exposes multiple examples of sub-optimal strategic leadership by politicians and government departments, including the Ministry of Defence. The responsibility for this is Prime Minister Tony Blair's, as was the 2006 decision to increase British strength in Afghanistan before forces had reduced as planned in Iraq. As the top UK strategic leader, he failed to match ends, ways and means, failed to insist that his instructions were implemented and failed to properly assess the effects of British strategy. Often, he was not served as well as he might have been by his ministers and by senior civilian officials and military officers who could themselves display strategic incompetence, but the ultimate responsibility for the sub-optimal functioning of the British security machinery was his. Blair's strategic leadership of Britain's role in both wars should be judged a failure. And unlike President Bush he failed to recognize the collapse of the transition strategy in Iraq in 2006. Indeed he concluded that it was not relevant to British strategy.

Gordon Brown, Blair's successor as British prime minister, continued Blair's strategic trajectory in Iraq. He struggled to lead the British war in Afghanistan, in part because his relationship with the senior military leadership had been gravely damaged by a decade of cuts in defence spending, for which as Chancellor (finance minister) at the time, he bore responsibility. He was also caught between two irreconcilable forces, the need to support US strategy with a meaningful British military contribution and a British public, media and parliamentary opposition increasingly unsupportive of Britain's war in Afghanistan. Lacking Blair's considerable powers of persuasion he was an unsuccessful war leader.

The overall assessment must be that between the deposition of the Taliban at the end of 2001 and the end of 2006, the leadership displayed by President Bush, Defense Secretary Rumsfeld and UK Prime Minister Tony Blair was largely inadequate.

By the time President Obama was inaugurated the trajectory of US drawdown from Iraq was set. But US connivance in Prime Minister Maliki's refusal to step down after the 2010 Iraqi elections had the unforeseen consequence of Maliki's repression of Iraqi Sunnis, creating the conditions for the rise of ISIS. Obama sought to thoroughly examine the strategic options for the war he inherited in Afghanistan. But the US strategy of a time-limited surge and rapid handover of security to the Afghan underestimated the fragility of Afghan state institutions and their security forces. This resulted in the Taliban's offensive campaign regaining the initiative and pushing Afghan forces out of rural areas cleared during the Surge.

Obama inherited President Bush's war in Iraq, and sought to improve the situation in Afghanistan and to kill or capture Osama Bin Laden. He was also confronted with other security challenges, including the wars in Libya and Syria, the rise of ISIS and Russian interference in Ukraine. Commentators often criticized him for his actions, or non-actions over these and other crises. Obama himself was not reticent to use force, when he considered it justified. When he accepted the award of the Nobel Peace Prize, he said so, to the apparent discomfort of some of his hosts.

Later, on a spring 2014 trip to Asia, travelling on Air Force One Obama had an informal conversation with the press contingent in the plane. Ben Rhodes, a member of the National Security Council Staff, described Obama's conversation:

> He went on a long tangent about how failures of American foreign policy were ones of overstretch, complaining about the lack of accountability for Iraq War supporters who were still the tribunes of conventional wisdom. Finally, he reached the end of his lecture. 'What's the Obama doctrine?' he asked aloud. The silence was charged, as we'd always avoided that label. He answered his own question: 'Don't do stupid shit.' There were some chuckles. Then to be sure that he got his point across, he asked the press to repeat after him: 'Don't do stupid shit.'[7]

The US, UK and some of their key allies can all be judged to have made many strategic, operational and tactical decisions that qualify as 'stupid shit'. In many ways they were their own worst enemies, architects of self-inflicted strategic defeats. The Afghan Taliban and Iran should be judged as much more successful.

Indeed, the most successful strategic leader of the wars was the Iranian Revolutionary Guards Quds Force commander, General Qassim Soleimani. He displayed both ruthlessness and adaptability, creating a network of militias in Iraq that used both force and politics to further Iran's aims and increase its influence in Iraq. He showed considerable personal leadership skills in actively supporting militias and in manipulating Iraq political actors. He was the single point of authority over Iran's activity in Iraq, achieving much greater unity over political, diplomatic, military and economic activity than any senior US actor in Iraq and Afghanistan. And Quds Force appeared explicitly constructed as an interagency task force.

LESSONS FOR STRATEGIC LEADERSHIP

A strategy must balance ends, ways and means to produce a plan that can be used by military commanders, diplomats, development agencies and intelligence services to formulate an interagency operational level plan, from which tactical plans can be developed. There must also be a political strategy to provide the foundation for all operational and tactical activities.

It is just as important to have the means to monitor the implementation of strategy. The effectiveness of a strategy must be regularly reviewed, particularly to reassess the utility of the force. This should not only draw on reports from the operational theatre within the machinery of government, but also be tested against the assessments of outside experts who are not part of the government machine. This must include host-nation national, regional and local governments as independent actors. It must assess the risk that host-nation governments will act in ways that make them part of the problem rather than the solution, due to corruption, politicization, and the existence of parallel structures. Dealing with these issues is likely to require a 'carrot and stick' approach.

Throughout the wars considerable demands rested on the shoulders of strategic leaders: heads of government, key politicians, senior military officers and civilian officials. There were many successful military operations in the wars in Afghanistan and Iraq, but these tactical victories were too rarely converted into strategic effect. Many sub-optimal strategic decisions made by the Bush and Blair governments were the result of incomplete, incoherent and inconsistent processes for the formulation of strategy and then monitoring and assessing its implementation.

SETTLING THE ACCOUNT

Despite his best intentions, President Obama was unable to meet his own objective of ending the war in Iraq responsibly. Indeed, the country had been so damaged by the war and so poisoned by the blatantly sectarian leadership of Shia prime minister Maliki that Operation *Iraqi Freedom* quickly morphed into a prolonged and costly war against ISIS. The Iraq war reinforced Iran as the dominant influence in Iraq, a position of advantage it had gained because of earlier US strategic failures in its occupation of Iraq. These followed from the greatest strategic mistake of all, the US 2003 decision to attack Iraq. This decision also destabilized the war in Afghanistan. It squandered the international goodwill on which the efforts to stabilize and reconstruct Afghanistan so depended.

It also drew away the resources, troops and political energy that could have done so much to alter the downward trajectory in that country from which the Al Qaida terrorists had set out on their audacious 2001 mission against America.

The innocent victims of 9/11, including the brave airline passengers who fought back against the hijackers, the casualties suffered by the forces of the US and its allies and the much greater numbers of military and civilian casualties in both wars deserved better strategic leadership and competence than that displayed by the US and British governments of President Bush and Prime Minister Blair.

They deserved much better than for all the blood, metal and gold to be expended, only for them to turn to dust.

Glossary

AAV	Amphibious assault vehicle
Abrams	US Army tank
ANCOP	Afghan Civil Order Police
ANSF	Afghan National Security Forces
ARRC	Allied Command Europe Rapid Reaction Corps
ATACMS	Army Tactical Missile System
AWACS	Airborne Warning and Control Systems
Badr Corps	An Iranian-sponsored militia linked to SCIRI (see below).
Battle group	A term used by many NATO armies to designate a battalion-sized combined arms grouping, usually formed around an infantry or armoured battalion. The US Army uses task force as a similar term.
Bradley	US Army infantry fighting vehicle
CDI	UK Chief of Defence Intelligence
CENTCOM	US Central Command
CERP	Commander's Emergency Response Program. A US military fund that allowed commanders to spend money on short term reconstruction projects.
CIA	Central Intelligence Agency. The US secret intelligence agency, with a role in covert operations.
CJTF	Combined Joint Task Force. A multinational and joint HQ. Many were formed during the wars, with a wide

variety of names such as CJTF Mountain or CJTF 76.

CPA	Coalition Provisional Authority
COIN	Counter-insurgency
DfID	Department for International Development
EFP	Explosively formed projectile/penetrator
EOD	Explosive ordnance disposal
FARP	Forward Arming and Refuelling Point
FCO	UK Foreign and Commonwealth Office
GPS	(US) Global Positioning System
HQ	Headquarters
IED	Improvised explosive device
ISR	Intelligence, surveillance and reconnaissance
ISTAR	Intelligence, surveillance, target acquisition and reconnaissance
ISAF	International Security Assistance Force
IRA	Irish Republican Army
ISI	Inter-Services Intelligence. The Pakistani military's secret intelligence agency, with a role in covert operations.
ISIS	Islamic State of Syria and al Sham
JDAM	Joint Direct Attack Munition
JSOC	Joint Special Operations Command
JSOTF	Joint Special Operations Task Force
JSTARS	E-8 Joint Surveillance Target Attack Radar System. An enormous US Air Force aircraft carrying a large radar designed to locate and track vehicle movement
KFOR	Kosovo Force
LAV	Light armoured vehicle. An eight-wheeled armoured personnel carrier used by both the US Marines and Canadian Army. It had a turret armed with a 25mm cannon.
MEF	Marine Expeditionary Force. A divisional or corps sized grouping of US Marines.
MEU	Marine Expeditionary Unit. A unit of US Marines organized to deploy from US Navy amphibious shipping and

operate independently. Usually contains a Marine infantry battalion, tanks, amphibious assault vehicles, artillery, combat engineers and logistics, including 15 days' worth of supplies. It also has over 20 organic aircraft including Marine helicopters and fighters.

MiTT	Military transition team
MoD	Ministry of Defence
MLRS	Multiple Launch Rocket System
MNC-I	Multinational Corps – Iraq
MNF-I	Multinational Forces – Iraq
MNSTC-I	Multinational Security Transition Command – Iraq
MOG	Manoeuvre Outreach Group
MP	Military Police
MRAP	Mine-Resistant Ambush Protected vehicle
M113	A US tracked armoured personnel carrier. Used largely by the US Army as a support vehicle at the start of Operation *Enduring Freedom*, it was subsequently judged insufficiently protected to be used in Iraq. It was also used by the Iraqi Army, before, during and after the US invasion.
National Guard	The US Army and US Airforce both have National Guard units. These are reserve units, staffed by part-time personnel. In peace they are commanded by the governor of the state they are based in. The governor can mobilize them for civilian emergencies. Many units were rapidly mobilized after 9/11 to improve domestic security, for example at airports and railway stations. Units were also mobilized to fight in Afghanistan and Iraq
NATO	North Atlantic Treaty Organization
NDS	National Directorate of Security, the Afghan intelligence agency
OMLT	Operational mentoring and liaison team
OPPLAN	Operations Plan
ORHA	Office of Reconstruction and Humanitarian Assistance
Republican Guard	An elite component of the Iraqi ground forces
RAF	Royal Air Force
Rivet Joint	The US Air Force's largest signals intelligence aircraft,

	the RC135 Rivet Joint, which was used to intercept Iraqi radar transmissions and military communications.
RMA	Revolution in Military Affairs
RPG	Rocket-propelled grenade
SAS	Special Air Service
SCIRI	Supreme Council for the Islamic Revolution in Iraq. An Iranian-backed political party, strongly linked to the Badr Corps (see above).
SEAL	Sea Air Land. The US Navy's maritime SOF.
SOCOM	Special Operations Command
Shura	A word in the Afghan language Dari for a consultative meeting. These would be called by Afghan and NATO military commanders and officials to consult local communities.
SOF	Special Operations Forces
Stryker	An eight-wheeled armoured personnel carrier used by the US Army in Iraq and Afghanistan. Units and formations so equipped were known as Stryker battalions and Stryker brigade combat teams.
SOFA	Status of Forces Agreement
Technical	Term describing an improvised fighting vehicle, such as a pick-up truck or 4x4 fitted with a heavy machine gun or cannons. Often used by the Taliban in 2001.
TF	Task force. The US Army uses this term to describe battalion-sized combined arms groupings, similar to NATO battle groups. The term is also used to describe various ad hoc groupings. It is also used by US and NATO SOF to describe battalion-sized groups.
TOC	Tactical operations centre
T72	A model of Russian tank used by Iraqi forces
UAV	Unmanned aerial vehicle
UN	United Nations
UNPROFOR	UN Protection Force
UNSCOM	UN Special Commission
USAF	United States Air Force
USAID	US Agency for International Development

Recommended Reading

BOOKS

Anderson, Ben, *No Worse Enemy: The Inside Story of the Chaotic Struggle for Afghanistan*, Oneworld, 2012

Atkinson, Rick, *In the Company of Soldiers: A Chronicle of Combat*, Henry Holt and Co, 2004

Bailey, Jonathan, Iron, Richard and Hew Strachan (eds), *British Generals in Blair's Wars*, Ashgate, 2013

Ballard, John R., Lamm, David W. and Wood, John K., *From Kabul to Baghdad and Back: The US at War in Afghanistan And Iraq*, US Naval Institute Press, 2012

Bellavia, David, *House to House: An Epic of Urban Warfare*, Simon & Schuster, 2007

Bird, Tim and Alex Marshall, *Afghanistan: How the West Lost its Way*, Yale University Press, 2011

Braithwaite, Roderick, *Afghantsy: The Russians in Afghanistan 1979–1989*, Profile Books, 2012

Brands, Hal, *What Good is Grand Strategy? Power and Purpose in American Statecraft from Harry S. Truman to George W. Bush*, Cornell University Press, January 2014

Briscoe, Charles H.; Kiper, Richard L.; Schroder, James A. and Sepp, Kalev I., *Weapon of Choice: U.S. Army Special Operations Forces in Afghanistan*, US Army Combat Studies Institute Press, 2003. https://www.armyupress. army.mil/Portals/7/combat-studies-institute/csi-books/WeaponOfChoice_ cmhPub_70-100-1.pdf

Bush, George W., *Decision Points*, Crown, 2010

Casey, George W., *Strategic Reflections; Operation Iraqi Freedom July 2004–February 2007*, US National Defence University Press October 2012. https://ndupress. ndu.edu/Portals/68/Documents/Books/strategic-reflections.pdf

Chandrasekaran, Rajiv, *Little America: The War Within the War for Afghanistan*, Knopf Doubleday, 2012

Coll, Steve, *Directorate S: The CIA and America's Secret Wars in Afghanistan and Pakistan 2001–2016*, Penguin Random House, 2018

Cowper-Coles, Sherard, *Cables from Kabul: The Inside Story of the West's Afghanistan Campaign*, HarperPress, 2011

Dannatt, General Sir Richard, *Leading from the Front*, Bantam, 2010

Dempsey, Martin E. and Ori Brafman, *Radical Inclusion: What the Post-9/11 World Should Have Taught Us About Leadership*, Missionday, 2018

Dobbins, James; Jones, Seth G.; Ruckle, Benjamin and Mohandas, Siddharth, *Occupying Iraq; A History of the Coalition Provisional Authority*, RAND Corporation, 2008 https://www.rand.org/content/dam/rand/pubs/monographs/2009/RAND_MG847.pdf

Dodge, Toby, *Iraq: From War to A New Authoritarianism*, International Institute for Strategic Studies, 2013

Dodge, Toby, *Iraq's Future: The Aftermath of Regime Change*, International Institute for Strategic Studies, 2005

Fairweather, Jack, *The Good War: Why We Couldn't Win the War or the Peace in Afghanistan*, Jonathan Cape, 2014

Farrell, Theo, *Unwinnable*, Bodley Head, 2017

Franks, Tommy, *American Soldier*, HarperCollins, 2004

Fraser, David and Hannington, Brian, *Operation Medusa: The Furious Battle That Saved Afghanistan From the Taliban*, Penguin Random House, 2018

Gates, Robert, *Duty: Memoirs of a Secretary at War*, Alfred A. Knopf, 2014

Gentile, Gian; Johnson, David E.; Saum-Manning, Lisa; Cohen, Raphael S.; Williams, Shara; Lee, Carrie; Shurkin, Michael; Allen, Breen; Soliman, Sarah and Doty III, James L., *Reimagining the Character of Urban Operations for the US Army*, RAND Corporation, 2017. https://www.rand.org/pubs/research_reports/RR1602.html

Giustozzi, Antonio, *The Taliban at War 2001–2018*, Hurst and Co, 2019

Gordon, Michael R., Trainor, Bernard E. and Gordon, Michael, *The Endgame: The Inside Story of the Struggle for Iraq, From George W. Bush to Barack Obama*, Pantheon, 2012

Gordon, Michael R. and Trainor, General Bernard E., *Cobra II: The Inside Story of the Invasion and Occupation of Iraq*, Pantheon, 2006

Grindle, Douglas, *How We Won and Lost the War in Afghanistan: Two Years in the Pashtun Heartland*, Potomac Books, 2017

Guardia, Mike, *US Army and Marine Corps MRAPS: Mine Resistant Ambush Protected Vehicles*, Osprey, 2013

Harnden, Toby, *Dead Men Risen: The Welsh Guards and the Real Story of Britain's War in Afghanistan*, Quercus, 2011

Hennessy, Patrick, *The Junior Officers' Reading Club: Killing Time and Fighting Wars*, Penguin, 2010

Hooker, Richard D., Jr and Collins, Joseph J., *Lessons Encountered: Learning from the Long War*, US National Defense University Press, 2015. https://ndupress.ndu.edu/Portals/68/Documents/Books/lessons-encountered/lessons-encountered.pdf

Hughes, Kim, *Painting the Sand*, Simon & Schuster, 2017

Jackson, General Sir Mike, *Soldier: The Autobiography*, Bantam, 2007

Jones, Seth, *In the Graveyard of Empires: America's War in Afghanistan*, W.W. Norton & Co, 2009

Jowett, Adam, *No Way Out: The Searing True Story of Men Under Siege*, Sidgwick & Jackson, 2018

Junger, Sebastian, *War*, Twelve, 2010

Kavanagh, Jennifer; Frederick, Bryan; Stark, Alexandra; Chandler, Nathan; Smith, Meagan L.; Povlock, Matthew; Davis, Lynn E. and Geist, Edward, *Characteristics of Successful U.S. Military Interventions*, RAND Corporation, 2019. https://www.rand.org/pubs/research_reports/RR3062.html

Kilcullen, David, *Blood Year: Islamic State and the Failures of the War on Terror*, Oxford University Press, 2016

Kilcullen, David, *Out of the Mountains: The Coming Age of the Urban Guerrilla*, Oxford University Press, 2014

King, Anthony, *Command: The Twenty-First-Century General*, Cambridge University Press, 2019

Lambeth, Benjamin S., *Airpower Against Terror; America's Conduct of Operation Enduring Freedom*, RAND Corporation, 2006

Ledwidge, Frank, *Losing Small Wars: British Military Failure in Iraq and Afghanistan*, Yale University Press, 2011

Malkasian, Carter, *War Comes to Garmser: Thirty Years of Conflict on the Afghan Frontier*, Oxford University Press, USA, 2016

Malkasian, Carter, *Illusions of Victory: The Anbar Awakening and the Rise of the Islamic State*, Oxford University Press, 2017

Mansoor, Peter, *Baghdad Sunrise*, Yale University Press, 2008

Mansoor, Peter, *The Surge*, Yale University Press, 2013

Marston, Daniel and Malkasian, Carter, *Counterinsurgency in Modern Warfare*, Osprey, 2008

Mattis, James, *Call Sign Chaos: Learning to Lead*, Random House, 2013

McChrystal, Stanley, *My Share of the Task; A Memoir*, Portfolio/Penguin, 2013

McChrystal, General Stanley; Silverman, David; Collins, Tantum and Fussell, Chris, *Team of Teams: New Rules of Engagement for a Complex World*, Penguin, 2015

Mercer, Johnny, *We Were Warriors*, Pan Macmillan, 2018

Mockaitis, Thomas, *The Iraq War: A Documentary and Reference Guide*, Greenwood, 2012

Orchard, Ade and Barrington, James, *Joint Force Harrier*, Michael Joseph, 2008

Parker, Harry, *Anatomy of a Soldier*, Faber & Faber, 2016

Perry, Walter L. and Kassing, David, *Toppling the Taliban: Air-Ground Operations in Afghanistan, October 2001–June 2002*, RAND Corporation, 2015. https://www.rand.org/pubs/research_reports/RR381.html

Perry, Walter L.; Darilek, Richard E.; Rohn, Laurinda L. and Sollinger, Jerry M., *Operation Iraqi Freedom: Decisive War, Elusive Peace*, RAND Corporation, 2015. https://www.rand.org/pubs/research_reports/RR1214.html

Poole, Oliver, *Black Knights: On the Bloody Road to Baghdad*, HarperCollins, 2003

Rashid, Ahmed, *Descent into Chaos: The United States and the Failure of Nation Building in Pakistan, Afghanistan, and Central Asia*, Viking, 2008

Richards, General Lord David, *Taking Command*, Headline, 2014

Ricks, Thomas E., *The Gamble: General Petraeus and the Untold Story of the American Surge in Iraq, 2006–2008*, Allen Lane, 2009

Ricks, Thomas E., *Fiasco: The American Military Adventure in Iraq*, Allen Lane, 2006

Ripley, Tim, *Operation TELIC*, Telic-Herrick Publications, 2014

Robinson, Linda, *Masters of Chaos; the Secret History of the Special Forces*, PublicAffairs, 2004

Robinson, Linda, *Tell Me How This Ends*, PublicAffairs, 2008

Robinson, Linda; Miller, Paul D.; Gordon IV, John; Decker, Jeffrey; Schwille, Michael and Cohen, Raphael S., *Improving Strategic Competence; Lessons from 13 Years of War*, RAND Corporation, 2014. https://www.rand.org/pubs/research_reports/RR816.html

Romesha, Clinton, *Red Platoon*, Arrow, 2016

Russell, James, *Innovation, Transformation, and War: Counterinsurgency Operations in Anbar and Ninewa Provinces, Iraq, 2005–2007*, Stanford University Press, 2011

Sánchez, General and Phillips, Donald T., *Wiser in Battle: A Soldier's Story*, HarperCollins, 2008

Silverman, Michael E., *Awakening Victory: How Iraqi Tribes and American Troops Reclaimed Al Anbar and Defeated Al Qaeda in Iraq*, Casemate, 2011

The Staff of the US Army Combat Studies Institute, *Wanat: Combat Action in Afghanistan*, US Army Combat Studies Institute Press, 2010. https://www.armyupress.army.mil/Portals/7/combat-studies-institute/csi-books/Wanat.pdf

Streatfeild, Richard, *Honourable Warriors: Fighting the Taliban in Afghanistan – A Front-line Account of the British Army's Battle for Helmand*, Pen and Sword, 2016

Synnott, Hilary, *Bad Days in Basra: My Turbulent Time as Britain's Man in Southern Iraq*, I B Tauris, 2008

Tootal, Stuart, *Danger Close*, John Murray, 2010 West, Bing, *The Strongest Tribe*, Random House, 2009

West, Bing, *No True Glory*, Bantam Dell, 2005

Zacchea, Michael and Kemp, Ted, *The Ragged Edge: A US Marine's Account of Leading the Iraqi Army Fifth Battalion*, Chicago Review, 2017

Zoroya, Gregg, *The Chosen Few: A Company of Paratroopers and ilts Heroic Struggle to Survive in the Mountains of Afghanistan*, Da Capo, 2016

SELECTED ARTICLES, PAPERS, REPORTS AND ONLINE PUBLICATIONS

'Accountability determination of US commanders for the 14–15 September attack on the Camp Bastion, Leatherneck and Shoraback complex, Helmand Province Afghanistan', US Department of the Navy, September 2013. https://www.hqmc.marines.mil/Portals/142/Docs/CMC%20Memo%20for%20the%20Record%20in%20Bastion%20Investigation.PDF

'A Good Ally: Norway in Afghanistan 2001–2014', Norwegian Ministry of Foreign Affairs and Ministry of Defence, Norwegian original August 2016, English translation 2018. https://www.regjeringen.no/contentassets/09faceca099c4b8bac85ca8495e12d2d/en-gb/pdfs/nou201620160008000engpdfs.pdf

'CENTCOM releases investigation into airstrike on Doctors Without Borders trauma center', CENTCOM press release, unreleased, 29 April 2016. https://www.centcom.mil/MEDIA/PRESS-RELEASES/Press-Release-View/Article/904574/april-29-centcom-releases-investigation-into-airstrike-on-doctors-without-borde/

'Counterinsurgency Reader', *Military Review* special edition, US Army Command and General Staff College, October 2006. http://cgsc.contentdm.oclc.org/cdm/ref/collection/p124201coll1/id/418

'Counterinsurgency Reader II', *Military Review* special editions, US Army Command and General Staff College, August 2008. http://cgsc.contentdm.oclc.org/cdm/ref/collection/p124201coll1/id/243

'Enhancing Security and Stability in Afghanistan', US Department of Defense, December 2018. https://media.defense.gov/2018/Dec/20/2002075158/-1/-1/1/1225-REPORT-DECEMBER-2018.PDF

'Fact Sheet: The New Way Forward in Iraq', White House Office of the Press Secretary, January 2007. https://georgewbush-whitehouse.archives.gov/news/releases/2007/01/20070110-3.html

'Joint Press Conference by President Obama and President Karzai', White House Office of the Press Secretary, 11 January 2013. https://obamawhitehouse.archives.gov/the-press-office/2013/01/11/joint-press-conference-president-obama-and-president-karzai

'Operations in Iraq January 2005–May 2009. An Analysis from the Land Perspective', Ministry of Defence, 29 November 2010. https://assets.

publishing.service.gov.uk/government/uploads/system/uploads/attachment_
data/file/557326/20160831-FOI07003_77396_Redacted.pdf

'Remarks by President Trump on the Strategy in Afghanistan and South
Asia', Arlington, VA, 21 August 2017. https://www.whitehouse.gov/
briefings-statements/remarks-president-trump-strategy-afghanistan-
south-asia/

Report of Special Operations Review Group, 23 August 1980. https://
nsarchive2.gwu.edu//NSAEBB/NSAEBB63/doc8.pdf

'Statement of Admiral Michael Mullen, US Navy Chairman Joint Chiefs of
Staff before the Senate Armed Services Committee on Afghanistan and
Iraq, 22 September 2011,' United States Senate Armed Services Committee.
https://www.armed-services.senate.gov/imo/media/doc/Mullen%2009-22-
11.pdf

'Statement of General Joseph L. Votel, Commander, U.S. Central Command,
before the House Armed Services Committee on the Posture of US Central
Command Terrorism and Iran: Defense Challenges in the Middle East,
27 February 2018', CENTCOM. http://www.centcom.mil/Portals/6/
Documents/Transcripts/HASCVotel20180227.pdf

'The Situation in Afghanistan and its Implications for International Peace and
Security', Report of the Secretary-General to the UN General Assembly, 13
September 2012. https://unama.unmissions.org/sites/default/files/sg_report_
to_sc_as_published_13sept12.pdf

Alderson, Colonel Alexander, 'The Validity of British Army
Counterinsurgency Doctrine After the War in Iraq 2003–2009', PhD
thesis, Cranfield University, 2009. https://dspace.lib.cranfield.ac.uk/
bitstream/handle/1826/4264/100126-Alderson-PhD%20Thesis.
pdf;jsessionid=8741B3A1B1D0520EB1D9354C22DBEF43?sequence=1

Ali, Obaid, 'The 2015 Insurgency in the North (3): The fall and recapture of
Kunduz', Afghan Analysts Network, 16 October 2015 (last updated 9 Mar
2020). https://www.afghanistan-analysts.org/the-2015-insurgency-in-the-
north-3-the-fall-and-recapture-of-kunduz/

Ali, Obaid, 'The 2016 Insurgency in the North: Beyond Kunduz City – Lessons
(Not Taken) from the Taleban Takeover', Afghan Analysts Network, 30
January 2016 (last updated 9 Mar 2020). https://www.afghanistan-analysts.
org/the-2016-insurgency-in-the-north-beyond-kunduz-city-lessons-not-
taken-from-the-taleban-takeover/

Bensahel, Nora; Oliker, Olga; Crane, Keith; Brennan, Jr, Rick; Gregg, Heather
S.; Sullivan, Thomas and Rathmell, Andrew, *After Saddam: Prewar Planning
and the Occupation of Iraq*, RAND Corporation, 2008. https://www.rand.
org/pubs/monographs/MG642.html

Biddle, Stephen, 'Victory Misunderstood', *International Security*, Vol. 21, No. 2,
Fall 1996. http://www.comw.org/rma/fulltext/victory.html

Brown, Lieutenant General Chris, 'Iraq Study Team Observations', Ministry of Defence, May 28, 2010. https://assets.publishing.service.gov.uk/government/uploads/system/uploads/attachment_data/file/16787/operation_telic_lessons_compendium.pdf

Chilcot, J. 'The Report of the Iraq Inquiry', Her Majesty's Stationery Office, 2016. https://webarchive.nationalarchives.gov.uk/20171123123237/http://www.iraqinquiry.org.uk/

Crawford, Neta C. 'Update on the Human Costs of War for Afghanistan and Pakistan, 2001 to mid-2016', Boston University, May 2015. https://watson.brown.edu/costsofwar/files/cow/imce/papers/2016/War%20in%20Afghanistan%20and%20Pakistan%20UPDATE_FINAL_corrected%20date.pdf

Crider, Lieutenant Colonel James R., 'A View From Inside the Surge', *Military Review*, March–April 2009. https://www.armyupress.army.mil/Portals/7/military-review/Archives/English/MilitaryReview_20090430_art013.pdf

Fontenot, Gregory, Degen, E.J. and Tohn, David, 'On Point: The United States Army in Operation Iraqi Freedom', US Army Combat Studies Institute Press, US Army Combined Arms Centre, 2004. https://usacac.army.mil/sites/default/files/documents/cace/CSI/CSIPubs/OnPointI.pd

Forsberg, Carl, 'Counterinsurgency in Kandahar: Evaluating the 2010 Hamkari Campaign', Institute for the Study of War, December 2010. http://www.understandingwar.org/sites/default/files/Afghanistan%20Report%207_15Dec.pdf

Groen, Lieutenant Colonel Michael S. and contributors, 'With the 1st Marine Division in Iraq 2003: No Greater Friend, No Worse Enemy', History Division, Marine Corps University, 2006. https://www.marines.mil/Portals/59/Publications/With%20the%201st%20Marine%20Division%20in%20Iraq,%202003%20%20PCN%2010600000000.pdf?ver=2017-04-05-160920-517

Haddon-Cave, Charles, QC, 'The Nimrod Review: An independent review into the broader issues surrounding the loss of the RAF Nimrod MR2 aircraft XV230 in Afghanistan in 2006', The Stationery Office, October 2009. https://www.gov.uk/government/publications/the-nimrod-review

House of Commons Defence Committee, 'Afghanistan – Camp Bastion Attack', The Stationery Office Ltd, 16 April 2014. https://publications.parliament.uk/pa/cm201314/cmselect/cmdfence/830/830.pdf

Howard, Jeffrey T., PhD; Kotwal, Russ S., MD, MPH; Turner, Caryn A., DrPH; Janak, Jud C., PhD; Mazuchowski, Edward L., MD, PhD; Butler, Frank K., MD; Stockinger, Zsolt T., MD; Holcomb, Barbara R., MSN; Bono, Raquel C., MD and Smith, David J., MD, 'Use of Combat Casualty Care Data to Assess the US Military Trauma System During the Afghanistan and Iraq Conflicts, 2001-2017', JAMA Surgery, 27 March 2019. https://pubmed.ncbi.nlm.nih.gov/30916730/

Kagan, Frederick, 'Choosing Victory', American Enterprise Institute, January
    2007 https://www.aei.org/research-products/working-paper/choosing-victory-
    a-plan-for-success-in-iraq/

Krivdo, Michael E., PhD, 'CJSOTF-A Combined Joint Special Operations
    Task Force-Afghanistan: A Short History 2002–2014', *Veritas*, Vol. 12,
    No. 2, 2016, https://www.soc.mil/ARSOF_History/articles/v12n2_cjsotf_
    page_1.html

McPherson, Lieutenant Commander James A., 'Operation Anaconda:
    Command and Control through VTC', Naval War College, 14 February
    2005. https://apps.dtic.mil/dtic/tr/fulltext/u2/a464899.pdf

Rayburn, Colonel Joel D. and Sobchak, Colonel Frank K., 'The US Army
    in the Iraq War, Volume 1, Invasion, Insurgency, Civil War 2003–2006',
    US Army Strategic Studies Institute, January 2019. https://publications.
    armywarcollege.edu/pubs/3667.pdf

Rayburn, Colonel Joel D. and Sobchak, Colonel Frank K., 'The US Army in
    the Iraq War, Volume 2, Surge and Withdrawal 2007–11', US Army Strategic
    Studies Institute, January 2019. https://publications.armywarcollege.edu/
    pubs/3668.pdf

Special Inspector General for Afghanistan Reconstruction May 2018,
    'Stabilization: Lessons from the US Experience in Afghanistan'. https://www.
    sigar.mil/pdf/lessonslearned/SIGAR-18-48-LL.pdf

Steeb, Randall; Matsumura, John; Herbert, Thomas J.; Gordon IV; John and
    Horn, William W., 'Perspectives on the Battle of Wanat: Challenges Facing
    Small Unit Operations in Afghanistan', RAND Corporation, 2011. https://
    www.rand.org/content/dam/rand/pubs/occasional_papers/2011/RAND_
    OP329z1.pdf

Tunnell IV, Colonel Harry V., letter to US Army Secretary, 20 August 2010,
    Michael Yon Online Magazine. https://www.michaelyon-online.com/images/
    pdf/secarmy_redacted-redux.pdf

Wright, Donald P. PhD; Bird, James R.; Clay, Steven E.; Connors,
    Peter W.; Farquhar, Lieutenant Colonel Scott C.; Chandler Garcia,
    Lynne and Van Wey, Dennis F., 'A Different Kind of War: The United
    States Army in Operation Enduring Freedom October 2001–September
    2005', US Army Combat Studies Institute Press, Fort Leavenworth,
    Kansas, 2010. https://history.army.mil/html/bookshelves/resmat/GWOT/
    DifferentKindofWar.pdf

Wright, Dr Donald P. and Reese, Colonel Timothy R. with the Contemporary
    Operations Study Team, 'On Point II: Transition to the New Campaign: the
    US Army in Operation Iraqi Freedom May 2003 – January 2005', US Army
    Combined Arms Centre, 2008. http://cgsc.contentdm.oclc.org/cdm/ref/
    collection/p16040coll3/id/183

NEWS ARTICLES

'Leave Peacekeeping to others, Rumsfeld says at Senate Hearing', *Baltimore Sun*, 12 January 2001. https://www.baltimoresun.com/news/bs-xpm-2001-01-12-0101120154-storych_reports/RR816.html

'President Obama's statement about Afghanistan', *Stars and Stripes*, 15 October 2015. https://www.stripes.com/news/transcript-of-president-obama-s-statement-about-afghanistan-oct-15-2015-1.373441

'Report blames lapses on Stryker commander — 532-page report finds colonel ignored doctrine, proper procedure in leading undisciplined BCT', *Military Times*, 27 March 2013. https://www.militarytimes.com/2013/03/27/report-blames-lapses-on-stryker-commander-532-page-report-finds-colonel-ignored-doctrine-proper-procedure-in-leading-undisciplined-bct/

Hashim, Asad, 'Leaked Report Shows Bin Laden's "Hidden life"', Al Jazeera website, 8 July 2013. http://www.aljazeera.com/news/asia/2013/07/201378134126155311.html

Hawley, Caroline, 'The Story of the Fake Bomb Detectors', BBC News website, 3 October 2014. https://www.bbc.co.uk/news/uk-29459896

Schmitt, Eric, 'Iraq-Bound Troops Confront Rumsfeld Over Lack of Armor', *New York Times*, 8 December, 2004. https://www.nytimes.com/2004/12/08/international/middleeast/iraqbound-troops-confront-rumsfeld-over-lack-of.html

Wellman, Philip Walter, 'US has dropped more munitions in 2018 in Afghanistan than it has in any year in over a decade'. *Stars and Stripes*, 3 December 2018. https://www.stripes.com/news/the-us-has-dropped-more-munitions-in-2018-in-afghanistan-than-it-has-in-any-year-in-over-a-decade-1.558577

Endnotes

Please note that the final editing of this book took place during the spring and summer of 2020, during the UK lockdown in response to the COVID-19 pandemic. Libraries and archives were closed and therefore the author has been in some cases unable to provide specific page referencing.

PREFACE

1 Christopher Tyerman, *God's War: A New History of the Crusades*, Penguin, 2007, p. xvi. I am also grateful for his insights into alternative historical perspective on the same page.
2 General Lord David Richards, *Taking Command*, Headline 2014.

CHAPTER I

1 'Report of Special Operations Review Group', 23 August 1980.
2 Stanley McChrystal, *My Share of the Task: A Memoir*, Portfolio/Penguin, 2013, p. 52.
3 Author's observations from a 1988 visit to SOCOM.
4 One of the armoured cavalry troops that was in the thick of the fighting was commanded by a young cavalry officer, Captain H.R. McMaster. He would play a key role in Iraq in 2005.
5 See Stephen Biddle, 'Victory Misunderstood', *International Security*, Vol. 21, No. 2, Fall 1996.
6 A useful account of the battle is in Mark Bowden's book *Black Hawk Down*, Signet, 1999.
7 The author analysed the British Army's operations in Bosnia in 1996 in *The Road From Sarajevo*, The History Press, 2016.

8   These events are described in greater detail in Carl Bildt's book *Peace Journey*, Weidenfeld & Nicolson, 1998, and General Wesley Clark's book *Waging Modern War: Bosnia, Kosovo, and the Future of Conflict*, PublicAffairs, 2002.

9   Author's conversations with senior US Army officers in London and Bosnia 1998–2003.

10 A vivid account of the Sierra Leone intervention based on diary entries can be found in General Lord David Richards' memoir *Taking Command*, Headline, 2014, chapters 7 to 9.

11 Author's observations, 1998–2003.

12 Speech archived at https://www.globalpolicy.org/component/content/article/154/26026.html

13 Transcript of presidential debate between Governor Bush and Vice President Gore, *Washington Post*, 11 October 2000. https://www.washingtonpost.com/wp-srv/onpolitics/elections/debatetext10110ob.htm?mod=article_inline

14 Transcript of the second presidential debate, *New York Times*, 12 October 2000. https://www.nytimes.com/2000/10/12/us/2000-campaign-2nd-presidential-debate-between-gov-bush-vice-president-gore.html

15 'Leave Peacekeeping to Others, Rumsfeld Says at Senate Hearing', *Baltimore Sun*, 12 January 2001.

16 Donald Rumsfeld, 'Beyond Nation Building', Intrepid Sea-Air-Space Museum, New York City, 14 February 2003. https://www.hsdl.org/?abstract&did=1871

CHAPTER 2

1   Vividly described in chapters 17 to 19 of John Masters' book *Bugles and a Tiger*, Michael Joseph, 1956.

2   See Roderick Braithwaite, *Afghantsy: The Russians in Afghanistan 1979–1989*, Profile Books, 2012, chapter 3, pp. 57–82.

3   A useful account is in Brigadier Mohammed Yousuf's and Mark Adkins' book *The Bear Trap*, Leo Cooper, 1992. Yousuf was the Pakistan Army brigadier who managed operational support to the Mujahedeen in the mid-1980s.

4   See Toby Dodge and Nicolas Redman (eds), 'Afghanistan to 2015 and Beyond', International Institute of Strategic Studies, 2011. Analysis of Pakistan's Afghanistan policy is on pp. 167–86.

5   Walter L. Perry and David Kassing, *Toppling the Taliban: Air-Ground Operations in Afghanistan, October 2001–June 2002*, RAND Corporation, 2015, p. 23.

6   President George W. Bush, 'A Great People Has Been Moved to Defend a Great Nation', 9/11 Address to the Nation, Washington, DC, 11 September 2001. https://www.americanrhetoric.com/speeches/gwbush911addresstothenation.htm

7   Perry and Kassing, *Toppling the Taliban*, p. 16.

8 US Department of Defense news briefing presented by Deputy Secretary of Defense Paul Wolfowitz, 13 September 2001. https://archive.defense.gov/Transcripts/Transcript.aspx?TranscriptID=1622

9 Multiple sources report this. A detailed account is found in Michael R. Gordon and General Bernard E. Trainor, *Cobra II: The Inside Story of the Invasion and Occupation of Iraq*, Pantheon, 2006, pp. 15–17.

10 President George W. Bush, 'Address to the Joint Session of the 107th Congress', Washington, DC, 20 September 2001. https://georgewbush-whitehouse.archives.gov/infocus/bushrecord/documents/Selected_Speeches_George_W_Bush.pdf

11 President George W. Bush, 'Address to the Nation', Washington, DC, 7 October 2001. http://georgewbush-whitehouse.archives.gov/news/releases/2001/10/20011007-8.html

12 Author's conversations with British SOF commanders.

13 Steve Coll, *Directorate S: The CIA and America's Secret Wars in Afghanistan and Pakistan*, Allen Lane, 2018, p. 116.

14 Something the author saw for himself at the time in Bosnia.

15 Annex A to 'Letter dated 5 December 2001 from the Secretary-General addressed to the President of the Security Council', UN Security Council, 2001. https://peacemaker.un.org/sites/peacemaker.un.org/files/AF_011205_AgreementProvisionalArrangementsinAfghanistan%28en%29.pdf

16 Theo Farrell, *Unwinnable*, Bodley Head, 2017, p. 98.

17 There is a good account of the genesis and early role of ISAF in Farrell, *Unwinnable*, pp. 92–100.

18 See Lieutenant Commander James A. McPherson, US Navy, 'Operation Anaconda: Command and Control through VTC', Naval War College, 14 February 2005.

CHAPTER 3

1 President George W. Bush, 'Remarks at the Virginia Military Institute in Lexington, Virginia', Virginia Military Institute, 17 April 2002. http://www.presidency.ucsb.edu/ws/index.php?pid=73000

2 Later to return to Afghanistan as Commander Regional Command South in 2010 and Deputy Commander of ISAF in 2013. Now UK Chief of the Defence Staff.

3 Based on numerous sources, including author's visit to UK PRT in Helmand Province, May 2009. See also Carter Malkasian and Gerald Meyerle, 'Provincial Reconstruction Teams: How Do We Know They Work?', US Army Strategic Studies Centre, 2009. https://ssi.armywarcollege.edu/pdffiles/PUB911.pdf

4 David F. Mitchell, 'Blurred Lines? Provincial Reconstruction Teams and NGO Insecurity in Afghanistan, 2010–2011', *Stability, International Journal*

of Security and Development, March 2015. https://www.stabilityjournal.org/articles/10.5334/sta.ev/#B9

5 'Rumsfeld: Major combat over in Afghanistan', CNN website, 1 May 2003. http://edition.cnn.com/2003/WORLD/asiapcf/central/05/01/afghan.combat/

6 Private briefing to author by UK officials.

CHAPTER 4

1 Walter L. Perry, Richard E. Darilek, Laurinda L. Rohn and Jerry M. Sollinger, *Operation Iraqi Freedom: Decisive War, Elusive Peace*, RAND Corporation, 2015, p. 183.

2 McChrystal, *My Share of the Task*, p. 181.

3 Colonel Joel D. Rayburn and Colonel Frank K. Sobchak, 'The US Army in the Iraq War, Volume 1, Invasion, Insurgency, Civil War 2003–2006', US Army Strategic Studies Institute, January 2019; chapters 2 and 3 provide a clear and relatively short account of land component planning.

4 Nora Bensahel, Olga Oliker, Keith Crane, Rick Brennan, Jr., Heather S. Gregg, Thomas Sullivan and Andrew Rathmell, *After Saddam: Prewar Planning and the Occupation of Iraq*, RAND Corporation, 2008, fn p. 43.

5 General Tommy Franks, *American Soldier*, HarperCollins, 2005, pp. 415–16.

6 McChrystal, *My Share of the Task*, p. 52.

7 McChrystal, *My Share of the Task*, p. 53.

8 James Mattis, *Call Sign Chaos*, Random House, 2019, p. 85.

9 Rayburn and Sobchak, 'The US Army in the Iraq War', Vol. 1, p. 84.

10 Rayburn and Sobchak, 'The US Army in the Iraq War', Vol. 1, p. 85.

11 Gregory Fontenot, E.J. Degen and David Tohn, 'On Point: The United States Army in Operation Iraqi Freedom', US Army Combat Studies Institute Press, US Army Combined Arms Centre, 2004, p. 211.

12 Fontenot, Degen and Tohn, 'On Point', p. 301.

13 Fontenot, Degen and Tohn, 'On Point', p. 303.

14 The description of 1st BCT's advance to the airport and subsequent fighting draws on Fontenot, Degen and Tohn, 'On Point', pp. 299–310.

15 The discussion of 2nd BCT's two Thunder Runs draws on Gordon and Trainor, *Cobra II*, pp. 378–79, and 'On Point', pp. 336–82.

16 Fontenot, Degen and Tohn, 'On Point', p. 342.

17 Fontenot, Degen and Tohn, 'On Point', p. 346.

18 Fontenot, Degen and Tohn, 'On Point', p. 349.

19 Chilcot, J. 'The Report of the Iraq Inquiry' (hereafter 'Iraq Inquiry'), Her Majesty's Stationery Office, 2016, Executive Summary, p. 121. https://webarchive.nationalarchives.gov.uk/20171123123237/http://www.iraqinquiry.org.uk/

20 BBC Radio 4 documentary 'The Reunion', first broadcast 1 April 2018. https://www.bbc.co.uk/programmes/b09xctwq

21 General Charles C. Krulack, 'The Strategic Corporal: Leadership in the Three Block', *US Marine Corps Gazette*, January 1999. https://apps.dtic.mil/dtic/tr/fulltext/u2/a399413.pdf

22 BBC Radio 4,'The Reunion'.

23 Evidence given to the Iraq Inquiry by Major General Graham Binns, 2 June 2010. https://webarchive.nationalarchives.gov.uk/20171123123606/http://www.iraqinquiry.org.uk/the-evidence/witnesses/b/maj-gen-graham-binns/

CHAPTER 5

1   Toby Dodge, 'Iraq's Future: The Aftermath of Regime Change', International Institute for Strategic Studies, 2005.

2   Donald Rumsfeld and General Richard Myers, US Department of Defense news briefing, 11 April 2003. http://archive.defense.gov/Transcripts/Transcript.aspx?TranscriptID=2367

3   This chapter uses the invaluable chronology and analysis contained in Donald P. Wright and Timothy R. Reese with the Contemporary Operations Study Team, 'On Point II: Transition to the New Campaign: The United States Army in Operation IRAQI FREEDOM May 2003 – January 2005', US Army Combined Arms Centre, 2008. Like 'On Point', this is an in-house contemporary historical account of the US Army in Iraq.

4   George W. Bush, speech aboard USS *Abraham Lincoln* off San Diego, CA, 1 May 2003. https://georgewbush-whitehouse.archives.gov/news/releases/2003/05/20030501-15.html

5   Lieutenant General Ricardo S. Sanchez, *Wiser in Battle: A Soldier's Story*, HarperCollins, 2008, p. 186.

6   Mattis, *Call Sign Chaos*, p. 113.

7   Wright, Reese and COST, 'On Point II', p. 30.

8   Wright, Reese and COST, 'On Point II', p. 30.

9   McChrystal, *My Share of the Task*, pp. 101–02.

10 Observation made by author, April 2004.

11 President George W. Bush, 'Steps to Help Iraq Achieve Democracy and Freedom', Pennsylvania, 24 May 2004. https://2001-2009.state.gov/r/pa/ei/pix/prsdnt/32747.htm,.

12 Mattis, *Call Sign Chaos*, p. 123.

13 Mattis, *Call Sign Chaos*, p. 12.

14 Bing West, *No True Glory*, Bantam Dell, 2005, p. 137.

15 Mattis, *Call Sign Chaos*, p. 129.

16 Wright, Reese and COST, 'On Point II', p. 40.

17 Sanchez, *Wiser in Battle*, p. 351.

18 Peter Mansoor, *Baghdad Sunrise*, Yale University Press, 2008, p. 324.

19 See LTG Anthony R. Jones, 'AR 15-6 Investigation of the Abu Ghraib Prison and 205th Military Intelligence Brigade', and MG George R. Fay, 'AR 15-6

Investigation of the Abu Ghraib Detention Facility and 205th Military Intelligence Brigade', US Department of Defense, August 2004 https://www. hsdl.org/?abstract&did=451656. The executive summaries are of exemplary clarity. See also Paul T. Bartone, 'Lessons of Abu Ghraib: Understanding and Preventing Prisoner Abuse in Military Operations', *Defense Horizons*, November 2008. www.dtic.mil/dtic/tr/fulltext/u2/a490174.pdf

20 Jim Garamone, 'Rumsfeld Accepts Responsibility for Abu Ghraib', American Forces Press Service, 7. May 2004.

21 Thomas E. Ricks, *Fiasco: The American Military Adventure in Iraq*, Allen Lane, 2006, p. 290.

CHAPTER 6

1 This account draws on multiple sources, especially Bing West, *No True Glory* and Gian Gentile, David E. Johnson, Lisa Saum-Manning, Raphael S. Cohen, Shara Williams, Carrie Lee, Michael Shurkin, Brenna Allen, Sarah Soliman and James L. Doty III, *Reimagining the Character of Urban Operations for the US Army*, RAND Corporation, 2017.

2 Staff Sergeant David Bellavia, *House to House: An Epic of Urban Warfare*, Simon and Schuster, 2007, p. 71.

3 Bellavia, *House to House*, p. 107.

4 The Qayis al-Khazali Papers, published by the American Enterprise Institute. https://www.aei.org/the-qayis-al-khazali-papers/

5 McChrystal, *My Share of the Task*, p. 186.

6 Rayburn and Sobchak, 'The US Army in the Iraq War', Vol. 1, p. 456.

7 Author's interview, 2009.

8 Secretary of State Condoleezza Rice, testimony on Iraq and US policy to Senate Committee on Foreign Relations, 19 October 2005. https://www. foreign.senate.gov/imo/media/doc/RiceTestimony051019.pdf

9 'National Strategy for Victory in Iraq', National Security Council, November 2005, Executive Summary. https://georgewbush-whitehouse.archives.gov/ infocus/iraq/iraq_strategy_nov2005.html

10 McChrystal, *My Share of the Task*, p. 188.

11 Author's observations, 2011.

12 McChrystal, *My Share of the Task*, p. 155.

13 Robert Gates, *Duty: Memoirs of a Secretary at War*, Alfred A. Knopf, 2014, p. 267.

14 James Russell, *Innovation, Transformation, and War: Counterinsurgency Operations in Anbar and Ninewa Provinces, Iraq, 2005–2007*, Stanford University Press, 2011, p. 117.

15 Secretary of Defense Leon E. Panetta, 'Statement on Women in Service', Pentagon Press Briefing Room, Arlington, VA, 24 January 2013. https:// archive.defense.gov/speeches/speech.aspx?speechid=1746

CHAPTER 7

1 See Rayburn and Sobchak, 'The US Army in the Iraq War', Vol. 1 p. 446.
2 Field Manual 3-24 'Counterinsurgency', December 2006, US Army, pp. 2-1–2-2.
3 Thomas E. Ricks, *The Gamble: General Petraeus and the Untold Story of the American Surge in Iraq, 2006–2008*, Allen Lane, 2009, pp. 74–104; Linda Robinson, *Tell Me How This Ends*, PublicAffairs, 2008, pp. 30–36.
4 MNF-I, 'Campaign Progress Review', December 2006.
5 MNF-I, 'Campaign Progress Review', December 2006.
6 Frederick Kagan, 'Choosing Victory: A Plan for Success in Iraq', American Enterprise Institute, January 2007, p. 1.
7 The White House, 'Fact Sheet: The New Way Forward in Iraq', Office of the Press Secretary, 10 January 2007.
8 'General Petraeus's Opening Statement', *New York Times*, 23 January 2007 https://www.nytimes.com/2007/01/23/world/middleeast/24petraeustextcnd.html; General David H. Petraeus, 'The Way Ahead in Iraq', *Military Review*, March–April 2007, p. 3.
9 MNF-I 'Joint Campaign Plan', 26 November 2007, Preface.
10 For a more detailed description of the campaign plan see Robinson, *Tell Me How This Ends*, pp. 176–77.
11 Peter Mansoor, *The Surge*, Yale University Press, 2013, p. 67.
12 'Petraeus: The Islamic State isn't our biggest problem in Iraq', *New York Times*, 20 March 2015. https://www.washingtonpost.com/news/worldviews/wp/2015/03/20/petraeus-the-islamic-state-isnt-our-biggest-problem-in-iraq/?utm_term=.8e6a8ef4dc60
13 Brian Bennett, 'The General', *Time Magazine*, 30 November 2008. See also Ricks, *The Gamble*, p. 105.
14 Bing West, *The Strongest Tribe*, Random House, 2009.
15 Based on Lieutenant Colonel James R. Crider, 'A View From Inside the Surge', *Military Review*, March–April 2009 and on Colonel Alexander Alderson, 'The Validity of British Army Counterinsurgency Doctrine After the War in Iraq 2003–2009', PhD thesis, Cranfield University, 2009.
16 MNF-I 'Counterinsurgency Guidance', 19 June 2007.
17 MNF-I 'Counterinsurgency Guidance', 19 June 2007.
18 General David H. Petraeus, 'Report to Congress on the Situation in Iraq', 10–11 September 2007. Archived at the POLITICIO website: https://www.politico.com/pdf/PPM43_general_petraeus_testimony_10_september2007.pdf

CHAPTER 8

1 Williamson Murray, *Military Adaptation and War: With Fear of Change*, Cambridge University Press, 2012.

2 Schmitt, Eric,'Iraq-Bound Troops Confront Rumsfeld Over Lack of Armor' *New York Times*, 8 December 2004.

3 Author's observations, Helmand, June 2009.

4 Author's interviews, 2014.

5 Author's interviews, 2014.

6 US Army Capstone Concept 2009 TRAQDOC 525-3-0, p. 11.

7 Author's interviews with senior British Army intelligence officials, 2010.

8 Author's observation, Kabul, June 2013.

9 Author's observations, Helmand and Kandahar, June 2009.

10 McChrystal, *My Share of the Task*, p. 199.

11 Gage, W. 'The Baha Mousa Public Inquiry Report' (hereafter 'Baha Mousa Inquiry'), Her Majesty's Stationery Office, 2011, paragraph 7.208. http://webarchive.nationalarchives.gov.uk/20120215203912/http://www.bahamousainquiry.org/f_report/vol%20ii/Part%20VII/Part%20VII.pdf

12 McChrystal, *My Share of the Task*, p. 201.

13 This section draws heavily on Gates, *Duty*, pp. 115–48, 445–49.

14 Gates, *Duty*, p. 147.

15 Gates, *Duty*, pp. 266–67.

CHAPTER 9

1 Iraq Inquiry. https://webarchive.nationalarchives.gov.uk/20171123123237/http://www.iraqinquiry.org.uk/

2 Iraq Inquiry Chairman's Statement, 6 July 2016.

3 Iraq Inquiry Chairman's Statement, 6 July 2016.

4 BBC Radio 4, 'The Reunion'.

5 Evidence given to the Iraq Inquiry by Major General Andrew Stewart. http://webarchive.nationalarchives.gov.uk/20171123123302/http://www.iraqinquiry.org.uk/the-evidence/witness-transcripts/

6 Iraq Inquiry, p. 533.

7 Iraq Inquiry, p. 535.

8 Iraq Inquiry, p. 95.

9 Iraq Inquiry, p. 535.

10 Hilary Synnott, *Bad Days in Basra: My Turbulent Time as Britain's Man in Southern Iraq*, I B Tauris, 2008, p. 252.

11 Baha Mousa Inquiry.

12 Disappointingly the reasoning behind this decision was one of several issues that the Iraq Inquiry chose not to explore.

13 Colonel Alexander Alderson, 'The Validity of British Army Counterinsurgency Doctrine After the War in Iraq 2003-2009', Cranfield University PhD thesis, 2010, pp. 148–49.

14 Thomas Mockaitis, *The Iraq War: A Documentary and Reference Guide*, Greenwood, 2012, p. 11.

15 Evidence given to the Iraq Inquiry by Lieutenant General Sir Jonathon Riley, 14 December 2009. http://webarchive.nationalarchives.gov.uk/20171123123620/http://www.iraqinquiry.org.uk/the-evidence/witnesses/r/lt-gen-jonathon-riley/

16 Evidence given to the Iraq Inquiry by Lieutenant General John Cooper, 15 December 2009. https://web.archive.org/web/20160716225704/http://www.iraqinquiry.org.uk/media/230141/2009-12-15-transcript-rollo-cooper-s2.pdf

17 Evidence given to the Iraq Inquiry by Lieutenant General Richard Shirreff, 11 January 2010. https://web.archive.org/web/20160717194013/http://www.iraqinquiry.org.uk/media/95138/2010-01-11-Transcript-Shirreff-S2.pdf

18 Evidence given to the Iraq Inquiry by Lieutenant General Richard Shirreff, 11 January 2010.

19 International Police Advisors were provided by Armor Group, a private security company, and were to provide the specialist advice and mentoring to the Iraqi Police Service.

20 Taken from 'Operations in Iraq January 2005–May 2009, An Analysis from the Land Perspective', Ministry of Defence, 29 November 2010.

21 Iraq Inquiry Chairman's Statement, 6 July 2016.

22 Author's researches, 2009–10. Analysed in the Iraq Inquiry, pp. 228–41.

23 Lieutenant General Chris Brown, 'Iraq Study Observations', Ministry of Defence, May 28, 2010.

24 Sentiment expressed at closed Army conferences by a number of senior leaders.

25 The author saw this for himself while working in two different branches of the UK Ministry of Defence between 2004 and 2009.

26 Richards, *Taking Command*, p. 300.

27 Précis by author from *The Infantryman*, 2008, an in-house British Army journal.

28 Author's observations in UK Ministry of Defence, 2006–07.

29 Evidence given to the Iraq Inquiry by Air Chief Marshal Sir Jock Stirrup, 1 February 2010. https://webarchive.nationalarchives.gov.uk/20171123123302/http://www.iraqinquiry.org.uk/the-evidence/witness-transcripts/

30 BBC Radio 4,'The Reunion'.

31 Richard Iron, 'Basra 2008: Operation Charge of the Knights', in Jonathan Bailey, Richard Iron and Hew Strachan, *British Generals in Blair's Wars*, Ashgate, 2013.

32 Evidence given to the Iraq Inquiry by Air Chief Marshal Sir Jock Stirrup, 1 February 2010.

33 Author's interviews, 2009–10.

34 See pp. 134–35 of the Iraq Inquiry Executive Summary, for analysis of weaknesses in UK decision making and implementation in the post-conflict period.

35 Iraq Inquiry Executive Summary, p. 110.
36 Iraq Inquiry Executive Summary p. 136.

CHAPTER 10

1 See Rayburn and Sobchak, 'The US Army in the Iraq War', Vol. 2, pp. 500–06.
2 See Caroline Hawley 'The Story of the Fake Bomb Detectors', an account of the fraud and jailing of the perpetrators by a British court, BBC News website, 3 October 2014.
3 Rayburn and Sobchak, 'The US Army in the Iraq War' Vol. 2, p. 527.
4 Chronicled by Professor Toby Dodge in his book *Iraq: From War to A New Authoritarianism*, International Institute for Strategic Studies, 2013.

CHAPTER 11

1 Observations by the author while serving in the UK Ministry of Defence 2004–06.
2 Jonathan Bailey, Richard Iron and Hew Strachan (eds), *British Generals in Blair's Wars*, Ashgate, 2013, pp. 218–19.
3 An excellent summary of the growth of the Taliban in Helmand and southern Afghanistan is found in Theo Farrell, *Unwinnable*, and in Carter Malkasian, *War comes to Garmser: Thirty Years of Conflict on the Afghan Frontier*, Oxford University Press, USA, 2016.
4 'UK troops "to target terrorists"', BBC News website, 24 April 2006.
5 *Danger Close* is also the title of a vivid account of 3rd Battalion, the Parachute Regiment in the 2006 battles in Helmand, written by the then-commanding officer, Stuart Tootal.
6 David Fraser and Brian Hannington, *Operation Medusa, the Furious Battle that Saved Afghanistan from the Taliban*, Penguin Random House, 2018. Fraser commanded the Regional Command South multinational brigade in 2006 and was the overall commander for Operation Medusa.
7 Haddon-Cave, Charles, QC, 'The Nimrod Review. An independent review into the broader issues surrounding the loss of the RAF Nimrod MR2 aircraft XV230 in Afghanistan in 2006', Her Majesty's Stationery Office, October 2009.
8 In 2012 the 1st Battalion, 3rd US Special Forces Group, who had provided the leadership for Task Force 31, became the first non-Canadian unit to receive a Canadian Commander in Chief's Commendation.
9 Fraser, *Operation Medusa*, p. 197.
10 A gripping account of the defence of the isolated British base at Musa Qala by the commander of an ad hoc infantry company thrown together

to defend the outpost is in Adam Jowett's book *No Way Out*, Sidgwick & Jackson, 2018.

11 An insightful account of the role of the Grenadier Guards OMLT role is Patrick Hennessy's book *The Junior Officers Reading Club Killing Time and Fighting Wars*, Penguin, 2010.

12 Farrell, *Unwinnable*, p. 365.

13 This account of Taliban adaptation and weaknesses is based on discussion in Antonio Guistozzi, *The Taliban at War 2001–2018*, chapters 5 and 6.

14 Author's observations from a 2009 visit to Lashkar Gar and Sangin.

15 The battle of Wanat was analysed in depth in by the US Army Combat Studies Institute in *Wanat: Combat Action in Afghanistan*, US Army Combat Studies Institute Press, 2010.

16 The battle was analysed by the RAND Corporation who used computer modelling and simulation to better understand the outcome of the battle. See Steeb, Matsumura, Gordon and Horn, 'Perspectives on the Battle of Wanat: Challenges Facing Small Unit Operations in Afghanistan', RAND Corporation, 2011.

17 The author was second in command of a British infantry battalion in South Armagh in 1992.

18 Malkasian, *War Comes to Garmser*.

19 Both soldiers who earned the Medal of Honor have described the battle: see Clonton Romesha, *Red Platoon*, Penguin Random House, 2016.

20 'AR 15-6 Investigation re: Complex Attack on COP Keating - 3 Oct 09', CENTCOM, 2010. http://graphics8.nytimes.com/packages/pdf/world/AR15-6Sum.pdf

CHAPTER 12

1 'A New Strategy for Afghanistan and Pakistan', White House blog, 27 March 2009 https://obamawhitehouse.archives.gov/blog/2009/03/27/a-new-strategy-afghanistan-and-pakistan

2 McChrystal, *My Share of the Task*, p. 310.

3 President Barack Obama, 'Remarks by the President in Address to the Nation on the Way Forward in Afghanistan and Pakistan', Washington, DC, 1 December 2009. https://obamawhitehouse.archives.gov/the-press-office/remarks-president-address-nation-way-forward-afghanistan-and-pakistan

4 John F. Sopko, 'Stabilization: Lessons From the US Experience in Afghanistan', Office of the Special Inspector General for Afghanistan Reconstruction, May 2018. https://www.sigar.mil/pdf/lessonslearned/SIGAR-18-48-LL.pdf

5 Author's observations, 2009–10.

6 'Statement of Admiral Michael Mullen, US Navy Chairman, Joint Chiefs of Staff before the Senate Armed Services Committee on Afghanistan and Iraq, 22 September 2011', Senate Armed Services Committee.

7 Asad Hashim, 'Leaked Report Shows Bin Laden's "Hidden Life"', Al Jazeera, 8 July 2013.

CHAPTER 13

1 'The Situation in Afghanistan and its Implications for International Peace and Security', report of the Secretary-General to the UN General Assembly, 13 September 2012.

2 'Accountability Determination of US Commanders for the 14–15 September Attack on the Camp Bastion, Leatherneck and Shoraback Complex, Helmand Province Afghanistan', Department of the Navy, 30 September 2013.

3 House of Commons Defence Committee, 'Afghanistan–Camp Bastion Attack', The Stationery Office Ltd, 16 April 2014.

4 Douglas Grindle, *How We Won and Lost the War in Afghanistan: Two Years in the Pashtun Heartland*, Potomac Books, 2017.

5 'Joint Press Conference by President Obama and President Karzai', White House Office of the Press Secretary, 11 January 2013.

6 See Obaid Ali, 'The 2015 Insurgency in the North (3): The Fall and Recapture of Kunduz', Afghan Analysts Network, 16 October 2015 (last updated 9 Mar 2020) and 'The 2016 Insurgency in the North: Beyond Kunduz City – Lessons (not Taken) from the Taleban Takeover', Afghan Analysts Network, 30 January 2016 (last updated 9 Mar 2020).

7 'CENTCOM releases investigation into airstrike on Doctors Without Borders trauma center', CENTCOM press release, unreleased, 29 April 2016.

8 'President Obama's statement about Afghanistan', *Stars and Stripes*, 15 October 2015.

9 Andrew Quilty, 'Static War: Helmand after the US Marines' return', Afghan Analysts Network, 23 April 2020. https://www.afghanistan-analysts. org/en/reports/war-and-peace/static-war-helmand-after-the-us-marines-return/

10 President Donald Trump, 'Remarks by President Trump on the Strategy in Afghanistan and South Asia', Arlington, VA, 21 August 2011.

11 President Donald Trump, 'The United States has foolishly given Pakistan ...', Twitter, 12.12pm, 1 January 2018. https://twitter.com/realDonaldTrump/status/947802588174577664

12 'Statement of General Joseph L. Votel, Commander, U.S. Central Command, before the House Armed Services Committee on the Posture of US Central Command Terrorism and Iran: Defense Challenges in the

Middle East, 27 February 2018', CENTCOM. http://www.centcom.mil/Portals/6/Documents/Transcripts/HASCVote120180227.pdf

13 Philip Walter Wellman, 'The US has dropped more munitions in 2018 in Afghanistan than it has in any year in over a decade', *Stars and Stripes*, 3 December 2018.

14 Private conversation with State Department and Pentagon officials, autumn 2018.

15 'Enhancing Security and Stability in Afghanistan', Department of Defense, December 2018.

16 Published on the US State Department website. https://www.state.gov/wp-content/uploads/2020/02/Agreement-For-Bringing-Peace-to-Afghanistan-02.29.20.pdf

CHAPTER 14

1 US casualty figures taken from Department of Defense website, 7 April 2019. https://dod.defense.gov/News/Casualty-Status/

2 https://www.iraqbodycount.org/

3 Neta C. Crawford, 'War-related Death, Injury, and Displacement in Afghanistan and Pakistan 2001–2014', Boston University, 22 May 2015: https://watson.brown.edu/costsofwar/files/cow/imce/papers/2015/War%20Related%20Casualties%20Afghanistan%20and%20Pakistan%202001-2014%20FIN.pdf, augmented by post-2014 figures from the UN Mission in Afghanistan (UNAMA): https://unama.unmissions.org/

4 Contained in US Senate Committee on Armed Services, 'The Situation in Iraq and Progress Made by the Government of Iraq in Meeting Benchmarks and Achieving Reconciliation.', US Government Publishing Office, 8, 9 and 10 April 2008. https://www.govinfo.gov/content/pkg/CHRG-110shrg45666/html/CHRG-110shrg45666.htm

5 Mansoor, *The Surge*, p. 223.

6 For an excellent strategic analysis of Iraq in the context of previous US military interventions see Jennifer Kavanagh, Bryan Frederick, Alexandra Stark, Nathan Chandler, Meagan L. Smith, Matthew Povlock, Lynn E. Davis and Edward Geist, *Characteristics of Successful U.S. Military Interventions*, RAND Corporation 2019.

7 Ben Rhodes, *The World As It Is: Inside the Obama White House*, Penguin Random House, 2018, p. 278.

Index

References to maps are in **bold**.